THEOLOGY AND IDENTITY

The Impact of Culture upon Christian Thought in the
Second Century and in Modern Africa

THEOLOGY AND IDENTITY

The Impact of Culture upon Christian Thought in the Second Century and in Modern Africa

Kwame Bediako

B.A. Hons. French (Legon, Ghana), B.A. Hons. Theology (London: CNAA), M.-ès-L. (Bordeaux), Docteur 3ème Cycle (Bordeaux), Ph.D. (Aberdeen)

OXFORD
REGNUM BOOKS

REGNUM BOOKS is a two-thirds world publishing
company on behalf of the International Fellowship of
Evangelical Mission Theologians (INFEMIT), formed
of the Africa Theological Fraternity, the Latin American
Theological Fraternity, and Partnership in Mission Asia.
It works in co-operation with major western Christian
organisations and is based at the Oxford Centre for
Mission Studies, P.O. Box 70, Oxford, U.K.

ISBN 1 - 870345 - 10 - X

British Library Cataloguing-in-Publication Data
Bediako, Kwame
    Theology and identity : the impact of culture upon
    Christian thought in the second century and in modern Africa
    I. Title
    248.4

Published by
Regnum Books
in association with
Lynx Communications

Cover design: Lawrence Littleton Evans
Typeset in India by Wordmakers, Bangalore.
Printed in Singapore by Stamford Press Pte. Ltd.
for Regnum Books, P.O. Box 70, Oxford, U.K

Contents

Abbreviations   ix

Preface   xi

Summary   xv

INTRODUCTION

The question of identity as a key to understanding
the concerns of Christian theology in modern Africa
and in the second century AD   1

PART ONE
THE CHRISTIAN GOSPEL AMID GRAECO-ROMAN CULTURE: BARBARISM, HELLENISM AND CHRISTIAN IDENTITY

Chapter 1

The problem of Christian identity in the context of
Graeco-Roman culture of the early Roman Empire   15

Chapter 2

The Gospel as the triumph of Barbarism? (1):
Tatian, or, the vindication of the Barbarians
against the Greeks   64

Chapter 3

The Gospel as the triumph of Barbarism? (2):
Tertullian, or, the vindication of a new identity
within Graeco-Roman culture   100

Chapter 4

Christ and the Hellenistic heritage (1):
Justin, or, Christ as "the Expectation of the Nations" 137

Chapter 5

Christ and the Hellenistic heritage (2):
Clement of Alexandria, or, Christ as the unifying
principle of all knowledge   174

PART TWO
THE MODERN AFRICAN PREDICAMENT:
IDENTITY AND QUESTS FOR INTEGRATION

Chapter 6

Christianity as "Civilisation": the legacy of
"the third opportunity" and the making of a modern
identity problem   225

Chapter 7

A variety of African responses (1):
Bolajo Idowu, or, the continuity of God in African
experience   267

Chapter 8

A variety of African responses (2):
John Mbiti, or, Christ as the Redeemer of the
African heritage   303

Chapter 9

A variety of African responses (3):
Mulago gwa Cikala Musharhamina, or, the entry of
Africa into the "Catholica"   347

Chapter 10

A variety of African responses (4):
Byang Kato, or, theology as Bibliology   386

Chapter 11

Conclusion: Africa and the Fathers – the relevance
of the achievement of early Hellenistic Christian
theology for the theological enterprise in modern
Africa   426

Bibliography   445

Indexes   480

Abbreviations

AACC	All Africa Conference of Churches
AAS	*Asian & African Studies*
AEAM	Association of Evangelicals of Africa & Madagascar
AFER	*African Ecclesiastical Review*
AIM	Africa Inland Mission
ATJ	*African Theological Journal*
BJRL	*Bulletin of the John Rylands Library*
CACSS	*Corpus Apologetarum Christianorum Saeculi Secundi*
CAH	*Cambridge Ancient History*
CCL	*Corpus Christianorum, Series Latina*
CMS	Church Missionary Society
CRA	*Cahiers des Religions Africaines*
DCB	*Dictionary of Christian Biography*
DL-FAC	*Dictionnaire Latin-Français des Augeurs Chrétiens*
DNB	*Dictionary of National Biography*
DTC	*Dictionnaire de Théologie Catholique*
EMQ	*Evangelical Missions Quarterly*
ERE	*Encyclopaedia of Religion and Ethics*
ERT	Evangelical Review of Theology
ET	English translation
Eusebius, *HE*	Eusebius, *Historia Ecclesiastica*
Eusebius, *PE*	Eusebius, *Praeparatio Evangelica*
FRLANT	*Forschungen zur Religion und Literatur des alten und neuen Testaments*
GCS	*Die Griechischen Christlichen Schriftsteller der ersten drei Jahrhunderte*
GNB	*Good News Bible*
Goodspeed, *Index*	E.J. Goodspeed (ed.), *Index Apologeticus sive Clavis Iustini Martyris Operum aliorumque Apologetarum pristinorum*
HTR	*Harvard Theological Review*
IRM	*International Review of Missions*
JICH	*Journal of Imperial and Commonwealth History*
JRA	*Journal of Religion in Africa (Religion en Afrique)*
JTS	*Journal of Theological Studies*

JTSA	*Journal of Theology for Southern Africa*
LCC	*Library of Christian Classics*
LCL	*Loeb Classical Library*
LMS	London Missionary Society
LSJ	*A Greek-English Lexicon,* ed. by H.G. Liddell & R. Scott; rev. edn. by Sir H.S. Jones
LXX	Septuagint (Greek translation of the Old Testament)
NCB	*New Century Bible*
NovT	*Novum Testamentum*
NRT	*Nouvelle Revue Théologique*
NSH	*The New Schaff-Herzog Encyclopaedia of Religious Knowledge;* based on 3rd edn of *Real-Encyklopädie für protestantische Theologie und Kirche*
OCD	*The Oxford Classical Dictionary (2nd edn)*
PACLA	Pan-African Christian Leadership Assembly
PG	J.P. Migne, *Patrologia Graeca*
PGL	*A Patristic Greek Lexicon,* ed. by G.W.H. Lampe,
PW	A. Pauly and G. Wissowa, *Real-Encyklopädie der classischen Alterumswissenschaft*
RAC	*Reallexikon für Antike und Christentum*
RCA	*Revue du Clergé Africain*
RHE	*Revue d'Histoire Ecclésiastique*
RHPR	*Revue d'Histoire et de Philosophie Religieuses*
RSR	*Recherches de Science Religieuse*
SIM	Sudan Interior Mission
TNDT	*Theological Dictionary of the New Testament* (ET of *Theologisches Wörterbuch zum Neuen Testament*)
TU	*Texte und Untersuchungen zur Geschichte der altchristlicher Literatur*
VC	*Vigiliae Christianae*
WCC	World Council of Churches
ZNW	*Zeitschrift für die Neutestamentliche Wissenschaft*

PREFACE

This book is, with the exception of editorial revisions in parts, the substance of a thesis which I presented for the Degree of Doctor of Philosophy at the University of Aberdeen in July 1983.

My interest in the theme of Gospel and Culture, which forms the background to the treatment I have given, is rooted in the development of my own Christian self-understanding. From quite early in my Christian conversion experience, I have felt the need to seek a clarification for myself of how the abiding Gospel of Jesus Christ relates to the inescapable issues and questions which arise from the Christian's *cultural* existence in the world, and how this relationship is achieved without injury to the integrity of the Gospel.

In the theological circles of my formative years as a Christian convert, the usual approach to the question of Gospel and Culture was to seek the appropriate response solely from the Scriptures, particularly of the New Testament. Only gradually did it become obvious to me that this important Scriptural orientation needed to be given an equally valid *historical* dimension, historical to the extent that it took serious account of the developments and responses of Christians of other periods in the Christian story, quite apart from the historical realities that link the problems of our modern context to other contexts in the Christian past. The weakness for me of the "purely" Scriptural orientation is the assumption that the historical tradition of the Church has little value in interpreting the realities of our modern Christian existence.

My discovery of the value of Christian history for understanding the questions of modern Christianity had a lot to do with the writing and teaching of the person who eventually became the supervisor of my research, Professor Andrew F. Walls, Head of the Department of Religious Studies and Director of the Centre for the Study of Christianity in the Non-Western World, then at the University of Aberdeen. From its inception to its completion, my research enjoyed Prof. Walls' continuous and sustained interest

xi

and guidance. I came to see the work in one sense as a tribute to him; and my earnest hope was that the finished product would be worthy of one who was in every way a great teacher, a truly *reverendissimus magister*. It was from Prof. Walls that I learnt to appreciate that if I looked closely enough into the concerns of modern African theology, it was possible to wake one day and find myself in the second century of the Christian era! Since the completion of the work for this book, I have often returned to that realisation.

It is a special delight for me that Prof. Walls warmly welcomed the results of my research, and I wish to record my deepest gratitude to him for his generous commendation of my book.

In preparing the thesis text for publication, I wondered whether the discussions of the second-century thinkers and the modern African writers might be interlaced. The benefit of such a presentation would have been to keep the parallels, analogues and comparisons between the two eras consistently fresh in the reader's mind. In the end, I decided that the chapters should be left in their present order. Whilst the book seeks to make a contribution to the understanding of modern African Christianity, it seeks to do so by situating twentieth-century African theology within the organic tradition of Christian theology as a whole. Accordingly, the book attempts to remove African theology from the historical limbo in which it has often been held, caught between African "non-Christian" beliefs and values on the one hand, and Western "Christian" ideas on the other. By focusing on the problems of forging Christian identity in the context of the religious pluralisms of the second century of the Christian era and modern Africa, I wish to suggest that it is possible to read the Christian Fathers in their contexts with new eyes! It is possible to ask fresh questions of the Christian tradition of the past, questions which can in turn illuminate the task of constructing local theologies and the doing of theology in our religiously pluralistic modern world.

In a work of this nature, the author's debt to others is always extensive. My indebtedness to Prof. Andrew Walls has already been noted. I also enter a word of gratitude to Prof. Adrian Hastings of Leeds University (then of the Department of Religious Studies, Aberdeen) for much stimulation and a keen interest in my subject, and for making available material on the Roman Catholic "side" of the African Christian story. I must also thank the staff of the Aberdeen University Library, particularly of the Inter-Library Loan Department, for the dedication with which they pursued for me material not available locally. In this same connection I also record my gratitude to my friend Rev. Philip Kivuva Muinde of Aberdeen, through whose kindness I was able to have access to some of the writings of Rev. Prof. John Mbiti. Prof. Mbiti himself kindly granted me an interview, and I hereby return thanks. It is profoundly gratifying that Prof. Mbiti has accepted my interpretation of his intellectual career and theological writings.

I trust that all the other authors whose works formed the subject of my study – both those who have already joined "the cloud of witnesses" and those yet to do so – will find my interpretation just. It is a happy feeling to know that with my own calling into Christian ministry, I was being associated with such an honourable company of advocates and witnesses of the eternal Gospel of our Lord and Saviour Jesus Christ.

A special word of thanks goes to the Presbyterian Church of Ghana in which I am a minister, and to the church's partners in Germany, the Evangelisches Missionswerk in Südwest-deutschland (EMS), the Evangelical Lutheran Church of Württemberg, both in Stuttgart, for their generous assistance and support through the several years spent on research and writing in Aberdeen, and subsequently for grants awarded to make this publication possible. I mention in particular, for their interest in the "career" of this book in its various phases from research to publication, the following persons: the late Moderator, Very Rev. G.K. Sintim-Misa, former Moderator, Very Rev. I.H. Frempong, former Synod Clerk, Rev. A.K. Sah, former Secretary for Inter-Church and Ecumenical Relations, Rev. S.K. Aboa, former Africa Secretary at EMS, Rev. Dr. Hans-Jürgen Becken, the General Secretary of EMS, Rev. Dr. Jorg Schnellbach and the current Africa Secretary, Rev. Dorothea Margenfeld, and Oberkirchenrat, Dr. Walter Arnold and Rev. Albrecht Hauser, both of the Department of Mission and Ecumenical Relations of the Church of Württenberg.

My thanks also to the Board of Mission of the Netherlands Reformed Church in Oestgeest for their assistance towards the costs of publication. I mention especially the Africa Secretary, Rev. Pier Magré, for his consistently keen interest in my work. The Board of Mission was particularly desirous of seeing that the book is made easily available to seminaries and theological colleges in Africa.

I record also my gratitude to my friend Dr. Iwan Russell-Jones who helped me with proof-reading of the original thesis. The administrative burden of preparing the thesis text for publication was energetically undertaken by Rev. Dr. Christopher Sugden of Regnum Books, Oxford. Through the several years which this task was to involve, Chris kept the process on track in the face of technical difficulties and frustrations which, at one point, included the loss in the post of the whole edited manuscript! To Chris, my fellow directors of the Oxford Centre for Mission Studies and the International Fellowship of Evangelical Mission Theologians, owners of Regnum Books, I record my gratitude for their unfailing encouragement and for the acceptance of my book in the new series of studies in mission.

I am also most grateful to Helen Nunn at the Oxford Centre who "keyboarded" the manuscript for printing, and to the Rev. Norman Hillyer for creating the indexes and for proof-reading.

It is customary in all writing to acknowledge one's indebtedness to one's spouse. In this case, I do so with full gladness. Throughout the whole research period I enjoyed Gillian's constant encouragement and comfort. In the midst of her varied responsibilities, which included her own research obligations, she managed to make time to transform often untidy manuscripts into superb typescripts. When it came to preparing the thesis for publication the task of the initial editing of the text again fell upon her! Without her dedication and consistent labour of love on my behalf, the book would have taken much longer to produce.

Towards the end of the original writing period in Aberdeen, our son Timothy Yaw was born, bringing his own dose of delight and delay to the completion of the thesis. Subsequently, upon our return to Ghana, our second son, Daniel Kwabena, was born, whilst Gillian was engaged on the editing of the thesis. Both, together with Mama, have had active roles in affecting Dada's work! Appropriately then, to a most devoted wife and to two very delightful sons, this book is dedicated.

Akropong-Akuapem, Ghana   ***Kwame Bediako***
September 1991

SUMMARY

This book seeks to bring together two eras and contexts of Christian history and attempts to show the relevance of the insights and achievements of the one context for the other. It is hoped that, in the process, the work makes a contribution to the study of Christian history as an organic entity.

The basic argument which underlies the various chapters is that the development of theological concern and the formulation of theological questions are closely linked as an inevitable by-product of a process of Christian self-definition. In this sense, how certain problems assume a priority of a group of writers, is illuminated by the view of Christian self-identity that a particular writer takes, or which is shared by that group of writers. Christian identity, therefore, emerges as an essential ingredient of the whole process that results in clearly defined theological interests. The argument of the thesis, accordingly, attempts to validate the claim that theology is called to deal always with culturally-rooted questions. Furthermore, the approach adopted makes it possible to study theological ideas through the questionings and encounters in the lives and achievements of particular Christian writers; in this way also the theoretical conclusions that are drawn are derived from actual Christian existence.

In a brief *Introduction*, an attempt is made to establish the validity of the basic argument of the book for the two eras of Christian history treated, namely, modern African Christianity and Graeco-Roman Christianity of the second century. The parallels between the two contexts are set forth, and the importance of the correlation, particularly for a correct interpretation of modern African theology in the post-missionary era, is shown.

In line with the methodological principle of setting the authors' theological ideas in the contexts in which they were developed, in *Chapter One* I make a study of the cultural and "ideological" framework in which early Hellenistic Christian self-definition was achieved. The specific questions with which Hellenistic Christian thinkers had to struggle are shown, therefore, to have been closely related to the intellectual and spiritual forces that operated in their world. It is against this historical and cultural background that the viewpoints and achievements of the individual writers are assessed in the remaining chapters of *Part One* of the book.

Tatian (*Chapter Two*), though in one sense belonging to Syriac Christianity, yet belongs to Hellenistic Christianity by virtue of his *Oration Addressed to the Greeks*. In spite of his intense renunciation of Hellenistic culture, he bequeathed to Hellenistic Christianity his chronological demonstration of the priority of Moses and the Old Testament (hence of the Christian tradition connected with it) to Greek institutions and learning. By thus vindicating the Barbarians against their "cultured despisers" the Greeks, Tatian enabled Christians of Hellenistic culture to feel at home in their world for he provided the intellectual grounds for countering the charge of Christian rootlessness in history.

Tertullian's concerns (*Chapter Three*) in relation to the cultural witness to Graeco-Roman culture move in a similar direction to Tatian's, but with a difference. Unlike Tatian, Tertullian belonged well within Graeco-Roman culture and yet he maintained an equally profound and religiously-motivated distance from the culture. Tertullian's major concern was not so much how the Christian Gospel might be made relevant to the world, as how Christian truth was to be defended, and protected from the world conceived of as "demonic". Tertullian, therefore, represents the "negative" response of the Christian to the cultural tradition in which he stands.

Justin and Clement of Alexandria (*Chapters Four and Five*) represent the more "positive" response to Graeco-Roman tradition. Whilst Justin did the basic ground-clearing work aimed at securing the rights of Christian revelation in the context of rival claims and against its misrepresentations, it fell to Clement to seek to unify Christian insights and what he considered worthy in the Hellenistic tradition into an integrated account of reality, with Christ at its head as the ultimate hermeneutical key to the entire religious history of mankind.

The modern African story which forms the subject of *Part Two* presents some peculiar characteristics, in view of the quality of European-African relations reaching back into the era of the Slave Trade, the corresponding effect of this "inhuman traffic" on the European image of Africa and its eventual transference into European scholarship relating to African peoples. Accordingly, in

Chapter Six, I discuss the intellectual and spiritual forces that shaped the missionary outreach into Africa from the modern West and seek to show, particularly, the *theological legacy* of this missionary enterprise on the emergent African theological consciousness. The main argument of the chapter is that the ethnocentricism of a large part of the missionary enterprise not only prevented sufficient understanding of African religious tradition, but also led to a *theological* misapprehension of the nature of the Christian Gospel itself. African theology in the post-missionary era, therefore, is as much a response to missionary underestimation of the value of African pre-Christian religious tradition, as it is an *African* theological response to the specific and more enduring issues of how the Christian Gospel relates to African culture. Thus modern African Theology emerges as a theology of African Christian identity.

In the "variety of African responses" studied, E. Bolaji Idowu (*Chapter Seven*) represents most distinctly the affirmation of the continuity of God in African experience from the pre-Christian heritage into Christian confession. It is around this major thrust of his literary career that, it is suggested, his fiercely "African" churchmanship and his concern for indigeneity generally, are to be understood. Idowu's greatest achievement is in his vindication of an internal monotheism underlying African pre-Christian religious tradition.

John S. Mbiti (*Chapter Eight*) presents a more settled and eirenical approach to the theological legacy of the missionary past. Accordingly, whilst he is equally keen that an authentically African appropriation of the Christian Gospel should take place, his literary output has been in the direction of an elucidation of the theological meaning of the pre-Christian heritage as an integral part of the African Christian consciousness. By his sustained argument that the religious heritage constituted a *praeparatio evangelica,* Mbiti is able to root the unity in African experience not so much in the pre-Christian religion and its possible affinities with Christian ideas, as in the unity and "geographical" universality of Christ. By this "elevated Christological perspective", Mbiti's outlook approaches that of Justin and Clement in the earlier period.

Mulago gwa Cikala Musharhamina (*Chapter Nine*) is eminently suited to represent the African francophone response to the missionary history and the Christian Gospel within the Roman Catholic tradition of Christianity. With a literary career which reaches into the very beginnings of creative theological initiative among Africa's Catholic intellectuals, Mulago's major achievement has been to show consistently that African pre-Christian tradition does possess a coherent body of beliefs and symbols and interpretations of life which alone can provide the foundation for an authentic African Catholic Christianity. The case for an *African* Theology, of which he emerges as an acknowledged promoter, therefore also implies the acceptance of this African (or Bantu, in his particular instance) *vision du monde.*

Byang Kato (*Chapter Ten*) was most notable as the dissenting voice in the chorus of positive evaluations of the African pre-Christian religious heritage. But in Kato's case, his response was complicated by a theological posture which rendered his appreciation of the heritage from the past problematic. His great achievement, however, consisted in a persistent affirmation of the centrality of the Bible in the theological task. Kato thus contributed a viewpoint of cardinal importance, even though his own acultural conception of theology in fact defeated the very purpose of theology as the struggle with culturally-rooted questions.

In the Conclusion (*Chapter Eleven*) I bring together the theological concerns of the early and the modern contexts into an analogous relationship and use the achievements of the former as a means of clarifying what may yet need to engage the attention of African Theology in the future. In particular, pursuing the analogy with the achievement of early Hellenistic Christian thought, I indicate the need for a response to the emergent African intellectual anti-Christian heritage in a way that should achieve greater interpretative depth and especially set in better perspective the blemishes of the African religious past.

The "Tertullianic" viewpoint of Byang Kato must be given due weight here; but so also must the evidence of a firmly established *Christian* religious commitment in the African Church. In other words, African "academic theology" may need to pay even greater attention to the Church "at the grass roots" where the discovery of Christianity as "a historical category" in the African experience, as in the early Hellenistic experience, seems already to have been made at the specific level of religious apprehension.

It can be expected that a fuller integration of this discovery into African Theology is only a matter of time, thus confirming that the early Christian experience amid Graeco-Roman culture and the modern African Christian experience belong to one and the same story.

Introduction

The Question of Identity as a Key to Understanding the Concerns of Christian Theology in Modern Africa and in the Second Century AD

Modern African Theology and its agenda: the meaning of the pre-Christian heritage as a prime concern.

Since the early 1960s saw "the first flowering of 'African Theology'",[1] one of the more difficult problems which this literature has raised has been how to account for the fact that "the chief non-Biblical reality with which the African theologian must struggle is the non-Christian religious tradition of his own people", and that African Theology soon became "something of a dialogue between the African Christian scholar and the perennial religions and spiritualities of Africa".[2] There is no issue so crucial as the understanding of this heightened interest in the African pre-Christian religious tradition, if Africa's theologians are to be interpreted correctly and their achievement duly recognised.

The concern with the meaning of the African religious heritage quite early assumed such proportions that Adrian Hastings ventured to suggest that one effect of this concentration of interest was that "areas of traditional Christian doctrine which are not reflected in the African past disappear or are marginalised".[3] In an article published in 1974, Prof. Kwesi Dickson (of Ghana), himself a Biblical scholar with interests in the relation of the Bible to African life and thought, urged that "African theologians who are searching for an African Theology can... hardly afford to base their exercise solely on African religion and culture and Western theology".[4] Dickson argued that "methodological guide-lines for those seeking to relate Christianity to African life and thought" lay to hand in "the questionings and rejections and adaptations that brought about the shaping of the distinctive Hebrew religion which provided the setting for the Gospel", and so finally felt able to insist that African students of theology should not only "be *au fait* with African life and thought and with Western theology", but "equal-ly... be at home in the Biblical material".[5]

In spite of Dickson's claim about the links between African Theology and Western theology, the departure of the modern African theological interest from modern Western theology could not be more pronounced. It is not hard to see what had happened; the very religious tradition which was generally deemed unworthy of serious theological consideration in missionary times, now oc-cupied a central place on the African theological agenda.Conse-quently, even though Africa's theologians would make use of categories of description inherited from the Western Christian theological tradition, they were obviously setting themselves to give to the African pre-Christian religious heritage an interpreta-tion which the European missionary understanding of Africa was, on the whole, unable to achieve. The real significance of modern African theological writing lies in the attitude that is taken towards the African religious past.

Adrian Hastings has rightly observed that "the central theme of this literature" has been "the nature of the traditional religion of Africa and its relationship of continuity rather than discon-tinuity with Christian belief".[6] This fact is important and has been underscored by Archbishop Desmond Tutu in his appreciation of the achievement of "African Theology":

"African theologians have set about demonstrating that the African religious experience and heritage were not illusory and that they should have formed the vehicle for conveying the Gospel verities to Africa... It was vital for the African's self-respect that this kind of rehabilitation of his religious heritage should take place. It is the theological counterpart of what has happened in, say, the study of African history. It has helped to give the lie to the supercilious but tacit assumption that religion and history in Africa date from the advent in that continent of the white man. It is reassuring to know that we have had a genuine knowledge of God and that we have had our own ways of communicating with deity, ways which meant that we were able to speak authentically as ourselves and not as pale imitations of others. It means that we have a great store from which we can fashion new ways of speaking to and about God, and new styles of worship consistent with our new faith."[7]

This fact alone should suffice to make African theologians interesting for what they are in themselves, and should also lead to an investigation of the theological significance that attaches to the issues with which they have had to struggle.

Towards a new interpretative paradigm (1): the "Christian identity" problem

It is arguable that by developing their interest in the African pre-Christian religious heritage into a major theological concern, Africa's theologians have moved in the direction anticipated by some for Christian theology in Africa in the post-missionary era. Writing in 1960, Bishop Bengt Sundkler, who had served the cause of Christian mission in Southern and Eastern Africa, suggested:

> "A theologian who with the Apostle is prepared to become to the Jews as a Jew, to them that are without law, as without law, and *therefore*, unto Africans as an African, must needs start with the fundamental facts of the African interpretation of existence and the universe."[8]

It is true that Sundkler was in no doubt that "theology, in essence, is to understand the fact of Christ". But he was careful enough to point out that "theology in Africa has to interpret this Christ in terms that are relevant and essential to African existence". Consequently, it was in "the myths of African religions" that Sundkler believed could be found "certain broad patterns of which theology in Africa must take account".[9] What Sundkler's suggestion amounted to, in fact, was that the interpretation, albeit from a *Christian* stand-point, of the African pre-Christian heritage of ideas and wisdom, was an essential and integral part of the task of theology in the African Church. It is perhaps not surprising, therefore, that whereas Sundkler saw the kind of theological encounter he described as emerging "not in tones of academic theology, but in tones, and overtones, of preaching and song and movement",[10] it was the practitioners of "academic theology" who seem to have taken him most seriously.[11]

To the extent that African Theology's attempt at "rehabilitating Africa's rich cultural heritage and religious consciousness"[12] has been made as a self-consciously Christian and theological effort, it can be said to have been an endeavour to demonstrate the true character of African Christian identity. Had this realisation been more to the fore in the debate about the *possibility* of an African

Theology, it is conceivable that some of the scepticism that greeted the first fruits of African theological scholarship would have been found to be unnecessary. It has not been generally recognised that the kind of study that the African theologian makes of African religious tradition cannot be compared with "a clinical observation of the sort one might make about Babylonian religion; he is handling dynamite, his own past, his people's present".[13] One effect of thus failing to appreciate the dynamics of African theological scholarship has been a corresponding inability to grasp the significance of African theological writing in its own terms.

Looked at from the standpoint of the context of modern African theologians (that is, as *Christian* scholars), the traditional religions of Africa belong to the African religious past; but this is not so much a chronological past as an "ontological" past. The theological importance of the religious past therefore consists in the fact that together with the profession of the Christian faith, it gives account of the same entity – namely, the history of the religious consciousness of the African Christian. It is in this sense that the theological concern with the African religious heritage becomes an effort aimed at clarifying the nature and meaning of African Christian identity. What is involved is the quest for what Bishop Kenneth Cragg has described as "integrity in conversion, a unity of self in which one's past is genuinely integrated into present commitment. Thus the crisis of repentance and faith that makes us Christians truly integrates what we have been in what we become".[14]

In view of the importance that the issue of African Christian identity has in the development of African theological literature, one might have assumed that the interpretation of the religious heritage from the past through the use of Christian theological categories needed no apology. Since, as has been noted, the concern with the theological meaning of the pre-Christian tradition has taken the form of a dialogue between the African Christian scholar and the religious tradition of his own people, there could be no antecedent inadmissibility relating to the use of concepts and insights from Christian theology for understanding the encounter that was taking place. However, it is precisely on the question of the validity of applying Christian theological categories to the elucidation of African religious experience, that the debate over "African Theology" has been most intense. Thus, whereas sociological, anthropological, as well as purely phenomenological approaches have generally been welcomed, theological perspectives have tended to be treated with suspicion.[15] This has had the effect of obscuring the contribution of Africa's theologians towards the interpretation of what is, in fact, their own religious heritage.

In this regard, Dr Hastings is less helpful when he suggests that the methodology of African Theology has amounted to an attempt to interpret African religious tradition "within the structures of Western theological thought",[16] as if the achievements of Christian scholarship hitherto were intrinsically Western. If "African Christianity has in fact and rightly, two primary sources of inherited wisdom and continuity – Christian revelation and tradition upon the one hand, and African traditional religion upon the other"[17] – then it follows that "Christian revelation and tradition" cannot be conceived of as an autonomous and foreclosed entity, and precluded from African theological thought. Surely the choice must lie with African Theology as to the descriptive categories and the criteria of judgment that it brings to bear upon African reality.[18] Consequently, the distinction made by J.K. Agbeti between "African Theology" as the systematic arrangement of the religious ideas and perceptions derived from African pre-Christian (and pre-Islamic) experience on the one hand, and African Christian Theology on the other,[19] though helpful in theory, is not compelling. This is not to discount the probability that such a systematisation of African pre-Christian religious experience can be achieved. However, that distinction cannot be applied to the highly committed churchmen who constitute the body of Africa's academic theologians so far. It is worth noting that the very writers who have been preoccupied with the nature and meaning of the African religious past are the ones who have been just as concerned to explore ways in which African *Christian* experience may establish its identity within African life itself, and in the Church world-wide. It is the importance of both these concerns as well as their close interrelation in modern African theological writing that effectively argues for the view that the African theologian's concern with the traditional religions of Africa must find its fullest interpretation within the framework of *Christian* theology.

Towards a new interpretative paradigm(2): African theology and Christian history

The methodological framework required for understanding the concerns of African Theology is therefore, *mutatis mutandis,* what Harold W. Turner has outlined for the religious study of African primal religions:

"Cultural, anthropological, psychological, sociological, political and other models have proved their value in the elucidation of the interaction between religions and their milieux. Religion, however, cannot be equated with culture, society, morality, psychic processes or political systems and the distinctive features of religion escape us if we reduce it to any or all of these other categories, no matter how intimately it is interwoven with these aspects of the total reality. We need therefore a religious model for the study of the 'religion' of African religions..."[20]

Behind Dr Turner's methodological recommendations here, there lies his more general concern that African primal religions be recognised and included in the study of the varieties in the human response to the revelations of the Transcendent, on the grounds that "African primal religions form part of the common spiritual heritage of mankind".[21]

Similarly, if "the nature of the field of study must provide the major control over the methods employed",[22] then it would seem that one of the more helpful ways of seeking to understand African theologians is to place them in continuum with the historical movement that has produced and is likely to produce in the future, people like them, that is, in Christian history. In other words, we are likely to gain greater insight into the nature and scope of the issues with which Africa's theologians have been wrestling, if we acknowledge that we are studying part of the history of the interaction of the Gospel of Christ with the religious traditions and experiences of men and women. If one maintains an organic view of Christian history,[23] then the study of the variety of modern African responses to the Gospel of Christ in relation to, say, earlier patterns, is legitimate. It allows us to examine and appreciate some of the urges of "essential Christianity"[24] as these manifest themselves in different cultural contexts. The "particular" is within the "universal", and by studying the dynamics of African Christian self-understanding, and earlier responses in other historical milieux, each in its own context, we are also learning something about Christian self-understanding as a whole. This means that it becomes necessary to inquire into the extent to which the theological concerns of the modern African Christian writers reflect some of the fundamental questions and dilemmas which are raised for the Christian consciousness as such. Only then shall we also understand what is unique in the African experience. Looked at from the perspective of an organic view of Christian history, therefore, the encounter of the Christian faith with the African religious heritage ceases to be the meeting of *Western* culture and *African* values. Rather, since we have to do with "Christ... conversing with the soul of Africa",[25] it becomes important to insist that some of the criteria for understanding the nature of that encounter can be discovered in the history of the people of God and His Christ. In the process, the theological questions thrown up by the modern African context may be found to be not "qualitatively new" but rather new manifestations of phenomena which are "identifiable elsewhere in the Christian story".[26]

The phase of Christian history which offers the most instructive parallels to the modern African context is the beginning of Hellenistic Christianity in the early Roman Empire. With Christianity virtually transposed from its original Jewish matrix and fast becoming a predominantly Gentile phenomenon, it was from the circles of Gentile Christian thought that a significant body of Christian literature emerged, in which the problem of Christian identity and the nature of continuity with the pre-Christian tradition began to be faced in earnest.

Traditionally, the early Christian writers with whom we shall be concerned have been studied largely for their contribution or otherwise to the development of Christian doctrine. Accordingly, their careers have tended to be assessed in terms of their relation to orthodoxy or heresy. However, looked at from the standpoint of the Christian identity problem and how it was faced in relation to the issues raised for the Christian consciousness by Graeco-Roman culture in which they all shared to varying degrees, these writers become more interesting in themselves as persons. Their careers gain a significance beyond questions of dogma alone; they become important as witnesses to a more enduring problem: the Christian's response to the religious past as well as to the cultural tradition generally in which one stands, and the significance of that response for the development of theological answers to the culturally-rooted questions of the context.

Like their counterparts in the African Church of the twentieth century, the Christian writers of the early period manifested all the signs of being the product of and belonging to a period of transition. They displayed bold initiatives in actual theological production, but were also marked by a certain polemicism, and some uncertainty as to their methods of argumentation. With their clearly defined religious convictions, there went a cautious feeling after a sound basis for ways of integrating "old" and "new" in the light of their new faith. As with the African context, the reader comes upon material which derives from more than a merely intellectual exercise; confronted with the task of vindicating Christian identity in relation to Graeco-Roman culture which had its own religious and intellectual heritage, they were having to work out that identity in terms of a religious conviction whose very ground of appeal appeared to lie outside of their culture. It was in the process of the adjustments, adaptations and rejections that took place, that some of the formative factors in the Christian theological tradition were clarified and bequeathed to later generations.

The suggestion that parallels do exist between early Christianity and modern manifestations of the Christian faith, particularly in the Churches of Africa and Asia, has been made by other students of Christian history and Christian thought, and I am grateful to those scholars for their insights into the nature of my subject. As early as 1920, Campbell N. Moody drew parallels between early Gentile converts on the one hand, and Chinese Christians of the early twentieth century.[27] John Foster, one-time professor of Ecclesiastical History in the University of Glasgow, not only considered "the Younger Churches [of Africa and Asia] the Early Church of our day",[28] but also consistently used insights from the nature of Indian Christianity in the twentieth century in his interpretation of the missionary preaching of the first three centuries of the Christian era.[29] The relevance of the patristic context and achievement for the study of modern Christian history has also been urged by André Benoit,[30] whilst J.D.Y. Peel has pointed to some earlier models (including Christian expansion within the early Roman Empire) for understanding the comparable process in modern Africa.[31] But it is to two seminal studies by A.F. Walls[32] that I owe my understanding of the dynamics of the encounter in life and thought between the Christian Gospel and culture, and especially the interplay of the two forces which Walls describes as "making Christianity at home in the life of a people" and "the conforming of a Church's life to standards outside of itself",[33] and how these forces manifest themselves in the theology of early Hellenistic Christianity and in modern African theology. I have developed some of the ideas and insights I have received, and also offered some contributions of my own. With the exception of a passing reference to the relevance of "the kind of re-interpretation" of the Christian faith in the Graeco-Roman world to the modern African theological enterprise, in an essay by Samuel G. Kibicho (of Kenya),[34] I am not aware of any African student in the field of Christian history and theology who has brought together detailed studies of early patristic and modern African theological thought in the way that I have attempted.

Celsus and all his friends: the significance of anti-Christian polemic

In investigating the parallels between the two groups of Christian writers, I have concentrated upon the Christian material; anti-Christian polemic has been introduced only incidentally. Paradoxically, it is the development of an African anti-Christian polemic in response to African Theology that further heightens the value of the correlation between early Hellenistic Christian theology and modern African theology. It is one of the most extraordinary features of the African scene that the bitterest critics of African Theology are non-Christian African intellectuals who, feeling no affinity with the quest for African Christian identity, can comfortably dismiss the Christian interpretation of African religious tradition as irrelevant to Africa. For Okot p'Bitek, by far the most incisive of these critics, the Christian interpretation of African religious tradition involves inevitably the introduction of "Greek metaphysical conceptions into African religious thought" and is the work of "intellectual smugglers".[35] He singles out a leading African theologian, John Mbiti, for criticism, in view of Mbiti's efforts at systematising African religious ideas into a "philosophy"; if Mbiti considers that being African is a sufficient justification for his endeavour,[36] Okot p'Bitek has a ready response:

> "The writer did not add that he was also a Christian and a priest, which is more important, as what comes out of his works is more Christian than African."[37]

In the epilogue which he contributed to Okot p'Bitek's book, Ali Mazrui, the former Professor of Political Science at Makerere University, Uganda, formulated his own criticism of African Theology for Christianising African religious tradition:

> "Why should there be a constant search to fit African conceptions of God into notions like omnipotence and omnipresence and omniscience? Why should there be a constant exploration for one super-god in African societies, as if one was trying to discover an inner monotheism in traditional African belief systems? Why should African students of religion be so keen to demonstrate that the Christian God had already been understood and apprehended by Africans before the missionaries came?"[38]

What both Okot p'Bitek and Ali Mazrui demonstrate by their searching criticism, is that they have understood the essential thrust of the African theological enterprise of the last two decades.

Their perceptive observations of the Christianisation of African pre-Christian tradition may be taken as an indication of the success that African Theology has in fact achieved.

However, Okot p'Bitek and Ali Mazrui are not offering a commendation; to the extent that African Theology has succeeded in "distorting" African religious tradition, they dissociate themselves from its achievement, and so indirectly they force Africa's theologians to consider all the more seriously the problem of Christian identity in the African context. Here, Christian history comes full circle and Africa's Christian theologians are brought to confront the modern African counterparts of Celsus and other informed critics of the Christian movement in the Graeco-Roman world. There is some evidence that Celsus wrote his book, *The True Doctri*ne, in response to Justin's Christianisation of the Hellenistic philosophical traditions.[39] To Celsus, Christianity was unacceptable fundamentally because of its foreign-ness to the Hellenistic outlook. The note of the foreign-ness of Christianity will be sounded again and often in Africa. If African theologians are to answer their critics effectively, a clear definition of African Christian identity and how it integrates into an adequate sense of African selfhood will doubtless form part of the response. The theological quests of the last two decades will thereby have been vindicated.

******

Considerations of space make it necessary that only a restricted number of Christian writers from the two contexts be included in this study. As a result, some interesting personalities have been omitted from the treatment.

However, the choice of Tatian, Tertullian, Justin and Clement of Alexandria for the early period, and of E. Bolaji Idowu, John Mbiti, Mulago gwa Cikala Musharhamina and Byang Kato, for the modern period, has been made to provide sufficient breadth and diversity of interest to ensure that the study is as far as possible representative of the two contexts. The order in which the authors are treated is not meant to indicate chronological sequence. The specific points of interest and significance which each author exhibits have been argued in the appropriate chapters.

The Conclusion (Chapter Eleven) seeks to assess the relevance of the achievement of the early period for the modern effort.

Footnotes to the Prolegomena

1. Adrian Hastings, *A History of African Christianity, 1950-1975*, Cambridge: Cambridge University Press, 1979, p.231.

2. Adrian Hastings, *African Christianity – An Essay in Interpretation*, London: Geoffrey Chapman, 1976, pp.50f.

3. *Ibid.*, p.52.

4. K.A. Dickson, "'Hebrewisms in West Africa' – The Old Testament and African Life and Thought", in *Legon Journal of the Humanities*, vol.1, 1974, pp.32f.

5. *Ibid.*, p.33. Cf. Prof. Dickson's survey article on "Research in the history of religions in West Africa" in *Religion*, August 1975, in which he expressed regret that West Africa had not produced enough researchers in the area of "Biblical Ideas and Customs". The favoured fields of study and research according to Dickson were African Traditional Religion and Ethics, Interaction of Religions and Independent Churches.

6. Adrian Hastings, *A History of African Christianity, 1950-1975*, p.231.

7. Desmond Tutu, "Whither African Theology?" in Edward Fasholé-Luke *et al.* (eds), *Christianity in Independent Africa,* London: Rex Collings, 1978, p.366.

8. Bengt Sundkler, *The Christian Ministry in Africa,* London: SCM Press, 1962, p.100. Emphasis in original. This book is the abridged version of the book of the same title published in 1960 as a study of theological education in Africa.

9. *Ibid.*, p.99.

10. *Ibid.,* p.116.

11. See Harry Sawyerr, *Creative Evangelism – Towards a New Christian Encounter with Africa,* London: Lutterworth Press, 1968. Prof. Sawyerr, who begins his first chapter by recalling the words of Bishop Sundkler quoted above, then goes on to end the paragraph as follows: "We shall in the following pages attempt a synoptic consideration of the problems involved in adopting his [Sundkler's] approach to which we fully subscribe" (p.13).

12. Desmond Tutu, *op.cit.*, p.367.

13. A.F. Walls, "The Gospel as the Prisoner and Liberator of Culture" in *Faith and Thought*, 108 (1-2), 1981, p.49; also in *Missionalia*, vol.10, no.3, November, 1982, p.103.

14. Kenneth Cragg, "Conversion and convertibility – with special reference to Muslims" in John R.W. Stott and Robert Coote (eds), *Down to Earth – Studies in Christianity and Culture,* Grand Rapids: Eerdmans, 1980, p.194.

15. See, for instance, Benjamin C. Ray, *African Religions – Symbols, Ritual and Community,* Englewood Cliffs, New Jersey: Prentice Hall Inc., 1976, pp.14ff.

16. Adrian Hastings, *African Christianity – An Essay in Interpretation,* p.52. My emphasis. Cf. Benjamin C. Ray, *op.cit.*, p.15. To that extent, one wonders whether the call by Harold W. Turner in his "The Way forward in the religious study of African primal religions" in *JRA*, vol.12, fasc.1, 1981, p.12, for the use of the "specialist contributions of the phenomenology and history of religions" in order to achieve "interpretative depth" in the study of African religious traditions, might not also be seen as yet another instance of the use of the structures of Western thought applied to African religion.

17. Adrian Hastings, *African Christianity – An Essay in Interpretation,* p.52.

18. The rightness of applying *theological* categories to African reality has

been defended by Harold W. Turner, *op.cit.*, p.12: "There is... a place for theologically orientated studies (Western or any other) of all aspects of reality and African religions can claim no exception from this."

19. J.K. Agbeti, "African Theology: What it is" in *Presence*, vol.5, no.3, 1972, p.7. For a discussion of Agbeti's view, see Aylward Shorter, *African Christian Theology*, London: Geoffrey Chapman, 1975, p.27.

20. Harold W. Turner, *op.cit.*, p.13.

21. *Ibid.*, p.14.

22. *Ibid.*, p.1.

23. See the wide-ranging introductory essay, "The Study of Church History" in Hubert Jedin *et al.* (eds), *History of the Church*, vol.1 (= Karl Baus, *Handbook of Church History, 1*), London: Burns and Oates, 1965.

24. John Foster, *Then and Now – The Historic Church and the Younger Churches*, London: SCM Press, 1942, p.63 and passim.

25. John V. Taylor, *The Primal Vision – Christian Presence amid African Religion*, London: SCM Press, 1963, p.7.

26. A.F. Walls, "The Anabaptists of Africa? The Challenge of the African Independent Churches" in *Occasional Bulletin of Missionary Research*, vol.3, no.2, April 1979, p.48.

27. See Campbell N. Moody, *The Mind of the Early Converts*, London: Hodder and Stoughton, 1920.

28. See John Foster, *Then and Now – The Historic Church and the Younger Churches*, p.65.

29. See John Foster, *After the Apostles – Missionary Preaching of the First Three Centuries*, London: SCM Press, 1951. Professor Foster observed, commenting on his work: "Perhaps one of my original contributions may be keeping in mind throughout, the light thrown upon the Early Church by situations... in the Younger Churches" (preface, p.11).

30. André Benoit, *L'Actualité des Pères de l'Eglise* (Cahiers théologiques, 47), Neuchâtel: Editions Delachaux et Niestlé, 1961.

31. J.D.Y. Peel, "The Christianisation of African Society: some possible models" in Edward Fasholé-Luke *et al.* (eds), *op.cit.*, pp.443-454.

32. See A.F. Walls, "Towards understanding Africa's place in Christian history" in J.S. Pobee (ed), *Religion in a Pluralistic Society (Essays presented to Professor C.G. Baëta)*, Leiden: E.J. Brill, 1976, pp.180-189; and "Africa and Christian Identity" in *Mission Focus*, vol.6, no.7, November 1978, pp.11-13.

33. A.F. Walls, "Towards understanding Africa's place in Christian history", *op.cit.*, pp.188.

34. See Samuel G. Kibicho, "The Continuity of the African Conception of God into and through Christianity: a Kikuyu case-study" in Edward Fasholé-Luke *et al.* (eds), *op.cit.*, pp.387f.

35. Okot p'Bitek, *African Religions in Western Scholarship*, Kampala: East African Literature Bureau, 1970, p.88.

36. See John S. Mbiti, *African Religions and Philosophy*, London: Heinemann, 1969, pp.1-2.

37. Okot p'Bitek, *op.cit.*, p.108.

38. *Ibid.*, p.125.

39. Carl Andresen, *Logos und Nomos: Die Polemik des Kelsos wider das Christentum*, Berlin: Walter de Gruyter, 1955.

Part One

THE CHRISTIAN GOSPEL AMID GRAECO-ROMAN CULTURE: BARBARISM, HELLENISM AND CHRISTIAN IDENTITY

"To any student primarily concerned with the other religions of the Empire, Christianity stands out as curiously uncompromising, in spite of the attempts of the apologists to represent it as a reasonable Greek philosophy. Against deliberate compromise there stood firmly the intense personal devotion of the many who had found the certainty which they craved, the peace which the Roman Liturgy stresses to this day. *Pax Domini sit semper vobiscum... dona nobis pacem... Domine Jesu Christe qui dixisti Apostolis tuis, Pacem meam relinquo vobis.*"

A.D. Nock, *Early Gentile Christianity and its Hellenistic Background,* p.101

Chapter 1

The Problem of Christian Identity in the Context of Graeco-Roman Culture of the Early Roman Empire

I. "Enemies of the Roman Order"

In *The History of the Decline and Fall of the Roman Empire*, Edward Gibbon pointed to a fundamental distinction between Jews and Christians in the eyes of Graeco-Roman traditionalists, a distinction which laid bare some of the assumptions underlying the attitudes of the critics of Christianity, and which eventually determined the State policy of persecution:

> "The difference between them is simple and obvious, but according to the sentiments of antiquity, it was of the highest importance. The Jews were a *nation*; the Christians were a *sect*; and if it was natural for every community to respect the sacred institutions of their neighbours, it was incumbent on them to persevere in those of their ancestors. The voice of oracles, the precepts of philosophers and the authority of the laws unanimously enforced this national obligation. By their lofty claim to superior sanctity, the Jews might provoke the Polytheists to consider them as an odious and impure race. By disdaining the intercourse of other nations they might deserve their contempt. The laws of Moses might be for the most part frivolous or absurd; yet, since they had been received during many ages by a large society, his followers were justified by the example of mankind; and it was universally acknowledged that they had a right to practise what it would have been criminal in them to reject. But this principle which protected the Jewish synagogue afforded not any favour or security to the primitive Church. By embracing the faith of the Gospel, the Christians incurred the supposed

guilt of an unnatural and unpardonable offence. They dissolved the sacred ties of custom and education, violated the religious institutions of their country, and presumptuously despised whatever their fathers had believed as true, or had reverenced as sacred... It was in vain that the oppressed believer asserted the inalienable rights of conscience and private judgment. Though his situation might excite the pity, his arguments could never reach the understanding, either of the philosophic or of the believing part of the Pagan world."[1]

Thus, whilst the relation of Christians to Jews was for Christians an important factor and "a necessary component of what it meant to be a Christian",[2] in the eyes of their enemies it looked problematic. The unavoidable dilemma to be faced by Christians of Graeco-Roman culture well into the third and even the fourth century AD lay in the fact that, prejudice apart, their most informed critics and opponents considered their religious outlook and very existence in the society as a sheer impossibility. Theirs was seen as a "new and solitary vagary of which there is no trace in Hellenism or Judaism".[3] Jews may be regarded as loathsome, the "basest of peoples",[4] "famous for their insults to the gods";[5] Jewish religion, in spite of its being "ancient and well established", was included in those that the Emperor Augustus held in contempt.[6] Nevertheless, the Jews were a people with a history and might at worst, insurrection excepted, be left to their own devices.[7] They had a right to exist according to the traditions of their ancestors, even if they "regard as profane all that we hold sacred, and permit all that we abhor".[8] Christianity was a newcomer, with no land to call its own, no history.[9]

It was obvious, therefore, that if Christians of Graeco-Roman culture were to achieve any real measure of valid and settled identity, they needed to come to terms with the various facets of that culture from which they themselves had emerged. For this reason there is more to the study of the fortunes of the Christian movement in the Graeco-Roman world than the political and legal questions which have generally dominated investigations and interpretations of the field. W.H.C. Frend has shown in *Martyrdom and Persecution in the Early Church* that the attitude of Christians themselves and Christian doctrines had as much to do with the titanic conflict which ensued as did the outlook of the authorities and the legal system of the Empire. To that extent, the conflict was more than the encounter of different systems of thought and belief, or a clash of cultures, though these features are found and form part of the story. However, they can be properly understood and appreciated in their dynamism only when we recognise their essentially human and personal dimension.[10] The eventual triumph of Christianity over Graeco-Roman Paganism was more than the unification of disparate elements in a higher religious syncretism;[11] nor is it adequate to suggest that Christianity acquired "the vital power to make it the world movement it became"[12] by adapting itself to the Graeco-Roman world through a break with an earlier identity as a Jewish sect and by the assumption of "the character of one of the salvation-cults of the Hellenistic world". For there is also the fact that men and women of Graeco-Roman culture were willing to identify with, and make their own, a religious tradition and a teaching which were seen as alien to traditional Graeco-Roman values: the *mos maiorum*, the ways of the ancestors, the inherited tradition. The Christians were virtually "turning the world upside down" [ἀναστατῶσαντες], that is, upsetting traditional and accepted patterns of religious allegiance and practice.[13] It is revealing of this upheaval that Tacitus' comments on the champion of republican ideals, Thraesea Paetus, who was forced to commit suicide under Nero, could be applied to the Christians: *Spernit religiones, abrogat leges.*[14]

Thraesea Paetus had refused to take the solemn oath of loyalty to the Emperor at the beginning of the year, and he would not offer sacrifice for the safety of the Emperor, nor did he believe in the divinity of the Emperor's wife, Poppaea, any more than he cared for the deeds of the deified Augustus and Julius.[15] But if Thraesea "spurned the religious rites and broke the laws", his action was the logical result of a political attitude towards Nero, and what that Emperor represented in his eyes. For quite different reasons, the Christians inherited the legacy of Thraesea and others like him, and came to be included among the "enemies of the Roman order".[16] R.M. Grant comments succinctly on this strange Christian inheritance:

"The religious disaffection which in Thraesea's case was apparently a symptom of his political attitude, was for Christians the heart of the matter. They could not accept the gods or the rites of the Graeco-Roman world. They were not concerned with restoring the Roman republic or with any particular form of governmental order. On the practical question of cultus, however, they rejected the demands of Roman civic life."[17]

Therefore, an inescapable element of Christian identity in the early Empire was that they were out of step with the society in general at some vital points. It is this fact, more than anything else, which, as Gibbon suggested, explains "the surprise of the pagans which was soon succeeded by resentment":[18] the Christians "dissolved the sacred ties of custom and education, violated the religious institutions of their country, and presumptuously despised whatever their fathers had believed as true, or had reverenced as sacred".[19] The precarious character of the situation of the Christian has been aptly compared with that of the Gentile proselyte in the Graeco-Roman world; he lacked recognised status in society.[20] By becoming virtual "outsiders" or at best "marginals", Christians easily attracted accusations of crimes bordering on the treasonable, which so often attached to non-conformists in Roman society. Christianity, as it appeared to Roman traditionalists, was "un-Roman".[21] How it was so, and why a religious movement of "the most pious of men" was "exposed to the unjust but dangerous imputation of impiety"[22] is best understood in the light of what their Pagan critics and opponents believed they saw in Christians and in their movement.

II. Through Pagan eyes... a new "superstition"

One might possibly date the first and most important encounter between Christianity and the Roman government in the year AD 30, when Jesus was crucified under the administration of Pontius Pilate in Judaea.[23] It is interesting that the Roman prefect accepted the accusation laid against Jesus, that he claimed to be "the King of the Jews".[24] John's Gospel makes it explicit that the accusing priests set against the alleged claims of Jesus the rule of the Emperor: "We have no king but Caesar".[25] We can only suppose that the charge of sedition implied here may have contributed to Pilate's eventual willingness to hand Jesus over for crucifixion. The Jews had a record of insurrection and religious revolt; Jesus appeared to be in that tradition. Other New Testament references to the encounter of the Christian movement with the Roman authorities reveal a similar tendency on the part of the latter to treat the movement as a sect within Judaism but as harmless, on the whole.[26]

It is probable that *Acts* 18:2 can be correlated with the reference by Suetonius to the expulsion of the Jews from Rome under the Emperor Claudius.[27] If Suetonius' phrase *impulsore Chresto*, in fact indicates the Pagan confusion over *Christus*,[28] then it is not unlikely that the "constant disturbances" among Jews may have centred on discussions about Jesus as the Messiah and related issues. At any rate, a Christian community existed in Rome before

Paul's arrival in the city (cf. *Acts* 28:15), and it seems fair to conclude that to Roman authorities "Christians" were still simply a sect within Judaism. The book of *Acts* closes with Paul in Rome, living "at his own expense", preaching the Kingdom of God and teaching about the Lord Jesus Christ quite openly and unhindered, thus well within what was acceptable in Roman law.[29]

The evidence from *Acts* suggests, therefore, that for the first three decades after the crucifixion of Jesus, Christians appeared to pose no threat to the Roman system. Suspicions of disloyalty, as in the case of Paul and Silas in Macedonia (*Acts* 16:20ff; 17:6f), were apparently soon dispelled. This first Christian record of the expansion of the new movement within the Empire does not give any evidence of hostility from the Imperial authorities towards the people of "the Way".[30] In so far as they were generally regarded as a Jewish religious sect,[31] they would also have enjoyed the favour shown to Jews in general.[32]

It must be supposed, therefore, that the genesis of hostile Pagan attitudes and their hardening into harassment and eventual persecution are related to the emergence and growth of a distinctive Christian identity, distinctive, that is, in Pagan eyes, from the early Jewish connection. This development must in turn be related to the spread of Christianity among non-Jews. Already in the New Testament there are indications of relatively early conversions among Gentiles, even as far as the Imperial household.[33] As Adolf von Harnack notes, Paul indirectly suggests that some who were wise and mighty and of good birth had become Christians[34] (cf. *1 Corinthians* 1:26f). However, it was generally the case that well into the second century people of the lower and depressed classes predominated in the Christian community.[35] The important fact is that the Gospel preaching had been more successful among non-Jews than among Jews[36] and it was only a matter of time and circumstance for this reality and its implications to dawn on Pagan public opinion. The Pagan identification of Christianity will, accordingly, be instructive.

The first reference in Pagan sources which shows that Roman opinion was becoming more "informed" on the identity of Christians, is the punishment of Christians for allegedly causing the fire of Rome in AD 64.[37] Tacitus, writing about fifty years after the event in *ca.* AD 115 was not convinced by the hated Nero's claim that the Christians were in fact responsible for the fire. However, he too disliked the Christians, charging them with criminal intentions and activities.[38] Tacitus does not elaborate on what crimes were imputed to the Christians. However, his designation of the movement as a pernicious superstition is instructive. It is an idea on which the official Pagan attitude to Christianity will come to depend and we must return to it later. It is equally interesting that Tacitus takes pains to point out the Judaean origins of this "evil", thereby linking the movement with an already deeply resented people; the Christians were for Tacitus simply an offshoot of the "basest of peoples" and so were, like them, stigmatised for their hatred of the rest of humanity.[39] Tacitus may well have understood "humanity", *humanum genus,* as the Roman Empire and Graeco-Roman values.[40]

   In point of fact, Tacitus' diction, as Wuilleumier notes, is reminiscent of Sallust's account of the conspiracy of Catiline.[41] If the historian's claim regarding the numbers involved – "a huge crowd" – is to be credited and not treated as "a rhetorical exaggeration",[42] then we have an important Pagan reference to an early rapid growth of the Christian movement.

A similar designation of the Christians, equally marked by personal hostility, is in Suetonius' *Life of Nero.* Suetonius, commenting on Nero's actions in dealing with various abuses in the City, mentions the punishment of Christians. Interestingly, however, without saying anything about the fire of AD 64, he also applies the name superstition to the Christian movement.[43]

   Though he shows less interest in following up the genesis and history of the movement, Suetonius nonetheless notes its novelty. Perhaps even more significant is his association of the new *superstitio* with anti-social and possibly even magical conspiratorial intentions.

   Before we examine what was understood by the term *superstitio* and why it was applied to the Christian movement, a third source for this Pagan designation of Christianity must be mentioned. It occurs in the correspondence of the Younger Pliny, Governor in Bithynia, with the Emperor Trajan. In the well-known exchange relating to what to do about the Christians,[44] the Governor describes the movement as nothing more than "a degenerate sort of cult carried to extravagant lengths".[45] It is worth noting that though the Governor resorted to torture of two women called *ministrae,* probably "deaconesses", he was more puzzled than hostile. This is confirmed by other factors. On the one hand, the Governor associates the unusual phenomenon with possible political agitation and this is attested by his earlier banning of "political societies" and voluntary clubs and associations which could become seed-beds of political disaffection and conspiracy.[46] On the other hand, Pliny seems quite inclined to the view that the Christians might be harmless and innocent persons, and that no crimes might attach to the name Christian.[47] Nevertheless Pliny then asks whether in fact crimes are not associated with the name and this shows just how deeply rooted was the Roman apprehensiveness when faced with any departure from traditional values. It is of no little interest that as well as describing Christianity as a "superstition", Pliny should make specific mention of their "stubbornness and unshakeable obstinacy", meaning thereby the "madness" which he believed he saw in the Christian display of the will to martyrdom. When Pliny's attitude towards this Christian "madness" is taken with similar views expressed by Celsus and the Emperor Marcus Aurelius,[48] then we begin to appreciate what Graeco-Roman Pagans understood by "superstition" as applied to the Christians.

III. "Superstition" and "Religion"[49]

From the three testimonies to the Christian movement as *superstitio*, it is evident that all three writers have in common the underlying attitude of aversion and suspicion to foreign cults and their presumed association with social and moral deviations – which endangered the stability and harmony of society. Consequently, a key factor in the Pagan view of Christianity as *superstitio* is provided by Cicero's explicit statement of the fundamental principles governing religion from the Roman standpoint:

> "No-one shall have gods to himself, either new gods or alien gods, unless recognised by the State. Privately they shall worship those gods whose worship they have duly received from their ancestors."[50]

Religion, therefore, was a matter not of personal belief and devotion, but of social duty and ancestral practice. By thus tying national (or racial) identity so closely to religion as national cult, the Roman outlook made it impossible for a Roman citizen or a born Roman to hold a "new", foreign or alien religion.[51] Depth of conviction on this point must have been matched by Roman punctiliousness. Cicero's Stoic interlocutor, Balbus, in *De Natura Deorum*, declares:

> "If we care to compare our national characteristics with those of foreign people, we shall find that, while in all other respects we are only the equals or the inferiors of others, yet in the sense of religion, that is in reverence for the gods, we are far superior."[52]

Roman "reverence for the gods" was not only a cause of national pride; it was also the ultimate explanation for the political and social ascendancy of the Roman people, as Polybius had believed a century before Cicero.[53] The Roman scrupulousness in religion, public and national reverence for the gods, was held to account for the greatness and stability of Roman power; wars of conquest had been "won by those commanders who obeyed the dictates of religion".[54] Vergil was to provide the deepest foundation for the belief that Imperial prestige was the outcome of Roman piety, reverence for the gods and for ancestral values. The "piety" of Augustus mirrors an identical quality in Aeneas.[55] With the formal establishment of the cult of the Imperial genius under the Principate, Roman religion was from then on associated with the Imperial mission of Rome, affording sacral sanction for Roman values, *Romanitas*,[56] and its proper observance having far-reaching consequences for the prosperity and advancement of the commonwealth founded upon the fortunes of the Eternal City.

The association of religion with the well-being of the Roman commonwealth and its validation on the grounds of ancestral custom, also meant that religious piety was the ground for social morality;[57] departure from the traditional, ancestral piety was held to imply thereby a relaxation in commitment to the ideals of *Romanitas,* and to the social virtues which promoted and strengthened those ideals of Roman grandeur.[58] It is in this sense of the "ontocratic"[59] alliance of religion and its concomitant piety with the promotion of the ideals of *Romanitas*, that we are to understand the Roman distinction of religion from superstition.

Cicero states what must have been the general position, attempting in the process to provide the respective etymologies of the two terms.

"Religion has been distinguished from superstition not only by philosophers but by our ancestors. Persons who spent whole days in prayer and sacrifice to ensure that their children should outlive them were termed "superstitious" and the word later acquired a wider application. Those, on the other hand, who carefully reverenced and, so to speak, retraced all the lore of ritual were called "religious"... Hence superstitious and religious came to be terms of censure and approval respectively."[60]

The passage occurs in Balbus' defence of the existence of the traditional gods, against Epicurean strictures. It is interesting that as a Stoic, he himself had little regard for the myths and stories in which the traditional theology had been transmitted, and instead resolved the gods into physical elements and natural forces. But Balbus would not completely abandon religion; this would be unthinkable for a self-consciously proud Roman. His philosophical reconciliation with traditional piety required that he should argue for "the best and also purest, holiest and *most pious* way of worshipping the gods"; and this involved venerating them "with purity, sincerity and innocence both of thought and of speech".[61] Even more significantly, this philosophical defence of *religio* was made upon the grounds of ancestral tradition.[62] In terms of the argument, therefore, true *religio,* right "reverence for the gods", hence also genuine piety, set forth the appropriate devotion to the traditional gods in accordance with the ideals and social virtues which had been passed on from one generation to the next for centuries. Cicero indeed considered that if the gods did not exist, or did not exercise any providential care over human affairs, then not only would "piety", "reverence" and "religion" disappear, but loyalty, social union and justice, the queen of the virtues, would be lost as well. Piety towards the gods, the fundamental concomitant of true religion, was essential for the social cohesion and moral stability of the State.[63]

At this point, Cicero's view on religion is, in effect, identical with Varro's third variety of "theology", namely, "civil theology".[64] In contradistinction to the other two – the mythical (or fabular) and the natural (physical) or philosophical – civil theology was best suited to national, political purposes. This was because it consisted in knowing what gods state and citizen should worship, and with what rites. There was no reason why the three varieties might not exist side by side. Varro's *penchant* for classification simply led him to put his finger on the distinguishing mark of the general Roman understanding of religion and its function. Fundamentally, it was a political binding force and a means of social control. It was this characteristic of Roman religious life which Polybius saw and admired in the second century BC.[65] Since religion was less a matter of personal belief and more the maintenance of ancestral custom, it left no room for idiosyncratic or private judgment.[66] It was first and foremost a matter of national interest. It is an indication of the depth of this well-held view among the Romans that the national reconstruction undertaken by Octavian, following the disruption of the civil war, was to include the reform and the proper ordering of religion.[67] Understood primarily as loyalty to ancestral custom and especially public and private devotion to the traditional gods, religion was considered integral to the best and highest in *Romanitas*, and a characteristic mark of Roman civilisation and virtues in relation to un-Roman "barbarism".

A striking example of the tenacity of this attachment to religion is seen in Lucius Annaeus Seneca. In the judgment of Samuel Dill, he "had broken completely with paganism". His Stoicism, removed from the old, hard, cold and detached Stoicism of Cicero's Balbus, became for him virtually a religion. His conception of God, though starting with the Stoic creed, yet did not reconcile him to the traditional gods of the pantheon.[68] In Seneca we find the most emphatic expression of the function of philosophy as purely ethical, reforming, guiding and sustaining character and conduct.[69] Having found in philosophy the firm and sure way of striving towards the highest good (*i.e.*, wisdom – σοφία)[70] the great tutor of Nero nevertheless did not quite abandon the "old" outlook. Like his fellow Stoics who "had not enough feeling for the past to satisfy the pious and patriotic, nor the resolution to be done with it",[71] Seneca fell between two stools. Whilst his Stoic philosophical ethics furnished him with an integrative principle for his search for the truth about things divine and human (*Epistle* 90.3), Seneca remained tied to the traditional gods and the requirement of "piety" towards them. His description of the nature of the philosophic life is reminiscent of Cicero's statement of the social and moral necessity of *religio:*

> "From her [*philosophy's*] side religion (*religio*) never departs, nor duty (*pietas*), nor justice (*iustitia*), nor any of the whole company of virtues which cling together in close-united fellowship."[72]

The suggestion that Seneca failed to break completely with traditional religion even though he rejected image worship and despised the rites of the civil theology,[73] is not intended to diminish the moral stature of the eminent philosophic director. His attachment to and encouragement of religion simply shows how integral it was to being Roman to maintain a devotion of sorts to the "immortal gods". It seems quite a reasonable assumption that the Stoic rational approach to the quest for union with the divine in the universe may have been pursued in conscious opposition to the promises of ecstasy and emotional release offered by the mystery cults of Oriental and Egyptian origin, which were invading the empire.[74] It was partly due to the underlying cultural difference between Roman (and Greek) on the one hand, and "barbarian" or non-Roman (and non-Greek) on the other, that *religio* was seen to be a distinguishing mark of *Romanitas*, and *superstitio* was seen to belong to "barbarism". Liebeschuetz' observation expresses the Roman understanding generally:

"Religion is unemotional. Emotional religion, particularly when kindled in the masses, is objectionable and dangerous, and among foreigners a sign of barbarism."[75]

But by far the most illuminating treatment of the distinction between "true", or right "religion" on the one hand, and its "false" counterpart, "superstition", was provided by Plutarch of Chaeronaea in Boeotia.[76] Though "Greek by blood, birth, home and instinct, proud of his race, his land, their history, their art and their literature",[77] Plutarch yet felt at home in the political constitution of the Graeco-Roman world. For all his patriotic regard for the old achievement of the Hellenic name, he was as firmly convinced of the divine mission of Rome as ever was Vergil or any other patriotic Roman.[78] Keenly concerned to retain continuity with the past, Plutarch would have been "an admirable co-worker with Maecenas in carrying out the religious reforms of Augustus".[79]

However, Plutarch's deep feeling for religion and his broad sympathies with every well-held religious tradition, wherever it may be found[80] enabled him to see in the distinction between "true religion" and "superstition" more than the social and cultural differences between Graeco-Romans and barbarians, and the divergences in their religious practices. He devoted a book to the subject, entitled *On Superstition*.

Plutarch was a persistent defender of the claims of the inherited religion and piety against philosophical scepticism and Epicurean criticisms of the gods of traditional mythology,[81] and in his book he brought to his attack on "superstition" a moral fervour which shows that he recognised in the "infirmity" of superstitious devotion, an important weapon of the critics of religion in general.[82] Moreover, the expression of vehement abhorrence for "superstition", coming from one who was himself so deeply committed to religious belief and observance, is an important index as to what learned Pagans thought of the Christian movement when they applied to it the term *superstitio*.

Plutarch was just as opposed to "atheism" as he was to "superstition", for he saw both as cognate evils, springing from an identical source, namely "ignorance and blindness in regard to the gods".[83] But whereas atheism, as in Epicurean materialism, is simply an intellectual error, superstition was the worse enemy in its entanglement with emotion; the problem is further accentuated when emotion is accompanied by derangements of the soul, by which Plutarch meant some form of intellectual aberration in regard to the nature of the gods and of religion which resulted in unworthy and base views about the gods. For Plutarch, therefore, "superstition" is reprehensible as an intellectual error "touched with emotion".[84] The superstitious man is victim of an infirmity, a moral disorder which utterly crushes him. This "emotion engendered from false reason" produces an immobilising and paralysing effect on human action, because it is essentially, as the Greek δεισιδαιμονία (superstition) suggests, a fear or dread of the deities.

For Plutarch, a doctrine of the existence of daemons, good and bad, as intermediaries between ultimate Divinity and man, explains the less pleasant aspects of the traditional mythology.[85] Therefore in the religious scheme, the gods were essentially the source of all human happiness and joy,[86] and true religion was marked by dignified and sober piety, fidelity to ancestral custom, reasonableness and civility.

"Superstition", according to Plutarch, contradicts this viewpoint:

"... to find a god whom he [the superstitious person] shall not fear is impossible for him who fears the gods of his fathers and kin, who shudders at his saviours, and trembles with terror at those gentle gods from whom we ask wealth, welfare, peace, concord and success in our best efforts in speech and action."[87]

Superstition, accordingly, goes to "disgrace and transgress the god-given ancestral dignity of our religion".[88] The refusal of Jews to defend themselves against attack on the Sabbath is, for Plutarch, a sure indication of superstition.[89]

It so happens that several of Plutarch's instances of superstitious outlook and behaviour relate to "barbarian" peoples – Carthaginians, Gauls, Persians, Scythians – with particular reference to their alleged practice of human sacrifice. "Superstition" also describes the excesses of some Egyptian worship. However, it would be inaccurate to conclude that Plutarch simply held superstition as the essential charge against foreign cults from the Graeco-Roman standpoint. Greeks also, by their reactions to dreams and portents, according to Plutarch, were shown to have been victims of superstition.[90]

In Plutarch's understanding, therefore, superstition had to do with a kind of religious attitude and devotion, marked by excess of emotion and evident in bizarre and irrational practices; it generated fanaticism, based upon unworthy and base views about the gods. Superstition was derogatory to the gods and offensive to "true religion", which lies between "rough and hardened atheism" on the one hand, and the diseased condition of superstition on the other.[91] If total disregard of the gods was "unholy", it was even more reprehensible to hold superstitious beliefs about the gods. Such "more unholy opinions" about the gods implied the belief that:

> "... the gods are rash, faithless, fickle, vengeful, cruel and easily offended; and... the superstitious man is bound to hate and fear the gods... as he hates and fears the gods he is an enemy to them."[92]

Religion should serve practical ethical ends, so by linking "superstition" and "atheism" in terms of a common fundamental misapprehension of the nature of true religious piety, Plutarch follows the logic of his argument and charges both "superstition" and "atheism" with the tendency to promote impiety:

> "Hence it occurs to me to wonder at those who say that atheism is impiety and do not say the same of superstition."[93]

This close association of "superstition" with "atheism" and the indictment of both as "impiety" is at one with the general Roman suspicion of religious groups whose practices were at odds with Roman ancestral custom and so were considered not to promote genuine religion. Plutarch's understanding of piety is essentially the view that Cicero held about religion in the late Republic; and Seneca's expressed philosophy of religion in the early Empire would not have proved unacceptable to the ardent Greek apologist for ancestral piety.

Therefore, though neither Cicero, Seneca, nor Plutarch had any contact with the Christian movement,[94] they all contribute important insights, nonetheless, into the early hostile reaction to Christianity from Graeco-Roman traditionalists. For the Christian movement could be described as superstition and equally be accused of "atheism".[95] Both charges fitted into the picture which the Christian movement presented of itself to the Graeco-Roman Pagan world. As William Schoedel has pointed out, "to be an atheist was to deny the traditional state gods".[96] By their general refusal to participate in the cult of the Emperor which they considered incompatible with their understanding of God and man,[97] the Christians excluded themselves from a common loyalty to the State which became central in the Augustan renewal of religion and society. In that sense, the indictment held against the Christians was unanswerable.[98] But as with the designation superstition, the validity of the charge of atheism rested upon the

Graeco-Roman understanding of religion and piety. By describing the Christian movement as superstition, its critics, from the viewpoint of their religiosity, were declaring it to be, as Joseph Vogt aptly puts it, "the opposite of religion".[99] Therefore, the early Graeco-Roman designations of the Christian movement[100] reveal an underlying assumption borne out by the use of the key word, superstition. Robert Wilken's comment sums up appropriately its significance:

> "The terms superstition and impiety carry cultural and religious overtones. Reflecting a judgment drawn primarily from the realm of public religion, it asserts not only that Christians had foreign origins, but that their religious practices did not contribute to the well-being of society."[101]

In the course of the second century AD, earnest and better-informed critics of the Christian movement associated it with the flood of Oriental cults which were increasingly gaining a hold on the populations in the Empire. To Lucian of Samosata, a Cynic, Christ had simply introduced yet another new cult or rite into the world.[102] Celsus' book *The True Doctrine*[103] provides the first evidence of a sustained and serious literary anti-Christian polemic. It is clear that he saw Christianity as no different from the other foreign cults of Oriental provenance.

> "For just as among them [*the Oriental mystery cults*] scoundrels frequently take advantage of the lack of education of gullible people and lead them wherever they wish, so also this happens among the Christians."[104]

Celsus was no cold rationalist, and his opposition to Christianity arose out of the philosophical strand of Graeco-Roman religious piety which accepted the existence of a Supreme God along with a host of subordinate supernatural powers without seeking to reconcile them.[105]

Christianity was originally barbarian (by virtue of its connection with Judaism) and therefore contemptible. It was part of the same process whereby whatever was hideous and shameful from every part of the world converged on the Empire's capital and became popular.[106] But Celsus' criticism of the Christian movement stands in the Ciceronian tradition which associated political disruption and chaos with dissent from customary practice in religion. Quite apart from what he considered to be the folly and perversity of Christianity – in its doctrines[107] – Celsus was most concerned about the Christians' lack of national feeling. Consequently, Celsus recognised a vital difference between Christianity and the parallel phenomena of the other cults of Oriental provenance. Long before the State took action to deal with the problem, Celsus had seen in Christianity a mass movement of apostasy from tradition and well-established custom.[108] By his persistent and evidently sincere appeals to the Christians to recover a credible loyalty to the Emperor and the State,[109] he showed his awareness of the political danger to the Empire which issued from the Christians' abjuration of the ancient and tradition-al ways[110] of Graeco-Roman society. He understood, in the words of A.D. Nock, that "the Jewish reluctance to worship the Emperor seemed queer, but the Christian dangerous".[111] But what Celsus failed to grasp was the nature of the motive force of the Christian movement and of the Christians themselves.[112]

IV. Through Christian Eyes: Conversion and its Problems

Accordingly, whilst J. Vogt is right to insist that in the final analysis the eventual state persecution of Christians could be fully understood only in terms of the nature of Graeco-Roman "religiosity",[113] the strangeness of Christian conduct cannot be fully explained in terms of superstition but of what Christians self-consciously believed was offered them in their Gospel. In view of the fact that the adoption of the Christian stance implied a self-exclusion, in some sense, from the securities of Graeco-Roman society,[114] it is appropriate to inquire into the nature of that inward conviction; to find out what questions were raised for the Christian converts of Graeco-Roman culture, and to seek to appreciate how these questions illuminate the investigation into their problem of identity.

Since national identity and religion had the same basis in traditional Graeco-Roman understanding,[115] the Christian Gospel was to compel the world of Graeco-Roman culture, Christian and non-Christian alike, to face up to a specific element in the religious consciousness, namely, conversion, which, though present with Judaism, now came to assume an importance that was novel and unavoidable.[116] The acceptance of the Christian Gospel within Graeco-Roman culture forced into the open what A.D. Nock had called the "two opposing poles of religion".[117] To these two opposing poles, the "religion of tradition" and "prophetic religion", cor-respond respectively, "adhesion" and "conversion". Christianity, infinitely more than Judaism (for Judaism, as we have noted above, had a history and a tradition), accentuated the demands of "prophetic religion". A genuine acceptance of the Christian creed and stance not only indicated a "disaffection with things as they are" and a "desire to launch out on a new path", but also involved a certain amount of renunciation of aspects of the Graeco-Roman past. Conversion involved therefore:

"the reorientation of the soul of the individual, his deliberate turning from indifference, from an earlier form of piety to another, a turning which implies a consciousness that a great change is involved, that the old was wrong and that the new is right."[118]

Religion in Graeco-Roman Paganism, which existed as an intrinsic aspect of social organisation, made no missionary efforts outside its own society; its essential element was the practice and the sanctity of custom hallowed by preceding generations. With no religious frontier to cross, traditional Graeco-Roman piety, accordingly, had no difficult decision to make between two views of life.

"Adhesion" was produced by a meeting of cultures without "any definite crossing of religious frontiers in which an old spiritual home was left for a new once and for all". With adhesion, a person had "one foot on each side of a fence which was cultural not credal". The acceptance of new worships was seen as bringing useful supplements and not substitutes, and did not involve the taking of a new way of life in place of the old.[119] Consequently, traditional religion in the Empire offered the possibility of adhesion to a variety and multiplicity of cults; Christianity and Judaism were in the unique situation of insisting on conversion. Since therefore everything in regard to religion in Graeco-Roman Paganism made for the conservation of custom, "anything like conversion would be a breach of etiquette: it would mean superstition, unreasonable enthusiasm characteristic of the lower orders".[120]

There was an important exception to the general picture: philosophy, by the second century AD, had come to dominate the spiritual and intellectual life of educated people. Speaking in tones increasingly religious,[121] philosophers held a clear concept of two types of life, a higher and a lower; men were exhorted to turn from one to the other. Turning from luxury and self-indulgence and superstition to the disciplined philosophic life was, effectually, a conversion, a turning around of the soul, from this changing world, until its eyes could bear to contemplate reality and the supreme Good.[122] Philosophy produced some striking types, the saints of antiquity,[123] and conversion to philosophy became the nearest equivalent to what some educated Christians understood concerning their own conversion to the Christian stance.[124] Therefore, while regarding the "old" Graeco-Roman religion as unworthy and untrue, some Christian writers were eager to reconcile philosophy and their own teaching.[125] In later chapters we shall deal more fully with the subject of the philosophical tradition and seek to show how some Christians understood that tradition and why in several cases a high value was placed upon it.

It is reasonable to suppose that a radical experience of conversion as described above underlay Christian self-consciousness in the period we are considering. The emphasis placed upon conversion by some Christian writers indicates how important and significant this experience was for appreciating the dynamics of their new self-definition and outlook.[126] Justin's note of exuberant triumph would be sounded repeatedly in much of the Christian apologetic literature of the time:

"We have not been deceived and shall not cease to confess Him [*i.e. Christ*]... we have not believed empty fables, or words without foundation, but words filled with the Spirit of God, bursting forth with power and exuberant with grace."[127]

This experience was equally available to the masses of ordinary and illiterate Christians, who were, so to speak, enabled to live "philosophically".[128]

Given the particularly hostile context in which such convictions and affirmations were held and heard in the Graeco-Roman society of the early Empire,[129] it is important that we do not make an abstraction of the human and personal dimensions of the problem of identity for the Christians; the situation was as yet a far cry from one in which a Christian could, with ease, merge his "Roman" with his "Christian" identity.[130] The vindication of Christianity in the period had to do with more than the legal status of Christianity.[131] H. Richard Niebuhr is right in his judgment that "the story of Graeco-Roman civilisation's attack on the Gospel is told too often in terms of political persecution only".[132] The question as to what to do with Christianity was felt equally by Christians of Graeco-Roman culture. The Christian problem did not consist primarily in how to relate new with old *ideas*; there was, for Christians, a necessarily *inward* dimension to the problem of their self-understanding. They had to struggle to know how to come to terms (and how not to) with a world in which anti-Christian sentiment and policy were validated upon the grounds of a broadly cultural ideology that fused together religion and politics. The affirmation of the experience of conversion, therefore, by its very nature was

to be a vindication of the dimension of the distinctiveness of
personality in Christ, and a radical challenge to the "ontocracy"[133]
of Graeco-Roman *religio*. The Christian stance, therefore,
amounted to confrontation of the spirit of classical Paganism, the
religion of culture, with the culture of religion.[134]

> "In Christ... they [*the Christians*] claimed to possess a principle
> of understanding superior to anything existing in the classical
> world. By this claim they were prepared to stand or fall."[135]

At the same time we must acknowledge that culture, some of
whose elements the Christians so inflexibly repudiated, was not
outside of themselves. For all its uncompromising rejection of
whatever was considered from the Christians' standpoint to be
immoral, erroneous and ungodly, Christian conversion was largely
the conversion of persons of Graeco-Roman culture, in the context
of Graeco-Roman culture. This fact has been noted by Prof. Nock
to have been significant for the eventual triumph of the Christian
apologetic movement:

> "The apologists were without exception men who were not the
> sons of Christians, but had been converted to Christianity
> themselves. The *apologia* of each one was therefore, in a
> measure, an *apologia pro vita sua*."[136]

Accordingly, a further aspect of the inward character of the
problem of identity for Christians of Graeco-Roman culture was
that sooner or later the convert had to settle accounts with his past
and his own cultural tradition; either to reject them, or to integrate
them into the present. How to interpret the Pagan past – the entire
Graeco-Roman cultural heritage with its traditions, religious and
intellectual; what to do about it; how to situate oneself in relation
to it – these became major points of discussion for Graeco-Roman
Christians. The dimension of "inwardness" with regard to the
problem of identity for Christians of Graeco-Roman culture, involved, therefore, a struggle to make their Christian self-consciousness feel at home within that culture, whilst their identity
remained tied to, and primarily shaped by, a "doctrine which was
originally *barbarian*".[137]

Conversely, the process of integration of personality also compelled Christians of Graeco-Roman culture to seek ways of being
at home in a "barbarian" tradition. This meant coming to terms
with those elements of the Christian Gospel, teaching and history
which were deemed distasteful and unacceptable to Graeco-Roman
sensibilities and outlook.[138] Ultimately, this meant coming to terms

with the religious history of ancient Israel and the authoritative record of that history, the Scriptures of the Old Testament. The fact that the Hebrew Scriptures were available in the Greek language did not abrogate their "barbarian" connection. Paradoxically, it was upon the basis of the antiquity and priority of Moses and the Old Testament traditions to Graeco-Roman religious and intellectual traditions, that many Christians of Graeco-Roman culture were able to vindicate their place in the scheme of human history.[139] It was the "barbarian" heritage of the Christian Gospel that gave the new movement a *tradition* of its own.

The use of the method of allegorical interpretation of the Hebrew Scriptures in the literature of the apologetic movement answers to the same urge and cannot therefore be dismissed as "haphazard and unscientific".[140] It was part of the general process of the integration of Christian personality and identity. The logic of inwardness which Graeco-Roman Christian conversion brings to bear upon the interpretation of our authors indicates that the process of establishing the antiquity and authority of the Hebrew Scriptures as, in some sense, integral to Christianity, was consistent with the move to come to terms with the cultural problem that was raised for Graeco-Roman civilisation by Christ.[141] It is this same logic of inwardness which is affirmed by Richard Niebuhr's perceptive comment that the debate about Christ and culture takes place

> "not only in the open where parties calling themselves Christians and anti-Christians meet, but more frequently among Christians, and in the hidden depths of the individual conscience; not as the struggle and accommodation of belief with unbelief, but as the wrestling and reconciliation of faith with faith."[142]

Once this perspective is granted, it becomes clear that the historical development of the Christian religion during the early centuries witnesses to more than the interaction of Graeco-Roman and Christian *ideas*. The "process of continuous 'translation' of Christianity's sources aimed at giving the Graeco-Roman world an ever more accurate understanding of their context",[143] had an inward and infinitely more difficult aspect to it[144] in the life and thought of Christians of Graeco-Roman culture: to establish an authentic Christian identity within their culture, meaningful both for them and for the world as it was then known.

V. The Christian Movement as "the Third Race"

Marcel Simon[145] has shown the crucial importance of the dates AD 70 and AD 135 for the early development of the Christian movement. With the destruction of the Jerusalem Temple, and the dissolution of the Jewish community based on the Temple in AD 70, Judaeo-Christians who had generally associated themselves with the Temple ritual, were forced to emerge into independent existence. This event itself conferred on Christianity autonomy from Judaism, as well as a sense of a different destiny. When in AD 135, the last Jewish revolt against Roman power led by Simon Bar Kochba was quelled, some Christians believed that the event provided confirmation of a divine verdict on Israel for her rejection of the Messiahship of Jesus of Nazareth and the murder of James, the brother of Jesus.[146]

As the social life of the Church, together with the forms of its religious observance and the development of its intellectual outlook, increasingly took place outside of the Jewish milieu, the distinction of Christianity from Judaism, of church from synagogue, became more clearly defined.[147] Moreover, because Christianity assumed progressively (and massively) the character of a Gentile phenomenon, the meagre results of evangelisation among Jews was an important contributing factor in shaping the self-awareness of converts from a Graeco-Roman cultural background. Justin dwells on this fact with considerable persistence and even supplies Old Testament prophetic validation for his view that "the Christians from among the Gentiles are both more numerous and more true than those among the Jews and Samaritans".[148] Later in the same chapter, Justin designates Gentile Christians as "more true and more believing".[149] Therefore Justin's radical declaration to Trypho in favour of Christians must be appreciated in the context of the existence of a considerable body of Gentile Christians.[150]

> "The true spiritual Israel, and descendants of Judah, Jacob, Isaac and Abraham... are we who have been led to God through this crucified Jesus."[151]

It is interesting that in citing his Christian "ancestors", Justin works into the past from the more recent patriarchs, as if wishing to stress the importance of Christian roots in history and antiquity. And yet, for all its claim to be "the true spiritual Israel", Christianity remained essentially the church of the Gentiles.[152] Justin's statement evidently underlines the fact that there was no more pressing problem to be faced by Gentile Christians in the Graeco-

Roman world than the question of their heritage and historical roots. Whereas, in relation to Jews, the followers of Jesus felt able to describe themselves as the "true Israel" or "the true circumcision",[153] these terms were less meaningful to Gentiles. In a Gentile matrix, the Christians needed a new self-definition as they distinguished themselves from Judaism on the one hand, and distanced themselves from Graeco-Roman religious rites on the other. In the process, they emerged as a third entity, "the third race" (*tertium genus*) as they came to be called. However, "by separating itself from its Jewish milieu, the third race... lost the benefit of antiquity which alone had made the Jews traditionally acceptable in the Roman world".[154] It is appropriate, therefore, that we trace the history of the concept and seek to determine its significance.

Adolf von Harnack[155] has skilfully assembled the literary evidence for the historical development of the self-consciousness of the Christian movement from the tentative beginnings in apostolic times to the explicit, positive self-designation as "the third race of humanity" in the third century AD.[156]

Already in the New Testament writings Christian self-consciousness of constituting a "race... a nation... a people" becomes apparent.[157] However, as indicated above, this self-definition was worked out in relation to the nation of Israel and was most meaningful in the context of the anti-Judaistic polemic. Within Graeco-Roman, Gentile culture, new categories of self-definition were needed.

From the evidence of St Paul's letters, the apostle to the Gentiles shows awareness of the problem. In St Paul's mind, humanity comes to assume a triple division: Jews, Greeks and the Church of God.[158] The first two represented, for the apostle, the two generally accepted categories of barbarians and Greeks in the ancient Mediterranean world.[159] The apostle, however, does not designate the Church as a people; rather, it is a "new creation"[160] embracing both Jews and Greeks, on the common basis of faith in Christ.[161] Harnack sums up the evidence from the apostle's writings as follows:

> "The people of Christ are not a third people to him beside their neighbours. They represent the new grade on which human history reaches its consummation, a grade which is to supersede the previous grade of bisection, cancelling or annulling not only national, but also social and even sexual distinction."[162]

It is evident, therefore, that the basis for Christian self-definition was to be essentially a religious one, not national, nor cultural, nor social.

A similar triple division, but one which is more closely defined in terms of the conception of God and the nature of true worship, is found in *John's Gospel*. Jesus' words in 4:21ff make the following distinctions. Firstly, there are those who lack both the true knowledge of God and the right understanding of worship, namely, the Samaritans. Secondly, there are those who have access to the truth concerning God, and yet have erroneous and inadequate understanding of true worship, namely, the Jews. Finally, there is the third category of those who have both the right knowledge and also the proper spiritual understanding of true inward worship, namely, the Christians, for they alone worship the Father "in Spirit and in Truth".[163] It is this triple division, on the grounds of religion and worship, which comes to form the basis for the development of Christian self-consciousness in the Graeco-Roman world.

An important landmark in this development is the anonymous writing, *The Preaching of Peter*. This document must be considered as one of the first "Apologies" for Christianity in the early second century AD.[164] Unfortunately, only two passages from the entire work have survived, preserved in the writings of Clement of Alexandria.[165]

The value of this early piece of writing for our present discussion lies in what the unknown author makes of the distinctions between Jews, Greeks and Christians. After establishing that God is one and transcendent, he goes on to apply the Old Testament prophecy concerning the new covenant (*Jeremiah* 31:31ff) not only to Jewish religious history, but also to Greek institutions. He applies to both sets of values and traditions the same description; they are both now declared old and superseded. A new covenant, transcending both Greek and Jewish traditions and conceptions of worship, has come into operation. This new way of worship has come into the world with the rise of Christianity. Christians are those who worship God "anew, in a third way".

There can be little doubt that this early "apology" for the Christian movement found its way into the important centres of Christianity like Alexandria, Athens and Rome.[166] It is also argu-able that the work made an important contribution to that process whereby thoughtful Gentile Christians sought to articulate their identity in relation to Graeco-Roman culture and tradition. This is evident in the way Clement of Alexandria uses the passages he quotes.[167] The significance of the *Preaching of Peter* lies in the author's suggestion that there was, in the past, a divine covenant which dealt with both Greeks and Jews; the order is noteworthy. Consequently, the "new... third way" of worship, which is represented by Christianity, is related to the Greek (i.e. Gentile) tradition and heritage in a manner which, for boldness and originality, had not then found expression. The suggestion was to have a great future in the writings of later Gentile Christians.[168]

The triple distinction – Greeks, Jews and Christians – is found also in the second-century epistle *To Diognetus,* which equally belongs within early Hellenistic Christian apologetics.[169] The unknown author describes Christians as those who take no account of "those who are regarded as gods by the Greeks" neither observe "the superstition of the Jews".[170] However, the difference between Christians and the rest of mankind does not consist in their "locality or in speech or in customs".[171] Rather, claiming all spiritual insight and moral virtue in society for the Christian faith, the writer draws on the analogy of the soul's relation to the body to explain the nature of Christian existence in society.[172] The picture given of the Christians is of a community closely defined by its religious convictions and their effect on conduct. There is no question of separation from the rest of mankind, but of distinction from erroneous and misguided conceptions of Deity and worship. Christians are not fundamentally alien to the world, neither are they opposed to society as a whole. They simply believe differently about God and they conduct themselves differently, that is, with moral excellence and love.

Christian doctrine is "no earthly discovery",[173] but a divine communication of the original truth, through the agency of the Son of God who became incarnate for the purpose and for the benefit of all mankind. That Christianity is a new and recent development in human life and affairs[174] is only apparent. Far superior, and in no way comparable to philosophical speculations about God, this divine communication has inaugurated "the present season of righteousness", following human inability to live worthily by human resources alone.[175] Therefore, there can be no doubt about the abiding relevance of Christian doctrine for all mankind, neither can it really be spoken of as late in religious history. Rather, it is the case that "being convicted in the past by our own deeds as unworthy of life, we might now be made deserving by the goodness of God".[176] Christian doctrine consequently offers to all mankind "full knowledge" not only of the truth of God's nature, but particularly of his love towards mankind.[177]

A more explicit development of the triple division in the direction of the conception of the third race is found in the *Apology* of Aristides, the Athenian "philosopher",[178] a work which was addressed to the Emperor Antoninus Pius.[179]

Developing further the distinctions which have already been noted in the *Preaching of Peter*, Aristides specifies three categories[180] of people; there are, in the first place, worshippers of false deities, essentially polytheists, then Jews and finally Christians. The first category is further subdivided into Chaldeans, Greeks and Egyptians.[181] As was the case in the *Preaching of Peter*, the distinctions are made on the basis of religion – specifically, the conception of Deity and the manner of worship.

Polytheists are most in error since their worship is directed at created things and images;[182] moreover, for all their intellectual advance, the Greeks are discredited in the writer's estimation by the immoral accounts of the lives and careers of gods in their mythology.[183] Whilst the Jews are commended for their apprehension of the unity of God and for their exemplary social life (Syriac text), they are equally criticised on account of their rejection of Christ as the Son of God. From the writer's standpoint, their mistaken worship of angels, their observance of Sabbaths and other feast days, and such regulations as circumcision and food laws, are an indication that Jews have only partially grasped the truth.[184] It is the Christians who alone have the right understanding of the nature of Deity, and who also worship God aright. The proof of the claim, Aristides suggests, is seen in Christian moral and social life.[185]

Apart from the triple division of mankind upon the grounds of religion, an equally interesting feature of the *Apology* of Aristides is the attempt the writer makes to provide a doctrine of the religious ancestry of the various categories of worshippers. Accordingly, "the Christians trace their origin from the Lord Jesus".[186] The idea of the "genealogy" of Christians, established in relation to Jesus Christ as, in some sense, their Ancestor, was to reappear in Justin's writings.[187]

From the three documents of early Christian apologetics discussed so far, it becomes clear that by the middle of the second century AD, the understanding of the Christian faith as the "new... third way" of religious apprehension and manner of worship was of considerable influence in Christian centres of thought. Consequently, "the triad of Greeks (Gentiles), Jews and Christians" seems to have become "the Church's basal conception of history".[188]

However, it was in the Latin West that the explicit formula of *tertium genus* – "the third race" – was to emerge. When we meet it in Tertullian,[189] it is a term of abuse, hurled at Christians by their opponents. At least, this seems to have been the case in Carthage, towards the end of the second century, and in the early third century. Moreover, from Tertullian's acerbic retorts, the designation was used with exclusive reference to the Christians' religious stance in the eyes of their Graeco-Roman neighbours. The term was therefore employed to distinguish Christians from devotees of Roman religion and from Jews, as Tertullian explains:

> "But it is in respect of our religion and not our nationality that we are supposed to be the third race; the series being the Romans, the Jews and the Christians after them."[190]

It is hard to know whether Tertullian was being sarcastic in his use of *superstitio* to describe the Christian faith. There can be no doubt, however, that the expression *tertium genus* as applied to the Christians by their Pagan opponents, would have had the connotation of contempt in which un-Roman ways in religion were held. When one compares the expression of dislike for Christians with expressions of similar attitudes to Jews in Graeco-Roman society, it becomes clear that the hatred of Christians represented a heightened form of the resentment and pervasive fear and spite felt towards Jews.[191] Therefore, the term *tertium genus*, expressive of the sense that Christians were no more than the dregs and offscouring of society, is indicative of the depth of feeling and the fear which Christians inspired. Certainly, this interpretation is suggested by the way in which Tertullian uses and understands the term as he refutes it:

> "... if they who belong to the third race are so monstrous what must they be supposed to be who preceded them in the first and second place?"[192]

Tertullian appears to have been completely unaware of any positive Christian use of the concept of a "new... third way" or worship as it had developed in some circles of Hellenistic Christian apologetics and, consequently, he is wholly preoccupied with the negative, abusive connotation of *tertium genus*. Therefore when, in characteristic fashion, Tertullian retorts and seeks to give his opponents a taste of their own medicine, he applies *tertium genus* as a term of ridicule, to the institution of eunuch priests in Graeco-

Roman tradition:

"You have your third race, not indeed third in the way of religious rite, but a third race in sex, and made up as it is of male and female in one, it is more fitted to men and women."[193]

It is evident that Tertullian did not like the term and he did not return to the subject in his *Apology*, which must have been written very soon after *Ad Nationes*.[194] When the term next occurs in his writings,[195] it is again an expression of resentment uttered by the hostile masses in the circus! As Harnack remarks:

"What people saw... was a descending series, with regard to the numina and cultus; first Romans, then Jews, then Christians."[196]

Tertullian might have been ignorant of a positive Christian tradition regarding "the third race". However, it is less likely that he would have been unfamiliar with the historical precedent which had described the "great multitude" involved in the equally hated and feared Bacchanalia in 186 BC, as "almost constituting a second people".[197] In Pagan eyes the parallels were startling; it is not improbable that the crimes held against the third race may also have had a literary association in Graeco-Roman minds with what was generally believed to have been true of the "second people".[198] Therefore, Tertullian's visceral reaction to the jibe, "third race" – for so he took it – must be considered to have been as much a well-considered response to a deep and tenacious Graeco-Roman prejudice held on the basis of religion and piety, as a sign of his ignorance of other uses of the term.

However, it is interesting that an explicitly positive vindication of the self-designation as "the third race" is found in the Latin Christian literature of the mid-third century in a document associated with Carthage. The Pseudo-Cyprianic tract, *De Pascha Computus*,[199] which is concerned primarily with the problem of determining the date of Easter, clearly refers to Christians as "the third race of mankind".[200] The reference to the "mystery" of the Christian faith in the immediate context of the statement argues strongly in favour of understanding "third race" in the sense in which the author of the *Preaching of Peter* spoke of Christians as those who worship God "anew... in a third way". The negative connotation of the expression which we find in Tertullian must therefore represent the hostile Pagan response to a positive usage in some Christian circles.

It is reasonable, then, to link the usage of "third race" in the *De*

Pascha Computus to the apologetic tradition represented by the *Preaching of Peter,* the *Epistle to Diognetus* and the *Apology* of Aristides. The existence of this tradition of a positive Christian usage of the concept, whether as the tentative form in the Greek documents, or as the explicit self-designation in the third century Latin tractate, goes to show that some Christians of Graeco-Roman culture were sensitive to the need to relate their religious convictions and community traditions to the wider context of Graeco-Roman history and culture. If it is correct that the *Preaching of Peter* lies behind both the *Epistle to Diognetus* and the *Apology* of Aristides,[201] then the witness of Clement of Alexandria, who evidently perceived the potential of the concept for a religious history of mankind from a Christian standpoint, is an important index to the seriousness with which the effort to achieve a coherent and acceptable Christian self-definition was made.[202]

On the other hand, the evidence for a negative connotation given to "third race", as attested in Tertullian's writings, indicates that the attempt to integrate Christian self-consciousness into a wider human heritage was fraught with difficulties and was not without dangers. In view of Tertullian's general outlook, his testimony to the negative usage of "third race" is perhaps not surprising. As one for whom the Christian community was marked by a total way of life – defined by a religious conviction and knowledge, a divine rule of life and a bond of hope[203] – a postulate of radical distinctiveness was fundamental to his understanding of how Christian identity related to the Graeco-Roman heritage. Consequently, Tertullian felt no necessity to justify his religious consciousness to his religious opponents. His uncompromising repudiation of "third race" must therefore remain an exception.

In any case, the existence of both positive and negative traditions regarding the use and understanding of the concept of "third race" in Christian literature is, perhaps, itself a pointer to the enigmatic nature of the problem of identity that faced Christians of Graeco-Roman culture in the early Roman Empire. Robert Wilken aptly describes the Christian predicament when he writes:

> "The Christians were not only unknown, but were themselves searching for a clearly defined identity."[204]

VI. "Christ... was partially known... by Socrates..." [205]

By making this bold assertion, Justin was initiating a tradition which was to have far-reaching consequences for the direction which Christian reflection took in the Graeco-Roman context.

Whilst Justin's intuition has a lot to do with the eventual "development of a rational theology in the Greek tradition" as part of the
process whereby Christian teaching and language came to be at
home in Hellenistic culture,[206] the more fundamental importance
of his declaration relates to the problem of identity for Justin
himself, and for others like him: converts to Christ from a Hellenistic background.

In two stimulating articles, Robert Wilken has shown that
Graeco-Roman attitudes to Christians provided the framework in
which Christian attempts to achieve identity were forced to
move.[207] According to this argument, the Christian apologists of
the second century AD, at home in the spiritual world of Graeco-
Roman tradition, understood the logic which led from "superstition" to impiety on the one hand, and from "philosophy" to piety on
the other.[208] The general foundations and validation of that logic
have been noted in the discussion of the views of Cicero, Seneca
and Plutarch, on religion and superstition. In order therefore to
avoid identification with the dreaded foreign cults which were
presumed immoral and socially subversive, and also to win a
hearing from thoughtful men and women, Justin and other Christian teachers attempted to present the Christian faith as a
philosophical teaching, which taught and promoted piety and
moral excellence.[209] The goal of the Christian effort became essentially identical with the philosophical religion of Lucius Annaeus
Seneca:

> "Philosophy's sole function is to discover the truth about things
> divine and things human. From her side, religion never departs,
> nor duty, nor justice, nor any of the whole company of virtues
> which cling together in close united fellowship. Philosophy has
> taught us to worship that which is divine, to love that which is
> human..."[210]

However, the Christian faith had a religious and ethical content
of its own, and it was not going to become easily reducible to the
religious philosophy of Graeco-Roman tradition.[211] The presupposition which lay behind Justin's claim can, therefore, be further
clarified in terms of the missionary challenge which Justin and his
successors understood as confronting them in their situation. Jean
Daniélou considers that the Christians' concern in this regard was
"above all to demonstrate the consonance of the Christian message
with human reason" and so "establish contact between the Christian message and Hellenism".[212] Daniélou sees this aim as the
essential basis of Justin's doctrine of the Logos – in its two aspects

of the fullness of knowledge which is a gift of grace through the Incarnate Word, Christ, and human reason, itself a participation in "the divine Word"[213] in his pre-incarnate activity. The fuller treatment of Justin's position will be the subject of a later chapter. For the present, it is enough to show that by claiming for "Socrates and those like him",[214] a previous activity of the divine Word, Christ, he introduced into the quest for coherent Christian identity in Graeco-Roman culture an entirely original element.

It is worth noting that the affirmation of Christian affinity with the philosophical tradition is not uniformly endorsed in the Christian literature of the period. Tatian and Tertullian stand out as the most important representatives of an attitude which must have been shared by other, perhaps less intellectually capable Christians.[215]

Tertullian was probably unaware of the thinking and usage of other Christian leaders of opinion and opposed to some of the developing trends, and sought defiantly to make capital out of the recent origins of the Christian movement:

"We are but of yesterday and we have filled every place among you – cities, islands, fortresses, towns, market places, the very camp, tribes, companies, palace, senate, forum – we have left nothing to you but the temples of your gods."[216]

Tertullian also rejected any suggestion that the Christian movement could be described as a school of philosophy. To him such a designation meant a diminution of the credentials of the Christian faith; it had the effect of reducing Christian teaching to the level of human speculative systems, which lacked any claim to certainty. The Christian faith was a divine revelation originating in the divine realm.[217] Philosophy was essentially the parent of heresy.[218]

Henry Chadwick has drawn attention to the fact that whilst Tertullian's postulate of radical discontinuity between Christianity and Greek philosophy[219] was the traditional position in the Latin West till the time of Marius Victorinus (converted from Neo-Platonism)[220] and Augustine, in the Greek East the question of the relation of Christianity to philosophy was felt and faced early, as from the second century AD, in the writings of the Apologists.[221] What Dr. Chadwick's comment leaves unexplained is why there was this difference in the Christian attitude to philosophy between the Latin West and the Greek East. It seems to me that what we have said so far about the attempts made by Hellenistic Christians to forge a credible and acceptable identity in relation to their own culture, offers some insights into that difference.

This same perspective helps to explain the case of Tatian. Werner Jaeger[222] has shown the importance and significance of Greek culture and education, *paideia*, for the expansion of Christianity in the early centuries and has rightly insisted that the career of Tatian was an exception to the general picture. Tatian was a disciple of Justin Martyr, whom he admired,[223] but though he was trained in Greek culture and education, he did not believe in it.[224] However, Jaeger is too quick to suggest that the Apologists were primarily concerned to present Christianity as the religion of the "cultured" world,[225] and this colours his interpretation of Tatian's stance. E.J. Goodspeed has also criticised Tatian for "a kind of cultural primitivism".[226] However, the search for an authentic Christian identity provides a better key for interpreting Tatian's outlook. It is clear that Tatian did not feel at home in Greek culture; in the first place, it did not belong to him. He had been born beyond the boundaries of the Empire and though he went through the schools of Greece and acquired a knowledge of its culture, as his *Oration* clearly shows, yet he rejected Greek culture as being to him "a foreign land".[227] He consequently felt no need nor desire to come to terms with Greek culture. The "philosophical" tradition he vindicated was not the Greek (and Roman), but the "Barbarian",[228] and on grounds which were just as firmly Christian and theological[229] as they may have been culturally motivated.[230]

Moreover, there was more to Graeco-Roman culture than the philosophical tradition, and Christian writers of Graeco-Roman culture were at one with Tatian in his criticism of certain features of that culture, even though there was a difference in intensity. We must not overstate the positive attitude of Justin and others to the intellectual tradition of Graeco-Roman culture. Some important modifications appear in their evaluation of the gains and insights of the philosophical tradition.[231] Henry Chadwick's cautious assessment of Justin indicates the significant emphasis in his outlook:

> "He knows what is true and judges accordingly. So with regard to the doctrine of God, he declares that the Stoics are wrong. Pantheism, materialism and fatalism are false. But the Stoics are excellent on morality. Plato, on the other hand, though right about God's transcendence and incorporeality, is wrong in his doctrine of the soul and in his acceptance of the cyclic fatalistic theory of transmigration. *In all these judgments, we see Justin's*

Christian faith impelling him to reject metaphysical positions that he thinks incompatible with the Bible."[232]

Thus it is necessary to recognise that the outlook which links Tatian with Tertullian in their common distrust of the Greek philosophical tradition belongs within Christian consciousness as indicative of a radically Biblicist apprehension of Christian truth and may be related to the apostolic injunction to beware of "the empty deception of philosophy, based on a man-made tradition of teaching... and not based on Christ".[233] The radically exclusivist perspective of Tatian and Tertullian on the relation of Christian teaching to the philosophical tradition, is uniformly underpinned by a conviction that the latter amounts to merely human speculation.[234] To the extent that they are correct in distinguishing "divine revelation" from "human reason", their outlook acts as a necessary counterweight which enables us to evaluate in their proper balance the more liberal attitudes of Justin and Clement.[235]

The tradition which Justin initiated must not, however, be hastily considered as a reduction of traditional Christian doctrine in favour of the gains and insights of the Greek philosophical tradition.[236] Neither was his admiration for Socrates, and hence the affirmation of Christian affinity with him, a sudden and unreflective gesture. The important question to ask at this point is: what was the contribution of the link with Socrates and the "philosophical" tradition he represented towards the achievement of Christian identity in Graeco-Roman culture? What relation does the vindication of Christianity as the "philosophy... alone safe and profitable"[237] have with the attempt to find for the Christians a place in the religious history of humanity as those who worship God "anew... in a third way"?[238]

Socrates was the most striking exemplar of the intellectual and rational protest against the traditional mythology elaborated by Hesiod and Homer, the conception of the divine which was based upon it, and the popular religion which issued from it. Further-more, by his resolute determination to endure suffering and death for what he considered to be right, Socrates became in the religious consciousness, the type of witness for truth and righteous sufferer and martyr.[239] The Christians, called to account for their rejection of traditional religiosity and to answer for their "impiety" and "atheism", were quick to recognise the significance of the Socratic precedent as a weapon against their accusers.[240]

But Justin vindicates the career of Socrates, not so much for the sake of Socrates, as for the sake of his own Christian position and convictions. By affirming that the outlook of Socrates was prompted and motivated by the activity, though partial, of the divine Word, Christ, Justin became the first person to seek to validate Graeco-Roman Christian identity in terms of Graeco-Roman tradition itself, at least in terms of a strand in that tradition. The special merit of Socrates, for Justin, lay in his application of true reason and inquiring insight to expose the fraud and deceptions of the popular religion which was basically inspired by evil spirits to enthral ignorant folk.[241] Since Christians are those who now have access to the full illumination granted by the divine Word Himself, they stand in the tradition of Socrates, hence in line with the most enlightened tradition in the Graeco-Roman heritage.[242] J. Daniélou rightly points to the important implications which Justin's intuition had for the missionary task:

> "To renounce idolatry and to accept Christianity ceases for the Greek to be a betrayal of his tradition, and becomes instead an act of loyalty to the best elements in it... Christianity is the plenary manifestation of something which the sages had possessed only in a partial revelation."[243]

One effect, therefore, of Justin's approach to the Graeco-Roman heritage is that the very difficulties involved in the Christians' attempt to achieve a valid and acceptable identity within the terms of the culture are now accounted for. The conflict between Christians and their opponents is in continuity with the old conflict between Socrates and his detractors; both struggles mirror the fundamental conflict between truth and falsehood. On the one side is the divine Word, in company with all those who have responded to His activity in them – in the past as in the present; on the other side, there are found the evil spirits, the originators and inspirers of the false theology in the Hesiodic and Homeric mythology.[244] The remarkable insight which informs this bold and imaginative treatment of Gentile religious tradition has been appropriately underscored by Prof. A.F. Walls, in relation to the history of the Christian world mission of later times:

> "Justin, in fact, has reached a place where many another missionary was to come over the next eighteen centuries: he has concluded that there was more than one type of non-Christian tradition. There is that which is palpably devilish; there is that which is compatible with the Gospel and strenuously opposed to what it opposes."[245]

Justin's insight, which amounts to a "theory of two traditions" in the Graeco-Roman heritage, the true as distinct from the erroneous, the enlightened perceived and disentangled from the corrupt, was crucial for Clement of Alexandria, who elaborated and applied it with even greater intellectual rigour and consistency than Justin would have been able to do.[246] That Clement considered the question so important is best explained by the fact that in him (as also in his greater successor, Origen), the Christian faith and the Greek philosophical tradition became embodied in one and the same individual in a manner as had not occurred before.[247] Clement, the "last and most important" of the Christian apologists, understood Christianity as the fulfilment of the divine education of the human mind and personality already evident in the Greek philosophical tradition.[248] The Christian faith summed up and brought together under one head a divine, universal training of mankind, of Greeks as well as of Jews (and Barbarians in general):

> "... to the Jews belonged the Law, and to the Greeks, philosophy, until the Advent; and after that came the universal calling to be a peculiar people of righteousness, through the teaching which flows from faith brought together by one Lord, the only God of both Greeks and Barbarians, or rather, of the whole race of men."[249]

It was therefore on the basis of this fundamental intuition that the Christian faith was heir to all that was worthy in the Hellenistic past, together with the chronological argument for the antiquity of the Old Testament and hence also of the *Christian* tradition – this latter being the greatest and most distinctive achievement of Tatian – that Graeco-Roman Christians were able to find a place to feel at home in their world.

It was the intuition of Justin as against the negative stance of Tertullian and Tatian which prevailed and continued to exercise the minds of thoughtful Christians. But their claim to be "philosophers" and to stand in the true philosophical tradition of Graeco-Roman culture caused the battle with Graeco-Roman tradition to be engaged in earnest; their opponents had no option but to dispute this claim.[250] Before the Christians became effectively a state within the State, they were threatening to rob Paganism of the latter's heritage. The very intellectual insights which had been attained through the long history of the philosophical and rational criticism of the popular religion, and on which Christians and non-Christians could agree,[251] the former claimed for themselves. "Whatever is well said by anyone is mine",[252] so had said Seneca, for, "the best ideas are common property".[253] But it was the little-known Christians who threw down the gauntlet: "Whatever things were rightly said among all men are the property of us Christians".[254] When, in bitter irritation, Celsus[255] wrote his book against the Christians and the Christian faith, it is hardly surprising that he entitled his work *The True Doctrine*.

VII. Conclusion

The aim of this chapter has been twofold: on the one hand, to understand the attitudes of Graeco-Roman critics of the Christian movement as the latter thrust into the Graeco-Roman world of the early Roman Empire; on the other, to trace the development of Christian self-awareness and identity in the context of Graeco-Roman tradition which produced the vast numbers of Christian converts of the period. The evidence has been drawn as far as possible from the primary sources representing the views and attitudes of the major personalities concerned.

As we have seen, the rise and spread of the Christian movement introduced into Graeco-Roman culture a novel and also disturbing phenomenon. The problem raised had implications for Christian converts as well as for non-Christians. That Christianity eventually became the political problem *par excellence* for the State is well known. Our interest has been directed more towards appreciating the "broadly cultural" problem which was raised by the incidence of Christian conversion and by religious convictions which were held and affirmed at the personal level and the need soon felt to validate Christian identity itself in terms relevant and meaningful for those who desired to be at home in the Graeco-Roman heritage.

Accordingly, as the earlier superficial and less informed Pagan views of the Christian movement gave way to more knowledgeable criticism, the intellectual and spiritual credentials of the Christian faith required to be shown for what they were. Graeco-Roman criticism fastened on to the novelty of Christianity, its upstart status in Graeco-Roman society, its "barbarous accents" and its disruptive posture in the religious and social traditions of mankind. The Christian writers, alive to the spiritual realities and intellectual outlook of their world, attempted to vindicate the Christian faith in ways which seemed to them both faithful to the tradition of Christian teaching itself and consistent with their own participation in the cultural dynamics of Graeco-Roman civilisation. Questions relating to the place of Christian self-consciousness in the religious and intellectual history of Graeco-Roman culture became central for Christian teachers and leaders of thought. How, for example, did the wider developments of their culture and heritage relate to their own specific experience which could not be spoken away? Moreover, were there ways in which their particular experience and world view as Christians could be validated for their non-Christian neighbours? In short, how were thoughtful Pagans to be helped to come to the same commitment, so long as the Christian outlook was considered intrinsically "barbarian" and irremediably alien? The missionary (or missiological) agenda which confronted the Christian movement in Graeco-Roman society could not be more fundamental and comprehensive. At the heart of the agenda was the viability of Christian identity itself in terms of the cultural inheritance in which the Christians also stood.

The problem of identity, therefore, resolved itself into a treatment of the past – its traditions, insights, no less than its perversities! A key was needed to interpret the past and stake claims on it, or to reject it as utterly unworthy, which some Christians did; Tertullian is the notable exemplar here.

On the whole, however, the positive attitude to the "old" tradition prevailed. Christians found in Christ the eternal and heavenly Word, now fully accessible through his incarnation and in apostolic teaching the key for their enterprise: to reap the harvest of philosophy and the best in the Pagan heritage for the Christian position. Justin and Clement of Alexandria represent this outlook and trend.

Paradoxically, it was one who did not himself belong to Graeco-Roman civilisation and who seemed unwilling to serve that culture, who rendered a most valuable service to Christians of Graeco-Roman culture. By his firm vindication and demonstration of the antiquity and priority of the "Barbarian philosophy" to the Greek philosophical tradition, Tatian bequeathed to Graeco-Roman Christianity a powerful instrument for carving a secure place for itself in the religious traditions of mankind. It meant not only that Christians could make a case for being allowed to feel at home in the world, but also that the very claim of the universal significance of the Christian Gospel was now grounded in historical tradition. Christians, therefore, had not only the means for vindicating their own historical identity, but also a basis for "theologising" in their world, and responding to the questions from within it.

And yet the impact of Tatian's elaboration of the chronological argument is only symptomatic of a much wider relevance. Tatian (with Tertullian) symbolises the outlook of those whom H. Richard Niebuhr has called the "representatives of exclusive Christianity".[256] Their significance for the problem of culture and Christian identity lies in the radical Biblicism which underpins their Christian self-understanding. Though they present an extreme and a somewhat negative posture, it is their radically Christian response to the identity problem which enables other Christian groups not to lose their balance.[257] It is appropriate, therefore, that we first take a close look at the vindicators of "Barbarism" against "Hellenism".

Notes

1. Edward Gibbon, *The History of the Decline and Fall of the Roman Empire*, vol. 2 (edited by J.B. Bury), London: Methuen and Co., 1897, pp.74-75. Cf. J. Geffken, *Der Ausgang des Griechisch-Römischen Heidentums*, Heidelberg: Carl Winter, 1929,p.19.

2. R.L. Wilken, "The Christians as the Romans (and Greeks) saw them", in E.P. Sanders (ed), *Jewish and Christian Self-Definiton* (vol.1), *The Shaping of Christianity in the 2nd and 3rd centuries*, London: SCM,1980, p.104.

3. Harnack attributes these sentiments, expressed by Eusebius, *PE*, 1,2, to Porphyry, a third-century opponent of Christianity. See Adolf Harnack, *Mission and Expansion of Christianity in the First Three Centuries* (vol. 1) (ET by J. Moffatt), London: Williams and Norgate, 1908, p.276.

4. Tacitus, *Histories*, 5.8. All references from Greek and Latin classical writers, unless otherwise stated, are from the Loeb Classical Library (*LCL*).

5. Pliny (The Elder), *Natural History*, 13,4.

6. Suetonius, *The Deified Augustus*, 43. Augustus' attitude would say more about his attitude to the Jews as a people than about his knowledge of Jewish religion. Cf. R.M. Grant, *Augustus to Constantine, The Thrust of the Christian Movement into the Roman World*, London: Collins, 1971, p. 33. It seems the evidence is not conclusive; see W.H.C. Frend, *Martyrdom and Persecution in the Early Church. A study of a conflict from the Maccabees to Donatus*, Oxford: Blackwell, 1965, p.117.

7. Cf. the reaction of the proconsul Gallio in the controversy involving Paul and the Jews in Corinth, reported in *Acts* 18:12-17.

8. Tacitus, *Histories*, 5.4.

9. R.L. Wilken, "The Christians as the Romans (and Greeks) saw them", p.104.

10. See Gregory Dix, *Jew and Greek, A Study in the Primitive Church*, London: Dacre Press, 1953, pp.110f. He comments: "One has to remember that history happens through men and women, not through abstractions" (p. 110).

11. See Adolf Harnack, *Mission and Expansion* (vol.1), pp.312ff.

12. D.W. Riddle, "Environment as a Factor in the Achievement of Self-consciousness in Early Christianity", in *Journal of Religion*, 99, 1927, pp.162-163.

13. Cf. *Acts* 17:6 (cf.18:13, in reference to Jewish law; 16:20f. in reference to Roman Paganism.)

14. Tacitus, *Annals*, 16,22,3.

15. *Ibid.*

16. R. McMullen includes Christians in his study of dissent and deviation in ancient Rome; see his *Enemies of the Roman Order*, London: Oxford

University Press, 1967. It is interesting that Tacitus expressed the same feelings about the Christians as he did of the hated Jews (cf. *Histories*, 5.5 on Jewish hatred of non-Jews: *adversus omnes alios hostile odium*. Cf. *Annals* 15,44,4 on Christians' hatred of the rest of humanity: *odio humani generis*.

17. R.M. Grant, *op.cit.*, p.99.

18. Edward Gibbon, *op.cit.*, p.75.

19. *Ibid.*, p.75.

20. W.H.C. Frend, *op.cit.*, p.171.

21. Cf. R. McMullen, *op.cit.*, p.246.

22. Edward Gibbon, *op.cit.*, p.75.

23. See R.M. Grant, *op.cit.*, p.97.

24. See *Mark* 15:12,26.

25. *John* 19:15.

26. Cf. *Acts* 18:12-17; 24,25 *passim*.

27. Suetonius, *The Deified Claudius* 25,4. See William Neil, *The Acts of the Apostles (NCB)*, London: Marshall, Morgan and Scott, 1973, pp.194-195; F.F. Bruce, *The Acts of the Apostles* (the Greek text with Introduction and Commentary), London: Inter-Varsity Press, second edition, 1952, pp.342-343. See W.H.C. Frend, *op.cit.*, pp.160-161, for a more cautious view.

28. Tertullian obviously knew of this confusion and fully exploited the Greek meaning of χρηστός, good, pleasant; cf. *Ad Nationes*, 1,3; *Apology*, 3). Justin may also have been aware of the misunderstanding; cf. *1 Apology*, 4.

29. See F.F. Bruce, *op.cit.*, p.481, on ἀκωλύτως.

30. See F.F. Bruce, *op.cit.*, on this description of the Christian movement; cf. *Acts* 9:2; 19:9,23; 22:4; 24:14,22.

31. Evidently, whereas the Christians themselves may have preferred to refer to themselves as "the Way", their critics, most probably Jews, referred to them as a sect; see *Acts* 24:14, ἥν λέγουσιν αἵρεσιν, also *Acts* 28:22.

32. See Josephus, *Antiquities*, 20,8,11.

33. See *Philippians* 4:22; cf. *Romans* 16:11; would the reference be to the household of Narcissus, the powerful official of the Emperor Claudius?

34. Adolf Harnack, *op.cit.*, vol.2, p.34.

35. See Origen, *Contra Celsum*, 1,27; 8,75; cf. Caecilius' views in Minucius Felix, *Octavius*, 5,8,12; also Lucian in *Peregrinus*, 12,13. Christian writers readily acknowledged this fact; cf. Justin, *1 Apology*, 60; *2 Apology*, 10; Tatian, *Oration*, 32-33. Tertullian makes special mention of the presence of poor Christians at the community meals (*Apology*, 39, 14-19).

36. As *Romans* 9-11 shows, an early theological problem for the Church was "the unbelief of the Jews".

37. Tacitus, *Annals*, 15,44. Interestingly, Tacitus says it is the masses who so designated the "Christians" by the name, quoting it as *Chrestiani*; cf. Suetonius, *Claudius*, 25,4; but he himself was more knowledgeable on Christian origins and writes the name correctly, *Christus*.

38. "... a class hated for their *scandalous behaviour* [whom] the common people called Christians. The originator of that name, Christus, had been executed by the governor Pontius Pilate during the reign of Tiberius. This *pernicious superstition*, afer being suppressed for a while, again broke out, not only *in Judaea, the source of that evil*, but even in Rome, to which all things foul and shameful from every quarter of the world gather and are practised. Accordingly, arrest was first made of those who confessed [*sc.* to being Chris-

tians]: then, on their evidence, an *immense multitude* was convicted, not so much of the charge of arson as for their *hatred of the human race*." Tacitus, *Annals,* 15,44,3-4. My emphasis.

39. Cf. Tacitus, *Histories,* 5.5 (said of Jews).

40. See W.H.C. Frend, *op.cit.,* p.162.

41. Tacite, *Annales,* 13-16, Texte établi et traduit par P. Wuilleumier, Paris: Editions Belles Lettres, 1978, p.171. See Sallust, *The War with Catiline,* 37,3, where he associates the "conspiracy" of Catiline with the alleged anti-establishment sentiments of the plebian class: "Invariably in a state those who have no money envy the respectable and exalt trouble-makers; they dislike the established state of affairs and long for something new; out of discontent with their own position they are keen for everything to be changed." From Tacitus' patrician standpoint, the *Christiani* seemed just as despicable.

42. P. Wuilleumier, *op.cit.,* p.171. For a possible reference to the Neronian persecution, cf. *First Epistle of Clement to the Corinthians,* 6,1: "a great multitude of the elect", πολὺ πλῆθος ἐκλεκτῶν, perished. See J.B. Lightfoot, *The Apostolic Fathers,* London: Macmillan, 1898, p.8.

43. Suetonius, *Life of Nero,* 16,2.

44. Pliny, *Letters and Panegyricus,* vol.2, Book 10, 96-97. Also J. Stevenson (ed), *A New Eusebius (Documents Illustrative of the History of the Church to AD 337),* London: SPCK, 1957, pp.13-18.

45. Betty Radice's translation in *LCL.*

46. E.T. Merrill, *Essays in Early Christian History,* London: Macmillan, 1924, pp.52ff.

47. Cf. his question to the Emperor, "whether it is the mere name of Christian *(nomen ipsum)* which is punishable, even if innocent of crime *(si flagitiis careat)*", Pliny, *op.cit.,* 96,2.

48. W.H.C. Frend, *op.cit.,* p.231, n.76, cites Origen, *Contra Celsum* 8, 65, for an indication of how the Christian will to martyrdom struck educated Pagans of the time. For the only reference by the Emperor Marcus Aurelius to the Christians, see his *Meditations,* 11,3.

49. See the comprehensive treatment of Graeco-Roman traditional piety by D. Kaufmann-Bühler in article *"Eusebeia", RAC,* vol.6, coll.986-1023.

50. Cicero, *De Legibus,* 2,8,19, pp.392-3.

51. An interesting instance where this fundamental aspect of Graeco-Roman religiosity was given constitutional sanction was the *Constitutio Antoniana* of the Emperor Caracalla in AD 212, which tied Roman citizenship to participation in state religious practices. See W.H.C. Frend, *op.cit.,* p.312, for discussion of its implications for the Church. Cf. also J. Vogt, *Zur Religiosität der Christenverfolger im römischen Reich,* Heidelberg: Carl Winter, 1962, p.18.

52. Cicero, *De Natura Deorum,* 2,3,8 (ET by H. Rackham), p.130-131.

53. See Polybius, 6, 56: "The most important difference for the better (i.e. between Roman and Greek cities) which the Roman commonwealth appears to me to display, is in their religious beliefs... a scrupulous fear of the gods is the very thing which keeps the Roman commonwealth together..." cited in T.R. Glover, *Conflict of Religions in the Early Roman Empire,* London: Methuen, 1919, pp.3f. Polybius saw in religion the requisite means of ensuring social control and inculcating discipline; "their [Romans'] object is to use it as a check upon the common people". So religion was politically expedient as a binding force and socially useful for discipline; cf. Varro's views in Augustine, *De Civitate Dei,* 4,27; 6,5

54. Cicero, *De Natura Deorum,* 2,(3),8.

55. Vergil, *Aeneid*, 6,791ff.

56. See C.N. Cochrane's perceptive treatment of the Roman "religion of culture" which was the basis of the reconstruction of the Republic as attempted by Augustus, in *Christianity and Classical Culture (A Study of Thought and Action from Augustus to Augustine)*, London: Oxford University Press, 1939, revised edition 1957, ch.2.

57. See D. Kaufmann-Bühler, *op.cit.*, col. 993.

58. Cicero, *De Natura Deorum*, 1,2-4. "If there are no gods (as some philosophers hold) or the gods have no concern for men, how can piety, reverence or religion exist... with piety, reverence and religion must disappear, and with them loyalty, social union... justice" (pp.5-7).

59. See Arend van Leeuwen, *Christianity in World History: The Meeting of the Faiths of East and West* (ET by H.H. Hoskins), London: Edinburgh House Press, 1964, pp. 173ff and *passim*.

60. Cicero, *De Natura Deorum*, 2 (28), 72, p. 193. Whether Cicero's etymological explanation is correct or not does not affect our argument.

61. *Ibid.*

62. It is interesting that Cicero does not consider the religious laws of his ideal state as in any way at variance with the religious institutions of the hoary Roman antiquity of Numa. On the contrary, they are "in harmony with the character of our early state which was the best in the world". See *De Legibus*, 2, (10), 23.

63. See D. Kaufmann-Bühler, *op.cit.*, col.1000, on the relation of *eusebeia* (piety) and the state.

64. See Augustine, *De Civitate Dei*, 4,27; 6,5. (It is interesting that the pontiff Cotta in Cicero's *De Natura Deorum*, includes Publius Scaevola in his ancient authorities, and Scaevola is also mentioned by Augustine (4,27). See also Tertullian, *Ad Nationes*, 4,1, for further Christian criticism.)

65. Polybius, 6,56. It is worth noting that Polybius personally thought of Roman religion as superstition (δεισιδαιμονία). Moreover, his admiration was not unqualified. He considered the most distinctive quality of the Roman commonwealth as a necessary evil; it would perhaps not have been necessary, had it been possible to form a state composed of wise men. But the common people must be kept in check and their unruly passions curbed, hence the necessity of "invisible terrors and suchlike pageantry". What an ànticipation of the Marxian interpretation of religion, and possibly also an illustration of the adage: "What is religion to me is superstition to you". Cf. Alice Gardiner, "Superstition" in *ERE*, vol.12, pp.120-122.

66. Cotta in Cicero, *De Natura Deorum*, is willing to accept and perform the rituals of his office, even without asking questions, and without proof *(débeo... maioribus autem nostris etiam nulla ratione reddita credere)*, 3,2,6, whilst he himself is attracted by other, somewhat less orthodox views.

67. J.H.W.G. Liebeschuetz, *Continuity and Change in Roman Religion*, Oxford: Clarendon Press, 1979, especially ch.2, "The Augustan Revival".

68. Samuel Dill, *Roman Society from Nero to Marcus Aurelius*, London: Macmillan, 1904, 1910, pp.305,331. And yet Stoics on the whole remained vague on their concept of God. Seneca uses God, gods, nature, fate, almost synonymously; see J.H.W.G. Liebeschuetz, *op.cit.*, pp.113f; T.R. Glover, *op.cit.*, pp.72-73.

69. Samuel Dill, *op.cit.* p.298.

70. See Seneca, *Epistulae Morales*, 89,4-8.

71. T.R. Glover, *op.cit.*, p.71.

72. Seneca, *Epistulae Morales*, 90,3. Cf. Cicero, *De Natura Deorum*, 1, (2), 3-4.

73. According to Augustine, *De Civitate Dei*, 6,10; (also Tertullian, *Apology*, 12), Seneca wrote a book, *On Superstition (De Superstitione)*, no longer extant, in which he castigates the traditional civil religion in a way which Varro could not. Seneca's freedom from the civil theology Augustine puts down to his philosophical outlook. But note Augustine's strictures on Seneca, "But this man whom philosophy had made, as it were, free, nevertheless, because he was an illustrious senator of the Roman people, worshipped what he reproached, because, forsooth, philosophy had taught him something great, namely, not to be superstitious in the world, but on account of the laws of the cities and the customs of men, to be an actor, not on the stage, but in the temple, conduct the more to be condemned that those things which he was deceitfully acting he so acted that the people thought he was acting sincerely".

74. T.R. Glover, *op.cit.*, p.56.

75. J.H.W.G. Liebeschuetz, *op.cit.*, p.60.

76. See Plutarch, Περὶ Δεισιδαιμονίας in *Moralia*, 2.

77. T.R. Glover, *op.cit.*, p.78.

78. See his *De fortuna Romanorum* in *Moralia*, 4; also his *Praecepta gerendae Republicae* in *Moralia*, 10.

79. John Oakesmith, *The Religion of Plutarch*, London: Longmans, Green and Co., 1902, pp.78ff.

80. In his treatise on Egyptian cults, *De Iside et Osiride (Moralia*,5), he developed his important idea that differences in conception of Deity were due to geographical and cultural differences between nations.

81. See, for example, his *Adversus Colotem*, 31(112-15), in *Moralia*, 14, in which he argues for the existence of gods from the consensus of mankind and the existence of religious rites in all human societies. See also *Amatorius*, *Moralia* 9,13 (756), for a firm statement of the argument in favour of the ancient traditional faith, against philosophical scepticism.

82. See his *Non posse suaviter vivi secundum Epicurum*, in *Moralia*, 14,21, (1101-2). The description of the "pleasantness" of religion is here set against that "element of tremulous fear" which underlies and supplies the major factor of superstition which is literally "fear of the daemons". Plutarch's argument in Περὶ Δεισιδαιμονίας focuses on this element of superstitious fear or dread.

83. *De Superstitione*, in *Moralia*, 2 (1,164,E).

84. J. Oakesmith, *op.cit.*, p.180.

85. See *De Defectio Oraculorum*, *Moralia*, 5,9 (414,F.)

86. See *Non posse suaviter* (21,1101,1102); also *De Superstitione* (9,169,D).

87. *De Superstitione* (4,166,D).

88. *Ibid.*, (3,166,B).

89. *Ibid.*, (8,169,D). See *1 Maccabees* 2:29ff on the reactions of Jews to the troops of Antiochus Epiphanes in 168 BC; cf. Josephus, *Antiquities*, 12,6,2.

90. Plutarch instances the suicides of Midas and Aristodemus, and the career of the Athenian general Nicias (see *De Superstitione*, 8,168,F).

91. *Ibid.*, (14,171,F).

92. *Ibid.*, (11,170,E)

93. *Ibid.*, (10,169,F).

94. On Seneca, see J.N. Sevenster, *Paul and Seneca*, Leiden: E.J. Brill, (Supplement to *NovT* vol.4), 1961. On Plutarch, see R.C. Trench, *Plutarch, his*

Life, his Parallel Lives and his Morals, London, 1873, p. 13.

95. See Justin, *1 Apology,* 5; Athenagoras, *Legatio,* 4-30.

96. William R. Schoedel, "Christian Atheism and the Peace of the Empire" in *Church History,* vol. 42, no.3, 1973, p.310.

97. See C.N. Cochrane, *op.cit.,* ch.3.

98. William Schoedel, *op.cit.,* helpfully shows how Athenagoras makes a distinction between theoretical and practical levels of the question of atheism, and that whilst Athenagoras is convincing on the theoretical level, the real problem was the practical "atheism" of the Christians, so far as their Pagan accusers were concerned.

99. J. Vogt, *op.cit.,* p.12.

100. Tacitus, *Annals,* 15, 44, 3-4; Suetonius, *Life of Nero,* 16,2; Pliny (the Younger), *loc.cit.* It is not unlikely that Tacitus' description of the Christian *multitudo ingens* harks back to Livy's account of the suppression of the Bachanal cult in 186 BC (cf. Livy, 39, 8-19). It is equally probable, from Pliny's sense of alarm, that the Governor saw the Christians in a similar light. That Christians were aware of the designation, see Minucius Felix, *Octavius,* 9: *vana et demens superstitio* (vain and senseless superstition).

101. R.L. Wilken, "The Christians as the Romans (and Greeks) saw them", pp.106-107.

102. Lucian, *Peregrinus,* 11.

103. Substantial excerpts are in Origen's response to Celsus in *Contra Celsum,* translated and edited by Henry Chadwick, Cambridge: Cambridge University Press, revised edition, 1965.

104. Origen, *Contra Celsum,* 1,9.

105. Note Henry Chadwick's interesting comment: "Celsus is no second-century Voltaire. That is a title perhaps appropriate to Lucian, but not to Celsus, who, had he been writing his book in the 20th century, might well have entitled his work, *A Recall to Religion.* See his *Origen: Contra Celsum,* xxii.

106. Cf. Tacitus, *Annals,* 15,44,3.

107. Particularly scathing on Virgin Birth, deity of Christ, Resurrection; see Origen, *Contra Celsum,* 1, 28ff; 1,69ff; 2,55; 5,14.

108. A.D. Nock, *Conversion (The Old and the New in Religion from Alexander to Augustine),* Oxford: Clarendon Press, 1933. See also C. Andresen, *Logos und Nomos: Die Polemik des Kelsos wider das Christentum,* Berlin: Walter de Gruyter, 1955.

109. See Origen, *Contra Celsum,* 8,67,69,73.

110. The Edict of the Emperor Gallienus (311) revoking the edicts of persecution provides an interesting insight into what the grounds of persecution were: "We wished previously, acting for the good of the commonwealth, to correct all things according to the ancient laws and public discipline of the Romans". R.A. Markus comments as follows: "Christians were to be brought to their senses and conform to the ancient laws and discipline. The persecution was nothing more nor less than part of a pagan revival." See R.A. Markus, *Christianity in the Roman World,* London: Thames and Hudson, 1971, p.86.

111. A.D. Nock, *op.cit.,* p.228.

112. Cf. T.R. Glover, *op.cit.,* p.259.

113. J. Vogt, *op.cit.,* p.12. "They left the room for expressions of different kinds of metaphysical experience of existence, for Apuleius with his longing for redemption and belief in mysteries, as much as for the deep wisdom of Plutarch and the lofty skepticism of Tacitus. But for Christianity this Roman

religion had no room. Pliny's actions and the Emperor's judgment backing them up cannot be completely understood unless their religious attitude is appreciated as the phenomenon of a belief which is both self-contained and also affects the outside world."

114. Particularly evident in the accounts of trials of the martyrs, see *Acts of Justin and Companions;* the prefect, Rusticus, declares, 5.8: "Those who have refused to sacrifice to the gods and to yield to the emperor's edict are to be led away to be scourged and beheaded in accordance with the laws." H. Musurillo, *The Acts of the Christian Martyrs,* Oxford: Clarendon Press, 1972, p.53.

115. G.E.M. de Ste. Croix, "Why were the early Christians persecuted?" in *Past and Present,* 26, November 1963, pp. 6-38, especially pp.24ff. Cf. Simeon L. Guterman, *Religious Toleration and Persecution in Ancient Rome,* London: Aiglon Press, 1951, p.26.

116. Cf. J. Speigl, *Der römischen Staat und die Christen,* Amsterdam: Verlag A.M. Hackert, 1970, p.250. Cf. G.E.M. de Ste. Croix, *op.cit.,* p.27: "... the problem posed by Christianity, its exclusiveness, was something Rome had never encountered before – except under very different conditions, in the Jewish national religion."

117. A.D. Nock, *op.cit.,* pp.2ff, on whose study I have depended for this aspect of my discussion.

118. *Ibid.,* p.7.

119. *Ibid.,* p.7.

120. *Ibid.,* p.162. An interesting instance of conversion to "religion" would be the conversion of Lucius to devotion to Isis, in the picaresque novel by Apuleius of Madaura, *Metamorphosis (The Golden Ass).*

121. On "philosophy" in the context of religious quests of the period, see S. Angus, *The Religious Quests of the Graeco-Roman World – A Study in the historical background of early Christianity,* London: John Murray, 1929, ch.4, "Greek Moral and Mystical Philosophy", pp.58-75. Cf. A.D. Nock, *op.cit.,* pp.179ff.

122. Plato, *Republic,* 518,D (ET by Cornford), Oxford: Clarendon Press, 1941.

123. Socrates was by far the most illustrious exemplar. Note Justin's sincere and warm admiration for him (cf. *2 Apology,* 13). Clement of Alexandria held Plato in very high esteem (cf. *Stromateis, passim*); when Tertullian spoke of Seneca as *saepe noster (De Anima,* 20), he was evidently making a distinction between that philosopher and much that he criticised in Roman culture.

124. Cf. Justin, *Dialogue,* 8, Christianity as the only "safe and profitable philosophy". An interesting instance of conversion to philosophy preceding Christian conversion was the young Augustine, through his reading of Cicero's now lost *Hortensius* (see Augustine, *Confessions,* 3,4). See Jean Daniélou, *Gospel Message and Hellenistic Culture* (ET by J.A. Baker), London: Darton, Longman and Todd, 1980, pp.10f, for the influence of Aristotle's now lost *Protreptikos,* with its call to conversion to philosophy, on Christian apologetic writing.

125. A.D. Nock, *op.cit.,* p.186.

126. Justin, *Dialogue,* 8; Tatian, *Oration,* 29,35; Clement, *Paidagogos,* especially "Hymn to Christ" at the end; Tertullian's vindication of martyrdom on grounds of finding favour with God (*Apology,*50).

127. Justin, *Dialogue with Trypho,* 9.

128. Note the interesting comment on Christians by Galen: "They include

not only men, but also women who refrain from cohabiting all their lives; and they also number individuals who, in self-discipline and self-control in matters of food and drink, and in keen pursuit of justice, have attained a piety not inferior to genuine philosophers" (in R. Walzer, *Galen on Jews and Christians*, London: Oxford University Press, 1949, p.15; quoted in J. Stevenson (ed), *A New Eusebius: Documents illustrative of the history of the Church to AD 337*, London: SPCK, 1957, p.133.

129. The accounts of the trials and deaths of the early Christian martyrs must be among the most moving documents from Graeco-Roman Christianity. See F.L. Cross, *The Early Christian Fathers*, London: Duckworth, 1960, pp.192ff.

130. In the fifth century AD, Orosius, a Christian from Roman Spain, would write in his *Historiarum adversus paganos*, 5,2: "When I, a refugee from disturbance and upheaval, flee to a haven of security, I find everywhere my native land, everywhere my law and my religion... As a Christian and as a Roman, it is to Romans and to Christians I come." Quoted in R.A. Markus, *op.cit.*, p.9.

131. Jean Daniélou makes this his starting point in regard to the Apologists and subsequently places the emphasis on their wider missionary purpose, namely, their attempt to present the Gospel to the Pagan world in ways which "reveal the distinctive character of the Kerygma in its Hellenistic form" (*op.cit.*, p.7). The eminent schòlar describes a result – I am more interested in the process of achieving that result.

132. H. Richard Niebuhr, *Christ and Culture*, New York: Harper and Row (Harper Colophon Books), 1975, p.4. Niebuhr quotes Geffken, *op.cit.*, p.1. See H. Lietzmann in *CAH*, 12, p.515, for an emphasis on the political question.

133. For the word "ontocracy" describing a totalitarian union of "throne and altar", see Arend Th. van Leeuwen, *op.cit.*, pp.173f.

134. C.N. Cochrane, *op.cit.*, p.29.

135. *Ibid.*, vi.

136. A.D. Nock, *op.cit.*, p.250.

137. The taunt by Celsus (cf. Origen, *Contra Celsum*, 1, 2).

138. Celsus' reaction to the Christian movement and to the intellectual and political outlook of Christians provides a useful indication as to what an educated and concerned Graeco-Roman traditionalist found objectionable in Christianity. His views can be summarised under three heads:

1) Christianity was unacceptable to reason, in view, for instance, of its insistence on faith as the ground for knowledge and experience; consequently, Christianity could only be for fools and the illiterate (1,9; 3,44,55).

2) The new teaching was unacceptable to good taste for its "stories" of virgin birth (for Celsus, a case of illegitimacy) (1,28), and of God coming down to earth (4,2,3); Christian confidence in God and hope of resurrection is the hope of worms and frogs! (4,23).

3) The Christian movement was objectionable in regard to the political interests of the state – Christians were lacking in patriotic sentiment – and the growth of Christianity threatened the social cohesion of the Empire (8,68,69,73ff).

139. This was precisely the point of the argument from chronology, which, already used in the apologetics of Hellenistic Judaism (cf. Josephus, *Contra Apionem*) came to be massively exploited by the Christians. See Justin, *1 Apology*, 44,59,60; Tatian, *Oration*, 31,36ff; Theophilus of Antioch, *Ad Autolychum*, 2,30; 3,20ff; Tertullian, *Apology*, 19,47; Clement of Alexandria, *Stromateis*, 1,15,21 *et passim*; Eusebius, *Praeparatio Evangelica*, 10,11; Lac-

tantius, *Divine Institutes*, 4,5.

140. T.R. Glover, *op.cit.*, p.184. See Philip Carrington, *Christian Apologetics of the Second Century (in their relation to modern thought)*, London: SPCK, 1921.

141. H. Richard Niebuhr, *op.cit.*, p.4.

142. *Ibid.*, p.10.

143. Werner Jaeger, *Early Christianity and Greek Paideia*, London: Oxford University Press, 1961, p.36.

144. Cf. J. Geffken, *op.cit.*, p.1.

145. Marcel Simon, *Verus Israel, Etude sur les relations entre Chrétiens et Juifs dans l'empire romain (135-425 AD)*, Paris: E. de Boccard, 1964, pp.87ff.

146. See Origen, *Contra Celsum*, 1,47; 2,13; Eusebius, *HE*, 2,23; Tertullian, *Adversus Judaeos*, 13.

147. At Antioch in Syria, the followers of Jesus the Christ acquire the now common name "Christians" (cf. *Acts* 11:26). It is worth noting that the first occurrence of the term "Christianity" is in the writings of Ignatius, Bishop of Antioch (died *ca.* 115); see his *Epistle to Magnesians*, 10; *Epistle to Philadelphians*, 6, for his distinction of Christianity (Χριστιανισμός) from Judaism (Ἰουδαϊσμός) in J.B. Lightfoot and J.R. Harmer, *The Apostolic Fathers*, London: Macmillan, 1898.

148. Justin, *1 Apology*, 53. Justin obviously associates Samaritans and Judaeans together as descendants of the earlier tribes of Israel.

149. Justin's Old Testament authorities are *Isaiah* 54:1 and *Jeremiah* 9:26, which he mistakenly attributes to Isaiah.

150. See Adolf Harnack, *op.cit.*, vol.2, pp.94-96. If the *Dialogue* was actually based on a meeting in Ephesus, then the massive expansion of Christianity in Asia Minor provides an interesting sidelight on Justin's assertion.

151. Justin, *Dialogue*, 12.

152. Marcel Simon, *op.cit.*, p.91.

153. *Philippians* 3:3. As Adolf Harnack points out, the New Testament usage of the polemical claim to be the "Israel of God" (*Galatians* 6:6) was done against the background of resisting Judaisers; see his *op.cit.*, vol.1, p. 242. The same must be said of such texts as *John's Gospel* 4:23, and possibly *1 Peter* 2:9ff.

154. R.A. Markus, *op.cit.*, p.25.

155. Adolf Harnack, *op.cit.*, vol.1, pp.240-278. I am indebted to Harnack for the outline history of the concept, though I interpret the material differently in parts, in view of my subject and my perspective on the history.

156. Pseudo-Cyprian, *De Pascha Computus;* the work is dated *ca.* 242-243; see E.J. Goodspeed, *A History of Early Christian Literature* (revised and enlarged by R.M. Grant), Chicago: Phoenix Books, 1966, p.177.

157. *1 Peter* 2:9.

158. *1 Corinthians* 10:32.

159. Cf. *Romans* 1:14; *Colossians* 3:11, seem to define other sub-divisions. On the persistence of Greek-Barbarian antithesis, in the ancient Mediterranean world, see Martin Hengel, *Jews, Greeks and Barbarians: Aspects of the Hellenization of Judaism in the pre-Christian period* (ET by John Bowden), London: SCM Press, 1980, especially ch.7.

160. *2 Corinthians* 5:17.

161. Cf. *Ephesians* 2:14ff.

162. Adolf Harnack, *op.cit.*, vol.1, p.243; cf. *Galatians* 3:28.

163. See the Pauline expression in *Philippians* 3:3: "we are the true circumcision who worship *in the spirit of God*" (οἱ πνεύματι Θεοῦ λατρεύοντες). (My emphasis.)

164. See Aimé Puech, *Les Apologistes grecs du deuxième siècle de notre ère,* Paris: Hachette, 1912, pp.33ff.

165. See Clement of Alexandria, *Stromateis,* 6,5.

166. Cf. Philip Carrington, *The Early Christian Church* (Vol.2, *The Second Christian Century*), Cambridge: Cambridge University Press, 1957, pp. 17-18.

167. Clement's use of the *Preaching of Peter,* as I shall seek to show in a later chapter, fits in perfectly with his own desire to elaborate a scheme of divine self-disclosure and a history of redemption, which takes Greek tradition into account from the start. Clement's purpose, therefore, throws an interest-ing sidelight on what the earlier Christian writer may have been attempting to establish.

168. It is quite possible that behind this courageous effort lies the method and trend of St Paul's own missionary preaching among Gentiles (cf. *Acts* 14:15-18, in Lystra; 17:22-34, in Athens; also *Romans* 2:14ff). Aimé Puech makes the link with Paul explicit, especially in regard to the two speeches in Lystra and Athens: "The two speeches in Lystra and Athens stand indeed at the beginning of all apologetic literature; they predesign its main lines with perfect precision." (*op.cit.*, p.24).

169. F.L. Cross, *op.cit.*, p.27; text in J.B. Lightfoot and J.R. Harmer, *op.cit.*, p.487.

170. *To Diognetus,* 1.

171. *Ibid.,*5.

172. *Ibid.,* 6.

173. *Ibid.,* 7.

174. *Ibid.,* 1.

175. *Ibid.,* 9, 7.

176. *Ibid.,* 9.

177. *Ibid.,* 10.

178. Aristides, *Apology,* Greek text as edited by J.A. Robinson, *Texts and Studies* 1 (i) (ET by J.R. Harris), Cambridge: Cambridge University Press, 1891, pp.100-112.

179. *Contra,* Eusebius, *HE,* 4 (3), who placed the work earlier and suggested that it was addressed to the Emperor Hadrian; see Philip Carrington, *op.cit.*, p.95.

· 180. The Syriac and Armenian versions speak of four categories: 1) Bar-barian, 2) Greeks, 3) Jews, 4) Christians.

181. Aristides, *Apology,* 2 (Greek version).

182. *Ibid.,* 3-7 (Greek); 3-7 (Syriac); also 12-13 (Greek).

183. See *ibid.,* 8-9 (Greek); 8-13 (Syriac).

184. *Ibid.,* 14 (Greek); 14 (Syriac).

185. *Ibid.,* 15ff (Greek); 15ff (Syriac).

186. *Ibid.,* 15 (Greek). The Syriac version (2) gives a fuller treatment of the subject: "The Barbarians... trace the origin of their kind of religion from Kronos and from Rhea and their other gods... The Greeks... from Hellenos, who is said to be sprung from Zeus... The Jews... trace the origin of their race from Abraham who begat Isaac, of whom was born Jacob... The Christians trace the

beginning of their religion from Jesus the Messiah; and he is named the Son
of God Most High..."

187. Justin, *Dialogue*, 123; cf. *Martyrdom of Justin and Companions*,
declaration of Hierax, "Christ is our true Father, and our faith in him is our
mother" (Ch.4,8), in H. Musurillo, *op.cit.*, p.51.

188. Adolf Harnack, *op.cit.*, vol.1, p.250. The most impressive exemplar of
the Christian conception of universal history within the scope of our subject,
is Clement of Alexandria. He was to build upon the earlier insights by
suggesting that the rise of Christianity specifically signifies the inauguration
of "the universal calling (ἡ κλῆσις ἡ καθολική) to be a peculiar people of
righteousness, through the teaching which flows from faith brought together
by one Lord, the only God of both Greeks and Barbarians, or rather of the whole
race of men" in *Stromateis*, 6,17.

189. Tertullian, *Ad Nationes*, 1, 8, 20; *Scorpiace*, 10.

190. Tertullian, *Ad Nationes*, 1,8.

191. Only a couple of examples in each case, from the several well-known
expressions will suffice: Apollonius Molon criticised Jews as "atheists and
misanthropes... cowards... the most witless of all barbarians... consequently
the only people who have contributed no useful invention to civilisation"; see
Josephus, *Contra Apionem*, 2,148. Tacitus, *Histories*, 5,8. describes Jews as
"the basest of peoples". On Christians, the Christian writer from Carthage,
Minucius Felix, provides an index of Pagan opinion in the words attributed to
the Pagan Caecilius in his dialogue *Octavius*. Christians are described as
latebrosa et lucifuga natio (ch.8).

192. Tertullian, *Ad Nationes*, 1,8.

193. *Ibid.*, 1,20.

194. Both works are dated *ca.* AD 197. See B. Altaner, *Patrology* (ET by
H.C. Graef), Freiburg: Herder, London: Nelson, 1960, p.169.

195. Tertullian, *Scorpiace*, 10.

196. Adolf Harnack, *op.cit.*, vol.1, p.269. My emphasis.

197. Livy, 39,13,14. Livy's *multitudinem ingentem* ominously foreshadows
Tacitus' *multitudo ingens* said of the Christians; see Tacitus, *Annals*, 15,44,4.

198. This may possibly have been the case with Pliny the Younger, in
Bythinia, who resorted to the torture of some Christian women to ascertain
the truth of the rumours concerning Christian secret misdeeds (see his *Letters*,
Bk. 96). The attack by Marcus Cornelius Fronto (of Cirta in Africa), against
the Christians, and reported by Minucius Felix in his *Octavius*, 9,6; 31,2, might
have rested on some such similar association of "Christians" with groups like
the "Bacchanalia cult".

199. Text in Migne, *PL*, 4, 930,D - 968,A.

200. *Ibid.*, 962,B.

201. J.A. Robinson, "The Remains of the Original Greek of the *Apology* of
Aristides" in J.A. Robinson (ed), *op.cit.*, pp.86ff.

202. Cf. R.A. Markus, "The Problem of Self-Definition: From Sect to
Church" in E.P. Sanders (ed), *op.cit.*, pp.1-15.

203. Tertullian, *Apology*, 39.

204. R.L. Wilken, "The Christians as the Romans (and Greeks) saw them",
p.102.

205. Justin, *2 Apology*, 10.

206. See R.A. Norris, *God and World in Early Christian Theology*, London:
A. & C. Black, 1965, 1966, pp.4f.

207. R.L. Wilken, "Toward a Social Interpretation of Early Christian Apologetics" in *Church History*, vol.39, no.4, 1970, pp.437-458; also, "The Christians as the Romans (and Greeks) saw them", pp.100-125.

208. R.L. Wilken, "The Christians as the Romans (and Greeks) saw them", p.108.

209. *Ibid.*, p.108. It is noteworthy in this regard that the Christian literature produced in the context made a lot of the excellence of Christian moral and social life, no less than of Christian teaching; cf. Justin, *1 Apology*, 15,29; *2 Apology*, 1,6; Athenagoras, *Legatio*, 11, 32-33; Tatian, *Oration*, 32ff; *Ad Diognetum*, 5; Clement of Alexandria, especially *Paidagogos*.

210. Seneca, *Epistulae Morales*, 90,3. Interestingly the quest for an integrated knowledge of all "things divine and human" becomes central to the theological task which Clement of Alexandria set for himself; cf. *Paidagogos*, 2,2; also *Stromateis*, 1,5.

211. The physician Galen, who made favourable comments on the "philosophical" conduct of Christians, nonetheless stumbled at the Christian insistence on faith as a principle for the knowledge of truth. (See R. Walzer, *op.cit.*, in J. Stevenson, *op.cit.*, pp.132-133.)

212. Jean Daniélou, *op.cit.*, p.31.

213. *Ibid.*, pp.41f. (Cf. Justin, *1 Apology*, 46; *2 Apology*, 10,13.2)

214. Justin, *2 Apology*, 7; cf. *1 Apology*, 5: 46.2

215. See, for example, the *Hortatory Address to the Greeks* (*Cohortatio*) falsely attributed to Justin. Also, *The Mockery of the Heathen Philosophers* (*Irrisio*) (Διασυρμὸς τῶν ἔξω φιλοσόφων) by Hermias; text in Otto, *CACSS*, vol.2, pp.1-31.

216. Tertullian, *Apology*, 37; *PL* 462, A - 463, A.

217. *Ibid.*, 46ff.

218. See Tertullian, *De Praescriptione Haereticorum*, especially ch.7.

219. Tertullian, *Apology*, 46-49.

220. The conversion of Victorinus was a major event in Augustine's "spiritual" pilgrimage; see his *Confessions*, Bk.8, Ch.2.

221. Henry Chadwick, *Early Christian Thought and the Classical Tradition*, London: Oxford University Press, 1966, pp.1-3.

222. Werner Jaeger, *op.cit.*

223. Tatian, *Oration against the Greeks*, 18. He speaks of Justin as "most admirable Justin" (θαυμασιώστατος Ἰουστίνος). The comment is quoted in Eusebius, *HE*, 4,16,7.

224. Werner Jaeger, *op.cit.*, pp.3-5.

225. *Ibid.*, p.27.

226. E.J. Goodspeed, *op.cit.*, p.107.

227. Louis Duchesne, *Early History of the Christian Church (From its foundation to the end of the third century)* (ET), London: John Murray, 1910, p.156.

228. See Tatian, *Oration against the Greeks*, 29; 35.

229. Aimé Puech, *Les Apologistes grecs*, p.156.

230. May we not have to allow the possibility that Tatian saw in Christianity, especially in view of its "barbarian" roots, a powerful tool for warding off the imposition of Greek culture which he felt to be alien to him, and for affirming his own Assyrian identity?

231. Cf. Justin's remarkable statement, "I confess that I both boast and

with all my strength strive to be found a Christian; not because the teachings of Plato are different (ἀλλότρια) from those of Christ, but because they are not in all respects similar (ὅμοια)as neither are those of the others, Stoics and poets and historians" (*2 Apology*, 13). The context is Justin's claim for the fullness of Christian knowledge as against the partial and inadequate character of the insights of philosophers, such inadequacy being seen in the inconsistencies in their views.

In this regard, see Athenagoras, *Legatio, 7,* for the judgment that the fundamental flaw in the intellectual adventure of Greek thinkers lay in the fact that rather than learn from God concerning God (παρὰ θεοῦ περὶ θεοῦ) they simply sought, each one, to learn from himself (παρ' αὐτοῦ ἕκαστος). Contradictions and inconsistencies are again the consequence of their speculative theology.

Cf. Clement of Alexandria, *Protreptikos*, 5, 6, for the view that some philosophical speculation could in fact be considered as no more than vanity (κενοδοξία), and amounted to seeing the truth in a dream (ὀνειρώττουσαν τὴν ἀλήθειαν); cf. *Stromateis*, 2,2, for the view that faith (πίστις), rejected by educated Greeks (Celsus?) as futile and barbarous (κενὴν καὶ βάρβαρον) as an essential element in all true intellectual apprehension.

232. Henry Chadwick, *Early Christian Thought and the Classical Tradition*, p.21. My emphasis.

233. *Colossians* 2:8

234. Tatian repeatedly emphasises the arrogance (ἀλαζονεία) of the Greeks in their self-portrait of cultural superiority.

235. See H. Richard Niebuhr, *op.cit.*, pp.65ff, for his perceptive treatment of the *necessity* and yet *inadequacy* of the radical, anti-cultural Christian outlook.

236. Werner Jaeger, *op. cit.*, p.35. Cf. Henry Chadwick's observation: "Justin does not merely use Greek philosophy. He passes judgment upon it", in *Early Christian Thought and the Classical Tradition*, p.20.

237. Justin, *Dialogue with Trypho*, 8.

238. *The Preaching of Peter*, cited in Clement of Alexandria, *Stromateis*, 6,5.

239. E. Benz, "Christ and Socrates in the early church" in *ZNW*, vol.43, 1950-51, pp.195-224. It is possible that, as Benz suggests, "the Socratic characteristic of fearlessness in the face of death gave him the impulse to study the teaching of the Christians" (p.200).

240. Cf. Justin, *1 Apology*, 5,46; *2 Apology*, 7,10. Also, Athenagoras, *Legatio*, 31; and Tertullian, *Ad Nationes*, 1,4; *Apology*, 14. According to the Cynic, Lucian of Samosata, the calamities of Peregrinus caused Christians to treat him for a time at least, as a "new Socrates" (καινὸς Σωκράτης); see his *Passing of Peregrinus*, 12.

241. Justin, *1 Apology*, 5.

242. Justin, *2 Apology*, 10. Clement of Alexandria considered that it was from Socrates that the Greeks had "received their most important dogmas" (*Stromateis*, 6,2).

243. Jean Daniélou, *op.cit.*, p.33.

244. E. Benz, *op.cit.*, pp.198f. Athenagoras (*Legatio*, 31), who, unlike Justin, refrained from calling Socrates a Christian, nonetheless saw in the ancient sage's suffering and death in the cause of what he held to be true, an analogy of the Christian predicament of his own time.

245. A.F. Walls, "The first chapter of the Epistle to the Romans and the

Modern Missionary Movement" in W. Gasque and R.P. Martin (eds), *Apostolic History and the Gospel (Biblical and Historical Essays presented to F.F. Bruce)*, Exeter: Paternoster Press, 1970, p.348.

246. See especially *Protreptikos*, 5,7,10, and *Stromateis, passim.*

247. Cf. Henry Chadwick, *Early Christian Thought and the Classical Tradition*, p.65, on Clement: "His entire character and personal achievement constitute in themselves an answer to Celsus' thesis that between Christianity and the Hellenic tradition there can be no reconciliation".

248. Werner Jaeger, *op.cit.*, p.47.

249. Clement of Alexandria, *Stromateis*, 6,17.

250. Cf. J. Speigl, *op.cit.*, p.254.

251. See E.R. Dodds, *Pagan and Christian in an Age of Anxiety (Some aspects of religious experience from Marcus Aurelius to Constantine)* Cambridge: Cambridge University Press, 1965, pp.118ff.

252. Seneca, *Epistulae Morales*, 16,7.

253. *Ibid.*, 12,11.

254. Justin, *2 Apology*, 13.

255. For the examination of the evidence in support of the view that Celsus had Justin's work in mind, see Carl Andresen, *op.cit.* For a summary of the main points, together with further evidence, see Henry Chadwick, *Early Christian Thought and the Classical Tradition*, p.133, n.59.

256. H. Richard Niebuhr, *op.cit.*, p.66.

257. *Ibid.*, p.68.

Chapter Two

The Gospel as the Triumph of Barbarism? Tatian, or, the Vindication of the Barbarians against the Greeks

I. Tatian: the traditional view – one who broke with the church

Of our authors, Tatian is the one on whom the witness of early Christian tradition was most unfavourable. His reputation for heresy is owed not only to the authority of Irenaeus, who links Tatian with Marcion, Valentinus and Saturninus,[1] but also to Tatian's own espousal of extreme ascetic and Encratite views, as well as to his idiosyncratic exegesis of the Scriptures.[2] Eusebius, in his *Church History*, cites Irenaeus' strictures on Tatian, together with other equally unfavourable testimonies.[3] Later writers repeated Irenaeus' criticisms, and even extended them into making Tatian the founder of a heretical sect.[4]

This view of Tatian proved quite tenacious as is shown by the persistent tendency later, even among Syriac-speaking theological writers of the East from where Tatian had come in the first place, to speak of Tatian as a heretic, and a Greek one too![5] Most probably, it was through the Syriac translation of the *Church History* of Eusebius in the fourth century that Tatian came to the general attention of Syrian theologians.[6] In this connection, the observation made by A.-S. Marmardji is interesting:

"It is from Rome...that he got his name Tatian. His long stay in the West, and particularly in Greece and his knowledge of the language and science of the Hellenes, prompted his own compatriots, the Syrians, to give him the surname, 'the Greek'."[7]

Tatian's renown among Syriac-speaking Christians was due in large measure to his great editorial work, the Gospel harmony *Diatessaron*, which most probably served as the first Syriac language text of the New Testament Gospel events.[8] Though this work was eventually banned from liturgical use by Rabbula, bishop of Edessa (died 435), a policy followed by Theodoret of Cyrrhus (died 457), it continued to be respected and consulted by Syriac-speaking exegetes and theologians well into the Middle Ages.[9] The work maintained its renown by virtue of the fact that the great *doctor* of the Syrian Church, Saint Ephrem, wrote a commentary on it in the middle of the fourth century.[10]

However, even in the framework of the apologetic literature of the second century, Tatian has continued to suffer. On the one hand, his life has had pre-heretical and heretical periods assigned to it. Thus, there has been a tendency to study his major extant work, the *Oration Addressed to the Greeks*, with a view to ascertaining its consistency or otherwise with orthodox Christian doctrines. For instance, J. Lebreton, in his study of the early history of trinitarian doctrine, regarded Tatian's contribution as "mediocre", considering it as "coming from a man halfway into heresy".[11] On the other hand, Tatian's association with "the most admirable Justin"[12] has not been completely in his favour. Irenaeus' statement reported by Eusebius, that Tatian "broke with the Church" after the martyrdom of Justin, is closely linked with his assertion that Tatian did not dare express heretical opinions whilst Justin was alive.[13] The effect of this view of Tatian was not only to place him under suspicion generally, but also to make it difficult to appreciate Tatian for himself and for his contribution to Christian self-understanding.[14] Since Tatian presents us with an important and necessary perspective on the question of Christian identity, it is only fair that he should be heard on his own terms, and not as the "unworthy disciple" of Justin.[15]

II. Christian Identity as a new perspective on Tatian

As Aimé Puech observed in his *Recherches sur le Discours aux Grecs de Tatien*, apart from the few testimonies to Tatian in the early patristic literature, "Tatian is known to us only through his own writings, that is, through his *Oration to the Greeks*".[16] In spite of the limitations which such a restricted field of investigation imposes, one can, nonetheless, as Martin Elze concludes, arrive at "a clear picture of his spiritual stature".[17]

The *Oration* does not by any means give us a full presentation of contemporary Christian belief and doctrinal understanding. It is notable that the name of Jesus Christ is not once mentioned in the entire work. Moreover, the use of Scripture is more often by suggestion than by explicit statement. However, these omissions need not indicate that Tatian was already on his way towards a rupture with the Catholic Church. Puech, who studied the problem, suggested a solution which took into account the nature and purpose of the *Oration*.[18] What Tatian's *Oration* does give us is an insight into a radical apprehension of the Christian faith from the standpoint of one who did not share in the eirenic and accommodating attitude to the pre-Christian intellectual and religious tradition of Graeco-Roman culture, such as one would find in Justin and in Clement of Alexandria.

Some scholars do not take sufficient account of Tatian's Syriac background;[19] on the other hand it is not necessary to postulate the existence of a thoroughgoing Syriac theology in contradistinction to Judaistic and Hellenistic theologies,[20] in order to appreciate the relevance of different cultural outlooks.[21] The polemical thrust of the *Oration* compels us to take seriously not only the author's fierce identification with the "Barbarians" against the "Greeks", but also his own explicit assertion that his place of birth was "the land of the Assyrians" – a statement implying that his conversion to the Christian faith may have been understood by him as a return to his roots. His intellectual and spiritual pilgrimage which took him out of "Barbarism" through the "waste-lands" of "Hellenism", eventually brought him to discover the truth, not in the lofty deliverances of the Greek philosophical and ethical tradition, nor in the popular religion of the "cultured" Greeks, but in the "unpretentious" and "artless" certainties of writings which have their origin and development in "Barbarian" tradition.[22] It is significant that it is from this point on in the *Oration,* after Tatian has made explicit the connection between his conversion experience and the "barbarian writings" (i.e. the Old Testament), that the claims for Christianity as philosophy are most vigourously urged.[23] The discovery of Christianity as philosophy, the only "true and profitable philosophy",[24] will not be for Tatian as it was for Justin the discovery of what the Greek philosophical tradition had sought and groped after. For Tatian, the assertion is made as the vindication of a radical alternative to the Graeco-Roman tradition.[25]

It is the assertion of the claims of "our Barbaric philosophy"[26] with its certainties, unity and coherence, against the speculations of the Greek tradition, with its uncertainties, divergencies and incoherences. It is the opposition of the claims of a unified divine revelation, the Word of God, against the vagaries of divergent human tenets.[27] On the one hand are the "harmonious" Christians; on the other, the "inharmonious" Greeks.[28]

At the heart of this sharp and uncompromising opposition between Christians (as Barbarians) and Greeks, is Tatian's conception of truth as the truth of God and the truth about God. Martin Elze recognised that it is Tatian's understanding of truth which stamps his whole way of thinking and motivates his life with the pursuit of truth – "the striving after truth" – and, consequently, makes Tatian see himself as a herald of the truth to the Greeks.[29] Tatian's use of his firm apprehension of the certainty of the Christian knowledge of God will be studied more closely later. However, at this point, it is important to note not only that Tatian feels superior to the entire Greek intellectual and moral tradition, but also that the basis of this feeling which causes him to address his readers "as from an eminence"[30] is his Christian self-consciousness. The radicality of Tatian's fundamental outlook which would manifest itself in his unmitigating distinctions between, on the one hand, the truth of the Christian tradition – divine, ancient and indivisibly one – and, on the other hand, the error inherent in the Greek tradition – human, derived and irremediably contradictory[31] – is first and foremost the radicality of a Christian self-identity which stubbornly refuses to give credence to the cultural and intellectual superiority which Greeks and Romans claimed for themselves.

In its outlook and thrust, Tatian's *Oration* is in the tradition of the great apologetic work of Josephus and other Jewish historical apologetic writers who were alive to the intellectual and cultural tensions of their world, and sought to respond to the contemptuous views held about Jewish society and mores.[32] Tatian's purpose, basically, is the defence of the Christian faith and the Christian community, without naming them in these terms, and within this purpose the historical antecedents of the faith in the religious history of ancient Israel carry tremendous significance. Tatian understood very well that the Christian faith was in direct historical continuity with a "Barbarian" tradition. From this apprehension, it was relatively easy for him to understand the superiority of the Christian faith, as the vindication of the worth of Barbarian self-identity, and as the utmost demonstration of the primacy of "Barbarism" over the cultural pretensions of "Hellenism". Tatian, therefore, extends his vindication of the Christian position into the broader issues concerning the validation of Barbarian peoples, presumed uncultured, in the face of the arrogance of Graeco-Roman claims. Thus, whilst it would be inaccurate to say that Tatian was merely continuing the tradition of Hellenistic Jewish apologetics, nevertheless, it was Tatian, of all the second-century apologists, who entered most firmly and with the least reserve, into the heritage of the achievement of Jewish apologetics in Hellenistic times. Puech's observation on the extent to which the Christian apologists were indebted to their Jewish predecessors is perhaps most evident in the case of Tatian:

> They [i.e. Jewish apologists to the Hellenistic world] taught them not to give way without discussion before Greek and Roman pride, before *civilisation*, but on the contrary to reclaim for the *Barbarians* the credit for all the ideas exploited by the Greeks.[33]

The high point of Tatian's contribution to this vindication of the "Barbarians" would be his chronological argument in the latter part of his *Oration*. But we can say with a reasonable degree of certainty that Christian conversion was experienced by Tatian as, *inter alia,* a liberation from the incubus of a culture which he felt to be alien and arrogant.

III. The "Renunciation" of Hellenistic tradition

The note of "renunciation" of Graeco-Roman tradition in its entirety, as much as in its particular aspects, is sounded quite early in the *Oration*,[34] and subsequently often enough to make it a major element of Tatian's outlook. The terms in which this rejection is expressed, echoes the Christian convert's repudiation and renunciation of the Devil in baptism[35] and suggests that there is more involved than merely cultural hostility or national feeling. The fact that Tatian frequently uses the first person plural of the pronoun and of the verb raises the question as to the meaning of this usage not only in those instances of the "repudiation" of Graeco-Roman tradition but also where the author affirms the Christian alternative. As Martin Elze has shown, Tatian's use of the pronoun or of the verb in the plural falls into two main categories; namely, a periphrastic manner of designating himself, and a reference to human beings in general.[36] It is evident from those instances in the first category, that Tatian's usage is not meant to be taken merely as a rhetorical device for himself alone. The persistence with which he speaks of Christianity or Christian practices in contradistinction to Greek philosophy and values, as "ours",[37] points to the vindication of a community of people with a common understanding. He calls for attention to his teaching as to *our* teachings;[38] the intellectual and spiritual insight thus gained, being "far beyond the apprehension of the world" is of the nature of an entirely different culture; it is *our* culture.[39] Against the mythological fictions of the Homeric theology, Tatian sets "*our* narrations";[40] and the Christian doctrine of God is *our* apprehension of God.[41] In what is, according to the context, evidently a reference to Old Testament social organisation and legislation, Tatian speaks of "*our* polity and the history of *our* laws".[42] The predictions of future events, as recorded in the Old Testament, came through *our* prophets.[43] Christianity itself, as the acme of a radically alternative tradition and philosophy, is *our* philosophy.[44]

Moreover, when Tatian prefaces his statements of Christian doctrine with expressions like "we have learnt"[45] and "we have received",[46] he is also to be understood as speaking on behalf of a community. There is no basis for presuming that the community in this case is only in tenuous connection with orthodox Christianity. In all the instances noted, as in his portrayal of the Christian community in general, Tatian emerges as a spokesman for the mainstream "Catholic" Christianity of the second century.[47] His staunch defence of a cardinal article of faith like the belief in the bodily resurrection at the consummation of all things,[48] sets him apart from Gnostic teachers.[49] The evidence bears out abundantly Martin Elze's view that "Tatian speaks here from within orthodox Christianity and is its spokesman".[50]

If Tatian's affirmation of Christian belief is made in the name of the mainstream Christian movement, then his renunciation of the Greek philosophical tradition and whatever he considers incompatible with Christianity, ought also to be taken as made on behalf of "Catholic" Christianity.

It is difficult to understand the intensity of Tatian's antipathy to Graeco-Roman tradition without recognising in him one who also had pursued the attractions of that culture and assimilated its achievements. His statements claiming the right to speak from the position of a participant who possessed personal knowledge of Graeco-Roman religion and culture, bear the marks of authenticity. His admission into the mysteries[51] may be a reference to the Eleusinian mysteries at Athens, the mysteries *par excellence*, as Otto indicates.[52] His claim to Greek scholarship,[53] as Puech has pointed out, must not be understood as simply indicating that he "studied rhetoric", that he may have been no more than "a mere declaimer". Tatian taught the disciplines which he studied.[54]

Moreover, Puech's meticulous examination of Tatian's style, syntax and vocabulary demonstrated that Tatian was not an ignorant person.[55] The *Oration* does show signs of negligence and a lack of systematic approach in composition; but the work as a whole indicates remarkable erudition and extensive knowledge in Greek studies, as Tatian himself claims:

> "The things which I have thus set forth before you I have not learnt at second hand. I have visited many lands; I have taught your disciplines; I have acquainted myself with many arts and inventions... for I do not attempt, as is the custom with many, to strengthen my own views by the opinions of others, but I wish to give you a distinct account of things with which I have personally acquainted myself.[56]

This assertion about his excellence in Greek learning recalls a similar statement made in the first chapter, which has lent itself to a variety of renderings. In concluding a catalogue of claims in favour of Barbarian cultural superiority to Graeco-Roman civilisation, and a criticism of the diversity of Greek dialects, Tatian declares: "On this account, we [I] have renounced your wisdom, though I was once thoroughly proficient in it".[57] Aimé Puech, who, like earlier editors,[58] gave to the passage the sense just described,[59] later modified his view. In an appended note to his more extensive study of the second century Apologists, Puech[60] suggested that on the basis of a possible ellipsis in the sentence, he made the latter part of the sentence refer, not to Tatian, but to a venerable figure in the philosophical tradition, like Plato. In sum, Tatian is here not claiming excellence in his knowledge of Greek studies; he is asserting the repudiation of an entire tradition, even if it included such an outstanding man as Plato.[61]

The passage is interpreted differently by Martin Elze.[62] He does not consider that Tatian is referring to any particular individual, such as Plato, because this would imply that Tatian was giving an implicit recognition to the philosophical tradition which he has just condemned.[63]

Elze rightly points to Tatian's explicit criticism of Plato in the next chapter of the *Oration*,[64] and this weakens Puech's modified position. Rather, Tatian's attitude to his past association with the Graeco-Roman intellectual tradition is that: "He wants to have nothing more to do with his past".[65]

The root of Tatian's self-understanding is his sense of certainty and confidence, sometimes to the point of self-esteem, in his new Christian self-identity; this note of exultant, and almost irritating self-assertion is intensely conveyed in the *Oration*. His claim to have reached a high level of proficiency in his mastery of Graeco-Roman culture is often coupled with a sense of moral and intellectual superiority, as a Christian, to the achievements of that culture.[66] Having transcended Graeco-Roman culture, he has reached finally a position of personal conviction and settled assurance in his intellectual outlook.[67] He who had ample reason for speaking highly of the Graeco-Roman tradition has now found it utterly bankrupt. His deep confidence in the Barbarian (Christian) tradition enables him to make a radical renunciation of the Greek intellectual tradition. But this is not as a result of being uninformed. On the contrary, in his new Christian self-identity he has discovered a firm intellectual and spiritual anchorage for his Barbarian self-worth. Moreover, in the Christian faith itself, and in its antecedents in a Barbarian history, Tatian has found an alternative tradition which is historically more ancient, internally harmonious and unmistakeably divine. It is upon these grounds which, for Tatian, are unshakeable, that his Christian self-understanding comes to rest.

IV. Christianity as the alternative tradition

Once the profoundly religious motivation of Tatian's outlook is granted, then it is inadequate to ascribe his renunciation of Graeco-Roman culture to some "kind of cultural primitivism".[68] That Graeco-Roman culture was to him "a foreign land"[69] cannot be ignored; being originally an Oriental, he felt no need to come to terms with Graeco-Roman tradition as other Christians must have done.[70] And yet the basis on which Tatian makes his criticisms of the Graeco-Roman tradition will be found also, as we shall see, in Christian writers who were more at home in that tradition. One important area in which this is the case is in the critique of the theology which underpinned the traditional religion of the Greeks – namely the Homeric theology.[71]

In chapter 21 of the *Oration*, having already consigned the gods of Graeco-Roman religion to the category of the fallen angels which have become the demons of the Christian schema,[72] Tatian now launches a frontal attack on the theology which rationalised the worship of such entities. Beginning with a defence of the Christian doctrine of the Incarnation, Tatian proceeds to expose the extent to which the Greek theology can be shown to be morally and spiritually despicable. It all hangs, for him, on the distinction between Christian doctrines and Greek myths.[73] The former denote clear statements, with their anchorage in historical events, whilst the latter indicate invented fables, being the speculation of men. But Tatian takes the argument into the moral turpitude of the Homeric gods, drawing upon the Greek mythology itself to demonstrate his claim that the gods manifest the characteristics and passions of fallen and depraved creatures; hence the deceiving of Hector by Athene, who assumes the appearance of his brother Deiphobus,[74] and Apollo, who, in love with Admetus, feeds the latter's bulls.[75] The dealings of the gods with men hardly redound to their credit. Tatian is also aware of the philosophical rationalisation of the gods into elements of nature and so he forces the ultimate conclusion upon the Greeks. Either the gods are allegorical names for natural forces, in which case here the very conception of divinity is overthrown;[76] or they are gods (demons, for Tatian), in which case their actions condemn them as morally despicable:

> "Believe me now, O Greeks, and do not resolve your myths and gods into allegory. If you attempt to do this, the divine nature as held by you is overthrown by yourselves; for, if the demons with you are such as they are said to be, they are worthless as to character."[77]

By stating his polemic in this form, Tatian wishes to force his opponents to admit the moral unacceptability of their gods and to recognise their unworthiness to receive religious devotion. He cannot worship natural elements, any more than he can pay religious homage to immoral divinities. But Tatian pushes the argument further yet by pointing to human personages in the Homeric epic – Hector, Achilles, Agamemnon, together with the Trojans (Barbarians) – and insists that if these human characters cannot be allegorised away, it is equally unacceptable to proceed in like manner with regard to the gods.[78] Tatian's purpose seems to be to push the Greek position to utter absurdity. In this way he seeks to affirm the superiority and truth of the Christian apprehension of God[79] as a radical alternative. For the sake of argument, but only as an abstract intellectual supposition,[80] one might consider a comparison with Greek concepts. However, this is, in fact, impossible; because the Greeks, who wallow in matter and mud[81] are far removed from rightly apprehending the true nature of divinity.

We have dwelt at some length on Tatian's criticism of the theological assumptions which underlie Greek religion as he saw them, because much in his outlook derives from here. The heart of his criticism of the Graeco-Roman tradition is his view that it offers no light whatsoever in the quest for the knowledge of God. His verdict on Greek philosophers is categorical: "You do not know God..."[82] And whatever light the Graeco-Roman tradition might have received, by borrowing and plagiarism from Barbarian sources, particularly from Moses, it has perverted by conceit, and misrepresented by its failure rightly to understand its meaning and character.[83]

Consequently, when Tatian isolates some particular aspects of Graeco-Roman culture for scathing criticism,[84] this must be seen as part of a unified perspective he has formed on the culture, from the standpoint of his religious (Christian) apprehension. When he attacks the stage, he is aware that the stage had religious associations, and especially that it featured prominently in the sacred festivals. But he insists that these solemnities are held at the instigation of wicked demons; in this way the moral corruption and ill-repute[85] of the stage are connected with the evil beings who are thus shown to control it. Tatian then directs his attention to an individual, most probably an actor on stage,[86] and uses him as an illustration of all that is morally corrupted and debasing in the culture of the stage. What Tatian so deeply detests is not simply the corrupting influence of the ribaldry and impiety of the stage, but also the very fact of acting a part – that the actor is "one thing internally, but outwardly counterfeits what he is not".[87] In characteristic fashion, Tatian ends his catalogue of offensive actions and gestures by summing them up in the man himself. And yet the criticism is not meant merely for an individual actor, but for the entire Graeco-Roman culture given over as enlightened. It is this culture which advertises itself in such degrading terms which he so uncompromisingly repudiates.[88]

In his attack on the games, he mentions boxing and gladiatorial shows. Of these two, he esteems boxing the lesser evil. But the gladiatorial shows are utterly reprehensible, involving a trading in human bodies and lives, and indicating, to Tatian, a deep depravity in the Graeco-Roman cultural outlook. The real point of his criticism lies in his comparison of this applauded and well-established pastime with the slaughter of beasts. For the gladiatorial shows amount to "cannibal banquets for the soul".[89] They simply demonstrate Tatian's fundamental contention: Graeco-Roman tradition is utterly bereft of a proper understanding of the nature of God and of the destiny of human life. Even what one might regard as "serious" culture such as the tragic drama with its sober treatment of human problems, music and literature, belongs for Tatian equally to the category of things of no value or

worth[90] from a religious and moral point of view. Christian revelation and tradition provide a totally other culture and way of life,
and Christian tenets need no supplement from Graeco-Roman
sources.

It is evident, therefore, when Tatian takes on the philosophical
schools and criticises their mutual divergences,[91] that he is simply
dealing with an unavoidable element in Graeco-Roman culture and
education of which he wholly disapproves. For Tatian, there is no
distinction between acceptable and unacceptable features of
Graeco-Roman tradition, such as we would find in Justin and in
Clement of Alexandria. Having discovered in the Christian faith a
totality of world-view, and all the ingredients for apprehending the
truth as belonging essentially to the Christian tradition, Tatian
then sees nothing extraordinary[92] in the achievements of Greek
philosophers. It is true that Tatian delights in attacking
philosophers for their personal faults and weakness[93] and consequently manifests a tendency to be unfair towards fellow human
beings.[94] However, it must be recognised that what Tatian is so
often pointing to is the discrepancy between words and deeds, the
failure to achieve sufficient integration of life and thought. Here,
in his view, is the fundamental weakness of the intellectual and
academic tradition of Graeco-Roman culture:

"Why do you busy yourselves with words, while you keep
yourselves aloof from deeds... Finding you to be such men as
these, we have abandoned you, and no longer concern ourselves
with your tenets, but follow the Word of God."[95]

The real target of Tatian's criticism is the inability of Graeco-
Roman intellectual tradition to give an accurate account of God, a
failure which, in his view, is connected with an inadequate self-
knowledge. "While inquiring what God is, you are ignorant of what
is in yourselves".[96] It is important to realise the essentially personal basis on which he makes this criticism. The speculative
tradition had failed to provide him with an answer to the riddle of
life; instead, it had contributed to its own disarray. When he
describes the effect of Graeco-Roman studies on the inquiring
student as "walking through a labyrinth", it is quite probable,
therefore, that we are meant to understand the statement as
autobiographical. At least we know he came to the conclusion that his
efforts in that field amounted to vain toil, hence the comparison with
the Danaids, damned for ever to draw water with a leaking jar![97]

For this reason, it is doubtful that the brief aside on the
question of time,[98] must be pressed into a discussion of "empirical"

and "metaphysical" time, as Martin Elze does.[99] As R.M. Grant has suggested,[100] a passage of the Christian Scriptures may well lie behind Tatian's thinking. Moreover, the immediate context of Tatian's expostulation on time is a criticism of grammarians, and in view of his previous training in grammar and rhetoric, he might have in mind grammatical discussions on tenses.[101] Having turned his back on these pursuits in order to devote himself to Christian life and teaching as he understood them, that is, to "follow the Word of God",[102] Tatian does not feel any need to validate his convictions on the terms of his critics. Rather, it is presumptuous of those who have no true knowledge of the unifying purpose and wisdom of God[103] to claim not only to assign elements of knowledge and wisdom to diverse intellectual disciplines, but also to explain time and its phases. The essential thing is to reckon with the One at whose will the totality of the ages exists.[104] As Martin Elze rightly observes: "It is the one and only God who is the measure and ruler of truth".[105]

It is from this fundamental apprehension that true knowledge is unified,[106] and is, moreover, the knowledge of God, that one can understand Tatian's utter repudiation of the Graeco-Roman intellectual and speculative tradition; for all its exalted claims, this latter failed to find God. This end of all seeking, the knowledge of God, Tatian came upon in the "Barbarian" (Christian) Tradition. Consequently, Tatian's critique resolves itself into an assertion of the utter irrelevance of the concerns and achievements of Graeco-Roman intellectual tradition:

"And what avails the Attic style, the sorties of philosophers, the plausibilities of syllogisms, the measurements of the earth, the positions of the stars, and the course of the sun? To be occupied with such inquiries is the work of one who imposes opinions on himself as if they were laws."[107]

The Graeco-Roman intellectual tradition is taken up with questions which are of wholly peripheral interest. For Tatian, it is the knowledge of God and the manifestation of that knowledge in life and conduct which count. To pursue secondary concerns amounts to imposing on oneself what are essentially human speculative tenets as though they were absolute laws.

Thus, when Tatian condemns one final element of Graeco-Roman culture, legislation,[108] his perspective is that of one who has found in the Christian faith and Scriptures a divine and hence superior legislation.[109] So far as he is concerned, there is no basis for considering Graeco-Roman legislation as superior to any other.

Thus, in the same context in which he condemns the Persian custom of honouring incest,[110] he also reproves the practice of pederasty among Romans.[111] Tatian is not concerned to discuss the merits and demerits of human legal systems; it is enough for him to set forth his contempt for Graeco-Roman cultural arrogance. Fundamentally, his outlook reflects a firm conviction that the Christian tradition constitutes in its totality a valid and higher alternative to the entire Graeco-Roman tradition, and for that matter, to any other merely human tradition.

V. The "two varieties of Spirit" as theological grounds for the Alternative Tradition

That there is more than simply cultural animosity to Tatian's renunciation of Graeco-Roman tradition, is seen also in his understanding of the origins and destiny of humanity, and hence, his view of salvation. It is not quite the case that Tatian's is "a theology without soteriology",[112] though his understanding of the question and his approach to it are not without obscurities and his language is sometimes difficult to interpret.[113]

In chapter 4, Tatian, affirming the Christian understanding of God as Creator and Spirit, seems intent on refuting Stoic immanentism;[114] in the process, he postulates a doctrine of "two Spirits":

"God is Spirit, not pervading[115] matter, but the maker of material spirits, and of the forms that are in matter; He is invisible, impalpable, being Himself the Father of both sensible and invisible things. Him we know from His creation, and apprehend His invisible power by His works. I refuse to adore that workmanship which He has made for our sakes. The sun and moon are made for us. How, then, can I adore my own servants? How can I speak of sticks and stones as Gods? For the spirit that pervades matter is inferior to the more divine Spirit; and this, even when assimilated to the soul,[116] is not to be honoured equally with the perfect God."[117]

This passage, which seems to recall at least two, and possibly more, Scriptural texts,[118] points in the direction of a further distinction which is more fundamental, because it underlies a basic differentiation among people. The clue to Tatian's thought lies in what he says about the assimilation or union of "the more divine Spirit" to the (human) soul, to which he returns later.

When Tatian takes up again the theme of "two spirits" in chapter 12, it is not to distinguish the transcendence of God from the created order as His workmanship; instead, it is to discuss the nature of the Fall, and to indicate its implications for human destiny. Since Tatian's thought is often led along by association of ideas, it is important to realise the context in which his discussion takes place. Tatian is concerned with the deities of Graeco-Roman religion, whom he insists on identifying with the "demons" of the Christian schema.[119] He is at pains to demonstrate the error of the theories and beliefs held about them, for he considers these deities to be irretrievably evil and of no use whatever to those who truly seek God. Tatian's theory of two spirits, at this point, is really meant to conclude in the utter discrediting of these "evil beings".

The "two spirits" are designated "soul", and the spirit which is "greater than soul"; this latter is properly "an image and likeness of God".[120] Both "spirits" existed in "the first men", that is, before the Fall, so that in one sense they might be material and in another, superior to matter.[121] Therefore, "soul", as the inferior "spirit", animates the created order and is present in stars, angels, plants and the waters, in men and in animals.[122] But the "more divine Spirit" which is greater than the soul, was available only to angels and men, who, through a proper use of freewill, would have derived the principle of "immortality"[123] from a continuing participation in the divine Spirit. However, just as the fall of man brought about the separation of "the more powerful Spirit" (the same as the more divine Spirit) from man, who thereby became mortal,[124] the rebellion of some angels – the occasion for the Fall in the first place – resulted in "a host of (evil) demons" who are worshipped by fallen mankind in error and ignorance.[125] According to Tatian, then:

"These beings, produced from matter, but very remote from right conduct, you, O Greeks, worship..."[126]

It is not necessary to maintain that it is only the divinities of Graeco-Roman religion who fall within this category for Tatian; his polemical attitude towards Graeco-Roman culture is sufficient to explain his statement. However, against what he considers to be "the trickeries of frenzied demons",[127] he opposes "doctrines... far beyond the apprehension of the world",[128] and derived from the "Barbarian" Scriptures,

"those most divine explanations which in the course of time have been consigned to writing, and make those who study them great lovers of God."[129]

Thus Tatian's Christian "absolutism" finds a theological validation in his understanding of the Biblical tradition itself, in that it is the Scriptures which provide the explanations for the world and teach the truth about men and about true worship. By the same token, the Scriptures explain the origin and nature of the errors of Graeco-Roman religion. But this radical Biblicism does more than serve Tatian's polemical purposes against Graeco-Roman culture; for it also informs his presentation of a doctrine of salvation which consistently refuses to yield on the fundamental distinction between those who follow "mere hearsay, probable conjectures and sophistical reasonings", and those who pay attention to words of a divine revelation;[130] it is the uncompromising distinction between belonging within the Christian (Barbarian) tradition where men acquire "intimacy with God" and "wallowing in matter and mud",[131] through the misguided worship of demons.

Tatian's conception of salvation, therefore, is essentially based on two foundations. The first is the doctrine of creation which makes the existence of all created entities, including the human soul, dependent on God, through His Word.[132] The second foundation is eschatology, involving the prospect, either of "death by punishment in immortality"[133] or "union with God".[134] The crucial factor is whether man acquires a knowledge of the truth, that is, of God[135] in the earthly existence. As Puech points out, Tatian's presentation does carry a certain Gnostic flavour about it, but it is "an attenuated and harmless gnosticism".[136]

Since Tatian approaches salvation from the perspective of human psychology, it becomes necessary for him to deal with the nature of the human soul. Against a well-held contemporary notion, he affirms that the soul (that is, of fallen man) is not in itself immortal, "though it is possible for it not to die".[137] This psychological approach to the question explains his use of *John* 1:5 in chapter 13:[138]

"In itself it [that is, the soul of fallen man] is darkness, and there is nothing luminous in it. And this is the meaning of the saying: 'the darkness does not comprehend the light'. For the soul does not preserve the Spirit, but is preserved by it, and the light comprehends the darkness. The Word in truth is the light of God, but the ignorant soul is darkness. On this account, if it continues solitary, it tends downward towards matter, and dies with the flesh; but if it enters into union with the Divine Spirit, it is no longer helpless, but ascends to the regions whither the Spirit guides it: for the dwelling place of the Spirit is above, but the origin of the soul is from beneath."[139]

Tatian shares in the general lack of clarity on the distinction of the Word from the Spirit in the theological reflections of the

Apologists;[140] when he goes on to speak of those who reject "the servant of God who has suffered",[141] it is not clear whether it is Jesus Christ who is meant, or, as the context might allow, the Spirit.[142] What is quite clear to Tatian is the overriding urgency and necessity for fallen men with darkened souls to find the light of the Divine Spirit who left them at the Fall. In thus finding salvation, men recover the condition they had when they were originally created through the Word. To this idea Tatian turns his attention in chapter 15 of the *Oration*.

The passage in question is one of the finest chapters of the *Oration*. It is evidently an effort to set out what the Christian Gospel, as he understood it, offers to fallen humanity and Tatian's "missionary" purpose in seeking the conversion of his readers becomes prominent:

> "It becomes us now to seek for what we once had, but have lost, to unite the soul with the Holy Spirit, and to strive after union [i.e. with the Spirit] according to God's design."[143]

Essential to Tatian's argument, as we have observed earlier, is the nature of man. Thus, reacting against well-known Graeco-Roman, particularly Stoic notions, he affirms the generally Biblical view of man as a psychosomatic unity,[144] and so denies the abstraction of mind as the totality of the human personality.[145] Man, fallen man, is body instinct with soul, and requires a third element, the Holy Spirit, as God's representative by whose presence man's constitution becomes truly a temple for God.[146] Without the presence of the Divine Spirit, man is distinguished from animals only by articulate speech.[147] By thus being complemented with the Holy Spirit, the human personality regains a full "trichotomist" constitution, and is thereby restored to being the image and likeness of God.[148] For,

> "man alone is the image and likeness of God, and I mean by man, not one who performs actions similar to those of animals, but one who has advanced far beyond mere humanity to God himself."[149]

The entry into salvation, as Tatian presents it, raises man thus constituted above the level of the existence of mere humanity; fallen men who remain at the level of mere humanity, "possess only soul",[150] not in any Gnostic sense as referring to ordinary Catholic believers, but in the Pauline sense, as referring to those who are not indwelt by the Holy Spirit.[151]

As always, Tatian makes his theological thought serve his

polemical purpose; and with a keen eye for basal issues, he relates the superiority of the person indwelt by the Divine Spirit (the Christian) not primarily to other persons, but to the divinities of Graeco-Roman tradition. If it is right that *1 Corinthians* 2:14f lies behind his description of unregenerate man as "possessing only soul", then it is probable also that the apostle's statement in the same context that whoever has the spirit, however, is able to judge the value of everything but no-one is able to judge him (*GNB*), may have provided the motivation for his bold assertion of the superiority of the regenerate person to the demons: "for the inferior has not the ability to apprehend the superior".[152]

Consequently, when Tatian introduces the text of *Psalm* 8:5[153] his interest at this point seems to be not so much the relation of men to angels in general but to the "demons" who are, in Tatian's scheme, fallen angels. Thus it is from this perspective that one can understand Tatian's use of the Scriptural reference. Men who originally were made a little lower than the angels, now through repentance and faith (and presumably the experience of salvation according to the Christian scheme), have been elevated above those angels who lost their original estate and now await irremediable punishment in immortality.[154]

"On this account, the nature of the demons has no place for repentance; for they are the reflection of matter and evil..."[155]

R.M. Grant has indicated that the phrase "place for repentance" is to be regarded as an allusion to the judgment of Esau in the *Epistle to the Hebrews* 12:17.[156] The use of "nature" and "reflection" to describe the demons would suggest equally an allusion to the early verses of that epistle. If this further reference is correct, then Tatian's aim seems to be to emphasise the utter contrast between the objects of worship in Graeco-Roman tradition and the object of worship in the Christian tradition, where Christ is spoken of as reflecting the glory of God, and bearing the very stamp of God's nature.[157] Graeco-Roman divinities are, therefore, not merely the epitome of all that is lowly and perishable, but also of all that is morally depraved and the very antithesis of the divine.

It is quite in character that in a passage which is so highly theological and soteriological, Tatian should maintain his fiercely polemical attitude to Graeco-Roman tradition. For the polemical stance is in his case also an intensely religious one. If the most vital issues of life have to do with the knowledge of God, and with restoration to the pristine constitution of man through union with the Divine Spirit, then the certainty of having apprehended the genuine divine revelation becomes the most prized possession.[158] He came upon this certainty of divine truth and the experience of its moral efficacy only in the Christian tradition. But if truth is not only divine but also one and unified, then it can only be found in the one tradition which alone has a divine character and origin. The absence of unity, the diversities and mutual contradictions, the confusion and strife in the Graeco-Roman philosophical tradition, confirm Tatian in his renunciation of that tradition. By the same token, the Homeric and Hesiodic mythology as an account of the gods becomes in his eyes the trickeries of the demons and consequently is to be reckoned as not original, not divine, and thereby not true.[159] In the light of Tatian's radical and firm contention for the definitive and unmistakeable superiority of the Christian (Barbarian) tradition, Martin Elze is certainly right that "there is for him no common ground between truth and error, between unity and plurality".[160] For according to Tatian:

"The Spirit of God is not with all, but taking up his abode with those who live justly, and intimately combining with the soul, by prophecies it announced things hidden from other souls."[161]

By thus confining the crucial activity of the Divine Spirit solely to the Biblical prophetic tradition, Tatian adds to the qualities of divinity and unity as distinguishing marks of the Christian tradition, the equally weighty dimension of antiquity.

VI. "We were here before you": the chronological argument

When Tatian begins to elaborate, as from chapter 31, his chronological argument for the superiority of the Christian tradition, he is clearly dealing with a subject which meant a great deal to him:

"But now it seems proper for me to demonstrate that our philosophy is older than the institutions of the Greeks."[162]

It is not central to our purposes to examine the details of this argument and its sources;[163] our concern is to understand the place and significance of the very concept of the chronological proof and its method, in the context of Tatian's Christian self-identity.

It is worth noting that as from this chapter, Tatian insists on speaking of the Christian faith, its ethical outlook and the special nature of the social interrelationships within the Christian community as a philosophy.[164] Whilst references to philosophy and philosophers [as such] are found in earlier chapters, the explicit claims for the Christian tradition as "philosophy" in its own right come to prominence in this latter section of the *Oration*. There seems to be more to the use of the word than merely competition with Graeco-Roman intellectual and spiritual tradition. Tatian's Christian teacher, Justin, was most emphatic on the use of it.[165] It gave account of the Christian apprehension of the nature of divinity and of the universe, thus of a total world-view and body of unified knowledge rooted in the knowledge of God.[166] In the closing chapter, when Tatian reasserts the motivation for his deliberate act of choosing the Christian tradition, and renouncing the Graeco-Roman tradition, it is upon convictions on these points that the stress is laid; knowing who God is and what is His work,[167] Tatian now possesses not only the personal apprehension of God, but also an enlightened understanding of His ways in the world and with men. Here, Tatian is asserting an insight into what was considered to be the sum of all philosophical knowledge and wisdom, namely, insight into that unity of knowledge of things divine and human which most high-minded persons of his age, Christians as well as Pagans, sought.[168]

From this perspective, the proof of the chronological argument does not, strictly, add to the convictions which Tatian holds as a Christian. His faith does not depend on it.[169] In his praise of the "Barbarian writings" which led to his conversion to the Christian outlook, Tatian indicates several factors other than their antiquity, and this makes it quite conceivable that he could have been persuaded to embrace Christianity for other reasons.[170] The chronological argument comes at the close of a vindication of Christianity of grounds which so far have had nothing to do with the antiquity of the Old Testament. Hitherto he has maintained an essentially dogmatic and even "ideological" posture. With this argument from chronology, Tatian abandons his earlier ideological stance; his aim remains the same, but the means of reaching it are now different. Curiously, it is when Tatian moves on to neutral ground, holding in abeyance, as it were, his apprehension of the truth far beyond mere human perception,[171] that his vindication of "Barbarism" takes on even greater boldness. For here, in fact, the ground was already prepared for Tatian's case,[172] and he did not need to draw on his own resources. Tatian, evidently aware of the evidence, could state regarding his approach:

> "I will not bring forward witnesses from among ourselves, but rather have recourse to Greeks. To do the former would be foolish, because it would not be allowed by you,[173] but the other will surprise you, when, by contending against you with your

own weapons, I adduce arguments of which you had no suspicion."[174]

The demonstration of "Christian" antiquity, therefore, may be seen as Tatian's *coup de grace*, the final decisive stroke to nail down the arrogant self-image of Graeco-Roman civilisation. He would achieve it by accepting the distinction which men of Hellenic, and eventually also of Roman, birth and culture made between themselves and other people; and by stretching fully some of the implications of that distinction, he would turn the tables upon the "cultured despisers" of the Barbarians.

The demonstration falls essentially into two parts. The first sets out to establish the comparative dates of Moses and Homer. Each of these figures is made to represent the *terminus a quo* of a set of institutions – the one "Barbarian", and the other Hellenic in its classical age. Tatian finds to hand evidence from Greek studies on Homer to establish the dates of Homer, disposing of the subject in one rapid chapter; he does not fail, though, to turn the lack of consensus on Homer into a criticism of what he considers to be the Greek propensity for fabulation and invention.[175]

As from chapter 36, the antiquity of Moses becomes the central theme. Committed to not resorting to Biblical evidence as grounds of proof, Tatian draws on historical records of three ancient and "Barbarian" peoples who had significant contact with "the Jews", as he calls ancient Israel.[176] What he is seeking to prove[177] is in effect quite simple. From the Babylonian evidence of Berosus, the essential fact is not only that the reign of Nebuchadnezzar indicates a crucial point of reference for Israelite (for Tatian, Jewish and hence Christian) anteriority to the rise of Greek imperial power,[178] but also that the military campaigns of the great Babylonian king, actually predicted by "*our* prophets",[179] took place "much later than the age of Moses". Similarly, the Phoenician evidence enables Tatian to establish the significant point that not only are the reigns of Solomon and the Phoenician king Hiram approximately contemporaneous with the Trojan war, celebrated in the *Iliad* of Homer, but that these dates are themselves "considerably later than the age of Moses".[180] The Egyptian evidence is obviously the most solid, since Tatian can thereby cite an independent source for linking the age of Moses, specifically, the Exodus of the Israelites from Egypt, with an ancient ruler of Argos, Inachos.[181]

It is quite conceivable, as Puech suggests, that Tatian himself may have considered the Egyptian evidence as the most weighty,

and that the other two were merely subsidiary and intended only
to impress his critics.[182] From this firm base, Tatian sets forth a
chronology of rulers of Argos between Inachos and Agamemnon,
with a corresponding list of rulers of Athens.[183] By tracing this
chronology, though without naming his sources,[184] Tatian is in fact
indicating the chronological distance that lies between Moses and
Homer; for behind the mention of Agamemnon, there lies always
the sack of Troy,[185] the central event of the *Iliad*.

From his summing up, in chapter 40, it becomes clear that the
proof of Moses' antiquity resolves itself into showing not only his
anteriority, but also his influence as the source of Greek learning
and institutions. It is important to demonstrate, on independent
grounds, that the *literary* records on which Greek institutions and
culture pride themselves – and Homer is the towering figure in the
Classical age – in fact come later and are therefore inferior to the
records on the Christian tradition, that is, the Old Testament,
whose origins are linked with Moses. Moses' position sets him and
the tradition associated with him above the entire Greek literary
tradition of mythology and history of heroes, wars and superhuman beings (as in Homer and Hesiod). It is from "Moses and
from those who have philosophised like him"[186] that the Greek
intellectual tradition has derived its insights. In other words, it is
from Moses and his successors in Hebrew prophecy and the Biblical
tradition generally, that the Greek tradition has learnt its lessons.
And yet, even this plagiarising from Moses and the Old Testament
tradition only succeeded in distorting their teaching. In this
category of "debased" *Mosaica,* Tatian evidently includes the
Hesiodic and Homeric theogony and theology as well as the later
philosophical tradition. It is also important to add that from
Tatian's standpoint, the true and original "philosophy" is found
only in the Christian, and hence "Barbarian" tradition. This is
what explains his confident conclusion:

"Therefore, from what has been said, it is evident that Moses
was older than the ancient heroes, wars and demons. And we
ought rather to believe him, who stands before them in point of
age, than the Greeks, who, without properly understanding his
teachings, drew from them as from a fountain. For many of the
sophists among them [the Greeks] stimulated by curiosity,
endeavoured to adulterate what they learnt from Moses and
from those who have philosophised like him, first that they
might be considered as having something of their own, and
secondly, that covering up by a certain rhetorical artifice
whatever they did not understand, that they might mis-

represent the truth as it if were a fable."[187]

The two reasons which Tatian gives to explain the distortions of the original and true teaching of Moses and his successors, are highly revealing of his view of Hellenistic culture as a whole. The first reason is the Greeks' conceit and desire to make borrowed knowledge appear inherently Greek; the second is the actual attempt to cover up what they have thus failed to understand under a heap of rhetorical artifices.[188] One is immediately reminded of what Tatian has said earlier, in chapter 21, on the differences between Christian and Hellenistic conceptions of divinity – the former derive from clear, verifiable statements and accounts, whereas the latter bear the stamp of falsification and invention, essentially "myth", which Tatian takes in the general sense of fiction.[189] A similar distinction, therefore, lies behind the opposition here between "truth" and "mythology". Tatian's conviction is that the very characteristic outlook – described "as idle and vain curiosity" – shaping the Hellenistic literary and intellectual tradition, leads to distortion when applied to the Christian tradition. At his conversion to Christianity, he came to the conclusion that Greek literature led to condemnation whilst the Christian "Barbarian" writings brought him not only moral but also spiritual and intellectual liberation.

"... my soul, being taught of God, discerned that the former class of writings [i.e. Greek literature and philosophical tenets] led to condemnation, but that these [i.e. Christian Scriptures] put an end to the slavery that is in the world, and rescue us from a multiplicity of rulers and ten thousand tyrants, while they give us, not indeed what we had not before received, but what we had received but were prevented by error from retaining."[190]

The second part of the chronological argument, which, as Puech suggests,[191] may have been inserted as an afterthought, consists in demonstrating the anteriority of Moses equally to the pre-Homeric personages who have made any significant contribution (chapter 41). On some of those named hardly any tradition has survived,[192] although there is no reason to assume that Tatian is seriously mistaken, or that the demonstration thereby ceases to have value. Again, it seems most likely that Tatian is drawing upon "source-books" on the subject under consideration, whilst his own negligence is not to be ruled out. But at this point in the argument, Tatian considers his conclusion fully established: Moses, the parent of the Christian tradition in its historical continuity with the Old Testament tradition, and a "Barbarian" one at that, is

shown to have been not only the founder of all "Barbarian wisdom",[193] but also the fount from whom all significant Hellenistic
knowledge has been derived.[194] In this sense the claim first made
in chapter 1, about Barbarian pre-eminence in almost every area
of culture and civilisation, is finally reasserted through the
chronological argument.

VII. "The best and most useful of all his works"[195]

In paying this tribute to Tatian, Eusebius had in mind the
chronological argument for the antiquity of Moses and his priority
to Hellenistic learning. For, on this score alone, it is possible to
maintain that for all his fierce antipathy to Hellenistic culture,
Tatian served Hellenistic culture by serving Hellenistic Christians. As Aimé Puech observed:

> "This aspect of his work is what appeared the most original to
> his successors; from Clement of Alexandria up to Eusebius, they
> did not cease to praise its importance and its originality."[196]

Clement of Alexandria, who certainly did not share Tatian's
antipathy to Hellenistic culture, acknowledged Tatian's work and
used his findings in setting forth his own case for the antiquity of
the historical tradition of the Old Testament.[197] Origen, arguing
against Celsus on the question of the antiquity of nations, whilst
he mentions Josephus, pays sterling tribute to Tatian and
speaks of his work as accomplished "with great learning".[198]
Theophilus of Antioch used the results of the chronological argument,[199] though he did not name Tatian. But it is Eusebius of
Caesarea who makes the most extensive use of Tatian's work by
reproducing, in his *Praeparatio Evangelica*,[200] the relevant chapters substantially as Tatian had composed them. In the literature
of Latin Christianity, the chronological argument is found in
Tertullian's most important work, the *Apology*,[201] in a form which
may well owe some of its material to Tatian;[202] the use of it will
reappear in the writings of Lactantius[203] and Augustine.[204]

It is evident from the passages in which Origen pays
tribute to Tatian that the work of Jewish apologists seeking
to establish Jewish antiquity was known in some Christian
circles of his time and possibly earlier. In any case, Tatian's
Christian teacher, Justin, had affirmed in his writings the
priority of Moses to Hellenistic learning and asserted the
indebtedness of Greek thinkers to him.[205] Yet, even if the
major conclusions of the argument had been known from
Jewish apologetics in the Hellenistic world,[206] it is important,

nonetheless, to recognise that it was Tatian who provided the first *Christian* demonstration of the evidence, and that he did it in the interests of the Christian faith. Tatian, for all his excesses, offered a remarkable gift to Christian tradition, as Puech's comment affirms:

"acclaimed after his own time, preserves the merit of being an attempt at demonstration in an area where Justin was content to confirm."[207]

Seen from this angle, Tatian's *Oration* also finds meaning within the missionary purpose of the Christian apologists in the Graeco-Roman world and represents a notable example of an "Exhortation to conversion" (*Protreptikos*); for the conversion of their hearers and readers was the aim which the Christian apologists, like their contemporary Hellenistic philosophic preachers, set out to achieve.[208]

And yet, Tatian's very perspective on the questions involved was bound to set him apart from his colleagues. His call to people of his day was not simply to abandon the error in the world and to embrace a higher and nobler truth. By limiting the target of his invective to a culture and a tradition which he so deeply resented, he made it virtually impossible for those who belonged to that culture and who stood in that tradition, to accept much of what he had to say. His conclusions on the question of Mosaic antiquity have been compared to those of the more extreme representatives of Jewish apologetics in the Hellenistic world.[209] Thus, whilst it is far from certain that Tatian actually depended on Jewish sources without acknowledging them,[210] the general tendency and aims of Jewish apologetics in the Hellenistic world must have been attractive to him; only he sought to achieve those aims as a Christian, and like them, as a "Barbarian": to vindicate the "Barbarians" of whom he was one:

"In order to rehabilitate the Barbarians it was important to prove that they had contributed their share, indeed the chief share, to the progress of humanity; but it was even more important to establish that the one authentic religion justified its claims, not only by its obvious truth but by its origins as well. Having existed before all cults like it, it was superior to them, and it would show by going back through the ages that it emanated from God himself. The cornerstone of the system was the fact that Moses had preceded all known founders of religions."[211]

It is interesting that in Edwyn Bevan's article on "Greeks and

Barbarians", he should describe the rise and expansion of the Christian movement, like the impact of Hellenistic Judaism, as part of a process whereby "the barbarian world gets a *revanche* upon Hellenism", and that he should recognise Tatian as a distinctive exemplar of this process.[212] Bevan's insight argues for the value of seeking to understand Tatian from the perspective of Christian identity. Tatian had no use for the concept of Christians as "the third race" or of the Christian faith as a "third manner of worship".[213] Otto must be right in his observation that Tatian was particularly sensitive to the charge of novelty held against the Christian movement and that he was keen to refute it, this being the motive behind the demonstration of the chronological evidence, namely, to refute the charge of novelty.[214] To that extent, the chronological argument, no less than the entire *Oration* with its intensely pro-Barbarian outlook, was part of a desire to establish the grounds for Christian identity. The "third race" argument, as we saw in the earlier chapter, was also part of that same desire as it was felt in some circles of Christian thought. The weakness of the "third race" proposition lay in the charge of novelty and the stigma of rootlessness. The argument from chronological antiquity sought to answer the charge of novelty and to do more: to vindicate the credentials of Christians in the history of mankind. This, then, is the measure of Tatian's achievement for Christian tradition in the "best and most useful of all his works". It took a Barbarian Christian to provide what was needed so that Hellenistic Christians could be at home in their world.[215]

VIII. Conclusion

From our study we can only conclude that the traditional view of Tatian's *Oration* as being the work of one who was mainly interested in giving vent to his deep anti-Greek feelings, is inadequate. When the *Oration* is taken, as we have done in this chapter, as the sustained and sincere effort of a serious Christian advocate to establish the grounds of the self-identity of his co-religionists, then its intrinsic value becomes more evident.

Besides, Tatian's later career as Encratite Christian cannot be allowed to obscure his achievement as apologist for the Christian cause. Whilst through his Gospel harmony, the *Diatessaron*, Tatian belongs to Syriac Christianity, the *Oration Addressed to the Greeks* assures him a place in the early history of the Christian apologetic movement amid Hellenistic culture.

On the other hand, one has to describe Tatian's achievement as paradoxical. Certainly he did not seek to serve the interests of Hellenism. He set out ostensibly to promote and validate the claims of "Barbarism" and to provide religious and historical foundations for Barbarian self-worth. But this somewhat narrow, polemical intent must be placed within a wider context, particularly in view of what Tatian actually achieved for Christian tradition. For if the religious basis for his claims lay in the evident spiritual and intellectual dynamic of the Christian faith in the Hellenistic world,[216] the historical validation of its Barbarian roots was also to hand in the Old Testament. Thus, on both counts, Tatian was not adducing new evidence or original data. Tatian's originality consisted in the fact that he fused the two realities into a coherent whole.

His affirmation that the Christian Gospel and its lights were in no way related to the philosophical and intellectual tradition of Hellenistic culture, would not be accepted by all Christians who were more at home in that culture, and who sought ways of coming to terms with their own cultural heritage. Nevertheless, Tatian's interpretation of Christianity cannot be set aside as though it were simply the projection of cultural animosity. At a more profound level, Tatian represents the view that the faith and the tradition within which it is confessed, form a unity, and that the one cannot be severed from the other. For obvious reasons, the fact that the faith and the history of its tradition were "originally barbarian",[217] held great significance for the Assyrian Christian, but in affirming that fact, Tatian was also making a religious claim. As Werner Jaeger has commented:

"The Assyrian Tatian who wrote Greek... and possessed Greek culture... did not believe in it. He violently disapproved of the direction in which the Christian trend of his time was moving; he warned Christians that the future of their cause did not lie in their gradual assimilation to Greek culture but would depend entirely on their keeping it immaculately pure as a barbarian cult."[218]

It is also important to realise that there were some Christians who belonged well within Graeco-Roman culture and who would have understood what Tatian was seeking to convey. One such was Tertullian of Carthage.

Notes

1. See Irenaeus, *Against all Heresies,* 1,28 (i); 3,23 (viii).

2. For a discussion of Tatian's exegetical method, see, for example, R.M. Grant, "Tatian and the Bible", in *TU,* 63, 1957, pp.297-306.

3. See Eusebius, *HE,* 4,28,29; Migne, *PG,* 20, 397C-401B.

4. Jerome, in the preface to his commentary on the *Epistle to Titus,* describes Tatian as "Encratitarum patriarches". See lists of *Fragmenta* and *Testimonia* in E. Schwartz' edition of Tatian's *Oration* in *TU* 4, (i), pp.48ff. For a discussion of the witnesses to Tatian in the Church Fathers, see Martin Elze, *Tatian und seine Theologie,* Göttingen: Vandenhoeck und Ruprecht, 1960, pp.106-124.

5. For the Syriac witnesses, see Martin Elze, *op.cit.,* pp.120ff.

6. *Ibid.,* p.121.

7. A.S. Marmardji, O.P., *Diatessaron de Tatien – Texte arabe établi, traduit en français, collationné avec les anciennes versions syriaques, suivi d'un évangeliare diatessarique syriaque et accompagné de quatre planches hors texte,* Beyreuth: Imprimerie Catholique, 1935, viii. It has been suggested that Tatian's parents may have been Greek officials of the Roman administration of Syria; see J.M. Fuller, art. "Tatianus" in *DCB,*vol.4, p.783. This argument for Tatian's Greek parentage and nationality was also put forward by Adolf Harnack; see his "Die Überlieferung der griechischen Apologeten des zweiten Jahrhunderts in der alten Kirche und im Mittelalter" in *TU,* 1(1-2), Leipzig, 1882, pp.199ff.

8. A.S. Marmardji, *op.cit.,* p.ix; also J. Hamlyn Hill, *The Earliest Life of Christ Ever Compiled from the Four Gospels, being the Diatessaron of Tatian,* Edinburgh: T. & T. Clark, 1910.

9. A.S. Marmardji, *op.cit.,* pp.x-xi.

10. *Ibid.,* p.xi.

11. J. Lebreton, *Histoire du dogme de la Trinité* (tome 2), Paris: Beauchesne et Cie, 1928, pp.487- 488. Elsewhere Lebreton has described Tatian's *Oration* as marked by "the weakness of a mind which thinks it is strong because it is severe". See his "L'apologétique chrétienne au 2ème siècle" in A. Fliche and V. Martin (eds), *Histoire de l'Eglise depuis ses origines jusqu'à nos jours* (tome 1– *L'Eglise Primitive*), Paris: Bloud et Gay, 1946, p.454. G. Bardy rejects Lebreton's estimation of Tatian, though without allowing him full "official" status: "He is certainly a witness to the faith, but he does not have the value of an official representative of tradition. On the contrary, it could not be said that he was not already half sunk in heresy even when he was writing the *Oration.*" See his article "Tatian" in *DTC,* vol.15, col.65. For positive assessments of Tatian, see also Aimé Puech, *Recherches sur le Discours aux Grecs de Tatien suivies d'une traduction française du Discours avec Notes,* Paris: Felix Alcan, 1903, pp.94ff; *Les Apologistes grecs du 2ème siècle de notre ère,* Paris: Hachette, 1912, pp.148-171; also, Martin Elze, *op.cit., passim.*

12. This is Tatian's own appreciation of his teacher – in his *Oration,* 18 (p.20.15f).

13. Eusebius, *HE,* 4,29. *PG,* 20,400B.

14. Aimé Puech must have been aware of this problem when he wrote: "my chief aim was to make Tatian comprehensible." See his *Recherches,* vii. One of the conclusions from Martin Elze's study of Tatian has been that Tatian, in his time, was largely misunderstood; see Martin Elze, *op.cit.,* pp.128f.

15. E.R. Hardy, "Introduction" to *1 Apology* of Justin Martyr, in *LCC* (vol.1), p.237. An indication of the tenacity of the traditional view is given by the judgment of an assiduous student of Tatian, R.M. Grant, "The Chronology of the Greek Apologists", in *VC,* vol.9, 1955, p.28: "Tatian wrote not in the name of Christianity but as an individual gnostic teacher". Cf. his "The Heresy of Tatian" in *JTS,* n.s. vol.5, 1954, pp.63f.

16. Aimé Puech, *Recherches,* v. As well as the *Oration* and the Gospel

harmony, *Diatessaron*, Tatian wrote other books. These are now lost, and it is not known whether some of those projected were actually written. *On Perfection according to the Saviour* is mentioned by Clement of Alexandria in *Stromateis* 3,13; a work on *Animals (Living Creatures?)* is mentioned by Tatian in the *Oration*, ch.15; *On the Nature of Demons* was also projected, according to *Oration*, 16; so also was a work on Greek writers on questions of divinity, according to *Oration*, 40. According to Eusebius, *HE*, 5,13, quoting Rhodo, a pupil of Tatian, the "master" also composed a book dealing with difficulties in the Scriptures!

17. Martin Elze, *op.cit.*, p.127.

18. See Aimé Puech, *Recherches*, p.80: "Tatian had the precise idea that his Logos could not and should not be any more than an *exhortation* to faith (προτρεπτικός) and not an exposition of doctrine." See also p.41.

19. On Tatian's explicit identification with "Barbarism" against "Hellenism", Elze states: "it will not then be quite so easy just to attribute Tatian's fondness for the Barbarians to his own nationality as a Syrian." See Martin Elze, *op.cit.*, p.26.

20. As is done by Heinrich Schlier, "Religionsgeschichtliche Untersuchungen zu den Ignatiusbriefen", in *ZNW*, 8, 1929.

21. Gregory Dix, *Jew and Greek – A Study in the Primitive Church*, London: Dacre Press, Westminster, 1953; see especially ch.1, "The conflict of the Syriac and Greek cultures". •   •

22. See *Oration*, ch.29; (p.30.3ff).

23. See *Oration*, chs. 31,32,33,35,42.

24. See Justin, *Dialogue with Trypho*, ch.9.

25. It is important to note that it is the whole of Graeco-Roman culture with its values that Tatian rejects; thus he criticises both the boasting (μεγαλαυχία) of the Romans and the vain speculations (ψυχρολογία) of Athenians (i.e. Greeks) in ch.35, (p.37.6f). Cf. Robert Joly, *Christianisme et Philosophie - Etudes sur Justin et les Apologistes grecs du deuxième siècle*, Bruxelles: Editions de l'Université de Bruxelles, 1973, pp.79f.

26. See, for example, *Oration*, ch.35, (p.37.7f).

27. *Ibid.*, ch.26, (p.28.3ff).

28. *Ibid.*, ch.25, (p.27.4).

29. Martin Elze, *op.cit.*, p.13; cf. *Oration*, ch.17, (p.18.22).

30. *Oration*, ch.17, (p.18.21).

31. See Martin Elze, *op.cit.*, especially ch.2 – "Tatians Auffassung von der Wahrheit".

32. The most outstanding work of this kind was the response of Josephus to the literary opponents of the Jews in his work *Contra Apionem*, although it replies to other critics besides Apion. For a treatment of the content and significance of the Jewish apologetic literature addressed to the Graeco-Roman world, see Emil Schürer, *A History of the Jewish People in the Time of Jesus Christ* (ET by Sophia Taylor and Peter Christie), Division 2, vol.3, Edinburgh: T. & T. Clark, 1886, pp.195-270. See also, M. Friedländer, *Geschichte der jüdischen Apologetik als Vorgeschichte des Christentums*, Amsterdam: Philo Press, 1973 (1st published Zurich, 1903).

33. Aimé Puech, *Les Apologistes grecs*, p.11.

34. *Oration*, ch.1, (p.2.9): "...we have renounced your wisdom..."

35. See G.W.H. Lampe (ed), *PGL*, pp.215ff.

36. Martin Elze, *op.cit.*, pp.54f.

92   THEOLOGY AND IDENTITY

37. For instance, chs.4 (p.5.15); 30 (p.31.2); 32 (p.33.13); 33 (p.34.2).

38. *Oration*, ch.12 (p.14.4).

39. *Ibid.*, ch.12 (p.14.8); cf.ch.35 (p.37.12).

40. *Ibid.*, ch.21 (p.23.7f).

41. *Ibid.*, ch.21 (p.24.15f).

42. *Ibid.*, ch.40 (p.41.11f); cf.ch.34 (p.36.23f).

43. *Ibid.*, ch.36 (p.38.9).

44. *Ibid.*, ch.31, (p.31.5).

45. *Ibid.*, ch.9 (p.10.9). The reference is to the existence of one Lord (δεσπότης).

46. *Ibid.*, ch.5 (p.5.16), affirming the pre-existence of the Word (λόγος) in God.

47. For example, Tatian's exalted portrayal of Christian morality, and especially of Christian womanhood, is parallelled in Athenagoras, *Legatio*, chs.33-34, and Justin, *1 Apology*, ch.19, and *2 Apology*, ch.2.

48. *Oration*, ch.6.

49. Martin Elze, *op.cit.*, p.56. But see R.M. Grant, "The Heresy of Tatian", pp.62-68, for a view which links Tatian's *Oration* with aspects of Valentinianism.

50. Martin Elze, *op.cit.*, p.56. See also Aimé Puech, *Recherches*, pp.94f. For a different view, see R.M. Grant, "The Chronology of the Greek Apologists", p.28.

51. *Oration*, ch.29 (p.29.26).

52. Otto, *CACSS*, vol.6, p.113, n.1.

53. *Oration*, ch.35 (p.36.26).

54. Aimé Puech, *Recherches*, p.15.

55. Aimé Puech, *Recherches*, especially ch.3, "Tatian et la Sophistique".

56. *Oration*, ch.35 (pp.36.25-37.4); I follow, in parts, Puech's French rendering.

57. *Ibid.*, ch.1 (p.2.9f).

58. Otto, who appears to have seen no difficulty in the passage, rendered it into Latin as: "Quamobrem valediximus vestrae sapientiae, quamvis omnino spectatus aliquis in ea essem". See *CACSS*, vol.6., p.7.

59. Aimé Puech, *Recherches*, p.109.

60. Aimé Puech, *Les Apologistes grecs*, pp.318-321.

61. *Ibid.*, p.320.

62. Martin Elze, *op.cit.*, pp.20-21.

63. *Ibid.*, pp.20f. According to Elze, the expression σεμνός τις "refers rather to Greek philosophy in general and should be understood ironically..." (p.21).

64. *Oration*, ch.2 (p.2.22f): "Plato, a philosopher, was sold by Dionysius for his gormandising propensities." Cf. ch.3 (p.4.7f).

65. Martin Elze, *op.cit.*, p.20.

66. For example, see *Oration*, chs.26,29-30.

67. Conveyed his frequent use of the Greek word κατάληψις. It is interesting that of 11 uses of κατάληψις and its cognate forms assembled in E.J. Goodspeed's *Index*, p.147, 9 are found in Tatian's *Oration*.

68. The criticism is made by E.J. Goodspeed in *A History of Early Christian Literature* (revised and enlarged by R.M. Grant), Chicago: Phoenix Books,

1966, p.107.

69. Louis Duchesne, *Early History of the Christian Church (from its foundation to the end of the third century)* (ET), London: John Murray, 1910, p.156.

70. On the contrast with Justin's attempts to trace and identify affinities between Christian faith and the Greek philosophical speculation, Aimé Puech writes: "He (Tatian) could not close his eyes to these obvious affinities, but because he did not feel them as Justin did he forgets them easily and does not bother to mention them one by one. He just indicates them as a body, attributing them to borrowings which the Greeks made from Moses." See his *Les Apologistes grecs*, p.156.

71. Cf. Athenagoras, *Legatio*, ch.17; also Clement of Alexandria, *Protreptikos*, ch.4.

72. *Oration*, chs.7-8.

73. *Ibid.*, ch.21 (p.23.7f).

74. Homer, *The Iliad*, Bk.22,11.224-231.

75. Callimachus (of Cyrene), *Hymn (2) to Apollo*, 9.11.47-49.

76. Tatian is evidently aware of the philosophical tradition of the rational critique of the Homeric theology, and the attempts to rehabilitate this latter by resolving the gods into abstract concepts and virtues; cf. Plato, *Ion* (or *On the Iliad*), where some interpreters of Homer are mentioned, such as Metrodorus of Lampsacus, Stesimbrotus of Thasos and Glaucon

77. *Oration*, ch.21 (p.24.2).

78. *Ibid.*, ch.21 (p.24.10ff).

79. *Ibid.*, ch.21 (p.24.15f).

80. *Ibid.*, ch.21 (p.25.15).

81. *Ibid.*, ch.21 (p.24.16).

82. *Ibid.*, ch.26 (p.28.5f); cf. ch.25 (p.26.25).

83. *Ibid.*, ch.40 (p.41.4ff).

84. Especially in chs.22-24 where he criticises, in turn, the stage, the games and gladiatorial shows, and the tragic drama.

85. *Ibid.*, ch.22 (p.24.19ff).

86. As Otto points out (*CACSS*, vol.6, p.96), earlier commentators were wrong in seeing, at this point, an attack on the Cynic, Crescens, who is criticised in ch.19. It is more appropriate to follow Dom Maran and to see here a description of an actor on stage. The profound disapproval and dislike of the stage by early Christians is found also in Tertullian, *Apology*, 15; *De Spectaculis*, 10 and Clement of Alexandria, *Paidagogos*, Bk.3, ch.4.

87. *Oration*, ch.22 (p.24.23f).

88. *Ibid.*, ch.22 (p.25.2). Augustine, approaching the problem of *mimesis* in the theatre from a psychological angle, rather than a cultural one, reached a more revealing critique of its harmful effects on him. See his *Confessions*, Bk.3, ch.2: "I did not seek the kind of sorrow which would wound me deeply, for I had no wish to endure the sufferings which I saw on the stage; but I enjoyed fables and fictions, which could only graze the skin. But where the fingers scratch, the skin becomes inflamed. It swells and festers with hideous pus. And the same happened to me"; cf. C.N. Cochrane, *Christianity and Classical Culture – A study of thought and action from Augustus to Augustine*, London: Oxford University Press, 1939 (reprinted 1957), pp.391f.

89. *Oration*, ch.23 (p.26.4).

90. *Ibid.*, ch.24 (p.26.16).

91. As he does in ch.25.

92. *Oration*, ch.25 (p.26.18).

93. See, for instance, his strictures in chs.2 and 3, as also in the early section of ch.25, were he seems deliberately to isolate the Cynic, as a philosophical type, for criticism – his unkempt appearance and ill repute. On the Cynic and pseudo-Christian, Peregrinus (Proteus), see Lucian of Samosata, *On the Death of Peregrinus*. On the shamelessness of Cynics, see Augustine, *De Civitate Dei*, Bk.14, ch.20.

94. See the view of E. Preuschen: "No educated Christian has more consistently separated from paganism; but by overshooting the mark, his scolding and blustering philippic lost its effectiveness because it lacks justice". See his article "Tatian" in *The New Schaff-Herzog*, vol.11, p.274. For a different view, see Aimé Puech, *Recherches*, p.40. Commenting on chapters 2 and 3 of the *Oration*, Puech writes: "Instead of criticising doctrines Tatian preferred to make personal attacks; ...but it should be remembered that early on *biography*, particularly in the hands of the Peripatetics, and even when it was dealing with philosophers, had adopted the form which we see given to it by Suetonius; and the work of Diogenes Laertius, who does no more than summarise his predecessors, shows us with how little in the way of critical approach and in what spirit of banal or malicious curiosity the most suspect anecdotes had been introduced into these memoirs. There is nothing in Chapters 1 and 2 which could not have come from similar sources; Tatian doubtless displays less high-mindedness than his master Justin in accepting all this gossip without editing it, but he certainly did not invent anything."

95. *Oration*, ch.26 (p.28.9ff). For similar sentiments expressed by a Christian of Greek culture, see Athenagoras, *Legatio*, ch.33.

96. *Oration*, ch.26 (p.27.19).

97. *Ibid.*, ch.26 (p.27.20f). See H.J. Rose, article "Danaus" in *OCD*, pp.311-312.

98. *Oration*, ch.26 (p.27.22-28).

99. Martin Elze, *op.cit.*, pp.103-105.

100. R.M. Grant, "Tatian and the Bible" in *TU*, 63, 1957, p.298. While he accepts that Tatian's discussion seems to be related to the Stoic idea that the past and future do not exist while the present does, he also suggests that Tatian might be referring to the discussion of "today" in the *Epistle to the Hebrews*, chs.3 and 4, based on *Psalm* 95:7. "Tatian apparently is hinting that the true division of time is into two ages, this one and the one to come..."

101. R.M. Grant, "Studies in the Apologists: Tatian's theological method", in *HTR*, 51, 1958, p.124.

102. *Oration*, ch.26 (p.28.14f). In view of the high value which Tatian places on his discovery of the Christian Scriptures (the Old Testament in particular), (cf. ch.29), it is likely that the Scriptures are meant here.

103. For they "are cut off from the true wisdom" (τῆς κατὰ ἀλήθειαν σοφίας ἀπετμήθητε), *Oration*, ch.26 (p.28.4).

104. *Ibid.*, ch.26 (p.27.27f).

105. Martin Elze, *op.cit.*, p.39.

106. On the nature of this unified truth as Tatian understands it, Elze notes further: "The unity is unifying not only externally, producing one exclusive doctrinal form of truth and not several, partial forms of truth which differ from one another; it is also internally unifying, showing conciseness in itself." (p.40).

107. *Oration*, ch.27 (p.29.13-17).

108. *Ibid.*, ch.28.

109. Cf. ch.13 (p.14.4) where it is spoken of as βαρβαρικὴ νομοθεσία.

110. *Ibid.*, ch.28 (p.29.20f). Cf. Clement of Alexandria, *Stromateis*, 3,2; Dio Chrysostom, *Discourses*, 10. 29-30, quoted in George Boas and A.O. Lovejoy (eds), *Primitivism and Related Ideas in Antiquity (Contributions to the history of Primitivism)*, New York: Octagon Books, 1973, p.135.

111. *Oration*, ch.28 (p.29.22f). Cf. Justin, *1 Apology* ch.27.

112. Martin Elze, *op.cit.*, p.105.

113. Aimé Puech, *Recherches*, pp.69f. Cf. R.M. Grant, "The Heresy of Tatian", pp.62-68.

114. Cf. Aimé Puech, *Recherches*, p.54: "What seemed essential to him was to distinguish God not only from matter but from the force which resides in matter. He is evidently desirous of refuting Stoicism, which he seems to know well."

115. A Stoic term (διῆκων) see "Index Graecus" in Schwartz, *Tatiani Oratio ad Graecos*, in *TU*, vol.4, pt.1, 1888, p.72.

116. I read ὥσπερ ψυχῇ παρωμοιωμένον, as in Otto, *CACSS*; cf. Aimé Puech, *Recherches*, p.113, n.4.

117. *Oration*, ch.4 (p.5.2-12).

118. For instance, *John* 4:24 for "God is Spirit"; *Romans* 1:20 for God's invisible power revealed by His works in creation; and possibly *1 Corinthians* 15:44 for the view that material substances do have "spirit".

119. See *Oration*, ch.7.

120. *Ibid.*, ch.12 (p.12.19f); cf.ch.15 (p.16.13).

121. *Ibid.*, ch.12 (p.12.21).

122. *Ibid.*, ch. 12 (p.12.26ff).

123. *Ibid.*, ch.7 (p.7.6-19).

124. *Ibid.*, ch.7 (p.7.30f).

125. *Ibid.*, ch.7 (p.8.2). There is little doubt that Tatian is here giving his own general understanding of the Biblical story of the Fall in *Genesis* 3 in a way that links the Fall with the onset of false worship, that is, the misguided worship of fallen angels, here identified with the divinities of Graeco-Roman worship. See Aimé Puech, *Recherches*, pp.64f.

126. *Oration*, ch.12 (p.13.19-21).

127. *Ibid.*, ch.12 (p.14.7).

128. *Ibid.*, ch.12 (p.14.8f).

129. *Ibid.*, ch.12 (p.13.13-14).

130. *Ibid.*, ch.12 (pp.13.31-14.1).

131. *Ibid.*, ch.21 (p.24.16f).

132. *Ibid.*, ch.5.

133. *Ibid.*, ch.13 (p.14.14).

134. *Ibid.*, ch.15 (p.16.6).

135. *Ibid.*, ch.13 (p.14.16f).

136. Aimé Puech, *Recherches*, p.68.

137. *Oration*, ch.13 (p.14.10-12).

138. Cf. R.M. Grant, "Tatian and the Bible", p.300.

139. *Oration*, ch.13 (p.14.16-26).

140. See J.N.D. Kelly, *Early Christian Doctrines*, London: A. & C. Black, 4th edition, 1968, pp.101-104.

141. *Oration*, ch.13 (p.15.5f).

142. If διάκονος in the passage is taken to refer to Christ, then Tatian's statement may be pointing in the direction of the later concept of *communicatio idiomatum* (ἀντίδοσις ἰδιωμάτων), whereby what is predicated of the Son in the Godhead may also be applied, by the principle of participation, to the Father. That this concept is already anticipated in Ignatius of Antioch, see J.N.D. Kelly, *op.cit.*, p.143. On the other hand, since Tatian speaks of Christ as "God... in the form of man", ch.21 (p.23.6), it is quite probable that "the God who has suffered" is a reference to Christ, in which case His διάκονος to effect human salvation, in Tatian's understanding, would be the Holy Spirit. In the light of ch.15 (p.16.23), where God is said to dwell in man διὰ τοῦ πρεσβεύοντες πνεύματος, Otto takes the present statement as a reference to the Spirit; see Otto, *CACSS*, Vol.6, p.63, n.19; (cf.p.69, n.10).

143. *Oration*, ch.15 (p.16.14-16), following Aimé Puech's rendering; see *Recherches*, p.128.

144. Edmond Jacob, *Theology of the Old Testament* (ET by Arthur W. Heathcote and Philip J. Allcock), London: Hodder and Stoughton, 1958 (orig. 1955) pp.157ff.

145. *Oration*, ch.15 (p.16.10-13). Cf. Marcus Aurelius, *Meditations*, 12,3. Otto, *CACSS*, vol.6, p.63, n.3 refers to Sextus Empiricus. However, for an interpretation of Tatian which sees his view of man as "*en plein stoïcisme*", see Michel Spanneut, *Le Stoïcisme des Pères de l'Eglise: De Clément de Rome à Clément d'Alexandrie*, Paris: Editions du Seuil, 1957, pp.138-140.

146. *Oration*, ch.15 (p.16.20ff). As Schwartz rightly notes, Tatian here seems to be drawing on Pauline ideas, as in *1 Corinthians* 3:16; 6:19; *2 Corinthians* 6:16; *Ephesians* 2:22. Moreover, the use of σκηνώματος in the same context may recall *2 Corinthians* 5:1 (τὸ σκῆνος); see R.M. Grant, "Tatian and the Bible", p.302.

147. *Oration*, ch.15 (p.16.24f).

148. Cf. Aimé Puech, *Recherches*, p.68: "Thus salvation for man means recovering possession of the Spirit. The Spirit has abandoned him and the soul, left to itself, has wandered off in pursuit of false gods. The soul must be reunited once more with the Holy Spirit, making with him 'a couple according to the will of God' (τὴν κατὰ θεὸν συσυγίαν)."

149. *Oration*, ch.15 (p.16.13-16).

150. *Ibid.*, ch.15 (p.16.30f).

151. Cf. *1 Corinthians* 2:14f.

152. *Oration*, ch.15 (p.16.31).

153. *Ibid.*, ch.15 (p.17.7f).

154. Cf. *ibid.*, ch.14.

155. *Ibid.*, ch.15 (p.17.1-3).

156. R.M. Grant, "Tatian and the Bible", p.303.

157. *Epistle to the Hebrews* 1:3.

158. Cf. *Oration*, ch.30, where Tatian makes an allusion to the parable of the hidden treasure in *Matthew* 13:44ff.

159. Martin Elze, *op.cit.*, pp.58-59.

160. *Ibid.*, p.62.

161. *Oration*, ch.13 (pp.14.31-15.3). The rendering of the passage as given is in view of ch.20 (pp.22.29-23.3).

162. *Oration*, ch.31 (p.31.4f).

163. For these sources, see Aimé Puech, *Recherches*, pp.82ff.

164. See *Oration*, ch.31 (p.31.5), "our philosophy"; ch.32 (p.33.5) converts to the Christian faith "pursue philosophy" (φιλοσοφοῦσι) and (p.33.27) becoming a Christian is an entry into a life of "philosophising" (φιλοσοφεῖν); ch.33 (p.37.19f) Christian women "pursue philosophy", as shown in their higher moral calibre to Greek courtesans depicted in statuary sculpture; ch.35 (p.37.7f) Christian faith is "our Barbarian philosophy" (τῆς καθ᾽ ἡμᾶς βάρβαρου φιλοσοφίας); ch.42 (p.43.9f) his own Christian conversion was an entry into a discipline in Barbarian philosophy (κατὰ βαρβάρους φιλοσοφῶν).

165. Cf. Justin, *Dialogue with Trypho*, ch.8 (Migne, *PG*, 6, 492C).

166. Cf. Robert Joly, *op.cit.*, p.79.

167. *Oration*, ch.42 (p.43.12f).

168. Cf. Justin, *Dialogue with Trypho*, ch.3; Clement of Alexandria, *Stromateis*, Bk.2, ch.2; Seneca, *Epistulae Morales*, 90,3.

169. In relation to Tatian's identification of Christianity with "Barbarian" tradition as part of his proof of the antiquity of the Christian faith, Martin Elze, *op.cit.*, p.36, does not seem to me to be quite right in his view that "it is not the standpoint of faith but the particular concept of truth which characterizes Tatian's attitude". For the point is not the claim that "Barbarians" as such are in the truth, but rather that the tradition of the Christian Faith, as the Truth, lies in Barbarian history. It is not necessary to insist that Tatian's view of the antiquity of Truth was also held in Greek intellectual circles (Elze, *op.cit.*, p.36), as though Tatian was deriving his convictions from Greek sources. If they agree with him, so much the better!

170. See *Oration*, ch.29 (p.30.4-16).

171. Cf. *ibid.*, ch.12 (p.14.5-9).

· 172. Cf. the interesting observation by Adolf Harnack: "Nothing more clearly characterises the position of things in the second century than the agreement between two men so radically different as Tatian and Celsus. Tatian emphatically declares that salvation comes from the Barbarians, and to Celsus it is also a "truism" that the Barbarians have more capacity than the Greeks for discovery of valuable doctrines. Everything was, in fact, prepared, and nothing was wanting"; see Adolf Harnack, *History of Dogma*, vol.2 (ET. from 3rd German edition, is also by Neil Buchanan), London, Edinburgh, Oxford: Williams and Norgate, 1896, p.176. For Celsus' views, see Origen, *Contra Celsum*, 1,2; 6,1. Would Celsus have read Tatian's *Oration*? See R.M. Grant, "The Chronology of the Greek Apologists", p.28.

173. Reading ὑφ᾽ὑμῶν as in Otto's edition, instead of ὑφ᾽ἡμῶν, as given by Schwartz; cf. Aimé Puech, *Recherches*, p.147, n.3.

174. *Oration*, ch. 31 (p.31.11-16).

175. *Ibid.*, ch.31 (p.32.15- 23).

· 176. *Ibid.*, ch.36 (p.38.9). The three sources are Babylonian history, Phoenician records and Egyptian chronicles.

177. On the problem of the identity of the authors cited and the value of their evidence, see Aimé Puech, *Recherches*, pp.83ff.

178. This may, possibly, be the significance of Tatian's specific mention of the later rise of the Persian Empire, which preceded the rise of Greek power under Alexander the Great.

179. *Oration*, ch.36 (p.38.9f).

180. *Ibid.*, ch.36 (p.39.6).

181. *Ibid.*, ch.38.

182. Aimé Puech, *Recherches*, p.84: "Ptolemy of Mendes and Aion are his two real authorities, and it is thanks solely to them that he can establish the

synchronism: Moses - Amosis - Inachos, which is the basis of his entire chronology." The respect for Egyptian lore and sources was reflected in Greek tradition itself; see Plato, *Timaeus*, 22,B, for the view of an Egyptian priest, speaking to Solon, that "Greeks are always children" (παῖδες) in relation to "Barbarian" civilisation. See Clement of Alexandria, *Stromateis*, 1,29, where this statement is quoted and discussed.

183. *Oration*, ch.39.

184. It is quite likely that Tatian is depending on handbooks available to him; see Aimé Puech, *Recherches*, p.85, n.1.

185. *Oration*, ch.39 (p.39.24; 40.27).

186. *Ibid.*, ch.40 (p.41.5f).

187. *Ibid.*, ch.40 (p.41.1- 10).

188. *Ibid.*, ch.40 (p.41.7ff). With regard to these strictures on the Greek intellectual tradition, it is worth noting a statement made by Edwyn Bevan in the context of a discussion of the Greeks' self-perception in relation to "Barbarians": "The Greeks liked statements which sounded logical and effective, and if they got that, they did not bother much to examine the facts"; see Edwyn Bevan, "Greeks and Barbarians" in F.S. Marvin (ed), *Western Races and the World* (The Unity Series,5), London: Oxford University Press, 1922, p.60.

189. See definitions in LSJ, *Lexicon*, p.1151.

190. *Oration*, ch.29 (p.30.11-13).

191. Aimé Puech, *Recherches*, p.85.

192. *Ibid.*, p.85.

193. *Oration*, ch.31 (p.31.8).

194. *Ibid.*, ch.40 (p.41.2ff).

195. Eusebius, *HE*, 4,29. Migne, *PG*, 20, 401A.

196. Aimé Puech, *Recherches*, p.82.

197. Clement of Alexandria, *Stromateis*, 1, 21 (cf.ch.15).

198. Henry Chadwick, *Origen: Contra Celsum* (Bk.1, ch.16), Cambridge: Cambridge University Press, 1953, p.18.

199. Theophilus of Antioch, *Ad Autolycum*, Bk.2, ch.30 (cf.Bk.3, ch.20).

200. Eusebius, *PE*, Bk.10, ch.11; Migne, *PG*, 21, 817A-825D.

201. Tertullian, *Apology*, ch.19, cf. ch.47. Elsewhere Tertullian is found criticising Tatian for his ascetic practices and teachings; see Tertullian, *De Jejunio*, ch.15.

202. See J.P. Waltzing, *Tertullien: L'Apologétique: Apparat critique et traduction littérale revue et corrigée*), Bibliotheque de la Faculté de Philosophie et Lettres, Université de Liège, Liège: H. Vaillant-Carmanne, 1919, pp.86-88.

203. Lactantius, *Divine Institutes*, Bk.4, ch.5.

204. Augustine, *De Civitate Dei*, Bk.18, ch.37. But Augustine, in view of the Scriptural text (*Acts* 7:22) which states Moses' education in Egyptian lore, and aware no doubt of the awe in which Egyptian traditions were held, reaches further back, to Abraham! "Yet not even the wisdom of the Egyptians could be antecedent in time to the wisdom of our prophets, because even Abraham was a prophet."

205. See Justin, *1 Apology*, chs.44,59,60.

206. Aimé Puech, *Les Apologistes grecs*, p.11. See Moriz Friedländer, *op.cit.* pp.420f.

207. Aimé Puech, *Recherches*, p.85. Cf. J.M. Fuller, *op.cit.*, p.804: "By his [Tatian's] very faults he served the Church."

208. See Jean Daniélou, *op.cit.*, pp.10f. Cf. Aimé Puech, *Recherches*. pp.97ff.

209. Here, one thinks especially of a certain Artapanus, who claimed not only that it was Abraham who taught the Egyptian monarch astrology, and Joseph who taught better agriculture to the Egyptians, but also that "Moses was the real founder of all the culture and even of the worship of the gods in Egypt". See Emil Schürer, *op.cit.*, 2/3, pp.206-8. As Schürer observes: "However strange this may appear, it is explained by the tendency of the whole. Moses was the introducer of all culture, even of religious culture" (p.207). Cf. Paul Kruger, *Philo und Josephus als Apologeten des Judentums*, Leipzig: Verlag der Dürr'schen Buchhandlung, 1906, pp.20-22; cf.Martin Elze, *op.cit.*, p.14. For fragments of Artapanus, see Eusebius, *PE*, Bk.9, chs.18 (Migne, *PG*, 21, 709B-C), 23 (725B-C), 27 (727D-736B).

210. Cf. Aimé Puech, *Recherches*, pp.85-87.

211. Aimé Puech, *Les Apologistes grecs*, p.12.

212. Edwyn Bevan, *op.cit.*, pp.66f.

213. Cf. Martin Elze, *op.cit.*, p.25. However, I consider that Martin Elze goes too far when he asserts that Tatian's self-understanding "is in no way orientated according to the standpoint of faith!" It is important also to look for what Christianity meant to a person who was not a Greek; cf. T.R. Glover, *Conflict of Religions in the early Roman Empire* (8th edition), London: Methuen and Co., 1919, pp.145ff.

214. Otto, *CACSS*, vol.6, p.119, n.5.

215. In my view, therefore, Martin Elze, *op.cit.*, p.25, is not right in saying that the opposition of Barbarism to Hellenism in Tatian "is simply a question of the opposition between education and lack of sophistication, and he lines up on the side of lack of sophistication". It is true of course that Tatian rejects any so-called "philosophical" attempts to treat some categories of persons as incapable of intellectual activity. According to Tatian, Truth, that is, Christian truth, is accessible to all, as Elze rightly emphasises (p.39).

216. See A.D. Nock, "Early Gentile Christianity and its Hellenistic Background", in A.E.J. Rawlinson (ed), *Essays on the Trinity and the Incarnation*, London: Longman, Green and Co., 1928, pp.51-156, reprinted in Zeph Stewart (ed), *A.D. Nock: Essays on Religion and the Ancient World*, Oxford: Clarendon Press, 1972, pp.49-133. Also published by Harper and Row (Harper Torch Books), New York, 1964.

217. Celsus is quick to insist on this point, for quite other reasons, of course. See Henry Chadwick, *Origen: Contra Celsum*, Cambridge: Cambridge University Press, 1953; for instance, Bk 1,2 (p.7).

218. Werner Jaeger, *op.cit.*, p.34.

Chapter Three

The Gospel as the Triumph of Barbarism? (2): Tertullian, or, the Vindication of a Radical Christian Identity within Graeco-Roman Culture

I. Tertullian: Saint or Heretic? Tertullian as an isolated figure in early Graeco-Roman Christianity

Tertullian, unlike Tatian, was no outsider to Graeco-Roman culture. By parentage, circumstance and education, he belonged within it and so by taking a negative and rejectionist posture to Graeco-Roman tradition, Tertullian raises more fundamental questions than Tatian's repudiation of that same tradition could ever do.

Nevertheless, the affinities between the two personalities are real, and have generally been noted.[1] In his lengthy article in the *Dictionary of Christian Biography*, J.M. Fuller wrote:

"The 'Assyrian Tertullian' [Tatian] and the African were not unlike in temperament and training, as their lives were not unlike in their fitful vicissitudes. Once convinced of the darkness of that with which their early life and culture had been associated, they sprang out of it towards the light, and consecrated to the truth the energies of full manhood and the powers of ripened intellects. But also, once convinced that the Encratites or the Montanists were sounder than the teachers of the Church they had joined, they seceded from what they counted lax in practice and erroneous in tenet to die 'not of the fold'."[2]

No interpretation of Tertullian can ignore those "fitful vicissitudes" of his life yet Fuller's last statement raises the question as to whether there might not be a more helpful approach to Tertullian's Christian career and achievement (as we have seen in Tatian's case) than the traditional distinction between Catholic and Montanist (heretical?) periods.

Quintus Septimus Florens Tertullianus – to give his name in full – emerges as one of the most colourful and controversial characters in the whole of early Graeco-Roman Christianity. He has been recognised as one who stands "at the beginning of the entire Latin Church history" and "appears beyond dispute as the first Latin Father of the church".[3] Yet he has not received uniform interpretation by the testimony of Christian tradition.[4] In a recent helpful study of the theological motivation and outlook of the great North African Christian, Gerald Lewis Bray rightly observes:

> "then as now, Tertullian has been a borderline figure, neither officially recognised as a saint, nor explicitly condemned as a heretic."[5]

However, the attempts to arrange his extant works in a chronological order to fit his alleged development from orthodoxy into an increasingly rigorist, Montanist outlook, reflecting Catholic and schismatic (heretical?) periods, have not proved entirely satisfactory.[6] G. Bardy, who treats Tertullian's career under these rubrics, is forced to recognise that the polemical *Adversus Praxean*, which is placed in the "Montanist period" is no less significant for the development of doctrine in the Great Church, even if its author is presumed to have been beyond the official boundaries of the Catholic Church. The fact is, Tertullian's doctrinal orthodoxy could not easily be impugned, even as a Montanist.[7] As Hans von Campenhausen tersely states: "As a Montanist, Tertullian did not become other than he had always been".[8]

In fact, doubts have been raised as to the accuracy of the view that Tertullian embraced "Montanism" at all. Douglas Powell,[9] challenged the traditional view that Tertullian's Christian career ended in a rupture with the Church, by drawing attention to the fact that the term "Montanism" does not appear before the fourth century.[10] He argued convincingly that Tertullian never really broke fellowship with the African Church.

> "Nowhere does he (Tertullian) refer to Montanist bishops, nowhere does he deny that the African bishops were genuinely bishops, nowhere does he say that the *ecclesia numerus episcoparum*[11] is not the true Church, that the *unius Christi unica sponsa*[12] is to be found only with those who accept the New

Prophecy. Nowhere does he say that the Montanists have been cast out, driven from the Churches, condemned by the definitive sentence of bishops; that they refuse the catholic eucharist and refuse to meet with *psychici* in common assembly. Lightfoot said of Hippolytus and his *disiunctio* from Callistus, 'his very vagueness is the refutation of the solution of a rival papacy'; we may similarly say of Tertullian that his very ambiguity is the refutation of a theory of a formal schism from the African Church."[13]

Furthermore, Pierre de Labriolle's study of Tertullian's language has shown that even in his use of the pronominal designations *nos* and *nostri, nobis* and their cognates in his designation of those with whom he identifies, Tertullian is not necessarily to be taken as defending a "sectarian" position.[14] He points to instances in "Montanist" works where Tertullian makes a distinction between Christians in general and non-Christians.[15] It is interesting that in one such instance he indicates an identity of viewpoint between Tertullian and the decision of the Church Council at Carthage about AD 225.[16]

G.L. Bray has also demonstrated that Tertullian's use of *psychici* ("carnal") and *spiritales* ("spiritual") to distinguish those he disapproved of from those whom he associated with, cannot be appealed to as conclusive proof of his "Montanism". The meanings implied have a sufficiently New Testament ring about them not to require a recourse to Montanist or "gnostic" influences.[17] Tertullian may simply have intended *psychici* as a criticism of those Christians who were allowing their thinking and actions to be influenced by non-Christian forms of thought which from his standpoint were worldly.[18] The distinction between *spiritales* and *psychici* (occasionally *animales*)[19] need not have meant more than the distinction, within one Christian community, between those who considered the more rigorous discipline taught by the *Paracletus*,[20] as binding on all, and so embraced it, and those who, in the eyes of the *spiritales*, were willing to settle for less than the full requirements of Christian teaching. Powell describes the situation as one of an *ecclesia in ecclesia*, and likens the smaller group to the Puritan classes in the Church of England in the sixteenth century, and also to the early Methodist societies.[21] The pattern will be found in many other places, and at other points in Christian history. It is also likely that Tertullian's knowledge of the movement was obtained from Montanist writings.[22] It is significant that some features considered distinctively Montanist are absent from Tertullian's writings; certainly there is a difference in emphasis.[23]

In Bray's view, therefore, the most reasonable way to take Tertullian's interest in, and identification with, "the New Prophecy" would be that:

"Tertullian backed the Montanists because he saw in them fellow *spiritales*, whose thirst for holiness and concern for discipline equalled his own... It is clear that Tertullian's real interest was not in prophecy or eschatology, but in sanctification and discipline. To the extent that the Montanists shared this overriding concern, Tertullian was prepared to welcome and defend them from attack. Apart from that, he was not interested."[24]

Tertullian may therefore have been less deeply influenced by the Phrygian movement than has been assumed in the past.[25] However, the fact that he identified with it and defended some of its stances is enough to explain how he himself came under a cloud once the Montanists were condemned and repudiated by the Great Church. Yet the evident worth of his writings secured for him an outstanding place in the history of Christian thought and literature. The paradoxical attitude of the early church to Tertullian is well expressed by Pierre de Labriolle:

"Tertullian became for the early ages of Christianity a famous example of the lamentable falling away to which men of rare intelligence are exposed. If a man like him fell into the snares offered by the wild speculations of Montanism, who could dare to feel sure of himself? They gave expression to words of grave pity in his regard not altogether lacking in bitterness. And they took advantage of his unsound reputation to copy from his writings abundantly – without giving his name!"[26]

II. "One becomes Christian, one is not born such": Tertullian and permanent "apologia" for a radical Christianity.

But if Tertullian "as a Montanist... did not become other than he had always been", then a more helpful approach is required for appreciating him. We need to discern an integrating principle which, arising from his own self-understanding, would allow him to speak as far as possible on his own terms. In this connection, G.L. Bray's work achieves remarkable success and makes an important contribution towards the elucidation of the outlook and significance of Tertullian for Christian self-understanding.[27]

The integrating principle that Bray identifies as determining Tertullian's approach to theology was his preoccupation with sanctification; this pursuit of holiness constituted the main theme of his writings.[28] Insisting rightly that Tertullian's extant works do not permit the construction of a complete picture of his intellectual and cultural background,[29] Bray points to Tertullian's profound sense of "the impermanence of the world's glory" as a factor to be taken seriously. Tertullian's reticence on "his own record and achievements" in this world is, therefore, consistent with his overriding aim as a Christian, namely:

> "... to know God in the person of His Son Jesus Christ, and as St Paul says in *Philippians* 3:9, to be found in him, not having his own righteousness, but that which is through faith in Christ. The student who would understand Tertullian must understand above all that his life was the pursuit of holiness in the presence of the living God."[30]

Tertullian's writings are the essential *locus* for discovering "the living power of his mind",[31] since they constitute virtually in their entirety "a battle cry"[32] on behalf of the Christian faith as he apprehended it. Tertullian's conversion was, as Bray affirms, "without doubt the single most important event in his life..."[33] Whatever else may be ascertained about Tertullian's social background, his familiarity with the contemporary culture and his knowledge of Graeco-Roman tradition, it is his Christian commitment which gives coherence and meaning to the total picture.[34] There can be no more eloquent testimony to the sense of a radical self-identity as a Christian than in Tertullian's assertion, in the face of his non-Christian critics: "We were of you: One becomes Christian, one is not born such" (Christians are made not born such!).[35] There can be little doubt that becoming a Christian and living self-consciously as one for the rest of his life was a fact of immense significance for Tertullian. His forceful vindication of the Christian cause derived not just from the fact that he possessed the literary and intellectual abilities commensurate to the task; in Tertullian we find a conjunction of intellectual ability and radical conviction to a degree that makes his defence of the Christian faith, especially in his great *Apologeticum,* "not quite the work of the fuller or baker at whom Celsus sneered".[36]

Tertullian's preoccupation with maintaining a distinct Christian self-consciousness shows its inner consistency in the persistence of themes, reflections and argumentation in writings which obviously span several years. Pierre de Labriolle,[37] drew attention to some of these concerns which give unity and a feeling of purpose to Tertullian's whole literary career as a Christian. Working from the *Apologeticum,* which is generally recognised as Tertullian's masterpiece, de Labriolle indicated themes which are resumed, refined or enlarged in other works. Accordingly, the entire argument for the universal validity of the Christian faith on the grounds of human intuition and psychology in the *De Testimonio Animae* can be related to the exultant outburst in the *Apologeticum*: "*O! testimonium animae naturaliter Christianae!*"[38] The brief and hurried statement on the nature of Christ in terms of Trinitarian doctrine in *Apologeticum*[39] is given fuller treatment in the polemical *Adversus Praxean*. *Apologeticum*[40] deals with the problem which the Jewish community and its religious traditions posed for Graeco-Roman Christianity, only in outline in terms of the Christian position on the vexed question of the identity of the Messiah and of his coming; but in the *Adversus Judaeos*[41] Tertullian, who elsewhere calls Jewish synagogues *fontes persecutionum*[42] lays out more extensively the whole basis of the bitter disputes with the Jews. In similar vein, the fearless assertion of Christian freedom of conscience in the *Apologeticum* (27,1) finds its full vigour in the cautionary tract, *Ad Scapulam,* addressed to the proconsul Scapula. The dire consequences that overtook some persecutors of Christians (*Ad Scapulam,* 3) had been hinted at in the threats of desertion from the Empire, and the consequent prospect of increased demonic activity as Christian exorcists withdrew their services.[43]

We find a similar continuity in Tertullian's treatment of some elements of Graeco-Roman culture. In one vigorous flourish, in the *Apologeticum*, he repudiates the entire paraphernalia of the circus shows, the theatre and the athletic games, undermining their very religious and social foundations:

"Equally we renounce your public spectacles as much as the matters which gave rise to them, which we know to be conceived of superstition, in that we have got clear of the very things about which these performances are concerned."[44]

The fuller exposition of his attitude to these unavoidable aspects of contemporary society becomes the subject of a separate volume: *De Spectaculis.* The treatise *De Idolatria* also witnesses to the persistence of the same concern in an even more enlarged and more radical perspective. It is also evident that Tertullian's unwillingness to describe the Christian faith as "a form (school) of philosophy"[45] and his profound mistrust of philosophical speculation for formulating Christian theology[46] are the ingredients which provide the basis for his fierce attack on Gnostic groups and their teachers in the *De Praescriptione Haereticorum.*

Even the subject of martyrdom, traditionally taken as an indication of his Montanist sympathies,[47] can be traced through the *Ad Martyras*, the *Ad Nationes* and the *Apologeticum*. It is interesting that in each of these works, Tertullian's argument is substantially the same. For instance, he appeals to examples of fortitude in the face of death in Graeco-Roman tradition, both as a defence of the Christian example against its critics (*Ad Nationes*, 1,18) and as an exhortation to fellow Christians facing the prospect of martyrdom (*Ad Martyras*, 4; *Apologeticum*, 50).[48] In this connection all that the *De Fuga in Persecutione* adds to Tertullian's treatment of the question is a further clarification and refinement of an already deeply held view, namely, the high value of martyrdom in persecution, which is now explicitly stated as originating with God, even though it strikes Christians "by the agency of the devil".[49] The rigorist arguments contained in the *De Fuga* are already found, also in the *Apologeticum*.[50] Consequently, it is not the case that Tertullian now makes a *volte face*, turning from earlier moderate positions.[51] Irrespective of the merits of Tertullian's arguments, it will be hard to deny his inner consistency with regard to the major preoccupations which remained with him throughout his Christian career.

Is it possible to ascribe any significance to this pattern of themes, concerns and reflections in which the *Apologeticum* emerges, not just as the masterpiece of composition and coherence – in view of the diversity of subjects that it holds together – but also as the centre-piece of Tertullian's literary output? The *Apologeticum* is generally dated quite early in Tertullian's Christian career and it is remarkable that it is also the work in which he seems to have given of himself most completely. Pierre de Labriolle made no more of this fact than simply to note that "it sometimes happens to writers to put their best selves in their first works".[52] However, the fact that Tertullian's most enduring literary work was his *Apologeticum* may itself be symbolic.

If Joseph Lortz is right that "apology means vindication",[53] then Tertullian comes closest to being the most eloquent, if also the most provocative, vindicator of the distinctiveness of Christian self-understanding in early Graeco-Roman culture. Lortz criticises, rightly, the tendency to treat Tertullian as apart from the Greek apologists. For him, the truth of the matter is that Tertullian builds on their foundations, and carries their work further. Consequently, they and Tertullian form "a spiritual unity".[54] But the vehemence both of his response to the hostile environment and of his defence of Christian self-identity, represents a considerable advance on his Greek counterparts. In so far as it is true that early Christian apologetics was not so much a positive intellectual movement, self-conscious and primary, as, essentially, "a product of the struggle which was forced upon Christians through the attack of a hostile paganism",[55] then it was Tertullian who embodies that struggle in its most uncompromising terms for his time. It is possible to understand the entirety of Tertullian's Christian career (including his sympathy with "the new prophecy") as the unrelenting battle of a man for whom the struggle to establish the rights of Christian identity had become the single most important reality in life. The fact that Tertullian lived in a period of religious transition and of syncretism,[56] lends added poignancy to his struggle. Jean-Claude Frédouille is right in suggesting that what so often passes for a negative attitude in Tertullian towards "the other side", is to be understood more accurately as a *defensive* posture, in favour of the faith that he has so unreservedly embraced.[57] It is in this twofold sense that Tertullian's work attains the quality of a permanent *apologia* for a radical Christianity.

The enigmatic and somewhat humorous tract, *De Pallio,* is of particular interest in this connection. On a superficial level the *De Pallio* was intended to justify Tertullian's decision to don the Greek philosopher's *pallium* in preference to the Roman *toga.* This change of garment was not in itself of great significance; there was evidence of widespread preference among Romans, including some emperors, for the less cumbersome *pallium.* If Frédouille is right that "to wear the *pallium* was not in effect to make oneself stand out by wearing special dress; it was, on the contrary to align oneself with an ever more widespread custom,"[58] then the composition of a literary justification for his action may itself be revealing of Tertullian's state of mind.

Fundamental to Tertullian's case in the *De Pallio,* which seems to be a personal *apologia,*[59] is the extensive argument concerning the universal law of mutations. It is to this that he appeals in defence of his own spiritual progression, symbolised in the move *a toga ad pallium*. But coupled with this argument is an important distinction namely, the distinction between permanent divine realities and the provisional, temporary realities of existence. His decision to wear the *pallium* falls in the category of "custom" which is subject to change, in time. However, "religion" – hence we have to understand his own religious conviction – like "nature", is fixed and belongs in the realm of divine realities:

> "The transfer of dress approximates to culpability just in so far as it is not custom but nature which suffers the change. There is a wide enough difference between the honour due to time, and religion. Let custom show fidelity to time, nature to God."[60]

If Tertullian has donned the Greek philosopher's *pallium*, it is not because his own Christian faith has been attenuated;[61] on the contrary, the *pallium* is ennobled by being worn by one who professes "a better philosophy".[62]

The distinction which Tertullian maintains here reappears frequently in his other writings and in varying degrees of radicality; but it remains basic to his entire outlook. It is used, for instance, in the *Apologeticum* to argue for a change in the law which is shown to be unjust in its application to Christians;[63] it is employed also in the argument urging the veiling of Christian maidens.[64] Thus, in what may well be one of the last of Tertullian's extant works,[65] his postulate of radical discontinuity between the religious consciousness of the Christian and his cultural environment abides.

III. "The devil's pomp": Christian identity amid a "demonic" universe

> "When entering the water, we make profession of the Christian faith in the terms prescribed by its law, we bear public testimony that we have renounced the devil, his pomp and his angels."[66]

When one considers the scope of Tertullian's conception of the Christian's renunciation, one appreciates how his religious outlook could have within it the potential for provoking a social revolution in the Empire.[67] It is easy enough to understand that Tertullian should condemn "the pleasures of the public shows" – the theatre, just as much as the circus and gladiatorial shows – for being "not consistent with true religion and true obedience to the true God"[68] (*non competant verae religioni et vero obsequio erga verum Deum*). But Tertullian means by the "devil's pomp" (*pompa diaboli*) more than the evident cruelty and perversity of the shows. These were merely the external manifestations of a more sinister reality with which the Christians to whom he addresses himself must learn to contend. As J.H. Waszink[69] has demonstrated, what "the devil's pomp" (*pompa diaboli*) denotes in Tertullian – who is the first witness to the explicit use of the expression in the baptismal rite – is no less than the very religious foundations and practices which undergirded and accompanied the social and cultural life of Graeco-Roman society, both individually and collectively, with particular application to the pomp and pageantry of the circus shows.[70]

The heart of Tertullian's contention is the identification of the deities of Graeco-Roman religion with fallen angels which have since become the evil demons of the Christian scheme.[71] Consequently, in so far as the near totality of the social life of the State and society in general is intimately linked with devotion to these presumed deities, it follows that for him "the whole of the public life in the pagan city is impregnated with the demonic".[72] The one word which sums up and condemns the entire phenomenon is "idolatry" (*idolatria*).[73] It is enough, for instance, that there was literary evidence which related the origins of the seasonal games to "festal days, and temples, and religious rituals".[74] For Tertullian, "the *ludi* are nothing but a form of idolatry".[75]

It is important to recognise the basis on which Tertullian proceeds to set aside the social claims which, in his view, society wrongly makes upon the Christian conscience. In the *Apologeticum*, he states categorically:

"We do not worship your gods, because we know that there are no such beings. This, therefore, is what you should do: you should call on us to demonstrate their non-existence, and thereby prove that they have no claim to adoration; for only if your gods were truly so, would there be any obligation to render divine homage to them."[76]

Tertullian goes on to give this proof by invoking the Euhemeristic theory concerning the human origin of the gods,[77] and by pointing to histories of the presumed gods.[78] Furthermore, with characteristic sarcasm, he not only insists that the actual objects of Graeco-Roman worship are mere statues – works of human art made from material substances – but also appeals to Seneca's treatise on Roman popular religion in which the respected philosopher was known to have been quite critical[79] of aspects of the same civil religion which the Christians are now being accused of dishonouring.[80]

But there is more to Tertullian's outlook than sarcasm or Christian "arrogance"; he believed profoundly that the religious devotion which the society insists on is fundamentally misguided, having arisen, as he says, from error:

"... does it not merit praise instead of penalty that we have rejected what we have come to see is error?"[81]

Therefore, in order rightly to appreciate Tertullian's uncompromising outlook, it is essential to realise that in common with the articulate vindicators of the Christian faith in his time, he was conscious of a moral and intellectual transformation in his own life and thought. This consciousness of an experience of "conversion"[82] must be borne in mind when one seeks to understand the attitudes which the early Christian apologists, of both Greek and Latin worlds, brought to bear on their relation to their pre-Christian religious and intellectual traditions.[83]

Accordingly, when Tertullian comes to deal with the social claims of Roman civil religion, he brings to the task not just a rigorist temperament,[84] but above all a religious attitude.[85] Because he is so profoundly convinced that it is evil demons who masquerade behind the names of Graeco-Roman deities,[86] Tertullian confronts the problem of the public shows as essentially a religious problem. How can the Christian who has made a choice for obedience to the true God participate in activities which honour the very beings he has now recognised to be evil? The overriding aim of these "spiritual beings" under the leadership of "Satan, the head of this evil progeny",[87] is "the ruin of mankind".[88] Through devices like "false healings" and "false divinations", their principal intent is to turn men's minds away from the true God and from obedience to His will.[89] This intent is also at work in the shows; and Tertullian even traces the skills and artistic gifts displayed in the shows to diabolic inspiration:

"... the demons predetermining in their own interests from the start, among other evils of idolatry, the pollutions of the public shows, with their object of drawing man away from his Lord, and binding him to their own service, carried out their purpose by bestowing on him the artistic gifts which the shows require."[90]

In and behind the cruelties of the gladiatorial shows – "the most noted and most popular of all"[91] – and the corrupting influences of the theatre,[92] Tertullian sees the activity of evil demons. If "the performances of the theatre have the common patronage" of Venus and Bacchus, then "the immodesty... which so specially and peculiarly characterises the theatre"[93] merely shows these two deities to be none other than the patron demons of drunkenness and lust.[94]

Thus, the whole outfit of the public shows, with their impressive ceremonial and procession,[95] as well as the dramatic arts, in Tertullian's view:

"... were instituted entirely for the devil's sake and have been got up entirely with the devil's things... in them you have that pomp of the devil which in the 'seal' of our faith we abjure."[96]

There is almost a military ring about Tertullian's language: Christians have enlisted under the "seal" and banner of God, and have no part in the activities of persons in a rival camp, under a rival "seal".[97] It is, perhaps, not surprising that Tertullian should therefore exclaim:

"Would that we did not even inhabit the same world with such [wicked persons]! But yet, in regard to what is of the world (*in saecularibus*), we are separate from them; for the world (*saeculum*) is God's but the worldly (*saecularia*) is the devil's."[98]

In view of the noted consistency with which Tertullian retained his basic concerns, it stands to reason that he should take up some of the specific questions surrounding Christian participation in the wider and more pervasive dimensions of social life. He does this in the *De Idolatria*. Unlike the *De Spectaculis*, the *De Idolatria*[99] seeks to bring the near totality of the political and administrative activities in Roman society under the rubric of "idolatry", this being "the principal crime of the human race, the worst guilt incurred by the world and the fundamental reason for divine judgment".[100] Tertullian's repudiation of vast areas of Roman social, civil, political and professional life will be validated virtually entirely on this one basis, that:

"If you have forsworn the devil's pomp (*diaboli pompam*) you should know that whatever you touch connected with it is idolatry."[101]

After quickly disposing of considerations regarding the scope of idolatry – for "every offence against God constitutes idolatry"[102] – and concerning the etymology of the term itself, Tertullian comes to the questions of practical import which are his major interest, and he devotes a predominant portion of the treatise to these. Tertullian is evidently aware of the professional implications of his position, even for some Christians.[103] However, for him, not only is the business of the manufacture of effigies of the gods obviously inadmissible, but also all contributory trades and crafts are to be shunned. Incense may have uses in medicine and even serve Christian funerary purposes; but incense is what "fattens every demon".[104] This is enough to render the business of dealing in incense at best ambiguous. Moreover, the duties of schoolmasters require not only that they teach the content of the mythological literature concerning the gods, but also that they participate in solemnities in their honour. Seen from this angle, the profession of the schoolmaster contributes to building up the rudiments of belief for the devil from the early stages of education. The professor of literature is unwittingly guilty of idolatry![105]

But whilst he so vehemently opposes the teaching of the literature by Christians, Tertullian is aware that literary studies are essential. His solution is a distinction between teaching and learning. A believer may *learn* these things if he is already capable of understanding the nature of idolatry. The student is here compared to one who "knowingly accepts poison but does not drink it".[106] And yet, the fact that Tertullian thus describes what is learnt, is sufficient to indicate the persisting difficulty he has with the system as a whole.

Some professions are less ambiguous. One such is astrology; but should one claim Scriptural sanction in the example of the Magi,[107] Tertullian has a ready rejoinder: the dream-message ordering them to go home, but by a way other than that by which they came, means that they should not continue in their former persuasion.[108] Thus magical arts of every sort, as well as all professions and trades which are connected however remotely with devotion to the gods, are firmly excluded from the *discipline*[109] of the Gospel:

> "... no art... no profession, no trade which administers either to equipping or forming idols, can be free from the charge of idolatry."[110]

But when, in the latter chapters of the treatise,[111] Tertullian decides to draw attention to the danger of committing idolatry in speech as well as in silent acquiescence, in greetings, no less than in written contracts, it becomes evident that Tertullian's concern reaches beyond the dubious connections of professional activity. What is at issue in fact is how the Christian may live in the world (*saeculum*) and preserve his Christian identity. The problem emerges in its most critical form when it has to do with service in the civil administration of the State, and in particular military service. How can the Christian serve in any administrative capacity when "demons are the magistrates of this world"?[112] It is above all a problem of conscience[113] and not a case of Tertullian's "egotistic preoccupation with the future life".[114] On the one hand, there is the problem of how the Christian, "a servant of God", can avoid contamination with "idolatry" in view of its pervasiveness:

> "Let us grant that it is possible for anyone to succeed in moving, in whatsoever office, under the mere name of the office neither sacrificing, nor lending his authority to sacrifices; neither con-

racting for sacrificial victims, nor delegating the care of temples; not looking after their tributes; not giving shows at his own expense or at the State's, or presiding over the giving of them; ... not even taking oaths; moreover, what comes under the terms of power, neither sitting in judgment on any one's life or character, ... neither condemning nor forecondemning, binding no one, imprisoning or torturing no one – if it is credible that all this is possible."[115]

But there is another aspect to the problem of civil office, and which is hinted at in the passage just quoted: Tertullian is deeply convinced that all forms of worldly power and dignity are not only alien to, but enemies of, God.[116] To validate his claim, Tertullian develops several arguments. For one thing, the ensigns of power are associated with the demons who are the real rulers.[117] It is also through the channels of worldly power that persecution comes upon Christians, God's servants, whilst the wielding of power blinds the impious to the punishments awaiting them.[118] But, more significantly, he draws attention to the example of Christ, who lived "in humility and obscurity"[119] and who, "though conscious of his own Kingdom... shrank back from being made a king" and so, "in the fullest manner, gave his own an example for turning coldly from all the pride and garb, as well of dignity as of power".[120] For, if the paraphernalia of worldly office and dignity were meant for Christians:

"who would rather have used them than the Son of God? What kind and what number of *fasces* would escort him? What kind of purple would bloom from his shoulders? What kind of gold would beam from his head, had he not judged the glory of the world to be alien both to himself and to his? Therefore, what he was unwilling to accept, he has rejected; what he rejected he condemned; and what he condemned, he has counted as part of the devil's pomp."[121]

It is essential that we understand the importance of the example of Christ for Tertullian. Tertullian does recognise instances in Scripture where positions of considerable influence in civil administration fell to "servants of God". Such are the cases of Joseph in Egypt and Daniel in Babylon. Tertullian's solution is twofold and revealing. In the first place, these men belonged to an old and rudimentary pre-Christian era in God's dealings with mankind, and so cannot be invoked to overthrow his case.[122] In the second place, whereas these men, despite their elevation, remained "slaves" of their rulers, the Christian is "slave" only of Christ, a possible reference to *1 Corinthians* 7:23 and to the favourite

Pauline self-designation.[123] But it is the example and teaching of Christ which finally weighs with Tertullian. The position he vindicates is, in his eyes, the truly *Christian* one.

This attitude emerges clearly in the short chapter in the *De Idolatria* devoted to the question of military service. Tertullian sees no significance in the fact that Biblical characters like Moses and Joshua and even the Israelite nation as a whole in the Old Testament had military careers; nor does he consider the faith of a Roman centurion[124] as sufficient to overturn his basic conviction on the question. To appeal to such instances really amounts to sporting[125] with the subject. For him, the question is settled on the strength once again of the example of Christ: the Lord, "in disarming Peter, unbelted every soldier".[126] According to Tertullian, then:

"There is no agreement between the divine and the human sacrament,[127] the standard of Christ and the standard of the devil, the camp of light and the camp of darkness; one soul cannot be indebted to two [masters], to God and to Caesar."[128]

In the *De Corona*, which is inspired by the bold example of a Christian soldier who refused to wear the laurel crown on the occasion of an imperial *donativum* in the camp, Tertullian presents much the same outlook as one finds in the *De Idolatria*. In the early chapters he seeks to prove the inadmissibility of the wearing of crowns, by appealing, in the absence of Scriptural injunction, to Christian "tradition",[129] and also by pointing to the association of crowns with the deities of Graeco-Roman religion.[130] However, the real issue at stake is not the military crown, but the military life itself; it has to do with whether "warfare is proper at all to Christians".[131] He appeals to the argument about the conflict of oaths,[132] and to the inevitability of transgressing God's law in the exercise of camp duties which are of a religious character.[133]

The demands of Christian discipleship and the requirements of military allegiance are fundamentally opposed: "the very carrying of the name [of Christian] from the camp of light to the camp of darkness is a violation of it."[134] But Tertullian is sensitive enough to perceive that the antinomy reaches beyond the simple consideration of religious commitment. The necessity for violence and the duty to kill which are incumbent upon the soldier, constitute a major stumbling block to Tertullian who understands the Christian life as one of peace and non-violence. Tertullian could thus ask, almost hauntingly, about military victories which were the occasions for wearing the laurel crown:

"Is the laurel of triumph made of leaves, or of corpses? Is it

adorned with ribbons, or with tombs? Is it bedewed with oint-
ments, or with the tears of wives and mothers? It may be of some
Christians too; for Christ is also among the barbarians."[135]

The Christian has no part in promoting the worldly interests of
the State, since he is "a foreigner in this world, and a citizen of
Jerusalem, the city above". Consequently, he has "nothing to do
with the joys of the world".[136]

By removing Christian discipleship so resolutely from the realm
of military life, as from much of the social life of the time, Tertullian
was undermining the stability of the Empire at a crucial point.[137]
But he was also giving expression to a genuinely Christian outlook
on the issues of violence, war and "patriotism"; and it is interesting
that the position which Tertullian seeks to champion in the context
of the beleaguered Church will find equally convinced advocates in
the era of the imperial Church.[138]

Is it the case that in the *De Spectaculis*, the *De Idolatria* and
the *De Corona*, Tertullian has come a long way from an earlier
"moderate" position on the questions discussed?[139] It is necessary
to recall a famous passage in the *Apologeticum* where Tertullian
claims the active presence of Christians in virtually every area of
Roman society:

> "We are but of yesterday, and we have filled every place among
> you – cities, islands, fortresses, towns, market-places, the very
> camp, tribes, divisions, palace, senate, forum – we have left you
> only [your] temples!"[140]

It is rightly suggested[141] that Tertullian is here making hyper-
bolic claims for Christian numerical strength. And yet an interesting element in these "rhetorical details" is Tertullian's deliberate
point that the one area of Roman civic life which Christians have
not filled are the temples! This fact shows the importance Tertullian attaches to the grounding of Christian identity on an essentially *religious* basis; it underscores his fundamental apprehension
that the irreconcilable differences between the Christian community and Graeco-Roman society were of a religious nature.
Because of the radical and "revolutionary" character of Tertullian's
religious outlook,[142] Tertullian's later statement:

> "We sail with you, *serve in the army with you,* live in the
> countryside with you and do business with you... we mix our
> crafts."[143]

should not be taken to suggest that Tertullian ever was in favour
of military service for Christians. The point of Tertullian's obser-

vation is simply that Christians are not the antisocial characters they are popularly alleged to be. In other words, beyond his apologetic purposes in the context, the fact that Christians are found in those areas of civic life is not binding on his perception of Christian discipleship.[144]

The consistency of Tertullian's outlook emerges when he seeks to show in *Apologeticum* 38 that Christians do not pose a threat to public order or to the unity of the Empire. In an earlier chapter he sought to demonstrate that there is such a thing as a proper Christian reverence and loyalty to the Emperor, since "he is instituted in office by our Lord".[145] However, Christians do not constitute a political danger, in the first place because they have no desire for political power or fame or place in society, and have no interest in vying for public office. They also possess a universal citizenship which renders their participation in affairs of state irrelevant.[146] In the second place, Christians have no need to take part in the public religious rituals in so far as they hold them to derive from error and superstition, whilst they abstain from the amusements of theatre, arena and gymnasium on moral grounds, preferring other pleasures.[147]

It is hard to find a more vigorous exponent than Tertullian of what Professor A.F. Walls has called "the 'pilgrim' principle", which consists in defining Christian authenticity in terms of factors that lie outside of one's natural culture and society.[148] R.A. Markus is certainly right to suggest that Tertullian's viewpoint is understandable in his historical context, which was characterised by the twin dangers of religious and intellectual syncretism and heretical Christianity.[149] Tertullian is evidently aware of these attendant dangers when he specifically defines the canons of Christian truth, as we shall see. However, his outlook also represents a profoundly religious response to the more pervasive problem of Christian self-understanding in a sinful world. Deeply convinced that the Christian faith held within itself the only fully reliable insights into the nature of religion and of human experience, Tertullian saw all else, and especially whatever opposed it, as demonic, inspired by Satan and calculated to rob the Christian of his priceless possession. If all the things which were of the world (*saecularia*) were of demons, Tertullian saw the evidence for it quite close at hand, in the religious outfit which sustained the Empire and its entire life. To that extent, Tertullian's outlook reflects remarkably the early fortunes of Latin Christianity as a whole. As Jean Daniélou has pointed out, Latin Christianity, being closer to the heart of the Empire, was led early to tackle the concrete issues raised in the Church's historical confrontation with the ideology of the Empire:

> "The religion of Rome was above all social and juridical, its essential aim being to maintain the *pax deorum* as the necessary guarantee of success in whatever was undertaken both by individuals and by the city as a whole. In the Latin world, Christianity for its part also displayed more particularly its social aspect, that of an institution founded in its turn on religion, and expressed primarily in loyalty to a society. From the start, therefore, conflict between the two societies was inevitable."[150]

What Daniélou's observation and analysis do not make clear is the fact that this "Latin" perspective on the Christian faith with its community, was, above all, of African inspiration, and that in this African tradition Tertullian had a pride of place.[151]

IV. "What has Athens to do with Jerusalem?" The source and measure of truth

With such radicality of outlook to society generally, it is not surprising that Tertullian should turn his attention to the task of defining the proper grounds for Christian certainty and the criteria for distinguishing Christian truth from its perversions. He sets out explicitly to do this in the *De Praescriptione Haereticorum.*[152]

It is obvious that, for Tertullian, a proper understanding of Christian truth requires the firm rejection of whatever is derived form the Graeco-Roman philosophical and intellectual tradition. But it is important to recognise Tertullian's overall concern. The trouble with philosophy is its association with heresy.

It is this fact – that Tertullian is so often at pains to emphasise "the relations existing between heresy and philosophy"[153] – which needs to be borne in mind when one comes upon his outbursts against philosophy:

> "What indeed has Athens to do with Jerusalem? What has the Academy to do with the Church? *What have heretics to do with Christians?* Our instruction comes from the porch of Solomon, who had himself taught that 'the Lord should be sought in simplicity of heart'. Away with all attempts to produce a Stoic, Platonic and dialectic Christianity! We want no curious disputation after possessing Christ Jesus, no further enquiry after receiving the Gospel. With our faith, we desire no further belief. For this is our first article of faith, that there is nothing which we ought to believe besides."[154]

The important questions which these declarations raise have not to do, as has been assumed by some commentators, with Tertullian's "anti-rationalism"[155] or otherwise.[156]

As Richard Norris has pointed out in a very perceptive study, Tertullian brings to his theological task as a Christian thinker and writer not so much "a theological system, but... a religious attitude... an outlook or perspective which is more elusive for the fact that it is presupposed rather than formulated in plain language".[157] Tertullian is not interested in any intellectual "quest" or "seeking" for its own sake. But this position is not prompted by a preference for obscurantism. Rather, it stems from a firm conviction that in the Christian Gospel, every honest seeker can find the fullness of divine revelation concerning the essential questions of life, which, for Tertullian, resolve themselves into the knowledge of truth and the certainty of faith in Christ. Thus, in a lengthy commentary on the Gospel saying "Seek and you will find",[158] Tertullian insists that the saying can only legitimately apply to *finding* the truth as taught by Christ, in order to arrive at a firm apprehension of *faith* in this truth.[159] Therefore, there is a limit to all "seeking", namely, "finding", just as there is an end also to all knocking and asking.[160] Seeking for its own sake is thus ruled out from a truly Christian mental attitude:

> "... there can be no indefinite seeking for that which has been taught as one only definite thing. You must seek until you find, and believe when you have found; nor have you anything further to do but to keep what you have believed, provided you believe this besides, that nothing else is to be believed and therefore nothing else is to be sought after you have found and believed what has been taught by Him who charges you to seek no other thing than what He has taught."[161]

When it is realised that Tertullian's overriding concern is to defend what he calls the Christian "rule of faith" – which embodies the Christian community's basic credal convictions on God, Jesus Christ, salvation and the ultimate destiny of men[162] – and to protect the Christian from falling away from these convictions, then his attitude to philosophy becomes clearer. It is also interesting that he addresses his remarks not only to heretical groups, but also to "orthodox"[163] Christians, who may be in danger of declining from the rule of faith.[164] What Tertullian criticises in philosophy – quite apart from the uncertainty and divergence of views among different schools[165] and the failure of philosophers to match their words with deeds[166] – is its attitude and approach to questions which, for Tertullian, are definitely settled by divine revelation as given in the Scriptures of the Christian Church. Philosophy brings to the question of God and His relation to men and the world and related issues, an outlook of speculative curiosity and excessive human enquiry,[167] rather than the attitude of faith. It is this mood and mental attitude derived from philosophy which in Tertullian's view characterises heretics.

Tertullian has forcefully argued this case in the *Apologeticum.*[168] There, he begins by pointing out, in the tradition of Christian apologetics of the time, that the antiquity of the Christian Scriptures, the Old Testament,[169] makes them the source of all later wisdom. It is from Christian sources, therefore, that philosophers have derived their semblance of truth comparable to Christian ideas.[170] But, whereas philosophers aspire to Christian doctrines, their overweening desire for personal glory and eloquence proves to be their undoing. Proceeding on the basis of speculative curiosity, they fail to believe in the divine character of the teaching of the Scriptures and so fail to understand them.[171] The great failing of the philosophical outlook lies in its attitude of contempt and disdain for faith and its dependence on human inquiry. But this attitude of mind leads philosophers into uncertainties and contradictions on questions on which the Scriptures are clear, certain and simple.[172]

The connection with heresy is obvious. In so far as the Scriptures (Old Testament) have been perverted through the speculations of philosophers, it is from the ranks of philosophers that heretics rise. Heretics are the intellectual offspring of philosophers; their work consists in adulterating the truth, and by applying their personal opinions, they seek to fit the teachings of the Christian Scriptures (the New Testament) to views derived from philosophy.[173] The way of truth is one and simple, from which both heresy and philosophy differ by being characterised by a multiplicity and intricacy of pathways, divergent from the one true way.

It is against the views of heretics, therefore, that Tertullian invokes the "rule of faith" (here called *regula veritatis* – rule of the truth), which originated with Christ Himself, and was transmitted by His own companions, the apostles, in relation to whom heretics are mere innovators and commentators who draw on their own speculations.[174] Consequently, there is no compelling reason to discuss the claims of heretics, inasmuch as being heretics, they deviate from the truth anyway.

Behind all travesty of the truth, in Tertullian's view, there lies the activity of demons, the spirits of error which seek to rival the claims of Christian truth.[175] Furthermore, it is from the truth itself that the material for its falsification is derived. For it is upon the truth that the demons operate, seeking to subvert the truth by instigating imitations of various Christian teachings, in the form of poetic fables and philosophical tenets, with a view to discrediting the integrity of Christian teachings.[176]

In essence, this chapter of the *Apologeticum* contains the major ingredients of the argument of the *De Praescriptione Haereticorum*; the most important new element in the latter work is a fuller treatment of the principles of exclusion.[177] And yet, even here, it is the *praescriptio novitatis* which is most prominent.[178] It is interesting that it is this very argument from priority – that is, the priority of truth to error – which is particularly stressed in the chapter of the *Apologeticum* we have just examined.

From our analysis, it is evident that Tertullian's view of philosophy is determined not only by his understanding of truth, which, for him, is fully available only within the Christian tradition and as preserved in the "orthodox" apostolic churches, but also by his view of the heretical groups and their teachers, who belong to the philosophical tradition, characterised by speculative *curiositas* and human *scrupulositas*.[179] Therefore the fact that Tertullian does not hesitate to make use of the philosophic knowledge which he had acquired before he became converted to Christianity in explaining or demonstrating Christian beliefs, does not necessarily lend a "contradictory" character to his statements on philosophy.[180] Tertullian's critique of philosophy has not to do so much with the specific teachings of particular schools; his concern lies deeper. As Richard Norris has observed, Tertullian sees in philosophy

"... an alien influence, a source of attitudes and ideas which corrupt the Rule of Faith. ... Philosophy, as Tertullian sees it, is not merely a set or sets of opinions. It is a historically identifiable tradition of thought embodied in a continuing series of human communities which perpetuate the original teaching of their founders. And Christianity necessarily stands outside this tradition. For Christianity is, in fact, itself *another* tradition, living on in a distinct community, the Church, and perpetuating not the views of Plato or Aristotle, but the revealed teaching of God Himself. The Gospel is therefore an *alternative* to philosophy, and its truth can only be preserved when it is kept free from adulteration with the principles of any rival tradition."[181]

If Norris' interpretation is correct, then it shows that it is in Tertullian's estimation of the Graeco-Roman philosophical tradition that he comes closest to Tatian,[182] and it is not sufficient to explain the latter's attitude as due to his origins outside Graeco-Roman culture.[183] For the great stress which both place on the all-sufficiency and utter "otherness" of the Scriptures suggests that their attitude answers to a common profound motivation in the Christian consciousness.

Perhaps more significant, however, is the fact that not only can literary parallels be established between the *De Praescriptione* and Irenaeus' *Adversus Haereses*,[184] but also that Tertullian's basic theological and pastoral concerns in the treatise can be related to those of the great bishop of Lyons.[185] Indeed when Tertullian warns of the dangers which result from an unbridled "curiosity" and speculation outside the rule of faith, he almost echoes similar admonitions from Irenaeus. Tertullian directs:

"So long, however, as its form remains in its proper order, you may seek and discuss as you please, and give full rein to your curiosity in whatever seems to you to hang in doubt, or to be shrouded in obscurity. You have at hand, no doubt, some learned brother gifted with the grace of knowledge... In any case, it is better to remain in ignorance than to know what you ought not to know, once you have acquired the knowledge of what you know. 'Your faith,' Christ said, 'has saved you', not your skill in the Scriptures. Faith resides within the rule; it has its law and in the observance of this law consists salvation. Skill, however, consists in curiosity, having for its glory the readiness which comes from knack. Let such curiosity give place to faith; let the glory yield to salvation... to know nothing in opposition to the rule [of faith] is to know all things."[186]

To appreciate Tertullian's thought in this passage, it is necessary to recall the relevant text of Irenaeus:

"It is better and more profitable to remain simple and ignorant, and by means of love to attain to nearness to God, than by imagining ourselves learned and skilful to be found blasphemous against [our] God... For this reason Paul exclaimed, 'Knowledge puffs up, but love edifies', not that he meant to inveigh against a true knowledge of God, for in that case he would have accused himself; but because he knew that some, puffed up by the pretence of knowledge, fall away from the love of God, and imagine that they themselves are perfect... It is therefore better, as I have said, that one should have no knowledge whatever of any one reason why a simple thing in creation has been made, but should believe in God, and continue in His love, than that, puffed up through knowledge of this kind, he should fall away from that love which is the life of man; and that he should search after no other knowledge except [the knowledge of] Jesus Christ the Son of God, who was crucified for us, than that by subtle questions and hairsplitting expressions he should fall into impiety."[187]

Irenaeus, like Tertullian, is eager to expose the errors of Gnostics and other heretics; but equally, like Tertullian, his concern is to discourage, among the orthodox "the rash ambitions of those who believe they are able, through their eloquence, to enrich the faith".[188] According to H.J. Carpenter, Irenaeus here is making "a distinction between essential faith and theology – and his is the first attempt to make it". By "taking his stand as a Christian pastor on the ground of popular theology", he refuses to allow speculative questions within the range of theology as such. Rather, for Irenaeus, theology has to do with seeking "a deeper understanding of the Biblical story of salvation"; he "cannot contemplate any conflict with the faith of the ordinary Christian".[189]

It is doubtful whether the distinction which Irenaeus makes can be accurately described in the terms that Carpenter employs. In any case, by designating Irenaeus' position as "popular theology", he weakens somewhat the presumed antinomy between "essential faith and theology". Moreover, it is doubtful whether it is the case that "in the *De Praescriptione* he [Tertullian] exalts the merits of uninquiring faith in the articles of the rule of faith with hardly a word of encouragement for anyone who exhibits curiosity even within the limits of the 'rule'.[190] Tertullian, it is true, warns about the dangers of curiosity. But he does allow a "seeking" which he considers proper:

"Let our seeking, therefore, be in that which is our own, and from these who are our own, and concerning that which is our own – that, and only that which can become an object of inquiry without impairing the rule of faith."[191]

It is important to understand the concern which prompt Tertullian to make these strictures – a concern which he shares with Irenaeus. Immediately Tertullian has explained the character of the true Christian enquiry, he follows up with a summary of the rule of faith.[192] It is significant that he describes the articles of faith as "what we defend",[193] for this reveals an important dimension of

Tertullian's mental posture as a Christian apologist and theologian. Tertullian is above all concerned to defend and protect the body of beliefs which he has inherited in the Church, and on which he holds firm personal convictions regarding their adequacy to answer the essential puzzles and questions of life.[194] This also means that even in his "speculative and dogmatic treatises"[195] he is mostly dealing "with problems which arise when one or another of the positions affirmed in the rule of faith is attacked". As Norris notes, "his attention is engaged not by the theological problems for their own sake, but by the necessity for preserving unaltered the doctrinal basis of the life of the Christian community", his purpose being always to show "his opponents wrong and the tradition as he has received it right".[196] This is also to say that Tertullian cannot really be held to break his own law on curiosity, so to speak, in these "speculative" works.[197] It is true that when he sets out to elaborate his theory of "economic" Trinitarianism, Tertullian finds that he is out of step with the "simple" – he would not call them "unwise and ignorant" – who always constitute the majority of believers.[198] But there is no suggestion that in stating what appeared a novel concept, he is aware of stepping beyond the rule of faith.

It is doubtful, therefore, whether Tertullian would have seen himself as caught in a "split between popular faith and scholarly theology" in his time, at least not in the sense in which "theology" would be said to belong outside the range of the rule of faith.[199] Like his Hellenistic predecessors in Christian apologetics,[200] Tertullian believed that the fullness of the revelation of truth was granted to humanity in the Christian Gospel. But unlike them, he was not interested in seeking anticipations of this revelation in the most noble insights within the intellectual and philosophical traditions of the pre-Christian, Graeco-Roman past. Where he appears to do so,[201] one gets the impression that it is a passing concession and that he places little confidence in such arguments.

Indeed, as is shown by his short tract, *De Testimonio Animae*, for Tertullian, the most convincing grounds for the validity of the truth of the Christian Gospel outside the Scriptural tradition, are not in comparable deliverances of philosophers, but in the basic universal apprehensions granted in human experience. Tertullian is aware that in charting this new course in apologetics[202] he is departing from the approaches adopted by other Christian writers.[203] His own approach is to reach, by appeal to the unselfconscious, ejaculatory sayings, wishes and fears of men in normal human experience, to what he calls the "common consciousness".[204] As applied, for instance, to the doctrine of God, Tertullian's approach makes no appeal to the results of philosophical inquiry[205] because, for him, the perception of the oneness and majesty of God is not arrived at by speculative reasoning, but is apprehended intuitively by every human soul everywhere, without distinction in culture or language, or even religious commitment.[206] So Tertullian declares with characteristic pithiness of style:

> "God is everywhere and the goodness of God is everywhere; demons are everywhere and the curse upon demons is everywhere; the calling down of divine judgment is everywhere; death is everywhere and the consciousness of death is everywhere, and the witness to it is everywhere. Every soul of its own right proclaims aloud those things which we are not permitted even to whisper."[207]

It is in the validity of this "common consciousness" that consists, for Tertullian, the primal truth of the Christian apprehension of God, as indeed of all reality. For this proof is the witness of nature itself: "O testimony of the human soul by nature Christian!"[208]

In taking this approach, it might well be that Tertullian draws upon the Stoic concept of "common notions".[209] But to leave it there is to misunderstand Tertullian; his is not an attempt to construct a "Stoic Christianity"! The divine revelation which is granted in Christian tradition is at no point indebted to any human speculative system. On the contrary, the testimony borne to its validity by the "common consciousness" serves to undermine the pretentious claims of the philosophical and intellectual tradition,[210] and to expose it for what it is. R.A. Norris rightly observes:

> "If anything, philosophy succeeds... only in introducing confusion and distortion into a knowledge which is the natural endowment of every man. It is Christian faith which clarifies, articulates and completes this knowledge."[211]

V. Conclusion

Seen from this angle, Tertullian's view of the theological task of the Christian Church, particularly in terms of its "cultural witness", is essentially defensive and negative. He is more concerned to protect the truth from being adulterated by the world, than to validate the relevance of the truth to the world. The prominence of anti-heretical writings in his total literary output is an interesting indication of this outlook.[212] But so also is his support for, and identification with, the "new prophecy". For if the source of the truth was God's revelation in the Scriptures committed to the Christian Church, the measure of that truth involved equally those Scriptures and the community of faith to which they were entrusted. In those Christians whom he castigated as *psychici.*, Tertullian saw an unwarranted separation between the exclusiveness of the truth of the Scriptures and the separateness of the community required to embody that exclusiveness. Tertullian could not accept such a compromise with the spirit of the world, certainly not with a world (*saeculum*) so patently under the power of demons and evil spirits.

It has been said that "consistency was not a strong point with this great advocate".[213] And yet, Tertullian's outlook is not lacking in consistency. Only, unlike his Hellenistic predecessors and contemporaries in the task of defending the claims of Graeco-Roman Christian self-consciousness, "the coherence he looks for in his theology is its coherence with the Rule of Faith, not its systematic intellectual coherence as a speculative creation".[214] Coming to terms with the world held little interest for him. To Christians held in prison and faced with the prospect of martyrdom, Tertullian could write:

"The Christian outside the prison has renounced the world, but in the prison he has renounced a prison too. It is of no consequence where you are in the world – you who are not of [the world]."[215]

However there is more to Tertullian's attitude than rhetoric: "One becomes Christian, one is not born such",[216] "The soul must become Christian, it is not born such" (not birth, but rebirth is what makes the Christian soul),[217] "Let them *become* [in the context of baptism] Christians when they have been able to know Christ",[218] "... to whom belongs the very Faith; whose are the Scriptures; by whom and through whom and when and to whom was that rule delivered whereby people become Christians?"[219] The importance of the theme for Tertullian is unmistakeable. It all hangs on *becoming* a Christian, a radical Christian. For him, therefore, everything came to rest on the continuous affirmation of a *Christian* conscience and outlook, which were ever more deeply determined and guided by the Rule of Faith conceived as a radical alternative to "all that was of the world". The fact is, Tertullian genuinely believed that the truth of the Christian Gospel meant that only such a response was possible and viable in a demonic universe. Consequently, it is impossible to separate his view of the world from his exclusivist conception of Christian truth and the

Christian life. To that extent, his response to his context was a fundamentally *religious* one. When this is granted, then everything else in his *vision du monde* hangs together. This very quality of "massive intransigence", as Markus has well observed, is what makes Tertullian's outlook "one of the permanent archetypes of possible Christian attitudes to the profane".[220]

Notes

1. See for instance, Louis Duchesne, *Early History of the Christian Church (from its foundation to the end of the 3rd century)* (ET of 4th edition), London: John Murray, 1910, p.156. Also R.A. Markus, *Christianity in the Roman World*, London: Thames and Hudson, 1974, pp.48f.

2. J.M. Fuller, "Tertullianus" in *DCB*, vol.4, p.819.

3. Hans von Campenhausen, *Fathers of the Latin Church* (ET by Manfred Hoffmann), London: A. & C. Black, 1964 (orig. 1960), pp.5,35.

4. For a succinct review of this testimony, see G. Bardy, "Tertullien" in *DTC*, vol.15, colls. 168-169.

5. G.L. Bray, *Holiness and the Will of God: Perspectives on the theology of Tertullian* (Marshall's Theological Library), London: Marshall, Morgan & Scott, 1979, p.1.

6. However, Frédouille has used the chronological scheme given by René Braun, as the framework for his study of Tertullian's spiritual evolution and the encounter in him of Graeco-Roman culture and Christian faith. See Jean-Claude Frédouille, *Tertullien et la conversion de la culture antique*, Paris, 1962. Cf. T.D. Barnes, *Tertullian: A Historical and Literary Study*, Oxford: Clarendon Press, 1971, Ch.5 – "Chronology". Barnes attempts to work out, on largely literary grounds, a chronology which is intended to make comprehensible "Tertullian's literary, intellectual and moral and theological development" (p.56). It is doubtful whether his "rational speculation" achieves better results for the understanding of Tertullian. See G.L. Bray, *op.cit.*, pp.30ff.

7. See G. Bardy, *op.cit.*, coll.138. His comment on the treatise is revealing: "It can be said that it constitutes the oldest theological treatise on the Trinity. The author clearly affirms the unity of God and the existence of three equal divine persons in one single substance".

8. Hans von Campenhausen, *op.cit.*, p.31, on the question of Tertullian's rigorist views on marriage.

9. Douglas Powell, "Tertullianists and Cataphrygians" in *VC*, 29, 1975, pp.33-54.

10. The reference is to Didymus the Blind, *De Trinitate* 3, 41 *(PG* 39, 983Bff)*.

11. Tertullian, *De Pudicitia*, 21, 17 *(CCL* 2, p.1328)*.

12. Tertullian, *De Monogamia*, 11, 2 *(CCL* 2, p.1244)*.

13. Douglas Powell, *op.cit.*, pp.37f.

14. Pierre de Labriolle, *La Crise Montaniste*, Paris: Ernest Léroux, 1913, p.356: "To tell the truth, even in those works of his which are indubitably Montanist, *nostri (nos, nobis* etc.) does not always have 'sectarian' meaning, and it must be studied quite closely..."

15. *De Virginibus Velandis* 17,3 *(CCL* 2, p.1226) on the dimensions of veils for Christian maidens; *De Monogamia* 9,8 *(CCL* 2, p.1242) on the contrast between Roman standards regarding wedlock and divorce and remarriage, and

his view of the Christian standards by opposing *illi* to *nobis*. *Adversus Praxean* 5,3 *(CCL* 2, pp.1163f) distinguishing the Greek understanding of the Λόγος as divine rational principle inherent in God, and the general Christian understanding (*in usu... nostrorum*): cf. the same as Word (*Sermo*), though he accepts the validity of the Greek conception to account for the nature of God before the generation of the Word for the purpose of Creation.

16. Pierre de Labriolle, *op.cit.*, p.356. The reference is to *De Pudicitia* 19,5 *(CCL* 2, p.1320) where *apud nos* seems to distinguish between Christians in general on the one hand, and a non-Christian (*ethnicus*) and a heretic *(hereticus)* on the other. It is also interesting that Tertullian sounds opposed to the recognition of heretical baptism.

17. G.L. Bray, *op.cit.*, pp.57f (cf. Paul's *First Epistle to the Corinthians*, 2:14-16). See Albert Blaise, *DL-FAC*, under *psychicus*, p.682.

18. G.L. Bray, *op.cit.*, p.58.

19. See the analytical table in de Labriolle, *op.cit.*, pp.360-361.

20. This is, by far, the most important of Tertullian's designations for the movement with which he identified. See de Labriolle, *op.cit.*, p.323.

21. Douglas Powell, *op.cit.*, pp.38f.

22. *Ibid.*, p.50. It was de Labriolle's view that Tertullian knew Montanism "in its historic reality and not a version of Montanism for export which had been systematically touched up" (*op.cit.*, p.299). G.L. Bray appears to have misunderstood de Labriolle on this point; see Bray, *op.cit.*, p.161, n.45.

23. See for instance, V.C. de Clercq, "The Expectation of the Second Coming of Christ in Tertullian", *Studia Patristica*, 11,2, 1972 (= *TU* 108, 1972), pp.146-151, especially p.147.

24. G.L. Bray, *op.cit.*, p.62..

25. In discussing Tertullian's rigorist views on marriage, which he takes as one of the points of controversy between "Montanists" and "Catholics" in Carthage, de Labriolle has to admit: "Fundamentally, Montanism hardly modified Tertullian's ideas... Montanism thus did no more in this case than make his thought more categorical and more brutally arrogant" *(op.cit.*, p.393).

26. Pierre de Labriolle, *History and Literature of Christianity – from Tertullian to Boethius* (ET by Herbert Wilson), London: Kegan Paul, Trench, Trubner and Co., 1924, p.56.

27. In his chapter 1, "Past and Present", Bray, *op.cit.*, gives a useful, critical review of the major studies on Tertullian since the 19th century.

28. G.L. Bray, *op.cit.*, pp.63f.

29. D. Barnes, *op.cit.*

30. G.L. Bray, *op.cit.*, p.31.

31. *Ibid.*, p.31.

32. Jean-Claude Frédouille, *op.cit.*, p.20.

33. G.L. Bray, *op.cit.*, p.38.

34. *Ibid.*, p.37.

35. *Apologeticum*, 18,4 *(CCL* 1, p.118).

36. T.R. Glover, *The Conflict of Religions in the Early Roman Empire*, London: Methuen and Co. (8th edition), 1919, p.336. For Celsus' views on the Christian faith, see Henry Chadwick, *Origen: Contra Celsum* (3,55), Cambridge: Cambridge University Press, 1953, pp.165f.

37. Pierre de Labriolle, *The History and Literature of Christianity from Tertullian to Boethius*, pp.70-74.

38. *Apologeticum*, 17,6 (*CCL* 1, p.117).

39. *Ibid.*, 21, 11-12 (*CCL* 1, p.124).

40. *Ibid.*, 21, 15 (*CCL* 1, p.125).

41. The genuineness of the latter chapters (9-14) of this work is held in some doubt; see Malte Åkerman, *Über die Echtheit der letzteren Hälfte von Tertullians Adversus Judaeos*, Lund: C.W. Lindstroms Bokhandel, 1918. But for a different view, see H. Tränkle, *Tertullians Adversus Judaeos*, 1964 (liii). It is quite conceivable, as Barnes has suggested, that Tertullian left the book unfinished considering the Jewish question as not central to the more fundamental problem of vindicating the credentials of Christianity in Graeco-Roman society. Certainly Tertullian's lack of interest, as we have seen, in the *tertium genus* argument would indicate how little impact Jewish religion and the Jewish community made on his thinking as a Christian. In any case, the *Adversus Judaeos* was intended to win, not Jews, but Graeco-Romans, possibly proselytes, to the Christian faith (see *Adversus Judaeos*, 1).

42. *Scorpiace*, 10, 10 (*CCL* 2, p.1089).

43. *Apologeticum*, 37.

44. *Ibid.*, 38,4 (*CCL* 1 p.149).

45. *Ibid.*, 46,2 (*CCL* 1, p.160).

46. See *ibid.*, 47,9 (*CCL* 1, p.164).

47. See Pierre de Labriolle, *La Crise Montaniste*, pp.363-458; G.L. Bray, *op.cit.*

48. T.D. Barnes, *op.cit.*, p.52, using evidence of fuller references to heroic deeds of the personages of the past in the *Ad Martyras* and in the *Apologeticum*. places the *Ad Nationes* earlier than the other two works. However, chronology has little effect on our argument

49. *De Fuga (in persecutione)*, 2,2 (*CCL* 2, p.1137).

50. Especially in chapter 50.

51. De Labriolle *(op.cit.*, pp.371-373), lays this charge upon Tertullian and points to moderate views in his *Ad Uxorem* 1 (3), and the *De Patientia* 13,6. For a different view, see G.L. Bray, *op.cit.*, p.60.

52. Pierre de Labriolle, *The History and Literature of Christianity*, p.70.

53. Joseph Lortz, *Tertullian als Apologet* (1 Band), Munster: Aschendorffsche Verlagsbuchhandlung, 1927, p.2.

54. *Ibid.*, p.1.

55. *Ibid.*, p.16. Cf. C.J. Cadoux, *The Early Church and the World (A History of the Christian attitude to pagan society and the State down to the time of Constantinus*, Edinburgh: T. & T. Clark, 1925, p.317. Karl Baus, *From the Apostolic Community to Constantine* (Handbook of Church History, 1) (trans. from 3rd revised German edition), London: Burns and Oates, 1965, pp.111f.

56. Charles Guignebert, *Tertullien: Etude sur ses sentiments à l'égard de l'Empire et de la société civile*, Paris: Ernest Léroux, 1901, pp.226ff.

57. Jean-Claude Frédouille, *op.cit.*, p.484.

58. *Ibid.*, p.471.

59. Jean-Claude Frédouille, *op.cit.*, pp.477f.

60. *De Pallio*, 4,2 (*CCL* 2, p.742).

61. "The *De Pallio* is not the literary expression of a belated conversion to philosophy", Jean-Claude Frédouille, *op.cit.*, p.471.

62. *De Pallio*, 6,2 (*CCL* 2 p.750).

63. See *Apologeticum* 4,5ff (*CCL* 1, p.93).

64. Tertullian, well aware that he might be upsetting some time-honoured customs or usages, forestalls criticism by invoking Jesus' self-designation as Truth, and opposing it to Custom: "But our Lord Christ called himself Truth, not Custom", *De Virginibus Velandis* 1,1 (*CCL* 2, p.1209).

65. Jean-Claude Frédouille, *op.cit.* p.444. Cf. B. Altaner, *Patrologia* (ET by Hilda Graef), Freiburg: Herder: Edinburgh, London: Nelson, 1960, p.178.

66. *De Spectaculis* 4,1 (*CCL* 1, p.231).

67. Charles Guignebert, *op.cit.*, pp.277f. "... it seems impossible to make a social revolution more radical than that which Tertullian's religion produces in the pagan world. Into a society founded itself on religion, tolerant, but resting on a tacit agreement with every belief and on their official subordination to a state religion, it throws this principle of dogmatic intolerance which destroys everything outside itself... It changes, if you will, not morality, but the moral life, the place of morality in its understanding as in its behaviour; it is not just a transformation, it is a turning upside down."

68. *De Spectaculis* 1,4 (*CCL* 1, p.227).

69. J.H. Waszink, *"Pompa Diaboli"* in *VC* 1, 1947, pp.13-41.

70. *Ibid.*, pp.34-36. Cf. W. Caspari & Geo. W. Gilmore, "Renunciation of the Devil in the Baptismal Rite" in *The New Schaff-Herzog*, vol.9, pp.488-489. Also, Ph. Oppenheim, "Apotaxis Lossagung im Taufritus" in *RAC*, Bd.1, colls. 559-562.

71. See *Apologeticum* 22 and 23.

72. Jean Daniélou, *The Origins of Latin Christianity* (ET by David Smith and John Austin Baker), London: Darton, Longman and Todd, 1977, p.412.

73. Cf. *De Spectaculis* 4,3: "... the entire apparatus of the shows *(universam spectaculorum paraturam) stems from idolatry (ex idolatria)...* our renunciatory testimony in the laver of baptism has reference to the shows, which, through their idolatry, have been given over to the devil, and his pomp and his angels."

74. *De Spectaculis* 5,3 (*CCL* 1, p.232). For a discussion of Tertullian's sources, see J.H. Waszink, "Varro, Livy and Tertullian on the history of Roman dramatic art" in *VC* 2, 1948, pp.224-242.

75. J.H. Waszink, *op.cit.*, p.224.

76. *Apologeticum* 10,2 (*CCL* 1, p.105).

77. This theory had been popularised in Rome by the poet Quintus Ennius (239-169 BC); see article "Quintus Ennius" in *PW*, 5, colls. 2589-2628. The theory is also used polemically by Lactantius, *Div. Inst.* 1,11.

78. *Apologeticum* 10 and 11.

79. Waltzing (*op.cit.*, fasc.24, p.64, n.6) suggests *verbis* to clarify the sense of the statement.

80. *Ibid.*, 12. Seneca's *De Superstitione* is used also by Augustine (*De Civitate Dei*, 6, 10) in his criticism of Roman religion.

81. *Apologeticum*, 12,7 (*CCL* 1, p.110). Cf. *ibid.*, 15,8 (*CCL* 1, p.114).

82. A.D. Nock has given as one of the reasons for the effectiveness of the early Christian apologetic movement of the second century: "The Apologists were without exception men who were not sons of Christians, but had been converted to Christianity themselves. The *apologia* of each of them was therefore in a measure the *apologia pro vita sua*." See his *Conversion: Old and New in Religion from Alexander to Augustine*, Oxford: Clarendon Press, 1933, p.250.

83. Guignebert is of the view that though we do not have from Tertullian an account of his spiritual and intellectual pilgrimage (as we do for Justin, *Dialogue with Trypho* 2 and 2; Tatian, *Oration* 29; and Cyprian, *Epistle to Donatus*, 5), nonetheless: "it is easy to guess from the totality of his writings that it must have been similar to that of Justin, Tatian and Cyprian". See his *Tertullien...* p.228, n.1. Tertullian himself declares: "We come from the same stock as you; Christians are made, not born", *Apologeticum* 18,4 (*CCL* 1, p.118).

84. Gaston Boissier's interesting study of Tertullian is spoilt somewhat because he dwells rather unduly and perhaps unjustly, on Tertullian's *nature de feu*. Consequently, he misses completely the genuinely religious dimension of Tertullian's outlook in the *De Spectaculis* and *De Idolatria*. See his *La Fin du Paganisme*, Paris: Hachette, 1894 (vol.1), pp.222-239.

85. Gilbert Murray's observation of "religion" and the "religious" outlook applies very much to Tertullian: "Religion is... all-encompassing and demanding of total allegiance – infinite in its application to life. The man who makes terms with his conscience is essentially non-religious." See his *Five Stages of Greek Religion*, London: Watts and Co., 1935, p.6. However, his negative strictures on religion and its "dangers" are purely subjective and quite arbitrary (pp.7-6).

86. See *Apologeticum* 23.

87. *Ibid.*, 22,2 (*CCL* 1, p.128).

88. *Ibid.*, 22,4 (*CCL* 1, p.128).

89. *Ibid.*, 22,12 (*CCL* 1, p.130).

90. *De Spectaculis* 10,12 (*CCL* 1, p.237).

91. *Ibid.*, 11,1 (*CCL* 1, p.238). Cf. *Apologeticum* 38,4 (*CCL* 1, p.149), "... *atrocitate arenae*".

92. *Ibid.*, 10; cf. *Apologeticum* 38,4 (*CCL* I1 p.149), "*impudicatia theatri*".

93. *Ibid.*, 10,8 (*CCL* 1, p.237).

94. *Ibid.*, 10,6 (*CCL* 1, pp.236-237).

95. *Ibid.*, 7,2 (*CCL* 1, p.233).

96. *Ibid.*, 24,2 (*CCL* 1, p.248).

97. Cf. another declaration of the same outlook in *Ad Martyras* 3,1 (*CCL* 1, p.5): "We are called to join the army of the living God at that moment when we repeat the words of the Sacrament [oath]..." The usage of the idea of *signaculum diaboli* is attested in Jerome; see his *Translatio homiliarum Origenis in Ezechielem* (homily 13), "Beware, Man, lest, while you leave that age, you be marked with the sign of the devil" (*PL* 25, 780D).

98. *De Spectaculis* 15,8 (*CCL* 1, p.241).

99. He refers (in *De Idolatria* 13,1 (*CCL* 2, p.1112)) to a volume already devoted (*suum iam volumen implevimus*) to "the shows and pleasures of that sort" (*De spectaculis... et voluptatibus eiusmodi...*)

100. *De Idolatria*, 1,1 (*CCL* 2, p.1101).

101. *Ibid.*, 18,8 (*CCL* 2, p.1120).

102. "Thus it emerges that in idolatry all [crimes] are detected and in all [crimes] idolatry", *ibid.* 1,5 (*CCL* 2, p.1101). Cf. Adhémar d'Alès, *La Théologie de Tertullien* (Bibliothèque de théologie historique), Paris: Beauchesne et Cie, 1905, pp.416f.

103. See *De Idolatria* 5, 8 and 12.

104. *Ibid.*, 11,2 (*CCL* 2, p.1110).

105. *Ibid.*, 10,6 (*CCL* 2, p.1110).

106. *Ibid.*, 10,6 (*CCL* 2, p.1110).

107. See *Gospel according to Matthew* 2:1-12.

108. *De Idolatria*, 9,5 (*CCL* 2, p.1108).

109. This is Tertullian's favourite term for the Christian life.

110. *De Idolatria* 11,8 (*CCL* 2, p.1111).

111. See chapters 20-23.

112. *De Idolatria*, 18,3 (*CCL* 2, p.1119).

113. On the significance of the dimension of "Christian" conscience, especially on the question of military service, see Jean-Michel Hornus, "Etude sur la pensée politique de Tertullien" in *RHPR*, 38, 1958, pp.1-38; especially pp.33ff.

114. Charles Guignebert, *op.cit.*, p.203.

115. *De Idolatria*, 17,3 (*CCL* 2, p.118). Cf. *De Spectaculis*, 8,9 (*CCL* 1, p.235): "Even the streets and the market-place, and the baths and the taverns, and our very dwelling places, are not altogether free from idols. Satan and his angels have filled the whole world".

116. *Ibid.*, 18,8 (*CCL* 2, p.1120).

117. *Ibid.*, 18,3 (*CCL* 2, p.1119).

118. *Ibid.*, 18,8 (*CCL* 2, p.1120).

119. *Ibid.*, 18,5 (*CCL* 2, p.1119).

120. *Ibid.*, 18,6 (*CCL* 2, p.1119).

121. *Ibid.*, 18,7 (*CCL* 2, pp.1119-1120).

122. "... you who argue about Joseph and Daniel know that things old and new (*vetera et nova*), rude and polished (*rudia et polita*), begun and developed (*coepta et explicata*), slavish and free (*servilia et liberalia*) are not always comparable" (*ibid.*, 18,4 (*CCL* 2, p.1119).

123. See for instance, *Romans* 1:1; *Philippians* 1:1.

124. See for instance, *Gospel according to Matthew* 8:5.

125. *De Idolatria*, 19,2 (*CCL* 2, p.1120).

126. *Ibid.*, 19,3 (*CCL* 2, p.1120).

127. Tertullian, by using *sacramentum*, is playing on the different meanings of the word, one of which is the classical sense of the military oath taken by the new recruit. For a study of these various meanings, as found in Tertullian, see Emile de Backer, *Sacramentum: Le mot et l'idée representée par lui dans les oeuvres de Tertullien*, Bruxelles: Albert Dewi; Paris: A. Picard et Fils, 1911, especially ch.2.

128. *De Idolatria*, 19,2 (*CCL* 2, p.1120).

129. See *De Corona*, 3-4.

130. *Ibid.*, 7. It is obvious that for Tertullian, this association is enough to condemn the wearing of crowns: "What sort of thing, then, must that be counted among the people of the *true God*, which was brought in by the nations in honour of the devil's candidates..." (7,8, *CCL* 2, p.1050) (my emphasis).

131. *Ibid.*, 11,1 (*CCL* 2, p.1056).

132. "Do we believe it lawful for a human oath to be added unto one divine (*sacramentum humanum divino superduci*), for a man to come under promise to another master after Christ..." (11,1, *CCL* 2, p.1056).

133. *Ibid.*, 11,2-4 (*CCL* 2 pp.1056-1057).

134. *Ibid.*, 11,4 (*CCL* 2, p.1057).

135. *Ibid.*, 12,4 (*CCL* 2, p.1059).

136. *Ibid.*, 13,4 (*CCL* 2, p.1061).

137. Charles Guignebert, *op.cit.*, pp.189f. Cf. Celsus' fears for the stability of the Empire in view of the Christian "menace". See H. Chadwick, *Origen: Contra Celsum*, 8,68-69, pp.504f.

138. See J.-M. Hornus, *op.cit.*, pp.33ff; he cites among others, the notable case of John Chrysostom. On the persistence of this strain of "detachment" from the promotion of imperial interests and from worldly power, Hornus observes: "The same attitude continues without changing appreciably after the Empire became Christian, which proves that we have here not a reaction to circumstances but a well-considered attitude appropriate to the Christian faith." (p.36)

139. Adhémar d'Alès, *op.cit.*, p.415. On the question of military service, for instance, d'Alès observes: "Previously he sanctioned it; now he rejects it, alleging that military service is incompatible with the service of Christ..." Cf. Emile de Backer, *op.cit.*, p.7, for a similar view.

140. *Apologeticum*, 37,4 (*CCL* 1, p.148).

141. T. Herbert Bindley, *Tertullian: Apologeticus adversus gentes pro Christianis*, Oxford: Clarendon Press, 1889, p.115, n.16: "There is some exaggeration in the accumulation of these rhetorical details." J.-P. Waltzing, *op.cit.*, (fasc.24), p.154, n.4: "This sentence is a cry of triumph. It is moreover stamped with some exaggeration: the hyperbole is in *implevimus*."

142. Charles Guignebert, *op.cit.*, p.277.

143. *Apologeticum*, 42,3 (*CCL* 1, p.157). (my emphasis)

144. Cf. Charles Guignebert's comments: "His thought is not, however, like that. There are Christians in the army; that is a fact which he confirms, and which provides him with a useful argument as he develops his reasoning: it is then for him a question of establishing that Christians are not useless creatures and that they resemble everybody else; but he does not approve of Christians being soldiers any more than he approves of their becoming involved in commerce, while confirming that they do." (p.192)

145. *Apologeticum*, 33,1 (*CCL* 1, p.143).

146. *Ibid.*, 38,3 (*CCL* 1, p.149).

147. *Ibid.*, 38,5 (*CCL* 1, p.150).

148. A.F. Walls, "The Gospel as the prisoner and liberator of culture" in *Faith and Thought*, 108, (1-2), 1981, pp.39-52; especially pp.45f.

149. R.A. Markus, *op.cit.*, pp.50f.

150. Jean Daniélou, *op.cit.*, p.405; cf. p.xvi.

151. See R.A. Markus, *Saeculum: History and Society in the Theology of Saint Augustine*, Cambridge: Cambridge University Press, 1970; especially ch.5, "*Afer scribens Afris*: The Church in Augustine and the African Tradition".

152. Jean-Claude Frédouille argues that Tertullian's aim was to put forth a number of specific principles (*praescriptiones*) excluding the claims of heretical schools, and that this consideration together with the manuscript evidence requires the title: *De praescriptionibus adversus haereses omnes*. See his *Tertullien et la conversion de la culture antique*, pp.228-230. We retain the traditional title as conveying adequately Tertullian's meaning, for in the final analysis the principles of exclusion resolve themselves into one: Heretics have no right to the Christian name, and consequently are debarred from Christian tradition, especially the use of Scripture. Further on the title, see Pierre de Labriolle, *Tertullien: De Praescriptione Haereticorum* (Textes et Documents), Paris: A. Picard et Fils, 1907, (vi), n.1; also Jean Daniélou, *op.cit.*, p.179:

"Tertullian was less concerned in the *De Praescriptione* to refute one particular heresy than to search for a criterion which would allow him to judge between what is in accordance with faith and what is not."

153. J.H. Waszink, *Quinti Septimi Florentis Tertulliani: De Anima*, Amsterdam: J.M. Meulenloff, 1947, p.113.

154. *De Praescriptione...* 7,9-13 *(CCL* 1, p.193) (my emphasis) Cf. *Apologeticum*, 46,18 *(CCL* 1, p.162).

155. Cf. Charles Guignebert, *op.cit.*, p.256; also, p.437: "On philosophy Tertullian expresses the most rigorous opinion, or very nearly, which is to be found among Christians." J. Quasten, *Patrology* (vol.2 – *The Ante-Nicene Literature after Irenaeus*), Utrecht-Antwerp: Spectrum, Publishers, 1964. On Tertullian's famous paradoxes in ch.5 of *De Carne Christi (CCL* 2, pp.880ff), Quasten writes: "...he is not concerned with building a bridge between religion and reason, but wants to emphasise that not even the apparent conflict between the facts of redemption and the human mind prevent him from believing in them... He was not interested in bringing harmony between faith and philosophy... Unlike Clement of Alexandria, he [Tertullian] was convinced that philosophy and faith have nothing in common" (p.320).

156. See H.A. Wolfson, *The Philosophy of the Church Fathers* (3rd edition revised), Cambridge, Mass.: Harvard University Press, 1970, pp.102-105. Cf. Robert Joly, *Christianisme et Philosophie (Etudes sur Justin et les Apologistes grecs du IIe siècle)*, Bruxelles: Edition de l'Université de Bruxelles, 1973, pp.33-36.

157. Richard A. Norris, *God and World in Early Christian Theology (A Study in Justin Martyr, Irenaeus, Tertullian and Origen*), London: A. & C. Black, 1965, p.97.

158. *Gospel according to Matthew* 7:7. It is interesting that Clement of Alexandria will give a quite different interpretation to this saying in *Stromateis*, 5,3.

159. See *De Praescriptione...* 10,1-4 *(CCL* 1, p.195).

160. *Ibid.*, 11,6 *(CCL* 1, p.196).

161. *Ibid.*, 9,4 *(CCL* 1, p.195).

162. *Ibid.*, 13.

163. The question of the relative positions of "orthodoxy" and "heresy" in the early centuries of Christianity is not important for our study. On this, see W. Bauer, *Orthodoxy and Heresy in Earliest Christianity* (ET), London: S.C.M., 1972 (orig. German, 1934), and H.E.W. Turner, *The Pattern of Christian Truth*, London: Mowbray and Co., 1954 (reprinted, AMS Press, New York, 1978).

164. *De Praescriptione...* 8,1 *(CCL* 1, p.193).

165. See *Apologeticum*. 47,5-8 *(CCL* 1, pp.163-164).. Cf. *Ad Nationes*, *(CCL* 1, p.42): "...that pure and simple wisdom of the philosophers which attests its own weakness *(infirmatem)* mainly by that variety of opinion which proceeds from an ignorance of the truth *(de ignorantia veritatis)*."

166. See *Apologeticum*, 46,5 10-16 *(CCL* 1, pp.161-162). Needless to say, Tertullian exposes these failings in heretics as well; see *De Praescriptione...* 42,6 *(CCL* 1, p.222): "... it is [supposed] that schisms seldom happen among heretics, because even when they exist, they are not obvious *(cum sint, non parent)*: their very unity, however, is schism *(schisma est enim unitas ipsa)*". On the conduct *(conversatio)* of heretics, see *De Praescriptione...* 41 and 43.

167. Cf. *ibid.*, 8,1 *(CCL* 1, p.193).

168. Particularly in *Apologeticum*, ch. 47.

169. *Apologeticum*, 47,1 *(CCL* 1, p.163).

170. "Which poet, or sophist has not drunk at the fount of the prophets? (*de prophetarum fonte potaverit*)." It is not unlikely that the image is taken from Tatian; see his *Oration*, 40. Moses is πηγή of Greek intellectual tradition.

171. *Apologeticum*, 47,3 (*CCL* 1, p.163).

172. *Ibid.*, 47,4 (*CCL* 1, p.163).

173. *Ibid.*, 47,9 (*CCL* 1, p.164).

174. *Ibid.*, 47,10 (*CCL* 1, p.164).

175. Cf. *De Praescriptione...* 39,1 (*CCL* 1, p.219) with references to *Ephesians* 6:12 and *1 Corinthians* 11:18ff.

176. *De Praescriptione...* 47,11 (*CCL* 1, p.164).

177. On these principles, see the thorough analysis by Jean-Claude Frédouille, *op.cit.*, pp.195-234.

178. *Ibid.*, p.230: "If then our treatise looks like a sort of compilation of *praescriptiones*, that is, arguments *a priori*, objections on principle, irrefutable proofs permitting Christians to avoid long scriptural discussions with heretics, one of these *praescriptiones* enjoyed a particular importance and efficacy in Tertullian's eyes: the *praescriptio novitatis*."

179. Cf. *De Praescriptione...* 7, 5 (*CCL* 1, p.192): "The same subject matter (*eadem materia*) is discussed over and over again by the heretics and the philosophers; the same arguments are involved (*idem retractatus implicantur*). Whence comes evil, and why [is it permitted]? (*unde malum et quare?*) What is the origin of man, and how [does he come]? ...Whence comes God? (*unde deus?*)."

180. H.A. Wolfson, *op.cit.*, p.104. Wolfson mentions *inter alia* Tertullian's explanation of the concept of the Logos as creator of the world (*Apologeticum*, 21), and argues that "his explanation [of the Trinity in the *Adversus Praxean*] is couched in terms and notions borrowed from philosophic literature" (p.105).

181. R.A. Norris, *op.cit.*, p.86.

182. It is interesting that J.-C. Frédouille, who links Tertullian's use of *curiositas* and *scrupulositas* with a philosophical tradition which condemned intellectual activity that only concerned itself with vain and sterile questions (*op.cit.*, pp.412-426), finally suggests that the main source for Tertullian's critique of philosophy in these terms is Tatian! (p.426). See Tatian's *Oration*, 40: Greek philosophers, actuated by περιεργία, attempted to adulterate Mosaic and other Old Testament teachings. See E. Schwartz, *Tatiani Oratio ad Graecos*, p.41.5.

183. See Louis Duchesne, *op.cit.*, p.156. Cf. Werner Jaeger, *Early Christianity and Greek Paideia*, London: Oxford University Press, 1961, p.34, also p.123, n.29.

184. See Adhémar d'Alès, *op.cit.*, pp.201-213. On ch.36 of the *De Praescriptione...* which sets forth the claims of the apostolic churches, d'Alès comments: "This eloquent page is visibly inspired by St Irenaeus, III,3" (p.210). Cf. S.L. Greenslade in *LCC*, vol.5, "Early Latin Theology", pp.31ff; also Appendix 1: "Irenaeus", pp.65ff.

185. J. Lebreton, "Le Désaccord de la foi populaire et de la théologie savante dans l'Eglise chrétienne du IIIe siècle" (i) in *RHE*, 19, 1923, pp.481-506, continued in *RHE*, 20, 1924, pp.5-37. See also H.J. Carpenter, "Popular Christianity and Theologians in the early centuries" in *JTS* (new series), 14, 1963, pp.294-310.

186. *De Praescriptione...* 14, 1-5 (*CCL* 1, p.198). The Scripture reference is to *Gospel according to Luke* 18:42.

187. Irenaeus, *Adversus Haereses*, 2, 26,1; Migne, *PG* 7, 810A.

188. J. Lebreton, "Le Désaccord de la foi populaire et de la théologie savante..." in *RHE*, 19, p.484.

189. H. J. Carpenter, *op.cit.*, p.302.

190. *Ibid.*, p.302.

191. *De Praescriptione...* 12, 5 (*CCL* 1, p.197).

192. *Ibid.*, 13.

193. *Ibid.*, 13,1 (*CCL* 1, p.197).

194. Adhémar d'Alès (*op.cit.*, p.36) rightly remarks: "Tertullian believes so strongly in the power of Christian truth aided by divine grace, that having ascended the slope which leads to faith he guarantees success to all those who embark upon it after him: "... the man who has heard will find God, and the man who has made the effort to understand will be compelled also to believe" (*Apologeticum*, 18,9).

195. H.J. Carpenter (*op.cit.*, p.302) indicates *Adversus Praxean* and *De Anima*, though without naming them.

196. R.A. Norris, *op.cit.*, p.97.

197. Cf. J. Lebreton, *op.cit.*, p.487: "And he himself did seek: his theological efforts have been much attacked, and he is not independent of those philosophies which are so severely judged."

198. *Adversus Praxean*, 3,1 (*CCL* 2, p.1161).

199. Cf. A. Harnack's comment: "The Gnostics were in short, the theologians of the first century", in his *History of Dogma*, Vol.1 (ET, from 3rd German edition, by Neil Buchanan), London: Williams and Norgate, 1894, p.227.

200. He speaks warmly of Justin as *philosophus et martyr* among a list of Christian writers, including Irenaeus, whom he proposes "to follow in every work of faith" (*in omni opere fidei...adsequi*), *Adversus Valentinianos*, 5,1 (*CCL* 2, p.756).

201. For example, in *Apologeticum*, 21, on the doctrine of the Λόγος.

202. *De Testimonio Animae*, 1,5 (*CCL* 1, p.175).

203. Cf. "Indeed, some [of our people] (*nonnulli*) who still continue their investigative labours in ancient literature, and still occupied [their] memory with it (*de pristina litteratura et curiositatis labor et memoriae tenor perseveravit*) have published works... from which it may be seen at once that we have embraced nothing new or monstrous, nothing for which we cannot claim the support of ordinary and well-known writings..." (*communes et publicae litterae*), *De Testimonio...* 1,2 (*CCL* 1, p.175). It is not as evident as Frédouille suggests (*op.cit.* p.417, n.28) that Tertullian is here full of "admiration" for his Hellenistic predecessors. See, for instance, Henry Chadwick, *Early Christian Thought and the Classical Tradition*, London: Oxford University Press, 1966, pp.1-3.

204. *De Jejunio adversus psychicos*, 7,1 (*CCL* 2, p.1261).

205. See *De Testimonio Animae*, 1,4 (*CCL* 1, p.175).

206. *Ibid.*, 1,6-7 (*CCL* 1, p.176); the basis for the claim is the "universality of nature" (*naturae universitas*), 6,3 (*CCL* 1, p.182).

207. *Ibid.*, 6, 4f (*CCL* 1, pp.182-183).

208. See *Apologeticum*, 17, 4-6 (*CCL* 1, p.117-118); cf. *De Testimonio...* 5,1-2 (*CCL* 1, p.1180): "These testimonies of the soul (*haec testimonia animae*)... I do not think [they] can appear frivolous or feeble to any one... if he reflect on the majesty of nature, from which the soul derives its authority. If you acknowledge the authority of the mistress (*magistrae*) you will own it also in

the disciple (*discipulae*). Nature is the mistress, her disciple is the soul. But everything the one has taught or the other learned, has come from God (*a deo traditum est*), the Teacher of the teacher (*magistro... magistrae*). And what the soul may know from its chief instructor (*principali institutore*) you can judge from what is within you."

209. See M. Spanneut, *Le Stoïcsme des Pères de l'Eglise (de Clément de Rome à Clément d'Alexandrie)*, Paris: Editions du Seuil, 1957, pp.278-279. Spanneut concludes, on Tertullian's argument in *De Testimonio*... "We are still well into the Stoic atmosphere" (p.279).

210. Cf. *De Testimonio*... 5,7 (*CCL* 1, p.182): "Why then, O man, will you maintain a view so groundless as that these [testimonies of the soul] have gone forth from the mere human speculations (*de humanis sententiis*) of your literature, and become established in common usage?"

211. R.A. Norris, *op.cit.*, p.87. Cf. *De Anima*, 3,1 (*CCL* 2, p.785): "the apostle as far back as his own time foresaw, indeed, that philosophy would do violent injury to the truth (*concusso veritatis*)." The reference is to St Paul in Athens, in *Acts of the Apostles* 17; there is also a possible reference to *Colossians* 2:8, warning of the dangers of philosophy.

212. B. Altaner, *op.cit.*, pp.169-178.

213. H.J. Carpenter, *op.cit.*, p.302.

214. R.A. Norris, *op.cit.*, p.104.

215. *Ad Martyras*, 2,5 (*CCL* 1, p.4).

216. *Apologeticum*, 18,4 (*CCL* 1, p.118).

217. *De Testimonio Animae*, 1,7 (*CCL* 1, p.176).

218. *De Baptismo*, 18,5 (*CCL* 1, p.293).

219. *De Praescriptione*... 19,2 (*CCL* 1, p.201).

220. R.A. Markus, *Christianity in the Roman World*, p.50. Cf. H.R. Niebuhr, *Christ and Culture*, New York: Harper (Colophon Books), 1975 (orig. publication, 1951), pp.51ff.

Chapter Four

Christ and the Hellenistic Heritage (1): Justin, or, Christ as "The Expectation of the Nations"

I   "I being one of them": the importance of Justin's self-definition

Justin, though Samarian by birth,[1] was most probably of Hellenistic parentage.[2] Several indications in his own writings give evidence of such a background.

In the *Dialogue with Trypho* (the Jew), he not only speaks of Jews as "your people", or "your nation", but also describes himself as "an uncircumcised man".[3] He identifies himself with "the Gentiles, namely us, who in every place offer sacrifices to Him, that is, the bread of the Eucharist and also the cup of the Eucharist, affirming both that we glorify His name and that you profane [it]".[4] In other words, his Christian self-identity is intimately linked with a heightened Gentile consciousness. In an important passage in the first *Apology*, when he sums up his proof from prophecy that Jesus is the Son of God and the final judge of the entire human race, Justin again includes himself among those believers from the Gentiles who are not only more numerous, but also more true in their commitment than Jewish and *Samaritan* Christians.[5] Justin is conscious that he belongs to a growing mass of people drawn "from every race of men" who have abandoned their former traditional devotions[6] to embrace faith in one who "was no sophist, but whose word was the power of God".[7] In addition, from his conversation with the old man who was instrumental in Justin's conversion to Christianity, Justin does not appear to have had previous knowledge of the Old Testament or of its contents.[8]

Consequently, it cannot be the case that, as Aimé Puech has argued, Justin interpreted his "philosophical" pilgrimage[9] as a religious quest, because "Jewish monotheism had, since his earliest years, made quite a profound impression upon him".[10] Justin's Hellenistic intellectual background in middle Platonism, as shown by Carl Andresen,[11] provides sufficient explanation for his conception of philosophy as essentially concerned with questions of theism, God's government of the world, and with ethics.[12] Nowhere in Justin's writings are we given the impression that he came to his Christian convictions through Judaism, even if it is the case that he had "a good working knowledge of post-biblical Judaism".[13] His belonging within Hellenistic culture, by birth and by upbringing, must be given its full weight for his work to be properly understood.

It is not surprising, therefore, that interpretations of Justin Martyr's Christian career and achievement have generally been concerned with his supposed attempt at merging the Christian faith and the Greek philosophical tradition, or at least as much of this latter as he considered compatible with the Christian Gospel. Whilst this concentration on Justin's positive estimation of philosophy is important, the approach often adopted has the effect of distorting Justin's attitude. Not only is the discussion not seriously related to "the missionary purpose of the apologists",[14] but also it fails to ask whether Justin's outlook has any significance for the universal mission of the Church in history.[15] Accordingly, appreciations of Justin have ranged from blaming him for initiating an unwarranted alliance between Christian faith and Greek philosophy perceived to be alien to the faith,[16] to pronouncing him ignorant of the Greek philosophical tradition beyond a superficial acquaintance.[17]

Justin Martyr remains "a figure of perennial fascination in the history of emergent Christianity".[18] However, this significance reaches beyond the fact that "he is the first Christian to make a serious attempt to determine the relations between Christianity and philosophy, between faith and reason".[19] We have already shown[20] that efforts to link the emergent movement and its understanding of reality with some strands in the Hellenistic philosophical tradition belong to a wider range of concerns felt by thoughtful Christians like Justin, who were converts to Christ from a Hellenistic background. Alive to the spiritual outlook of their world, they understood the logic which connected the designation of Christianity as "superstition" to the imputation of impiety whereas "philosophy" was considered to promote piety and teach moral excellence. Though he never tires of pointing to the non-racial and universal character of Christian allegiance,[21] the prominence of the Gentile element in the movement was a fact whose significance was not lost on Justin, who was "himself one of them".[22] Justin's writings give ample evidence that he was eminently aware of the kind of questions raised (for Hellenistic Christians like himself) by the Christian faith amid Hellenistic tradition, and that he attempted to find answers to some of those questions. It is in this broader context that one can adequately understand his efforts at linking Christian faith with Greek philosophy.

II. The true philosophy: the discovery of a hermeneutical key

Any attempt to explain Justin's distinctive and personal understanding of the relations between the Christian faith and the philosophical tradition in Hellenistic culture must deal with the opening chapters of the *Dialogue with Trypho*.[23] Justin, on a walk and wearing his philosopher's cloak,[24] is accosted by Trypho who desires to engage in a discussion on matters of philosophical interest. Trypho turns out to be a Jew, which causes Justin some surprise since, to his mind, the Old Testament Scriptures should provide Trypho with all the answers to the kind of problems which philosophers might be supposed to handle. Trypho's retort that philosophy should also be concerned with the question of God, His nature and relation to the world, is acknowledged by Justin, but he offers the explanation that the Greek philosophical tradition has, in fact, failed to deal consistently with this central question, and so has missed the path of "true philosophy".[25] Asked then to give an account of his own philosophy, Justin responds by distinguishing a unified and original God-given philosophy from the deliverances of the diverse philosophical schools, which are, in his view, degenerations from the original.[26] This is followed by an outline of Justin's own intellectual and spiritual pilgrimage which took him from one philosophical teacher to another – Stoic, Peripatetic, Pythagorean and finally Platonist. It was during his Platonist phase that he encountered an old man, evidently a Christian, who, in the course of a conversation on the nature of philosophy and the means of acquiring the knowledge which affords understanding of things human and divine, undermined his Platonist beliefs, pointed him to the prophetic writings (Old Testament), and urged him to pray for spiritual insight, for these things are not perceived nor comprehended by all, but only by the man to whom God and His Christ give understanding.[27]

In the next chapter (8,1-2), Justin recounts his conversion; Christian allegiance has given him a firm conviction that he now has come into the inheritance of the "only safe and profitable philosophy".[28] Following Justin's own exhortation to Trypho to make a commitment similar to his, the rest of the *Dialogue* proceeds to deal with the interpretation of the Scriptures and the Messiahship of Jesus.

Commentators are not unanimous on the historicity of these early chapters of the *Dialogue*, since these appear to have literary parallels in antiquity.[29] However, it is important to realise that such considerations, interesting as they are, do not take us far in our understanding of Justin and of his concerns. Drawing attention to A.D. Nock's observation that the *apologia* of each of the Christian apologists was "in a measure an *apologia pro vita sua*",[30] Oskar Skarsaune has rightly argued that "in defending his conversion, Justin is defending Christianity and vice versa", and that this close connection in Justin between apology on behalf of Christianity and on behalf of his conversion, gives to Justin's conversion story "more than biographical interest".[31] E.F. Osborn's comment is, therefore, apposite:

> "It is unlikely that Justin would approach the story of his conversion with an excursion into fantasy... He was writing a defence of his whole life before the hostile criticism of the Jews."[32]

But it is evident that through the *Dialogue*, as much as through the *Apologies*, Justin's overriding aim is to communicate his Christian convictions to his fellow Gentiles.[33] For it is the Gentile, rather than the Jew, as is shown by the well-known case of Celsus, who is more likely to be dismayed or angered by the ease with which Christians of Hellenistic culture like Justin, abandoned time-honoured custom in order to embrace the tenets of a novel community which, to all appearances, lacked any basis whatsoever in history and tradition. Thus Justin is concerned with more than the defence of the Christian community; and in this respect he differs significantly from Tertullian. With Justin, *apologia* becomes above all witness, intended to win the hearer to a commitment similar to his own. Accordingly, what Justin says to Trypho is meant for all who do not share his convictions:

> "If you are willing to listen to an account of Him, how we have not been deceived, and shall not cease to confess Him – although men's reproaches be heaped upon us, although the most terrible

tyrant compel us to deny Him – I shall prove to you as you stand here that we have not believed empty fables, or words without any foundation, but words filled with the Spirit of God, and mighty with power and flourishing with grace."[34]

When Justin's Hellenistic background is set alongside the courageous and uncomplicated affirmations of his Christian identity, it becomes possible to appreciate his estimation of the philosophical tradition under a new light. Henry Chadwick has rightly noted that for all his warm and positive evaluation of Greek philosophy, "there is nothing whatever in the traditional pattern of Christian teaching which he [Justin] feels it necessary to explain away or even to mute", and that "there is no sign in Justin of any tendency to mitigate or to attenuate traditional beliefs... in order to meet philosophical criticism".[35] Prof. Chadwick draws attention particularly to Justin's doctrines of Creation,[36] revelation in history,[37] and eschatology, which includes "a full-blooded and extremely literalistic doctrine of the resurrection of the flesh" and "a strictly earthly hope for a millennial reign of Christ at Jerusalem".[38]

However, Chadwick's suggestion that Justin's attitude is explained by "the optimism and extrovert confidence of Justin's programme for harmony and co-operation between faith and reason",[39] seems to me to be inadequate. It is doubtful whether Justin was working with the categories of "faith" and "reason" as though these represented for him different, and by implication, divergent modes of apprehending and setting forth truth. When Justin expresses his confidence in the Christian Gospel as the "only safe and profitable philosophy", he does not thereby mean that a tradition of philosophical enquiry based on rational "demonstration"[40] is harmonised with divine revelation communicated by the prophets in the Old Testament.[41] For in view of Justin's testimony, quoted earlier, he evidently agrees with the old man that:

"*These* [the prophets] *alone* both saw and announced the truth to men, neither reverencing nor fearing any man, not influenced by a desire for glory, but speaking those things alone which they saw and which they heard, being filled with the Holy Spirit."[42]

The implied criticism of those who are "reckoned philosophers" echoes Justin's own earlier strictures on the founders of the various philosophical schools, "each of whom thought the truth to be what he learnt from his teacher", and so distorted the original, unified knowledge into a many-headed hydra.[43] The point then is that Justin, as a convinced Christian thinker, even with his philosophical past, does not conceive of truth as having more than one source, namely, philosophy *and* Biblical tradition, or Christianity.[44] It is the latter which Justin understood to be the true philosophy; not as the best among other philosophies, but as the only one worthy of the name and identifiable with the primordial and unified philosophy.[45]

In expressing himself in this way, Justin does not suggest that in Christianity he found the "fulfilment" of the Greek philosophical tradition as such; Justin is not, in fact, arguing for a "continuity" between the philosophical tradition and the Christian faith as the rationale of his own conversion. Oskar Skarsaune has rightly drawn attention to the literary *hiatus* in the text of the *Dialogue*, between chapters 6 and 7, which indicates a real "break" in Justin's story:

> "The philosophic itinerary does not lead to Christianity, it ends in *Platonism*. Nor does the anti-Platonic argument of the old man lead Justin to Christ... The itinerary leads up to Platonism, the dialogue with the old man destroys Platonism. The combined effect is to give Platonism a prominent position among the schools of Greek philosophy, but not as a "bridge" or a "preparation" for Christianity. There is no smooth passage from Plato to Christ in Justin's story. Instead there is a complete break, marked by a literary break in the *Dialogue* between chapters 6 and 7. The prominent place of Platonic philosophy is not that of a "bridge", it is that of the only serious rival to True Philosophy (i.e. Christianity). It is not Platonism itself but its destruction that prepares Justin for conversion."[46]

One cannot, therefore, invoke Justin's lack of philosophical sophistication in order to explain his conversion,[47] for, when finally Justin describes his apprehension of Christian revelation as philosophic truth itself, philosophical subtleties have ceased to be relevant.[48] Justin's account leaves us in no doubt that it was the forcefulness of the prophetic revelation, particularly its predictive element regarding Christ, together with his own observation of Christian steadfastness in persecution, which proved potent in effecting his conversion.[49]

If it is right to link the text of *Dialogue* 8,1 with Justin's expression of admiration for the "philosophic" conduct of Christians in *2 Apology* 12,1,[50] then it becomes clearer what Justin understood by philosophy, and how the Christian faith would become for him "the only safe and profitable philosophy". The certainty[51] which the fulfilment of the prophetic predictions conveyed to Justin is corroborated by his own empirical observation which confirms to him that Christian conduct, arising from Christian doctrine, provides the fullest manifestation of genuine "philosophy", namely, the honour and love for only what is true, as he confidently declares to the "pious and philosophical" rulers of the Empire:

> "Reason directs all who are truly pious and philosophical to honour and love only what is true, declining to follow traditional opinions if these be worthless. Not only does sound reason direct us to refuse the guidance of those who did or taught anything wrong, but it is incumbent upon the lover of truth by all means and even if death be threatened, even before his own life, to choose to say and to do what is right.[52]

In the light, then, of Justin's statements and outlook, it would be misleading to conclude that Justin's "was a religious, not an intellectual quest. He adopted Christianity at the end because it was able to give satisfaction to a fundamentally unphilosophical mind."[53] It is not likely that Justin postulated this kind of dichotomy. On the other hand, the view that "Justin measures the value of philosophy by practical results",[54] does not go far enough either. The fact is, Justin, in making his appeal for the love of truth at whatever the cost, is arguing for common ground between the Christian and the genuine philosopher; and "that which joins them is not a mere name, but is a devotion to something more important than life itself".[55] An interesting illustration of this conviction is in Justin's strictures on his Cynic opponent, Crescens, whom he describes as ostentatious, a lover of bravado and vainglory, because he does not risk his life in the quest for truth, nor in the declaration of it.[56] Crescens is opposed to what, in Justin's estimation, is the true philosophic type, namely, Socrates, who is quoted accordingly: "A man must in no wise be honoured above the truth".[57]

Justin's conviction here may have arisen in part at least, from his view of philosophy and the task of the philosopher. In any case, the connection with Socrates was an important one for Justin, as it was for early Christian apologetics generally.[58] There can be little doubt that behind Justin's "open and whole-hearted admiration of Socrates",[59] there lies a deep reverence for the philosopher martyred for his witness to what he perceived to be truth; and, conceivably, this "may have been part of Justin's philosophical ideal before his conversion".[60] Skarsaune is certainly right in suggesting that such a philosophical ideal explains why Justin was "puzzled by and interested in the Christian martyrs", whilst it may also "have created a sympathy that helped Justin on his way to Christianity".[61] However, it is the fact that Justin, now a Christian, makes such ample use of the figure and career of Socrates[62] that gives the theme even greater significance in the context of Justin's concerns.[63]

The clue is found among the last words of the old man to Justin. After informing Justin of the prophetic predictions concerning Christ, the old man then warns:

"... the false prophets, filled with the lying unclean spirit, neither have done nor do [i.e. make these predictions], but venture to work certain wonderful deeds for the purpose of astonishing men and glorify the spirits and demons of error."[64]

It is interesting that on the reference to "the spirits and demons of error", both Otto and Goodspeed draw attention to 1 Timothy 4:1, and so relate the thought as in Justin to the belief in the activity of demons that was held among the Christians and others too.[65] However, the Christians introduced important differentia into this shared belief.[66] For many religious philosophers of the Graeco-Roman world, especially those of the Platonist tradition, "demons" did not have the same meaning they had for the Christians. Plutarch of Chaeronaea,[67] a representative in the early Empire of the concern for continuity in traditional piety, provides an interesting contrast. In Plutarch's religious philosophy, the demons (or daemons) are conceived as having on the whole a positive function: they safeguard the gods from contact with matter and so remove the absolute Author of good from evil,[68] whilst they also provide the means of relating men to the divine, which was essential for man's well-being.[69] Against this positive "daemonic" theology, which Glover describes as "pleasant rather than compulsive and inevitable",[70] the Christians opposed a radical reduction of "daemons" to the rank of fallen angels and evil spirits under Satan, the adversary of the purposes of God. They did this by drawing upon their sources in the Old Testament and Jewish pseudepigrapha, as well as upon Christian tradition itself.[71]

This new Christian daemonology had an important consequence: the Christian apologist had at hand an effective weapon not only for explaining the problem of evil in general, but particularly for dealing with the many difficulties as to the origin and power of religious error.[72] Thus, knowledge of "the truth about things divine and human" through the Christian revelation, leads at the same time to an apprehension of the nature and manifestation of error and deviation from truth. This aspect of Christian understanding which is prominent in the affirmations of the Christian writers of the period, is seen particularly in their persistent recourse to the view that behind the presumed deities of Graeco-Roman religion, in actual fact, lie demons in the Christian sense. For Justin this new Christian daemonology becomes crucial,[73] and his most enduring contribution to Christian theological thought is directly related to his use of this insight.

Having learnt from "that old man"[74] that the Saviour who lately – in Justin's words elsewhere, "took shape and became man"[75] – came in fulfilment of prophecies proclaimed in a distant antiquity, Justin understood also that such a Saviour had therefore been active all along in the vindication of truth among men. As this vindication of truth has a history in the past, so also must the "demonic" activity of seduction and opposition to truth. The career of Socrates who was martyred for denouncing just such a demonic deception,[76] now finds a heightened significance in an entirely new frame of reference. For the concept of an ancient and mortal conflict between truth and error, between God (with His Word) and His prophets, on the one hand, and "the lying, unclean spirit" with his "spirits and *demons* of error" and "false prophets" on the other hand, is a specifically Christian insight.[77] It is interesting that the comment passed on St Paul by the Athenians that he "seems to be talking about foreign gods" (*GNB*),[78] has been seen as an allusion to the charge brought against Socrates.[79] Since Justin does, in fact, use in his Christian scheme Plato's account of the accusation levelled at Socrates,[80] it is also likely that he made a link between Paul's proclamation of "the unknown God" and Socrates' exhortation to his fellow Athenians to seek "the God who was to them unknown".[81]

The value of such correspondences to Justin must have been immense. In the Christian revelation, which therefore was the "only safe and profitable philosophy", he found certainly "the true philosophy theoretically, and the right law of life practically".[82] But he discovered more: in the whole Christian schema, through his conversion, he came to apprehend an interpretative framework, a "hermeneutical key" for understanding the character of the ways of God with mankind. It is not just the Gentile tradition which can be brought into such a framework, though the Gentiles' past is particularly important to him and, in the circumstances, called urgently for an interpretation. Racial and cultural distinctions cease to be relevant and the religious history and conduct of people from every nation now come under one rule and measuring principle. Justin's most notable contribution to Christian thought lay in what he perceived to be this measuring principle: the universal activity of the "seminal Word",[83] who "took shape and became man and was called Jesus Christ".[84]

It is now possible, therefore, to understand how Justin's theological efforts, far from being aimed at "Hellenising" the Christian tradition, may have been in the direction of "Christianising" Hellenistic tradition.[85]

III. Testing the key: He who has enlightened all mankind

By making the bold assertion implied in this statement from the *Second Apology*,[86] Justin linked every human destiny to Christ and brought the disparate appearance of human experiences under a single viewpoint. Every human thought and action and every movement of the human spirit are placed under one criterion of judgment, namely Christ, the seminal Word of God, who has sown[87] "seeds of truth among all men".[88] For it is evident that in saying that the incarnate Christ was the full manifestation, body, reason and soul of the divine Word "for our sakes", Justin does not mean for the sake of Christians alone, but rather for the sake of all mankind.[89] Accordingly, it is essential to recognise from the start that at the heart of Justin's theory of the universal activity of Christ as the "seminal Word", the Word who sows, there lies a deep concern with human redemption.

The importance of Justin's theory of the Logos/Word, for our present purposes, has not to do with its dogmatic formulations, or how it relates to later Trinitarian and Christological orthodoxy.[90] Rather, it has to do with how Justin elaborates his insight to deal with a more urgent and "contextual" question. It is probable that Justin had considered deeply the thrust and major emphases of St Paul's missionary preaching,[91] and was sensitive to the universalist stirrings at work within the apostle, particularly to the effect that nowhere and at no time had the Living God left Himself without witness among men.[92] If such is the case, then St Paul's understanding seems to have led Justin towards a quest for a way to give account of this witness which the Living God had indeed borne to Himself in the Hellenistic past.[93] It was the theory of the Logos/Word which came to meet that need in Justin, and answered to the quest for integration of his Hellenistic self-consciousness and his Christian commitment.

Henry Chadwick has rightly pointed out that "Justin combines a radical rejection of the pagan religious tradition with a positive optimism towards classical philosophy".[94] But when Justin's attitude is made to rest simply on the rejection of "anthropomorphic myths and superstitious cults as unworthy of God", on the one hand, and on the acceptance of some philosophical intimations of theological truth, on the other, this obscures the fact that Justin's attempt to claim insights from the philosophical tradition for the Christian faith amounts to a practical (though thoughtfully conceived) solution and not a logical system. It is important to realise that Justin's treatment of the seminal Word is quite often more concerned with describing His function among men than with exploring His being in terms of abstract thought. Much of the time Justin is at pains to draw attention to evidences in human conduct which, he believes, are indications of the activity of the Word among men, rather than to elaborate his doctrine in its relation to specific philosophical tenets.[95] Seen from this angle, Justin's theological interest would appear to be much less concerned with the vindication of "Christianity as an attestation of rational truth"[96] than has hitherto been realised, and his orientation may have been – in the language of our time – more "praxeological" than theoretical.[97]

Carl Andresen has helpfully shown that one has to look to Justin's intellectual background in second-century Middle Platonism with its markedly religious and ethical orientation, in order to appreciate his "religious philosophy" and hence his use of the seminal Word to denote a dynamic force at work in men.[98] In his well-documented discussion of the antecedents of the idea, Andresen connects the Word who sows with Cicero's treatment of the "seeds of justice" which are implanted by nature in the human soul, and from which (as first principles) developed the moral virtues which contribute to social well-being and harmony.[99] In subsequent philosophical speculation, then, the term, which is of Stoic origin, escapes from the Stoic metaphysical sense as the rational World-principle, and is given a predominantly ethical and even "spiritual" meaning;[100] it becomes linked with the Stoic concept of "innate ideas" or "common notions" which form the basis of moral and religious intuitions common to all mankind.[101] Consequently, when Justin speaks of the "seeds of the truth present in all men", he is to be understood in terms of the Middle Platonist tradition which gave moral and ethical interpretation to the metaphysical and intellectual terminology of Stoicism.[102]

However, whilst Andresen's article has contributed immeasurably towards clarifying the meaning of Justin's vocabulary, he is mainly interested in the influence of the tenets and view-points of the *Schulplatonismus* upon the theological thought of the Apologist.[103] Our own interest consists in taking more seriously the fact that the Justin who is known through his extant works is first and foremost a *Christian* thinker, and that this fact must be given due significance in order to arrive at a fair estimation of him. As Barnard has observed:

> "It must be emphasised that he [Justin] is a biblical thinker, and whatever the philosophical influences to which he was exposed, this remained a primary influence."[104]

Furthermore, Ragnar Holte[105] has shown that Andresen's study has considerable relevance for the term "the seed of the Word" (especially in connection with the idea of seeds of virtues) but not to the term "the Word who sows", which is not attested in Middle Platonism.[106] Holte's distinction between the two terms as they relate to Justin's usage is an important step forward in helping to explain Justin's theological thinking. In Holte's view, "the term 'the seed of the Word' does not mean that *Logos* or some part of him is sown in man. The meaning is, on the contrary, that a seed is sown in Man by the personal *Logos*".[107] If Holte is right in reversing the passive rendering of the Word who sows into an active sense "*Logos*... sowing his seed in an actual religious and moral illumination"[108] – then it is evident that the term "in Justin denotes Christ, and it is probable that he [Justin] is influenced by Jesus's parable of the Sower who sows the Word of God (*Matt*. 13. 3ff)."[109]

It is important to recognise, therefore, that for Justin, "the Logos is not merely something implanted in man. He is a living person who is known and loved."[110] Whether or not Justin was directly indebted to the prologue of the *Gospel of John*,[111] it is evident that Justin's usage, particularly his firm equation of the whole or entire Logos with Jesus Christ,[112] would indicate that he "was dependent on earlier Christian use of the term and assumes that his readers will understand his ideas".[113] One can argue, then, that Justin's identification of the Word who sows with Jesus Christ is in itself not as revolutionary as it has sometimes been taken to be.[114] The real breakthrough afforded by Justin's thinking on the subject comes in his ability, through this identification, to provide a "Christian" or Christ-centred interpretation of Hellenistic tradition of the past.

The clue to Justin's insight is given in a fragment – probably from a lost work – preserved by Irenaeus. It is obvious that Irenaeus

is using Justin's statement as part of his own argument against
the Gnostics; yet his interpretation of Justin's thought is so accurate that part of it must be quoted with the fragment itself:[115]

> "Truly has Justin remarked that 'before the Lord's appearance
> Satan never dared to blaspheme God, inasmuch as he did not
> yet know his own sentence' because it was contained in parables
> and allegories; but that after the Lord's appearance, when he
> had clearly ascertained from the words of Christ and His
> apostles that eternal fire had been prepared for him as he
> apostasised from God of his own free will, and likewise for all
> who unrepentant continue in the apostasy, he now blasphemes
> by means of such men, the Lord who brings judgment [upon
> him] as being already condemned, and imputes the guilt of his
> apostasy to his Maker, not to his own voluntary disposition..."[116]

The immediate argument put forward by Irenaeus, that heresies
were a demonic counterblast to the revelation of the truth by Christ
to all mankind through His incarnation, is also found in Justin.[117]
However, the essential point which this Irenaean passage makes
in respect of Justin's thinking is that with the appearance of Jesus
Christ, "the Word of whom every race of men partakes",[118] there is
now given the understanding that "something extraordinary has
happened",[119] which clarifies the entire history of all the religious
traditions of mankind, and in a way that exposes the distinction of
truth from its parody. It is upon this fundamentally Christological
basis that Justin considers he has found a means for discerning,
in the Hellenistic pre-Christian past, "that which is palpably
devilish" from "that which is compatible with the Gospel..."[120] But
it is important to realise that for Justin this distinction between
truth and falsehood is not to be conceived of in chronological terms;
rather, it is essentially eternal and contemporary. Thus in interpreting the past, Justin is also explicating the present.

    It means that Justin's positive attitude to the philosophical
tradition is not to be taken as indicating that he saw in philosophy,
strictly, a *praeparatio evangelica*. The true character of Justin's
thinking has been well stated by Jean Daniélou:

> "Just as it is the Word himself who is the source of that partial
> knowledge of the truth which is given to every man, so too it is
> he who is the object and the norm of this knowledge. When
> Justin writes that Socrates or Heraclitus lived in accordance
> with the Word,[121] he does not mean in accordance with reason,
> but in accordance with the Word. That which Socrates and

Heraclitus knew is in fact the Word, who is Truth itself. They, however, only knew it obscurely,[122] partially."[123]

It is consistent, therefore, for Justin to claim that there were "Christians" before Christ,[124] and to insist that he and the Christians of his own day had a common cause with those of the past.[125] Through the power and grace imparted by Christ,[126] he can now give a proper account of the true nature of the achievements in the past and also offer adequate explanation for the limitations of former insights.

IV. How, then, did they know?

The evidence which Justin adduces to validate his claims falls broadly into two categories. On the one hand, he gives instances of anticipations of some specific biblical doctrines and Christian beliefs. These are traced through the works of ancient writers, poets and philosophers. On the other, Justin points to personages in the past, and nearer to his own time, who, acting upon the inward impulse given by the Word, took a stand against what they considered and Justin now affirms was religious error. The following discussion will show that the decisive emphasis in Justin's thinking falls on the second category.

The case for seeing in the speculative formulations of the past approximations of Christian and Biblical tenets is argued basically on two grounds. One of these is the chronological argument, which was to be exploited most fully by Justin's disciple, Tatian, as we have seen.[127] Thus Plato's cosmology in the *Timaeus* is, for Justin, indebted to the early verses of the book of *Genesis*.[128] In the same way, the Platonic speculations on the cruciform distribution of the "world soul" throughout the universe,[129] indicates Plato's inadequate apprehension of his readings from Moses![130] From this flows Plato's failure to truly understand the concept of the Cross and the doctrine of the Trinity![131] But it is important to note that this argument for the Platonic dependence on the Old Testament, based on the chronological priority of Moses, which is twice asserted,[132] does not have in Justin an anti-Hellenic edge[133] as it does in Tatian. Rather, it is appealed to as part of a comprehensive attempt to show that in one important sense, Christian doctrines were not as novel and unheard of as they were feared to be.

"If therefore on some points we teach the same things as the poets and philosophers whom you honour, and on other points [we] are fuller and more divine [in our teaching] and if we alone produce proof of what we assert, why are we unjustly hated more than all others?"[134]

Thus, there are analogies to Christian beliefs in the intimations of thoughtful persons everywhere and there is no essential difference of content between their approximations and the full reality, beyond the major distinctions of vagueness from clarity and evident proof of certainty.[135] These anticipations are found in the works of philosophers, poets and playwrights,[136] but the unity of the Truth itself argues for considering them as having been derived from those sources which alone possess the fullness of truth:

> "Whatever both philosophers and poets have said concerning the immortality of the soul, or punishments after death or contemplation of heavenly things or doctrines of that kind, they have received such suggestions from the prophets as have enabled them to understand and interpret these things. And hence, there seem to be seeds of truth in all men. But they are proved not to have accurately understood [the truth] when they contradict themselves."[137]

It is tempting to interpret the last statement as meaning that the failure to accurately understand the truth is proved by the mutual contradictions among the various thinkers.[138] However, this idea is not used by Justin, and the immediate context does not require it either. When Justin goes on to criticise a specific tenet, namely, the ultimate destiny of human beings, his criticism seems directed against the Stoic idea of fatalism.[139] On the basis of my own translation of the last sentence quoted[140] Justin must be understood as suggesting that the various thinkers and writers were unable to apprehend the true dimensions of the insights which they received because they "shared in" only "seeds of the truth" and not in the full revelation of the Truth as given in the Scriptures (properly understood only in the Christian community) and through the Incarnate Word.[141] Accordingly, they were bound to assert contradictions against the truth in relation to which their partial insights were merely approximations. In other words, the various thinkers and writers were unable to avoid inconsistencies since they had only partial apprehension of the Truth.

The implied suggestion that dependence on the Old Testament is in itself evidence of the presence of "seeds of truth" implanted by Christ, the seminal Word, brings us to the second ground on which Justin validates the claim that the speculative formulations of thoughtful persons were in effect approximations of Christian doctrines. For he argues that the persons concerned owed such insights to the direct, inward operation of the divine Word who enlightened them:

> "Whatever either legislators or philosophers expressed well and
> elaborated, they owed to their partial knowledge and con-
> templation of the Word. But since they did not know the
> whole of the Word, who is Christ, they often contradicted
> themselves."[142]

The similarities between this statement and the previous one
are striking, and they raise the question as to how dependence on
the Biblical literature relates to the partial inward knowledge of
the Word. It is evident that in Justin's mind there is little distinction between the two modes of partial apprehension of truth. It is
worth noting that in his interpretation of the Scriptures, in both
the *Apologies* and in the *Dialogue,* it is the way the Old Testament
points to Jesus Christ as the divine Word and Redeemer of
mankind that really interests him.[143] This means that for Justin,
there is an identity of content between the knowledge derived from
the Scriptures and the inward participation in the Word, for both
sets of apprehension lead to the same end, and so have the same
source, the Word Himself. But this partial knowledge, in either
case, is ineffectual to lead to the apprehension of the fullest
implications of the insights involved, hence the inconsistencies at
many points.

Justin makes this point most explicitly in a concluding passage
in the *Second Apology* where he brings together the theory of
dependence on the Scriptures and the inward operation of the
Word:

> "I both boast and with all my strength strive to be found a
> Christian; not because the teachings of Plato are different from
> those of Christ, but because they are not in all respects similar
> as neither are those of the others, Stoics, and poets and his-
> torians. For each one spoke well in proportion to the share he
> had of the divine spermatic Word seeing what was related to it.
> But persons who contradict themselves on the points of central
> importance appear not to have possessed the insight into hid-
> den meanings nor to have gained irrefutable knowledge.
> Whatever things were rightly said among all men, are the
> property of us Christians. For next to God, we worship and love
> the Word who comes from the unbegotten and ineffable God,
> since also He became man for our sakes, that becoming a
> partaker of our sufferings, He might also bring us healing. For
> all the writers were able to perceive Reality dimly on account
> of the innate seed of the Word that was implanted in them. For
> the seed and the copy given in proportion to [the recipient's]

capacity is one thing; and quite another is the thing itself, in which participation and imitation take place according to the grace which is from Him."[144]

In this very important passage, the centrality of Justin's concern with human redemption is most evident; it shows how profoundly he held that the entire history of the intellectual and religious quest of men centred upon bringing human beings into fellowship with God.[145] But it is crucial to Justin's whole argument that all this history, properly understood, is "both a work of Christ and an anticipation of Christ."[146] In other words, Justin effectively blocks off the possibility of interpreting the speculations and deliverances of past thinkers and writers on any other grounds than Christ alone. By the same token, he pronounces their insights limited and inadequate, considering them ineffectual on their own to lead to a full apprehension of the Truth.[147] For this to occur, one must make the kind of commitment to Christ (i.e. "worship and love the Word") that brings about that participation and growth into His likeness which takes place according to the grace imparted by Him, the Word.[148] Jean Daniélou is right, therefore, to stress that:

"He [Justin] is not in the least tempted by the idea of an order of natural truth which is the proper object of reason on the one hand, and an order of supernatural truth, the object of revelation, on the other. There are only an obscure knowledge and a clear knowledge of the one Truth, which is the Word."[149]

V. Who, then, were those who knew?

It is interesting that the personages of the past who were, in the eyes of Justin, "Christians" before Christ, were those who, in his estimation, witnessed to their knowledge, though partial, of the "one Truth which is the Word". We come here to Justin's second category of evidence which is meant to vindicate the Christian presence amid Hellenistic tradition.

It may well be the case that in his "endeavour to drive a wedge between pagan religion and Greek philosophy and to make common cause with the latter",[150] Justin was inserting himself consciously in the tradition of the philosophical criticism of the popular religion and of the Homeric and Hesiodic mythologies in particular.[151]

As early as the sixth century before Christ, the post-philosopher Xenophanes of Colophon had expressed criticism of the way the gods had been presented in the works of Homer and Hesiod: these poets "have attributed to the gods all things that are shameful and a reproach among mankind: theft, adultery and mutual deception. They have narrated every possible wicked story of the gods".[152] Xenophanes himself postulated a God beyond the gods – "one god, among gods and men the greatest, not at all like mortals in body or mind".[153] Xenophanes' purpose, therefore, was not to make sport of Homer and Hesiod, nor to banish religion altogether;[154] however, it is evident from the kind of questions he raised about the classical mythology that the anthropomorphism of the Homeric "reform" had rendered the gods "morally contemptible".[155] What seems to have been an attempt to humanise the "primitive" gods and to bring intellectual order into the chaos of religious concepts and worship inherited from the times of *Urdummheit* (primeval stupidity),[156] in fact provided the weapons for the criticism of the religion and for its eventual overthrow in the later Greek intellectual tradition.[157]

This rationalist criticism of the traditional religion and its gods reached its highest point in the agnostic and atheistic theories of the Sophists, for whom "man is not the creature, but the creator of his gods".[158] Even for Plato, "commonly regarded as the most bigoted and ruthless of theists",[159] the religion which is deemed necessary for the life and ordering of society is not constructed on the "traditional" Homeric account of the divine, but on a philosophical postulate of a cosmic God.[160] It is not surprising that Justin drew attention to the fact that Socrates (and Plato) set aside the claims of Homer and other poets to give authoritative teaching on religious realities and on the nature of divinity.[161] The critique made by early Christian apologetics of Graeco-Roman religion and of the "theology" on which it was based, can be said, therefore, to have had antecedents in the "discrediting of traditional Greek religion" in the history of the Hellenistic philosophical tradition itself.[162]

However, it would be inappropriate to regard the theological enterprise that Justin initiated as no more than a continuation of the Greek speculative tradition which had preceded him.[163] To the extent that he may have been inserting himself in that tradition, and seeking to answer some of the questions which it had raised about God and his relations to mankind and the world, Justin was steering the tradition along quite different lines. He was, at the same time, raising new questions for Hellenistic tradition. In other words, Justin was conscious that the Christian faith to which he gave unreserved allegiance, had a religious and intellectual content of its own,[164] and that it provided him with a framework for assessing the Hellenistic past in a way in which the latter had never been viewed before, that is, by seeking specifically Christian meanings within it. Justin's approach, in essence, is to read the history of Hellenistic tradition "backwards", and to interpret the past by the present. In an illuminating paragraph on Justin's apologetic, E.R. Goodenough pointed to this "retroactive" feature in Justin's interpretation of Hellenistic tradition:

"Christianity was accused of being a novel innovation, was ignored or sneered at by philosophers as beneath the notice of intelligent men, and it was this sort of attack to which Justin chiefly devotes his attention. The general scheme of his defence was first to deny the novelty of Christianity by demonstrating its continuity with Judaism, then to show parallels between the teachings of the Pentateuch and of the Greek philosophers, and then boldly to assert *post hoc ergo propter hoc,* that since Moses antedated Socrates and Plato, any common ideas must have been taken by the philosophers from the Jewish Scriptures. Granted thus the superior dignity of Christianity over philosophy because it was the legitimate completion of Judaism, the original source of knowledge of supermundane matters for all mankind, *Justin takes a new course and works from Christianity backwards to philosophy.* The system of Judaism achieved its long expected perfection in the person and teaching of Jesus Christ, who was the incarnation of that Spirit of Revelation which alone could guide the human mind to knowledge of the Truth. But this spirit of wisdom was present in every man as his highest intellect, so that not only does Christ represent the culmination of the prophecy of a single religion, even though that is the most ancient religion, but He is the incarnation of the Universal Intelligence which it has been the hopeless struggle of every philosopher to understand. The answer to the sneers of the philosophers that Christianity was not worthy of an intelligent man's consideration was thus the counter-attack that philosophy had failed, and that only in Christianity was the end of philosophy to be found."[165]

Yet in working from "Christianity backwards... to philosophy", to justify his claim for Christianity as philosophic truth itself, Justin was doing more than seeking to answer the sneers of the educated; he was attempting to establish the grounds for Christian self-consciousness in terms meaningful to the cultural and intellectual tradition which he shared with his Hellenistic opponents.[166] It is by this means that he is able to inject new significance into the lives of persons whose careers testify that they shared, even if only partially, in the spiritual inheritance which has now become his own. Consequently, he feels confident enough to claim them as fellow-witnesses to the Truth, and accordingly, as companions of Christ.

Here Justin's pre-Christian "Socratic motif",[167] his Christian demonology,[168] and his profoundly Christocentric emphasis meet and produce his most remarkable contribution to the interpretation of every "non-Christian" tradition. Justin firmly grasped the Pauline insight that the truth of the Christian Gospel is the truth of the person rather than of the religious tradition to which one belongs.[169] It is then only a short step for Justin to argue that authentication of one's knowledge of the Truth necessarily involves testimony and confrontation with falsehood, even at the risk of one's life. Thus Justin's postulate of common ground between the Christian and the genuine philosophers after the Socratic type, becomes clear.[170] However, when it comes to identifying the personages of the past, whom one might describe as "companions of Christ" in their time, Justin does not dwell on Socrates.

"... those who lived in accordance with the insights granted by the Word are Christians, even though they were reckoned atheists; such as, among the Greeks, Socrates and Heraclitus and others like them; among the Barbarians, Abraham, Ananias, Azarias, Mishael and Elijah and many others, whose deeds and names I decline to recount, knowing that it would be tedious... and among those of our own time, Musonius and others."[171]

What common thread links these persons who seem to be chosen at random? The clue to Justin's perception lies in his demonology. Whilst Justin is willing to claim the partial apprehensions of the Truth in the philosophical tradition as positive indications of the activity of the pre-incarnate Word, he refuses to treat in the same favourable light parallels and similarities to Christian beliefs in the actual ideas and practices of Graeco-Roman religion. Whatever approximations there are, as may be found in the mythological accounts of the gods, have been produced "at the instigation of the wicked demons to deceive and lead astray the human race".[172] In so far as the tales recounted of the presumed deities bear comparison with some events in the life and career of Christ, they are parodies and caricatures of them, anticipated by the evil spirits who, learning of the prophetic predictions concerning Christ's earthly life and ministry, put forth the imitations to obscure the real truth that would be revealed:

"For when they heard it predicted through the prophets that Christ was to come, and that impious men would be punished by fire, they put forward a number of so-called sons of Zeus, thinking that they could thus make men suppose that what was said about Christ was a mere tale of wonders like the stories told by the poets... though [the demons] heard the words of the prophets, they did not understand them accurately, but made mistakes in imitating what was told about our Christ."[173]

Instances of this demonic imitation are the story of Perseus as a parody of the miraculous virgin birth of Christ, and the activity of the healing god Asclepius as a caricature of Christ's healing ministry; and Justin links the story of Dionesus and the symbols of his worship with the messianic prophecy in *Genesis* 49:10ff, with its associations of blood and wine.[174] The dishonourable deeds of the "gods" prove conclusively that they were not gods at all, but in point of fact, wicked demons,[175] who deceived men into calling them gods and giving each of them the name which each of the demons had chosen for himself.[176]

The demons, thus, are the enemies of the Truth and work in opposition to the activity of the Word.[177] Accordingly, the all-important distinction between those who lived according to the Word, and hence might be described as companions of Christ,[178] and those who lived against the Word and so were enemies of Christ,[179] turns virtually entirely on their attitude towards the religious outlook of their day. The decisive evidence for Justin is that those persons in the past who dissented from a religious tradition which they considered misguided – and which Justin insists was devised by the wicked demons – incurred the displeasure of the demons thus unmasked,[180] and generally suffered for their stand. A variation of the argument is that earnest persons such as Socrates suffered persecution, whereas "disreputable" characters like Sardanapalus and Epicurus enjoyed favour.[181] Thus, just as Christ, the Word, is the source, object and nqrm of all knowledge of truth,[182] so the predicament of Christians provides an explanation of the careers of those persons who knew Christ partially.

The common thread that links "companions of Christ" among Greeks and Barbarians – Socrates, Heraclitus, Musonius... Abraham, Ananias, Azarias, Mishael, Elijah – becomes clear. In the words of Oskar Skarsaune:

"The uniting feature of all these men is obvious: they all – in

Justin's eyes – *denounced idolatry*, they were 'atheists' and were persecuted or even martyred by the demons and pseudogods (and their worshippers)."[183]

To the prominent example of Socrates, Justin adds that of Heraclitus, whose career in Ephesus he considers to have been not dissimilar to Socrates' in Athens.[184] In the Old Testament, Abraham is noted for his willingness to abandon the religious tradition of his past in obedience to the summons of the Living God; Ananias, Azarias and Mishael are mentioned for their refusal to bow to the golden image set up by King Nebuchadnezzar,[185] whilst Elijah's significance lies in the fact that he took a firm stand against religious syncretism and suffered persecution for doing so.[186]

Justin's inclusion of the Stoic philosopher Musonius Rufus in his catalogue of martyred witnesses to truth[187] might be considered puzzling. In Blunt's view, Justin is in error here, and suggests that for Justin to say that Musonius was murdered is an exaggeration.[188] But even if Musonius (and Heraclitus) suffered banishment and not execution, and ostensibly on political grounds, due weight must be given to Justin's general observation which shows where his emphasis falls:

"For as we have intimated, the demons have always effected that all those who to any degree live earnestly in accordance with insight given by the Word and shun vice, be hated."[189]

In view of this principle, the career of Musonius, who suffered under Nero,[190] makes his inclusion in Justin's catalogue quite understandable. According to Tacitus, Musonius was one of two "teachers of wisdom" who in AD 60 encouraged Rubellius Plautus, in exile and soon to be murdered by Nero's agents, to face death with courage.[191] Five years later, on the discovery of the conspiracy of Piso, Musonius owed his own banishment to his reputation as a teacher of wise precepts among the youth.[192] His career showed him also to be a Socratic type!

It is quite probable, as Ernst Benz has argued, that in invoking the example of the three men who were thrust into the fiery furnace in *Daniel* 3, Justin was drawing upon an earlier Christian tradition attested in the *Epistle of Clement to the Corinthians* 45:4ff.[193] If this is the case, the remarkable feature of Justin's use of the tradition lies in the sense of freedom he displays in applying the same tests both to Biblical characters and to persons in Hellenistic tradition whom he considered to have been equally valid witnesses to the one fundamental Truth, given to all mankind through the

Word, who took human form as Jesus Christ. As Benz comments:

"The outlook which Clement attributes to the three men in the fiery furnace is applied by Justin not merely to a large number of other Old Testament men of God, but also to the witnesses to truth in Greek philosophy."[194]

The difference between Clement (of Rome) and Justin at this point is symbolic, for it draws our attention to J.N.D. Kelly's considered judgment that "the Apostolic Fathers appear as witnesses to the traditional faith rather than interpreters striving to understand it".[195] From the kind of concerns which Justin (and his successors) brought to their vindication of Christianity, it was inevitable that the course of the Christian theological enterprise would be charted along different lines.

VI. Conclusion

From his meticulous study of Justin's life and work, Karl Semisch concluded that "most probably... Justin's labours conduced far more to the internal edification of the Christian Church than to its extension outwardly".[196] If this judgment is correct, it need not be considered as being to Justin's discredit. For if it was the case that the outward extension of the Church was taking place, as Justin argued, more evidently among Gentiles than among Jews,[197] then surely such "internal edification" would have had its own value. If one was to make good the claim that "we who keep the commandments of Christ, are, by virtue of Christ who begat us unto God, both called and in fact are, Jacob and Israel and Judah and Joseph and David, and true children of God",[198] then, sooner or later, there would be needed a new hermeneutic, not only of the records of Israelite tradition, but also of the Hellenistic tradition out of which the new, "true Israel"[199] was now being so massively drawn. The outstanding achievement of Justin's writings was to provide some of the basic ingredients for just such a hermeneutic, and to indicate some of the ways in which the task involved might be carried out.

But Justin was not thereby "hellenising" the Christian Gospel. By holding firmly to the centrality of the Old Testament Scriptures and Christian tradition,[200] he avoided the Gnostic option of eliminating whatever was "Barbarian" in the new faith.[201] More important still, for Justin, the centrality of the Old Testament consisted in its prediction of the incarnation of the Saviour, the Word of God, who took human form and was called Jesus Christ and who came, not as the fulfilment of the exclusive, nationalist aspirations of Jews, but supremely as "the expectation of the nations".[202]

It is hard to exaggerate the excitement that Justin must have felt at the prospect that it was Gentiles (people like himself) who were increasingly finding their spiritual home in the inheritance of Israel;[203] and the importance he attached to this fact is evident on almost every page of his writings that have come down to us.[204] The explanation for this remarkable turn of history Justin found in the universal significance of Jesus Christ as the divine Word, the source and norm of all truth and knowledge wherever it may be found. Accordingly, his attempt at elaborating the prior activity of Christ in the history of Hellenistic (and Barbarian) traditions was intended to clarify that fundamental apprehension. The fact that later Christian apologetics never retreated from the Christological axiom which he postulated, is an indication of the enduring quality of his insight. As R.A. Norris has observed:

"It was the apologetic merit of Justin's Logos doctrine that it explicitly claimed the history of Greek thought, the common cultural heritage of the Mediterranean world, as a part of the story of Christ's revelation of God. Christ as Logos becomes the universal mediator of the knowledge of God, and as such the culmination of the history not merely of Israel but of the entire 'inhabited world'."[205]

What is particularly interesting in this universalising of "salvation-history" is that it involves the Christianising not only of Hellenistic tradition, but the Jewish also; "holy pagans" and Jewish saints become "Christians before Christ", on the same terms; and the Old Testament, by virtue of Christ foreshadowed therein, becomes a Christian book.[206] Two centuries on, Eusebius of Caesarea is found writing that "it would be no departure from the truth, to assert that all those who have enjoyed the testimony of righteousness, from Abraham himself back to the first man, were Christians in fact if not in name".[207] Hans von Campenhausen's judgment of Justin is apposite:

"Nearly all the Greek Fathers of the Church were, consciously or unconsciously, his imitators."[208]

Notes

1. See *1 Apology* 1,1; *Dialogue* 120,6. Cf. *2 Apology* 15,1 on Simon Magus "of my own nation".

2. From his grandfather's Greek name (Bacchius) and his father's and his own Latin names (Priscus, Justinus), it is suggested that the family may have been of Italian origin. See G. Bardy's article, "Saint Justin" in *DTC*, vol.8, coll.2228-2277.

Cf. E.F. Osborn, *Justin Martyr* (*Beiträge zur historischen Theologie*, 47), Tübingen: J.C.B. Mohr, 1973, p.6.

3. *Dialogue* 28,2.

4. *Ibid.*, 41,3.

5. *1 Apology* 53,3.

6. *Ibid.*

7. *Ibid.*, 14,5.

8. See *Dialogue* 7 and 8.

9. As given in *Dialogue* 2.

10. Aimé Puech, *Les Apologistes grecs du IIe siècle de notre ère*, Paris: Hachette, 1912, pp.50,144f.

11. Carl Andresen, "Justin und der mittlere Platonismus" in *ZNW*, 44, 1952-53, pp.157-195.

12. L.W. Barnard, *Justin Martyr: His Life and Thought*, Cambridge: the University Press, 1967, pp.27-38. Cf. J.C.M. van Winden, *An Early Christian Philosopher: Justin's Dialogue with Trypho chapters one to nine* (Introduction, Text and Commentary), Leiden: E.J. Brill, 1971, p.23.

13. L.W. Barnard, *op.cit.*, p.52; also A. Lukyn Willians, *Justin Martyr: the Dialogue with Trypho* (Translation, Introduction and Notes), London: S.P.C.K., 1930, xxxiii.

For the view that Justin's doctrine of the Λόγος, for instance, was derived from Philo Judaeus, see E.R. Goodenough, *The Theology of Justin Martyr*, Jena: Verlag Frommansche Buchhandlung, 1923, pp.139-175. Cf. Karl Semisch, *Justin Martyr: His Life, Writings and Opinions*, vol.2 (ET by J.E. Ryland), Edinburgh: T. & T. Clark, 1843, p.207: "It [Justin's Λόγος doctrine] was of pure Biblical origin and consistency, but of a Philonic shape."

For a refutation of Goodenough's view, see L.W. Barnard, *op.cit.*, pp.92-96. Barnard observes appositely: "It is a fact often forgotten that Justin never mentions Philo, while he does mention his philosophic environment in Middle Platonism from which he passed into Christianity." (p.96)

14. See Jean Daniélou, *Gospel Message and Hellenistic Culture* (ET by John Austin Baker), London: Darton, Longman & Todd, 1973, pp.7-15.

15. The kind of approach we are criticising is seen in J.C.M. van Winden's initial observation in the introduction to his valuable study of the early chapters of the *Dialogue*. "The works of Justin Martyr have already been the object of intensive study... The main reason for this interest stems from Justin's appearance in Western history at a time when the two currents determining the course of this history merged, namely, Greek philosophy and Christian faith" (van Winden, *op.cit.*, p.1). Cf. L.W. Barnard, *op.cit.*, p.169: "It cannot be said that the Church has yet fully explored Justin's insights, although there are signs, in the contemporary encounter with the non-Christian faiths, that these are proving relevant again." An interesting study of the early Church which moves in the direction I am urging, is John Foster, *After the Apostles – Missionary Preaching of the first three centuries*, London: SCM, 1951: "Perhaps one of my original contributions will be keeping in mind throughout, the light thrown upon the Early Church by situations... in the Younger Churches" (preface, p.11). See also Campbell N. Moody, *The Mind of the Early Converts*, London: Hodder & Stoughton, 1920; André Benoit, *L'Actualité des Pères de l'Eglise* (*Cahiers théologiques*, 47), Neuchâtel: Delachaux et Niestlé, 1961.

16. See Adolf von Harnack, *History of Dogma*, vol.2 (ET by Neil Buchanan), London: Williams & Norgate, 1896. On the Apologists as a whole, and their

162   THEOLOGY AND IDENTITY

contribution towards a "Hellenising of Christianity", see pp.169-229.

17. See R.M. Grant, article "Justin Martyr" in *New Schaff-Herzog* (suppl. vol.14): "The extent of Justin's acquaintance with philosophy can easily be exaggerated... In fact it does not amount to a great deal" (p.620); cf. his "Aristotle and the Conversion of Justin" in *JTS* (n.s.), 7, 1956, pp.246-248. Grant responds to Carl Andresen, *op.cit.*

18. Henry Chadwick, "Justin Martyr's defence of Christianity", in *BJRL*, 47, 1964-65, p.275.

19. *Ibid.*, p.275.

20. See above, Chapter 1: *"Non licet esse vos:* The problem of Christian identity in the context of Graeco-Roman culture of the early Roman Empire".

21. Some relevant passages are *1 Apology* 1,1; 15,6; 31,7; 32,4; *Dialogue* 52,4; 131,5. Cf. L.W. Barnard, *op.cit.* p.169: "He was... the first thinker after St Paul to grasp the universalistic element in Christianity."

22. *1 Apology* 1,1. Commentators on the *Dialogue* have generally drawn attention to the theme of "Christians as the new people of God" which features prominently in the latter section of the *Dialogue*, as from chapter 109. See Otto, *op.cit.* (tom.1), 48-54; cf. A. Lukyn Williams, *op.cit.*, pp.xxxv–xxxvii; also P. Prigent, *Justin et l'Ancien Testament*, Paris: J. Gabalda et Cie, 1964, esp. chapters 9 and 10, "L'ancienne et la nouvelle alliance, *Dial.* 10 à 29", and "L'Universalisme, *Dial.* 117 à 140". In his introduction, Prigent reviews the divisions of the *Dialogue* as proposed by other commentators (pp.14-17).

The relevant chapters, 1-9, have been analysed in great detail in some recent studies.

23. See J.C.M. van Winden, *op.cit.;* Robert Joly, *Christianisme et Philosophie – Etudes sur Justin et les Apologistes grecs du deuxième siècle*, Bruxelles: Editions de l'Université de Bruxelles, 1973, pp.9-74. I have not had access to Niels Hyldahl, *Philosophie und Christentum. Eine Interpretation der Einleitung zum Dialog Justins*, Copenhagen: Munksgaard, 1966, but both van Winden and Joly discuss his work extensively.

24. According to Eusebius *(HE* 4,11,8; Migne, *PG*, 20,329C), "Justin... in a philosopher's garb (ἐν φιλοσόφου σχήματι) preached the divine word, and contended for the faith in his writings."

25. For this rendering of the meaning of *Dialogue* 1,4, I follow J.C.M. van Winden, *op.cit.*, pp.30f.: "Trypho's question and Justin's agreement are concerned with the true rather than with the actual philosophy, in other words: with philosophy properly so called. The actual Greek philosophy is opposed to it. *Justin states that the actual philosophy does not do what it should do."*

26. J.C.M. van Winden, *op.cit.*, p.42, accepts Hyldahl's hypothesis that Stoic ideas on a "primordial philosophy" lie behind Justin's words and that when Justin later speaks of Christianity as "the only safe and profitable philosophy" he means a recovery of what Hyldahl has called "the recovered primordial philosophy". Van Winden however, rejects Hyldahl's view that the *Urphilosophie* must not be identified with the Old Testament revelation (pp.111f).

27. *Dialogue* 7,3.

28. *Ibid.*, 8,1.

29. Robert Joly, *op.cit.*, who argues for the historicity of Justin's philosophical background (*contra* Niels Hyldahl, *op.cit.*), concludes that these chapters amount to " an *a posteriori* justification, and not the faithful record of an actual encounter" (p.72); cf. J.C.M. van Winden, *op.cit.*, pp.52,127.

30. A.D. Nock, *Conversion – The Old and the New in Religion from Alexander the Great to Augustine of Hippo*, Oxford, 1933, p.250, quoted in Oskar Skarsaune, "The conversion of Justin" in *Studia Theologica*, 30, 1976, p.55.

31. Oskar Skarsaune, *op.cit.*, p.55.

32. E.F. Osborn, *op.cit.*, p.7. On the whole question, Henry Chadwick's view seems to be the most accurate: "It is much more probable than not that we are being given an essentially veracious autobiography, even if Justin's memory, looking back some twenty years, is likely to have foreshortened and compressed the story. Like the rest of us, Justin is remembering the past in a way that the present requires". See his "Justin's defence of Christianity", p.280.

33. Cf. Henry Chadwick, *Early Christian Thought and the Classical Tradition, Studies in Justin, Clement and Origen*, Oxford: Clarendon Press, 1966, p.10.

34. *Dialogue*, 9,1.

35. Henry Chadwick, *Early Christian Thought and the Classical Tradition*, pp.18,19.

36. See *1 Apology* 10.

37. *Ibid.*, 31ff.

38. Henry Chadwick, *Early Christian Thought and the Classical· Tradition*, p.19. See in Justin, *1 Apology* 18-19; *Dialogue* 80; cf. L.W. Barnard, *op.cit.*, pp.163-166.

39. Henry Chadwick, *Early Christian Thought and the Classical Tradition*, p.18.

40. See *Dialogue* 7,2.

41. Equally, one must set aside Robert Joly's suggestion, *op.cit.*, p.72, that Justin "being an ancient philosopher and continuing to wear the dress of one... wanted to justify himself by writing this *Prologue*". There is no evidence that Justin wished to allay the fears and suspicions "*de ses co-religionnaires plus simples*". Whilst Joly refers to J. Lebreton's article of "Le désaccord de la foi populaire et de la théologie savants dans l'Eglise du IIIe siècle" (*RHE*, 19, 1923, pp.481-506; 20, 1924, pp.5-37), Lebreton himself does not include Justin in the history of this "*désaccord*".

42. *Dialogue* 7,1. (My emphasis.)

43. *Ibid.*, 2,1-2.

44. J.C.M. van Winden (*op.cit.*, pp.43-45), who, following Hyldahl (*op.cit.*) traces Justin's idea of a primordial, unified philosophy to Stoic influence, suggests that what is of interest to Justin is not so much the "philosophical scheme", as the similarity he sees between the history of philosophy and that of the heretical schools! Evidently, Justin imagines the evolution of philosophy as having gone the same way. The different philosophical schools are like heresies; they do not represent the one true philosophy. Their adherents are Platonists, Pythagoreans, etc., not philosophers. The "first men" i.e. the founders of the schools, were the first heretics. "Thus it becomes also understandable why, to him, the one true philosophy was *sent down*... to mankind... Just as the one Christianity, in the person of Christ, was *sent down* to mankind, so true philosophy appeared to men." (p.45).

45. See Ragnar Holte, "*Logos spermatikos*. Christianity and ancient philosophy according to Justin's Apologies" in *Studia Theologica*, 12, 1958, pp.164-165.

46. Oskar Skarsaune, *op.cit.*, p.56. Cf. J.C.M. van Winden, *op.cit.*, pp.110-111, on the end of chapter 6 and the beginning of chapter 7. "One may not conclude from this discussion that this philosophical argument actually caused Justin's conversion... [Justin is] 'reduced to a condition of argumentative helplessness'" (van

Winden quotes from A.D. Nock, *Conversion*, p.256).

47. According to R.M. Grant, "Aristotle and the Conversion of Justin", p.247, it was the old man's anti-Platonic arguments which "deprived the soul of immortality and powers of vision and transmigration" and "produced Justin's conversion". Oskar Skarsaune is right in urging, against Grant, that "the anti-Platonic argument prepared Justin's conversion, it did not produce it" (*op.cit.*, p.56, n.13).

48. See *Dialogue* 8,1-2. As Grant himself notes, Justin's major concern in his philosophical itinerary must have been a quest for "a source of ultimate truth" (*op.cit.*, p.248). And would not this, precisely, be the point of Justin's criticism of the philosophical schools for neglecting to pursue seriously the question of God? See *Dialogue* 1,4-5.

49. In *2 Apology* 12,1, Justin speaks of the impression made on him by Christians, "fearless of death and of all other things which are counted fearful..." when he was still a Platonist (τοῖς Πλάτωνος χαίρων διδάγμασι). Then he "perceived that it was impossible that they [the slandered Christians] could be living in wickedness and pleasure" (ἐν κακίᾳ καὶ φιληδονίᾳ).

50. J.C.M. van Winden, *op.cit.*, pp.118-119, links the two passages. Cf. Oskar Skarsaune, *op.cit.*, p.58, n.16. An interesting parallel to Justin's verdict on the Christians (in *2 Apology* 12,1) is the well-known observation by the second-century physician, Galen. See R. Walzer, *Galen on Jews and Christians*, London: Oxford University Press, 1949, p.15.

Quoted in J. Stevenson (ed), *A New Eusebius: Documents illustrative of the history of the Church to AD 337*, London: S.P.C.K., 1957, p.133.

51. Aimé Puech has rightly emphasised the significance of certainty for Justin: "Primarily, Christianity gave him certainty; why had philosophy not satisfied him? Because it is an endless quest... It [Christianity] gave him the most complete revelations on the divine essence. It put into his hands books which illuminated the entire history of the world from the beginning." See his *Les Apologistes grecs du IIe siècle de notre ère*, p.145. Cf. Hans von Campenhausen, *The Fathers of the Greek Church* (ET), London: A. & C. Black, 1963, p.7: "Justin's Christianity is marked by an urge to give practical expression to his faith, and by the absolute certainty of his ultimate convictions."

52. Cf. *1 Apology* 2,1. On the importance of the love of truth to Justin, see E.F. Osborn, *op.cit.*, pp.77-86.

53. E.R. Goodenough, *op.cit.*, p.72: "Justin found Christianity an escape from speculation... Revelation, as he understood it, satisfied all doubts, settled all problems" (*ibid.*, p.293).

54. Van Winden, *op.cit.*; "The same rationalistic verdict could be applied to a considerable part of the philosophy of the period. It seems, therefore, more correct to leave Justin in his historical environment, stating that his practical attitude to philosophy was an authentic one and dominant at the time. Philosophy was the guide of life and practical ethics its most important object" (p.119). A more just appreciation of Justin is given by Henry Chadwick (*Early Christian Thought and the Classical Tradition*), who contrasts him, on the one hand, with Lucian of Samosata, the "'rationalist', who is cynical equally about traditional religion and about philosophy", and on the other hand, with Numenius of Apamaea, for whom "everything is right and true" and so has "no criterion of judgment". For his part, "Justin stands between Lucian and Numenius. He knows what is true and judges accordingly" (pp.20f).
On the intellectual and religious climate of the period, see E.R. Dodds, *Pagan and Christian in an Age of Anxiety – Some aspects of religious experience from Marcus Aurelius to Constantine*, Cambridge University Press, 1966. Also Gilbert Murray,

Five Stages of Greek Religion, London: Watts & Co., 1935, esp. chapter 4: "The Failure of Nerve".

55. E.F. Osborn, *op.cit.*, pp.77f.

56. *2 Apology* 3,1,6.

57. The quotation is from Plato, *Republic* 10, 595C.

58. See the important article of Ernst Benz, "Christus und Sokrates in der alten Kirche" in *ZNW*, 54, 1950-51, pp.195-224

59. A.W.F. Blunt, *The Apologies of Justin Martyr*, Cambridge University Press, 1911, xiii.

60. Oskar Skarsaune, *op.cit.*, p.60. Skarsaune cites, in support, Hans von Campenhausen's concept of a contemporary "popular-philosophische Märtyrerideal", according to which "The Christian martyr who desires 'to enlighten the inner eye' of his judges appears in the role of Socrates and bases himself explicitly on this model." See Hans von Campenhausen, *Die Idee des Märtyriums in der alten Kirche*, Göttingen: Vandenhoeck und Ruprecht, 1936, p.153. The reference is to *The Martyrdom of Appollonius*, 44; See H. Musurillo, *Acts of the Martyrs* (Introduction, Texts and Translations), Oxford: Clarendon Press, 1972, pp.102-103.

61. Oskar Skarsaune, *op.cit.*, p.66.

62. See *1 Apology* 5,3; 46,3; *2 Apology* 3,6; 10,5,8.

63. Whilst Skarsaune *(op.cit.)* follows Benz *(op.cit.)* and draws attention to the importance of Socrates in Justin's outlook, he does not, in my view, stress sufficiently the fact that Justin is reflecting on Socrates self-consciously, as a Christian. I hope to show later that Socrates is more than a "conversion motif".

64. *Dialogue* 7,3.

65. On the common belief among Christians and others, see E.R. Dodds, *op.cit.*, esp. chapter 2: "Man and the Daemonic World", also p.177.

66. See M.P. Nilsson, *Greek Piety* (ET by H.J. Rose), Oxford: Clarendon Press, 1948, pp.170-175: "The Daemonisation of Religion".

67. T.R. Glover, *The Conflict of Religions in the Early Roman Empire* (8th ed), London: Methuen & Co., 1919, pp.75-112.

68. See Plutarch, *De Defectu Oraculorum* (9,414E) on the role of the deity in oracles: "If he [the god] allows himself to become entangled in men's needs, he is prodigal with his majesty (τῆς σεμνότητος) and he does not observe the dignity and greatness of his pre-eminence (τὸ μένεθος αὐτῷ τῆς ἀρετῆς)", in *Moralia* 5 *(LCL)*, pp.376-377.

69. See Plutarch, *De Iside et Osiride* (26,361C). "Plato calls this class of beings an 'interpretative and ministering class' (ἑρμενευτικὸν... γένος καὶ διακονικὸν) midway between gods and men (ἐν μέσῳ θεῶν καὶ ἀνθρώπων) in that they convey thither the prayers and petitions of men and thence they bring hither the oracles and the gifts of good things", in *Moralia* 5 *(LCL)*, pp.64-65. Cf. *De Defectu Oraculorum* (13,416E): "Those who refuse to leave us the race of demigods (δαιμόνων γένος) make the relation of gods and men remote and alien by doing away with the interpretative and ministering nature, as Plato has called it", in *Moralia* 5 *(LCL)*, pp.388-389. The reference is to Plato, *Republic*, 260D; *Symposium*, 202E.

70. T.R. Glover, *op.cit.*, p.110. Glover's concluding comments on Plutarch's religion are illuminating for the present study: "... every inherited and acquired instinct within him conspired to make him cling to tradition and authority as opposed to independent judgment. His philosophy was not Plato's, in spite of much

that he borrowed from Plato, for its motive was not the love of truth... He does not really wish to find truth on its own account, though he honestly would like its support... He cannot firmly say that anything with which religious feeling has ever been associated has ceased to be useful or has become false" (p.110).

71. See Werner Foerster, article "Δαίμων" in *TDNT*, 2, pp.1-20. Justin takes *Genesis* 6:2 to mean the "fall" of angels, see *2 Apology* 5,3.

72. Louis Duchesne, *Early History of the Christian Church (from its foundation to the end of the third century)* (ET of 4th ed), London: John Murray, 1920, pp.143-144. Heinrich Wey, *Die Funktionen der bösen Geister bei den griechischen Apologeten des zweiten Jahrhunderts nach Christus*, Winterthur: Verlag P.G. Keller, 1957, esp. pp.252-273, on comparison of Christian demonology with Hellenistic demonology.

73. One can get an idea of how dominant and pervasive the subject was by examining the number of times that words related to δαίμων are found in Justin's writing. Goodspeed, *Index Apologeticus*, lists no less than 85 such references. Oskar Skarsaune (*op.cit.*), has ably demonstrated the importance of the Christian demonology in Justin's definition of philosophy, which, he argues, is "to reveal the true nature of the demons (pretending to be gods) and to bring men to the only true God" (p.64). Whilst I appreciate Skarsaune's insights and I have made use of some of his ideas, my own contribution is to go further in expounding Justin's perception as it relates to the historical dimension of the problem of Christian (particularly Gentile) identity.

74. A casual reference to the old man later in the *Dialogue*, 23,3, which Skarsaune (*op.cit.*) cites as an indication that the old man of "meek and venerable manners" may, in point of fact, have been a person whom Justin had met and who, (like Pantaenus for Clement of Alexandria), "made him take the decisive step over to Christianity" (pp.70f).

75. See *1 Apology* 5,4.

76. Ibid., 5,3.

77. See Werner Foerster, *op.cit.*, p.18.

78. *Acts of the Apostles* 17:18.

79. Werner Foerster, *op.cit.*, p.19. Cf. F.F. Bruce, *The Acts of the Apostles (the Greek text with introduction and commentary)*, London: I.V.P., 1951, p.333.

80. See *1 Apology* 5,3; also *2 Apology* 10,5-6. Cf. Plato, *Apologia* 11, 24B: "... recognising the gods which the state recognises, and considering others to be new-fangled spirits."

81. *2 Apology* 10,6. Goodspeed (*Die ältesten Apologeten*, p.86) links Justin's text with *Acts of the Apostles* 17:23. See also, E. Benz, *op.cit.*, pp.206f. If, in fact, Paul's speech was in the context of an interrogation by the Areopagus Council to ascertain the acceptability or otherwise of Paul's teaching in Athens, then there is added poignancy to Justin's reference to Socrates; see Bertil Gärtner, *The Areopagus Speech and Natural Revelation*, Uppsala: C.W.K. Gleerup, 1955, pp.52-65.

82. A.W.F. Blunt, *op.cit.*, p.xiv.

83. See *2 Apology* 8,3; 13,3.

84. *1 Apology* 5,4.

85. Cf. Oskar Skarsaune, *op. cit.*, p. 65: "What is striking in Justin is not a supposedly 'philosophical' conception of Christianity, but a very unphilosophical conception of philosophy!"

86. *2 Apology* 10,1.

87. I follow R. Holte in taking σπερματικὸς Λόγος in an active sense, as implying "the Word who sows", on the analogy of the parable of the Sower, "who goes forth to sow". See R. Holte, "*Logos Spermatikos*: Christianity and ancient philosophy according to St Justin's *Apologies*", pp.109-168.

88. *1 Apology* 44,10.

89. Cf. *1 Apology* 10,2, where God's creation of the universe was for the sake of mankind (δι᾽ ἀνθρώπους).; also *2 Apology* 13,4, where Christ the Word is said to have become incarnate for our sakes (δι᾽ ἡμᾶς). Here may be happy anticipations of the later credal statement: "*who for us men and because of our salvation*, came down from heaven... and became human". See John H. Leith (ed), *The Creeds of the Churches: A Reader in Christian Doctrine from the Bible to the Present*, Richmond: John Knox Press, 1973, p.33.

90. See J.N.D. Kelly, *Early Christian Doctrines* (4th ed), London: A. & C. Black, 1968, pp.101-104; 145-149.

91. Cf. Henry Chadwick, "Justin's defence of Christianity", p.295.

92. See *Acts of the Apostles* 14:15-17; 17:22-31; *Epistle to the Romans* 1 & 2. Cf. "Is God the God of Jews only? Is he not the God of the Gentiles also? Yes, of the Gentiles also, since God is one" (*Romans* 3:29f).

93. Cf. Aimé Puech, *Les Apologistes grecs...*, p.147: "Justin was too honest and too sincere... not to be aware of the value of right intentions and not to recognise truth where it appeared to him. He was not resigned to thinking that almost the whole of humanity had one day quite recently been abandoned by God without remedy to ignorance and vice; he would not agree to shut his eyes to all that Platonism and Stoicism had produced in the way of noble ideas and generous acts... he regarded the exclusive spirit of Judaism with horror." Perhaps I may venture to add that Justin is less concerned with "Platonism" and "Stoicism" as such, than with evidences for his intuition in Hellenistic tradition as a whole and particularly in the lives of persons.

94. Henry Chadwick, "Justin's Defence of Christianity", p.294.

95. In this regard, an important passage is *1 Apology* 60,10. For all his admiration for what he considers are Platonic approximations of the Christian conception of the Cross and doctrine of the Trinity (see Plato, *Timaeus*, 36,B-C, Pseudo-Plato, *Epistle* 2, 312E), Justin declares: "It is not then that we hold the same opinions as others, but that all speak in imitation of ours (τὰ ἡμέτερα μιμούμενοι λέγουσι), cf. *2 Apology* 13,2. Justin has clearly perceived that Christian views are not derived from philosophical ones, nor identical with them.

96. A.W.F. Blunt, *op.cit.*, p.xiv.

97. Modern "theologians of liberation" have brought to the forefront concerns with concrete actions as the major task of theology. Cf. comment by Gustavo Gutierrez, *A Theology of Liberation, History, Politics and Salvation* (ET by Sister Caridad Inda and John Eagleson), London: S.C.M., 1974 (original 1971), p.6: "The function of theology as critical reflection on praxis has gradually become more clearly defined in recent years, but it has its roots in the first centuries of the Church's life."

98. Carl Andresen, *op.cit.*, p.170: "Justin understands the *Logos spermatikos* not as world spirit in the sense of the cosmological pantheism of the Stoa but as an intellectual-ethical principle." Andresen recognises, of course, a "cosmological" significance (*Bedeutung*) of the Word for Justin, in that the Word has a part in the creation of the world, and that He is active in non-Christian tradition (*Heidentum*) as he is, generally, in the world (p.174).

99. See Cicero, *De Finibus Bonorum et Malorum*, 4,7,17-18 (*LCL*, pp.317-321).

Cicero draws upon the views of the contemporary head of the Academy of Plato, Antiochus of Askalon. See "Antiochos von Askalon" in *PW*, 1/2, coll.2493-4.

100. Carl Andresen, *op.cit.*, pp.172ff.

101. Andresen points to instances in Origen who also held this view on the "seeds of virtue" in human nature. See *Contra Celsum* 4,25. Answering Celsus' insult that Christians are comparable to "a cluster of bats, or ants, or frogs or worms", Origen writes: "Whatever is the nature of the rational being, it would not be reasonable to compare it to a worm, since it possesses tendencies towards virtue. These general inclinations towards virtue prohibit us from comparing with a worm those who potentially possess virtue, and who cannot entirely destroy its seeds" (H. Chadwick's translation, p.201).

102. L.W. Barnard, *op.cit.*, pp.98f; cf. Jean Daniélou, *op.cit.*, pp.43.

103. Carl Andresen, *op.cit.*, pp.181ff.

104. L.W. Barnard, *op.cit.*, p.91.

105. Ragnar Holte, "*Logos Spermatikos*: Christianity and ancient philosophy according to St Justin's *Apologies*", pp.109-168.

106. *Ibid.*, p.145. Holte also makes a strong case for Justin's "unreserved attachment to the Christian doctrinal position" (pp.111ff).

107. *Ibid.*, p.146.

108. *Ibid.*, p.147.

109. *Ibid.*, p.128. This view is accepted by Henry Chadwick, "Justin Martyr's defence of Christianity", pp.294-295, n.11.

110. E.F. Osborn, *op.cit.*, p.38.

111. Aimé Puech, *Les Apologistes grecs*.., argues for a direct dependence on the *Gospel of John:* "For the doctrine of the Word in particular, they (the Apologists) could not have expounded and developed it without the aid of philosophy; but they found it in the Prologue to the Fourth Gospel... it is highly doubtful whether any of them would have dared to take such a bold initiative on his own."

112. See *2 Apology* 8,3; 10,1-3.

113. L.W. Barnard, *op.cit.,* p.99.

114. See J. Lebreton, *Histoire du dogme de la Trinité des origines au concile de Nicée*, Paris: Beauchesne et Cie, 1928, p.434. Cf. L.W. Barnard, *op.cit.*, p.170: "Justin, the philosopher, was not conscious that he was grafting on to the biblical basis of Christianity a philosophical interpretation which was bound to modify it – even in essentials... The heart of Christianity, for Justin, was God's care and love for man revealed in the Bible and supremely in Jesus Christ. It places him in the mainstream of the Christian tradition and not on the outskirts as one who grievously distorted the Christian kerygma by his excursions into philosophy."

115. The statement is reproduced by Eusebius, *HE*, 4, 18 (*PG* 20, 376C).

116. Irenaeus, *Adversus Haereses*, 5, 26,2 (*PG* 7, 1194C-1195A).

117. See for instance, *1 Apology* 26 & 56.

118. *1 Apology* 46,2.

119. E.F. Osborn, *op.cit.,* p.42.

120. A.F. Walls, "First Chapter of the Epistle to the Romans and the Modern Missionary Movement", in W. Gasque and R.P. Martin (eds), *Apostolic History and the Gospel*, Exeter: Paternoster Press, 1970, pp.346- 357.

121. See *1 Apology* 46,3; cf. *2 Apology* 8,1.

122. *2 Apology* 13,5.

123. Jean Daniélou, *Gospel Message and Hellenistic Culture*, p.44; cf. Ragnar Holte, *op. cit.*, p.147.

124. *1 Apology* 46,3; cf. *2 Apology* 10.

125. *2 Apology* 8,2-3.

126. *1 Apology* 60,11; *2 Apology* 13,6.

127. See above, chapter two: "The Gospel as the Triumph of Barbarism? (1): Tatian, or the Vindication of the Barbarians against the Greeks".

128. See *1 Apology* 59,1-5.

129. Plato, *Timaeus*, 32 B-C.

130. See *1 Apology* 60,1ff. The Old Testament reference is generally taken to be *Numbers* 21:5ff; see A.W.F. Blunt, *op.cit.*, p.88, n.12.

131. The Platonic source Justin appeals to is Pseudo-Plato, *Epistle* 2, 32E.

132. See *1 Apology* 44,8; 59,1.

133. Henry Chadwick, *Early Christian Thought and the Classical Tradition*, p.15.

134. *1 Apology* 20,3.

135. Cf. Jean Daniélou, *op.cit.*, p.44.

136. *1 Apology* 20,4-5.

137. *Ibid.* , 44,9-10.

138. See E.R. Hardy's translation in *LCL* 1, p.270: "...since they contradict each other."

139. Cf. *2 Apology* 7,3, where he makes a similar criticism. Cf. Carl Andresen, *op.cit.*, pp.183ff, though Andresen also interprets Justin's statement (*1 Apology* 44,10) to mean the mutual contradictions between various thinkers: "When Justin attributes the mutual contradictions among philosophers and poets..." (p.170).

140. My own translation of the passage at this point is on the basis that the indirect object is to be understood in a reflexive sense. See usage in *LSJ* (on the reflexive sense of ἑαυτοῦ), p.466.

141. For a discussion of the distinction between "sharing in" and "possessing" in Justin's thinking and its Middle Platonist terms of reference, see R.A. Norris, *God and World in Early Christian Theology. A study in Justin Martyr, Irenaeus, Tertullian and Origen*. London: A. & C. Black, 1965, p.43. See also, E.F. Osborn, *op.cit.*, pp.38f. Cf. Jean Daniélou, *op.cit.*, p.44: "the thought of the philosophers was no more than a seed. The word seed... automatically implies the expression 'partial' which Justin also uses".

142. *2 Apology* 10,2f.

143. W.A. Shotwell, *The Biblical Exegesis of Justin Martyr*, London: S.P.C.K., 1965, pp.8ff.

144. *2 Apology* 13,2-6.

145. Cf. *Dialogue* 1,3f; 2,6.

146. R.A. Norris, *op.cit.*, p.45.

147. *Ibid.*, p.44: "Justin is not saying that to read the philosophers is to know Christ. He is saying that to know Christ is to be able to dispense with philosophy."

148. On this statement, E.F. Osborn, *op.cit.*, comments: "... grace plays always the decisive role and can alone lead to participation in the Logos himself" (pp.39f).

For my interpretation of *2 Apology* 13,2-6, I am indebted to Osborn's discussion of the significant distinctions between μίμημα and μίμησις and the Platonic concept of participation μέθεξις (pp.38ff).

149. Jean Daniélou, *op.cit.*, p.44. It is doubtful, therefore, whether Ragnar Holte (*op.cit.*, p.151) is right to speak of Justin contrasting "natural revelation" with "Christian revelation".

150. Henry Chadwick, *Early Christian Thought and the Classical Tradition*, p.30.

151. Cf. R.A. Norris, *op.cit.*, pp.10-12,34.

152. H. Diels & W. Kranz (eds), *Die Fragmente der Vorsokratiker*, vol. 1 (5th ed), Berlin: Weidmannsche Buchhandlung, 1934-37. I have made use of the English translation of the fragments in Kathleen Freeman, *Ancilla of the Pre-Socratic Philosophers* (A Complete Translation of the Fragments in Diels' *Fragmente der Vorsokratiker*), Oxford: Basil Blackwell, 1952, p.22.

153. Kathleen Freeman, *op.cit.*, p.23.

154. R.A. Norris, *op.cit.*, p.11.

155. Cf. Gilbert Murray, *Five Stages of Greek Religion*, p.126: "A religious belief that is morally contemptible is in serious danger."

156. *Ibid.*, pp.1-38.

157. M.P. Nilsson, *The History of Greek Religion* (ET by F.J. Fielden, with preface by J.G. Frazer), Oxford: Clarendon Press, 1925, pp.178f. Cf. W.K.C. Guthrie, *A History of Greek Philosophy* (vol.3, *The Fifth Century Enlightenment*), Cambridge University Press, 1969, p.228: "Criticism of the gods on moral grounds came early. It needed no scientific speculation nor logical subtlety to be scandalised by Zeus' castration of his father or his many amours, the thefts and deceits of Hermes, or the jealousy of Hera and the malicious and vengeful character of the immortals in general."

158. E. Zeller, *A History of Greek Philosophy: From the earliest period to the time of Socrates*, vol.2 (ET by S.F. Alleine), London: Longmans, Green and Co., 1881, p.483. See also, W.K.C. Guthrie, *op.cit.*, esp. chapter 9: "Rationalistic theories of religion: Agnosticism and Atheism".

159. W.K.C. Guthrie, *op.cit.*, p.246.

160. Cf. A.-J. Festugière, *Personal Religion among the Greeks*, Berkeley: University of California Press, 1954, p.49: "God exists, but there is no longer any question of the Olympians. Plato does not suppress them. Indeed he suppresses nothing that was part of the religion of his forebears. But... he speaks of them with disdain. God exists, and he is the Soul of the Cosmos."

161. *2 Apology* 10,6. Cf. Plato, *Republic* 2, 377; 10, 595.

162. R.A. Norris, *op.cit.*, p.11.

163. Cf. Paul Wendland, *Die hellenistisch-römische Kultur in ihren Beziehungen zu Judentum und Christentum*, Tübingen, 1907, p.159 (= p.404 in 1912 edition, Tübingen: J.C.B. Mohr), quoted in Jaroslav Pelikan, *The Emergence of the Catholic Tradition (AD 100-600), (The Christian Tradition: A history of the development of doctrine*, vol.1), Chicago: University of Chicago Press, 1971, p.46: "They [the Christian Apologists] claim to be fighting for the new faith against the old world; in fact they are partly continuing the battle of intellectual currents which were already at war in the ancient world, only adding to them some new issues and weapons."

164. Cf. G. Bardy, article "St. Justin" in *DTC*, vol.8, coll. 2274f: "he [Justin] is happy that he can show when the need arises the agreement between ancient

wisdom and the teaching of Christ. But he never tries to place the Gospel in a framework which was not intended for it, nor to bring down the doctrine of the Word to fit into human systems. If he likes to demonstrate the action of the Word in the whole of humanity... this is because he is generous enough to desire the salvation of all men." See also, H. Chadwick, *Early Christian Thought and the Classical Tradition*, pp.21-22, and L.W. Barnard, *op.cit.*, pp.169f.

165. E.R. Goodenough, *op.cit.*, pp.105-106. My emphasis.

166. Justin's interest in the "Jewish" question is found particularly in the *Dialogue with Trypho*, and appears much less in the *Apologies*, which are largely concerned with the "Gentile" dimension of the vindication of Christian identity. Since we are dealing, in the main, with the "Gentile" question, it is the *Apologies* that have provided most of the material for this study.

167. Ernst Benz, *op.cit.*, p.200.

168. Oskar Skarsaune, *op.cit.*, pp.64f.

169. Bishop Kenneth Cragg has well observed on the Gospel preaching in the *Acts of the Apostles*, and particularly by St Paul: "Accidents of birth, race or culture do not now obtain in what is a personal discovery of a new sort of collective recruited by the common energies of grace and the common denominator of faith". See Kenneth Cragg, *Christianity in World Perspective*, London: Lutterworth Press, 1968, p.48.

170. Cf. Oskar Skarsaune, *op.cit.*, p.64: "The true philosopher is a potential martyr, a potential Socrates."

171. *1 Apology* 46,3; *2 Apology* 8,1.

172. *1 Apology* 54,1.

173. *Ibid.*, 54,2-4.

174. *Ibid.*, 54,5-6; *ibid.*, 22, entire.

175. *Ibid.*, 21,4-6.

176. *Ibid.*, 5,2.

177. Cf. E.F. Osborn, *op.cit.*, p.61: "Demons are the enemies of the logos and wherever they see his influence they attack."

178. Cf. Jean Daniélou, *op.cit.*, p.44: "When Justin writes that Socrates and Heraclitus lived in accordance with the Λόγος, he does not mean in accordance with reason, but in accordance with the Word."

179. *1 Apology* 46,3-4.

180. *Ibid.*, 5,3.

181. *2 Apology* 7,3. It is interesting that Justin does not criticise Epicurus for his "atheism", but rather for his "hedonism". For the view that Justin's treatment of Sardanapalus and Epicurus unites Hellenistic and Christian motifs, see Ernst Benz, *op.cit.*, pp.204ff. "Evidently Sardanapalus and Epicurus belonged to the traditional types of behaviour and attitude in which the early Church saw their demonic counterpart." (p.206)

182. Jean Daniélou, *op.cit.*, p.44.

183. Oskar Skarsaune, *op.cit.*, p.65.

184. This view of Heraclitus was also held by Athenagoras; see his *Legatio*, 31, (Migne, *PG* 6, 961C).

185. See *Daniel* 3.

186. See *1 Kings* 18-19 (LXX, *3 Kings* 18-19).

187. See *2 Apology* 8,1.

188. A.W.F. Blunt, *op.cit.*, p.116,n.11.

189. *2 Apology* 8,2.

190. See Otto, *op.cit.*, p.189, n.3, for a reference to Suidas who held *(narrat)* that Musonius, on account of his outspokenness, his critical outlook and his high sense of personal freedom, *a Nerone interfectum*. On Musonius, see *PW* 16, pp.893-897.

191. Tacitus, *Annals* 14, 59. Cf. *1 Apology* 46,4: "... those who lived according to the Word (μετὰ λόγου), and those who so live now, are Christians, fearless and unperturbed (καὶ ἄφοβοι καὶ ἀτάραχοι)."

192. Tacitus, *Annals* 15, 71. It is interesting that Epictetus who, originally a slave, became a great Stoic teacher himself, was a pupil of Musonius.

193. Ernst Benz, *op.cit.*, p.203.

194. *Ibid.*, p.203.

195. J.N.D. Kelly, *op.cit.*, p.90.

196. Karl Semisch, *op.cit.*, p.51.

197. See *1 Apology* 53,5.

198. *Dialogue* 123,9.

199. Cf. *Dialogue* 11,5: "For we are the true and spiritual Israelitish nation, and the race of Judah and of Jacob and Isaac and Abraham...we I say, are all this, who were brought nigh to God by Him who was crucified, even Christ..." There is no more exultant declaration of Justin's understanding of Christian identity in the *Dialogue*, and the thought is resorted to often enough (cf.119,5-6), to suggest that it was, probably, meant to strengthen the confidence of Gentile Christians. It is hardly surprising that Trypho should ask: "Are you Israel?" (123,7).

200. See, for instance, *1 Apology* 10,1-2 for a remarkable testimony to Justin's clear insistence on deriving his theological understanding from Christian tradition: "We have learned (received) (προσειλήφαμεν).. we have been taught and are convinced and believe (δεδιδάμεθα καὶ πεπείγεθα καὶ πιστεύομεν)... we have also been taught (δεδισάμεθα)... we have learned (received) (προσειλήφαμεν)."

201. Cf. A. von Harnack, *The History of Dogma*, vol.2, pp.170-175. "Viewed superficially, the Apologists were no doubt the conservatives; but they were so, because they scarcely in any respect meddled with the contents of tradition" (p.173).

202. See *1 Apology* 32, 104; Justin refers to *Genesis* 49:10-11. Cf. *Dialogue* 11,4; 52,2,4; 120,3,5.

203. Cf. *Dialogue* 29,1: "Let all of us Gentiles come together and glorify God, because he has looked down upon us; let us glorify Him by the King of Glory, by the Lord of Hosts. For he hath taken pleasure even in the nations, and He receives the sacrifices more gladly from us than from you [Jews]." (A. Lukyn Williams' translation)

204. It is an interesting indication of Justin's association of unbelief with Jews that in one of the fragments, *On the Resurrection* (now regarded as genuine), he blames the corruption of Christian doctrine primarily on Jews: "Because the prince of wickedness could in no other way corrupt the truth [i.e. concerning the doctrine of the Resurrection] he sent forth his apostles (evil men who introduced pestilent doctrines) choosing them from among those who crucified our Saviour; these men bore the name of the Saviour, but did the works of him that sent them, and on account of these persons the name itself [i.e. of the Saviour] has been spoken against". Greek text in Otto, *CACSS* (tomus 2, vol.3), p.244. Otto refers to similar sentiments expressed by Justin in *Dialogue* 35,2, and he comments: "It is obvious from our passage that most of these men were Jews, or at least Samaritans."

(*ibid.*, n.13). On Justin's final idea, cf. *Paul's Epistle to the Romans* 2:24. On the authenticity of the fragments, see P. Prigent, *op.cit.*, pp.50-61; cf. E.F. Osborn, *op.cit.*, p.146.

205. R.A. Norris, *op.cit.*, p.44.

206. See *Dialogue* 29,2. Justin insists, to Trypho's evident discomfiture, that the prophecies concerning Christ "are laid up in your Scriptures, or rather not in yours but in ours, for we obey them, but you [Jews], when you read, you do not understand their sense."

207. Eusebius, *HE* 1,4,6 (Migne, *PG* 20, 77C). Cf. *1 Apology* 46, 3ff.

208. Hans von Campenhausen, *The Fathers of the Greek Church*, p.15.

Chapter Five

Christ and the Hellenistic Heritage (2): Clement of Alexandria; or, Christ as the Unifying Principle of all Knowledge

I. Alexandria and the making of Clement the Scholar

Jerome's description of Alexandria is as a centre of Christian learning from the earliest period of its Christian history,[1] and this provides a fitting point of departure for approaching the career and achievement of Clement of Alexandria. For though it is generally agreed that his birthplace was Athens,[2] it was in the Egyptian city which had become a major centre of intellectual activity in the Graeco-Roman world, that Titus Flavius Clemens – to give his full name – found "his appropriate sphere of labour".[3] Here Clement, who portrays himself in his *Stromateis*[4] as a wandering student in quest of knowledge, finally "found rest" in the teaching of his Alexandrian master, Pantaenus,[5] settled, and through his teaching and writing made his contribution to Christian theology as a master in his own right. There is a certain inevitability in the fact that the work of "the first great Christian scholar"[6] is associated with the great cultural and intellectual centre of Alexandria,[7] but Clement's own interests and concerns also contributed greatly to effect a shift in the Christian centre of gravity to Alexandria for a century or more.[8] There is no certainty regarding the identity of the earlier teachers of Clement; but it is significant that those to whom he pays tribute in the passage in the *Stromateis* – "blessed and truly remarkable men" – were all Christians.[9] Accordingly, the Clement we know is the "converted Clement".[10] Clement's known intellectual biography situates him firmly, therefore, in the developing history of Christian thought, and this gives added significance to the particular emphases exemplified in his work.

That Clement, converted and a fully convinced Christian, should search out, starting from his native Greece, notable Christian teachers wherever they may be found, is an indication of his attitude of mind to the task of Christian theology. Tollinton has given a suggestive sketch of the kind of cultural and intellectual furniture that Clement would have brought with him from the Greek environment of his pre-Christian past.[11] This comprised not only training in the "encyclical subjects" – music, geometry, grammar, rhetoric, astronomy – but also his high estimation of the value of philosophy, his evident love of Greek literature, his understanding of religion as the gradual training of a person's best nature, and his view of salvation as the divine education of humanity. Thus Clement bore within him some of those essential ingredients which André-Jean Festugière summed up under the term "the Greek ideal".[12]

However, for all his unmistakeable Hellenism,[13] Clement also exemplifies to a remarkable degree, the freshness and the moral and spiritual dynamic of the Christian Gospel in its own terms as light and truth.[14] If there are in Clement's writings the combinations of Greek philosophical ideas with Christian doctrines, it is because Clement is able, through his Christian understanding, to see affinities between the various positions which he seeks to harmonise.[15] Thus, while it is true that he remains Hellenic "in every fibre of his nature",[16] it is conceivable that his intellectual career, as we know it, would have been still-born had he not become a Christian. A.-J. Festugière[17] has sought to show that part of the explanation for the phenomenal expansion of the Christian movement in the Graeco-Roman world lies in the fact that the Christian proclamation of salvation through Christ met the religious aspirations for deliverance in Hellenistic tradition – deliverance from the weight of the misery of the human condition, from the tragic sense of life which was intensely portrayed in the dramatic literature, from fate and the inflexible decrees of the old gods, as well as from the uncertainties of philosophical opinions.[18] If this argument is accepted,[19] then it is evident that we cannot adequately understand Clement, or any of the early Christian writers like him, unless we give due place to the significance of such a "deliverance" in his experience. Clement's entire outlook argues in favour of the observation that "the Greek soul felt the need for the light and power which it was to find in the Gospel but which it was powerless to formulate".[20] Clement's first major work, the *Protreptikos*, is essentially one sustained exhortation to his fellow educated Greeks to be willing to make the same discovery that he had himself come upon in his acceptance of the Christian message.

It is not surprising, therefore, that Clement has been described as one who was "above all things a missionary",[21] deeply concerned to win adherence to the way of life and mode of thought which he had embraced with his whole being, and particularly anxious to demonstrate that the Christian Gospel was, in fact, no alien phenomenon to the Hellenistic tradition in which he and his audience stood. The whole of Clement's career as a Christian doctor and apologist[22] can be summed up under this one guiding principle: to demonstrate the relevance and the significance of the Christian Gospel to the quests and aspirations – religious, philosophical, intellectual and ethical – in Hellenistic tradition, as indeed in all human history.

Accordingly, it is quite probable that Clement's decision to set off in search of Christian teachers was prompted predominantly by what we may describe as "methodological" considerations. In other words, equipped with the literary and philosophical training of his cultural background, and committed to the Christian message in which he had come to believe, Clement then felt the need for the kind of intellectual framework and theological understanding which together would enable him to elaborate a theory of redemption consistent with both the inner meanings he discerned in the religious and philosophical speculations of Hellenistic tradition, and the universalist claims of the Christian Gospel. But it would be misleading to see Clement as seeking here primarily an abstract intellectual construct – though he does engage in a certain amount of intellectual speculation, especially in the *Stromateis*.[23] There is a more abiding emphasis in Clement which can be missed when his intellectual interests are interpreted solely in terms of the quest for esoteric knowledge.[24] This emphasis consists in a continual effort to clarify and to elaborate a conception of the religious history of mankind that at once ensures the meaningfulness of all genuine quests for God and truth, and also secures the universal significance of the Christian revelation, particularly the centrality of the Incarnation of the Logos, Christ, the Saviour of all humanity. As Claude Mondésert has observed:

> "His method is based primarily on a religious history of humanity where the successive steps of God's divine pity become apparent. The Creator of all things reveals himself gradually to men and thus leads them to that unique and marvellous manifestation of the Logos, the only Son of the

Father, come down in flesh to be Master and Model, the Saviour of mankind."[25]

There is little doubt that the methodological tools for elaborating this account of the religious history of humanity were among the riches that Clement culled from the teaching of Pantaenus, himself a convert from Stoicism. Although it is not possible to establish the content of the curriculum of studies given by Pantaenus,[26] it is a fair assumption that the method and content of instruction as practised by Origen in Caesarea,[27] (after he had moved from Alexandria), are a reliable guide to the Alexandrine practice in the late second century.[28] In a letter of Origen's preserved by Eusebius, Origen justifies his method of examining the views of various philosophers on theological questions by appealing to the example of "Pantaenus, who benefited many people before our time by his thorough preparation in such things".[29] From Origen's testimony, the description by Eusebius of Pantaenus' varied abilities,[30] as well as Clement's own profound admiration for his teacher and for his instruction,[31] there is every indication that there was at Alexandria an orthodox tradition and a context which exemplified the sort of comprehensive synthesis that Clement was seeking.[32] Pantaenus must have been for Clement an embodiment of such a reality.[33] The basic thrust of this "Alexandrine tradition" of Christian theological scholarship[34] is aptly described by a modern historian of the Church:

"This teaching... is not exclusively religious; nor is it simply an apologetic preparation as was Justin's teaching in Rome; it is an encyclopaedic teaching, presenting first the entire range of profane learning, rising from there to religious and moral philosophy, and finally to Christian theology, set out in the form of a commentary on sacred books. This encyclopaedic concept of teaching was an Alexandrian tradition; ... it ensured the continuity of intellectual education, ensured in its entirety by the same master and leading through all disciplines, human and divine, to the one goal: the knowledge of God."[35]

Thus in the "school" of Pantaenus,[36] Clement found a ready welcome for his deep intuitions; but it is probable also that he there acquired some of the skills and insights which enabled him to make his own distinctive contribution to Christian thinking on the problem of harmonising the religious, ethical and intellectual forces inherent in Hellenistic tradition with the claims of Christian universalism.[37]

II. "The discovery of the appropriate framework": Clement and the task of Christian scholarship

It is evident that in bringing to his Christian career the interests and concerns we have noted above, Clement was following in
the trail of Justin.[38] However, whereas the great Christian
"philosopher and martyr" does little more than suggest hints and
leave us with his intuitions regarding the comprehensive nature
of the Christian Gospel, Clement, equipped with considerably
greater erudition, and also perhaps a keener Hellenic self-consciousness, is able to go much farther in validating the outlook that
they had in common; namely, that no worthy moral insight, intellectual achievement, or religious thought in Hellenistic tradition
lay outside of the activity and impulse of the divine Logos, Christ.[39]
Justin, writing a generation before Clement's time, had argued the
case essentially in its apologetic dimensions, in an attempt to
secure a hearing for the Christian message in a cultural context
that was hostile to it from a specifically religious, as well as a
generally ideological standpoint. By Clement's time, towards the
close of the second century,[40] the Christian Church had become "a
definite and recognised reality"[41] in the Graeco-Roman world, even
if it remained officially a *religio illicita*. The apologetic task aimed
at validating the Church's right and title to exist was accomplished. The expansion of Christianity was a fact;[42] now pres-
sures of a different sort exerted themselves upon the Church,
concerning her own life, mission and self-definition – in relation to
the wider world. In the words of Tollinton, "a more constructive
era is opening".[43]

In connection with this new "era", it is significant that, unlike
Justin and Tertullian, Clement does not seem to have written a
book against Jews. In the impressive list of Clement's writings,
given by Eusebius,[44] only one could be said to have dealt specifically
with the Jewish question. However, this work, the *Ecclesiastical
Canon*, was directed not against Jews, but as its subtitle indicates,
"against Judaisers", that is, Judaising Christians. In the view of
Theodor Zahn, Clement would have represented in this work the
ecclesiastical or "Catholic" position on some ritual practices and
observances, against tendencies towards Ebionitism.[45] This is not
improbable, and Clement's high estimation of the *Epistle of Barnabas*,[46] for instance – quite apart from his own viewpoints – shows
that he shared the attitude of the Christians of Graeco-Roman
culture who took the Old Testament to be essentially a Christian
book, and did not feel any need to apologise for doing so. If Walter

Bauer is right in suggesting that in Egypt, at the beginning of the second century, there existed Gentile Christians and Jewish Christians who were "not... united in a single community",[47] it is evident, nonetheless, which group had gained ascendency by Clement's time. Christianity had now attained "its complete independence from Judaism",[48] and for a Christian teacher, particularly in Alexandria, the theological task no longer included the necessity of facing up to the challenge of Judaism.[49] Clement is a notable witness to the fact that there had now emerged a Gentile Christian consciousness which was self-confident and free, and aware of no threat to its Christian identity, "for everything that was best in the world pointed to Christianity and found a home in the Church".[50] With Clement, the apologetic hints and intuitions which we have noted in Justin Martyr become the justification for the actual task of integrating all the scattered fragments of the eternal truth – in both barbarian and Hellenistic traditions – into that unity of the whole Truth inherent only in "the theology imparted by the ever-living Word".[51]

In order to execute his task, Clement needed an intellectual framework which had not hitherto been elaborated in the Christian community. Eugène de Faye may have gone too far in claiming that Clement "is the true creator of ecclesiastic theology";[52] in Irenaeus' five-volume *Adversus Haereses*, we see already the outlines of a coherent *théologie ecclesiastique*.[53] Yet it is a fact that the Christian literature of the second century had been mainly apologetic and anti-heretical, and had not gone far in formulating Christian beliefs in relation to each other, and especially in relation to alternative intellectual viewpoints represented by the philosophical tradition of Graeco-Roman culture. It was Clement's merit to have been the first to see the importance of providing such a theological construction.[54] Thus, Wilhelm Bousset's observation is apposite:

> "With Clement begins the history of really great Christian literature. Anything in the way of Christian writing which precedes him can be regarded more or less as occasional literature."[55]

Clement's great intellectual achievement in the development of early Christian literature is usually associated more closely with the *Stromateis* than with either of his two other major extant writings, the *Protreptikos* or the *Paidogogos*.[56] This view of Clement's work is based not only on the form and content of the *Stromateis*, with their evident heightened intellectual interest, but also on the fact that Clement therein[57] justifies to his Christian readers,[58] his decision to compose a work devoted specifically to the exposition of his more advanced ideas on how the intellectual treasures of Hellenistic tradition might be incorporated into the Christian understanding of reality. This view is a plausible one, since "he makes no such apology in the *Protreptikos,* or in the *Paidagogos,* and it could hardly be the reception of these works that inspired his defense".[59] However, if the real departure and innovation was "the scale and character of Clement's purpose,[60] it can be argued that these concerns are found also in the earlier works.[61]

In the *Protreptikos,* Clement states what the coming of Christ, and with Him the Christian revelation, has meant for the world; and Clement expresses himself in terms which already point to the concerns which the *Stromateis* will raise:

> "wherefore, since the Word Himself has come to us from heaven, we need not, I reckon, go any more in search of human learning to Athens and the rest of Greece, and to Ionia. For if our teacher is the One who has filled the universe with his holy energies in creation, salvation, beneficence, legislation, prophecy, teaching, we have the Teacher from whom all instruction comes; and the whole universe has already become an Athens and a Greece through the Word."[62]

In one bold stroke Clement concludes that the Christian account of reality, in cosmology and redemption, as in social teaching and ethics, supersedes the entire history of intellectual and philosophical speculation in Hellenistic tradition. But for Clement the Christian revelation achieves this feat, not by opposing Hellenistic tradition, but rather by absorbing it. The coming of the heavenly Word, and the account of divinity (*theologia*)[63] available through Him, have taken away from the Greek philosophical tradition any claim and pretension to finality; but the Word's coming has also made the universe into "one universal Hellas, one comprehensive Athens".[64]

It is evident that Clement understood the Christian Gospel in terms of the essential quest of the Hellenistic philosophical and intellectual tradition; namely, the quest for an account of reality – of God, man and the world – which was instinct with reason, coherent with experience, and consistent with the chief end of life, godliness.[65] The Christian Gospel for Clement represents the sum of that "really true wisdom which the most eminent of philosophers only managed to guess at" but which "the disciples of Christ grasped and proclaimed".[66] In so far as the Christian proclamation gives not only this comprehensive account of reality, but also the means of realising the chief end of life, godliness, through the transforming Holy Spirit of God,[67] it outstrips philosophy. Philosophy is a lengthy deliberation which pursues a never-ending love of wisdom,[68] and so, by implication, it offers no certainty or firm foundation for intellectual conviction. In contrast to the unresolved questions of philosophical speculation, the Christian Gospel offers a more satisfying intellectual framework for understanding the universe, and man, and man's relation to God. This seems to be Clement's understanding of St Paul's expression "the new creation".[69] In other words, the Christian Gospel has introduced into the world an entirely new and coherent way of understanding ourselves, and has provided a more satisfying focus for human existence with the specific goal of a heavenly life – the ultimate stage in our salvation and redemption.

The fact that the passage we have been discussing occurs in the *Protreptikos* is significant. For it indicates that Clement's interest in "a comprehensive synthesis of all that is of worth as arising from the one source of truth",[70] covered his entire Christian literary career. It is curious therefore that Tollinton, who in an evident reference to this passage in the *Protreptikos*, speaks of Clement's "fundamental Hellenism",[71] should single out the *Stromateis* as alone exemplifying what he calls the fusion of "the Christian spirit with elements that had origin elsewhere".[72] In our view, Wilhelm Bousset is right to include all three major writings in his assessment of the innovative character and purpose of Clement's work:

"With Clement's [*Protreptikos*], *Paidagogos* and *Stromateis* we enter the field of real literature for the first time; a literature which bears its purpose within itself and exists for its own sake, which consciously sets itself the task of embracing and presenting Christian life as a whole.."[73]

However, Bousset's observation can be modified; it is doubtful whether one can seriously maintain that Clement's writing "exists for its own sake". Henry Chadwick has argued that "the chief problem confronting Clement was a pastoral one"; namely, how to mark decisively the distinction between heresy and orthodoxy without surrendering to the anti-intellectualism of the mass of Christians in Alexandria.[74]

But an even more compelling motivation arising from Clement's own self-consciousness, can be isolated. The deliverance[75] which the Christian Gospel effected within Clement was pre-eminently an intellectual one. Through the Gospel, the universe became, for Clement, "sleepless light".[76] He believed that he had found the answer to the quest which, long before his time, set philosophers and thoughtful men on the path of an intellectual and moral criticism of the old gods and the "traditional" religion – namely, the quest for a truly noble and rational account of what the Divine really is.[77] His method of exhorting his fellow educated Greeks to embrace the Christian faith[78] clearly shows that he also identified with that tradition of criticism. Accordingly, Clement's concern to integrate into his Christian commitment his sympathies with Hellenistic tradition answered to a profound urge within him. When Clement eventually defends the view that the Hellenistic philosophical and intellectual tradition is virtually on a level with the Old Testament revelation, as preparatory training (*propaideia*)[79] for the Christian era in the Graeco-Roman world, it is quite clear that he is expressing a conviction which "had its origin and counterpart in his own intellectual and spiritual development."[80]

The fact that Clement would be prepared to argue that prior to the Incarnation, the "dawn of light", all knowledge and experience of the divine disclosure of truth – in Barbarian (i.e. Jewish) no less than in Hellenistic tradition – amounted to mere portions of the truth,[81] indicates how far Clement was willing to go to avoid the suggestion that for the Christian Gospel to be at home in Hellenistic tradition that tradition had to be "barbarised".[82] If the validity of the Christian faith was to be seen in terms of the needs and aspirations of Hellenistic tradition, then, according to Clement, there had to be a "wider framework", the appropriate framework within which a convincing demonstration of the faith[83] could be given. It is Clement's firm conviction that the Christian faith is "the account of the really true philosophy",[84] and so it ought to be capable of a coherent and cogent intellectual defence. Even though, as we have noted, the outworking of this fundamental intuition is evident early in Clement's Christian literary career, it is in the *Stromateis* that he develops extensively the theoretical justification for this deeply-held conviction that the highest moral, religious and intellectual insights in Hellenistic tradition, especially in philosophy, were compatible with the Christian Gospel.[85]

A close examination of the first chapter of *Stromateis* (Book 1) reveals the salient points in Clement's entire argumentation. It is only to be expected that Clement, reflecting within the terms of his Greek background and education, should be especially drawn to

suggestions confirming his intuitions with regard to that particular cultural tradition.[86] But the fact that Clement defends his
thesis so forcefully in the interest of a specific endeavour in
Christian scholarship, also shows how deeply he must have
thought about the problem. Clement is convinced that the more
profound intellectual apprehension of Christian truth which lies
beyond the simple faith of the new convert or simple believer, is
integral to the total impact of the divine Word upon men. For such
understanding has one source, the one and same Word, working
"by divine providence". The divine activity produces, and leads the
person so encountered through grades of transformation, all of
which are integral to salvation, described as a process:

> "the beginning of faith, readiness for adopting a right mode of
> life, the impulse towards the truth, a movement of enquiry, a
> trace of knowledge, in short, the means of salvation."[87]

Clement insists, therefore, that the most profound intellectual
apprehension, namely, the contemplation of God, is granted only
to those who respond in faith to the Word, and follow His instruction on the way of eternal life.[88] This primacy of faith in the Word
is essential for Clement and he returns to the idea very often
throughout the *Stromateis*.[89] In this first chapter of the book, the
importance of the principle is underscored by Clement's reference
to *Isaiah* 7:9, which in the LXX reads: "If you do not believe, neither
will you understand".[90] Thus, faith becomes not only the basis for
every apprehension of God and necessary condition for the life of
the enlightened Christian, but also the grounds on which any form
of knowledge at all can be gained.[91]

But Clement's insistence on faith as an "epistemological" principle is significant in another direction. Aware that he could not
admit in its entirety the "Hellenic philosophy", the whole of which,
like nuts, is not edible",[92] Clement needed to establish a criterion
for discriminating between philosophical tenets, and for disentan-
gling the true and worthwhile from the false and the worthless.
Interestingly, it was to faith in the Word, and what ensued from
such a commitment, that he looked to provide this rule:

> "Whoever chooses to banquet on faith, is steadfast for the
> reception of the divine words, having acquired already faith as
> a power of judging according to reason. Hence ensues to him
> conviction in abundance."[93]

Clement was therefore very critical of Epicurean philosophy
for its "atheism";[94] this is an indication, as de Faye notes, that "our

author... judges [philosophies and their systems]... according to their theology."[95]

Clement was also convinced that his efforts towards a coherent account of Christian understanding which integrated the appropriate insights of the Greek intellectual tradition were not new; he was simply developing ideas and approaches he had learnt from his teachers. Tatian and Athenagoras have always figured in any discussion of the identities of the six Christian teachers that Clement had in the course of his travels.[96] If Tatian was in fact one of them, Clement was not influenced by his antipathy towards Hellenism, but it is probable that he admired Tatian's chronological argument for the antiquity of Moses.[97] However, from Athenagoras, himself an Athenian who had seen the need to provide a reasoned demonstration for the Christian faith,[98] Clement would have derived the confidence to face up to the challenge of philosophy with the full conviction that the Christian Gospel possessed sufficient resilience to allow an educated Christian account for Greek intellectual insights without modifying the Gospel in its essential character. Clement would therefore have been right to believe that he was continuing a tradition inaugurated by Christian teachers who were adjudged reliable, because they preserved "the tradition of the blessed doctrine derived from the holy apostles".[99] Clement saw himself in the line of Christian teachers who had also been convinced that there were depths of knowledge within Christian understanding which could be developed from the common foundation of faith, and would yield nothing in intellectual cogency and attractiveness to the Greek philosophical tradition.

In order to realise this objective, Clement does not shrink from making use of what is best in philosophy and other preparatory training.[100] He postulates this principle for two reasons, both of which he derives from his reading of St Paul:

> "For not only for the Hebrews and those under the Law, according to the apostle, is it right to become a Jew. But also a Greek for the sake of the Greeks, that we may gain all. Also in the *Epistle to the Colossians* he writes, 'Admonishing every man, and teaching every man in all wisdom, that we may present every man perfect in Christ'. In this respect the resources of learning are like a relish mixed with the food of an athlete who is not indulging in luxury, but entertains a noble desire for distinction."[101]

If the first reason seems obvious enough, the second is an

instance of Clement's enigmatic style in the *Stromateis*. In fact the clue to Clement's meaning here is given in the next chapter. Pursuing the justification of his effort to set forth the Christian faith in such terms as are congenial to the educated Greek outlook, Clement again finds the validation for it in St Paul. For he sees in the apostle's expression: "the Greeks seek after wisdom",[102] an indication that the Greek apprehension of the Gospel comes through the kind of intellectual demonstration of the faith for which he is pleading. In Clement's view, therefore, it was proper to seek to bring the Greeks to faith in the Gospel by an appeal to what was cognate and by finding "a middle point of transition in their own intellectual possessions".[103]

Clement must have found most striking the apostle's insistence on the *universal* significance of the Gospel in *Colossians* 1:28; it is *every* man who is to be admonished, taught and brought to perfect salvation *in Christ*. Clement therefore justifies his sense of obligation "to become a Greek for the sake of the Greeks" on the grounds of this truly Christian and Biblical view of the unity of humanity, conceived concretely in terms of humanity's common participation in the same historical destiny leading to salvation in Christ.[104] This high view of the unity of mankind in all its vicissitudes is simply a corollary of an equally firmly held belief in the unity of all divine disclosure of the truth in Christ.[105]

Thus, for an educated Christian of Hellenistic culture like Clement, the major objective of his endeavour is now evident: to make a positive use of material from Hellenistic tradition in order to demonstrate that not only is conversion to the Christian faith appropriate for Greeks, but also that the true insights within Greek tradition necessarily converge upon Christ:

> "To us [Christians] belongs the word spoken to many before the [common] tradition. Wherefore, we must set forth the opinions and utterances which cried individually to them, by which those who hear shall more readily turn."[106]

The interpretation of this passage depends on what Clement means by "the word spoken to many before the [common] tradition". If he means the sum of philosophical tenets of the past, this will fit in with his method of seeking to expound the Christian meanings inherent within those philosophical tenets of which he approves. If, however, he means the Old Testament Scriptures, then he must be indicating the latter's relevance for understanding Hellenistic tradition itself.[107] Whilst this passage may be just another instance of the studied ambiguities favoured by Clement as a theological writer.[108] The first interpretation is preferable; a few lines following the passage quoted, Clement defines his task as that of producing the fruit of Greek learning.[109] It is hard not to infer that this "fruit" of the Hellenistic intellectual tradition is what Clement also calls "the seeds of the truth" which it falls to only "the husbandmen of faith" like himself to discover and set forth.[110]

It is in the context of considerations such as these that one must understand Clement's views on the usefulness, to the Christian, of intellectual culture,[111] on the need to advance from simple faith to enlightened faith which is "knowledge",[112] as well as his highly positive estimation of the philosophical tradition. In two extensive studies on Clement's use of his intellectual and literary culture, Pierre Camelot[113] showed convincingly that Clement's persistent effort to make a place for the "encyclical subjects" of general literal education in the Christian life is always directed towards theological ends: to show its usefulness in giving an intellectual grasp of the Christian faith, and to demonstrate its value in the defence of the truth thus apprehended against attacks from heretics and sceptics. Commenting on two passages in the *Stromateis*,[114] Camelot writes:

"The first task which Clement assigns to the liberal sciences is as follows: forming and preparing the soul and helping it in a positive way in its ascent towards the truth; and there is another: defending the faith already held against the attacks of error and unbelief."[115]

Furthermore, it is Clement's conviction that from the standpoint of integrity, the thoughtful Christian cannot condemn the views of sceptics on the grounds of "only a mere hearsay knowledge of their opinions".[116] The Christian needs to demonstrate the rightness of his case, and show the wrongness of the opponent's case in order to convince him: "For the refutation which is based on experience is entirely trustworthy, and the knowledge of what is condemned is found the most complete demonstration."[117]

But if, through the Word, the universe became for Clement an Athens and a Greece,[118] this did not have the effect of making him wish to bend over backwards to accommodate every whim of Hellas. His scathing attack on the Sophists for their delight in verbal cavilling[119] is an indication of how clear-sighted Clement was that in his concern to "become a Greek for the sake of the Greeks", the essential meaning of the Christian Gospel should not be lost. He even refuses to write in studied Greek style lest weightier dimensions of what he seeks to convey be missed.[120] It is evident that in his fervour and optimism about the possibility of a comprehensive synthesis of all that is worthy in the religious and intellectual history of mankind, Clement does not lose his Christian moorings. We have already noted his insistence on faith as a fundamental principle of knowledge, a position maintained in the face of the *penchant* in circles of Greek *paideia*, to exalt "reason" and to treat "faith" as the lowest grade of cognition, the state of mind of the uneducated who believe without demonstrable evidence.[121] Nor does Clement consider that the value of an intellectual and philosophical demonstration of the faith thereby implies an inherent deficiency in the Christian tradition available to the mass of Christians in the Church:

> "The teaching which is according to the Saviour is complete in itself and without defect being 'the power and the wisdom of God'; and the admission of Hellenic philosophy [into our Christian endeavour] does not make the truth more powerful; but rendering powerless the assault of sophistry against it, and frustrating the treacherous plots laid against the truth, [philosophy] may be said properly to be the 'fence and the wall of the vineyard'. The truth which is according to faith is as necessary for life as bread; while the preparatory training is like sauce and sweetmeats."[122]

Clement's intellectual interests ever remain with him, but they are now integral to his Christian self-consciousness, and are required by his understanding of his task as a Christian *doctor* among educated Greeks. It is hardly surprising that Clement's portrait of the "enlightened man", his "true Gnostic", is quintessentially that of the *Christian* scholar. Conversant with all kinds of wisdom – both Hellenic and Barbarian – such a person seeks to bring again together the separate fragments [of knowledge] and to make them one.[123] If Clement believed so strongly in the necessity of the enlarged intellectual framework for articulating the Christian faith, it was not only because he believed that such an endeavour would serve the interests of the faith intrinsically; he also held firmly to the view that the Christian faith itself had an appeal and a relevance to every cultural context. He saw it as his task to demonstrate that this was true of his own Hellenistic tradition.

III. The one great obstacle: The deadly drug of "custom" !

It has been said that it was a mark of Clement's Christian

optimism that he saw no danger in urging an intellectual accommodation between Christianity and Hellenistic culture.[124] But it can also be argued that it was on the basis of such optimism that Clement felt able to encounter head-on the most devastating charge held against the Christian movement in Graeco-Roman society. This charge, stated in its classic form by Celsus,[125] was that the Christians represented a social novelty, were outside the established patterns of normal religious allegiance and observance, and so constituted a grave and dangerous defiance of customary law.[126] Christian conversion within Hellenistic culture, therefore, was an anomaly. Raoul Mortley,[127] in a study of some passages in the *Stromateis*,[128] where Clement seeks to answer the charge by a historical argument, has well summed up the fundamental thinking behind the charge:

> "Christian social behaviour is unrecognisable, and the movement can lay claim to no historical justification for the idea that it has a traditional place within the Roman empire."[129]

In the *Stromateis*, Clement's response is in the form of a sober and painstaking effort to demonstrate that "Christians are recognisable historically, morally and intellectually"[130] by linking them with Old Testament history and religion. The response is part of the wider argument for the chronological priority of Moses and for the antiquity of Christian tradition which is thus derived from him. To this aspect of the problem we shall come later. For the moment, it is Clement's handling of the problem in the *Protreptikos* with which we shall be concerned. What gives the treatment in the *Protreptikos* particular significance and shows Clement's originality, is the fact that he confronts the idea of custom in the very terms in which the critics employed it, that is, as an intellectual principle for interpreting human existence. By undermining what was virtually a sacralised principle, namely, that it was not reasonable to abandon inherited custom,[131] Clement was seeking to weaken the suggestion that Christian conversion in the context of Hellenistic culture was an aberration.

Clement devotes the whole of the tenth chapter to the problem and then returns to it in the last chapter of his book, which shows how crucial he must have felt the issue was. From the standpoint of the identity question, the challenge of custom is probably the single most important subject that Clement treats in the *Protreptikos*. It is part of the total appeal to his fellow educated Greeks to embrace the Christian Gospel, and for many this implied the subversion, however minimally, of some elements in the wisdom of their cultural past.[132]

It is in itself significant that Clement chose the literary genre of the *Protreptikos* for his argument in favour of Christian conversion. For Clement was consciously identifying his own efforts with a notable strand in Hellenistic intellectual tradition. Initiated by Aristotle, the *Logos Protreptikos* was, as H.I. Marrou explains, "an inaugural lesson which seeks to recruit disciples to attract young people to the life of philosophy".[133] It was exemplified in the late Roman Republic by Cicero's *Hortensius*, the reading of which caused the young Augustine to be converted to philosophy.[134] Thus, the "exhortation" (*protreptikos*) to the philosophic life with its demand for "a break with the common culture"[135] was well suited to Clement's purpose. Indeed, an attack on custom and unreflective habit as obstacles in the way of intellectual development and the philosophic life was "characteristic of the whole protreptic tradition".[136]

Nonetheless, however relevant culturally the form adopted for his exhortation, Clement knew very well that his appeal was not simply a call to the philosophic life as was generally understood. Consequently, the argument urging the abandoning of custom and the adoption of the Christian life required more than the exposure of the worthlessness of popular opinion.[137] Therefore, before we examine Clement's reasons for discarding inherited wisdom of the past, we must pay attention to how he prepares the ground for his appeal in the earlier chapters of the *Protreptikos*.

An extraordinary feature of Clement's approach is his frequent and optimistic use of the Scriptures. He must have known that to attempt to vindicate the Christian position on the basis of documents derived from Hebrew (i.e. from Barbarian) tradition was bound to appear suspect to Graeco-Roman traditionalists. But as he observed the increasing impact of the Christian Gospel upon Gentiles, Clement may have felt a sense of confidence in the ability of the Christian message to commend itself intrinsically to Greeks. It is only such an outlook which explains his bold efforts at integrating Christian ideas into traditions which were already prevalent in Hellenistic religious history.

A notable feature of Clement's argument is his concept of "New Song" which he applied to Christ. Whether this had its source in Hellenistic or Biblical tradition,[138] it seems likely that he merged various traditions and read Christian meanings in the Hellenistic material.[139] Thus, against the admiration for the minstrels of legend, Amphion, Arion, Orpheus, Eunomus, Clement sets the excellence of Christ. The former belong to worthless legends whilst Christ (and Christian revelation) present the bright face of truth.[140] The sacred places of Greek religion, associated with the mysteries, are temples of initiation into error. Against the sacred associations of Mt Cithaeron (sacred to Zeus) and Mt Helicon (sacred to the Muses), Clement opposes the truth of the Christian Gospel "with wisdom in all her brightness from heaven", bringing light and "understanding for the salvation of those who walked in darkness".[141] Clement's use of the Isaianic passage: "for out of Zion shall go forth the law, and the Word of the Lord from Jerusalem",[142] indicates his confidence that Greeks could apprehend the message of the Scriptures, if they would only appreciate that the Old Testament expressed a truth meant for all mankind. Clement therefore declares that the word which comes from Jerusalem is "the heavenly Word, the true champion now crowned upon the stage of the whole world",[143] combining images derived from Hellenistic life with Biblical doctrine in a quite remarkable way.

Clement obviously relies on the relevance of the Scriptures to establish his case, but he also feels free to draw upon Hellenistic literary and mythological tradition; so that he even quotes Homer's *Odyssey*[144] in support of the saving power of the New Song, thereby supplanting the heroes of Greek religious tradition. These latter were in fact deceivers through whom demons produced illusions to procure the ruin of men, leading them into idolatry. This destructive activity of demons in the religious tradition is compounded by the sanction of custom. It is the hold of custom which, to Clement, constitutes the "lowest slavery" of men who ought to be enjoying "that truly noble freedom which belongs to those who are citizens under heaven".[145] It is in order to effect the liberation of men[146] that Christ came into the world as the New Song and Minstrel.[147]

Clement sees the liberation of men from tyrannical demons essentially in terms of moral and intellectual transformation. Christ brings men under the influence of a "mild and kindly yoke of piety".[148] It is in regard to this moral transformation that the heroes of the "old" religion and the mysteries failed. As deceivers their error consisted in using music and the arts to sacralise human passions. In this way they outraged human life, brought upon men demonic destructiveness, and so led men into idolatry.[149]

Christ, on the other hand, transforms human lives. Clement transposes the inanimate objects and wild beasts who were alleged to have been charmed by Orpheus, into human beings transformed by Christ, the new Minstrel – "for God is able of these stones to raise up children unto Abraham",[150] as He is able to make "men of God" from the "offspring of vipers".[151] In Clement's understanding, the stones and wild beasts of the Orphic myth and those of the Biblical sayings refer to the same reality, namely, human beings, who for the present purpose are Graeco-Romans, or Gentiles. By such allegorical penetration into what he saw to be the spiritual meanings both of the Scriptural texts and of the myths, Clement is able to argue for the validity of Christian conversion in Hellenistic culture without surrendering the Scriptures as alien.

Clement's sensitivity to the identity question of Hellenistic Christians is seen in his recognition that there might be a flaw even in the argument that the transforming power of the New Song was evidence for His universality. How could the novelty of the Christian Gospel be defended in view of the theories of Phrygian,[152] Arcadian,[153] or Egyptian[154] antiquity and prestige in religious history? Rather than disputing these theories, he takes his position on the basis of Scriptural declarations,[155] and argues that the truth he is putting forth only *appears* to be recent and new.[156] In one bold stroke, Clement sweeps away all these traditional theories:

"Not one of these nations existed before this world. But we were before the foundation of the world, we who, because we were destined to be in Him, were begotten beforehand by God. We are the rational images, formed by God's Word, or Reason, and we date from the beginning on account of our connection with Him, because 'the Word was in the beginning'."[157]

The entire argument hinges on the statement: "In the beginning was the Word".[158] Clement, shortly before, had appealed to the Biblical doctrine of the creation of man in the image of God as a further argument in favour of the universality of the New Minstrel;[159] now he draws out further implications from that doctrine. In view of the doctrine of Christ as the Word of God, the agent of man's creation, and the pattern of the perfect human personality, all converts to Christ have an eternal connection with Him. They thus become what the whole of humanity was intended to be from the beginning – rational images of the divine Word.[160] By virtue of this faith-connection with the heavenly Word, Christians are prior, dating from the beginning.[161] Therefore the Christian tradition of the "New Song" is new and recent only in so far as the heavenly Word has lately assumed, through Incarnation, the name of Christ; but this name is itself one which was consecrated in antiquity – in the Old Testament Scriptures – and speaks of power.

The ground for Christian priority and antiquity in religion lies, then, in this profound predestined connection with Christ, the eternal Word, and the expression "New Song" is justified, and with Scriptural validation, in view of the recent manifestation of the pre- existent Word.[162] The pre-existent Saviour of all men appeared by Incarnation as the Teacher of mankind.[163]

In the light of this fundamental availability of Christ to all humanity, and of the universal relevance of Christian tradition, Clement is able to associate "error" in Hellenistic religious tradition with the Biblical Fall and with Satanic deception. For what befell Eve in the primeval era is what the "one and the same deceiver now does to the rest of mankind".[164] Similarly, the Saviour of all mankind, "our rescuer and helper", has communicated to the world in the prophetic literature; but now, that is, since His Incarnation, He summons all plainly to salvation.[165] Thus, the saving activity of Christ is placed at the very beginning of the history of humanity, and is linked with present experience as one continuous activity of one and the same Saviour. Hellenistic Christian conversion is placed in line with the experience of the Hebrews in the Old Testament. In much the same way, the warnings against disobedience and unbelief addressed to the Hebrews[166] are now parallelled by the apostolic call to the Gentiles.[167] The means of divine self-disclosure through the prophetic oracles in the Old Testament is now matched by the "appeal to reason" which is intended to win Greeks. But the end of each method is the same, namely, to bring about a conversion to the Word.[168]

Clement's concern to urge the relevance of the Christian message (and of Biblical history as a whole) to Hellenistic culture, reaches a high point in a curious use of the story of John the Baptist.[169] John's preaching of repentance as preparation for Christ is related to the angelic visitation to the Baptist's aging parents.[170] Since Clement is more interested in the barrenness of Elizabeth than in the angelic visitation itself, he transposes her into the place of Zechariah. This becomes clear when he quotes *Isaiah* 54:1, which he severely allegorises (possibly in view of *Galatians* 4:27),[171] in order to yield the appropriate meaning. The barrenness of the wilderness and the barrenness of Elizabeth are linked by the thought that the response of faith to John's preaching, on the one hand, and the birth of a child to Elizabeth, consequent on her believing the promise, on the other, are both responses to one and the same Word, who speaks in both instances.

Hence those who refuse to believe in the Word remain barren and desolate and without access to the "salvation" which is "the fruit of productiveness, namely, eternal life".[172]

Once it is recognised that the productiveness of the barren woman is really the allegorical designation for the harvest of Gentile Christians,[173] it becomes clear what Clement is doing. Concerned to show that Biblical history, as the history of the saving activity of the Word in the past, has a relevance for the religious history of Hellenistic culture, Clement finds the appropriate symbolism in the ministry of one who was the "forerunner of the Word".[174] Thus for Clement, the dumbness of Zechariah symbolises the "mystic silence of the enigmatic Scriptures".[175] But just as John's birth ends his father's dumbness, so his ministry leads to a solution of the "enigma" of the Old Testament. For with the ministry of John, the long line of prophetic proclamation of salvation in history is brought to a head, and immediate witness is borne to the manifestation of the Word – the light of truth – who "becoming good news" brings to an end once and for all the "riddle" of the Hebrew Scriptures and clarifies their meaning for the religious history of all mankind. Thus, using the language of the mysteries, of which he otherwise severely disapproves, Clement urges his audience to "seek diligently after Christ" through whom alone, by the key of faith, mankind can see God.[176]

The preceding discussion on the *Protreptikos* has concentrated substantially on the introductory chapter of the book in order to show how, very early, Clement lays the basis for the argumentation in the rest of the book. Whilst the succeeding chapters will give much evidence of Clement's vast erudition, every significant point to be made is already touched upon in this first chapter. The lengthy and scathing attack on the gods and rites of the popular religion and on the mysteries, which follows,[177] is intended to establish essentially one point, that is, all that belongs to "the region of legends now grown old",[178] a view which is implied in the vigourous *apologia* for "the New Song of Salvation". With characteristic insight, Clement recognises that he is not dealing with isolated features of Hellenistic culture. Rather, he is confronting custom,[179] the cumulative tradition in rite and practice, to which men have become accustomed over several generations and which the vast majority of people never question in any serious manner. He sees it as his task to discredit this custom of inherited erroneous tradition about Divinity and worship which is inherent in Hellenistic culture.

Clement's position is seen very clearly in his sustained criticism, in chapter 4, of image-worship, and of the use of art generally in religion. In a passage which seems to be an echo of the Old Testament prophetic denunciations of idolatry,[180] Clement sets his new Christian understanding of God against the popular conception presupposed by the artistic representations of deities, and declares:

"For a statue is really lifeless matter shaped by a craftsman's hand; but in our view the image of God is not an object of sense made from matter perceived by the senses, but a mental object; God, that is the only true God, is perceived not by the senses but by the mind."[181]

G.W. Butterworth, who argues that Clement derives his strictures on artistic representation also from Platonic intellectualism,[182] admits, nonetheless, that though "by nature he is a Greek and not a Hebrew", Clement "feels justified in condemning... statues with all the sarcasm of an Isaiah".[183] The fact is, Clement finds it difficult to separate art from idolatry and religious error.[184] Because he approaches the problem from a religious and moral standpoint, he cannot accept the portrayal of the amours of gods in the Homeric myths,[185] even though he feels a sincere admiration for Greek poetry; it may be excellent poetry, but it lacks beauty if its content is morally reprehensible.

It is consistent with Clement's view of the popular religion, particularly of its deities, as the product of custom which legend and the lapse of time have consecrated, that he thought highly of the philosophical "quest" for a nobler conception of God.[186] What most impressed Clement was the fact that thoughtful persons and the philosophically minded, from as early as Heraclitus, had expressed disapproval of the popular religion, and had rejected the theology on which it was founded.[187] A fuller treatment of Clement's assessment of the philosophical tradition will be given later. It is sufficient to note at this point the place of Clement's understanding in his total thinking. Like Justin, Clement is brought to realise that with regard to the truth as known in Christian teaching, the Hellenistic heritage presents two divergent traditions. There is, on the one hand, a corrupt and erroneous one, seen in the popular religion and its account of divinity; whilst, on the other, there is a noble and enlightened one, witnessed in philosophy. It is not the case that Clement will seek to wed philosophy as such to the Christian Gospel. Rather, in his view, the questions which philosophers, turning their backs on the popular religion, sought to answer, are finally resolved only by the Christian Gospel.[188] Thus, if the popular religion and the mysteries, with their immoral deities, can be explained as the evidence of Satanic deception in Hellenistic tradition, the enlightened quest of philosophers indicates the reality of a divine activity in the same Hellenistic tradition:

> "For there is a certain divine effluence instilled into all men without exception, but especially into those who spend their lives in thought; wherefore they admit, even though against their will, that God is One, that He is unbegotten and indestructible, and that somewhere on high in the outermost spaces of the heavens, in His own private watch-tower, He truly exists for ever."[189]

There is little doubt that behind these lofty sentiments lies Clement's profound admiration for Platonic transcendentalism, and for what he considered were Plato's intimations of monotheism. The same theory of two traditions in the Hellenistic background also explains his view of the Greek heritage in poetry and literature.[190] The false and corrupt tradition consists in the acceptance of the popular religion and its mythology, whereas the noble and true tradition is manifested in the criticism of the false and in the quest for a more sublime conception of divinity.[191] Clement is well aware that the concerns of literature have been shaped, on the whole, by its form and method of composition, and that these have been generally in the realm of fiction. But this has not prevented some literary persons from bearing witness to the truth, whilst some have even conceded the errors into which the poetic myths have often led the public.[192] Thus the criticism mounted against the popular religion by the classical dramatists becomes an important element in Clement's argument. Euripides in particular, by his critique of the gods of the popular religion, becomes "indeed a worthy disciple of the Socratic school".[193]

The value of the philosophical and intellectual tradition in the Hellenistic heritage, for Clement, is that it produced people like Plato who, because they were thoughtful persons and followed the intuition inspired by the divine effluence in them, boldly presented the truth as they were able to perceive it.[194] Clement is fully convinced that these "glimmerings of the divine Word" and these "expressions of the truth" found in the Hellenistic tradition "even if only in scraps",[195] were given by divine inspiration and represent a sufficient guide to the full knowledge of God.[196] Nowhere does Clement declare unequivocally that the philosophical tradition by and of itself constitutes a complete revelation of God. In fact, by his own explicit statement in the next chapter, it is the Scriptures which, being "the oracles which exhibit in the clearest light the grounds of piety, lay a firm foundation for the truth".[197]

However, this positive evaluation of an aspect of the Hellenistic heritage is of great significance for Clement's defence of Christian conversion and for his commendation of the faith to fellow educated Greeks. On the one hand, the existence of this Hellenistic witness to Christian truth argues in favour of the evident power of that truth and clearly demonstrates that God never left Himself without witness in Hellenistic tradition. On the other hand, this Hellenistic witness also argues for the weakness and inadequacies of the philosophical and intellectual tradition, since it shows that the quest failed to reach its goal,[198] the full apprehension of which is Christ.

The reason for this failure, Clement suggests, was the lack of access to "the word of the truth".[199] Certainly these words cannot mean a total absence of divine promptings in Hellenistic tradition, since the reality of "glimmerings of the divine Word" has already been proved. But in the light of the early statements of chapter 8, it seems a fair assumption that Clement's words here refer to the Scriptures. For it is the "divine" Scriptures[200] – divine as against the merely human precepts of philosophers – which exhibit most distinctly the sure means for piety, lay a firm foundation for the truth, and constitute "short roads to salvation.[201] If Stählin's suggestion is correct, that it is the Cynic definition of philosophy as "a short road to virtue" which lies behind Clement's last statement, then it provides a clue to Clement's meaning. The Scriptures may be lacking in literary and stylistic elegance, but they have moral and spiritual power; "they raise up man when he is fast bound in the grip of evil", healing his moral ills; they speak with consensus and "with clear guidance", lead to salvation,[202] which is the true goal of human existence. The goal sought by philosophy is fully realised in Christian conversion; the Scriptures guide a person away from the delusion of the popular religion, and the philosophical objective of virtue is integrated into a truly godly piety.[203]

The Scriptures, therefore, address themselves to the human condition in Hellenistic culture and to Hellenistic religious history and experience. It is this conviction that Clement brings to his attempt to show, in chapters 8 and 9 that the Scriptures can be seen to make sense to Greeks, and that some portions speak specifically to Greeks. Clement does this by bringing together a battery of Old Testament prophetic denunciations of idolatry which for him is the hallmark of Hellenistic popular religion.[204] When, at the end of this indictment of idolatry, Clement invokes Paul's strictures on idolatry in *Romans* 1:20ff, he is fully confident that he is appealing to a verdict which applies specifically to Hellenistic religion.[205]

For Clement, whose devotion and loyalty to ecclesiastical tradition on Scripture is unmistakeable,[206] the establishment of the relevance of the Scriptures for interpreting Hellenistic religious history is important. For him, the immense attractiveness of the Christian Gospel lies in the belief that it fulfils the aspiration which lay behind the intellectual and moral critique by philosophers of the popular religion and its mythology. The Gospel not only confirmed that rejection of the conception of divinity offered by the mythmakers, but also provided converts with the spiritual dynamic and the intellectual integrity to pursue the life of godly piety which was the goal of the quest for the truth. This godly piety, conceived as "making man as far as possible resemble God",[207] is the work of God Himself, who accomplishes it by means of the divine Scriptures. Here Clement makes a precise use of *2 Timothy* 3:15. The exhortation (*Protreptikos*) to faith in Christ, therefore, has universal application because:

> "The Word was not hidden from any; He is a universal light; He shines upon all men... Let us hasten to salvation, to the new birth."[208]

The outcome of this wide ranging demonstration of the relevance of the Christian Gospel to Hellenistic tradition is that the call, in chapter 10, to abandon custom and inherited error is seen to be not as outrageous as it may sound, coming from a Christian. Christians have their predecessors within Hellenistic tradition, in those thoughtful persons who, following the divine impulse at work in them, turned from common opinion and custom and instead sought after God.[209] If the final goal of their quest, that is Christ, eluded them, it was because they did not have access to the comprehensiveness and evident clarity of the divine self-disclosure which Christian tradition now makes available.

Clement's response to Graeco-Roman traditionalists is, therefore, essentially a simple one. In the first place, he shows that the practice of abandoning old ways for new is part of the processes of life, growth and maturity,[210] so setting aside any suggestion of the antecedent inadmissibility of change. Secondly, he has already established the grounds for considering the "old" religion as belong-

ing to the region of outdated legends,[211] and so Clement now seeks
to argue for the propriety of religious change, where such change
involves a departure from ignorance of the true God to a knowledge
of Him. To do this, Clement insists on the inherent goodness of the
Christian proclamation of salvation for all people. Consequently,
he denies that the problem is a cultural one at all. Rather, it is a
matter of moral choice; between darkness and light, godlessness
and godliness; between "the old way, that is custom, which is
wicked, full of passion and without God", and bending "our course
towards the truth and... our real Father".[212] If, indeed, the Christian message is true, then it must be embraced even at the risk of
displeasing our human fathers; custom thus becomes "a deadly
drug".[213] Since salvation in Christ is the greatest boon that God has
ever bestowed upon humanity, it is more appropriate for men to
live in accordance with God's provision than in conformity to
custom.[214] The coming of Christ into the world has shone light upon
the earth, and filled the universe with the seed of salvation,[215]
transforming it into a sea of blessings.[216]

Therefore, for Clement, it is inconceivable that custom could be
urged in any serious sense against such a beneficent reality:

"Custom strangles man; it turns him away from the truth; it
leads him away from life; it is a snare, an abyss, a pit, a
devouring evil."[217]

If Clement seems unable to restrain this heightened abhorrence
for adhering to custom for its own sake, neither can he hide an
equally profound sense of exultation in Christ as Good News for
the world. In the first book of the *Paidagogos*, he declares:

"Dead, we need life; sheep, we need a shepherd; we who are
children need a tutor, and all humanity stands in need of Jesus;
so that we may not continue intractable sinners to the end, and
thus fall into condemnation, but may be separated from the
chaff, and stored up in the paternal garner."[218]

This idea that Christ's coming into the world is central and
crucial for the destiny of all mankind, has been rightly recognised
as the most dominant theme in Clement's scheme of human
religious history. In the judgment of B.F. Westcott:

"This thought of the Incarnation as the crown and consummation of the whole history of the world is perhaps that which is
most characteristic of Clement's office as an interpreter of the
faith. It rests upon his view of human nature, of the providential
government of God, and of the finality of the Christian dispen-

sation."[219]

But it is also worth noting that Clement's understanding of the universality of Christ as Saviour, is firmly linked with his view of the Scriptures. For Clement, the Scriptures, particularly the Old Testament, through an allegorical hermeneutic, can be shown to yield meanings that carry far-reaching significance for explaining the religious history of mankind as a whole.[220] It is this aspect of Clement's work that Claude Mondésert has rightly emphasised in his study of Clement's religious thought:

"It is the Scriptures which, first and foremost, inspire and guide Clement – present history before anything else... a history which unfolds, progresses and arrives at a supreme act (Incarnation), but arrives there only to set off again, but without departing thereafter from the influence of this central point and summit which it had reached... at the centre of this explanation [of the religious history of humanity], there is the Logos incarnate, the Christ who is the revealer of God and Saviour of men, promulgator and embodiment of the Scriptures."[221]

And yet it seems as though Clement was also haunted by the thought that the Old Testament might belong more exclusively to the religious history of the Hebrews.[222] For this reason, Clement felt the need to give account of divine self-disclosure in the Hellenistic past in a way that took more seriously the "Barbarian" character and origin of the Old Testament. It was in response to such a concern that, in the *Stromateis*, Clement came to argue that to the Greeks also, prior to the Incarnation, God had given "a covenant, peculiar, as it were, to them" to serve as "a steppingstone" to lead to the fullness that was to come with the Incarnation of the Word.[223]

IV. For Jews, the Law; for Greeks, Philosophy: The theory of "peculiar" covenants

Clement's views on the origin and positive value of the Greek philosophical tradition have probably been the most intensively studied,[224] and so will not be focused on here. Rather, we intend to examine how this positive evaluation of the philosophical tradition in Hellenistic culture fits into his overall scheme of the religious history of mankind, and illuminates his understanding of the history of redemption. Viewed from this angle, Clement's attempt to make room for the insights of philosophy in the divine activity of redemption through Christ, emerges as his most significant contribution towards resolving the crisis of identity that faced early Hellenistic Christians.[225]

The fact that Clement frequently speaks of the Christian faith as "philosophy" is itself significant. The Christian Gospel is "the true philosophy",[226] the only "really perfect and true philosophy".[227] He refers to the Old Testament as the "Barbarian philosophy",[228] or simply as "the Mosaic philosophy".[229] Affirming, therefore, the "Barbarian" connection of the Christian Gospel, Clement describes the latter as "the divine and barbarian philosophy";[230] the full apprehension of truth to which genuine intellectual investigation ought to lead the enquirer is "the philosophy according to Christ".[231] This "philosophical" conception of the Christian faith so pervades Clement's thinking that he uses the verb φιλοσοφεῖν to designate embracing the Christian life when quoting the well-known saying of Jesus:

"It is easier for a camel to go through the eye of a needle, than for a rich man to lead a philosophic life (φιλοσοφεῖν)."[232]

In explaining this Clementine emendation of the dominical saying, Einar Molland suggests that Clement is here "quoting from memory".[233] But even if this was the case, the alteration is significant. It is likely too that Clement, with characteristic freedom, deliberately re-writes the words of Jesus in order to make his point that there is an essential equivalence between accepting the call of the Gospel and a genuine commitment to the moral and intellectual ideals of philosophy. Entering "the Kingdom of God" has as its analogue in Hellenistic tradition the turning to philosophy. This analogous relationship between the philosophical outlook and Christian discipleship is not simply an apologetic device, nor is it fortuitous. Behind it lies one of Clement's most fundamental intuitions, namely, that the philosophical tradition in Hellenistic culture is a divine provision bestowed upon the culture – in much the same way as the Law was for the Hebrews – to illuminate the path that should lead to Christ.[234] As Molland observes:

"Clement recognises the Greek philosophy as a covenant parallel to the covenant of the Hebrews. The Greek paideia is the covenant of the Greeks."[235]

Clement's position is therefore to be understood against the background of what we have called "the theory of two traditions", namely, the true and the false. For it was in philosophy and kindred pursuits that thoughtful persons of the past found a spiritual home in their quest for the truth which is now available through the Gospel. What philosophy offered, and what the Gospel now provides, are therefore in historical continuum, like the Law and the Gospel of the Old and New Testaments.

Clement elaborates this idea when he expounds a passage from the apocryphal *Preaching of Peter*,[236] a document which, as we have already shown, constitutes an important landmark in the development of Christian self-identity in the Graeco-Roman world.[237] It is consistent with Clement's intuition that he bases his argument on a postulate of the essential unity of God, and His providential self-disclosure in Greek tradition, no less than in Hebrew tradition. Consequently, even if the knowledge of God in Hellenistic tradition was imperfect as compared with the positive perfect knowledge[238] which is conveyed by the incarnate Son of God, it was still knowledge of the same God. The Christian Gospel therefore introduces into the world a new manner of the worship of God but does not announce "another God".[239] In the light of the perfect knowledge which is provided by Christ, Clement feels free to criticise the religious traditions of both Jews and Greeks. Whilst Greeks fell into idolatry and polytheism, Jews mistook ceremonialism for true worship. Against the errors of both Greeks and Jews, Clement elaborates the theory of the new third manner of worshipping God through Christ, which is the characteristic mark of the Christians. The argument is in fact a statement of Clement's account of the religious history of mankind. But this account is Scriptural to the extent that Clement applies the Old Testament prophecy of the new covenant[240] equally to Greeks and Jews:

> "He [God] made a new covenant with us [that is, all mankind];
> for what belonged to the Greeks and Jews is old. But we who
> worship Him in a new way, in the third form, are Christians.
> For clearly... the one and only God was known by the Greeks in
> their [Gentile] way, and by the Jews in their [Judaistic] way,
> and in a new and spiritual way by us."[241]

For Clement, then, one can speak of different covenants, for Jews and for Greeks – both of which are fulfilled in the perfect, full revelation in Christ, to whom Jew and Greek alike are summoned to come in faith:

> "The same God that furnished both the covenants (i.e. Old and
> New Testaments) was the giver of Greek philosophy to the
> Greeks, by which the Almighty was glorified among the
> Greeks... Accordingly, then, from the Hellenic training and also
> from that of the Law are gathered into the one race of the saved
> people those who accept faith: not that the three peoples are

separated by time, so that one might suppose three natures, but trained in different covenants of the one Lord, by the Word of the one Lord."[242]

Even more remarkable, Clement reaches to the period prior to the Incarnation, and equates the prophets of the Old Testament with philosophers and thoughtful persons in Hellenistic tradition, as those whose careers witnessed to the divine self-disclosure among Greeks: "For as God wished to save the Jews by giving to them prophets, so also by raising up prophets of their own in their own tongue, as they were able to receive God's beneficence, He distinguished the most excellent of the Greeks from the common herd."[243]

Following the same intuition, Clement projects the saving activity of "the one Lord" into the region of the departed, arguing, on the strength of *1 Peter* 3:19, that the dead of past generations did hear the Gospel. Only whereas it was Christ in spirit who preached to departed Hebrews, to departed Greeks were sent the Apostles, and,

"God being good, and the Lord powerful, they save with a righteousness and equality which extend to all that turn to Him, whether here or elsewhere."[244]

Behind this parallelism in the activity of Christ and his apostles in the realm of the departed, there lies a projection of the actual historical circumstances of Christ's ministry in Palestine and the subsequent apostolic mission to the Gentiles. What took place on the one level of existence finds its counterpart in the other. But equally evident is Clement's own deep sense of the unity of mankind, which we have already noted. So that, since God is no respecter of persons,[245] "one righteous man does not differ, as righteous, from another righteous man, whether he be of the Law or a Greek. God is not only the Lord of the Jews but of all men, and particularly the Father of those who know Him."[246]

It would be unjust, however, to conclude from such arguments that Clement equates the Greek philosophical tradition with Biblical revelation, *simpliciter*. His thought on the subject is much more subtle and complex. To the extent that the Christian Gospel can be called philosophy, "the true philosophy", it is a coherent body of "systematic wisdom which furnishes acquaintance with the things which pertain to life." This quality of knowledge constitutes "a sure and irrefragable apprehension of things divine and human, comprehending the present, past and future, which the Lord has taught us both by His advent and by the prophets".[247] This description of the Christian account of divinity, as of all knowledge, Clement does not apply to the Hellenistic philosophical tradition. This latter, being only "a quest for the truth", contributes to the apprehension of the truth. However, the actual discovery of the truth is through the Son,[248] so that "philosophers are children unless they have been made men by Christ".[249] Furthermore, "the truth held by us" is to be distinguished from "the Hellenic truth", by virtue of the former's "extent of knowledge", certainty of demonstration, divine power and in other ways – "for we are taught by God, and instructed in the truly sacred letters by the Son of God".[250] More important still, it is the biblical revelation which really illuminates the true significance and meaning of Hellenic thought and speculation. Clement states this viewpoint emphatically in the sixth book of the *Stromateis*:

> "The meaning of Hellenic thought is fully illuminated by the truth bestowed on us through the Scriptures."[251]

As we have already shown, Clement attempts in the *Protreptikos* to demonstrate the truth of this claim by interpreting Hellenistic religious tradition in the light of the Bible. But this statement receives added significance in that it occurs in the context of the discussion of Greek plagiarisms from Barbarian sources, particularly from the Old Testament. Among the various theories[252] that Clement adduces to explain the medium for the divine provision of the truth in "the Hellenic thought", the theory of plagiarism, according to Molland, is "one which in the eyes of modern historians is rather unworthy of a thinker like Clement".[253] Certainly some of Clement's admirers are embarrassed by the amount of space and energy he devotes to a theme which, for them, "is entirely destitute of historical and literary foundation".[254] However, Eugène de Faye showed the deeper insight when he observed that the involved demonstration of Greek cultural and religious dependence on Hebrew tradition, to which Clement returns frequently in the *Stromateis*,[255] is, in fact, crucial for his entire theological project:

> "This thesis is basically the cornerstone of his entire system. He needed this sort of material support for building the bold and risky edifice which he was planning."[256]

It is true that Clement's massive chronological argument was fundamentally intended to establish that Christians by virtue of their connection with the Old Testament and Moses, were part of an ancient nation, with laws and traditions which entitled them to a place in the common history of mankind,[257] a right that was being denied them by Graeco-Roman traditionalists.[258] But if it is also true that Clement saw his major task as that of integrating all the fragments of truth from both Barbarian and Hellenistic sources into their unity in Christian truth – "the necessary work of forming an alliance between philosophy and Christianity"[259] – then the argument about Greek plagiarism from, and Greek dependence upon, the Old Testament is simply one dimension of the broader theory of the "peculiar" covenants. This becomes so because, ultimately, this theory of the covenants "peculiar" to Greeks and to Jews is another way of affirming the "divine intention behind the Greek tradition... and the consequent unity of all the sources of truth in God".[260] For the important factor in the "peculiar" covenants is not their diversity but their common origin and inspiration.[261] But since it is the Scriptures which provide the authentic interpretation of Christ who is the Truth,[262] the theory of dependence serves to secure the unity and universal significance of the Biblical tradition. Thus the theory of "peculiar" covenants and the theory of Greek dependence on Hebrew tradition, reinforce each other and point to the same conclusion: "for Clement, as for Justin, any truth the Greek tradition may contain proves no historical independence in face of Christian universalism".[263] It is not surprising that Clement, like Numenius of Apamea, believed that Plato was really Moses speaking Attic Greek.[264]

Consequently, Molland is right to suggest that to Clement's way of thinking, "there are many covenants in the history of mankind, but they all lead up to the one covenant in Christ".[265] This outlook is illustrated in a passage of the seventh book of the *Stromateis*, in which Clement compares the prayers of the pious to the blended incense mentioned in *Exodus* 30:34-36:

> "Wherefore we ought to offer to God sacrifices... such as He loves, that composite incense of which the Law speaks, which consists of prayers of many tongues and voices, or rather of different nations and races, which are prepared for the unity of faith by the gift of the covenants and brought together into that unity, with praises, with a pure heart, with just and right conduct, grounded in holy actions and righteous prayer."[266]

The crux of the passage is "by the gift of the covenants". Hort and Mayor take the words to refer to "Old and New Testament (*sic*) certainly, perhaps different testaments under the old".[267] However, if Molland is right in suggesting that behind "the covenants" there lies the more extensive Clementine concept of the variety of divine dealings, through which God brings together a unified body of the redeemed in Christ,[268] then it is, probably, the same idea that is expressed, though much less obscurely, in *Stromateis* 6, chapter 17:

"Rightly then to Jews belonged the Law, and to the Greeks philosophy, until the advent; and after that came the universal calling to be a peculiar people of righteousness through the teaching which flows from faith brought together by one Lord, the only God of both Greeks and Barbarians, or rather of the whole of mankind."[269]

V. Conclusion

Any estimate of Clement must pay tribute to his untiring efforts to establish in the Graeco-Roman world the claims of the Christian faith as a *religion savante*.[270] As we have sought to show, Clement did not see himself entirely as an innovator in this direction, and the early Christian tradition about the intellectual prestige of Alexandrine Christianity seems to have some basis in Clement's own eulogy of his teacher Pantaenus. The "encyclopedic conception of education"[271] as practised by his Alexandrian teacher also responded to some of Clement's own deepest intuitions. But Clement's advance on his teachers and his predecessors like Justin Martyr, in the movement for the vindication of Christianity in the Graeco-Roman world, is that he saw most clearly of all, and succeeded in articulating in writing, "that the religion in which he firmly believed could never have become a science, or assumed the shape of a philosophical system, without taking into account the best products of Greek thought".[272] His quest for the appropriately enlarged intellectual framework for what he considered to be the urgent task of his time, certainly places him in the forefront of the history of early Christian thought. R.B. Tollinton's observation is therefore very apt:

"For a positive exposition of Christian truth, challenging attention by its use of a secular method and meeting educated readers on ground that was their own, the time had not till now been ripe. Clement realised that the time for this had come."[273]

However, the appreciation of Clement's achievement in this regard – generally spoken of as "a process of Hellenisation of Christianity"[274] – has not been uniform. The theological agenda to which Clement devoted his entire Christian career has been criticised in modern times,[275] and has been described as an unwarranted and "illegitimate development of the teaching of Christ and His Apostles".[276] Indeed, his traditional claim to learning and scholarship – a claim recognised even by one who was critical of his theology and was the first to suspect Clement of heterodoxy[277] – has been challenged by other scholars who have sought to minimise Clement's first-hand acquaintance with the vast number of authors whom he quotes or alludes to in his writings.[278]

But Clement has also had his defenders. His place and prestige as "the first great Christian scholar" seems to have been largely vindicated by Tollinton who rightly points out that Clement "makes no claim to originality, inspiration, independence; rather tradition, collection, appropriation are the avowed characteristics of his work".[279]

There is little doubt that the trend in Christian scholarship which takes exception to Clement's attempt to integrate his sympathies with his Hellenistic background into his Christian commitment is, as Salvatore Lilla argues, generally based on the view that the Christian faith and Hellenistic intellectual culture represented two forces which were substantially alien to one another and between which no real synthesis was possible.[280] Even if this "ideological" resistance – in essence not dissimilar to the position of Celsus – to Clement's outlook may be said to rest, perhaps, on a misapprehension of his aim,[281] it may also be doubted whether Clement's writings are read closely enough. Eugène de Faye, whose work drew attention to the Christology of Clement as the *fulcrum* of his entire theological system, pointed to the failure, on the part of exponents of Clement's thought, to take seriously those passages, particularly in the *Protreptikos,* which constitute "a sort of profession of faith".[282] Commenting on the first chapter and the rousing appeal to conversion which concludes the *Protreptikos*, de Faye writes:

"Historians of Clement's thought do not often exploit passages like those. They seem to skim through them with the thought that it is not the thinker whom they are reading, it is only the preacher... And yet, is this right? You want to know precisely what part Christianity on the one hand, philosophy on the other, had in Clement's doctrines and ideas. Is he more of a Christian than a philosopher, or more of a philosopher than a Christian, that is the question which is being asked; and no account is taken of those passages where, as in the whole peroration of the *Protreptikos,* our author expresses his most intimate feelings and pours out his soul as a Christian! Where then can the tone of his faith be captured in greater purity?"[283]

It is because Clement, in the process of affirming his profound sympathies with his Hellenistic intellectual culture, remains "a singularly fervent Christian",[284] that his contribution to the ever renewed task of integrating Christian faith with culture is to be valued.[285] The fact that he felt free to attack the almost sacralised claims of "custom" in the interest of religious change,[286] and to commend to fellow educated Greeks conversion to a religious faith which was considered intrinsically, and not just historically, "Barbarian", is an indication that however deep his attachment to Hellenism, it cannot be said to have been uncritical. On the contrary, like Justin Martyr before him, he seems to have understood the truth of the Christian Gospel not as that of a religious system over against other systems, but rather as the truth of the one beneficent and loving God of all mankind, and capable of apprehension, however minimally, outside of, and prior to, the constituted Christian community. Advancing beyond the intuitions of Justin, Clement even postulated a tradition in Hellenistic culture which bore witness to an apprehension of the divine truth in the Hellenistic past.

John Patrick drew attention to the fact that in the *Protreptikos*, Clement "invites the Greeks to enter not into the fold of the Church but into the domain of truth".[287] This fact is not without significance. However, it is unlikely that Clement lived on the fringe of the Church as an intellectual and an individualist.[288] Rather, Clement saw the truth to be larger than the Church, and he viewed the Gospel of Christ fundamentally in its universal relevance.[289] The significance of Clement's conception of the theological task is as valid for the Christian Church now, on the threshold of a new era, in a new cultural matrix, as it was when F.J.A. Hort stated it nearly a century ago:

> "What he at once humbly and bravely attempted under great disadvantages at the beginning of the third century will have to be attempted afresh... if the Christian faith is to hold its ground among men; and when the attempt is made, not a few of his thoughts and words will probably shine out with new force, full of light for dealing with new problems."[290]

Notes

1. Jerome's observation occurs in his presentation of Clement's Alexandrian teacher, Pantaenus, who "... according to ancient customs in Alexandria where, from the time of the Evangelist Mark, there have always been Doctors of the Church, he was as well versed in ther divine Scriptures as in secular literature." See his *Liber de Viris Illustribus*, 36, in Migne, *PL*, 23, 651A. It is possible that Jerome is following Eusebius (*HE*, 5, 10), who dates the Alexandrian school of sacred learning "from the earliest times". For a treatment of the history, mission and achievement of this "school", see A. de

la Barre, "L'école chrétienne d'Alexandrie" in *DTC*, vol.1, coll. 805-824. Also, Gustave Bardy, "Aux origines de l'école d'Alexandrie" in *RSR*, vol.27, 1937, pp.65-90.

2. B.F. Westcott, "Clement of Alexandria" in *DCB*, vol.1, p.560. For evidence of early uncertainty, see Epiphanius, *Haer.* 32,6, "Clement, whom some say was from Alexandria, whilst others say from Athens" quoted in Stählin's edition of Clement's works, vol.1, xii.

3. R.B. Tollinton, *Clement of Alexandria: A Study in Christian Liberalism* (vol.1), London: Williams & Norgate, 1914, p.45.

4. *Strom.* 1,1; 11,1-2.

5. According to Eusebius (*HE*,5,11; 6,13), Clement, in his "Outlines", named Pantaenus as his teacher. This work now exists only in fragments. See Stählin's edition, vol.3, pp.195ff. There is little doubt that Pantaenus was that "Sicilian bee... concealed in Egypt... gathering the spoil of the flowers of the prophetic and apostolic meadows" (*Strom.* 1,1; 11,2).

6. Tollinton, *op.cit.*, p.164. Cf. F.L. Cross, *The Early Christian Fathers*, London: Duckworth, 1960, p.119.

7. L.G. Patterson, *God and History in Early Christian Thought – A study in themes from Justin Martyr to Gregory the Great*, London: A. & C. Black, 1967, pp.42f.

8. Eugène de Faye, *Clément d'Alexandrie: Etude sur les rapports du Christianisme et de la philosophie grecque au IIe siècle* (2nd ed), Paris: Ernest Léroux, 1906, p.15. "... the centre of gravity of Christianity is about to move. For about a century it is going to be neither in Asia Minor nor in Rome: it will be in Alexandria and in the regions going along with the impulse of the intellectual movement created by Clement and Origen."

9. See Theodor Zahn, *Forschungen zur Geschichte des neutestamentlichen Kanons und der altkirchlichen Literatur* (3 Theil: Supplementum Clementinum), Erlangen: Andreas Deichert, 1884, pp.156ff. Cf. John Patrick, *Clement of Alexandria* (The Croall Lecture, 1899-1900), Edinburgh and London: Blackwood & Sons, 1914, pp.7-8.

10. Claude Mondésert, *Clément d'Alexandrie: Introduction a l'étude de sa pensée religieuse à partir de l'Ecriture*, Paris: Aubier, 1944, p.222, n.3: "We know only that Clement (the convert); the other Clement, the Greek philosopher searching for the Truth (cf. *Strom.* 1,1; 11,1-2) is unknown to us..."

11. Tollinton, *op.cit.* (vol.1), Ch.1: "Clement", pp.1-30. On education in the Graeco-Roman world, see Henri-Irenée Marrou, *Histoire de l'éducation dans l'Antiquité*, Paris: Editions du Seuil, 1948.

12. A.-J. Festugière, *L'idéal religieux des Grecs et l'Evangile* (Preface by M.J. Lagrange), Paris: J. Gabalda et Cie., 1932. See especially "Introduction: L'idéal grec".

13. R.E. Witt has shown "the close connection that exists between his [Clement's] ideas and those of Greek philosophy", especially those of Clement's contemporary Plotinus and of Neo-platonism in general. See R.E. Witt, "The Hellenism of Clement of Alexandria" in *The Classical Quarterly*, vol.25, nos.3-4, July/October, 1931, pp.195-204.

14. Cf. C. Mondésert, *op.cit.*, p.226: "Few of the Fathers celebrated as Clement did the freshness and youth of the Gospel; that is because he sees the perfection of divine revelation, the supreme gesture which God made on behalf of doomed humanity."

15. For an exposition of this view of Clement's work, see Robert P. Casey, "Clement of Alexandria and the beginnings of Christian Platonism" in *HTR*,

16. R.B. Tollinton, *op.cit.* (vol.1), p.3.

17. A.-J. Festugière, *op.cit.* See especially, "Conclusion: La Délivérance'" pp.161-169.

18. *Ibid.* See especially Part 2, ch.1: "L'échec des philosophes" (pp.87-100), based on a study of Cicero's *De Natura Deorum*, and particularly of the inconclusive answers given by the representatives of the various philosophical schools to the question of God and religion.

19. Cf. A.D. Nock, *Early Gentile Christianity and its Hellenistic Background*, New York: Harper Torchbooks, 1964 (reprint), p.102: "Christianity satisfied both the religious and the philosophic instincts of the time."

20. M.-J. Lagrange, Preface to A.-J. Festugière, *op.cit.*, p.11.

21. Charles Bigg, *The Christian Platonists of Alexandria*, Oxford: Clarendon Press, 1886, p.47. Cf. A. de la Barre, "Clément d'Alexandrie" in *DTC*, vol.3, coll.139: "He (Clement) was above all an apostle, concerned to make himself all things to all men, a missionary..." For a study of Clement as a missionary theologian in the Hellenistic world, see Linwood Fredericksen, *A Christian Witness in a Non-Christian Culture According to Clement of Alexandria*, State University of Iowa, Ph.D., 1965, Ann Arbor: Univ. Microfilms.

22. For a view of Clement as the last and most important of the Apologists, see W. Jaeger, *Early Christianity and Greek Paideia*, London: Oxford University Press, 1961, p.57.

23. Cf. A. von Harnack, *History of Dogma*, vol.2 (ET by Neil Buchanan), London: Williams & Norgate, 1896, pp.234-235: "Here [in Clement] is found in form and content, the scientific Christian doctrine of religion which, while not contradicting the faith, does not merely support or explain it in a few places, but raises it to another and higher intellectual sphere, namely, out of the province of authority and obedience into that of clear knowledge and inward, intellectual assent emanating from love to God."

24. See J. Lebreton, "Le désaccord de la foi populaire et de la théologie savante dans l'Eglise chrétienne du IIIe siècle" in *RHE*, vol.19, 1923, pp.481-506. Lebreton's treatment of Clement's theology is spoilt by a tendency to exaggerate Clement's interest in a "higher religious knowledge due to a privileged revelation" (p.501). See also J. Lebreton, "La théorie de la connaissance religieuse chez Clément d'Alexandrie" in *RSR*, vol.18, 1928, pp.457-488.

25. C. Mondésert, *op.cit.*, p.223.

26. See W. Bousset, "Jüdisch-christlicher Schulbetrieb in Alexandria und Rom – Literarische Untersuchungen zu Philo und Clemens von Alexandria, Justin und Irenaeus" in *FRLANT*, vol.66, 1915, pp.155-271, on Clement. Bousset's attempt to isolate whole passages in Clement's writings as originating from Pantaenus has been overturned by other scholars. See especially, J. Munck, *Untersuchungen Über Klemens von Alexandria*, Stuttgart: Verlag von W. Kohlhammer, 1933, especially pp.127-204. Cf. Gustave Bardy, *op.cit.*

27. We owe this knowledge to the *Panegyric* (chs. 6-15) of Gregory Thaumaturgus, Origen's eminent pupil; Migne, *PG*, 10, 1068D-1096B.

28. Cf. John Patrick, *op.cit.*, p.6; Charles Bigg, *op.cit.*, pp.42f.

29. Eusebius, *HE*,6,19,13; Migne, *PG* 20, 568C. It is rather curious that Origen does not mention Clement in this connection.

30. Eusebius, *HE*, 5,10. He was "a man highly distinguished for his learning" in Migne, *PG*, 20,453C.

31. See *Strom.* 1,1; 11,1-2; cf. *Eclogae propheticae*, 56,1-2.

32. Admittedly, the situation regarding the boundary between "orthodoxy" and "heterodoxy" was somewhat unclear, as has been pointed out by Walter Bauer, *Orthodoxy and Heresy in Earliest Christianity* (ET), London: SCM, 1972, p.59: "... even into the third century, no separation between orthodoxy and heresy was accomplished in Egypt and the two types of Christianity were not yet at all clearly differentiated from each other". It is well known, however, that Alexandrian Gnostic teachers like Valentinus and Basilides elaborated a religious philosophy which, on the whole, was rejected by the Catholic Church. See A. von Harnack, *op.cit.*, p.170; Charles Bigg, *op.cit.*, pp.27-35. For a view of Clement's work as "an endeavour to mark more decisively" the line between heresy and orthodoxy, "but without surrendering to the anti-intellectual reaction with which some believers were expressing their opposition to Gnosticism", see Henry Chadwick, *Early Christian Thought and the Classical Tradition*, Oxford: Clarendon Press, 1966, p.33.

33. Cf. Henry Chadwick, *op.cit.*, p.32, on Clement's admiration for Pantaenus: "It appears that intelligence and orthodoxy were not commonly found together in second-century Alexandria."

34. See W.R. Inge, "Alexandrian Theology" in *ERE*, vol.1, pp.313-319.

35. J. Lebreton, "L'école chrétienne d'Alexandrie avant Origéne" in A. Fliche & V. Martin (eds), *Histoire de l'Eglise depuis les origines jusqu' à nos jours* (vol.2), Paris: Bloud et Gay, 1946, pp.226f.

36. It is still appropriate to speak of a "school", even if we accept Gustave Bardy's view (*op.cit.*, p.90) that it is Origen who strictly "deserves the name of founder" of the Catechetical School in its official capacity. Cf. J. Munck, *op.cit.*, p.185: "The Catechetical School in Alexandria was founded later than Clement. The schools of Pantaenus and Clement were enterprises which arose out of their personal work as teachers and died with them." In his final observation, Munck seems to me to have gone too far. As Origen's own tribute to Pantaenus shows, the latter's concerns and interests lived on. Bardy (*op.cit.*, p.89, n.79) acknowledges also that when Origen, in course of time, reorganised the official school into lower and higher grades (cf. Eusebius, *HE*, 6,15; Migne, *PG*, 20,553B), with personal responsibility for the advanced class, "he reassumes in some way the role which Clement played".

37. Cf. Tollinton, *op.cit.* (vol.1), p.150: "Pantaenus had taught him that the Gospel and Philosophy were not necessarily antagonistic and Clement probably learnt no more welcome lesson from his latest master."

38. Eugène de Faye, *op.cit.*, p.183: "What a road Christian thought has travelled since Justin Martyr! In this man we find the germ of almost all Clement's ideas."

39. Cf. Pierre Camelot, "Clément d'Alexandrie et l'utilisation de la philosophie grecque" in *RSR*, vol.21, 1931, pp.541-569. "What in Justin was only a generous longing becomes in Clement consciously worked out theory; what in Justin was indicated but barely outlined is in Clement developed at length." (p.563)

40. Clement's arrival in Alexandria is usually dated around the year AD 180; see Theodor Zahn, *op.cit.*, pp.156-176.

41. R.B. Tollinton, *op.cit.*, p.85.

42. See A. von Harnack, *The Mission and Expansion of Christianity in the First Three Centuries*, vol.2 (ET by James Moffatt), London: Williams & Norgate, 1908, pp.1-32.

43. R.B. Tollinton, *op.cit.*, p.85.

44. Eusebius, *HE*, 6,13; Migne, *PG*, 20,548B.

45. Theodor Zahn, *op.cit.*, p.37. Cf. A. von Harnack, *History of Dogma*, vol.1, pp.291f, n.2: "The Judaisers [referred to by Clement] were those Christians who, in principle, or to some extent, objected to the allegorical interpretation of the Old Testament."

46. Clement regards the author of this epistle as an authentic apostle (*Strom.* 2,6; 31,2), one of the seventy in the Gospels (*ibid.*, 2,20; 116,3), and quotes him several times. On its character and "Alexandrine mode of [Biblical] interpretation", see J.B. Lightfoot, *The Apostolic Fathers* (Part 1, vol.2), London: Macmillan & Co., 1890, pp.503ff.

47. Walter Bauer, *op.cit.*, p.53: "Each group congregated around a distinctive gospel, with the Jewish Christians at the same time also being influenced by the synagogue with regard to worship and organisation." The distinctive gospels, according to Bauer, are *The Gospel of the Egyptians* (for the Gentile Christians) and *The Gospel of the Hebrews* (used by Jewish Christians). On both of these "gospels", see E. Hennecke and W. Schneemelcher, *New Testament Apocrypha*, vol.1, (ET edited by R.McL. Wilson), Philadelphia: Westminster Press, 1963, pp.158-178. Schneemelcher comments on *The Gospel of the Egyptians*: "... we should be referred for its origin to an Encratite circle of the first half of the second century which cannot have comprised the whole body of the Egyptian Gentile Christians, i.e. Bauer's thesis would have to be somewhat modified" (p.177).

48. R.B. Tollinton, *op.cit.* (vol.1), p.85.

49. Marcel Simon, *Verus Israel – Etude sur les relations entre Chrétienne et Juifs dans l'Empire romain, AD 135-425*, (2nd ed.), Paris: E. de Boccard, 1964, pp.432-446. In *Strom.* 2,1; 2,1, Clement even expresses the view that his use of the Scriptures was also intended to aid a Jewish reader to turn "from the things he has believed [presumably falsely] to Him on whom he has not believed".

50. R.A. Markus, *Christianity in the Roman World*, London: Thames & Hudson, 1974, p.48.

51. *Strom.* 1,13; 57,6; cf.57,1. The "barbarian philosophy" meant here must be the Old Testament revelation.

52. Eugène de Faye, *op.cit.*, p.2.

53. Cf. Pierre Camelot, "Clément d'Alexandrie et l'utilisation de la philosophie grecque", p.564.

54. John Patrick, *op.cit.*, p.32: "Clement was the first to see the necessity of formulating a Christian theory of the universe, a Christian philosophy of history, a Christian code of ethics."

55. W. Bousset, *op.cit.*, p.155.

56. See R.B. Tollinton, *op.cit.* (vol.1), pp.183f; cf. John Patrick, *op.cit.*, pp.30f.

57. See *Strom.* 1,1.

58. See Eugène de Faye, *op.cit.*, pp.137-149, "Les Simpliciores". Also C. Mondésert, *op.cit.*, p.30.

59. John Patrick, *op.cit.*, p.30.

60. R.B. Tollinton, *op.cit.* (vol.1), p.183.

61. The chronology of Clement's three major extant writings has been much discussed, to no definite conclusion; see E.F. Osborn, *The Philosophy of Clement*

of Alexandria, Cambridge University Press, 1957, pp.5-7. The relation between the three works, based on *Paid*. 1,1; 3,3; and 3,12; 97,3-98,1, still seems to provide the most helpful chronological framework for understanding Clement's purpose and achievement. See J. Quasten, *Patrology* (Vol.2), *The Ante-Nicene Literature after Irenaeus*, Utrecht-Antwerp: Spectrum Publishers, 1964, p.7. Cf. Eugène de Faye, *op.cit.*, pp.51-60, "Le grand ouvrage de Clément".

62. *Protr.*, 11; 112,1.

63. Cf. *Strom.* 1,13; 57,6.

64. R.B. Tollinton, *op.cit.* (vol.2), p.273.

65. Cf. *Strom.* 1,7; 37,6: "Philosophy – I do not mean the Stoic, or the Platonic, or the Epicurean, or the Aristotelian, but whatever has been well said by each of these sects, *setting forth righteousness along with a doctrine pervaded by piety*, this eclectic whole I call philosophy. But such conclusions of human reasonings, as men have cut away and falsified, I would never call divine."

66. *Protr.* 11; 112,2. Cf. Justin, *Dialogue*, 2,1.

67. *Protr.* 11; 112,2; 113,1.

68. *Ibid.*, 11; 113,1.

69. *Ibid.*, 11; 114,3f. Cf. Paul's *Epistle to the Galations* 6:15.

70. R.B. Tollinton, *op.cit.* (vol.2), p.271.

71. *Ibid.*, p.274.

72. *Ibid.*, p.273.

73. W. Bousset, *op.cit.*, p.155.

74. Henry Chadwick, *op.cit.*, p.33; cf. John Patrick, *op.cit.*, p.32.

75. See A.-J. Festugière, *op.cit.*, pp.61-69.

76. *Protr.* 11; 114,2.

77. R.A. Norris, *God and World in early Christian theology – A study in Justin Martyr, Irenaeus, Tertullian and Origen*, London: A. & C. Black, 1965, pp.10f. On the history of this criticism, see P. Decharme, *La Critique des traditions religieuses chez les Grecs – des origines au temps de Plutarque*, Paris: A. Picard et Fils, 1904.

78. That this is what the *Protreptikos* especially was meant to achieve is well shown by Tollinton, *op.cit.* (vol.1), chapter on "An appeal to the educated".

79. An interesting indication of the importance of this concept in Clement's thinking is the fact that all the references for *propaideia* but the last, in Lampe, *PGL*, are taken from Clement.

80. R.B. Tollinton, *op.cit.* (vol.1), p.7; cf. p.13: "It is clear that in the main, Christianity was for him attained by advance and progress, as the stage of an even and gradual spiritual evolution, rather than by any hard-fought battle with his own nature, or by any painful and irrevocable abandonment of what had once been prized and dear."

81. See *Strom.* 1,13:57,1.

82. The criticism of the Christian faith as "essentially barbarian" was trenchantly stated by Celsus. See Origen, *Contra Celsum*, 1,2. Clement knew of some people who, trained in Greek philosophy, and believing in it, "shut their ears voluntarily to the truth, despising its Barbarian idiom" – see *Strom.* 6,8; 67,1.

83. *Strom.* 1,2; 20,2.

84. *Ibid.*, 1,2; 21,2.

85. In my view, there is much to commend the theory advanced by Eugène de Faye *(op.cit.*, pp.87-121), that the *Stromateis* do not constitute the projected *Didaskalos* (cf. *Paid.* 1,1), which was to be a systematic exposition of Christian doctrine, but is rather a parenthetical work, justifying the use of Greek philosophical ideas in the elaboration of Christian theology. Accordingly, the *Didaskalos* may never have been written. Cf. J. Quasten, *op.cit.*, p.12.

86. However, it is a mark of Clement's breadth of sympathy that he includes the wisdom of diverse peoples well beyond the boundaries of the Graeco-Roman world in his discussion of Barbarian cultural superiority to Greeks (cf. *Strom.* 1,15-16); and he is, possibly, the first Christian writer to mention Buddha *(ibid.*, 1,15; 71,6); cf. Henry Chadwick, *op.cit.*, p.32.

87. *Strom.* 1,1; 4,3.

88. *Ibid.*, 1,1; 5,4: "those who have been rightly reared in the words of truth and have received provision for eternal life, wing their way to heaven."

89. See especially, *Strom.* 2,2-6,11 and 5,1-3.

90. *Ibid.*, 1,1; 8,2.

91. See Eugène de Faye, *op.cit.*, pp.201-216. On the primacy of faith for Clement, de Faye comments: "On this major point he never varied. It was a fixed principle in his thought. He returns to it so often and with such insistence that it is clear that he holds to it absolutely. In fact it is the fundamental principle of his Christianity, the one which constitutes the originality of the idea which he constructs of the links between the Christian religion and philosophy."

92. *Strom.* 1,1; 7,3.

93. *Ibid.*, 1,1; 8,2.

94. See *ibid.*, 1,1; 1,2: "Epicurus the leader of atheism"; cf. 6,8; 67,2: "those who in the Hellenic philosophy preach the impiety and hedonism of Epicurus, and whatever other tenets are disseminated contrary to right reason exist among the Greeks as spurious fruits of the divinely bestowed gift". And yet, with characteristic breadth of sympathy, Clement finds worthy elements in Epicurean thought (cf. *Strom.* 4,8; 69,2-4, and *ibid.*, 5,14; 138,2).

95. Eugène de Faye, *op.cit.*, p.164.

96. See for instance, Theodor Zahn, *op.cit.*, pp.150ff.

97. See *Strom.* 1,21; 101,2.

98. See Athenagoras, *Legatio*, 8,1.

99. *Strom.* 1,1; 11,3.

100. *Strom.* 1,1; 15,3.

101. *Ibid.*, 1,1; 15,4-16,1. The references are to *1 Corinthians* 9,20-21 and *Colossians* 1:28.

102. *1 Corinthians* 1:22.

103. John Patrick, *op.cit.*, p.42.

104. C. Mondésert, *op.cit.*, pp.187-219. Mondésert draws attention to Clement's frequent use of the word ἀνθρωπότης, especially in the *Paidagogos* (22 times), a book which would seem to have been addressed to the Christian community, and he comments appropriately: "When it comes to mankind, one cannot but be struck by the insistence with which the concept is marked in Clement of the unity of the human race within itself, and the union of mankind

across all ages and in all places: in Creation, in the Fall, in the different stages of revelation and redemption, in the salvation by Christ and finally in the blessedness of the *pleroma*, the arrival at the divine Monad." (p.190).

105. See *Strom*. 6,2; 28,5: "The common (Father) God" invoked by Aecus; also, *Strom*. 7,16; 95,3 – "We have one source (ἀρχήν) of teaching, the Lord", operating πολυτρόπως καὶ πολυμερῶς (*Heb*.1:1).

106. *Strom*. 1,1; 16,2. My emphasis.

107. The effort to interpret Hellenistic tradition and religious history through Biblical history without resort to the theory of plagiarism, is very admirably done by Clement in the *Protreptikos*, as we shall show in the next section.

108. See Einar Molland, *The Conception of the Gospel in the Alexandrian Theology*, Oslo: Jacob Dybwad, 1938, pp.10-14.

109. *Strom*. 1,1; 17,2.

110. *Ibid.*, 1,1; 18,1.

111. See for instance, *Strom*. 1, chs.6,9-10,20.

112. See *Strom*. 1,12 & 20; 2,11; 5,1; 6,10.

113. See Pierre Camelot, "Les Idées de Clément d'Alexandrie sur l'utilisation des sciences et de la littérature profane" and "Clément d'Alexandrie et l'utilisation de la philosophie grecque" in *RSR*, vol.21, 1931, pp.38-66 and pp.541-569.

114. See *Strom*. 6,11;91,1f: "The studies of philosophy therefore and philosophy itself are aids in treating of the truth... Accordingly the soul must be prepared and variously exercised, if it would become in the highest degree good. For there is the scientific and practical element in truth; and the latter flows from the speculative and there is need of great practice and exercise and experience"; and *Strom*. 1,9; 43,4: "I call him truly learned who brings every-thing to bear on the truth; so that from geometry and music and grammar and philosophy itself, he guards the truth against assault."

115. Pierre Camelot, "Les idées de Clément d'Alexandrie sur l'utilisation des sciences..." p.51.

116. *Strom*. 1,2; 19,3.

117. *Ibid.*, 1,2; 19,4.

118. See *Protr*. 11; 112,1.

119. See *Strom*. 1,3.

120. *Ibid.*, 2,1; 3,1-2.

121. On the importance of this aspect of the "clash of cultures" involving Christians in the Graeco-Roman world, see E.R. Dodds, *Pagan and Christian in an Age of Anxiety – Some aspects of religious experience from Marcus Aurelius to Constantine*, Cambridge: Cambridge University Press, 1965, pp.118ff.

122. *Strom*. 1,20; 100,1-2. The references are to *1 Corinthians* 1:24, and possibly *Matthew* 21:33.

123. *Strom*. 1,13; 57-58. For a thorough study of "the true Gnostic" in Clement, see Walther Völker, "Der wahre Gnostiker nach Clemens Alexandrinus", *TU, 57*, 1952. On Clement's view of the nature and value of philosophy and intellectual culture generally, see especially, "Exkurs: Wesen und Wert der Philosophie", pp.332-352. However, Völker seems to suggest, wrongly in my view, that the philosophical and intellectual culture which Clement pleads for is really extraneous to him as an orthodox Christian theologian, and hence of little substantial importance for his theological

enterprise.

124. Cf. R.A. Markus, *op.cit.*, p.48: "Optimism is a by-product of self-confidence. The optimism distinctive of Alexandrian Christianity was based on the belief that everything that was best in the world pointed to Christianity and found a home in the Church. Men like Justin, Clement and Origen... saw no radical discontinuity between the culture of classical antiquity and... Christianity... Assimilating Greek thought and learning did not appear to them as likely to submerge their Christian faith beneath a culture felt to be alien or hostile."

125. See Origen, *Contra Celsum*, 5,34.

126. It is evident that in terms of Celsus' anti-Christian polemic, νόμοσ in the fragment from Pindar whom he quotes, means "custom". Interestingly, when Origen comes to deal with the saying, "custom (νόμος) is king of all" (5,40), he reverts to the less controversial sense of "law", and thus quietly avoids the really explosive issue that Celsus is raising. If this view is correct, then Clement's willingness to confront the problem of "custom" is all the more noteworthy. Clement also quotes, to his advantage, the same text from Pindar. See *Strom.* 1,29; 181,4.

127. Raoul Mortley, "The Past in Clement of Alexandria: A study in an attempt to define Christianity in socio-cultural terms" in E.P. Sanders (ed), *Jewish and Christian Self-Definition (vol.1): The Shaping of Christianity in the Second and Third Centuries,* London: SCM Press, 1980, pp.186-200.

128. *Strom.* 1,21-29.

129. Raoul Mortley, *op.cit.*, p.187.

130. *Ibid.*, p.200.

131. *Protr.* 10; 89,1.

132. See Pierre de Labriolle, *La Réaction Païenne: Etude sur le polémique anti-chrétienne du Ier au VIe siècle,* Paris: L'Artisan du Livre, 1948 (1st publ. 1943). On the criticisms of the Christian movement: "... few grievances emerge from the pens of his detractors as often as that of wrecking ancestral traditions." (p.13)

133. Henri-Irenée Marrou, *op.cit.*, p.284. Cf. Jean Daniélou, *Gospel Message and Hellenistic Culture* (ET), London: Darton, Longman & Todd, 1973, p.131: "Clement accepted the title for his own work, since this was a direct challenge to that of Aristotle, summoning men to the true philosophy; namely, Christianity."

134. Augustine, *Confessions*, 3,4. See Henri-Irenée Marrou, *Saint Augustin et la fin de la culture antique,* Paris: E.de Boccard, 1938, pp.161-173.

135. Henri-Irenée Marrou, *Histoire de l'Education dans l'Antiquité,* p.283.

136. L. Alfonsi, "La 'Consuetudo' nei 'Protrettici'", in *VC*, 18, 1964, p.32. See fragments from Cicero's *Hortensius*, quoted in Alfonsi's article (p.33).

137. Cf. Cicero, *Paradoxa Stoicorum*, 8: quoted in L. Alfonsi, *op.cit.*, p.33.

138. See the brief but illuminating study of F.H. Brigham, Jr., "The Concept of *New Song* in Clement of Alexandria's *Exhortation to the Greeks*", in *Classical Folia* (New York), vol.16, 1962, pp.9-13. Brigham discusses, as possible sources, the following: (a) the *Protagoras* of Plato, (b) *Moses 1* of Philo, (c) the *Psalms* (LXX) 32:2-4; 39:3-4; 97:1-3; 143:9-10; 149:1, (d) *Isaiah* 42:6, (e) *Revelation* (Apocalypse) 5:9; 14:2.

139. Cf. F.H. Brigham, *op.cit.* (pp.12f): "'New Song' was familiar to many in his Christian audience through the liturgical use of the psalms and would

at the same time recall the oracular tradition of the ancient poets for his pagan readers."

140. *Protr.* 1; 2,1.

141. *Ibid.*, 1; 2,3.

142. *Isaiah* 2:3.

143. *Protr.* 1; 2,3.

144. Homer, *Odyssey*, 4,217f (ET by A.T. Murray, *LCL*, pp.52f). It is evident that for Clement the words of Homer can be taken to apply to the experience of salvation produced by the God of the Scriptures. Pierre Camelot has found 190 instances of direct quotations or references relating to Homer. See his "Les idées de Clément d'Alexandrie sur l'utilisation des sciences..." p.60.

145. *Protr.* 1; 3,1.

146. With regard to the last statement, Stählin refers to *Philippians* 3:20, the heavenly citizenship of Christians. However, Clement could equally be referring to *Romans* 8:24ff, on the liberty of the children of God, as their state of salvation in Christ.

147. *Protr.* 1; 3,2.

148. *Ibid.*

149. *Ibid.*, 1; 3,1.

150. *Ibid.*, 1; 4,2. *Matthew* 3:9.

151. *Protr.* 1; 4,3; *Matthew* 3:7; *1 Timothy* 6:11.

152. See Herodotus, *Histories 2* (ET by A.D. Godley, *LCL*), pp.274ff.

153. See Apollonius Rhodius, *The Argonautik*a, 4,264 (ET by R.C. Seaton, *LCL*), pp.312f.

154. Herodotus, *op.cit.*, pp.274ff.

155. *Psalm* 109:3 (LXX); *John* 1:1.

156. *Protr.* 1;6,3.

157. *Ibid.*, 1; 6,4-5.

158. *John* 1:1.

159. *Protr.* 1; 5,4: "The Lord fashioned man a beautiful, breathing instrument after His own image; and assuredly He Himself is an all-harmonious instrument of God, melodious and holy, the wisdom that is above this world, and the heavenly Word."

160. Cf. Justin, *Dial.* 40,1 for use of τὸ πλάσμα (rational image) in describing Adam.

161. Cf. *Ephesians* 1:4, Christians are "in Him (i.e. Christ) before the foundation of the world".

162. *Titus* 2:11-13. Cf. *Strom.* 7, 16; 102,3.

163. *Protr.* 1; 7,3. Cf. *Paid.* 1,9; 83,3.

164. *Protr.* 1; 7,5f. In chapter 2 (12,2), Clement links the Bacchic serpent with the serpent in *Genesis* 3, by seizing on a verbal resemblance between the cry of the Bacchants (Eυα), Eve (Eυα) "through whom error entered into the world", and the transliteration of the Aramaic word for serpent *ḥiwyā*'. It is interesting moreover, that, according to Ludwig Koehler, *ḥiwyā*'is a derivation from *ḥawwâ* (Eve)! See Koehler-Baumgartner, *Lexicon in Veteris Testamenti Libros*, Leiden: E.J. Brill, 1958, p.280.

165. *Protr.* 1; 7,6.

166. *Ibid.*, 1; 8,1-2. Stählin cites *Exòdus* 7:3; 13:21; *Acts* 7:36.

167. *Protr.* 1; 8,1. Cf. *Ephesians* 2:2. Clement seems to imply that though the Old Testament has relevance for all men, the apostolic writings (the New Testament) apply particularly to Gentiles.

168. *Protr.* 1; 8,2.

169. *Ibid.*, 1; 9,1ff. 170. *Luke* 1:7-13.

171. Stählin associates the two texts.

172. *Protr.* 1; 9,2-3.

173. See for instance, *Strom.* 2,6; 29,1. Cf. Justin, *1 Apology*, 53,3.

174. *Protr.* 1; 9,2.

175. *Ibid.*, 1; 10,1.

176. *Ibid.*, 1; 10,3. Also 12; 120,1-5. Cf. John Patrick, *op.cit.*, p.61: "He represents Christianity as the true mystery of which the Greek mysteries were only a shadow, and calls on the Greeks to embrace Christianity in the very language of the mysteries which he urged them to abandon."

177. *Protr.* 2-4.

178. *Ibid.*, 2; 11,1.

179. *Ibid.*, 4; 46,1.

180. *Ibid.*, 4; 51,2ff

181. *Ibid.*, 4; 51,6.

182. Cf. *ibid.*, 10; 98,4.

183. G.W. Butterworth, "Clement of Alexandria and Art" in *JTS*, vol.17, 1916, pp.68-76.

184. *Ibid.*, p.70. See *Protr.* 4; 57,1.

185. *Protr.* 4; 59,2.

186. *Ibid.*, 6; 68,1. See chs.5 and 6.

187. Cf. *ibid.*, 4; 50,4f.

188. Clement is careful enough as a scholar to point out elsewhere that even the philosophical tradition never quite fully succeeded in overcoming the grip of the old deities. See *Strom.* 6,6; 44: "For to those who were righteous according to the Law [that is, Jews] faith was wanting... But to those who were righteous according to philosophy, not only faith in the Lord, but also the abandonment of idolatry was necessary."

189. *Protr.* 6; 68,2-3. Cf. "The thoughts of virtuous men are produced through the inspiration of God, the soul being disposed in the way it is, and the divine will being conveyed to human souls, with particular divine ministers contributing to such services. For regiments of angels are distributed over the nations and cities. And, perchance, some are assigned to individuals" *Strom.* 6,17; 157,4-5 (cf. *Deuteronomy* 32:8; *Hebrews* 1:14).

190. *Protr.* 7.

191. Cf. Pierre Camelot, "Les idées de Clément d'Alexandrie sur l'utilisation des sciences..." pp.60f.

192. *Protr.* 7; 73,1.

193. *Ibid.*, 7; 76,3.

194. Cf. *ibid.*, 7; 74,2.

195. *Ibid.*, 7; 74,7.

196. *Ibid.*, 6; 72,5.

197. *Ibid.*, 8; 77,1.

198. *Ibid.*, 7; 74,7.

199. *Ibid.*, 8; 77,1.

200. *Ibid.*, 8; 77,1.

201. *Ibid.*, 8; 77,1.

202. *Ibid.*, 8; 77,1.

203. *Ibid.*, 8; 77,1.

204. *Ibid.*, 8; 77,2-81,1.

205. "The holy apostle of the Lord... accuses the Greeks...", *ibid.*, 8; 81,2.

206. Cf. Henry Chadwick, *Early Christian Thought and the Classical Tradition*, p.64: "Clement is hellenised to the core of his being yet unreserved in his adhesion to the Church in the sense that he is opposed to Gnosticism and bound to the authority of Scripture as inspired revelation by which alone he has certitude concerning God's will and purpose."

207. *Protr.* 9; 86,2. Cf. Plato, *Theaetetus* 176,B (ET by H.N. Fowler, *LCL*), pp.128f.

208. *Protr.* 9; 88,2.

209. *Ibid.*, 6; 72,3.

210. *Ibid.*, 10; 89,1.

211. *Ibid.*, 2; 11,1ff.

212. *Ibid.*, 10; 89,2.

213. *Ibid.*, 10; 89,2.

214. *Ibid.*, 10; 89,3; 90,2.

215. *Ibid.*, 10; 110,1.

216. *Ibid.*, 10; 110,3.

217. *Ibid.*, 12; 118,1.

218. *Paid.* 1, 9; 83,3.

219. B.F. Westcott, "Clement of Alexandria" in *DCB*, vol.1 p.566. An interesting indication of how deeply Clement had come to understand himself in the light of Christ as an all-encompassing Reality of experience and thought is given by the "Hymn to Christ" which concludes the three books of the *Paidagogos,* celebrating the excellence of Christ's moral teaching.

220. On the hermeneutical problem affecting both Biblical and Hellenistic traditions that faced early Hellenistic Christian writers including Clement, see W. den Boer, "Hermeneutic problems in early Christian literature" in *VC*, vol.1, 1947, pp.150-167. On Clement as exegete, and his combination of "Greek allegorism" with "Biblical typology" to explain the universal history of salvation, see Jean Daniélou, *op.cit.*, pp.237-255.

221. C. Mondésert, *op.cit.*, pp.188-189. Cf. Eugène de Faye, *op.cit.*, p.179: "Clement likes to establish his doctrines by the witness of Scripture."

222. Cf. Clement's uncertainty on the relative positions of philosophy and the Scriptures in the history of salvation: "God is the cause of all good things; but of some primarily as the Old and New Testaments; and of others by consequence, as philosophy; perchance too, philosophy was given to the Greeks

directly and primarily till the Lord should call the Greeks" (*Strom.* 1,5; 28,2). For a view that the Gospel (NT) as distinct from the Law (OT) has a particular relevance for Hellenistic tradition, see *Strom.* 6,6; 44,2ff. Cf. Einar Molland, *The Conception of the Gospel in the Alexandrian Theology*, pp.71f.

223. *Strom.* 6,8; 67,1.

224. Recently, with particular reference to the intellectual and cultural background to Clement's ideas, Salvatore R.C. Lilla, *op.cit.*, pp.9-59. See also Einar Molland, *The Conception of the Gospel in the Alexandrian Theology*, pp.40-69; also his "Clement of Alexandria on the origin of Greek philosophy" in *Symbolae Osloenses*, fasc.15-16, 1936, pp.57-85. See also Thomas Finan, "Hellenism and Judeo-Christian history in Clement of Alexandria" in *Irish Theological Quarterly*, vol.28, 1961, pp.83-114. Eugène de Faye's monumental study of Clement is, as shown by its sub-title, inspired by the conviction that Clement provides an important response to one of the vital questions of his time: "The main one of the [pressing questions] the answer to which affected the very future of the new religion was to know what sort of attitude it would adopt with regard to Greek philosophy."; see his *op.cit.*, p.51. For de Faye this was "the main question of the epoch" (p.127)

225. See for example, R.A. Markus, *op.cit.*, ch.3, "The crisis of identity", pp.48-69.

226. *Strom.* 1,5; 32,4. Cf. *Strom.* 2,11; 48,1; *Strom.* 6,7; 56,2.

227. *Ibid.*, 2,2; 5,1.

228. *Ibid.*, 5,8; 51,1. Cf. the writers of the Old Testament are "philosophers of the Hebrews", especially, *Strom.* 1,21; 101,1.

229. *Strom.* 1,28; 176,1.

230. *Ibid.*, 1,20;99,1. Cf. *ibid.*, 2,2; 5,1: "The barbarian philosophy which we follow, is in reality perfect and true."

231. *Strom.* 6,8; 67,1.

232. *Ibid.*, 2,5; 22,3. See *Luke* 18:25; *Matthew* 19:24; *Mark* 10:25.

233. Einar Molland, *The Conception of the Gospel in the Alexandrian Theology*, p.41.

234. See *Strom.* 1,5,7; 6,5-8,17; 7,2.

235. Einar Molland, *The Conception of the Gospel in the Alexandrian Theology*, p.72.

236. For an analysis of the various fragments of this composition, see E. Hennecke & W. Schneemelcher (eds), *op.cit.*, vol.2 (ET by R. McL.Wilson), pp.94-102.

237. See Chapter One above: "*Non licet esse vos:* The problem of Christian identity in the context of Graeco-Roman culture of the early Roman Empire".

238. *Strom.* 6,5; 39,1. Cf. *Strom.* 1,19; 91,5.

239. *Ibid.*, 6,5; 39,5.

240. *Jeremiah* 31:31f.

241 *Strom.* 6,5; 41,7.

242. *Ibid.*, 6,5; 42,1-2.

243. *Ibid.*, 6,5; 42,3.

244. *Ibid.*, 6,6; 47,4.

245. *Ibid.*, 6,6; 46,4. cf. *Acts* 10:34; *Romans* 2:11.

246. *Strom.* 6,6; 47,2.

247. *Ibid.*, 6,7; 54,1.

248. *Ibid.*, 1,20; 97,1-2.

249. *Ibid.*, 1,11; 53,2.

250. *Ibid.*, 1,20; 97,4. Cf. *1 Thessalonians* 4:9; *2 Timothy* 3:15.

251. *Strom.* 6,2; 4,3.

252. These theories have been thoroughly analysed by Einar Molland in his "Clement of Alexandria on the origin of Greek philosophy", pp.62-75.

253. Einar Molland, *op.cit.* p.63.

254. John Patrick, *op.cit.*, p.48. Patrick plays down the importance of the theme for Clement: "The only original contribution by Clement to it is that though the truth was stolen, it was none the less true, a real possession however acquired. He did not invent the hypothesis, but he found in it a weapon at once to disarm the opposition of the narrower section in the Church, and a means of constructing a bridge between Greek thought and Christian truth" (pp.48-49). Cf. Thomas Finan, *op.cit.*, p.101: "It is not necessary to dwell at length on an apologetic *topos* which does not represent the best thinking of Clement on the subject."

255. See *Strom.* 1,11,14-16,21-29; *Strom.* 2,5,18; *Strom.* 5,1,10-12,14; *Strom.* 6,2-6. Cf. *Protr.* 6,70,1.

256. Eugène de Faye, *op.cit.*, p.186.

257. Raoul Mortley, *op.cit.*, especially pp.190-200.

258. Clement calls Moses "our Moses" (*Strom.* 1,24; 158,1), designates the Old Testament as ancient literature "ours" (*Strom.* 1,29; 180,2), and speaks of "the departure from Egypt of our kinsmen the Hebrews" (*Strom.* 1,22; 150,2). According to Salvatore R.C. Lilla, *op.cit.*, p.37: "It is difficult to resist the hypothesis that Clement has already read Celsus' *Alethes Logos* and bore in mind his charges against Judaism and Christianity when he wrote the *Stromateis.*"

259. Eugène de Faye, *op.cit.*, p.187.

260. Thomas Finan, *op.cit.*, p.100.

261. Cf. C. Mondésert, *op.cit.*, p.210: "Basically there is only one revelation of God who is also its Author." Also Salvatore R.C. Lilla, *op.cit.*, p.31: "What really mattered for Clement... was to show the substantial identity between the content of the Greek philosophical doctrines and the teaching of Scripture and in this way also the divine origin of Greek philosophy."

262. Cf. *Protr.* 8,77,1.

263. Thomas Finan, *op.cit.*, p.88.

264. *Strom.* 1,22; 150,4.

265. Einar Molland, *The Conception of the Gospel in the Alexandrian Theology*, p.73.

266. *Strom.* 7,6; 34,2.

267. F.J.A. Hort & J.B. Mayor (eds), *Clement of Alexandria: Miscellanies Book VII (The Greek Text, with introduction, translation, notes, dissertations and indexes)*, London: Macmillan & Co., 1902, p.250.

268. The idea of "the unity of faith", an evident reference to *Ephesians* 4:13, argues in favour of such an interpretation.

269. *Strom.* 6,17; 159,9.

270. The expression, as a description of Christianity, is used by H.-I. Marrou, *Histoire de l'Education..* p.418.

271. J. Lebreton, "L'école chrétienne d'Alexandrie avant Origène", in A. Fliche & V. Martin, *op.cit.* (vol.2), p.226.

272. Salvatore R.C. Lilla, *op.cit.*, p.9. Cf. Thomas Finan, *op.cit.*, p.93: "While Justin's problem is the larger, speculative historical problem of justifying the ways of God in history and the revelation of truth, Clement has the more delicate and complex task of integrating in a single *Weltanschauung* the two sets of values represented by the Greek and the Judeo-Christian traditions."

273. R.B. Tollinton, *op.cit.* (vol.1), p.183.

274. Salvatore R.C. Lilla, *op.cit.*, p.232.

275. See Adolf von Harnack, *History of Dogma*, vol.2; on Clement, see especially Chapter 6, "The Transformation of the Ecclesiastical Tradition into a Philosophy of Religion, or the Origin of the Scientific Theology and Dogmatic: Clement and Origen". Also Edwin Hatch *The Influence of Greek Ideas and Usages upon the Christian Church* (The Hibbert Lectures, 1888), London: Williams & Norgate, 1890. Hatch refused to admit a mediating position between "Greek elements in Christianity" and "the uncoloured majesty of the Gospels". In his view, "whether we accept the one or the other, it seems clear that much of the Greek element may be abandoned" (pp.351-352).

276. Hort & Mayor, *op.cit.*, p.xxii.

277. The ninth-century Church Father, Photius, cast doubt on Clement's orthodoxy, and yet was compelled to concede that Clement's work exhibited considerable erudition, *Bibliotheca* 110; Migne, *PG*, 103, 384D-385A), quoted in Stählin's vol.1, p.xv.

278. Hermann Diels, *Doxographi Graeci*, Berlin, 1879. Diels describes Clement as "... himself the most cunning purloiner of other people's material" (p.19). Also see the helpful note on "Les sources de Clément" in Eugène de Faye, *op.cit.*, pp.333-336.

279. R.B. Tollinton, *op.cit.* (vol.1), p.164. On the question of Clement's dependence on compilations and secondary sources for his knowledge of the history of philosophy, Camelot observes: "Whatever answer might be made to these questions, it is nonetheless certain that Clement was well acquainted with the history of Greek philosophy; this may have been an acquaintance at second hand, but in spite of that a well informed acquaintance." See his "Clément d'Alexandrie et l'utilisation de la philosophie grecque", p.542.

280. Salvatore R.C. Lilla, *op.cit.*, p.2.

281. Cf. Linwood Fredericksen, *op.cit.*, p.260: "Though he did aid in bringing about the Hellenisation of Christianity, his goal was the Christianisation of Hellenism."

282. Eugène de Faye, *op.cit.*, p.265.

283. *Ibid.*, p.69.

284. *Ibid.*, p.71. Cf. Pierre Camelot: "Clement is truly and profoundly Christian.." See his "Les idées de Clément d'Alexandrie sur l'utilisation des sciences.." p.66.

285. See H. Richard Niebuhr, *Christ and Culture*, New York: Harper & Row, 1975 (1st publ. 1951), pp.123ff.

286. Cf. *Paid.* 1,7; 54,3: "What is called by men an ancestral custom passes

away in a moment, but the divine guidance is a possession which abides for ever."

287. John Patrick, *op.cit.*, p.60.

288. G.W. Butterworth, *op.cit.*, p.75. Cf. Hans von Campenhausen, *The Fathers of the Greek Church* (ET), London: A. & C. Black, 1963, p.36: "... of all the Fathers of the Church, Clement was without any doubt the most unecclesiastical of all, in other words, the one who was most indifferent to the organised Church". However, according to *Paid.* 1,6; 37,3, Clement may even have been a presbyter in the Church of Alexandria.

289. On Clement's achievement as a "missionary theologian in Hellenistic culture", Linwood Fredericksen (*op.cit.*, p.12) writes: "Clement's lack of writing a systematic theology book for future generations to peruse does not diminish his importance to second-century Christianity. He provided a philosophical-theological framework in which Christianity could interpret itself to the Hellenistic culture. As such an apologist, he was a kind of missionary to a gradually increasing segment of the Church, the educated classes. Had it not been for the intellectual approach to Christian evangelism many of the cultured pagans would not have grasped the appeal of the Christian *kerygma*".

290. F.J.A. Hort, *Six Lectures on the Ante-Nicene Fathers*, London: Macmillan & Co., 1895, pp.90-91. Cf. R.B. Tollinton, *op.cit.* (vol.1), pp.x-xi: "... in a transitional age, he had a singular power of discerning spiritual affinities, and... on most of the problems of his time, his judgment was generous and sound. It is his temper, his attitude, his religious 'orientation' which are really worth preserving."

Part Two

THE MODERN AFRICAN PREDICAMENT: IDENTITY AND QUESTS FOR INTEGRATION

"The recognition that religions are not unitary mutually exclusive entities which replace each other in the process of religious change, but that a person's or a community's religious experience has to be taken in itself and within its own social setting, was perhaps more readily learned in Africa than elsewhere."

A.F. Walls, "A Bag of Needments for the Road: Geoffrey Parrinder and the study of religion in Britain", p.145.

Chapter Six

Christianity as "Civilisation": The Legacy of "The Third Opportunity"[1] and the Making of a Modern Identity Problem

I. "The Image of Africa": Antecedents and Formative Factors

To appreciate adequately the kind of agenda which Africa's theological writers have set for themselves in the post-missionary era, it is important to understand the image of Africa in the corporate European mind during "the Great Century"[2] of the Christian missionary advance. That image has been aptly described by Dr Adrian Hastings in his *Church and Mission in Modern Africa:*

> "In fact, neither in the nineteenth nor in the early twentieth centuries did missionaries give much thought in advance to what they would find in Africa. What struck them, undoubtedly, was the darkness of the continent; *its lack of religion and sound morals*, its ignorance, its general pitiful condition made worse by the barbarity of the slave trade. Evangelisation was seen as liberation from a state of absolute awfulness and the picture of unredeemed Africa was often painted in colours as gruesome as possible, the better to encourage missionary zeal at home."[3]

It is not surprising that, as a result of this perception of Africa, the European missionary approach tended to

> "treat everything pre-Christian in Africa as either harmful or at best valueless, and to consider the African once converted from paganism as a sort of *tabula rasa* on which a wholly new religious psychology was somehow to be imprinted."[4]

The impact of this largely negative early European evaluation of African tradition, particularly in religion, upon the African theological consciousness was to be immense and virtually every African Christian writer of modern times has responded in one form or other to this "European *Afrikaanschauung*".[5]

It is worth noting, however, that the character of this European view of Africa did not originate with Christian missionaries during the "Great Century". As Philip Curtin has ably demonstrated, the general image formed by the mid-nineteenth century of African racial, social and cultural inferiority to European peoples "was very largely drawn from Europe's first impressions taken during the earlier and formative decades".[6] It is significant therefore that "before 1800... the chief contact of Negro Africa with European peoples was through the traffic in slaves for the white man's economic enterprises in the New World".[7] To understand properly what went into making the missionary view of Africa, it is to the quality of European contact with Africa in the few preceding centuries that one must look.

In contrast to its economic advantages to European slaving interests, the trade in human beings from Africa could only produce loss to Africans, even if it enriched some individuals and for a time also some states, at the expense of others. After a thorough examination of the evidence, Henry Gemery and Jan Hogendorn came to the conclusion that "the economic costs of the trade [i.e. to West Africa] exceeded its gains on an overall basis", so that "the overseas slave trade had a detrimental economic impact even without considering its social costs".[8]

If the effect of this "uncommon market" in the economic sphere was to help widen the "technological gap" between African and European societies, the slave trade also entailed social and political disruptions within African societies themselves. As African societies were drawn more and more into slaving, either in order to survive economically or in order to avoid being enslaved, or both, social and political relationships and structures were undermined through wars fought now with European firearms.[9] The slave trade thus promoted the disintegration of African societies and prepared the conditions for eventual colonial occupation when the slaving partnership was terminated by some of the European nations which had derived the greatest prosperity through the trade. The slave trade thus became the prelude to the misfortunes of colonialism.[10]

Accordingly Basil Davidson is right in his judgment that "in a strict sense the European connection was a tragic one for Africa".[11] This was most devastatingly so in the formation of European attitudes towards Africa and Africans. Since European contact with Africans was largely limited to the trade in slaves from Africa, many Europeans knew Africans as little more than people who "might be had" with relative ease for servile tasks.[12] The concept of the "Great Chain of Being" became a fundamental part of the intellectual outlook in Europe in the eighteenth century,[13] ensuring that "the Negro" was last in the rank following "White", "Red" and "Yellow" races. The absence of scientific and biological justification for this conclusion was compensated for by criteria drawn from non-scientific assumptions.[14] When Anton Wilhelm Amo, the "Guinea African" as he was often described, became known as an outstanding scholar and philosopher in eighteenth-century Germany, he was praised by the Chancellor and Senate of the University of Wittenberg in 1734 as

"an excellent example of the fact that from amongst uncivilised nations, through special education, outstanding and important individuals could emerge."[15]

Amo was an exception that proved the rule.

At the end of the slave trade era, which coincided with the climactic stages of an awakening of humanitarian conscience in Europe,[16] the image of Africa was well-nigh fixed; Africans were not only savage and uncivilised, they were also "in the very depths of ignorant superstition".[17] The redeeming factor, however, was that the fault was "not in their nature but in their condition".[18] As the period of Christianity's third opportunity in Africa began to unfold, it was evident that the slave trade was a major factor shaping the new Christian enterprise, in that it was activated as much by a profound sense of grief at the harm done to Africa and Africans by the European trade for slaves from Africa as by a rediscovery of the Great Commission in the Gospel.[19]

The missionary enterprise thus became part of a much wider benevolent movement in Africa: to elevate the peoples of Africa to "assume their place among civilised and Christian nations".[20] In his programme for the "deliverance of Africa", Sir Thomas Fowell Buxton, a notable Christian humanitarian and Member of Parliament, included the impartation of "moral and religious instruction" as only one element in a comprehensive fourfold plan.[21] Nevertheless it was this element, the inculcation of the Christian

religion, which he and others[22] saw as the essential agent for the
"civilisation of Africa". Any doubts about the possibility of "savage"
and "barbarous" peoples ever becoming Christians without being
civilised first,[23] were soon dispelled by the strong contention that
the Gospel itself was "the great civiliser of barbarous men".[24]
Buxton's statement of the case has become famous:

> "Whatever methods may be attempted for ameliorating the
> condition of untutored man, *this* alone can penetrate to the root
> of the evil, can teach him to love and to befriend his neighbour,
> and cause him to act as a *candidate* for a higher and holier state
> of being... This mighty lever (i.e. Christianity) when properly
> applied, can alone overturn the iniquitous systems which
> prevail throughout the continent. Let missionaries and school-
> masters, the plough and the spade, go together, and agriculture
> will flourish; the avenues of legitimate commerce will be
> opened; confidence between man and man will be inspired
> whilst civilisation will advance as the natural effect, and Chris-
> tianity will operate as the proximate cause of this happy
> change."[25]

Here were all the ingredients of the confident compact for
effecting nothing less than a far-reaching culture-change in Africa
and her peoples: the Christian religion, the school (and eventually
higher education), technical and industrial training, new agricul-
tural skills and commercial enterprise – a whole package which,
in the new missionary encounter with Africa, it was sincerely
believed, would cause the "dark continent" to advance to that state
of prosperity and happiness which Europe enjoyed by divine
providence.

Christianity was the key, the "mighty lever", which brought it
all about. "True civilisation and Christianity are inseparable".[26]
Since the technical and cultural achievement of Europe were now
generally and confidently identified as the fruits of Christianity,
it seemed appropriate that to effect the salvation of Africa, Africans
must be given the total package of Christianity and (European)
civilisation.

II. Europe as Christendom: the West and the Rest

Long before the modern missionary movement fastened upon
the civilisation of Africa through the impartation of the Christian
religion, developments in Europe had brought about a virtual
identification of "European" with "Christian" in a way that was to
affect very deeply the Christian story of Africa in the nineteenth

and twentieth centuries. Owing to a number of factors, not least the Muslim threat to Europe in the European Middle Ages and the experience of the Crusades against the enemies of Christianity, there emerged "the consciousness of a concrete territorial Christendom".[27] The weakening of the Christian communities of the Eastern Mediterranean, as well as their isolation from the active Christian centres of the Latin West, helped towards the identification of *Christianitas* with Europe.[28]

That the conception of Christendom and its virtual interchangeability with Europe was not seriously questioned by the Protestant Reformation of the sixteenth century, is surely a testimony to the profound hold of the idea on the European self-consciousness.[29] Thus it can be argued that by putting their churches into the hands of national governments and rulers, the Protestant reformers intensified a belief which was already pervasive in the public imagination. Accordingly, the practical necessity of having to deal with the "natural enemy", the Muslim Turk, further deepened the religious assumptions common to Catholics and Protestants about the European homeland of the Christian religion.[30]

It is hardly surprising, therefore, that it will be in terms of Europe, the inheritor of Christianity – Japheth dwelling in the tents of Shem (following a long tradition of biblical exegesis) – that Europeans will look at the rest of the world.[31]

In itself, such an outlook was quite consistent with the cultural and economic self-confidence of Europe which had been growing steadily during the previous centuries. The revival of religion towards the end of the eighteenth century which produced the profound sense of missionary obligation, seems also to have intensified this European self-confidence.[32] More radical spirits, it is true, were not unaware of the religious blemishes of the Christian nations of Europe. William Carey, foremost protagonist of the missionary enterprise, was one who held no belief in the religious superiority of Europeans or of "those who bear the Christian name".[33] But this in no way undermined the general conviction that the civilised culture and institutions of Europe owed their enlightened status to Christianity, itself the most "civilised" of all religions.[34]

In the fourfold division of "Christian, Jewish, Mahometan, Pagan"[35] the fourth category was in a class of its own for being devoid of monotheism, a major consideration in the test of religion.[36] From what was known of the peoples of Asia and Africa, they came within the category of pagan. However, whilst the Indians and the Chinese could be accounted "civilised" pagans by virtue of being literate, Africans were believed to be without literature, arts, sciences, government, laws, and also cannibalistic and naked, and so were reckoned to be savage and barbarous pagans, "... as destitute of civilisation as they are of true religion".[37] These ideas formed part of the stock of knowledge[38] and persisted in the intellectual climate of Europe well into the nineteenth century,[39] when they became fused with evolutionary and racial theories of human achievement, civilisation, history and progress.[40]

Curiously, the task of classifying and theorising on the religion of African societies fell not to those who were the first to have close human contact with African peoples in the African context, that is, Christian missionaries, but to Europeans who only had a minimal contact with them and who were "at the time they wrote, agnostics or atheists".[41] In this category were some of the influential pioneers in the then new sciences of anthropology and comparative religion, both of which finally came into their own on the basis of Darwinian evolutionary assumptions.[42] British theoreticians like John Lubbock (Lord Avebury, 1834-1913), E.B. Tylor (1832-1917) and J.G. Frazer (1854-1951)[43] were products of the Christian civilisation of their time, but the nature of their own religious convictions and confession remains problematic.[44] Neither were these writers particularly concerned with the distinctly religious and theological objectives of the missionary movement.[45] Theirs was a quest for the origin of religion in the history of mankind, constructed on a strict evolutionary scheme of development from lower, simpler forms, to higher, more refined and complex levels of culture. Since they associated levels or stages of material culture with corresponding stages in mental and spiritual culture, lower material accomplishments of "primitive" peoples pointed naturally to equally backward levels of moral, religious and intellectual development. Consequently, "fetishism" or the later, more enduring term, "animism"[46] with its associated ideas was simply the religious counterpart to the general social and technical inferiority of uncivilised and savage peoples.

The extent to which these early anthropologists and their theories of human cultural history exerted an influence on the thinking of the missionary movement is not easy to assess. However, the fact that the attitudes and assumptions underlying their theories are found equally in the missionary view of African peoples and of African values, would suggest that these theoreticians on "other people" spoke for a sizeable proportion of European opinion, including the missionary element.

An indication of this is given in the proceedings of the World Missionary Conference, held at Edinburgh, Scotland, in 1910, "to consider missionary problems in relation to the non-Christian world".[47] The work of the Commission charged with reporting on the Christian Gospel as it related to non-Christian religions is of particular interest for our present purposes.[48] For by both implication and explicit statement, the Commission's report shows that it was Tylor's work which provided the theoretical framework for understanding, in the words of W.H.T. Gairdner, "the religious beliefs of more or less backward and degraded peoples all over the world".[49] Not only does Tylor's word "animism" serve as the generic term describing "the form of religion", but the report on "Animism" in fact starts thus:

"The form of religion dealt with in these papers is described as Animism. 'The theory of Animism', wrote Tylor, 'divides into two great dogmas; first concerning souls of individual creatures, capable of continued existence after death or destruction of the body; second, concerning other spirits, upward to the rank of powerful deities.' (*Primitive Culture*, (i), p.426)"[50]

"Animism" therefore, to all intents and purposes, constituted in the missionary understanding, a religious system[51] like the other categories treated: Chinese religions, religions of Japan, Islam and Hinduism. However, of all of them, Animism was probably the most difficult for the missionary to penetrate since it had neither literature nor scholars to expound its mysteries to the European mind. It is understandable therefore that many missionaries were hesitant to suggest that there existed any "preparation for Christianity" in this form of religion, whilst some even concluded that there was "practically no religious content in Animism".[52]

Tylor's work, it is true, is not explicitly cited again in the Report on Animism. Instead it is the pioneer missiological work of Johannes Warneck, *The Living Forces of the Gospel*[53] based on his experiences among the Batak people of Sumatra, which dominated and the eminent missionary scholar was himself available at the Conference to give further commentary on his findings. It seems fair to say that Warneck provided the missionary and theological validation for what Tylor had concluded on theoretical and evolutionary premises. It was held by some missionaries, for example, that among devotees of Animism "there is often no sense of sin: conscience seems hardly to exist... that the virtues of truth, thrift and purity are unknown".[54] Johannes Warneck added his authoritative testimony:

> "Immoral as the Animist is, he does not feel his immorality as such. Not even the cannibal and scalp-hunter who tortures his enemy in the most cruel manner, nor the adulterer and thief, will admit that he is doing wrong."[55]

So also did E.B. Tylor conclude; for him Animism characterises tribes very low in the scale of humanity,[56] and the "one great element of religion, that moral element which among the higher nations forms its most vital part, is indeed little represented in the religion of the lower races".[57] Tylor, who elsewhere criticises some writers on "the lower races", including the missionary Robert Moffat, for their failure to recognise "anything short of the organised and established theology of the higher races as being religion at all"[58] explained the absence of morality in Animism in a way that served well those who saw in their Christian civilisation the most refined manifestation of the moral conscience.

> "It is not that these races have no moral sense or no moral standard, for both are strongly marked among them, if not in formal precept, at least in that traditional consensus of society which we call public opinion, according to which certain actions are held to be good or bad, right or wrong. It is that the conjunction of ethics and Animistic philosophy, so intimate and powerful in the higher culture, seems scarcely yet to have begun in the lower."[59]

Thus Tylor who had no need for the postulate of revelation to find religion in "savage animism"[60] sees in this "earlier system in which began the age-long course of the education of the world",[61] the evidence for the conclusion "that the relation of morality to religion is one that only belongs in its rudiments, or not at all, to rudimentary civilisation".[62] The "savage animism" of the lower races is, consequently, "not immoral, it is unmoral", being "almost devoid of that ethical element which to the educated modern mind is the very mainspring of practical religion".[63]

It is not difficult to conclude that missionaries arrived, on the basis of their theological perspectives, at the same judgments about "the savage and the uncivilised" which Tylor had formed on the presupposition of evolutionary development. With little, if any, self-doubt regarding their apprehension of the Christian Gospel, no correspondent was found to indicate that missionary experience in the midst of Animism "had altered in form or substance their impression as to what constitutes the most important vital elements in the Christian Gospel".[64] It was not entirely ruled out that "the Christian faith itself may learn from even Animism, surely the humblest of all possible teachers... and the least sublime of all the five great creeds".[65] The Commission's own conclusion, showing greater sensitivity and moderation, was willing at least to raise the question whether "the Christian Church *in civilised lands* is using sufficiently the elemental truths of Revelation..."[66] In particular, the intense awareness of a world of spirits and personal powers, as Warneck had documented from Sumatra, was not missed. But its significance for the formulation of the relations between God and man and the world could as yet be estimated only in terms of a question.[67]

From the preceding analysis, one can say that missionary thinking in relation to Africa (at least its Protestant wing), at the beginning of the twentieth century, participated in the general European outlook more intimately than the missionaries would probably have realised. It has been argued that some of the changes in the missionary estimation of African competence in West Africa in the latter part of the nineteenth century were not unrelated to the ascendancy of British imperialist ideology and sense of inherent racial superiority, which was validated by anthropological theories on "the place of the negro in nature".[68] But any charge of outright racism against the modern missionary movement into Africa will be hard to prove and it is not our purpose to produce evidence to argue the case one way or the other.[69] By any reckoning Christian missionaries to Africa in the post-slave-trade era must be considered to belong to the humanitarian side of the European debate about other peoples.[70]

This view is not invalidated even when one allows for Philip Curtin's very judicious observation that a crucial weakness in the anti-racist and humanitarian case was the failure to distinguish between race and culture.[71] In this respect the missionary acceptance of the general European presupposition of African "savagery" and "primitivism" had more far-reaching significance than was perceived. Since the impartation of Christianity as understood in European terms was seen as the "mighty lever" without which other means were of no avail to effect "the elevation of the native mind"[72] and the civilisation of Africa, the result could only be achieved when Africans had become like their European mentors in culture. The aim was to produce as near replicas as possible of European models of Christian life and conduct – in effect, "Black Europeans".[73]

It is doubtful whether the famous mid-nineteenth century proposals for indigenous, self-governing, self-supporting and self-propagating churches, associated with the Church Missionary Society,[74] implied a substantial departure from this fundamental presumption. When the opportunity arose in the work of the Niger Mission for a consistent application of these proposals and ideas under the leadership of Samuel Ajayi Crowther, it was felt by some that the day of African ability had not yet fully come.[75]

Samuel Ajayi Crowther was a notable product of the process of acculturation which underlay the tie-up between Christianity and European civilisation[76] while at the same time giving evidence of a certain independence of thought. In the biography of the eminent Bishop of the Niger Territory, Jesse Page clearly indicates that Crowther's career and personal achievement constituted a major response to European critics who held suspicions about African capacity. Crowther's abilities, as well as the entire Christian establishment of Sierra Leone, literate and academically respectable,[77] provided "strong evidence of the progressive possibilities of the African mind and character".[78] And yet it would seem that the view held of Crowther by his European mentors never rose above paternalism; he remained merely, as was said of him as a youth, "a very useful instrument for carrying on the work in Western Africa".[79] When the question of his ordination came to be considered, one testimony borne of him was that "he would do honour to our Society".[80]

It is therefore not surprising that his persistent and profoundly sympathetic attempts to come to grips with the traditional religion of the Niger peoples and to work for religious change in terms meaningful to Africans, despite his generally negative view of Niger society,[81] were to a considerable degree lost on the CMS. His methods were eventually not considered adequately fit to produce "substantial Christianity", by which was meant, European Christianity.[82]

III. European ethnocentricism and its effects: the African religious past as a theological problem

From the standpoint of the post-missionary era, it would be easy to relate the negative attitudes to African traditional religions and world views to missionaries' ignorance born of unfamiliarity and unpreparedness.[83] Knowledge of African people has advanced significantly in the twentieth century, in some cases through missionary endeavour.[84] In a little over a decade after the Edinburgh Conference of 1910, the missionary image of Africa was already registering some marked changes which included "more respect for the Africans and for their past",[85] which it was now believed, contained "elements of a high religious value".[86]

However, the argument from ignorance of African peoples is not as weighty as it might appear in the first instance. Greater and more accurate knowledge of Africans would not necessarily have created more positive attitudes, for empirical knowledge of Africans and African values is not, in a strict sense, what lies at the centre of the problem of the missionary attitude. Rather it is the perspective from which the Christian enterprise was carried out during the phase of Christianity's "third opportunity" in Africa which is of greater significance. Behind the missionary unpreparedness for a serious encounter with academic or theological issues that would arise from the presence of Christianity in Africa,[87] there lay the long tradition of an unquestioned presumption of European value-setting for the Christian religion. Missionaries, on the whole, saw in Africans and the African environment what they expected to find. In other words, what was observed in Africa was understood and interpreted, not in terms of Africa, but in terms of Europe, that is, of the European value-setting for the faith.[88]

The pervasive nature of ethnocentric presuppositions in Western missionary writing may be illustrated from Raoul Allier's massive work, *Le Psychologie de la conversion chez les peuples non-civilisés*.[89] While Allier's work is not concerned exclusively with Africa, it does represent an important milestone in the attempt by a Westerner to understand the missionary enterprise from the angle of those who were its "victims" generally,[90] and draws largely from the accounts of French Protestant missionaries in Southern Africa. The interesting feature about this work is Allier's approach and his understanding of the process of Christian conversion for the "uncivilised". It is important to note that behind Allier's work there stands the philosophical and sociological theories of Lucien Lévy-Bruhl on the mentality and thought-patterns of primitive peoples.[91]

Lévy-Bruhl had postulated a fundamental and abiding distinction between civilised thought which proceeds by the logic of non-contradiction, and primitive thought which functions by means of participation and identification with the object of thought and thus knows no such critical distance.[92] Allier seeks to show, from the incidence of genuine religious conversion and moral and intellectual change among "uncivilised" peoples, that the primitive can become civilised. From this angle, Allier's book is a profound *apologia* for the Christian enterprise against its opponents and detractors at home.[93]

But the real point of interest for us is that in what is otherwise a very sympathetic piece of work, with fine insight into the dynamics of the religious consciousness, Allier uncritically assumes that conversion to Christianity for "uncivilised" peoples amounts to the development and acquisition of the mental processes of "civilised" peoples – their logic, their reason, their morality and their version of individuality – in effect the "ways of civilised people".[94] Roger Bastide's criticism of Allier is apposite:

> "Raoul Allier has not even faced up to the problem of seeing whether there could not be a conversion *sui generis* within a mentality governed by the law of participation. He assumes straight off that religious conversion presupposes our logic."[95]

Roger Bastide's comment is particularly significant in that it is placed in the general critique of what he calls "the confusion of the process of Christianisation with the process of westernisation".[96] This is all the more poignant because Allier has firmly grasped the fact, witnessed to by the missionary authorities he cites, that it is the Gospel in its own terms, rather than the appurtenances of European culture, which supplies the motive power for the "radical" changes he describes, with appropriate emphasis on the discovery of personality and human worth by converts.[97]

Thus, whilst Allier rightly emphasises the revolutionary character of the Christian Gospel among non-Western peoples, he nonetheless exemplifies the failure to conceive that Christianity among Africans or other non-Europeans could be different from the European manifestations of the faith, and that there could be other criteria than those provided by European civilisation to measure the attainments of the emergent Christianity.[98]

One may therefore isolate European ethnocentricism as a significant factor in the story of Christianity in Africa. From this has emerged one major issue for African theology in the post-missionary church, namely, the problem of identity in African Christian understanding. The measure of the problem posed for African Christians by European ethnocentricism is indicated in the following observation by John Mbiti:

"Mission Christianity was not from the start prepared to face a serious encounter with the traditional religions and philosophy or the modern changes taking place... the Church in Africa now finds itself in the situation of having to exist without a theology."[99]

Other African writers have echoed Mbiti's grief at this lack of theological consciousness and education in the numerous Christian communities of Africa; significantly, the problem is often associated with the missionary history.[100] By not allowing in the first place for the existence of a "heathen" memory in the African Christian consciousness, the widespread European value-setting for the faith created a Church "without a theology". The assertion made by E.B. Idowu that the Church in Nigeria was yet to develop "a theology which bears the distinctive stamp of Nigerian thinking and meditation"[101] is an indication of the nature of that *lacuna*. For theological memory is integral to identity;[102] without memory we have no past, and having no past, our identity itself is lost, for the "past is also our present".[103] The theological problem which has arisen from the missionary tie-up between Christianity and "civilisation" (that is, European culture), consists therefore in this, that it threatened to deny African Christians their own past and sought instead to give them a past which could not in any real sense become fully theirs.[104]

One natural result of this is that in the post-missionary era, when European value-setting for African Christianity has been generally discarded, the theological meaning of the pre-Christian past becomes an unavoidable element in all major African theological discussion. The main issue here is not the early anthropologists' concern to define "the negro's place in nature". Rather, it has to do with, as E.B. Idowu put it regarding his own people,

"whether in the pre-Christian history of Nigerians, God has ever in any way revealed Himself to them and they have apprehended His revelation in however imperfect a way; whether what happens in the coming of Christianity, and as a result of evangelism is that Nigerians have been introduced to a *completely* new God who is absolutely unrelated to their past history".[105]

That the question is posed in this form is itself an indication of unease with the theological implications of a view of the Christian faith which links it indissolubly with European civilisation and values.[106]

Another example of this dissatisfaction is found in J.S. Mbiti's *Concepts of God in Africa*, in which he summarises his researches into pre-Christian understandings of the Divine among a variety of African peoples; what is of particular interest is that he considers these concepts to "have sprung independently out of African reflection on God".[107] It is significant that from the evidence adduced, the differences between pre-Christian and Christian understandings are almost negligible.

Idowu and Mbiti are not alone in probing the lines of continuity from pre-Christian religious experience into African Christian confession. It is a fact that all specifically theological writing by Africans so far in the twentieth century has tended towards what Adrian Hastings has rightly described as "something of a dialogue between the African Christian scholar and the perennial religions and spiritualities of Africa".[108]

It is indeed extraordinary that one of the elements which would have been considered in an earlier age indicative of African "primitivism" and "heathenism", namely, the "old religion", should now become an unavoidable item in African Christian reflection and religious scholarship. But what raises this concern with the religious tradition of the past above antiquarian and anthropological interest is the theological significance which now attaches to that past in the African Christian self-understanding. In other words, the theological interest in the religious tradition of the African past relates to dimensions of African identity which the missionary enterprise, by its basic cultural presumptions, would have been incapable of reaching. A.F. Walls, with characteristic insight, has shown what lies at the heart of the modern African theological interpretation of the religious past:

"... no question is more clamant than the African Christian identity crisis. It is not simply an intellectual quest. This massive shift in the centre of gravity of the Christian world which has taken place cannot be separated from the cultural impact of the West in imperial days. Now the Empires are dead, and the Western value-setting of the Christian faith largely rejected. Where does this leave the African Christian? Who is he? What is his past? A past is vital for all of us – without it, like the amnesiac man, we cannot know who we are. The prime

African theological quest at present is this: What is the past of the African Christian? What is the relationship between Africa's old religions and her new one?"[109]

That a problem of such fundamental significance for the Christian churches of Africa should also be a direct legacy of the missionary enterprise which was so massively instrumental in bringing these communities into being raises an important question. One may ask whether "the unconscious arrogance of the Western mind"[110] which underlay the mood that made Christianity and civilisation into "opposite sides of the same coin",[111] was indicative not merely of a cultural partiality, but also of a theological *Problematik*. In other words, did the long tradition of the association of Christianity with European civilisation – "the vestigial remains of Europe's medieval heritage of ideas"[112] – have the effect in Africa of turning what might simply have been a cultural blunder into a significant theological misconception? Of the sincere and deep humanitarianism of the modern missionary enterprise to "elevate" and "civilise" the "savage" and "primitive", there can be no gainsaying; on the other hand, the theological problems which resulted from its ethnocentric presuppositions also need to be recognised in order to understand the concerns of African theological debate in the post-missionary era.

IV. "The fact is... Africa had no Paul"[113]

Kenneth Cragg has rightly called attention to this "falling short of world perspective in terms of theology and culture" in the modern missionary movement from the West, despite its "heroic attainment... in respect of adventure and travail".[114] But he is careful to point out that such critical assessment is made from a twentieth-century perspective, in an era which is post-imperial as it is post-missionary, and "in the light of subsequent experience and the vantage of time".[115] It is only fair, therefore, that any theological assessment of the modern missionary enterprise must be strictly within comparisons with the best ideals of the faith that it sought to impart. For, as Bishop Cragg writes:

"In the end, it is by its own, and not some external, insight that its compromises and failures are to be discerned and reproached."[116]

In this respect, "criticisms of the modern missionary movement in the light of St Paul's supposed missionary methods" are not as "irrelevant" as Max Warren pronounced them to be.[117] Whatever the contrasts in social conditions,[118] this does not obviate comparison in terms of the *theological* perspectives of the propagators of the faith. In the end, it is the apostolic mission to Gentiles which provides the most adequate paradigm for assessing "by its own insight", a similar massive transposition of the Christian faith. On the appropriateness of using the apostolic precedent, Bishop Cragg further explains:

> "This is no doubt part of the benediction of the Scriptural documentation of apostolicity, to which, in duty bound, our self-criticisms must continually return, lest we lose our bearings and obscure our temptations."[119]

Our concern here is to attempt to understand how the exertions of the modern missionary movement which has resulted in the present impressive geographical comprehensiveness of the Christian Church in the world, has entailed at the same time a sense of alienation which causes an African theologian to ask: "Why do we remain in the Christian fold?"[120]

In *Post-Christianity in Africa*, G.C. Oosthuizen attempts to show that conditions in mission-founded churches – including the element of "foreignness" – had much to do with the rise and proliferation of "separatist or indigenous movements".[121] In support of his argument he contrasts the first major historical transposition of the Christian faith with its modern analogue, the Western missionary movement. In the earlier transposition from the Jewish cultural milieu to that of the Greek world, "Paul, well versed both in Rabbinic Judaism and in all aspects of Hellenism, was in the centre of this transposition".[122] The effect of Paul's work therefore was an effective "process of translation and transposition" of "the Gospel with its prophetic and historical background" into Greek idiom and experience where Jesus found a home as *Kyrios* (Lord) as he was Messiah in the Jewish milieu.[123]

In the modern African context on the other hand, the need to get to grips with African world-views and experience of reality was not taken seriously or was simply ignored; but not by the leaders of the Independent Churches:

> "The independent movements accept the fact that they have to do with their own world and world-view, and this is in contradiction to many missionaries whose motto was, 'You must become like us.'"[124]

In Dr Oosthuizen's view, the fallacy in the Western missionary approach to Africa "has been due to the development of Western Christianity itself", the fallacy that "is alive in the concept of

Western Christian civilisation".[125]

If Africa had no Paul, whom then did she have? When Johannes van den Berg examined the motives of the modern missionary movement in the light of the Bible, the verdict he came to was, at best, ambiguous.[126] In Ruth Rouse's study of missionary vocation, out of three hundred accounts of call to the mission field, only one missionary "directly attributes his call to a missionary study of the Bible".[127] There is overwhelming evidence that the sheer misery and need, particularly of African peoples, in relation to Christian Europe was a most potent impulse to missionary vocation. It must have seemed right that achievement could only be on the side of Europeans, whilst Africans could only receive from them; nowhere did this seem more right than in the transmission of the Gospel. The threefold factors of circumstance isolated by Kenneth Cragg – the "fact of empire", the racial ambiguities of "white" agency and leadership among "coloured" races, and the European "managerial" superiority and competence – only served to reinforce and to distort further the "Western possessiveness" of the Christian faith as it was passed on to non-Western peoples.[128] All these, uncritically accepted and trusted, would have their cramping effect on the understanding of the missionary task, no less than on the human relationships so formed within their embrace.

At each of the points indicated above, the propagators of the Christian faith in the Graeco-Roman world were heirs to no such privileges. As Cragg points out, the Christian mission then was not pursued in "the context of privileged imperialism";[129] and evidently Paul's Roman citizenship could not be counted on to promote a religion which would eventually threaten the ideological foundations of the State.[130]

In the second place, "for all their sharpness, the Jew-Gentile, Greek-Barbarian tensions at the time of Christian beginnings were not of that exclusifying character".[131] Here one may note not only the emergence of the ingredients making for the outlines of *one* civilisation, as Harnack has indicated,[132] but also the existence of persons of Jewish parentage who, being at home in Hellenistic culture and in cultural solidarity with their world, were the first to perceive the universalist dimension of the Christian Gospel.[133] In contrast to this circumstance of virtual interpenetration as Cragg observes:

"Nowhere has this instinctive durability and pride of cultures been more disadvantaged than in the white and western invasions of other humanity under circumstances of political dominance, material power, economic strength and racial self-esteem."[134]

If the Christian communities in the Graeco-Roman world were not composed exclusively of the poor[135] nonetheless the "evidence covering the period between the primitive age and that of Marcus Aurelius, confirms the view that in the contemporary Christian communities, the lower classes, slaves, freedmen, and labourers, very largely predominated".[136] Fairly early in Christian history, Christians of the original Mother-Church of the faith in Judaea are described as "poor" and were receiving relief from Gentile Christian communities.[137] The result of that "paradoxical advantage of economic poverty and social simplicity"[138] was that the early Christian enterprise in the Graeco-Roman world was saved from the temptations of paternalism and the cultural arrogance of the Western mind which came to attach to the modern missionary movement.[139] And yet, the cumulative evidence of these contrasts of circumstance, helpful and interesting as they are, does not bring us to the point of theological contrast.

In the ecumenical context of a post-imperial world, it is easy to recognise that Christian mission, on the analogy of the outgoing love and saving activity of the Triune God, calls for a transcendence of particularity by universality and that such universality in outlook includes an openness to new theological insights as Christ, in effect, appears more and more to possess his universal inheritance. Therefore, Johannes Blauw rightly identifies "universalism" as the fundamental perspective of the Biblical teaching on mission.[140] To that extent, "the Gospel is no longer to be thought of apart from the lands which were once colonised: the name of Christ has been named, his Church established, and the Kingdom of God is at hand in the lands which were formerly 'far off.'"[141] John Taylor concludes his admirable study of the Christian Church in Buganda by posing the question:

"... whether in Buganda and elsewhere in Africa, the Church will be enabled by God's grace to discover a new synthesis between a saving Gospel and a total, unbroken unity of society. For there are many who feel that the spiritual sickness of the West, which reveals itself in the divorce of the sacred from the secular, of the cerebral from the instinctive, and in the loneliness and homelessness of individualism, may be healed through a recovery of the vision which Africa has not yet thrown away. The world Church awaits something new out of Africa."[142]

Such testimony to a broad outlook on the Christian mission must not obscure the fact that in the formative and major periods of the modern expansion of Christianity, there was little of such theological sensitivity and it was not evident to many that the Christianity of the West could learn theologically from the emergent churches in the "non-Christian" lands. We have already noted that at the first World Missionary Conference in Edinburgh in 1910, all the missionary correspondents who contributed material on "Animistic Religions" – which included the whole African field – were "unhesitatingly" certain that their missionary experience had not "altered in form or substance their impression as to what constitutes the most important vital elements in the Christian Gospel".[143] We have also seen that the conference took a generally low view of African heritage in religion and culture. But could the explanation for that have also been a dearth in theological understanding? G.H. Anderson has said of the Conference:

"Edinburgh was primarily concerned with strategy, and most participants seemed to take for granted that the Great Commission of Christ (*Mt.* 28:19) was the only basis needed for the missionary enterprise. It came at a time when missionary endeavour was at a high point of enthusiasm and the missionary obligation was considered a self-evident axiom to be obeyed, not to be questioned."[144]

The theme of the Jerusalem Conference of 1928 indicates that missionary thinking about the "non-Christian" world conceived of that world in terms of religious systems.[145] In this one particular respect the modern missionary enterprise revealed a fundamental difference in theological perspective from the Gentile mission of the primitive church as this was crystalised in the vision and achievement of Paul.

In his penetrating study of the missionary understanding of the first chapter of the *Epistle to the Romans* as this understanding related to the view of the modern "heathens", Prof. A.F. Walls has shown how, in the course of the Western encounter and study of the ways of the non-Western and non-Christian world, Western categorisations came to overlay the apostolic teaching:

"As systems, and ultimately the collective labels for systems which we call the world religions, have slipped into the place of ungodly men in the interpretation of *Romans* 1, so Christianity, also conceived as a system, has sometimes slipped into the place of the righteousness of God. The true system has been opposed to the false system condemned there. It has sometimes, but not always, been realised that "Christianity" is a term formally identical with the other labels; that it certainly covers as wide a range of phenomena as most of them; that if the principalities and powers work within human systems, they can and do work in this one. Man-in-Christianity lies under the wrath of God just as much, and for the same reasons, as Man-in-Hinduism. It was the realisation of this which saved the earliest generations of the modern missionary movement from the worst of paternalism. Man was vile everywhere, not only in Ceylon."[146]

For by the ungodly in *Romans* 1, the apostle means not systems at all, but men:

"It is men who hold down the truth in unrighteousness, who do not honour God, who are given to dishonourable passions. It is upon men, who commit ungodly and wicked deeds, that the wrath of God is revealed."[147]

A natural effect of the missionary outlook of modern times was a certain tendency to confuse their institutionalised Christianity with Christ, to make the former the bestower of salvation. This misapprehension also tended to obscure the truth that "it was not Christianity that saves, but Christ".[148]

By fastening so intently on the "sheer paganism" and awfulness of African "heathen superstitions"[149] Western missionaries were considerably less conscious of the "heathen" as men with their utterly *human* fears and joys, hopes and disappointments, and yearnings for salvation. Bishop Cragg describes the apostolic contrast with regard to Paul's firm apprehension of the universal need of all men, Greek as well as Jew, and on the same terms, for the one and the same universal Gospel:

"Through all there runs, as integral to the sense of the universal, the new dimension of the person, the sense of men as men, not of Jews as Jews, or Greeks as Greeks."[150]

For,

"What turns upon grace and personality cannot be racially received or culturally confined. It has to do with men as men, their sins and their fears, and not with Jews as Jews, or Greeks as Greeks. Thus its unity majestically transcends the most stubborn divisions in humanity."[151]

If we are to understand how the nineteenth- and early twentieth-century Western missionaries to Africa were so generally derogatory of African tradition, here is, at least, a beginning of an explanation which avoids the usually loaded racial and cultural theories. By failing to view man-in-African heathenism as man in the same terms as man-in-Christianity, Western missionaries failed to recognise that "there was more than one type of non-Christian tradition".[152] If Justin and Clement of Alexandria were right in postulating a "theory of two traditions" in the Graeco-Roman heritage,[153] that intuition and insight must be related to the approach and theological emphases which shaped the apostolic missionary preaching in their world. It is interesting that Luke's presentation of Paul's encounter with Greeks on Mars Hill in Athens has been interpreted as "the symbolic summit of the Apostle's mission".[154] It can rightly be said therefore that the apostle who grasped most firmly the significance of Christ for the entire universe,[155] and who strenuously preached Jesus to Jews as the fulfilment of the promises of the Old Testament,[156] proclaimed with equal conviction that Jesus was to Gentiles also the fulfiller of their deepest religious and spiritual aspirations.[157] In failing correctly to apprehend and follow the apostolic precedent in their understanding of African "heathenism", our modern missionaries, by the same token, deprived themselves of the means of recognising and articulating the universal nature and activity of Christ among the "heathen" they encountered.

There is evidence from missionary records themselves that such a recognition could have occurred. In a discussion of the dynamics of Christian conversion in the African encounter with missionary proclamation, Prof. Walls has observed:

"Probably no group, perhaps no person, is ever converted from one religion to another; they are more likely to be converted from agnosticism, after the old way has failed."[158]

In this connection the journal of the Rev. Thomas B. Freeman's two visits to Ashanti[159] provides an illuminating illustration. Some of the most touching accounts relate to Freeman's dealings with Korinchi (Korankye?), Chief of Fomunah (Fomean?). Korinchi seems to have struck a ready and deep friendship with the missionary.[160] Probably to Freeman's surprise, Korinchi was not eager to receive "presents according to the usual custom";[161] his wish was "rather to become acquainted with the Gospel".[162] Perhaps the most significant aspect of Korinchi's story relates to the ritual immolation of slaves and other underlings in Ashanti, a feature of life which Freeman had ample opportunity to document and even to discuss with some local people[163] Not long after Freeman arrived

Korinchi's sister died and since she was "an Ashanti of distinction" the ritual human sacrifices took place.[164] Then, ten days later, Freeman reports a meeting with Korinchi which reveals him as a quite remarkable man:

"Tuesday, 28th – I paid Korinchi a visit and reasoned with him closely on the painful consequences of human sacrifices, and the 'customs' for the dead. He readily acknowledged the evil, and expressed himself ready to abolish it, if he were at full liberty so to do; but he feared the King.[165] The only reason he could give for making 'customs' in addition to human sacrifices for the dead, was that they felt very unhappy when they lost their relatives and friends, and were glad to have recourse to drunkenness, or anything which would drive away gloomy thoughts from their minds for a season. As he thus gave me a good opportunity of directing him to the only refuge for a troubled mind – the consolation of true religion – I told him, God alone was able to sustain under afflictions and bereavements. He seemed affected with what I said to him. In the evening he sent me a present, consisting of a sheep, yams and plantains."[166]

Korinchi's story made an impact in London. His friendship with Freeman was remarked by the Rev. John Beecham, who in writing to commend mission to Ashanti in Methodist circles (he was at the time secretary of the Wesleyan Methodist Missionary Society), nursed the hope that Korinchi would have provided local support for the enterprise had his life not then come to a sad end. John Beecham's account of what happened to Korinchi is revealing:

"Mr Freeman congratulated himself on having found a friend in Korinchi, the Chief of Fomunah; but his aid cannot be anticipated; for Korinchi, having given some cause of offence, has been destroyed with deliberate cruelty – the King having ordered a certain stream to be diverted from its channel, until a hole should be dug in its bed, in which that unfortunate chief was placed, and then left to perish in the returning waters of the rivulet."[167]

The questions which may now be posed have to do with Korinchi's standing in relation to Asante tradition, in view particularly of his attitude to human sacrifice. Would the manner of his life's end, no less than his response to Freeman's preaching, qualify him as witness to what Nathan Söderblom called "the religion of good conscience"?[168] Does the career of Korinchi open up a wider perspective, which may be considered a "biographical" approach, related to the insights of Justin Martyr into pre-Christian Hellenistic tradition?[169] Was Korinchi a "Socrates" in his time and place in Asante religious tradition? Would Justin have seen in Korinchi what he saw in the careers of Socrates, Musonius Rufus and "many others like" the ancient sage? And could the words of Erasmus quoted by Söderblom and applied to "Socrates and the Teacher of China, Kong-fu-tse" (Confucius), be equally relevant to Korinchi and others like him in pre-Christian African tradition?

"It may be that the Spirit of Christ goes farther and wider than we think. And there are many in the fellowship of the Saints, who are not in our catalogue."[170]

However, all these questions must remain open. For it is unlikely that Freeman, Beecham or many Western missionaries of modern times either raised them or conceived of the universality of the Christian Gospel in the way the "vantage of time"[171] has taught us to do.

Because of the modern missionary misapprehension on this specific point of universality, fundamental questions on the possible positive meaning of Christ for the pre-Christian religious past could hardly surface or be taken with sufficient seriousness in the missionary era. The New Testament, on the other hand, shows an awareness of the problem,[172] and significantly, approaches a solution not from the standpoint of the nearness or otherwise of the Gentile religious heritage to the more "enlightened" Jewish tradition, but rather on the basis of the universality of Jesus Christ.

Here we must agree with S.G. Williamson in his view that in Africa Western "missionary work in general seems to have adopted an attitude at variance with the New Testament".[173] What he says of the missionary story of the Akan of Ghana could well summarise the stories of other African societies.[174] In the light of the Akan belief in a hierarchy of spirits and gods, as well as in a Supreme Being, Dr Williamson writes:

"It is conceivable that as pure faith Christianity might have spoken directly to the Akan in his apprehension of reality. The apostles and missionaries of the New Testament period seem to have approached their listeners on the basis of what they did believe, at least to the extent that they proclaimed Christ as the Saviour of men within a milieu which allowed the existence of 'gods many and lords many'. The missionary enterprise among the Akan did not take this line, but being Western in outlook and emphasis felt bound to deny the Akan world-view, not only on the basis of what was essentially Christian belief, but on the ground of what was, in effect, a European world-view."[175]

Consequently, as Dr Williamson notes further:

"The invitation to accept the Christian religion was also a call to participate in a Western interpretation of reality. Thus converts were not merely required to abandon the worship of many gods for the worship of the One God, but were taught to look upon traditional religion as the worship of nonentities. The missionary enterprise was seeking to implant its Christianity by the method of substituting for the Akan world-view what was a European world-view."[176]

This implied "theology of mission" did not allow for redemption in Christ within Akan world view and tradition, but only outside of them.[177] But if Christian redemption was held to be virtually impossible within African tradition, what then could be the nature of African Christian identity?[178] It is hardly surprising that some of the questions with which African theology is wrestling in the post-missionary Church are a legacy of the theology of the modern Western missionary enterprise – in that "what they (the Western missionaries) did not do still remains to be done..."[179]

That Africa had no Paul, therefore, had consequences beyond Oosthuizen's suggestion that:

"What Africa needs today is men thoroughly versed in the Bible, in contemporary theology, in world trends and social conditions, and in the African world and its thinking."[180]

Admirable and valid as this conception is, it does not get to the heart of the matter. There is a more subtle dimension to Paul's crucial role in the cultural and intellectual transposition of the Gospel from the Jewish cultural world into the Hellenistic world than he suggests.[181] In a strict sense, the fullness of that transposition could only be the work of Christians of Hellenistic culture themselves. In addition, for all his intense self-consciousness as apostle to the Gentiles, Paul remained as eager to preach to Jews as to Gentiles.[182] We have also seen that we misunderstand Paul when we read him as providing intellectual elaborations for one theological *system* against other systems. Thus, whilst it is true that Paul's missionary labours make him "the dramatic symbol of this whole passage between two worlds",[183] we should not imagine him as engaged in founding a new Gentile Christianity.[184] The great "mystery" revealed to the Apostle to the Gentiles has to do with their full participation through faith in Christ in the divine promises of the Old Covenant.[185] Thus the Church of Christ, uniting Jew and Gentile, in the "Israel of God".[186] Paul's whole approach is based on his conviction that, in the words of Gregory Dix, "the Gospel is no longer Jewish, but it was from the Jews".[187]

For Paul's achievement was not obtained without a struggle, a theological one primarily, with elements within the form of Christianity known and practised in the cultural milieu of the earliest Mother-Church. If Paul's adversaries, the so-called Judaisers, had had their way, Graeco-Roman Christianity and the nature of New Testament teaching might have taken a different turn.[188]

The great significance, then, of Paul in the early mission, and hence for all cross-cultural Christian mission, consists in his ministry as a facilitator and enabler for the Gentiles. It is Paul above all who ensured that Gentiles would feel at home in the Gospel, on the same terms as Jews like himself were accepted, that is, by faith in Christ Jesus and not by submitting to Judaising demands for circumcision.[189] Thus Hahn is right to link closely freedom from the Law and universality in Paul's conception of mission:

> "Freedom belongs just as much as universality to the Gospel. Here, of course, it is not a matter of a freedom based on man's essential nature, as it was regarded in Greek and Hellenistic thought, but of a freedom understood eschatologically, based on being free from all subjection to the powers of this age. It is a freedom to which Christ has set us free (*Gal.* 5:1). This freedom is the sign of those who belong to the heavenly Jerusalem, while the earthly Jerusalem with its children is still enslaved (*Gal.* 4:21-31). For even the Law itself if it is understood as the way of salvation, is servitude, and if it were imposed on the Gentiles it would simply lead from one slavery to another."[190]

Thus the great achievement of Paul in the early Christian mission was to have worked tirelessly to secure the conditions in which the Christian self-understanding of Gentiles could develop and flourish in the subsequent Christian centuries. By his firm grasp of the universality of the Gospel of Jesus the Messiah, and by his insistence on the all-embracing inclusiveness of this Gospel, and on the same terms for all men, he placed at the disposal of Christians of Graeco-Roman culture the basic tools for assessing their own heritage, for making their own contribution to Christian life and thought and also for testing the genuineness and Christian character of that contribution.

However, even if Africa may be said to have had no Paul[191] in the sense that she had no early facilitators for African theological freedom,[192] she cannot now be said to have no access to the Gospel according to Paul. For the apostolic achievement and precedent has validity also for Africa, and the Western missionary history may cease to be a determining factor in the growth of her freedom and Christian identity.[193]

V. Conclusion

One of the most significant developments within the African Experience in our time, has been the emergence of a widespread African theological literature carrying its own Christian and intellectual convictions, with its own agenda. But before this development can be understood in its own terms within African Christianity, it is important to appreciate the factors and influences which have contributed towards the shape and character of this emergent African theological consciousness. In other words, African theologians must find their place in the historical movement which has produced them, that is, the history of the expansion and growth of the Christian religion in Africa.

The planting and existence of Christianity in Africa cannot be separated from the history of the missionary outreach and exertions of the Christian Churches of the Western European world, even though it is also true that African initiative in the propagation of the Christian faith has been considerable.

But the history of Western Christian missions in Africa belongs to, and is a direct response to, a longer history of African contact with European peoples. The story of early African contacts with Europeans is a largely melancholy one. The conditions in which Europe met Black Africa and her people exercised a deleterious influence on the image of Africa in the European consciousness. Eventually, when the awakening of humanitarian conscience and of spiritual life in many Christian circles brought missionaries to Africa from the end of the eighteenth century onwards, the "elevation" and "civilisation" of barbarous and degraded Africa could not easily be separated from the impartation of the Christian faith to the "heathen". The forces which operated in the earlier formative period had become determining factors for the missionary programme of the important "third opportunity".

The emergence of a massive Christian presence in Africa through the modern missionary movement from the Western Churches constitutes one of the most spectacular success-stories in the history of the expansion of Christianity through twenty centuries. African "paganism" has been one of the most fertile soils for the Christian Gospel. At the beginning, it was not recognised that Africans could be responding to Christianity as a religious faith that appealed to them on its own terms, without the trappings of European civilisation. This was further complicated by a rather uncritical tradition in European Christianity which tended to associate the faith almost inseparably with European cultural achievement and its fruits. Consequently, missionary Christianity seemed, to all intents and purposes, bound to uproot the African from his "heathen" past with its barbarities, savagery and ignorance, in order to give him a new identity, constructed on the basis of the new, total package of Christianity and European civilisation. In its best form, this outlook was a genuine, humanitarian effort to offer Africans what was believed to be the best way of life conceivable.

It is such assumptions about the relationship between Christianity and European civilisation on the one hand, and about African "heathenism" and the meaning and value of the African religious past on the other, which become the most problematic dimensions in this success-story of the transposition of Christianity. I have sought to show that the cultural partiality which accompanied the Western missionary transmission of Christianity indicates a theological *Problematik* in missionary theology. I have pursued the examination of this *Problematik* into the suggestion that the Western missionary enterprise departed from New Testament and apostolic precedents at some crucial points. This probably happened as a result of a "theology of mission" which informed the missionary understanding of "heathenism", and a general failure to correctly apprehend the universality and the freedom inherent in the Gospel, for which the apostle Paul most persistently fought, on behalf of Gentile Christians, and against Judaisers.

Does this then leave us with the conclusion that the Western missionary enterprise in Africa was generally, if unwittingly, a "Judaising" enterprise? It has been suggested that this, indeed, was the case.[194] Certainly, the circumstances of contrast between the apostolic mission to Gentiles and the Western enterprise in Africa have a bearing on the consequences of the modern mission. Indeed, when one compares, in terms of outlook and temper, representative literature produced by Christians of Graeco-Roman culture in the second century with what corresponds to it in twentieth-century Africa, one comes away with the distinct impression that the latter have hitherto had to labour under an incubus which the former appear to have been spared. It is unfortunate that the quest for an African Christian identity in terms which are meaningful for African integrity and also adequate for Christian confession, should become so pervasively bedevilled by the missionary enterprise that was instrumental in bringing African Christianity into being, no less than by consequences of the melancholy history of African contact with the Christian peoples of Europe.

But if African theological freedom was generally not facilitated by the Western missionary movement, the contemporary task of African theology is not thereby rendered impossible; African theologians also now share in the inheritance of the Gospel. Theological freedom is the freedom of the Gospel. This means that to adequately appreciate the concerns of African theologians in the post-missionary era, one must inquire into their understanding of the significance of the Gospel for the interpretation of African realities and for the meaning of African Christian identity.

Notes

1. See C.P. Groves, *The Planting of Christianity in Africa* (vol.1, to 1840), London: Lutterworth Press, 1948, pp.vii f. The modern missionary enterprise of the 19th and early 20th centuries represents "the third opportunity of Christianity in Africa"; the first was in apostolic times, and ended with the Muslim invasions of North Africa in the 7th century; the second is taken to have begun with the Portuguese voyages of exploration in the 15th century, and it came to an end with the decay and collapse of Portuguese power in the 16th century.

2. The expression is used by K.S. Latourette as a description of the massive Christian missionary advance in the period between 1800 and 1914. See his *A History of the Expansion of Christianity* (vol.5, *The Great Century: The Americas, Australasia and Africa, AD 1800-1914*) New York: Harper and Brothers, 1943; *ibid.* (vol.6, *The Great Century: North Africa and Asia, AD 1800-1914*), New York: Harper and Brothers, 1944. (The entire set of 7 volumes reprinted by Zondervan, Grand Rapids, 1970.)

3. Adrian Hastings, *Church and Mission in Modern Africa*, London: Burns and Oates, 1967, p.60. My emphasis.

4. *Ibid.*, p.60.

5. The expression is from Philip Curtin, *The Image of Africa: British Ideas and Action 1780-1850*, Madison: University of Wisconsin Press, 1964, p.480.

6. *Ibid.*, pp.vi-vii.

7. K.S. Latourette, *op.cit.* (vol.3, *Three Centuries of Advance, 1500-1800*), New York: Harper and Brothers, 1939, p.240.

8. Henry Gemery and Jan S. Hogendorn, "The Economic costs of West African participation in the Atlantic slave trade: A preliminary sampling for the 18th century", in Gemery and Hogendorn (eds), *The Uncommon Market: Essays in the Economic History of the Atlantic Slave Trade* (Studies in Social

Christianity as "Civilisation"   253

Discontinuity series), New York: Academic Press, 1979, p.161.

9. See Basil Davidson, *Black Mother – Africa and the Atlantic Slave Trade* (revised and expanded edition), Harmondsworth: Penguin Books, 1970, 1980, p.242: "Huge quantities of firearms were poured into West Africa during the major period of the slave trade; and the state of Dahomey, increasingly a militarised autocracy, was among those that had the doubtful benefit. At the height of the 18th century commerce, gunsmiths in Birmingham alone were exporting muskets to Africa at the rate of between 100,000 and 150,000 a year, and it was common talk that one Birmingham gun rated one Negro slave. This last was Birmingham sales talk rather than a statement of fact... Yet the spirit of the saying was true enough. Firearms had become indispensable to the Guinea trade."

10. *Ibid.*, p.283. See also, J.D. Hargreaves, *Prelude to the Partition of West Africa*, London: Macmillan, 1963; Walter Rodney, *How Europe Underdeveloped Africa*, London: Bogle-L'Ouverture, 1972, Dar-es-Salaam: Tanzania Publishing House, 1972. For an illuminating study of the history of Dahomey (now Benin) from this viewpoint, see Alan Scholefield, *The Dark Kingdoms – The Impact of White Civilisation on Three Great African Monarchies*, London: Heinemann, 1975, pp.53-109.

11. Basil Davidson, *op.cit.,* p.271.

12. Sir John Hawkins, whose daring sea-faring adventures established English participation in the Triangular Trade, mentions as a major reason for his first voyage of 1562, the fact that he was "among other particulars assured that Negros (*sic*) were good merchandise in *Hispaniola*, and that store of *Negros* might easily be had upon the coast of Guinea". His second voyage in 1564 had the approval of Queen Elizabeth I, who lent a vessel of the Royal Navy, the "Jesus" for the expedition. See E.J. Payne and C.R. Beazley (eds) *Voyages of the Elizabethan Seamen: Select Narratives from the 'Principal Navigations' of Hakluyt*, Oxford: Clarendon Press, 1907, pp.6, 9.

13. See Arthur O. Lovejoy, *The Great Chain of Being: A Study of a History of an Idea*, Cambridge, Mass.: Harvard University Press, 1936, pp.183-207.

14. Philip Curtin, *op.cit.*, p.38.

15. Norbert Lochner, "Anton Wilhelm Amo: A Ghana Scholar in 18th century Germany" in *Transactions of the Historical Society of Ghana*, vol.7, Legon, 1965, pp.60-81.

16. For an illuminating exposé of the breadth of humanitarian interest in the African, in English thought and literature from the 17th to 19th centuries, see Eva Beatrice Dykes, *The Negro in English Romantic Thought: A Study of Sympathy for the Oppressed*, Washington, D.C.: The Associated Publishers, 1942. For a useful treatment of the extent and consensus between evangelical (mainly English) and humanist and rationalist (mainly French) humanitarians, see S.H. Swinny, "The Humanitarianism of the 18th century and its results", in F.S. Marvin (ed), *Western Races and the World*, London: Oxford University Press, 1922, pp.121-145. Swinny put forward the view that Lord Mansfield's judgment on slavery in England in 1772 was "perhaps more in consonance with the spirit of the age than with the law of the country" (p.140). Certainly the long history of British official acceptance of the institution would seem to argue in his favour, and this makes the humanitarian achievement all the more remarkable. For the full text of the judgment of Lord Chief Justice Mansfield in the famous case of James Somersett, see Stiv Jacobsen, *Am I Not a Man and a Brother? British Missions and the Abolition of the Slave Trade in West Africa and the West Indies (1786-1838)*, Uppsala: Gleerup, 1972, p.47.

17. T.F. Buxton, *The African Slave Trade and its Remedy*, London: Frank Cass, 1840, p.515.

18. *Ibid.*, p.457. See Philip Curtin, *op.cit.*, pp.252-258, for a discussion of the extent of agreement between humanitarians and their opponents on the "barbarism" of Africa and Africans. On the other hand, a thoroughgoing intellectual racism which held Africans to be inherently and permanently inferior to Europeans was to be put forth in the following decades, prominently espoused by men like the one-time army surgeon in South Africa, Robert Knox, *Races of Men* (1848), and in France by Arthur de Gobineau, *Essai sur l'inégalité des races humaines* (4 vols), (1853-55); see Philip Curtin, *op.cit.*, pp.377-382.

19. The sense of needing to atone for the wrongs of the slave trade was a potent motivation factor in the modern missionary enterprises. The instructions to the first two missionaries sent out in 1804 by the Church Missionary Society are revealing on this point: "though Western Africa may justly charge her sufferings from this trade (i.e. slave trade) upon all Europe, directly or remotely, yet the British nation now is, and has long been, most criminal. We desire therefore while we pray and labour for the removal of this evil, to make Western African the best remuneration in our power for its manifold wrongs." See Eugene Stock, *The History of the Church Missionary Society: Its environment, its men and its work* (vol.1), London: CMS, 1899, p.95. Cf. Max Warren, *The Missionary Movement from Britain in Modern History*, London: SCM Press, 1965, pp.49-50. For the American "side" of the story, see C.J. Phillips, *Protestant America and the Pagan World: The first half-century of the American Board of Commissioners for Foreign Missions, 1810-1860* (Harvard East Asian Monographs, 32), Cambridge, Mass., Harvard University Press, 1969, pp.206f. It is ironical, on the other hand, that in the year the institution of slavery was declared to be illegal in England, the one English clergyman who by then had served as missionary in West Africa, the Rev. Thomas Thompson, produced a defence of the slave trade, citing philosophical and Biblical authorities. Thompson's work was entitled: *The African Trade for Negro Slaves shown to be consistent with the principles of Humanity and the laws of Revealed Religion*, London, 1772. See E. Irving Carlyle, "Thomas Thompson" in *DNB*, vol.56, edited by Sidney Lee, London: Smith, Elder and Co., 1898, p.223. According to Carlyle, "Thompson, without considering the subject very deeply, draws his argument from Aristotle and his illustrations from the Pentateuch."

20. T.F. Buxton, *op.cit.*, p.458.

21. The full programme was to: (1) impede and discourage the slave traffic, (2) establish and encourage legitimate commerce, (3) promote and teach agriculture, (4) impart moral and religious instruction. See T.F. Buxton, *op.cit.*, p.518.

22. Buxton cites the testimonies of various missionary agencies which had come to conclusions similar to his own and he derives the use of the association of "the Bible and the plough" from the Rev. James Read of the LMS, who worked in South Africa and married a Hottentot woman. For an appreciation of Read, see Richard Lovett, *The History of the London Missionary Society, 1795-1895* (vol.1), London: Henry Frowde, 1899, p.571. See Buxton, *op.cit.*, p.483; cf. pp.505-510.

23. In the Church of Scotland, which was relatively late in engaging in foreign missionary outreach, as late as 1796, a speaker in General Assembly was expressing the view that "to spread abroad the knowledge of the Gospel among barbarians and heathen nations seems highly preposterous, in so far as it anticipates, it even reverses the order of nature", see Alec R. Vidler, *The Church in an Age of Revolution: 1789 to the present day* (Pelican History of the Church, 5), Harmondsworth: Penguin Books, rev. ed., 1977, p.248.

24. The expression is from a 19th-century work intended to stir missionary interest: John Beecham, *Ashantee and the Gold Coast, Being a sketch of the History, Social State and Superstition of the inhabitants of these countries with a notice of the state and prospects of Christianity among them* (with introduction and notes by G.E. Metcalfe), London: Dawson's of Pall Mall, 1968 (1st published, 1841), p.339. He refers to Buxton, *op.cit.*, p.502.

25. T.F. Buxton, *op.cit.*, pp.510-511.

26. The observation was made by the secretary of LMS, Rev. William Ellis, and is quoted by Buxton, *op.cit.*, p.507.

27. Denys Hay, *Europe: The Emergence of an Idea*, Edinburgh University Press, 1957, p.35.

28. *Ibid.*, pp.64-72.

29. For an interesting and widened restatement of the idea at the beginning of the 20th century, in the context of political disunity in Europe owing to war; see H.G. Wood, "Religion as a unifying influence in Western Civilization", in F.S. Marvin (ed), *The Unity of Western Civilisation*, London: Oxford University Press, 1915, pp.280-300.

30. Denys Hay, *op.cit.*, pp.98, 111-116.

31. See *ibid.*, pp.1-15, for the discussion of the contribution of the progeny of Noah to the emergence of the consciousness of European Christendom.

32. On the association of "Christianity" with "civilisation" in the thought of the modern missionary movement, Max Warren comments: "It is very easy to dismiss this as cultural *hubris* and theological illiteracy. What we ought to recognise is that in this close association of ideas we are seeing the vestigial remains of Europe's medieval heritage of ideas, among them the idea of Christendom." See his *Missionary Movement from Britain in Modern History*, London: SCM, 1965, p.60.

33. See William Carey, *An Enquiry into the Obligations of Christians to Use Means for the Conversion of the Heathens (reprinted from the edition of 1792)*, London: Hodder and Stoughton, 1891, p.65.

34. Cf. the judgment of the *Encyclopedia Britannica* of 1797: "When the different systems of religion that have prevailed in the world are comparatively viewed with respect to their influence on the welfare of society, we find reason to prefer the polytheism of the Greeks and Romans to the ruder, wilder, religious ideas and ceremonies that have prevailed among savages; Mahometanism, perhaps in some respects, to the polytheism of the Greeks and Romans; Judaism however to Mahometanism; and Christianity to all of them." See article, "Religion" in *Encyclopedia Britannica* (3rd edition), vol.16, Edinburgh, 1797, p.77.

35. See for instance, William Carey, *op.cit.*, p.38.

36. Cf. J. Hondius' map of world religions (1625), reproduced in Denys Hay, *op.cit.*, between pages 108 and 109.

37. William Carey, *op.cit.*, p.63.

38. Cf. the view of the *Encyclopedia Britannica*, in 1805, on African religion: "But though the Negroes have little speculative religion, they have much superstition, as appears from the great use which they make of what are called *fetiches*, of charms... any natural object which chances to catch hold of the fancy of a Negro;" in article "Africa", in *Encyclopedia Britannica* (4th edition), vol.1, pt.1, Edinburgh, 1805, p.267.

39. Cf. a mid-19th century missionary assessment of Black Africa: "At this day

the negro race stands before the world in a condition disgraceful to itself and to humanity. Divided into innumerable tribes and languages – without literature, laws or government, arts or sciences – with slavery for its normal social condition and the basest and bloodiest superstition in the world for religion – a religion without reference to God or their souls, to sin or holiness, to heaven or hell, and even without the outward insignia of temple, priest or altar, it has sunk so low as to be regardless alike of conscience and of shame, to reckon a man's life at his market value as a beast of burden, and to practise cannibalism, not from want but revenge, and a horrid lust of human flesh." See Hope Waddell, *Twenty-nine years in the West Indies and Central Africa – A Review of Missionary Work and Adventure, 1829-1858*, London: Frank Cass, 1863, 1970, p.227.

40. For a succinct treatment of the history of the racist idea applied to the achievement and progress of nations from the European standpoint, see R. Nisbet, *History of the Idea of Progress*, New York: Basic Books, 1980, pp.286-296. For a more comprehensive treatment of the development of European racist philosophy and the humanitarian opposition to it, see Philip Curtin, *op.cit.*, pp.363-387.

41. E.E. Evans-Pritchard, *Theories of Primitive Religion*, Oxford: Clarendon Press, 1965, p.15.

42. Eric J. Sharpe, *Comparative Religion: A History*, London: Duckworth, 1975, p.48.

43. John Lubbock, *The Origin of Civilization and the Primitive Condition of Man*, 1870; E.B. Tylor, *Primitive Culture, Researches into the development of mythology, philosophy, religion, art and custom* (2 vols) (3rd edition revised), London: John Murray, 1891. (1st published 1871); J.G. Frazer, *The Golden Bough*, London: Macmillan, 1890 (1st edition, 2 vols.); 1900 (2nd edition, 3 vols); 1922 (Abridged edition, 1 vol.).

44. E.E. Evans-Pritchard, *op.cit.*, pp.15-16; Eric Sharpe, *op.cit.*, p.87: "Frazer was in fact conventionally Christian all his life, and in no way wanted to see his work applied to the dismissal of religion. In all probability he gave little thought to the possibility of any "application" whatsoever, of his work."

45. Concerning Tylor, brought up as a Quaker, it may not be unfair to ask whether Evans-Pritchard's criticism of his work might not also be related to the fact that he linked the religious philosophy of "the savage fetish-worshipper" to that of "the civilised Christian" in a way which drove a wedge between all forms, stages and manifestations of religion (essentially and fundamentally Animistic) and materialism (*Primitive Culture*, vol.1, pp.501-502). Following a strict evolutionary schema, therefore, he undermined the intellectual respectability of religion in an age of science, the former having become the "remains of crude old culture which have passed into harmful superstition" (*op.cit.*, vol.2, p.453).

46. "Fetishism" as a description of the religion of African peoples was provided by the Frenchman, Charles de Brosses in *Du culte des dieux fétiches, ou Parallèle de l'ancienne religion de l'Egypte avec la religion actuelle de Nigritie*, (1760), republished by Gregg International Publishers Ltd., Westmead, Farnborough, 1972. According to de Brosses, "Fetish" was a "term coined by our merchants in Senegal from the Portuguese 'fetisso', i.e. *something magic, supernatural, sacred or oracular...* These sacred fetishes are nothing more than the first material object which any nation or any individual cares to choose and have ceremonially consecrated by his priests." The theory of "animism", as a description of the religious belief in spiritual beings, both animate and inanimate, as developed by E.B. Tylor in his *Primitive Culture*,

displaced "fetishism" and established itself as the convenient term for the religion of Africans and of others placed in the same category by European observers.

47. This was the Conference's brief, as stated in the subtitle to the official reports of the Conference.

48. The report was compiled from the responses of missionaries on the field, 60% of the answers relating to the African field, with occasional samplings from the Dutch (East) Indies and British India. See *World Missionary Conference 1910: Report of Commission IV – The Missionary Message in Relation to Non-Christian Religions*, Edinburgh and London: Oliphant, Anderson and Ferrier, 1910, p.7 (henceforth cited as *The Missionary Message in Relation to Non-Christian Religions*); for a list of the questions circulated, see p.2.

49. W.H.T. Gairdner, *Edinburgh 1910: An Account and Interpretation of the W.M.C.*, London: Oliphant, Anderson and Ferrier, 1910, p.139.

50. *The Missionary Message in Relation to Non-Christian Religions*, p.6.

51. See W.H.T. Gairdner, *op.cit.*, p.139.

52. *The Missionary Message in Relation to Non-Christian Religions*, p.24. Of the 14 missionary correspondents in Africa who sent answers to the questionnaire, a dozen were virtually certain that there was "no religion", meaning "formulated religious observances and doctrines", in evidence; and whatever there was could not be "prized as religious help or consolation". See *Answers to Questionnaire for World Missionary Conference, Edinburgh 1910* (Commission IV, *The Missionary Message in Relation to Non-Christian Religions*). Bound volumes of typescripts: vol.1, *Japan, Animistic Peoples, Indochina, etc.*, held in Christ's College Library, Aberdeen, Scotland. (On this missionary understanding of "Animism" in its relation to Christianity, see A.F. Walls, "The First Chapter of the Epistle to the Romans and the Modern Missionary Movement" in W. Ward Gasque and Ralph P. Martin (eds), *Apostolic History and the Gospel: Biblical and Historical Essays presented to F.F. Bruce on his 60th birthday*, Exeter: Paternoster Press, 1970, p.355.) I am indebted to Prof. Walls of the University of Aberdeen, for access to the Christ's College material.

53. Johannes Warneck, *The Living Forces of the Gospel: Experiences of a Missionary in Animistic Heathendom* (translated from 3rd German edition by Neil Buchanan), Edinburgh and London: Oliphant, Anderson and Ferrier, (n.d.).

54. *The Missionary Message in Relation to Non-Christian Religions*, pp.12-13.

55. *Ibid.*, p.13. Warneck, who would allow that among every heathen people there did exist "one or other delightful trait", nonetheless could conclude: "All the same, when we speak of a general perversion of morality among animistic peoples, we mean that the idea of morals is entirely absent or present only in a stunted form. They have a custom, a law, a fixed usage, but no morality. There are no moral standards. They have the idea of the permitted and the forbidden, but not that of good and evil." See *The Living Forces of the Gospel* (ET), p.126. For a different view of "animistic" morality espoused at the Edinburgh Conference, see *The Missionary Message*, pp.297-298.

56. E.B. Tylor, *op.cit.* (vol.1), p.426.

57. *Ibid.*, p.427.

58. *Ibid.*, p.420. On the "peculiar" heathenism of the Tswana, Robert Moffat wrote: "Satan has been too successful in leading a majority of the human race by an almost endless variety of deities... While Satan is obviously the author of the polytheism of other nations, he has employed his agency with fatal success, in erasing every vestige of religious impression from the minds of the Bechuanas, Hottentots, and Bushmen, leaving them without a single ray to guide them from

the dark and dread futurity or a single link to unite them with the skies." See his *Missionary Labours and Scenes in Southern Africa*, London: John Snow, 1842, pp.243-244.

59. E.B. Tylor, *op.cit.* (vol.1), p.427. My emphasis.

60. *Ibid.* (vol.2), p.356.

61. *Ibid.*, p.357.

62. *Ibid.*, p.360.

63. *Ibid.*, p.360.

64. *The Missionary Message in Relation to Non-Christian Religions*, p.35.

65. W.H.T. Gairdner, *op.cit.*, p.141. It is worth noting that at the next comparable missionary conference, at Jerusalem in 1928, the interest was on "non-Christian systems", and "the humblest... and least sublime of all the creeds" had given way to "secular civilisation" on the list of issues which deserved special treatment; see *The Christian Life and Message in Relation to Non-Christian Systems of Thought and Life* (vol.1 of Reports of the Meeting of the International Missionary Council at Jerusalem, Easter, 1928), London: Oxford University Press, 1928. (It is interesting that for the 1910 Conference, one missionary correspondent in South Africa had concluded that there were "no definite non-Christian religions in this part of South Africa"; see *Answers to Questionnaire for World Missionary Conference, Edinburgh 1910*, p.244)

66. *The Missionary Message in Relation to Non-Christian Religions*, p.220. My emphasis. "The elemental truths" meant here are stated as follows: "the unity, the omnipotence, the omnipresence, and the availability of God, as the Protector and Deliverer of His children, the hearer and answerer of prayer not only in the soul's inner experiences but in the outward environment and circumstances", (p.220). Warneck's work in Sumatra had highlighted these elements of the Biblical teaching, and the Commission was alert enough to recognise its implications for Christian theology. Earlier on the Report speaks of "the Christianity of Europe" being "recalled if not to forgotten truths, at least to neglected graces by the infant churches" (p.37). For Warneck's evidence and analysis, see *The Living Forces of the Gospel*, pt.3, pp.188-302.

67. See *The Missionary Message in Relation to Non-Christian Religions*, pp.220-221. Cf. W.H.T. Gairdner, *op.cit.*, p.141.

68. J.F.A. Ajayi, *Christian Missions in Nigeria, 1841-1891: The Making of a new elite*, London: Longman, 1965, pp.260-264. "The Negro's place in nature" was in fact the title of a paper presented by James Hunt to the Anthropological Society of London in 1863. See *Memoires Read before the Anthropological Society of London 1863-64* (vol.1), London, 1865, pp.1-64. For a different interpretation of the attitudes of the "new breed" of radical evangelicals, see G.O.M. Tasie, *Christian Missionary Enterprise in the Niger Delta, 1864-1918*, Leiden: E.J. Brill, 1978, pp.104f and 133-134. Also see A.F. Walls, "Black Europeans, White Africans: Some Missionary Motives in West Africa" in D. Baker (ed), *Religious Motivation: Biographical and Sociological Problems of the Church Historian*, Cambridge, Cambridge University Press, 1978, p.343; and Andrew Porter, "Evangelical Enthusiasm, Missionary Motivation and West Africa in the late 19th century: the career of G.W. Brooke" in *JICH*, vol.6, 1977, pp.23-46.

69. For a severe and possibly one-sided treatment of the problem, see P.J. George, "Racist assumptions of the 19th century missionary movement" in *IRM*, vol.59, 1970, pp.271-284. For the Catholic story, see Laënnec Hurbon, "Racisme et Théologie missionnaire", in *Présence Africaine*, vol.71, part 3, 1969, pp.35-47; Yves M.-J. Congar, *The Catholic Church and the Race Question*, Paris: Unesco, 1953.

70. See, for instance, J. van den Berg, *Constrained by Jesus' Love: An inquiry into the motives of the missionary awakening in Great Britain in the period between 1695 and 1815*, Kampen: J.H. Kok, 1956. Cf. M. Warren, *op.cit.*, pp.36-55. See also, C.J. Phillips, *op.cit.*, especially Ch.9, "The missionary image of the world". For an assessment by an African historian, cf. E.A. Ayandele, *The Missionary Impact on Modern Nigeria, 1842-1914: A Political and Social Analysis*, London: Longman, 1966, especially Ch.11, "The missionary impact on Society".

71. Philip Curtin, *op.cit.*, p.386.

72. T.F. Buxton, *op.cit.*, p.457; also p.511.

73. See A.F. Walls, "Black Europeans, White Africans: Some Missionary Motives in West Africa", pp.339-348.

74. The concept is credited particularly to the outstanding secretary of the Church Missionary Society, the Rev. Henry Venn. See Eugene Stock, *op.cit.*, (vol.2), p.412. For a comparable and contemporaneous development in the missionary thinking of the North American, Rufus Anderson, see R. Pierce Beaver (ed), *To Advance the Gospel: Selections from the Writings of Rufus Anderson*, Grand Rapids: Eerdmans, 1967.

75. The career and achievement of S.A. Crowther, the first African bishop of the Anglican Communion, has been variously assessed; the CMS decision to appoint a European successor, and so, in effect, reverse Henry Venn's proposals, is accepted by Stephen Neill, *A History of Christian Missions* (The Pelican History of the Church: 6), Harmondsworth, Penguin Books, 1964, pp.377-378. For different conclusions, see J.F.A. Ajayi, *op.cit.*, pp.245ff; E.A. Ayandele, *op.cit.*, pp.207ff; see also J.B. Webster, *Christian Churches among the Yoruba, 1888-1922*, Oxford: Clarendon Press, 1964. For a recent and helpful examination of the evidence, see G.O.M. Tasie, *op.cit.*, especially ch.3, "The Delta Revolt".

76. See Robert Joly, *The Origins of Modern African Thought. Its Development in West Africa during the 19th and 20th Centuries*, London: Faber and Faber, 1968, pp.177-195. Cf. A.F. Walls, "Black Europeans, White Africans: Some Missionary Motives in West Africa", p.341.

77. By the 1870s, Fourah Bay College, affiliated to the University of Durham, was offering degree courses in arts and theology, which was more than most early European missionaries to Sierra Leone had acquired. See A.F. Walls "Missionary vocation and the ministry: the first generation", in M.E. Glasswell and E.W. Fasholé-Luke (eds), *New Testament Christianity for Africa and the World, Essays in honour of Harry Sawyerr*, London: SPCK, 1974, pp.141-156.

78. Jesse Page, *The Black Bishop, Samuel Adjai Crowther*, London: Hodder and Stoughton, 1908, p.38. Crowther's achievement in the ordination examination, conducted by the Regius Professor of Greek at Cambridge, caused no little stir in learned circles used to discussing "the mental capacity of the negro", and concluding that it was "always deficient as regards logical faculty". See Jesse Page, *op.cit.*, p.71; also pp.35, 37, 249.

79. *Ibid.*, p.34.

80. *Ibid.*, p.69. My emphasis.

81. See P.R. McKenzie, *Inter-religious Encounters in West Africa, Samuel Adjai Crowther's Attitude to African Traditional Religion and Islam*, Leicester: Study of Religion sub-Dept., 1976.

82. *Ibid.*, p.74; cf. E.A. Ayandele, *op.cit.*, p.208, quoting Ashcroft to Hutchinson, 8th Jan.1880: "I feel it is a most difficult subject at present, this *purely native*

mission. But I feel more convinced that it will have to be a mixed Mission and that Europeans must lead if there is to be any genuine substantial Christianity in the Niger".

83. Cf. Adrian Hastings, *Church and Mission in Modern Africa*, pp.60f.

84. The careers of Edwin W. Smith and E. Geoffrey Parrinder are particularly interesting in this regard. On Smith, see the study of his thought on the relation of Christianity to African Traditional Religion by Malcolm J. McVeigh, *God in Africa: Conceptions of God in African Traditional Religion and Christianity*, Cape Cod, Mass. and Hartford, Vermont: Claude Stark, 1974. On Parrinder, see A.F. Walls, "A bag of needments for the road: Geoffrey Parrinder and the study of religion in Britain", in *Religion*, vol.10, pt.2, Autumn 1980, *Essays for Geoffrey Parrinder at 70*, pp.141-150. On the Catholic side of the story, see R.P. Placide Tempels, *La Philosophie Bantoue*, Paris: Présence Africaine, 1948; ET as *Bantu Philosophy*, by Colin King, with foreword by Margaret Read, Paris: Présence Africaine, 1959.

85. Thomas Jesse Jones, "New Forces in Africa", in E.W. Smith, *op.cit.*, p.132; also pp.36-43.

86. On the question of the existence of any preparation for Christianity in the African religious past, the Le Zoute conference struck a quite different note from Edinburgh 1910, affirming that it is now recognised more than before that Africans have been prepared by previous experience for the reception of the Gospel and that their experience contains elements of high religious value, in E.W. Smith, *op.cit.*, p.16. Cf. D. Westermann's views in an article specially written for the Le Zoute conference: "Can a system of life by which a race has lived through many centuries be entirely worthless? Must it not contain elements of divine education and guidance that should not be destroyed but be brought to full evolution? May it not be a preparatory stage for fuller life?" See D. Westermann, "The Value of the African's Past" in *IRM*, vol.15, 1926, pp.427-428.

87. J.S. Mbiti, *op.cit.*, p.232.

88. In February, 1839, Rev. T.B. Freeman on a visit to Kumasi, the capital of Ashanti (Asante in present orthography), wrote: "Sunday, 17th – Blessed by God, through whose good providence I was born in a Christian country!

'Thine's the Sabbath-peace, my land,
And thine the guarded hearth.'

How amazing the difference between England and Ashanti! Here no village bell, sweetly sounding 'across the daisied mead' invites the humble Christian to the sanctuary of God! Here (it may be presumed) no hymn of praise ascends from the natives of this country to their Creator; no house of prayer is seen standing with its doors wide open, inviting man to share in its sacred immunities!" (Freeman was part African himself, son of an African father and English mother.) See his *Journal of Two Visits to the Kingdom of Ashanti in Western Africa*, London: John Mason, Wesleyan Conference Centre, 1843, pp.23-24.

89. Raoul Allier, *La Psychologie de la Conversion chez les peuples non-civilisés*, Paris: Payot, 1925.

90. See S.C. Neill, "The History of Missions: An academic discipline" in G.J. Cuming (ed), *The Mission of the Church and the Propagation of the Faith*, Cambridge, Cambridge University Press, 1970, p.160.

91. See particularly, Lucien Lévy-Bruhl, *Les Fonctions mentales dans les sociétés inférieures*, Paris: Félix Alcan et Guillaumin, 1910; *La Mentalité Primitive*, Paris: Félix Alcan, 1922.

92. L. Lévy-Bruhl, *Les Fonctions mentales...* pp.37-38. For a criticism of Lévy-Bruhl, see E.E. Evans-Pritchard, *op.cit.*, especially ch.4, "Lévy-Bruhl".

93. Raoul Allier, *op.cit.*, 3ème partie, pp.449ff.

94. *Ibid.*, especially ch.8, "L'attention morale et l'intelligence"; also pp.423-428.

95. Roger Bastide, "Sociologies des Missions protestantes" in *Les Missions protestantes et l'histoire* (Actes du 11e Colloqué, 4-9 octobre, 1971, Université Paul Valéry, Montpellier, Etude des Colloques, vol.2), Paris: Société de l'Histoire du Protestantisme français, n.d. p.58.

96. *Ibid.*, p.58.

97. Raoul Allier, *op.cit.*, 3ème partie, pp.453-469.

98. His brief treatment of the "Ethiopian" Church movement in Southern Africa fastens unduly, in my view, on moral blemishes and ignores any serious considerations of the problem of cultural alienation and the possibility of an African quest for integrity and freedom from missionary control, as well as for a Christian life shaped by African understanding rather than by European models.

99. J.S. Mbiti, *African Religions and Philosophy*, London: Heinemann, 1969, p.232. With regard to "the modern changes taking place in Africa", it is worth noting that the important missionary conference in 1926, to consider African questions, had nothing special to say about the presentation of the Gospel to educated and civilised Africans; see E.W. Smith, *The Christian Mission in Africa: A study based on the work of the international conference at Le Zoute, Belgium, Sept.14th-21st, 1926*, London: Edinburgh House, 1926.

100. See, for instance, writers as diverse in their positions as: E.B. Idowu, *Towards an Indigenous Church*, London: Oxford University Press, 1965, pp.4, 22-23; Byang H. Kato, *Theological Pitfalls in Africa*, Kisumu, Kenya: Evangel Publishing House, 1975, pp.14-15.

101. E.B. Idowu, *Towards an Indigenous Church*, p.22.

102. See Robert L. Wilken, *The Myth of Christian Beginnings*, London: SCM Press, 1979 (1st published in the U.S.A. by Doubleday and Co., in 1971), pp.1-26, especially his discussion on "Memory as part of self-understanding" (pp.4-5).

103. This last statement was communicated to the author by Prof. Mbiti in the course of a meeting in August, 1980.

104. A.F. Walls offers some judicious comments on the new Krio (Sierra Leone) Christianity, which are apposite here: "The Krio Church was built on receptive Africans, uprooted from coherent societies and without the means of rediscovering their former cohesion. The only identity now open to them was a new identity. They took the only viable alternative open to them, European civilisation". See his "Black Europeans, White Africans: Some Missionary Motives in West Africa", p.341. Cf. A.F. Walls, "A Colonial Concordat: Two Views of Christianity and Civilisation" in D. Baker (ed), *Church, Society and Politics*, (Studies in Church History), Oxford: Blackwell, 1975, pp.293-302.

105. E.B. Idowu, *Towards an Indigenous Church*, pp.24-25.

106. *Ibid.*, pp.2-3.

107. J.S. Mbiti, *Concepts of God in Africa*, London: SPCK, 1970, p.xiii.

108. Adrian Hastings, *African Christianity: An Essay in Interpretation*, London and Dublin: Geoffrey Chapman, 1976, p.51.

109. A.F. Walls, "Africa and Christian Identity", p.13.

110. Max Warren, op.cit., pp.61, 166.

111. Ibid., p.60.

112. Ibid., p.60.

113. G.C. Oosthuizen, Post-Christianity in Africa – A Theological and Anthropological Study, London: C. Hurst and Co., 1968, p.235.

114. Kenneth Cragg, Christianity in World Perspective, London: Lutterworth Press, 1968, p.18.

115. Ibid., p.18.

116. Ibid., p.18.

117. Max Warren, op.cit., p.88.

118. Max Warren, op.cit., p.88.

119. Kenneth Cragg, op.cit., p.43.

120. It is Gabriel Setiloane, a South African Methodist clergyman, who has expressed this sense of estrangement the most acutely, to my knowledge. See his, "Where are we in African Theology?" in K. Appiah-Kubi and Sergio Torres (eds), African Theology en Route (Papers from the Pan-African Copnference of Third World Theologians, December, 1977, Accra, Ghana), Maryknoll: Orbis Books, 1979, p.64.

121. Ibid., pp.xi, 4ff.

122. Ibid., p.234.

123. Ibid., p.235.

124. Ibid., p.235.

125. Ibid., p.3.

126. See Johannes van den Berg, op.cit., pp.187-213.

127. Ruth Rouse, "A Study of Missionary Vocation", in IRM, vol.6, 1917.

128. Kenneth Cragg, op.cit., pp.19-28.

129. Kenneth Cragg, op.cit., p.41.

130. See Chapter 1 above: "Non licet esse vos..." It is ironical that the Christians survived also because they were little known and understood. When the State awoke to the threat and set about acting with vigour, as Duchesne observes: "It was too late: the Church escaped, and it was the Empire that fell". Louis Duchesne, Early History of the Christian Church: from its foundations to the end of the third century (ET of 4th edition), London: John Murray, 1910, p.84.

131. Kenneth Cragg, op.cit., p.41.

132. Adolf von Harnack, op.cit. (vol.1), pp.19-23.

133. It is important to note that Paul's mission to Gentiles had, in a real sense, its forerunner in the work of converted Hellenistic Jews who, as a result of their evangelistic zeal among non-Jews, were responsible for attracting the "Christian" name in the first place; (cf. Acts 11:19-26). On the significance of the Hellenistic Jews for the early Christian mission, see Ferdinand Hahn, Mission in the New Testament, pp.59-77; see also, Marcel Simon, St Stephen and the Hellenists in the Primitive Church, London: Longmans, Green and Co., 1958.

134. Kenneth Cragg, op.cit., p.41. My emphasis.

135. See Georg F. Vicedom, Missio Dei: Einführung in eine Theologie der

Mission, München: Chr. Kaiser Verlag, 1958; Johannes Blauw, *The Missionary Nature of the Church: A Survey of the Biblical theology of Mission* (Foundations of the Christian Mission series), London: Lutterworth Press, 1962; George Peters, *A Biblical Theology of Missions*, Chicago: Moody Press, 1972. For a useful survey of issues and concerns, see G.H. Anderson (ed), *The Theology of the Christian Mission*, London: SCM Press, 1961, especially G.H. Anderson's introductory essay, "The Theology of Mission among Protestants in the 20th Century", pp.3-16; also has a helpful bibliography.

136. Adolf von Harnack, *op.cit.* (vol.2), pp.33-34; see the whole chapter 2 – on the inward spread of Christianity; cf. *1 Corinthians* 1:26f.

137. *Acts* 11:27ff; *Galatians* 2:10, also *2 Corinthians* 8,9.

138. Kenneth Cragg, *op.cit.*, *passim*.

139. *Ibid.*, p.43; cf. Max Warren, *op.cit.*, p.166.

140. Johannes Blauw, *op.cit.*, *passim*.

141. *Ibid.*, pp.113-114.

142. John V. Taylor, *The Growth of the Church in Buganda: An Attempt at Understanding*, London: SCM Press, 1958, p.259. Cf. Norman J. Goreham, "Towards an African Theology", in *The Expository Times*, May, 1975, vol. 86, no.8, pp.233-236. "As the Gospel is preached in new languages and the Church is planted in new soil, there may well appear hitherto forgotten or hidden treasures of truth which will enrich the Church as a whole. Much of the magnificently positive theology in African Christianity may in years to come shine forth in full splendour and help to recover for us all something of the lost radiance of the Christian faith" (p.236).

143. *The Missionary Message in Relation to Non-Christian Religions*, p.35.

144. G.H. Anderson, "The Theology of Mission among Protestants in the 20th century", p.5.

145. As far as the "theology of mission" went, the Conference was concerned with "non-Christian systems of thought and life". Since "it was not true to speak of animism as a system", it did not feature in the list of major treatments, except in two interventions during discussion; see *The Christian Life and Message in Relation to Non-Christian Systems of Thought and Life*, pp.364-365.

146. A.F. Walls, "The First Chapter of the Epistle to the Romans and the Modern Missionary Movement", p.356.

147. *Ibid.*, p.356. Emphasis in original.

148. *Ibid.*, p.357.

149. Some accounts of missionary labours included as a matter of importance a section on the "heathen superstitions" and customs, their cruelties, or some such designation of the ways of "barbarous men"; see for instance, *A.M.MacKay – Pioneer Missionary of the Church Missionary Society to Uganda*, by his sister, (Missionary Researches and Labours and Travels, 14), London: Frank Cass, 1970 (1st published in 1890), especially ch.5, "Heathen Superstitions". Robert Moffat in Southern Africa considered that it "would be neither very instructive nor very edifying" to describe Bechuana customs; see his *Missionary Labours and Scenes in Southern Africa*, p.249.

150. Kenneth Cragg, *op.cit.*, p.62.

151. *Ibid.*, p.48.

152. A.F. Walls, "The First Chapter of the Epistle to the Romans and the Modern Missionary Movement", p.348.

153. See Chapter 1 above: "*Non licet esse vos...*"

154. J. Dupont, *Etudes sur les Actes des Apôtres*, Paris: Les Editions du Cerf, 1967, p.414. 155. See *Colossians* 1:15ff; *Ephesians* 1:10ff.

156. *Acts* 13:26ff.

157. *Ibid.*, 14:15ff; cf. 17:22ff.

158. A.F. Walls, "Ruminations on Rainmaking: The Transmission and Receipt of Religious Expertise in Africa", in J.C. Stone (ed), *Experts in Africa* (Proceedings of a Colloquium at the University of Aberdeen, March, 1980), Aberdeen: Aberdeen University African Studies Group, 1980, p.148.

159. Thomas B. Freeman, *op.cit.*

160. *Ibid.*, p.64.

161. *Ibid.*, pp.25, 27, 128.

162. *Ibid.*, p.24.

165. I.e. the King of Asante (Asantehene) in Kumasi.

166. T.B. Freeman, *op.cit.*, pp.27-28.

167. John Beecham, *op.cit.*, pp.343f; cf. T.B. Freeman, *op.cit.*, p.110.

168. Nathan Söderblom, *The Living God: Basal forms of Personal Religion*, (Gifford Lectures, 1931), London: Oxford University Press, 1933, pp.234-263.

169. See, especially, our Chapter 4 above, "Christ and the Hellenistic Heritage (1): Justin, or Christ, as the expectation of the nations".

170. Nathan Söderblom, *op.cit.*, p.263.

171. See Kenneth Cragg, *op.cit.*, p.18.

172. See *Romans* 2:11ff.

173. S.G. Williamson, *Akan Religion and the Christian Faith*, Accra: Ghana Universities Press, 1965, p.138.

174. See John S. Mbiti, *African Religions and Philosophy*, p.237.

175. S.G. Williamson, *op.cit.*, p.168.

176. *Ibid.*, p.170. Cf. Noel Smith, *The Presbyterian Church of Ghana, 1835-1960*, Accra: Ghana Universities Press, 1966, especially ch.5, "The Impact of Christianity upon Traditional Religion and Life".

177. S.G.Williamson, *op.cit.*, 171.

178. Cf. the question posed by Kenneth Cragg, *op.cit.*, p.57: "For if the old is taken away, to whom is the new given?" in response to D. Westermann's total rejection of the African religious past; see D. Westermann, *Africa and Christianity (Duff Lectures, 1935)*, London: Oxford University Press, 1937, pp.2,94.

179. Noel Smith, *op.cit.*, p.86.

180. G.C. Oosthuizen, *op.cit.*, p.235.

181. *Ibid.*, p.234.

182. W.D. Davies: *Paul and Rabbinic Judaism: Some Rabbinic Elements in Pauline Theology* (4th edition with new preface), Philadelphia: Fortress Press, 1980, p.85.

183. Gregory Dix, *op.cit.*, p.55.

184. *Ibid.*, p.56.

185. *Ephesians* 3:3ff; also 2:11ff: cf. *Colossians* 1:27.

186. *Galatians* 6:16.

187. Gregory Dix, *op.cit.*, p.112.

188. See *Acts* 15:1-33; cf. 11:2ff; *Galatians* 2:1-10; cf. 2:11-21. On the Judaisers and their views of the early Christian mission to non-Jews, see Ferdinand Hahn, *Mission in the New Testament* (Studies in Biblical Theology, 47), ET by Frank Clarke, London: SCM Press, 1968, especially ch.3, "The Mission in Early Christianity"; cf. Gregory Dix, *Jew and Greek – A Study in the Primitive Church*, London: Dacre Press, Westminster, 1953, especially ch.2, "The Jewish-Christian Church".

189. *Galatians* 5:2ff.

190. Ferdinand Hahn, *op.cit.*, pp.100-101.

191. Cf. John Mbiti's comment, written in 1968, on the dearth of theologians in Africa: "The tragedy goes further back, in that with a few exceptions, missionaries who established Christianity in the past one hundred years have not been theologians. The Church has now come into existence evangelistically, but not theologically", in his *New Testament Eschatology in an African Background: A Study in the Encounter between New Testament Theology and African Traditional Concepts*, London, SPCK, 1978, p.188 (1st published, London: Oxford University Press, 1971.) As an indication that Mbiti's criticism was not unfair, it may be noted that in 1926, the Le Zoute Conference was faced with the problem of the quality of missionary personnel: "Surely the day has gone when the best men could be picked out for India and China and the rest sent to Africa, as if any man or woman were good enough for Africa... Nothing is too good for Africa." See Edwin W. Smith (ed), *op.cit.*, p.46.

192. It has been argued that the transference of Christian faith from Europe and North America to Africa in the modern missionary movement has been "oppressive"; see Timothy M. Njoya, *Dynamics of Change in African Christianity: African Theology through Historical and Socio-Political Change*, Ph.D. thesis, Princeton Theological Seminary, N.J. 1975, Ann Arbor: University Microfilms, 1976, p.625. However, it is arguable that, in the course of time, facilitators for the African theological enterprise have emerged in the persons of Edwin Smith, Geoffrey Parrinder, John V. Taylor on the Protestant side, and Placide Tempels on the Catholic side. Certainly John Mbiti includes the writings of Parrinder, Taylor and Tempels among those that manifest "a change of approach and attitude..." to African religious tradition. See John S. Mbiti, *African Religions and Philosophy*, pp.10ff.

193. See Andrew F. Walls, "The Anabaptists of Africa? The Challenge of the African Independent Churches", in *Occasional Bulletin of Missionary Research*, vol.3, no.2, April 1979, pp.48-51. Prof. Walls observes: "In the end, the history of African Christianity will be a single story [i.e. as opposed to the distinction between so-called 'independent' and 'mainline' forms of African church life] in which the missionary period is only an episode" (p.51). Cf. Elliott Kendall, *The End of an Era – Africa and the Missionary*, London: SPCK, 1978, p.1: "The missionary period in Africa, as elsewhere, has come to an end".

194. Roland Allen, who served in the Anglican Society for the Propagation of the Gospel in China, and later devoted much of his writing to the theme, argued persistently that the modern missionary movement incorporated a not inconsiderable measure of "Judaising": "To find a parallel to our modern missions in the churches of St Paul, we should have to imagine a Judaistic church in Macedonia of Achaia divided into Pharisaic, Sadducean and Grecian parties. In fact we should have to imagine that St Paul and his fellow-workers were all Judaisers... A rule is made in London by a Conference of Western bishops and is applied indiscriminately

to China and to Africa, and none dares to say that the Chinese have already settled this question for themselves in their own way, and that, though their decision may not approve itself to Englishmen, still it is certainly not a sufficient reason for breaking communion.

With the alteration of a few titles, the same description would, I fear, be equally applicable to the missions of other Christian bodies. They too carry abroad their own organisation and forms. They too Judaise in exactly the same way." See Roland Allen, *Missionary Methods: St Paul's or Ours?* Grand Rapids: Eerdmanns, 1962, p.137 (1st published in 1912 by World Dominion Press).

Chapter Seven

A Variety of African Responses (1): Bolaji Idowu, or the Continuity of God in African Experience

I. Idowu and the advocacy of an African scholarship

The Rev. Professor Bolaji Idowu of Nigeria has long been recognised as a leading advocate of a "theology which bears the stamp of original thinking and meditation of Africans".[1] Among modern African theologians, Idowu is probably the one who has made particularly his own the plea for an authentic African theology and churchmanship, having devoted an entire book to the subject.[2] A vigorous academic, Idowu was for several years Professor and Head of the Department of Religious Studies at Ibadan, of which Geoffrey Parrinder had been the first lecturer.[3] In January 1976, he was installed as Patriarch of his church, the Methodist Church of Nigeria, a designation which is perhaps significant for one who possesses, to a remarkable degree, a keen sense of his Africanness and also a feeling for ancient African Church history!

Prof. Parrinder had also been the supervisor of Idowu's doctoral thesis presented to the University of London in 1955.[4] This connection with the one scholar in the field of religions whose life-work resulted in establishing the academic respectability and importance of African traditional religion is in itself interesting.

But Idowu has made a notable contribution towards this development in his own right. The Ibadan Journal of Religious Studies, *Orita*, with its stated purpose of understanding and interpreting African Traditional Religion, Christianity and Islam as "three Faiths" interacting with each other in the one cultural matrix of Nigeria, owes much to Idowu's inspiration and perception. His many articles in *Orita* provide as much an indication of his theological viewpoint as do his major books.[5] Through them, one realises that Idowu's chosen field of study and concern has remained very much the religious and cultural realities of his native Nigeria, even though he has entertained little doubt that his conclusions have a relevance for the whole of tropical Africa. It may justly be said that through the academic career of Idowu, as a scholar and as an advocate for a religious consciousness which is inherently African, there has come into existence a "school of thought" that carries its own intellectual convictions, is certain of its methodology, and reaches well beyond Ibadan.[6]

II. The basic issue: "the apparent foreignness of Christianity"

It is quite in keeping with Idowu's fundamental intuition about the post-missionary Christian presence in Africa, that for the seventh International African Seminar, organised by the International African Institute in Accra, Ghana, he wrote a paper on "The Predicament of the Church in Africa".[7] Idowu was alive to the fact that he was discussing the subject in the heyday of African nationalism in the decade of African political independence, and he felt a need to respond, on the one hand, to "the extreme nationalist who can now see no good at all in what the Church has been doing in Africa..." and, on the other, to "the loyal children of the Church who feel only gratitude and who regard anything that savours of criticism as disloyalty". Accordingly, he made common cause with "those who claim that they also are true children of the Church but realise that their house needs to be put in order".[8] This ability to be generally critical of the missionary planting of Christianity in Africa whilst yet remaining a staunch churchman has been a constant feature of Idowu's career.

But the strength of "The predicament of the Church in Africa", as Baëta noted in his introductory review, lay in Idowu's point that

> "the [African] Church is still a dependent one looking to missionaries from outside for manpower and material resources, dependent in its theology, its liturgy and its church discipline, in fact in its whole expression of the Christian life."[9]

In the catalogue of factors which, in Idowu's view, constituted "the present predicament" of the Church,[10] there is little doubt that the most potent is what he describes as the "result of prefabricated theology and traditions".

"It was a serious mistake that the Church took no account of the indigenous beliefs and customs of Africa when she began her work of evangelisation. It is now obvious that by a misguided purpose, a completely new God who had had nothing to do with the past of Africa was introduced to her peoples. Thus there was no proper foundation laid for the Gospel message in the hearts of the people and no bridge built between the old and the new; the Church has in consequence been speaking to Africans in strange tongues because there was no adequate communication. In consequence, the Church has on her hands communities of believers who, by and large, live ambivalent spiritual lives."[11]

Each of these statements carries far-reaching significance for the tenor of Idowu's theological concerns.[12] The importance of "the indigenous beliefs and customs of Africa" in his total theological outlook is not an antiquarian interest in the artifacts of African culture and how these may be integrated into the life of the Christian Church. Rather, it underscores Idowu's profound unease with the European missionary enterprise among African peoples as a whole: at the specific level of religious apprehension, in his view, Africans were somehow being required to shed their Africanness as part of the process of becoming Christians. Accordingly, he quotes John Taylor approvingly to the effect that missionary practice was demanding, wrongly, like the Judaisers of apostolic times,[13] "some cultural equivalent of circumcision".[14]

But what might appear to have been no more than a clash of cultures was in fact, for Idowu, a religious problem, the result of a theological misconception. The alleged ambivalence in the spiritual life of the African Christian – "being able to go out of Church straight to his diviner without feeling that he is betraying any principle"[15] – has been generally explained as a concomitant of the European value-setting for the Christian life in Africa's missionary history. In other words, if European missionaries had been more critical of the identification of European cultural values and the Christian faith, the occurrence of confusion in the African mind would have been less likely. Thus conceived, missionary error consisted essentially in a lack of sensitivity to the limitations of European culture on the one hand, and to the positive values of African cultural categories for expressing Christian realities, on the other; missionary religious understanding, accordingly, is left intact. Idowu cuts through this argument and locates the root of the problem in what he considers to be the heart of religion itself:

the apprehension of God.[16] To the extent that European missionary practice undervalued and ignored the sense of God and His
activity as perceived in African tradition,[17] it introduced unwittingly "a completely new God who had nothing to do with the past of
Africa..."

Why the continuity of God from the pre-Christian tradition into
the Christian consciousness is so important for Idowu, we shall
examine later. It is sufficient to note now that what Idowu means
here is certainly not that the God of African tradition is intrinsically different from the God of Christian proclamation and experience. On the contrary, Idowu rejects any such distinction,
affirming elsewhere that "Africa recognises only one God, the
Supreme, Universal God... one and the same God, the Creator of
all the ends of the earth..."[18] Furthermore, Idowu must have been
aware that in the vast number of cases, an already existing African
name for God was adopted into Christian preaching and into the
translation of the Church's Scriptures. What Idowu is seeking to
highlight, therefore, is the fact that European missionary practice
"seldom made any attempt to build on this [African sense of God]
or interpret its fundamental significance".[19] For Idowu, the failure
cannot be reduced to a merely incidental oversight or cultural
blunder carrying scant repercussions for the emergent African
Church. This is because the absence of what he considers "the
proper foundation" for integrating African past experience into
present reality renders the missionary proclamation theologically
inadequate – i.e. in Christian terms – and even suspect. Consequently, in Towards an Indigenous Church, after quoting C.H.
Dodd:

"Is the God of our redemption the same as the God of creation?
The inevitable answer is that He is the same God."[20]

Idowu then comments:

"Unless evangelism is based upon this foundation, it is difficult
to see how anyone can make an ultimate success of it."[21]

Idowu does not deny the reality of the Christian presence in
Africa in the wake of the missionary enterprise; what he is calling
into question is the ability of a westernised African Christianity
which does not seriously integrate the African religious past, to
truly appropriate the Gospel in African terms.

It is not surprising, therefore, that Idowu is the African
theologian who has been most vehement in his distrust of
European interpretations of African religious tradition.[22] Idowu is

not even sure that he can trust Western theological judgment *qua* Western. In his paper presented at the Consultation of African Theologians in 1966, he observed:

"Recent publications in Europe and America have come to indicate how much confusion there is in the minds even of the enlightened Westerners about God. If we take for example some of the writings of Dietrich Bonhoeffer, the writings of Paul Tillich, and *Honest to God* of Dr J.A.T. Robinson, we shall see at least two facts clearly emerging: the fact that the masses of Westerners appear to be losing their sense of God, and Western theology is in conflict because it has become too theoretical: God according to it has become largely an intellectual concept."[23]

This pervasive rejection of the normativeness of European Christianity is seen in how far Idowu is prepared to go to "marginalise" European mediation of the Christian Gospel to Africans. As one "to whom Jesus Christ is personal Saviour" he affirms:

"... that Christianity is a *Universal* Religion instituted of God through Jesus Christ the Saviour, of the *whole world*: that it came into being in consequence of the *invincible love of God for the world which He created* and in which *His redemptive purpose has always been at work*. If Christianity came to Nigerians through Europeans, that is only because God has used Europeans as vehicles and transmitters of His redemptive truth to Nigerians. It is of the nature of Christianity that it must be shared and passed on; and so it was imperative that when *Europeans received Christianity through Asians* they also must pass it on to, and share it with, others. This is the process by which *in the eternal purpose of God Christianity reached Nigerians*. Christian Nigerians will also find themselves in the position of those who transmit the Gospel once the Church in Nigeria attains true selfhood and is sufficiently alive and virile."[24]

Idowu's words seem to be well chosen, and it might be argued that this interpretation of missionary history as really redemptive history is also meant to answer the non-Christian critic. For, whilst Idowu is evidently embarrassed by "the European structure of the Church in Nigeria and the distinctive European complexion of its Christianity",[25] the nationalist critic might alarmingly seize on these very features to discredit Christianity as "a European Institution which has no beneficial relevance for Nigerians, but which has nevertheless been imposed upon them as an engine of colonial policy by their European overlords".[26] However, in the preceding discussion, I have attempted to show that Idowu's radical criticism of European missionary proclamation, and its outcome in the predicament of the Church in Africa, has a properly theological dimension to it. This will become clearer as we examine what Idowu means, theologically, by "a radical indigenisation of the Church".[27]

III. Towards an Indigenous Church... "where the old finds fulfilment in the new"

The small volume which bears this title, *Towards an Indigenous Church*, was probably the first and clearest statement by a leading African theologian of specific proposals that an African Church which found itself to be "heavily tinged with Western culture"[28] might consider, in order to transform itself into an authentic African Christian community. It is true that as far back as 1955, the Christian Council of Ghana (then Gold Coast) had sponsored a conference on "Christianity and African Culture";[29] three years later, the conference of African Protestant churchmen which was to lead to the All Africa Conference of Churches, had also shown interest in some aspects germane to the subject.[30] On the Roman Catholic side, there had appeared in 1956, *Des prêtres noirs s'interrogent*,[31] a collection of essays by African and Caribbean priests then studying in Europe, which was destined to be an important landmark in the development of African Roman Catholic theological thought.[32]

However, when Idowu's book was published, "in 1965, expressions like 'African Theology', 'African Christian Theology', *Theologia Africana*, were hardly, if ever, used".[33] Furthermore, within the limits of three short chapters, the author covered a wide spectrum of subjects. It is understandable that Idowu earned the accolade of "the doyen of West African theologians".[34] For these reasons, it is appropriate that we look more closely at his argument in *Towards an Indigenous Church*, as it relates to the subject of this study.

It is consistent with Idowu's noted interest in questions affecting his native Nigeria that he addressed himself primarily to the Church in Nigeria, which in his view, was "on trial":

"She is being called upon to justify her existence in the country; to answer in precise terms the question as to whether her purpose in Nigeria is not to serve as an effective tool of imperialism, a veritable means of softening up Nigerians for the purpose of convenient exploitation by Europeans, ... whether the aim of religious educators in Nigeria was to make Christians or to 'Westernise' Nigerians; whether in fact, Christianity and 'Westernism' are not synonymous in their evangelistic vocabulary... whether what we have in Nigeria today is in fact Christianity, and not in fact only transplantations from a European cult, the various ramifications of which are designated Methodists, Anglicans, Presbyterians, Baptists, Roman Catholics, Salvation Army, Seventh Day Adventists, and so forth."[35]

By posing these questions, Idowu was expressing some of the views which were put over in varying degrees of seriousness, as part of the explanation for the colonial history of a now independent Africa.[36] In other words, however minimal or total, the connection of the Christian missionary enterprise with the European colonial powers had in fact been, it was now an embarrassment for the African Church.[37] But whilst the specifically political aspect of the problem was by no means insignificant for Idowu, he was more deeply troubled by the psychological effects of the missionary history on Nigerian Christians. Idowu certainly did not consider Christianity as merely "a European cult", but he recognised nonetheless that the historical association of the Christian faith with Western cultural values

"succeeded in enslaving the mind, inasmuch as it inculcated that the only way to human dignity and full grown personality was to be in everything like Europeans and to despise their own [Nigerian] culture".[38]

Idowu traces this state of affairs to the fact that "the beginning of Christianity in its present history in Nigeria" was inextricably linked with "Nigerian ex-slaves" from Sierra Leone. It was these who, in his view, "were to a large extent instrumental in promoting among Nigerians the aspiration to be like Europeans in all things, they and their offspring being the nuclei of the sophisticated communities who set the fashion which the generality of impressionable and admiring Nigerians sought to copy or ape".[39] The adoption of European names and European dress was the least disturbing aspect of this psychological enslavement and cultural alienation. More ominous, for Idowu, was the observation that "in spite of the political independence of Nigeria, the way things are done in Europe and America still forms the norm and standard by which the life of the Church is ordered".[40] In this connection, it is interesting that Idowu recalls the discovery of his own "mistaken and limited... concept of Jesus Christ", which he describes as "... heavily impregnated with faulty notions or borrowed, second-hand and distorted European ideas", and that at a time when he was already "a trained minister and a University graduate".[41] This passing biographical detail provides a useful insight into Idowu's approach which might possibly be obscured by his characteristically passionate manner of communicating his views. It seems to me excessive, therefore, to say that "Idowu unsparingly and relentlessly attacked African theologians and ministers for failing to produce relevant and meaningful theologies which unmistakenly bear the hallmarks of the mature thinking and reflection of Africans".[42] While it is undoubtedly true that Idowu finds it easy to speak of the African Christian community as one that "has been spoonfed by Europeans all along",[43] nevertheless it appears that Idowu is willing to pose to himself the embarrassing questions which he raises for the African Church as a whole.

It is also important to appreciate the grounds upon which Idowu insists on "a radical indigenisation of the Church". If it is crucial that the Church in Nigeria "should bear the distinctive stamp of the country", it is in order that it may be effective in its life and mission in the country. If the Church "must respect, preserve and dedicate to the glory of God anything that is of value in the culture and institutions of the country", equally the Church "must preserve full allegiance to the Eternal, Cosmic, Unchanging Christ, who is her only Lord".[44] This association of indigenisation with evangelisation is important for Idowu,[45] and may explain why, when he comes to the heart of his treatment in the second chapter, he discusses not only the problems of theology in their intellectual dimensions, as one might expect, but also Bible translation and the language of evangelism.

It is a further indication of Idowu's theological and Christian concerns that he explicitly distinguishes his use of "indigenisation" from any non-Christian "nationalistic substitute" or parody of Christianity, and from any comparison with "the Nigerianisation of the civil service".[46]

"We mean by it simply that the Church should bear the unmistakeable stamp of the fact that she is the *Church of God in Nigeria*. It should be no longer an outreach or a colony of Rome, Canterbury or Westminster Central Hall in London, or the vested interest of some European or American Missionary Board... the Church in Nigeria should be the Church which affords Nigerians the means of worshipping God as Nigerians; that is, in a way which is compatible with their own spiritual temperament, of singing to the glory of God in their own way, of praying to God and hearing His Holy Word in idiom which is clearly intelligible to them... She should be... the spiritual home of Christian Nigerians, a home in which they breathe an atmosphere of spiritual freedom.

"At the same time, she should be a Church the keynote of whose life is the Lordship of Jesus Christ, the Church in which in all things He is pre-eminent. Thus, an indigenous Church in Nigeria must know and live in the watchful consciousness that she is part as well as 'presence' of the 'One, Holy, Catholic and Apostolic Church'."[47]

I have quoted Idowu at considerable length because here he expresses most clearly his concept of the indigenous church, indicating the two poles around which his thinking revolves. Idowu does not choose between the categories of "particularity" and "universality", but affirms both as intrinsic to the character of a truly "indigenous Church". And yet the basis of the "universality" of the indigenous Church is significant. Whilst he shows awareness of the Church's history and concrete, visible "presence" in other cultures, Idowu is careful to locate the links of the indigenous Church [in Nigeria] with the Christian "presence" elsewhere in the self-conscious confession of faith in Jesus Christ, and not in such cultural characteristics as may have been transmitted in the course of the expansion of Christianity in the world. Thus, against what he calls "hereditary structure", he sets "the full recognition of the absolute Lordship of Jesus Christ, Who is the Living Lord, in consequence of Whom the Church is a living and dynamic organism, sufficient for the present needs of each nation *in every age and generation*".[48] Idowu, of course, does not reject completely the legitimacy of elements which may historically and culturally lie outside of the "indigenous Church"; and he concedes that:

"To speak of an indigenous Church is not to ask that every mark of 'foreignness' attaching to her should be removed. For the Church in a nation to attempt to divest herself completely of all 'foreign' elements is to cut herself adrift from the stream of history and end in an eddy; it is to deny herself of the spiritual tonic which 'the Communion of Saints' affords. In short she will cease to be a living cell within the whole Body."[49]

And yet, this thought occupies a secondary place in Idowu's

overall position, and the fact that he finds it necessary to enter the qualification may be in itself significant. For the overwhelming emphasis to which he returns is "the absolute Lordship of Jesus Christ and total undivided allegiance to Him, cost it what it may..."[50]

The reasons which Idowu gives for this insistence are illuminating. In the first place, the affirmation of the Lordship of Jesus Christ as a living reality ensures that the Church will be a "truly living and virile" one. In the second place, "the full acknowledgment of the Lordship of Jesus Christ will make Him real to Nigerians".[51] The basic principle which Idowu thus establishes here – one which would seem to inform his entire theological outlook – is that the essential and constitutive element in an authentic African Christianity is not found in the latter's historical connection with European or Western Christianity, missionary history notwithstanding. Rather, it is to be found in the direct, deliberate and self-conscious appropriation of Jesus Christ as a living and present reality experienced in African terms. This principle sets aside the "tyranny of structural heredity"[52] exercised by Western traditions of Christianity over those African Christian communities which have come into existence through their instrumentality. It also frees the Church in Africa to draw upon the whole deposit of the Universal Christian Tradition according to African wishes and needs. Consequently, in the realm of liturgical reform, Idowu considers it appropriate that the Church in Africa should be free to derive benefit as much from the Eastern Orthodox Church and the Church of South India, as from the Presbyterian Church of Scotland.[53] The identity and self-understanding of African Christianity are therefore no longer to be determined by the history of European religious rivalries and divisions which Idowu calls "the darling sin of Europeans and Americans in the first instance".[54] Instead, they are to be shaped by an African Christian consciousness which claims as its due right a direct and primary access to the sources of Christian revelation and faith.

As a result the indigenisation for which Idowu pleads is more subtle and more complex than may be suggested by, for instance, his observation that "the title 'Anglican' is a misnomer for a Church in 1964 Nigeria".[55] If the necessity to replace "the European complexion of the Church" with "an indigenous complexion" bulks so large in Idowu's argument, it is because this imperative expresses a continuing and more fundamental burden, namely, that "Christian Nigerians... cease to see Jesus Christ as an imported divinity from a European pantheon" and that "they come to see Him as God's Messiah to Nigerians, their own personal Saviour and Lord".[56] Idowu attempts to lay down the foundation for achieving this all-important aim when he tackles the problem of "Theology".

When Idowu comes to discuss the "concrete examples" which, in his view, validate his contention that "the European structure of the Church has, to a large extent, made for spiritual sterility in her life",[57] it may appear somewhat strange that he does not begin with "Theology", since one might expect that "the debate over indigenisation will rage most furiously around the question of an African Theology".[58] And yet, by starting with the need for more accurate translations of the Bible, which in turn should undergird a more effective communication in evangelism, Idowu is proceeding in the more logical manner. After all, theology can be said to be "a form of critical thought, what is often called a second order intellectual activity".[59] Historically, Christian theology has been born of, and followed, Christian faith.[60] Accordingly, problems of the appropriate liturgy in the worshipping community, as well as questions affecting the dress and vestments for religious personnel, become meaningful only after the religious community has come into existence in its social setting and is conscious of its own identity.

Seen from this angle, Idowu's treatment of theology in third place, at the heart, as it were, of the five items, may carry some symbolic significance, and if so, further heightens its centrality. But the inclusion of Biblical research and translation in the agenda of the Church that seeks to be truly indigenous is of particular significance. For whilst Idowu bases his argument on the practical necessity of improving in the light of better knowledge work previously done,[61] this concern is entirely consistent with his view that Africans have to "hear God in Jesus Christ addressing Himself immediately to them in their native situation and particular circumstances".[62]

The words just quoted can be taken to indicate the essential thrust of Idowu's outlook on the theological question as it relates to the Indigenous Church. For it is of the nature of the theology which bears "the distinctive stamp of indigenous originality" that it arises from Christians in Africa doing their own thinking and grappling "spiritually and intellectually with questions relating to the Christian faith" as their own questions.[63] This presupposes that the Christians concerned have "discovered Christ for themselves".[64] As far as Idowu is concerned, this is not what has happened in Nigeria:

"Surely, the basic aim and the goal of evangelism is that Christ should become real to people as their Lord and Saviour. Evangelism has certainly failed where people call themselves Christians, set up edifices where they congregate for worship, and yet cannot say from their hearts and in their own words who Jesus is, and what He has done and is doing for them corporately and individually, and what He means to them as the absolute Lord of life – the whole of life – *within the context of the world in which they live.*"[65]

I emphasise the final statement because it seems to be the focus of Idowu's critique. His suggestion that the persons concerned are incapable of making adequate Christological declarations should not be taken at face value to mean that utterly no affirmation of any kind is to be found. In other words, to say that "the Church in Nigeria has not developed a theology which bears the distinctive stamp of Nigerian thinking or meditation",[66] is not the same as saying that she has no theology. Rather, the point of Idowu's criticism and distress is that:

"Her theology is book theology; that is, what she reads in books written by European theologians, or what she is told by Europeans, is accepted uncritically and given out undigested in preaching or teaching."[67]

The telling illustration which Idowu uses to describe by contrast the situation he is discussing is the encounter of Jesus with the Samaritan woman and her people as recorded in the Fourth Gospel.[68] There can be no doubt that Idowu finds particularly attractive in the Gospel the suggestion of a literary progression in the narrative, detailing the growing response of the Samaritans to Jesus. Beginning with the profession of faith by the inhabitants of the town "because of the woman's testimony", the narrative rises to a higher pitch when a further profession of faith is made "because of His (Jesus') word" now actually heard by the people themselves. It is the final stage in this crescendo of affirmation – "for we have heard for ourselves, and we know that this is indeed the Saviour of the world" – which, Idowu considers, is missing in the contemporary reality of Nigerian Christianity.

"Christian Nigerians must be able to say this if Christ has indeed become real to them. The Church in Nigeria can only develop a distinctive theology in consequence of their own personal knowledge of God and personal appropriation of the Lordship of Christ."[69]

Had Idowu left the question there, he would have contributed little beyond stating the obvious handicap of a Christian Church which has learnt the Gospel predominantly in "loan words".[70] However, it is the merit of Idowu's work that he elevated his observation of theological deficits in the African Church into a major item on the theological agenda. For, by transposing the problem of "a distinctive theology in consequence of personal knowledge of God and personal appropriation of the Lordship of Christ" in African terms into the wider issue of the "question of God's revelation" in the African pre-Christian past and its relation to the Christian present,[71] Idowu was posing the question of indigenisation in an entirely new light. He was also, perhaps unwittingly, answering his own query as to why the Church in Nigeria had not developed an indigenous theology. Could it have been also because, hitherto, "the revelation already vouchsafed to Nigerians" had not been "linked with Biblical revelation"?[72] It is understandable therefore, that, for Idowu, the problem of theology in the African Church comes to focus on "finding 'the bridge' between the old and the new" in African religious experience.[73] By conceiving of the problem in this form, Idowu brings the issue round to the identity of the African Christian. But behind the matter of identity, there lies the more insistent question of the continuity of God. For,

"What does God as revealed in the Biblical religion mean to Nigerians in their own native situation?"[74]

IV. "Where do we come in this one world which belongs to God?"

In saying "God", Idowu means "God as revealed in the Biblical religion" and who "so loved the world that He sent His only begotten Son to redeem" it.[75] But, for Idowu, "God" also means Olódùmarè, God as known and experienced in Yoruba pre-Christian religious tradition. It is in the interplay of these two concepts and how they in fact become one reality – albeit diversely apprehended – that we may locate Idowu's most enduring theological interest. For Idowu considers that it is in relation to the question of God – God in African pre-Christian tradition – that the problem of indigenisation is felt at its sharpest. This is the "fundamental question":

"Whether in the past pre-Christian history of Nigerians, God has ever in any way revealed Himself to them and they have apprehended His revelation in however imperfect a way; whether what happens in the coming of Christianity and as a result of evangelism is that Nigerians have been introduced to a *completely* new God who is absolutely unrelated to their past history."[76]

As we have already noted, Idowu has no difficulty in affirming the unity of God, hence the identity of God in all religions; he expresses his viewpoint forcefully in an article in *Orita*:

"Of the three religions in Nigeria – the Traditional Religion, Islam and Christianity – there is not one which has the right to speak as if there are many Gods of which each religion or nation takes its own exclusive choice. The basic theology of the Traditional Religion [as of Islam and Christianity] in each locality has always insisted on One God, one universe, one cradle and one point of dispersal of the members of the single family of mankind; ... neither of them can recognise another God or other gods without violating its own essence."[77]

In line with this, Idowu answers the "fundamental question" which he considers missionary evangelism has left the Church in Africa by appealing to the Bible!

"On the basis of the Bible, taken as a whole... there is only one God, the Creator of heaven and earth and all that is in them; *the God who has never left Himself without witness in any nation, age, or generation*; Whose creative purpose has ever been at work in this world; Who by one stupendous act of climactic self-revelation in Christ Jesus came to redeem a fallen world."[78]

By invoking the reputed source of missionary preaching, Idowu illuminates the theological grounds for his criticism of missionary evangelism.[79] But there seems to be more to Idowu's approach than just the desire to correct the theology of missionary preaching, and it is important to understand his methodological standpoint.

I have already shown how the attempt to provide a theological interpretation for African pre-Christian religion within the structures of Christian thought finds its consistency in the very process which makes such an effort unavoidable, namely, the quest for the unity of self in conversion that "truly integrates what we have been in what we become".[80] However, in Idowu's case, there is a further dimension which relates particularly to his understanding of religion itself, and it is this which clarifies his entire position on the question of God. In the article on "Faiths in Interaction", Idowu observes,

"It should have been clear to us by now that our concern is with persons, living men and women of different faiths, as they meet, mingle, live and act together, and interact on one another. *We are not studying religion in the abstract; for there is nothing like abstract religion, that is, religion apart from persons who practise it.*[81] Religion has to do inextricably with persons as individuals, and especially with peoples in their own homes – their domestic, cultural settings; it has to do with corporate bodies of peoples as clans, communities and nations; with men and women who believe and are inspired and actuated by their beliefs. A people's religious motives and habits, the way their religion conditions their behaviour and affects their relationship with other people, begin first with the fact that the religion is in them and forms the norm of their character. The interaction of religions is thus basically the interaction of peoples who practise the religions."[82]

I have quoted Idowu at some length here, because it seems to me that this essentially personalist thesis on religion is necessary for understanding his persistent affirmations of the continuity of God from the African pre-Christian past into the present Christian experience. Though Idowu's view of religion bears a striking resemblance to the equally personalist theory of Wilfred Cantwell Smith whom he quotes or refers to in several places,[83] Idowu does not follow Cantwell Smith in rejecting the designation "religion" as irrelevant.[84] For Idowu, the "acts of devotion and service" are just as significant in the religious life as is faith, "the personal trust in the living, transcendental Being and concommittal in self-surrender to the divine will".[85] If the inwardness of faith provides the common denominator of all religious apprehension, the external phenomena of worship point to the fact that such apprehension occurs within the categories of culturally appropriate "inborn capabilities".[86]

It follows therefore that on the subject of "revelation", Idowu firmly sets aside any notion that "religion could be divided into two categories: the religion based on God's climactic revelation in Jesus Christ, and... man-made religion, i.e. other religions besides Christianity". This would be a "deliberate or unwitting flying in the face of truth". For,

"If revelation indeed means God's self-disclosure, if he has left his mark upon the created order and his witness within man – every man – then it follows that revelation cannot be limited in scope and that it is meant for all mankind, all rational beings, irrespective of race or colour."[87]

A constant feature of Idowu's approach to this all-important question is to decisively eliminate whatever might suggest a European possessiveness of the Christian faith. But this fiercely polemical edge is balanced by what we have called his personalist view of religion. This enables him to argue for the universality of the divine self-disclosure. Therefore, when he appeals to apostolic doctrine on the question,[88] Idowu is simply securing this universal availability of God by exposing the theological groundlessness of any exclusivism of revelation conceived in racial or cultural terms. He can thus state categorically:

"In every part of the world, therefore, what in general terms is known as worship is a result of one central impulse – that of one divine personal will seeking all the time to make itself known."[89]

Idowu's twofold method of stating his position on the question of God is employed also in his paper on "God" presented at the Ibadan Consultation on "Biblical Revelation and African Beliefs".[90] Well before he actually discusses African experiences and under-standings of God, Idowu characteristically tackles the question at the sharp end, asking "whether every race has something of this knowledge [of God], however primary, or whether any peoples could be said to have been completely excluded from it".[91] Drawing upon the conclusions of Andrew Lang,[92] Nathan Söderblom,[93] and particularly Wilhelm Schmidt,[94] Idowu affirms the universal "belief in and worship of one Supreme Deity", against those European scholars who are, in his view, guilty of "emotional resentment and deliberate refusal to accept the facts", and who would rather postulate "an academic invention... a primitive high god" only to preclude so-called "primitive" peoples from a knowledge of revelation from the Living God.[95] In the final analysis, Idowu rests his case on Christian doctrine: the creation of the universe as "the primary stage of revelation – something through which the Creator is revealed", and the rationality of human nature, which makes the human being "someone address-able and therefore responsible (response-able): someone to whom God could communicate His revelation through his appreciation of the created order and with whose spirit the Divine Spirit could have immediate communication".[96]

But if Idowu can conclude that the whole universe is God's realm and that all peoples are His concern,[97] the Biblical doctrine of the inscrutability of God[98] requires that he should balance appropriately the affirmation of the universal availability of divine self-disclosure. But as might be expected, apart from a properly theological motive, Idowu is concerned also to state just as firmly that no "people or creed can claim to possess a *clear* knowledge of God in an absolute sense"; Idowu considers it essential to vindicate African experience and tradition against its European despisers:

"This point is very important for us; it is not infrequently that we hear it glibly stated that Africans have no clear concept of God. This arises largely from the unexamined premise that because Europeans have written systematic statements about God, therefore they have a clear concept of God."[99]

When Idowu examines various African understandings of God, his conclusions are hardly distinguishable from what may be assembled from the Biblical account of God. Indeed it would be a serious misapprehension of Idowu's thinking on the question to expect that what he calls Africa's "own distinctive concepts of God according to African traditional belief"[100] should differ significantly from Christian ideas. For his study of the African divine names which "are descriptive both of His [God's] nature and His attributes"[101] in order to establish the African sense of God's uniqueness, sole control of the world, and His universality,[102] is also meant to indicate how closely African experience comes to Biblical understandings. Consequently, Idowu has no difficulty in connecting the religious meanings expressed in the West African divine names, "Oriṣẹ", "Chukwu", and "Ọdomankoma", with the declaration about God and His relations to mankind as found in *Psalm* 104:29-30 and *Acts* 17:28.[103]

The effect of Idowu's argument, then, is to establish the legitimacy of an African experience and knowledge of God which yields nothing in significant detail to other comparable (particularly European) concepts. In other words, Africa's God is not "a loan-God from the missionaries".[104] But if the whole discussion tends to minimise and possibly even obliterate distinctions between Christian experience and African pre-Christian tradition, the explanation for this must be Idowu's unwillingness or inability to separate his theological affirmations from his cultural commitment. His basic premise is that "... African Traditional Religion is the master-key to the understanding of Africans *who in all things are religious*".[105] Idowu, consequently, contends that for African Christian theology to be indigenously African, it has to maintain a necessary continuity with the fundamental element of African self-identity. By reducing the culture he is intent on vindicating to its core – religion,[106] Idowu is able to identify this fundamental element as African Traditional Religion – "traditional because it has its own pattern which is its heritage from the past".[107] Whatever theological construction becomes necessary in Africa in the light of Christian revelation, it cannot be done by neglecting this African religio-cultural "heritage from the past". This explain why he considers that "the material gathered from the study of the indigenous beliefs [of Nigeria]", in order to ascertain "what God has done, in what way He has been known and approached in the past and present history of Nigerians", is what "will form the basic raw material for Christian theology in Nigeria".[108] At the specific level of theological reflection, therefore, Idowu's position resolves itself into a "strong cultural orientation to religion",[109] which makes the vindication of the integrity of an African cultural and religious consciousness the dominant factor in his entire thinking. Consequently, the spirited defence of the continuity of God in African religious experience is, in fact, the particular focus for his general and pervasive insistence on the continuity of African cultural and religious consciousness.

It is possible to form the impression that Idowu is interested in the theology of the Christian faith not in its own right but only in so far as it provides a means of establishing the grounds of African religious identity. One is most likely to be inclined to such a view on reading *African Traditional Religion – A Definition*.[110]

The result of "years of experience in the study of African traditional religion"[111] – of which fourteen were spent in lecturing on the subject in the University of Ibadan[112] – *African Traditional Religion – A Definition* .may rightly be considered as the mature treatment of questions that had been with Idowu for a long time. In a work that aims at being "definitive and interpretative" as well as "methodological",[113] Idowu is at his most combative, responding blow by blow to virtually every derogatory European evaluation of African religious tradition. Though drawing often upon non-African scholarship to establish his positions, Idowu's book carries its own conviction as a work done "from the inside",[114] and the author is proud to associate himself with "Africans who are prepared to wean themselves intelligently from prefabricated

scholarship and made-in-Europe academic tradition".[115] It is perhaps significant that this book remains to date the Nigerian
scholar's last major publication. Virtually every significant subject
which he has treated elsewhere is here taken up and amplified.

Idowu has here drawn out the full implications of the intuition
which had motivated his former teacher and mentor, Geoffrey
Parrinder, to the effect that the way African societies apprehended
spiritual realities possessed a coherence and a consistency which
argued for its recognition as a religious tradition alongside the
other so-called world religions.[116] By placing the study of African
religion in the context of a comprehensive (and sometimes ram-
bling) treatment of religion *per se*, Idowu makes an important
African contribution towards the study of Africa's religious
heritage as a subject for serious academic discussion.

From the perspective of its aims, then, it is not surprising that
the work displays a tendency towards reductionism in its assessment of Christianity (and Islam) in the total reality of African
religious life. For Idowu, "African traditional religion is *the* religion
practised today by the majority of Africans... nakedly in most cases;
but also, in some cases, under the veneers supplied by Westernism
and Arabism..."[117] Behind these two terms, an informed reader of
Idowu will discern Christianity and Islam, which continue to haunt
Idowu with the spectre of their foreignness to the African genius
in religion. It is extraordinary that Idowu can quote quite comfortably the Biblical statement: "It does not yet appear what we shall
be",[118] and apply it to the prospect of African Traditional Religion.
The vindication and affirmation of African selfhood which elsewhere[119] is laid upon the African Christian community, is here
more confidently entrusted to the revitalisation of Africa's "old"
religions, with their "God-given heritage" of "indigenous spiritual
and cultural treasures".[120]

But if Idowu appears to preclude any serious concern with the
Christian faith in its own right for African theology, this is because
he sees the *initial* task of African theology as one of providing the
appropriate interpretation of that revelation contained in the
"heritage from the past", so that the old and the new may find their
unity in the one and the same God who has acted in both. This then
gives added significance to the fact that his original and possibly
most valuable contribution to the African theological quest relates
to that aspect of African religion which caused Europeans in their
earlier encounters to underestimate the African sense of God,

namely, the African consciousness of a wider spirit world that was apparently unrelated to the One Supreme God.[121]

V. "Gods many and lords many"?

However intent Idowu is in arguing that "the basic theology of the Traditional Religion in each locality has always insisted on One God, one universe, one cradle and one point of dispersal of the members of the single family of mankind",[122] he is careful enough to recognise that in much of the African tradition (including the Yoruba variant in which he shares), objective phenomena in the religion[123] raise a specific problem which is as delicate as it is unavoidable. This is the problem posed by the incidence of a multitude of "divinities" who "so predominate the scene that it is difficult for the casual observer to notice that under them, there is one vital cultic basis".[124]

The fact that Idowu is prepared to deal with the problem is a further indication of his eagerness to take on those issues which have proved problematic in the European understanding of African tradition. It is also evident that Idowu does not consider that the phenomenon of "the One and the many" constitutes a *problem* for the worshippers in the particular religious tradition concerned; the difficulty in fact exists only for "the casual observer", who lacks access to the throbbing heart of the religion involved. In his attempt to answer the questions raised by the phenomenon of "gods many and lords many", Idowu ultimately draws his conclusions, not on the basis of the opinions of scholars, especially outsiders, in the field of religion, but rather in view of what the particular people concerned "know and believe".[125]

Idowu readily identifies the underlying problem posed by "gods many and lords many" as that of the vexed concept of "polytheism" which he rejects as an inappropriate description of the African tradition:

"African traditional religion cannot be described as polytheistic. Its appropriate description is monotheistic, however modified this may be. The modification, is, however, inevitable because of the presence of other divine beings within the structure of the religion."[126]

Idowu then goes on to discuss the derivative status of the divinities in relation to the Supreme God, and their ministerial functions, which show that "they have no absolute existence and [that] the African world is under a unitary theocratic government".[127] Whilst this general discussion is helpful and interesting, it is his more detailed study of the Yoruba situation in *Olódùmarè – God in Yoruba Belief,* which carries greater significance. For the Yoruba context provides one example of a highly advanced structure of divinities (orìṣà) under a well-known Supreme God, found in West Africa which "may be said to be the home of divinities".[128]

Idowu[129] derives the collective designation (Orìṣà) from its primeval application to the arch-divinity (eventually Orìṣà-nlá) of Yorubaland. According to Yoruba mythology, this arch-divinity through the deliberate mischief of his own servant, Àtọwọ́dá, "was crushed to bits and scattered" by a stone. From the collected pieces which were distributed "all over the world", there resulted not only "the cult of the arch-divinity 'all over the world'", but even more important, the emergence of a number of other divinities. Idowu interprets this myth as follows:

"The significance of this myth lies in its suggestion that Orìṣà was originally a unity; that this is the Yoruba way of giving recognition to the process of 'fragmentation' which comes as a result of giving concrete shapes in the mind to certain outstanding attributes of the Deity, or of that renaming, due to circumstances, by which one and the same divinity becomes apparently several divinities."[130]

In this atmosphere of ubiquitous divinities with overlapping characteristics, the way is thus open for seeing in the name Orìṣà a possible corruption of an original name of the Supreme God Olódùmarè, namely, Orìṣẹ (Head-Source).[131] Presumably it is this corruption of Orìṣẹ into Orìṣà that also explains the fact that "the name Orìṣà is applied to Him (Olódùmarè) in some parts of Yorubaland, even though He is indisputably *not* one among the divinities".[132]

The status of Olódùmarè in relation to the orìṣà, then, is one of absolute transcendence,[133] though they are also conceived as having been brought forth by Him, and, at least in the case of the principal divinities like Orìṣà-nlá, derived directly from Him.[134] Idowu then argues that the religion of the Yoruba, far from being a polytheism, is in fact a monotheism. But it is what he calls a "diffused monotheism" in which "the good Deity delegates certain portions of His authority to certain divine functionaries who work as they are commissioned by Him".[135] Accordingly the legion of orìṣà[136] can be conceived of, in effect, as the *manifestations* of Olódùmarè, His "ministers, looking after the affairs of the universe and acting as intermediaries between Him and the world of men."[137]

It is very tempting indeed to see Idowu's interpretation of Yoruba religion at this point as little more than an effort to rehabilitate theologically his own religious past in view of his present commitment. For as we have already noted, the question of identity forms an important element in Idowu's whole outlook. However, there is no reason to suggest that his theological commitment necessarily invalidates his conclusions.[138] On the contrary, an indication that Idowu's analysis may indeed be accurate is the fact that studies of African religion conducted elsewhere on the continent and without the presuppositions of an African Christian theologian, seem to confirm Idowu's conclusion on the Yoruba conception of the relation of Olódùmarè to the orìṣà. The anthropologist E.E. Evans-Pritchard, discussing the interrelations of the Nuer simultaneous belief in "God" as Spirit (*Kwoth*) with a belief in a multiplicity of spirits (*kuth*), as well as the Nuer habit of identifying other peoples' deities with their own, observes:

> "The Nuer attitude in this matter shows clearly the markedly monotheistic tendency of their religious thought. It is polyonymous but not henotheistic. The inference we can draw from this in considering the spirits of the air is that they are not thought of as independent gods but in some way as hypostases of the modes and attributes of a single God... The spirits of the air are, nevertheless, being Spirit, also God. They are many, but also one. God is manifested in, and in a sense is, each of them. I received the impression that in sacrificing or in singing to an air-spirit, Nuer do not think that they are communicating with the spirit and not with God. They are, if I have understood the matter correctly, addressing God in a particular spiritual figure or manifestation."[139]

This theory whereby the multiplicity of "spirits" or (as in the Yoruba case) "divinities" can be seen as manifestations or refractions of "a single God", constitutes one of Idowu's most valuable theological insights into African religious tradition. For it enables him to establish conclusively that "the religion of the Yoruba... consisted in a 'Primitive Monotheism'",[140] so that, finally, "if we speak of 'the religion of the Yoruba' we can only do so in reference to the fact that Olódùmarè is the core which gives meaning and coherence to the whole system".[141]

But the theory serves two other purposes. It helps account for

the "decay" in Yoruba religion, whereby "the cults of the hitherto
ever-increasing intermediary divinities who for practical purposes
often become ends in themselves have had an insidiously detrimental effect on His [Olódùmarè's] cult as a regular objective
phenomenon in the religious activities of the Yoruba".[142] Idowu
would presumably regard such a development as retrograde, since
what ought to be "means to an end which, technically, they are
according to Yoruba theology", have now become ends in themselves.[143]

It also helps explain why Idowu considers that "Christianity,
by its unique and universal message, stands the best chance of
fulfilling that which is implied in the Yoruba concept of God..."[144]
Idowu concedes that "a people's idea of God" can undergo "modification by way of enrichment and correction",[145] and this is what
Christianity with its peculiarly Trinitarian monotheism, as well
as its host of angels and archangels, has done to Yoruba religion,
since "it [Christianity] has helped to emphasise the belief of the
Yoruba in the Supreme God".[146] In other words, the "Diffused
Monotheism" of the "old" Yoruba religion acquires a sharper focus
in Yoruba Christianity, as human attention becomes directed more
intently towards "the one essential Factor by which the life and
belief of the Yoruba cohere and have sustenance".[147] If this were to
result in the multitude of divinities who, in any case, are no more
than "means to an end", finally receding into oblivion, Idowu would
probably welcome such an outcome. For all his spirited vindication
of an African religious consciousness which maintains its roots
firmly in the "heritage from the past", Idowu is not committed to
the unambiguous reality of the divinities:

"... to those who worship the divinities and derive succour from
belief in their existence, to such they are real: but to those who
have outgrown them, all reality is concentrated in the Deity."[148]

VI. Conclusion

Idowu may not be the most quoted African theologian, nor is he
the one with the weightiest bibliography. Nevertheless, his impact
on the African theological scene is significant. Idowu's importance
has registered most prominently in his contribution to African
scholarship in the field of religion; and he typifies and represents
above all an outlook, a standpoint, a position: African religious
tradition has a right to be recognised and vindicated on its own
terms, and without apology to those who, in the past, despised it
without knowing it intimately.[149] If the movement towards estab-

lishing the intellectual respectability of African Traditional
Religion began before Idowu's own academic career, his contribu-
tion to its growth has not been negligible.[150]   The work that
Geoffrey Parrinder initiated at the University of Ibadan, and which
Idowu pursued, continues under the current head, Dr J. Ọmọṣade
Awolalu who himself has been a research pupil of Idowu's.[151]

A cursory reading of Idowu's writings is likely to leave one with the
impression that the range of his theological concerns is somewhat
restricted. His books and articles[152] offer little evidence of serious
interest in the themes and issues which have usually constituted
the traditional fare of Christian (hitherto predominantly
European) theology. With the exception of the relevant sections in
Towards an Indigenous Church, Idowu's work contains scant
speculation on Christ, the Holy Spirit, the Church, the Sacraments, the Last Things, as items of doctrine in themselves. Even
his one sustained interest in the question of God is not dealt with
in any way recognisably akin to the standard approaches in
European systematic theologies.

But it may be this feature of Idowu's work which gives it its
significance. Among African theologians of his generation, perhaps
none is so clearly intent on determining his own agenda as Idowu.
If the unacceptable face of missionary Christianity in Africa consists in its "foreignness", nowhere is this more true than in the
"undigested" theology which the Church in Africa seemed to be
satisfied to give out in preaching and teaching.[153] Idowu refuses to
accept that the African Church should be theologically "spoonfed
by Europeans".[154]

If, therefore, as Idowu's contribution to the process whereby
Africans take "the initiative in constructing the formularies of
their faith as Christians",[155] he devotes his attention to the African
understanding and experience of God, this is because he believes
that:

"... in Africa, the real cohesive factor of religion is the living God
and that without this one factor, all things would fall to pieces.
And it is on this ground especially – this identical concept – that
we can speak of the religion of Africa in the singular."[156]

Here, "with regard to the concept of God", Idowu finds "a
common thread, however tenuous in places, running throughout
the continent".[157] He is even prepared to argue that phonetic
similarities in some of the names for God found in a variety of
African societies might possibly be proof that they constitute

variations of the same name.[158] Whatever the merits of Idowu's linguistic argument, the unmistakable effect of his general thesis is to challenge the early European assessment that African societies possessed little knowledge, let alone awareness, of a single, ruling Deity.

However, the question might justly be put: has Idowu over-stated his case? Was African pre-Christian (and pre-Islamic) tradition monotheistic? The answer to the question may well lie in the history of the naming of God in African tradition. In his important introductory chapter to the symposium, *African Ideas of God*, Edwin Smith noted that "with few exceptions, Christian missionaries in their teaching and translations of Scripture have adopted African names of God",[159] and went on to indicate a significant difference between the Christian mission in Africa and the earlier missionary story of Europe.

"Teutonic peoples had their own god-names – Wodan, god of the dead, Donar, god of thunder and the sky, Tyr, god of war. The Christian missionaries took over, not these personal names, but the class-word *god*, which denoted (according to the Oxford Dictionary) a superhuman person who was worshipped as having power over nature and the fortunes of mankind; and also an image or other object which was worshipped. Whatever it meant to our Teutonic forefathers it did not mean what it means to us today: Christianity took it and filled it with a new content.

"Christian missionaries in Africa differ from their predecessors in Europe for they have generally adopted not class-names like *theos* and *god* but personal names like Nyame, Leza, Nyambe."[160]

Whilst Edwin Smith sees in the two missionary stories essentially an identity of principle – "that of meeting pagans on their own ground..." – he is careful to point out in a footnote that "it would be doing violence to the language to make a plural of such a name as Leza or Nyambe; for they cannot have a plural; there is but one Leza, one Nyambe".[161] Furthermore, Hilda Ellis Davidson, commenting on the passing of the "old faith" of the peoples of Northern Europe when they came into contact with Christianity, has observed:

"The power of the Christian religion lay also in the welding together of the different aspects of the heathen faith into a united whole, with a God who was the father of all men, and not the fickle All-Father of Asgard [Odin]..."[162]

This is hardly the place to raise the question as to who were the polytheists, and who were the monotheists, the Europeans or the Africans. However, it does not seem out of place to ask whether Edwin Smith's note is not of more than linguistic interest; for words give account of meanings. As early as 1881, the great missionary scholar of the Basel Mission in the Gold Coast, Johannes Christaller, noted that the plural *anyame* (formed from the Akan divine name *Onyame*), had been "merely introduced", presumably by missionaries, to describe the religion of people who were generally believed to be polytheists. And he himself remarked:

> "The heathen negroes are, at least, to a great extent, rather monotheists, as they apply the term for God only to one supreme being."[163]

Whatever value one attaches to Christaller's intuition regarding Akan religious thought, it is noteworthy that Geoffrey Parrinder, who in his first book on African religion, considered that the religion of West African peoples could be "roundly called 'polytheism'",[164] in a subsequent article concluded that "the overall impression is that much of African thought is both theistic and unitary".[165] In a recent study, Patrick J. Ryan[166] has examined the history of the distinction of "God" from "gods" in Semitic, Graeco-Roman and Western Christian religious traditions, and compared the evidence with the understanding of the concept of "God and the gods" as found among the Yoruba and Akan of West Africa. In Ryan's view, "the Yoruba and the Akan are better equipped linguistically than are Semites, Greeks, Romans and their inheritors to express the absolute uniqueness of God".[167] Consequently, he is able to conclude:

> "It would seem, in fact, that even before Muslims and Christians arrived in the West African forest zone, where both the Akan and Yoruba peoples live, speakers of Yoruba and Akan were assured of the supremacy of the One Whom a modern theologian calls 'the incomprehensible term of human transcendence'."[168]

The precise nature of African pre-Christian religious thought and experience continues to be explored by African scholars in the field of religions.[169] But it seems to be well established that the designation of Africa's "old" religions as "polytheism" is virtually abandoned. For his part, Idowu has suggested that to find "proper polytheism", one would have to look, not in African religion, but rather in European tradition.[170]

Geoffrey Parrinder may well be right in the view that "the attempts [made by African scholars] to diminish the role of the lesser gods and claim a degree of monotheism for Africa" may be "influenced by preconceptions and misunderstandings" which arise from the theories of "such [European] writers as Tylor" who had branded polytheism as "the belief of savage tribes".[171] If Parrinder's interpretation of African theological scholarship is correct, it is understandable that Idowu, who resolutely rejects that designation for Africans, should also refuse to accept the accompanying term as the description of their religious heritage.

To speak of the achievement of Idowu's work, one has to consider it from two points of view. Negatively, it contributes to the process whereby an influential body of European opinion concerning African religious traditions is made to stand upon its head. Positively, it places the relationship of the Christian faith to the religious tradition which it inherits in Africa in an entirely new light, and affirms that Africa's "old" religions constitute a proper (though by no means sole) source of African Christian theology.[172] In 1974, Malcolm J. McVeigh reiterated Roland Oliver's earlier warning that Christianity in [East] Africa might disintegrate at the centre whilst expanding at the circumference.[173] and added, in relation to the continent as a whole:

"Much depends on the Church's willingness to assess the present position of God in African Christianity and its ability to reorient its message; so that the God who revealed Himself fully in Jesus Christ will be able to speak in a new way to the deepest needs of the African heart."[174]

However, the judicious observation by Janzen and MacGaffy with relation to Kongo religion, may indicate that McVeigh perhaps magnified somewhat the "danger... on the horizon" and that Idowu's fundamental intuition about the continuity of God in African religious experience is essentially valid:

"The parallel between the Biblical 'God' and the African *Nzambi* is sufficiently close that protracted scholarly debate has failed to discover how much the modern concept of *Nzambi* owes to missionary teaching, and the equivalence of the two terms has been universally accepted in Kongo for many generations."[175]

Notes

1. E. Bolaji Idowu, *African Traditional Religion – A Definition*, London: S.C.M. Press, 1973, p.xi.

2. See E. Bolaji Idowu, *Towards an Indigenous Church,* London: Oxford University Press, 1965.

3. See A.F. Walls, "A Bag of Needments for the road: Geoffrey Parrinder and the study of religion in Britain", in *Religion – Journal of Religion and Religions,* vol.10, Spring 1980, pp.141-150.

4. The thesis forms the basis of Idowu's important book, *Olódùmarè – God in Yoruba Belief,* London: Longman, 1962. In his preface, the author speaks of Prof. Parrinder as one "who inspired and supervised my thesis throughout", p.viii. (my emphasis)

5. Prof. Idowu served as Chairman of the Editorial Committee from 1967 to 1976 and contributed several articles to the Journal. Details of these articles are given in our Bibliography. *Orita* is explained as meaning "in the Yoruba language where major ways meet".

6. The kind of theological perspective Idowu exemplifies, and which we hope to clarify subsequently, is found in, for instance, Samuel G. Kibicho, "The continuity of the African conception of God into and through Christianity: A Kikuyu case study" in E.W. Fasholé-Luke *et al.* (eds) *Christianity in Independent Africa,* London: Rex Collings, 1978, pp.370-388; Gabriel Setiloane, "How the traditional world-view persists in the Christianity of the Sotho-Tswana", in Fasholé-Luke *et al.* (eds), *op.cit.,* pp.402-412; also Gabriel M. Setiloane, *The Image of God among the Sotho-Tswana,* Rotterdam: A.A. Balkema, 1976.

7. See C.G. Baëta (ed), *Christianity in Tropical Africa* (Studies presented and discussed at the seventh International African Seminar, University of Ghana, April, 1965), London: Oxford University Press, 1968, pp.417-440.

8. *Ibid.,* p.417.

9. *Ibid.,* p.353.

10. *Ibid.,* pp.427-435.

11. *Ibid.,* p.433. This section of the paper draws substantially on the author's more sustained discussion of the "Problem of the Indigenisation of the Church in Nigeria" in three broadcast talks given in 1961, which he eventually developed into the book, *Towards an Indigenous Church.*

12. An indication of the seriousness which Idowu attached to these sentiments is the fact that in his "Introduction" to the papers presented at the Ibadan Consultation of African Theologians (January, 1966), he felt able to write: "There is no doubt that the urgent predicament of the Church in Africa today is that of the apparent foreignness of Christianity. And this, as we have pointed out, has resulted from the erroneous notion with which evangelism was bedevilled from the start. By a miscarriage of purpose the church has succeeded in preaching to, and in teaching about a strange God whom they have somehow come to identify as the God of the white man. But what has happened to the God as known to their forebears – the God who is the foundation of their traditional beliefs? He remains still with them. And so we have left them with two Gods in their hands and thus made of them peoples of ambivalent spiritual lives." See Kwesi A.Dickson and Paul Ellingworth, *Biblical Revelation and African Beliefs,* London: Lutterworth Press, 1969, p.13.

13. See *Acts* 15:1-21.

14. C.G. Baëta (ed), *op.cit.,* p.434. See John Taylor, *The Primal Vision – Christian Presence amid African Religion,* London: S.C.M.Press, 1963, pp.109-111.

15. C.G. Baëta, *op.cit.*, p.433.

16. E. Bolaji Idowu, *African Traditional Religion – A Definition*, p.75: "Religion results from man's spontaneous awareness of, and reaction to, his immediate awareness of a Living Power, 'wholly other' and infinitely greater than himself; a Power mysterious because unseen, yet a present and urgent Reality, seeking to bring man into communion with Himself... Religion in its essence is the means by which God as Spirit and man's essential self communicate. It is something resulting from the relationship which God established from the beginning of (human) life between himself and man..."

Elsewhere Idowu writes: "The uniqueness of each religion lies in its conception of Deity and its apprehension of the divine will. Here is the heart of every religion, its essential theology and the motive of its ethical emphasis". See his "Faiths in Interaction", in *Orita*, vol.4, no.2, December, 1970, p.94.

17. Cf. Adrian Hastings, *African Christianity – An Essay in Interpretation*, p.51: "Europeans almost always underestimated the African sense of God in their earlier encounters, being much more struck by the strong consciousness of a wider spirit world – ancestors and natural forces – with its shrines and sacrifices."

18. E. Bolaji Idowu, "The Study of Religion, with special reference to African Traditional Religion" in *Orita*, vol.1, no.1, June 1957, p.12.

19. Adrian Hastings, *African Christianity – An Essay in Interpretation*, p. 52.

20. C.H. Dodd, *Gospel and Law*, Cambridge: Cambridge University Press, 1957, p.79.

21. E. Bolaji Idowu, *Towards an Indigenous Church*, p.25.

22. It is interesting that Idowu rejects what he calls "the obnoxious notion of a High God" (presumed remote, cf. Dietrich Westermann – *Africa and Christianity*, London: Oxford University Press, 1957, p.74), putting it down to "the refusal — deliberate refusal – on the part of foreign investigators to accept that Africans are as much entitled to a place with the Supreme God as they are". See his "The Study of Religion with special reference to African Traditional Religion", p.11; also his *Olódùmarè – God in Yoruba Belief*, p.140-143, and *African Traditional Religion – A Definition*, pp.61f.

23. E. Bolaji Idowu, "God", in Kwesi A. Dickson and Paul Ellingworth (eds), *op.cit.*, p.21. For a similar view of Western theological understanding from an African theologian who is an admirer of Idowu, see Gabriel M. Setiloane, *The Image of God among the Sotho-Tswana*, pp.229f: "In the whole discussion of MODIMO, and in what has been said above about the contrast between 'Being' and 'Supreme Being' (see his chapter 6: 'Attributes and Praise-Names of MODIMO') there is a suggestion that what missionaries have been able to offer to Africans is not GOD but "the god of the Europeans, who may well – perhaps rightly – be discarded with the coming of political independence and the reassertion of African culture which is its ideological counterpart. Indeed the whole discussion in the West – focused in *Honest to God* and the 'death of God' theology – suggests that the West itself has lost the image of God as *mysterium tremendum et fascinans* and deals at best, with a *creator abscondus*, a god of the gaps, or a saviour of individual souls destined for pie in the sky... It is indeed suggested that western theologians might go to school with the Sotho-Tswana if they wish to rediscover, in truth, the Yahweh whom they profess to serve."

24. E. Bolaji Idowu, *Towards an Indigenous Church*, pp.7-8. My emphasis.

25. *Ibid.*, p.2.

26. *Ibid.*, p.1.

27. *Ibid.*, p.6.

28. *Ibid.*, p.4. Idowu uses the expression to describe the Christianity of the Sierra Leone recaptives who later provided some of the earliest missionaries to Nigeria and the most prominent of whom was undoubtedly Samuel Ajayi Crowther, the first African bishop of the Anglican Communion. On the whole question of the "European" character of this Christianity, see A.F. Walls, "Black Europeans, White Africans: Some missionary motives in West Africa", in D. Baker (ed), *Religious Motivation: biographical and sociological problems of the Church historian*, Cambridge: Cambridge University Press, 1978, pp.339-348.

29. See *Christianity and African Culture*, Accra: Christian Council of the Gold Coast, 1955.

30. See *The Church in Changing Africa (Report of the All Africa Church Conference, Ibadan, January 1958)*, New York: International Missionary Council, 1958. Section 4 is on "The Church and Culture". See especially, J.H. Nketia, "The Contribution of African Culture to Christian Worship" (pp.59-65).

31. See *Des prêtres noirs s'interrogent* (Rencontres 47), Paris: Les Editions du Cert, 1956.

32. The volume is generally placed at the head of the history of African theology by African Roman Catholic theologians. See, for instance, Ngindu Mushete, "L'Histoire de la Théologie en Afrique: de la polémique à l'irénisme critique" in Kofi Appiah-Kubi *et al.* (eds), *Libération ou adaptation? La théologie africaine s'interroge* (Le Colloque d'Accra), Paris: Librairie-Editions l'Harmattan, 1979, pp.30-48.

33. E.W. Fasholé-Luke, "The Quest for an African Christian Theology" in *The Ecumenical Review*, vol. 27, no.3, 1978, pp.259-269. Quotation on p.259. But John Mbiti, "Some Current Concerns of African Theology" in *The Expository Times*, vol.87, 1975-76, pp.164-168, draws attention to the use of the term as early as 1956. See P.D. Fueter, "Theological Education in Africa", in *IRM*, vol.45, October 1956, pp.37f.

34. *Ibid.*, p.259.

35. E. Bolaji Idowu, *Towards an Indigenous Church*, p.1.

36. For an attempt by an African (Ghanaian) Christian historian "to present the facts, analyse the events in the light of the available evidence and so help readers understand the situation..." in the early years of Ghana's political independence when missionaries were "under fire", see S.K. Odamtten, *The Missionary Factor in Ghana's Development up to the 1880's*, Accra: Waterville Publishing House, 1978.

37. For further development of the idea that the European connections of the Church (in Africa) had "now become rather a handicap", see Idowu, "The Predicament of the Church in Africa", in C.G. Baëta (ed), *op.cit.*, pp.429-431.

38. E. Bolaji Idowu, *Towards an Indigenous Church*, p.5.

39. *Ibid.*, pp.3-4. On the adoption of European values by the recaptives, it is worth noting, as A.F. Walls has pointed out, that these were "... recaptive Africans, uprooted from coherent societies and without the means of rediscovering their former cohesion. The only identity now open to them was a new identity. They took the only viable alternative open to them, and adopted – and adapted – the package of Christianity and European civilisation". See A.F. Walls, *op.cit.*, p.341.

40. E. Bolaji Idowu, *Towards an Indigenous Church*, p.6.

41. *Ibid.*, p.3.

42. E.W. Fasholé-Luke, *op.cit.*, p.259.

43. E. Bolaji Idowu, *Towards an Indigenous Church*, p.22.

44. *Ibid.*, p.3.

45. Cf. E. Bolaji Idowu, "The Predicament of the Church in Africa", in C.G. Baëta (ed), *op.cit.*, p.436. Idowu's concern in this area seems to have been shared by his equally eminent contemporary, the late Harry Sawyerr, of Fourah Bay College, Freetown, Sierra Leone. See Harry Sawyerr, *Creative Evangelism: Towards a New Christian Encounter with Africa*, London: Lutterworth Press, 1968.

46. E. Bolaji Idowu, *Towards an Indigenous Church*, pp.9f.

47. *Ibid.*, p.11.

48. *Ibid.*, p.13.

49. *Ibid.*, p.12.

50. *Ibid.*, p.13.

51. *Ibid.*, p.13.

52. *Ibid.*, pp.12,13.

53. *Ibid.*, p.48.

54. *Ibid.*, p.53.

55. *Ibid.*, p.14.

56. *Ibid.*, p.49. It may seem odd that for all his insistence on the Church (in Nigeria) bearing "the stamp of originality", Idowu should decide that "ministers' vestments" are one area in which "the Church in Nigeria must preserve something as token of her being part and presence of the Universal Church" (p.40). And yet, may this in itself not indicate how much more profound and fundamental is the indigenisation for which Idowu is pleading?

57. *Ibid.*, p.15. These "concrete examples" are (a) the Bible in Nigerian languages, (b) the language of evangelism, (c) Theology, (d) Liturgy, (e) Dress and Vestments.

58. Philip Turner, "The Wisdom of the Fathers and the Gospel of Christ: Some notes on Christian adaptation in Africa", in *JRA*, vol.4, fasc.1.

59. *Ibid.*, p.56.

60. See Daniel von Allmen, "The Birth of Theology: Contextualisation as the dynamic element in the formation of New Testament Theology", in *IRM*, vol.64, January, 1975, pp.37-52.

61. E. Bolaji Idowu, *Towards an Indigenous Church*, pp.16f.

62. E. Bolaji Idowu, "Introduction" in Kwesi A. Dickson and Paul Ellingworth (eds), *op.cit.*, p.16.

63. E. Bolaji Idowu, *Towards an Indigenous Church*, p.23.

64. *Ibid.*, p.23.

65. *Ibid.*, p.23. My emphasis.

66. *Ibid.*, p.22.

67. *Ibid.*, p.23.

68. *John* 4:39-42.

69. E. Bolaji Idowu, *Towards an Indigenous Church.* p.24.

70. G.C. Oosthuizen, *Post-Christianity in Africa:- A Theological and Anthropological Study*, London: C. Hurst and Co, 1968, pp.235f: "The danger

is that the African Church may fail to communicate the Gospel to its own society, because it has learned the Gospel in loan words from the West. Loan words can be understood by the intelligentsia, but they do not speak to the heart of the nation. They do not reflect its own spiritual struggles, and, because of this, they fail to communicate the Word of God."

71. E. Bolaji Idowu, *Towards an Indigenous Church*, pp.24-26

72. *Ibid.*, p.26.

73. *Ibid.*, p.26. *Cf.* E. Bolaji Idowu, "The Predicament of the Church in Africa", in C.G. Baëta (ed), *op.cit.*, p.433.

74. E. Bolaji Idowu, *Towards an Indigenous Church*, p.26.

75. *Ibid.*, p.24; cf. *John* 3:16.

76. *Ibid.*, pp.24f. Idowu's emphasis.

77. E. Bolaji Idowu, "Faiths in Interaction", in *Orita*, vol.4, no.2, December, 1970, pp.93-94. Cf. E. Bolaji Idowu, "The Study of Religion with special reference to African Traditional Religion", p.12.

78. E. Bolaji Idowu, *Towards an Indigenous Church*, p.25. My emphasis; cf. *Acts* 10:34f, 14:14ff.

79. E. Bolaji Idowu, "The Predicament of the Church in Africa", p.433.

80. See "Introduction", above. Cf. Kenneth Cragg, "Conversion and Convertibility – with special reference to Muslims", in John R.W. Stott and Robert Coote (eds), *Down to Earth: Studies in Christianity and Culture*, Grand Rapids: Eerdmans, 1980, p.194.

81. My emphasis.

82. E. Bolaji Idowu, "Faiths in Interaction", pp.90-91. Cf. his *African Traditional Religion – A Definition*, p.12: "There can be nothing like religion in the abstract or religion considered apart from persons who worship and practise the tenets of their faith."

83. See, for instance, E. Bolaji Idowu, "The Study of Religion with special reference to African Traditional Religion", p.5; "Faiths in Interaction", pp.87,94; *African Traditional Religion – A Definition*, pp.5,9,13-16,18,19,23-25,104-105,136. An indication of Cantwell Smith's view is given in his classic *The Meaning and End of Religion*, London: S.P.C.K., 1978 (1st published in 1962 by Macmillan, New York), p.195: "Perceptive readers will have noticed that in the course of this present inquiry the adjective 'religious' has been retained in use even while the noun is rejected. This has to do with a contention that living religiously is an attribute of persons. The attribute arises not because those persons participate in some entity called *religion*, but because they participate in what I have called transcendence."

84. E. Bolaji Idowu, *African Traditional Religion – A Definition*, pp.23-25.

85. *Ibid.*, p.25.

86. E. Bolaji Idowu, *Towards an Indigenous Church*, p.25.

87. E. Bolaji Idowu, *African Traditional Religion – A Definition*, p.56. On the importance of getting "our theology right at this delicate point" (i.e. on "revelation"), Idowu writes elsewhere: "If we are true to the spirit of the Bible and of our faith, we must admit that God's self-disclosure is, in the first instance, to the whole world and that each race has grasped something of this primary revelation according to its native capability. To deny this as some have been trying to do, is to approach theology with a cultural bias and be traitors to truth." See his "Introduction" in K.A. Dickson and P. Ellingworth, *op.cit.*, p.12.

88. E. Bolaji Idowu, *African Traditional Religion – A Definition*, pp.56f. Cf. *Romans* 1:20f; *Acts* 17:26-28.

89. E. Bolaji Idowu, *African Traditional Religion – A Definition*, p.57. Idowu here quotes from H.H. Farmer, *Revelation and Religion*, London: Nisbet, 1954, p.105.

90. E. Bolaji Idowu, "God", in Kwesi A. Dickson and Paul Ellingworth (eds), *op.cit.*, pp.17-29.

91. *Ibid.*, p.18.

92. Andrew Lang, *The Making of Religion* (2nd ed.), London: Longmans, Green and Co., 1900.

93. Nathan Söderblom, *The Living God: Basal forms of personal religion* (Gifford Lectures, 1931), London: Oxford University Press, 1933.

94. Wilhelm Schmidt, *The Origin and Growth of Religion* (ET, 2nd ed.), London: Methuen and Co., 1935.

95. E. Bolaji Idowu, "God", pp.18f.

96. *Ibid.*, p.19.

97. *Ibid.*, p.20.

98. Idowu refers to *Isaiah* 45:15, and *Job* 11:7.

99. E. Bolaji Idowu, "God", p.21.

100. *Ibid.*, p.29.

101. *Ibid.*, p.24.

102. *Ibid.*, pp.26-29.

103. *Ibid.*, p.26. Orìṣè, Chukwu and Ọdomankoma are, respectively, Yoruba, Igbo and Akan divine names which generally express God's manifold bounty as the creator and source of all life. On Orìṣè, see E. Bolaji Idowu, *Olódùmarè – God in Yoruba Belief*, pp.61ff; on Chukwu, see Emefie Ikenga Metuh, *God and Man in African Religion: A case study of the Igbo of Nigeria*, London: Geoffrey Chapman, 1981; on Ọdomankoma, see J.B. Danquah, *The Akan Doctrine of God* (2nd edition), London: Frank Cass, 1968.

104. E. Bolaji Idowu, "God", p.29. Idowu here refutes the view of A.B. Ellis, *The Tsi-speaking Peoples of the Gold Coast*, 1887, p.24. On Ellis, see Geoffrey Parrinder, *West African Religion*, London: Epworth Press, 1969, p.13.

105. E. Bolaji Idowu, "The Study of Religion with special reference to African Traditional Religion", p.11.

106. Cf. E. Bolaji Idowu, *Olódùmarè — God in Yoruba Belief*, p.5: "The real keynote of the life of the Yoruba is neither their noble ancestry nor in the past deeds of their heroes. The keynote of their life is their religion. In all things they are religious. Religion forms the foundation and the all-governing principle of life for them.".

107. E. Bolaji Idowu, "The study of Religion with special reference to African Traditional Religion", p.11.

108. E. Bolaji Idowu, *Towards an Indigenous Church*, p.25.

109. The expression is used by Gabriel M. Setiloane in describing his own theological position, but it suits Idowu's just as admirably. See Gabriel Setiloane, "Where are we in African Theology?", in Kofi Appiah-Kubi and Sergio Torres (eds), *African Theology en Route* (Papers from the Pan-African Conference of Third World Theologians, December 17-23, 1977, Accra, Ghana), New York: Orbis Books, 1979, p.61.

110. Published by SCM Press, London, 1973.

111. *Ibid.*, p.ix.

112. *Ibid.*, p.204.

113. *Ibid.*, p.xi.

114. *Ibid.*, p.xi.

115. *Ibid.*, p.102.

116. *Ibid.*, p.ix: "The world still has to be convinced that there is an indigenous religion of Africa and that, by right, it deserves the name of religion." Cf. Geoffrey Parrinder, *Religion in Africa*, London: Pall Mall Press, 1969, pp.7ff.

117. E. Bolaji Idowu, *African Traditional Religion – A Definition*, p.x; cf. p.208.

118. *Ibid.*, p.208; cf. *1 John* 3:2.

119. E. Bolaji Idowu, *Towards an Indigenous Church*, pp.7f.

120. E. Bolaji Idowu, *African Traditional Religion – A Definition*, p.205.

121. See Adrian Hastings, *African Christianity – An Essay in interpretation*, p.51.

122. E. Bolaji Idowu, "Faiths in Interaction", p. 93.

123. E. Bolaji Idowu, *Olódùmarè – God in Yoruba Belief*, p.141.

124. *Ibid.*, p.141.

125. *Ibid.*, p.vii.

126. E. Bolaji Idowu, *African Tradition Religion – A Definition*, p.168.

127. *Ibid.*, p.168; cf. pp.169-173.

128. *Ibid.*, p.165.

129. E. Bolaji Idowu, *Olódùmarè – God in Yoruba Belief*, pp.59ff.

130. *Ibid.*, p.60.

131. *Ibid.*, p.60.

132. *Ibid.*, p.61; cf. p.62: "All together, the orìṣà form the Yoruba pantheon. Olódùmarè is not one among them. He is 'wholly other' than they. But they are under His constant vigilance and control, and to Him they owe absolute fealty."

133. *Ibid.*, p.54: "He [Olódùmarè] is supreme over all in an absolute sense; and His authority cannot be questioned by any one of the divinities, or by all of them together." Cf. Patrick J. Ryan, "'Arise O God!' The problem of 'Gods' in West Africa" in *JRA*, vol11, fasc.3, 1980, p.166: "The complete absence of any patrilineage dedicated to Olódùmarè (Olórun) as well as the almost total lack of any direct ritual worship of the Supreme Being may be taken not as an indication of Olódùmarè's otiose nature but of His absolute transcendence. He is not merely God above the gods." However, on the cult of Olódùmarè, see E. Bolaji Idowu, *Olódùmarè – God in Yoruba Belief*, pp.140-143.

134. E. Bolaji Idowu, *Olódùmarè – God in Yoruba Belief*, p.62.

135. *Ibid.*, p.62.

136. *Ibid.*, pp.67-69, for a discussion of the number of orìṣà.

137. *Ibid.*, p.62.

138. Cf. H.W. Turner, "The way forward in the religious study of African Primal religions", in *JRA*, vol.12, fasc.1, 1981, pp.1-15. "There is also a place for theologically orientated studies (Western or any other) of all aspects of reality and African religions can claim no exception from this" (p.12).

139. E.E. Evans-Pritchard, *Nuer Religion*, London: Oxford University Press, 1956, pp.49,51. For a similar conclusion on the religion of a neighbouring people, see Godfrey Lienhardt, *Divinity and Experience – The Religion of the Dinka*, Oxford: Clarendon Press, 1961, p.56: "All Dinka assert that Divinity is one, *nhialic ee tok...* Yet *nhialic* is also a comprehensive term for a number of conceptions which differ considerably from each other... This unity and multiplicity of Divinity causes no difficulty in the context of Dinka language and life."

140. E. Bolaji Idowu, *Olódùmarè – God in Yoruba Belief*, p.202. Cf. W. Schmidt, *op.cit.* pp.262ff; although Idowu does not refer to Schmidt's thesis in this instance, an approving reference is to be found in his "God", p.18.

141. E. Bolaji Idowu, *Olódùmarè – God in Yoruba Belief*, p.203.

142. *Ibid.*, p.143.

143. *Ibid.*, pp.32,63.

144. *Ibid.*, p.215.

145. *Ibid.*, p.32.

146. *Ibid.*, p.209.

147. *Ibid.*, p.202.

148. *Ibid.*, p.63.

149. An interesting indicator of his uncompromising vindication of Africans' right to define their own realities and the categories for dealing with them, is his spirited defence of the "reality" of witchcraft against non-Africans who might be tempted to offer reductionist theories of explanation. See E. Bolaji Idowu, "The Challenge of Witchcraft", in *Orita*, vol.4, no.1, June, 1970, pp.3-16.

150. On the development of African Traditional Religion as a subject for academic study among African theologians, it is interesting that in 1977 Gabriel M. Setiloane was extolling Idowu's *African Traditional Religion – A Definition* above what he described as John S. Mbiti's "apologetical works, coupling African religion with philosophy and much too simplistically drawing up similarities between African traditional understanding and the Christian faith". See Gabriel M. Setiloane, "Where are we in African Theology?", p.62.

151. See J. Omosade Awolalu, *Yoruba Beliefs and Sacrificial Rites*, London: Longman, 1979.

152. Idowu has also published a series of Bible studies on the *Book of Job*, which we have not considered essential to include in this study. See E. Bolaji Idowu, *Job: A Meditation on the Problem of Suffering*, Ibadan: Daystar Press, n.d.

153. E. Bolaji Idowu, *Towards an Indigenous Church*, pp.22-23.

154. *Ibid.*, p.22.

155. *Ibid.*, p.26.

156. E. Bolaji Idowu, *African Traditional Religion – A Definition*, p.104.

157. *Ibid.*, p.103.

158. *Ibid.*, pp.103-104. Idowu mentions, in this connection, names like Yamba, found in parts of Nigeria, Yambe or Yembe, attested in the Cameroons and the Congo, and Onyame or Nyame found among the Akan of Ghana!

159. Edwin W. Smith (ed), *African Ideas of God – A symposium* (2nd ed. revised and edited by E.G. Parrinder), London: Edinburgh House Press, 1950, p.34.

160. *Ibid.*, p.35.

161. *Ibid.*, p.35.

162. H.R. Ellis Davidson, *Gods and Myths of Northern Europe*, Harmondsworth: Penguin Books, 1964, p.222.

163. J.G. Christaller, *A Dictionary of the Asante and Fante Language Called Tshi (Chwee, Twi), with a grammatical introduction and appendices on the Geography of the Gold Coast and other subjects*, Basel: Evangelical Missionary Society, 1881, pp.342f.

164. Geoffrey Parrinder, *West African Religion – A Study of the Beliefs and Practices of Akan, Ewe, Yoruba, Ibo and Kindred Peoples* (with a Foreword by the Rev Dr Edwin Smith), 3rd ed. London: Epworth Press, 1969 (1st published in 1949), p.11.

165. E.G. Parrinder, "Monotheism and Pantheism in Africa", in *JRA*, vol.3, 1970, p.87.

166. Patrick J. Ryan, "'Arise O God!' The Problem of 'Gods' in West Africa", in *JRA*, vol.11, fasc.3, 1980, pp.161-171.

167. *Ibid.*, p.169.

168. *Ibid.*, pp.169-170. Ryan quotes from Karl Rahner, *Foundations of Christian Faith* (ET by William V. Dych), New York: Seabury, 1978, p.454.

169. See for instance, Emefie Ikenga-Metuh, "Religious Concepts in West African Cosmogonies", in *JRA*, vol.13, fasc.1, 1982, pp.11-23. However, why Ikenga-Metuh rejects the suggestion of "monotheism" in preference for "African theism" (p.23), is obscure to me.

170. E. Bọlaji Idowu, *African Traditional Religion – A Definition*, p.166: "The Olympian situation has always offered a veritable example of what may be described as proper polytheism. Here we have a system where the gods appear not to have transcended the universe of social cliques and inter-tribal conflicts. Not only were the gods all of the same rank in kind and passion, distinguished from one another only by a hierarchy of status or power among more or less equals; but also they shared in the passions of men and tended to use their divinity in competing with, and beating, men in 'superfluity of naughtiness'."

171. E.G. Parrinder, "Monotheism and Pantheism in Africa", p.83. Cf. E.B. Tylor, *Primitive Culture: Researches into the development of mythology, philosophy, religion, language, art and custom* (vol.2), 3rd edition, revised, London: John Murray, 1891, p.332: "... no savage tribe [in which he included Africans] of monotheists has been ever known."

172. Cf. Adrian Hastings, *African Christianity – An essay in interpretation*, London: Geoffrey Chapman, 1976, p.52.

173. Malcolm J. McVeigh, *God in Africa: Conception of God in African Traditional Religion and Christianity*, Cape Cod, Massachussetts and Hartford, Vermont: Claude Stark, 1974, p.182. McVeigh was referring to Roland Oliver, *The Missionary Factor in East Africa*, London: Green and Co., 1952, p.291.

174. Malcolm J. McVeigh, *op.cit*, p.182.

175. John M. Janzen and Wyatt MacGaffey (eds), *An Anthology of Kongo Religion: Primary texts from Lower Zaire* (University of Kansas Publications in Anthropology, 5), Lawrence, Kansas: University of Kansas, 1974, p.14.

Chapter Eight

A Variety of African Responses (2): John Mbiti, or Christ as the Redeemer of the African Heritage

I. "Erupt Your grace in me, O Lord..."[1]: Theology as spiritual freedom in the Gospel

These words of pure spiritual aspiration written by Professor John Samuel Mbiti occur not in a theological discussion, but in a collection of his poems, and this fact gives some indication of the many-sidedness that has marked his intellectual career as a Christian scholar and theologian. John Mbiti is the modern African theologian with by far the weightiest bibliography. His published writings cover a wide range of subjects, including African Christian theology, Biblical studies, the pre-Christian religious traditions of Africa, the world-view they imply and their encounter with the Christian faith, and creative writing in some European languages and in his own Kenyan mother-tongue, Kikamba.[2] Moreover, he has displayed a sustained interest in cultural questions generally as they affect Africa. At the first World Festival of Negro Art and Culture, Mbiti contributed a study on African oral literature,[3] and a decade later, for the second Festival, he was to add a study of African cosmology.[4] Nearly sixty of the entries in the *Oxford African Encyclopaedia*[5] are owed to him. It is consistent with such a varied literary output that well before he attained middle age,[6] Mbiti had, deservedly, gained "an international reputation as the leading African theologian",[7] and it is not going too far to suggest that his appointment in 1972 to the Directorship of the World Council of Churches Ecumenical Institute in Céligny, Switzerland, was perhaps a measure of his stature as a theologian in the wider

Christian world.[8]

In common with other theological writers in modern Africa, Mbiti shares the concern to affirm the integrity of an African point of view in religious apprehension where it has been underestimated or despised in Africa's missionary history. His numerous writings on African Traditional Religion establish this position beyond any shadow of doubt. But what Mbiti brings to this task is a profoundly settled Christian self-consciousness which makes his vindication of African religious values free from anti-European polemic. Though he would himself criticise "mission Christianity" for its failure to penetrate "sufficiently deep into African religiosity",[9] nevertheless, the subject of missionary errors and misconceptions concerning African religious life figures less prominently in Mbiti's work than in the writings of some other African theologians. In 1974 Mbiti was lamenting that "when African Christians take the microphone on the Church platform, they exhaust themselves with harping on the ills and mistakes caused by missionaries or Western Churches".[10]

As one whose Christian commitment provides the essential focus of his own self-understanding,[11] Mbiti does not invest the *Problematik* of Christianity in Africa, its allegedly "alien" character, with an overriding importance.[12] This does not mean that he fails to perceive the serious implications of the heavily Western bias in the nature of Christian understanding imparted to African converts.[13] Rather, Mbiti considers that "historically, Christianity is very much an African religion".[14] So far as Mbiti is concerned, Christianity's deep roots "in the history of our continent"[15] (even if only in parts of it), prior to the massive invasion of "the third opportunity", is a fact of great significance for an adequate understanding of the fortunes of the Christian faith in Africa. For it means that there is a sense in which the success of the modern missionary enterprise of the nineteenth and twentieth centuries may be seen as the fuller establishing of what, after all, "can rightly be described as an indigenous, traditional and African religion."[16] In other words, the European connections of the Christian presence in Africa in the more recent phase of its development, must not be overstated. Instead, due weight ought to be given also to the African antecedents and participation, in order to do justice to the place and significance of the Christian faith in African life.

But over and above the historical argument, Mbiti points to African confession of the Christian faith on its own terms. Very early in modern African Christian history, as if to parallel the ancient history, some Christian communities produced their martyrs, such as "among the Baganda and the Gikuyu as well as isolated individuals all over Africa who have a Faith for which they died or are prepared to die if need be".[17] It cannot be seriously maintained that these African Christian martyrs bore witness to an "alien" religion.

The same concern to vindicate the integrity of African Christian consciousness and experience is seen in Mbiti's attitude to the Independent Church movement in Africa. Mbiti is not an unreserved admirer of the African Independent Churches,[18] and yet he finds in them the outworking of a spiritual principle which he will himself seek to establish. To the extent that these churches are significant as "protest churches" – that is, protest against the domination which "has shown itself on the African scene in many forms: colonial, ecclesiastical, social, theological, cultural and administrative"[19] – they represent a massive African rejection of imported and imposed forms of the Christian life. At the same time, they bear witness to the fact that "African peoples have taken seriously to Christianity".[20] And Mbiti, in the expectation that the Independent Churches, in course of time, will not be "as far apart from the historical Churches as they are at present",[21] looks forward to the prospect of an African Christianity moulded and determined not by European and North American models of Christianity, but by the questions and the issues thrown up by the African context itself, as well as by the internal life of the African Church.

As an extension of the same concern, Mbiti makes a distinction between Christianity on the one hand, and the Christian Faith or the Gospel, on the other. Christianity, which "results from the encounter of the Gospel with any given local or regional community/society" is always indigenous and, by definition, culture-bound. The Gospel, on the other hand, is "God-given", eternal, and does not change.[22] Consequently, although Mbiti has spoken in a few places of the need to "africanise" and "indigenise" Christianity,[23] he soon comes to consider the very idea of the indigenisation of Christianity as less meaningful and even positively misleading:[24]

"To speak of 'indigenising Christianity' is to give the impression that Christianity is a ready made commodity which has to be transplanted to a local area. Of course, this has been the assumption followed by many missionaries and local theologians. I do not accept it any more."[25]

In rejecting the concept of the "indigenisation of Christianity", Mbiti rejects also the related idea of the "indigenisation of theology"; for theology is always indigenous, resulting from the effort to articulate the meaning of the Gospel in a particular cultural milieu in response to the realities of that milieu. But it is important to realise that what Mbiti is hereby seeking to establish is an essentially spiritual principle, and one which will consistently underpin the way he handles his theological concerns. In essence, that principle is the freedom of the African Christian conscience to define and formulate its own apprehension of the Christian faith, not only in terms of the positive content of the faith itself, but also in relation to the religious needs and aspirations of the African background and context. Elsewhere, Mbiti has observed that one aspect of the significance of the Independent Church movement in Africa is that these churches point to a way in which African Christians seek to "be or remain authentically African while at the same time being ecclesiastically universal".[26] In a profound sense, the statement applies also to Mbiti's own theological outlook, and to the outworking of his chosen theological agenda.

We shall presently examine the content of Mbiti's theological thinking. However, it is worth noting here that there may well be a parallel between the centrality of the principle of spiritual freedom as the condition for a creative African theology, and Mbiti's personal history, leading from his early upbringing in the Church of the Africa Inland Mission (the Africa Inland Church) into membership of, and ordination in, the Anglican Communion.[27] Finding that the AIM's lack of adequate rootage in a wider Christian history was compounded by a defective Christian fellowship and an absence of "a concrete theology" to deal with vital questions thrown up by the Christian presence in the African context, Mbiti chose to take leave of an atmosphere in which he felt unable to profess and experience the liberating faith in Christ. Within the world-wide communion of Anglicanism, Mbiti believes that he found catholicity, historicity and apostolicity.[28] One thing about which he had no doubt, was that the Gospel had been preached by the AIM; the weakness of that proclamation, however, consisted in its lack of serious encounter with the African religious heritage and social reality. The effect of this weakness in missionary proclamation on the theological development of the emergent Church, in

Mbiti's view, would be far-reaching, as he was eventually to indicate, applying the conclusion to African missionary history as a
whole:

"The missionaries who began this modern phase of Christian
expansion in Africa, together with their African helpers, were
devout, sincere and dedicated men and women. But they were
not theologians... These workers were more concerned with
practical evangelism, education and medical care, than with
any academic or theological issues that might arise from the
presence of Christianity in Africa. Mission Christianity was not
from the start prepared to face a serious encounter with either
the traditional religions and philosophy, or the modern changes
taking place in Africa. The Church here now finds itself in the
situation of trying to exist without a theology."[29]

Hinted at here is an important element in Mbiti's theological
agenda, namely, his concern that the communication of the Gospel
should manifest a cultural appropriation of it in African terms.
What this implies is that since theological self-consciousness is an
essential mark of the Church in any cultural context, a Church
which is "trying to exist without a theology" is an anomaly, and
indicates its uncertainty regarding its own self-understanding and
its own identity. In this connection, Mbiti's principle of spiritual
freedom acquires special significance. For what it implies above all
is the freedom to discern one's own questions, to formulate those
questions and to seek the appropriate answers to them, and to do
it all in the freedom of the Gospel. The kind of issues that Mbiti's
work highlights, together with his manner of responding to them,
exemplifies to a high degree, this principle of freedom in theology.
Whilst all African theologians exhibit in their work varying
degrees of Christian self-consciousness, none, perhaps, gives so
clear an indication that his theology grows out of his sense of joy
in the experience of the Christian faith.[30] It is therefore not surprising that, for Mbiti, the quest for an African theology is rooted in
the very process whereby the African Church communicates the
Gospel in the context of African existence.

II. Toward an African Theology (1): Speaking the
Gospel "in our local language"

Johannes Verkuyl has rightly noted in his *Contemporary Missiology:*

"It goes without saying that African theology does all the things
which theology in general does, but in African theology (as in

Asian) all these other functions are embraced in the missionary or communicative function. It is not primarily an intra-
ecclesiastical exercise, but a discipline whose practitioners
keep one question central: How can we best do our theology
so that the Gospel will touch Africans most deeply?"[31]

Much as this "communicative function" of theology is acknowledged and stressed by virtually all African theological writers, it
is Mbiti who seems to have gone farthest in making it a major
theological preoccupation. His many articles and essays on the
encounter of the Christian faith with African culture can be interpreted as having this one, all-embracing purpose: to discover and
set forth the most effective and appropriate ways in which the
Gospel of Jesus Christ may find deeper rootage in African religious
and cultural consciousness. Furthermore, the special merit of
Mbiti's approach to the subject is that he conceives of the communicative or missionary activity of the African Church as the very
process through which an "African Theology" will develop.

This viewpoint emerges quite clearly in a paper Mbiti presented
on "The Ways and Means of communicating the Gospel", at the 7th
International African Seminar, held in April 1965 at Accra,
Ghana.[32] It is not necessary for our purposes to rehearse the details
of the presentation. Our interest is simply to follow through the
argumentation which Mbiti employs to establish the claims of an
African theological viewpoint as arising from the experience of the
African Church.

That Mbiti introduced questions affecting an African theological approach and interpretation into a paper which might have
been limited simply to the "strategy of evangelism"[33] in Africa, was
perhaps, significant. At least, from Prof. Baëta's account of the
proceedings, Mbiti's use of the term "African theology" and his
advocacy on behalf of what it should entail, caused something of a
stir.[34] And yet, Mbiti was only suggesting that the "Gospel which
remains basically the same for all time" had to be communicated
in terms that were meaningful to African perception of African
needs:

"As on the day of Pentecost, the Gospel should be presented in
such a way that each person will hear it in his 'own language'.
We must now search for ways and means of communicating the
Gospel to make it intelligible to its hearers, and to bring out its
true depth effectively."[35]

Though Mbiti was obviously interested in the Church's communication to those who, for all practical purposes, were on the "outside", it soon becomes clear that he was just as concerned with those who were "inside", and it is here that his major emphasis seems to fall. His overriding concern appears to be how the Gospel is communicated within and to the African Church whose responsibility it is not only to *proclaim* the Gospel, but also to *embody* it:

> "The Church as the Body of Christ is herself the living channel, *par excellence*, of communicating the Gospel. Not only does she teach and proclaim the Gospel, but she is the embodiment of that Gospel; and her voice goes forth not only in audible words but in her very existence and life. As she makes her numerical expansion and spiritual growth, the Gospel is being proclaimed and communicated. She cannot be severed from her message, and neither can that message become meaningful except within the embrace of the Church."[36]

This stress on the Christian community as the essential bearer of the Gospel has important implications for Mbiti's entire approach. For instance, it helps to explain why he makes the rather puzzling distinction between "preaching" and "teaching".[37] Whereas "preaching" implies a certain degree of aloofness from the hearers, this is not felt to be the case with "teaching". At least, an explanation in this direction is suggested by Mbiti's reference to "our Lord" who not only preached but also "*taught*... especially those who followed Him, in order to make the people understand what He came to accomplish".[38] Accordingly, the theology developed in the very process of communicating the Gospel simply becomes the logical corollary to theological knowledge within the Christian community. What Mbiti seems to be saying, therefore, is that effective communication of the Gospel (by the Christian community) presupposes a properly *theological* awareness on the part of the communicators, who need to have an adequate and intelligent apprehension of the "true depth" of the Gospel.

The point of the emphasis on the Church becomes even clearer when Mbiti argues that since "by her very nature, the Church is a corporate Body", evangelisation must operate "in the context of our [African] corporate community life", the point being that it is in terms of the social structure of African existence-in-community that the Gospel of salvation is to be communicated in the context of African life.

Accordingly:

> "If we want him [the African] 'saved', then he must be allowed

to bring with him into the Body of Christ all his many relatives. African traditional religions are not compartmentalised areas of life: they are incorporated into the whole life of the people. If the ultimate goal of preaching and accepting the Gospel is to transpose allegiance from tribal religions to the Lord Jesus Christ, then the process of transposition should be entire and not partial, radical and not casual."[39]

In other words, the proclamation of the Gospel must create community comparable to the old, even if the basis of allegiance is different. The important thing is that the resultant community is seen to answer to the longings implied in the "old". Indeed, as the transference of allegiance is made from one set of symbols to another, the process does not entail a complete denunciation of the "old". On the contrary, as the "old" meanings find fulfilment in the "new", the new meanings are, in turn, understood in terms of the aspirations brought from the "old".[40] Theological consciousness grows as part of the interplay of this dialectic, reflecting the aspirations of the heritage from the "old" now realised in the new realities which therefore provide the anchorage for a new identity. The Church as the community of the redeemed, especially in its sacramental life, supersedes the "old" kinship group, not by way of obliteration, but rather, by way of fulfilment. We are quite close to another favourite theme in Mbiti's writings, and one which recurs frequently: the Christian Gospel, far from being opposed to African religious ideas is, in fact, the crowning fulfilment of African religiosity.

"We must therefore seek to make the Church the centre of existence from which African peoples may derive the fulfilment of their life's aspiration whether in time of need or in time of feasting, and where they may experience a communal life which has a vaster scope and meaning than tribal life without Christ could ever provide... The Church will become for them a community in which their corporate aspirations are not destroyed but fulfilled and intensified, in which tribal foundations are not simply shaken and replaced with a vacuum but are made more secure in Christ. The God who made man and provides him with children, life and rain, will now become man's light, and man will have fellowship with his Creator.

"In this way... Jesus Christ will so confront the peoples of Africa, that in Him and through Him they will find access to God whom they already acknowledge in their traditional ideas to be the Creator of all things, as the One who strengthens kinship between man and man, and the One who established kinship between man and God. In this manner, this eternal Gospel of the Incarnation will begin to accommodate itself in the African environment, making its challenges felt and its promises realised."[41]

From the statements above, it is evident that for Mbiti the terms in which the Gospel is communicated and the kind of theological approach and idiom which result from such communication, are very closely linked. Consequently, if the African Church is largely bereft of theological consciousness,[42] part at least of the explanation may be that the Church's communication of the Gospel is "in a foreign language". He reiterated this viewpoint when, in 1970, as Head of the Department of Religious Studies and Philosophy at Makerere University, Kampala (Uganda), he addressed leaders of the (Anglican) Church of Uganda, Rwanda and Burundi:

"We cannot effectively carry out mission in a foreign language. Just as missionaries from overseas had to learn our languages... so must we put mission in a language which makes sense to those whom we missionise. In other words, we have to sing the Gospel in our tunes, set to our music, played on our instruments. I speak metaphorically. We must drum it out with our great drums, on our tom-toms, on our waist-shaped drums, for only these can vibrate and awaken entire villages: the violin is too feeble to awaken the sleeping pagans of our society..."[43]

For all his insistence on the necessity to set forth the Gospel and African experience of it in unmistakeably African idiom, derived from African inspiration, Mbiti is aware that an African theology cannot be produced to order, and he said as much in 1965:

"We cannot artificially create an 'African theology' or even plan it; it must evolve spontaneously as the Church teaches and lives her Faith and in response to the extremely complex situation in Africa. It may well happen that there will not be one but several types of African theology, which, if it is of value, must be another expression of the theology of the Universal Church."[44]

And yet, by arguing that the African Church should reflect *theologically* on its evangelistic activity, Mbiti moves the discussion about "African Theology" in a direction which, hitherto, has not been explored. The clue to his approach must surely be his consistent distinction between the phenomenon of Christianity – especially in its cultural embodiment as the missionary religion brought to Africa – and the Christian Faith. This distinction also helps to explain Mbiti's generally positive evaluation of the connection between the Christian Gospel and African culture.[45] For it means that since it is the Christian Faith rather than European Christianity as such which fulfils the aspirations and intentions implied in Africa's indigenous cultures,[46] the task of constructing an African theology on the basis of African experience and communication of the Christian Faith can proceed without anxiety or self-justification. It is entirely consistent with this viewpoint that, on another occasion, mindful of the controversy surrounding not only the form and content of "African Theology", but even the possibility of its development, Mbiti should cut through the debate and use the term "without apology or embarrassment, to mean theological reflection and expression by African Christians".[47]

The position that Mbiti has thus maintained on the whole question of "African Theology" is of the utmost importance for assessing his true significance in modern African Christian thought. Moreover, it stamps his writings with a feeling of freedom which in the context of the quest by African theologians for an appropriate sense of identity, is quite remarkable.[48] It is particularly interesting, for example, that the vindication of an African theological point of view, reflecting African cultural sensitivities, which Idowu affirms largely as a concomitant of African religious self-consciousness generally, is defended by Mbiti on the basis of African Christian experience itself. The difference in approach is seen in Mbiti's readiness to take up themes which belong more closely within the mainstream of wider Christian tradition.[49]

Nevertheless, Mbiti, like his colleague Idowu, remains preeminently an exponent of the African theological viewpoint and an interpreter of the religious experience which goes to inform it. It is true that in Mbiti, the Christian insistence becomes more pronounced; but it is this fact itself which makes his approach to the African pre-Christian heritage all the more interesting and significant.

III. Toward an African Theology (2): The pre-Christian heritage as *Praeparatio Evangelica*

In concluding his *New Testament Eschatology in an African Background*,[50] Mbiti revealed what he considered to have been "one of the intentions" of the study, namely, "to raise the question regarding Christian Theology in Africa".[51] After discussing the views and expectations of several writers on the subject, Mbiti lists and expatiates briefly on four areas of engagement which he saw as fundamental in the production of such Theology. The first area named is Biblical Theology. In Mbiti's view, this "must be the basis of any theological reflection, otherwise we shall lose our perspectives and may not claim the outcome to be Christian theology".[52] Secondly, Mbiti names "Christian Theology from the major traditions of Christendom", which he considers essential for providing African theologians with their way into "the mainstream of ecumenical and apostolic heritage", and into "The Catholicity of the Church".[53] With respect both to Biblical Theology and to the theology from the major traditions of Christendom, Mbiti insists that the rich heritage from Christian tradition be understood and translated into the African milieu, and so be made relevant to the Church in Africa.

Whilst Mbiti obviously placed a high value on the two areas named, it was the third and fourth, in fact, to which he looked for "a uniquely African contribution to Christian theology at large".[54] These comprised a study of African Religions and Philosophy – in other words, the pre-Christian traditions of Africa in religion and thought – in dialogue with the Christian message as embodied in Christ Himself, and what Mbiti calls the "Theology of the living Church", that is, the actual life and experience of African Christian communities.[55] It is particularly interesting that in a work which focuses a great deal of attention on the New Testament world of ideas in their own terms, Mbiti already points the way to what will become his growing concern with the specifically *African* dimensions of the problem of Christian theology in Africa.

In course of time, Mbiti has come to consider two areas of African reality which he had not previously articulated clearly, namely, African culture and African history, as equally significant "sources of theological development in Africa".[56] Mbiti has not had much to say generally about African history. However, it is understandable that Mbiti should regard African history as theologically significant when it is realised that what he has in mind is the nature of the experience that has, for a long time, shaped African societies, and which continues to determine the contemporary African scene – largely a history of the experience of suffering, exploitation and liberation.[57] But behind the equally increased interest in culture, there lies, in fact, Mbiti's long-standing distinction between Christianity – conceived of as a social and cultural embodiment of the Gospel – and the Christian Faith. What this insistence on culture means is that the cultural embodiment of the Christian Faith in the African milieu is a subject for study in its own right, and not simply as cultural reaction to missionary imposition of European forms of Christianity. His most important treatment is provided by the two articles: "African Indigenous Culture in relation to Evangelism and Church Development"[58] and "Christianity and Culture in Africa".[59]

The first of these two studies represents the finest attempt by an African theological writer to articulate a theology of culture as applied to African life. After showing how early missionary attempts to evangelise African societies by ignoring or despising their cultures created problems not only for evangelisation, but also in the African Christian conscience, Mbiti goes on to examine some of the ways in which the Gospel might in fact be interpreted as the fulfilment of African cultural values and so be brought into fruitful contact with them to the benefit of African expression of the Faith. The concept of fulfilment, as Mbiti employs it, is taken from H. Richard Niebuhr's classic treatment of the variety of ways in which Christ might be related to human cultural values and ideals.[60] Thus part of Mbiti's argument involves a reversal of the earlier derogatory assessment of African culture and an inclusion of Africa in the general theory that Christ is the fulfiller of all human cultures. However, Mbiti does not rest the case in such general terms; he seeks to demonstrate such fulfilment by pointing to elements in African tradition, particularly in religion, which seem to anticipate dimensions of the Christian life and the Christian understanding of reality, though, in his view, earlier opportunities in this direction were missed:

"It is my contention that, even though officially Christianity either disregarded African religion altogether, or treated it as an enemy, it was in fact African religion more than anything else, which laid down the foundation and prepared the ground for the eventual rapid accommodation of Christianity in Africa, and for the present rapid growth of the Church in our continent. Without African religiosity, whatever its defects might be, Christianity would have taken much longer to be understood and accommodated by African peoples..."[61]

Mbiti then proceeds to give specific examples which indicate the extent to which the "new" reality of the Christian Faith was in fact in continuum with dimensions of African tradition, highlighting the African celebration of life and the corporate sense of existence:

"For example, African religion is deeply celebrational of life, and this keynote of celebration could have been incorporated into Church development thus making it unnecessary, ultimately, for so many of African Christians to revert to traditional methods of celebrating life. Indeed the Christian Faith is one of joy, and it is a great pity that Christian joy is suppressed among peoples who otherwise approach life celebrationally. Another example where African religiosity would have lent itself readily to Church development is its communality and corporateness. African religion and social life lay great emphasis on communal welfare, values, concerns, and kinship, both horizontally and vertically (to include the departed). On the whole evangelism has presented Christianity on an individualist basis, making individualistic appeals, and the development of the Church has tended to ignore the community dimensions of the Church's existence and concerns. This aspect of Church development is, however, beginning to be remedied in some countries of Africa, and is fairly evident in the Independent Churches."[62]

Through these wistful intimations of what "could have been", it is possible to form an impression of what the theological task within the Church in Africa ought to be. Mbiti himself had stated this in unmistakeable terms in an article published two years earlier in which he discussed the future prospects of the Traditional Religions in Africa and their implications for Christian theology in Africa:

"The number of full adherents of the Traditional Religions in Africa by AD 2000 will be almost negligible. In their traditional settings these religions will have dwindled numerically though not in their beliefs, but they will have bequeathed to Christianity some of the riches of African traditional religiosity. As such, Christianity will have become an agent of fulfilment in the sense that it will not destroy Traditional Religions as such, but it will have superseded them by bringing into them other dimensions of religion which they lack and which are not opposed to the traditional religiosity. *In missiological jargon, these Traditional Religions will have been a real 'praeparatio evangelica' (preparation for the Gospel); and it is now up to African theologians to interpret the meaning of that preparation for the Gospel, in the African context of not only the past but* today and tomorrow. "[63]

In this significant statement Mbiti reveals the fundamental rationale which underpins virtually his entire theological output. Furthermore, Mbiti had already begun to publish works which would become influential contributions towards this comprehensive synthesis of Africa's pre-Christian and Christian traditions, indicating, perhaps, that this perception of the African theological task must have answered to a fairly early intuition. *African Religion and Philosophy* had been published in 1969, and the following year was to see the publication of *Concepts of God in Africa*. It is perhaps significant that *New Testament Eschatology in an African Background*, the substance of his Cambridge doctoral thesis of 1963, was first published only in 1971. A few years later, in 1974, Mbiti's *corpus* on African Traditional Religion was augmented by *Prayers of African Religion*. Before we examine the contribution of this "trilogy" to Mbiti's theological aim, it is worth appreciating the significance of this concern with the meaning of Africa's pre-Christian religious heritage.

It is not hard to understand what was happening; if the nature and theological meaning of the pre-Christian heritage was to form such a major part of the African theologian's agenda, he could not possibly derive his models from a Western theological reflection which, on the whole, had little to say of positive value about African tradition.[64] The point is not that Western theology was intrinsically of no use to the African theologian *qua* Christian theologian. Rather, for the kind of task which the African context now pressed upon Africa's theologians, the traditional models of Western theological training offered little assistance. A.F. Walls has expressed succinctly what this meant. Commenting on the agenda of Africa's theologians of Mbiti's generation, he observes:

> "Each... was trained in theology on a Western model; but each has moved into an area for which no Western syllabus prepared him, for each has been forced to study and lecture on African traditional religion – and each has found himself writing on it."[65]

It is obvious that in "moving" from New Testament Theology into the area of African Traditional Religion, Mbiti, like other African theologians who have made similar shifts,[66] was entering a field which had been hitherto, at least from the standpoint of Western scholarship, the hunting-ground of anthropology, not theology.[67] Thus, the task of giving a theological interpretation to the pre-Christian African heritage must often involve translating anthropological material concerning African societies into theological terms and categories. Much of the controversy surrounding the possibility of an "African theology" explored from such a perspective, and the value attached to the theological meanings thus given to African Traditional Religion, will relate to this important circumstance which attended modern African theology at its birth. It is a sign of the extent to which Mbiti's work answered to the expectations and needs of a sizeable proportion of African educated opinion, that his books soon became standard textbooks for the teaching of African Traditional Religion all over the continent.[68]

In writing *African Religions and Philosophy*, Mbiti was in fact expanding on lectures to his students, both at Makerere University College, Uganda (as it was then), and at Hamburg University in West Germany, where he taught during the academic year 1966-67. Very early in the book, Mbiti acknowledge that he was probably venturing forth as an innovator:

"Our written knowledge of traditional religions is comparatively little, though increasing, and comes chiefly from anthropologists and sociologists. Practically nothing has been produced by theologians, describing or interpreting these religions theologically."[69]

But if one expects to find in *African Religions and Philosophy* a treatment in depth of the particular and complex religious traditions found all over Africa, one will be looking in the wrong place, for it was not the author's intention to provide such a study, and he says as much:

"In this study I have emphasised the unity of African religions and philosophy in order to give an overall picture of their situation. This approach does not give room for the treatment in depth of individual religious and philosophical systems of different African peoples. There is an increasing number of monographs coming out through which this aspect of study is being met, and I do not feel it necessary to duplicate the work when so many other fields remain scarcely harvested. I have therefore chosen to highlight both similarities and differences considering the African picture as a whole. For this reason, I have drawn examples from all over Africa, both making general observations and giving detailed illustrations."[70]

The strength of the book, however, seems to consist in the

author's perspective on the subject. For what Mbiti does is to draw on the relevant available ethnographic data on various African societies across the continent, to give a descriptive and interpretative study of African peoples through their philosophical worldviews and religious ideals and practices. Taking the view that "religion permeates into all departments of (African) life so fully that it is not easy or possible always to isolate it", Mbiti posits the methodological principle that "a study of these religious systems is therefore, ultimately, a study of the peoples themselves in all the complexities of both traditional and modern life".[71] And the merit of the book may well lie in Mbiti's perception of the close connection between the religious concepts and practices which he discusses and the peoples whose religious lives embody them.

When *African Religions and Philosophy* is seen from this angle, its true character becomes apparent. The work is not intended to examine the religious belief-systems of African societies for their own sake, or in abstraction from the overall developments within these societies. Indeed, a cursory glance at the chapter titles confirms that the author is not discussing religious systems at all, but rather themes in the religious lives of African societies. It is hard to see how a work which deals with not only "the worship of God" and the nature of "spiritual beings", but also "marriage and procreation" and "changing man and his problems", as well as modern secular ideologies, can be said to "reduce African religions to a set of 'doctrines' analogous in structure to Western faiths".[72] It seems more accurate to regard *African Religions and Philosophy* as seeking to approximate a religious history of African societies taken together as a cultural unit within mankind. The preponderance of material relating to so-called "traditional" Africa (as against Christian and Muslim Africa) is legitimate since it indicates what constitutes the main *substratum* of later developments in African religious tradition. It also means that the inclusion of Christianity, Islam and other religions in the treatment is justified, for they too flow into the overall history of African religion. Mbiti is therefore right to stress that "both Christianity and Islam are 'traditional' and 'African' in a historical sense, and it is a pity that they tend to be regarded as 'foreign' or 'European' and 'Arab'."[73]

In the final analysis, Mbiti's interpretative key is determined by his own theological commitment, which is Christian, and motivated by the thesis that all the religious traditions of Africa

other than the Christian, constitute, in their highest ideals, a
praeparatio evangelica. This emerges quite clearly in the closing
chapter, in which Mbiti attempts to evaluate the relative positions
of the various major traditions – Traditional Religions, Christianity and Islam – as well as the place of religion in general, in
modern Africa. Convinced that "the religious traditions of Africa
contain the only lasting potentialities for a basis, a foundation and
a direction of life for African societies",[74] it is through what the
Christian Faith offers that he thinks the African quest for identity
and "the freedom... of mature manhood and selfhood are at-
tainable".[75] And in what follows, the theory of *praeparatio evangelica* which initially serves to integrate the pre-Christian heritage
into present Christian self-consciousness, becomes also a basis for
affirming the validity of the Christian commitment for the present
as well as the future. The passage is so significant that we quote
it *in extenso*:

"In this schema of things, Christianity which is also
'indigenous', 'traditional' and 'African' like the other major
religious systems considered here, holds the greatest and the
only potentialities of meeting the dilemmas and challenges of
modern Africa, and of reaching the full integration and manhood of individuals and communities. It is highly doubtful that,
even at their very best, these other religious systems and
ideologies current in Africa are saying anything radically new
to, and different from, what is already embedded in Christianity. And yet, the strength and uniqueness of Christianity
do not lie in the fact that its teaching, practice and history have
all the major elements of the other religious traditions. The
uniqueness of Christianity is in Jesus Christ. He is the stumbling block of all ideologies and religious systems; and even if
some of His teaching may overlap with what they teach and
proclaim, His own Person is greater than can be contained in a
religion or ideology. He is the 'Man for others' and yet beyond
them. It is He, therefore, and only He, who deserves to be the
goal and standard for individuals and mankind, and whether
they attain that ultimate goal religiously or ideologically is
perhaps irrelevant. Attainment of that full stature and maximum identity demands that reference be made to an external,
absolute and timeless denominator. And this is precisely what
Christianity should offer beyond, and in spite of, its own
anachronisms and divisions in Africa. *I consider traditional
religions, Islam and the other religious systems to be
preparatory and even essential ground in the search for the*

Ultimate. But only Christianity has the terrible responsibility of pointing the way to that Ultimate Identity, Foundation and Source of security."[76]

If *African Religions and Philosophy* is an attempt to provide an "ontological" framework[77] within which the history of African religious experience finds a coherence – fully achieved only in relation to Jesus Christ – *Concepts of God in Africa* elaborates on one dimension of that experience, namely, "African reflection about God".[78] The two books are also closely connected in their production, in that *Concepts of God in Africa* was completed in the course of Mbiti's lectureship at the Theological Faculty of Hamburg University in the academic year 1966-67 – a period which, as we have noted, had an influence on the writing of *African Religions and Philosophy*. Furthermore, from the references made in *African Religions and Philosophy* to *Concepts of God in Africa*, it seems obvious that what the author has sought to do in this latter work, is to provide a more detailed study of the evidence which informs some of the conclusions he has drawn in the more general treatment in *African Religions and Philosophy*.[79]

By stating at the outset that "African peoples are not religiously illiterate",[80] Mbiti indicates quite clearly what the book is meant to achieve. From an impressive collection of information from no less than 270 different societies all across Africa, Mbiti provides a systematic study of the African pre-Christian experience and knowledge of God contained in African wisdom sayings, myths, ritual pronouncements and prayers. Perhaps no other work of Mbiti's shows so evidently the impact both of his own Christian commitment as an African scholar, and his Christian theological training; these elements of background are employed to admirable effect in *Concepts of God in Africa*. Accordingly, when he describes the attributes of God in African experience, Mbiti feels quite free to use terms and categories which are standard usage in Western Christian theological discussion, like "omniscience", "omnipotence", "omnipresence", "immanence" and similar concepts. But the use of these "classical" terms serves rather than dominates the material, and much of the book retains an anecdotal flavour that reflects the kinds of source-material which lie behind Mbiti's systematisation. As Mbiti proceeds by allowing various African peoples to speak for themselves through the available documentation, *Concepts of God in Africa* becomes a massive store of information; the list of African peoples, with their countries and names for God, at the end of the main body of the book, adds a further usefulness to the work.

The significance of *Concepts of God in Africa* lies in the fact that the author does not seek to *prove* the pre-Christian African knowledge of God; Mbiti offers no apology for suggesting that many of the African concepts bear striking resemblance to Biblical ideas, "particularly those of the Old Testament".[81] Several African societies speak of God as "Creator",[82] "Father" (and Grandfather), and a few as "Mother" and "Friend", while some understand themselves to be "Children of God".[83] Behind countless simple acts and expressions, especially in relation to worship,[84] there seems to lie the evidence for Mbiti's contention that religion is probably the most profound and the richest part of the cultural heritage of African peoples.[85] Mbiti is aware that African pre-Christian religion rarely manifests itself in creeds or formal definitions of "Faith". But for him, the evidence is overwhelming that:

> "African peoples are not spiritually illiterate, but the word 'faith' in its technical sense seems something foreign to them. To assert, however, that they have 'no faith' in God, would be absolute nonsense, and there are no atheists in traditional African societies. An Ashanti proverb seems to summarise the situation well; it says, 'No one shows a child the Supreme Being', because even the child knows of God almost automatically by instinct."[86]

Perhaps the finest illustration of Mbiti's consistently positive evaluation of African religious tradition as *praeparatio evangelica* is given in *The Prayers of African Religion*. As in the case of *Concepts of God in Africa*, Mbiti draws upon literary sources in the main, and so does not seek to achieve originality by introducing hitherto unrecorded prayers. The merit of his work lies elsewhere. For what Mbiti has said about the study of Africa's traditional religions generally, holds particularly in relation to the subject of prayer; whereas prayers used in African pre-Christian religious life have been recorded, these prayers have not been seriously interpreted theologically.[87] Thus, with the addition of a lengthy and useful introduction, and appropriate commentaries and notes providing essential background to the 300 prayer texts assembled, Mbiti transforms a work of compilation into a major account and presentation of African spirituality.

It is important for Mbiti that the majority of the prayers preserve religious traditions which date from well "before the penetration of Christianity into the interior of Africa".[88] For this means that the overwhelming theism of the prayers[89] constitutes a significant corrective to the more widespread assumption about the African sense of God, held by European interpreters of Africa in their earlier contacts with African peoples.[90] Thus, without polemical engagement, Mbiti is able to let the evidence of the prayer literature of African societies speak for itself; the result is a veritable psalter, covering a wide variety of occasions in life, a collection of the spiritual riches of the African religious tradition, and a worthy foundation for, and integral element of, African Christian spirituality.[91] Mbiti states such a viewpoint quite explicitly in his Charles Strong Memorial Lecture of 1978, which was devoted to the subject of African prayer and spirituality.[92] Quoting the words of a traditional prayer of the Pygmies of Zaire celebrating God as Spirit – words formulated long before the coming of the Christian Faith to their society[93] – Mbiti once again finds in the religious experience of pre-Christian Africa, evidence for considering Africa's heritage in religion as a preparation for the Christian Gospel in African religious history:

> "In the beginning was Khmvoum (God)
> Today is Khmvoum,
> Tomorrow will be Khmvoum.
> Who can make an image of Khmvoum?
> He has no body.
> He is as a word which comes out of your mouth.
> That word! It is no more. It is past and still it lives!
> So is Khmvoum."

And Mbiti comments significantly:

> "This vision takes us to great heights of human spirituality. *As a Christian I say Amen to this prayer. Amen.*"[94]

With regard to the three major works which form Mbiti's *corpus* on African Religion, there is without doubt a sense of movement and a sharpening of focus from *African Religions and Philosophy*, to *Concepts of God in Africa*, and finally to *The Prayers of African Religion*. It is in the subject-matter of the third book, that Mbiti considers one should look for "the most intense expression of African traditional spirituality".[95] For it is here in this "valuable dimension... of African religion... the core of African spirituality"[96] – in the yearning for holiness, purity and cleanliness of heart, in the pervasive sense of dependence, faith, trust and confidence in God, and in the immense capacity for joy and thanksgiving[97] – that perhaps the real *praeparatio evangelica* in African tradition lies.[98] If this is the case, then so much else that Mbiti's extensive writings contain can be placed in clearer perspective.

EXCURSUS: "The African Concept of Time" and its Implications

Perhaps no item in Mbiti's writings is better known, and consequently more commented upon, than his exposition of what he called "the African concept of time". The entire third chapter of *African Religions and Philosophy* is devoted to the subject. More important still, Mbiti focused on the concept of time as the basic intellectual framework for interpreting African life, though he seemed also to be aware of its limitations:

> "My approach in this book is to treat religion as an ontological phenomenon, with the concept of time as the key to reaching some understanding of African religions and philosophy. I do not pretend that the notion of time explains everything, but I am convinced that it adds to our understanding of the subject..."[99]

How Mbiti suggests that "the African concept of time" helps in understanding the African world-view and interpretation of reality, we shall come to presently. For the moment, it is only fair to recognise that he went on to write about the subject in several other contexts to an extent that helps explain the volley of reactions which it has attracted.[100] But to get the whole subject in perspective, it is worth noting that Mbiti's exposition of "the African concept of time" and related themes like "hope", "history" and "the hereafter", is rarely independent of his efforts to articulate also the sort of differentia – religious and social – which, in his view, the Christian Faith has introduced into African life. Ultimately, these come to centre on Christ and Christology, as we shall soon show. In view of this overriding theological purpose, and particularly, of this Christocentric emphasis, it is clear that the purely "temporal" aspect of the subject, as an abstract philosophical problem, is not what has interested Mbiti. It is not surprising, therefore, that in a discussion of eschatology in relation to Christian mission a few years ago, Mbiti dissented from the view that "eschatology provides the basis and impetus for early Christian missionary activity" and that it is "eschatology that provides the crucial part of the continuity between the early mission and that in the twentieth century".[101] Mbiti urged instead that "both mission and eschatology acquire new meaning and impetus from the Christology of the New

Testament".[102] Such a statement indicates that it is misleading to approach Mbiti's thinking on the subject of time as though he was primarily concerned with the technical question of time-scales.

Once it is granted that Mbiti's interest in the subject of time answers to his theological presuppositions about the significance of the Christian Gospel for Africa, then the important question becomes what place "the African concept of time" has in his overall theological thinking. It is my contention that the concept, in its technical sense, has a lesser place in Mbiti's theological thinking than is suggested by its apparent prominence in his published pronouncements and writings. In other words, Mbiti's theory of an "African concept of time" fulfils a *negative* function in his theology, and belongs to the background, rather than the foreground of his thinking.[103]

Francis Gillies is probably right to draw attention to the fact that since Mbiti's "detailed research into the nature of African time has been confined to the Bantu... it is more accurate to describe his research findings as pertaining to Bantu concepts of time".[104] Indeed, Mbiti himself is often at pains to point out that an important aspect of his theory, namely, the linguistic argument from the tense-pattern of African languages, derives essentially from "East African languages to which I have been exposed",[105] particularly Kikamba and Gikuyu.[106] Furthermore, the proper roots of Mbiti's concern with the concept of time are located in the research findings which provided the material for *New Testament Eschatology in an African Background*.[107] This brings us to the recognition that the fundamental issue concerning time in Mbiti's thinking, has to do with the effect of Christian missionary proclamation on "traditional" Africa; it is doubtful whether the question of time would bulk so large in Mbiti's writings were it not for the fact that he saw the preaching of Christian eschatology in Africa as effecting some important new realities which African peoples needed to confront and understand.[108]

From Mbiti's various discussions of the subject, "the African concept of time" has three main characteristics: firstly, it is "two-dimensional", comprising "a long *past*, a present and virtually *no future*".[109] Secondly, African reckoning of time is "concrete" and specific, and "related to events, but not mathematically".[110] African chronology, therefore, becomes "a composition of events".[111] Thirdly, as it relates to history, the African concept of time moves "backwards", into the "past"[112] (which Mbiti denotes by the Swahili

Zamani), from the "present", the "now-period" (*Sasa*).[113] An important implication of this third characteristic of the African concept
of time, flowing from the first mentioned above, is stated quite
boldly by Mbiti:

"In traditional African thought, there is no concept of history
moving 'forward' towards a future climax, or towards an end of
the world. Since the future does not exist beyond a few months,
the future cannot be expected to usher in a golden age or a
radically different state of affairs from what is in the *Sasa* and
the *Zamani*. The notion of a messianic hope, or a final destruction of the world, has no place in the traditional concept of
history."[114]

On each of the three points stated above, Mbiti's ideas have met
with criticism.[115] On the issue of a future-directed consciousness,
for instance, Francis Gillies observes:

"It is a universal category in man... [a] fundamental
anthropological category which directs consciousness, in its
interaction with the empirical, objective world, to the
chronological future. Every society possesses it."[116]

But Gillies, who cites Alexis Kagame[117] in support of his argument that Bantu time-consciousness is (as in Western understanding) "an ontological reality" even if "it is experienced only
along with event",[118] fails to point out that Kagame in fact agrees
with Mbiti on the question of "the future".[119] This goes to show that
in order adequately to appreciate Mbiti's thought on the subject,
one must take it as a whole, and not proceed by "atomising" it.

A close reading of Mbiti's discussion of the subject of time
reveals that behind it all there lies what he terms the "religious
ontology" of African society, and his contention that, from the
stand-point of traditional Africa, "to live is to be caught up in a
religious drama".[120] When one understands that the fivefold
divisions of this "African ontology" – God, spirits, man, non-human
animate and inanimate creation – are conceived of in terms of their
relations to man,[121] then it becomes clearer how human existence
in time – what Kagame calls "the trajectory of existence"[122] – ties
in with the demands of the essentially religious universe in which
man lives, moves and dies.

If the category "God" describes and explains the origin of man,
and the "Spirits" – supernatural beings and *the spirits of the dead*
– explain his destiny,[123] then there is already an indication why

man's "trajectory of existence" may be said to move "backwards" not "forwards". The clue lies in what Mbiti says about the nature of the "past" (or *Zamani*) to which the "present" (*Sasa*), the period "of intense experience" is always tending:

> "People constantly look towards the *Zamani*, for *Zamani* had foundations on which the *Sasa* rests and by which it is explainable or should be understood. *Zamani* is not extinct, but a period full of activities and happenings. It is by looking towards the *Zamani* that people give or find an explanation about the creation of the world, the coming of death, the evolution of their language and customs, the emergence of their wisdom, and so on. The 'golden age' lies in the *Zamani* and not in the otherwise very short or non-existent future."[124]

What Mbiti does not mention is that the *Zamani* is also the realm of the Spirits of the dead,[125] although it may be presumed that it is implied in the reference to the "evolution of... language and customs, the emergence of... wisdom..." In addition, Mbiti confuses his discussion somewhat by introducing notions like "belief in progress, long-term economic planning, and daydreaming";[126] it is these ideas that his critics, not least his African critics, have seized upon.[127]

However, it is possible to see in Kagame's statement about the fundamental importance of the past in Bantu culture,[128] a clarification of Mbiti's view concerning the significance of the *Zamani*. The past is important, not simply because without it the present generation would not exist, nor the institutions and customs of the community have their present meaning. The past is important also because it is properly the realm of the community ancestors whose goodwill and protection are crucial for the continuation of the generation of the living. The latter therefore:

> "... should turn to the former [the ancestors] to make certain of the tutelary intervention which they expect of them, but that does not in any way mean that they do not face up to the future, since the goal of man, in their philosophical system, is the perpetuation of the line. Thus they turn to the 'past' to assure the future both of the individual and of their posterity."[129]

Kagame, later on, in an explanation of the true objective of history in Bantu understanding, introduces ideas akin to Mbiti's discussion of an "African ontology", and shows how inextricably human existence in time is bound up with the preservation of the ancestral memory and the ancestral identity by the community of the living, hence the continuing "presence" of the ancestral "past":

"Some people imagine that a society is constituted by the members of that generation alive at present. In fact, the people alive now constitute only one element of their society; the territory which they occupy constitutes another, and in the same way the language which they speak, not forgetting the elements which distinguish them from other similar communities. But the most important, most definitive element is constituted by the ancestors of each generation, who have progressively created and handed on to their posterity the territory, language and all the cultural elements thanks to which and without which they would be totally different. Thus all the generations together form a living whole."[130]

If my use of Kagame's insights to elucidate Mbiti's discussion is accurate, it shows that the impact of a future-oriented religious message upon African society will involve more than the discovery of a new dimension of time! If "the traditional concept of time is bound up with the entire life of the people",[131] then the irruption of a concept of time which is as foreign to African thinking as Mbiti suggests, will entail a major social and psychological upheaval.[132] But, as Mbiti has ably shown, the important emphasis of the eschatological message of the New Testament is not a three-dimensional time-scale, but rather, its "Christological orientation".[133] It is because the eschatology of the New Testament is so "firmly grounded on Christology and hence capable of being conveyed and understood in other historical and cultural situations such as the African background..."[134] that Mbiti feels able to criticise the Africa Inland Mission teaching on Christian eschatology in his native Ukambani, for it seemed to stress inordinately and exclusively some futuristic aspects of Christian eschatology.[135] For this reason, it does not appear necessary to blame the absence of a future dimension in the time-consciousness of the Akamba (Africans) for their turning the future dimension of the Christian message and its significance for the present into a "pie-in-the-sky", futuristic type of religion.[136] May Francis Gillies not be right in asking:

"Were the Akamba not, in fact, presented with an eschatology which could only be understood in this way?"[137]

A possible solution to the problem is that Mbiti finds in the imbalanced Akamba Christian conduct, itself an outcome of a particular missionary misconception of Christian eschatology, a further indication of a time-consciousness which makes the assimilation of "theological concepts from the New Testament difficult".[138] And yet, it would be a misrepresentation of Mbiti's thinking on the question to take this suggestion too far. For, in the context of the same discussion, Mbiti comes to the firm conviction that "Christian Eschatology is a Christological phenomenon which, *ipso facto,* must be impervious to temporal limitations, whatever understanding of Eschatology we might derive from linear or other concepts of Time".[139]

Thus the discussion on time, beginning with "African ontology", leads in the final analysis, into "Christian ontology", into the Christian apprehension of the essence of things. Seen from this angle, the discussion centres not on time as a commodity that "must be utilised, sold and bought" or else "created or produced"[140] but on Christ as the ground and boundary of human existence. For in Him, the two dimensions of "past" and "present" merge and hold forth the promise of a "living" future, which is already anticipated in a dynamic "present" that makes all things new.[141] That Africa is called to apprehend and fully appropriate *this* Christ is, by far, the most distinctive contribution of Mbiti's theology.

IV. "What the Gospel brought was Jesus Christ": Theology as Christology

Christology has been close to the centre of Mbiti's concerns throughout his theological career. He has also achieved remark-able clarity on the importance of Christological understanding in the overall theological consciousness of the Christian Church. Thus, in the concluding remarks to his study of the eschatological message of the New Testament, which he considered as "an aspect of Christological Theology",[142] Mbiti observed:

> "The final test for the validity and usefulness of any theological contribution is Jesus Christ. Since His Incarnation, Christian Theology ought properly to be Christology, for Theology falls or stands on how it understands, translates and interprets Jesus Christ, at a give Time, Place and human situation."[143]

We have already noted Mbiti's view that it is in the Christian Faith, particularly in the unique personality of Jesus Christ, that is found the one "external, absolute and timeless denominator" which provides the "goal and standard for individuals and mankind".[144] It is in this sense of the fundamental and universal significance of Jesus Christ that the Christian Faith, in Mbiti's view, "holds the greatest and the only potentialities of meeting the dilemmas and challenges of modern Africa, and of reaching the full integration and manhood of individuals and communities".[145]

Yet, to date, Mbiti has not written a major study of Christology in relation to "the dilemmas and challenges of modern Africa".[146] What Mbiti has done on the subject of Christology, is to provide two important articles which set forth some features of African apprehension and experience of Christ as they are evident in African church life.[147] In both of these essays, he drew largely on evidence from the so-called "independent" churches, on the ground that "it is within these churches that African Christians have more freely externalised their experience of the Christian Faith than is otherwise the case in the mission-dominated or historical churches".[148] Although it is now possible to regard the distinctions between "independent" and "historical" churches as less meaningful than they were thought to be,[149] Mbiti's essays served a useful purpose, in that the Christian experience of African churches was being analysed and presented to the wider world by an African scholar and churchman with a recognised international reputation as a theological voice from Africa.

To appreciate Mbiti's own view of Christ in relation to African experience and realities, one has to recall the theological paradigm which he has consistently applied in his interpretation of African religious tradition, namely, the thesis that the African pre-Christian heritage in religion constitutes a *praeparatio evangelica*. And to understand the significance of Christ in such a framework, one must appreciate how Mbiti conceives of "the essence of the Gospel".

The theme is developed in a little-known article which is the substance of an address to the Christian Union of Makerere University College.[150] Rejecting the view of the Christian Faith as "a set of beliefs and worship" which leaves portions of African life "unoccupied", Mbiti elaborated on a concept which sees the Christian Gospel as, "not a religion but as a way of life."[151]

"Our Lord Jesus Christ did not start a religion – He is not a religious Founder, as He has been called – nor is Christianity a religion even though it has been presented as such. To preach or accept Christianity as a religion is to do it a great injustice and to undermine its impact."[152]

Then, after citing Biblical instances where discipleship is personalised as commitment to, and intimate spiritual union with, Christ who "came to bring the whole man, the entire parcel of man's total existence, into a deep and intimate relationship with God the

Father",[153] Mbiti concludes on the essence of this "Gospel which must be presented to Africa":

> "He [Jesus Christ] turned what was a physical life into a sacramental life, and He meant to leave nothing out. He challenged the whole man and all man's activities: He came to reclaim the entire person, the total history of the whole person, the sum total of his activities and aspirations... and in practical terms this means the whole community, the whole society, the whole humanity, the whole creation. So, in effect, He came to make man so totally and absolutely religious that no department of man should be left untouched by His Lordship, no department should be left outside the relationship between creature and Creator, between man and God, between the child and the heavenly Father."[154]

It is evident that the word "religion" is here used in two senses – in the conventional understanding which applies it to beliefs and ritual acts, and in a special connotation which gives account of the essential experience of what Rudolf Otto has called "the numinous".[155] But what is really extraordinary about this important statement of Mbiti's understanding of Christ and the Gospel, is that Mbiti here articulates his view of the Christian Faith by consciously drawing upon his conception of African religious tradition. For behind his insistence on the Gospel's characteristic of "wholeness" there lies his conviction about the totally religious character of African existence, a theme which he restates earlier in the article.[156] Deep calls to deep, and it is the "wholeness" of African existence to which the "wholeness" of Christ in the Christian Faith answers.

Thus, recalling the fivefold categories of "African ontology" in which God, Spirits, Man, Animals, Plants and inanimate creation exist in a "unity, so that to break up that unity is to destroy one or more of these modes of existence, and to destroy one of them is in effect to destroy them all", Mbiti is able to show how the divine invasion of the world of man in the Incarnation, far from upsetting that unity, in fact retains "those five modes of existence... in equilibrium". For though "God... in our traditional concepts lives in another mode of existence separated from ours", He "became one of us, and we can become one with Him". The mystery of the Incarnation is, therefore, illuminated as the mystery of "the mutual indwelling of God and Man in which no department of Man is segregated or left out".[157]

Seen from this angle, the "God-given preparation for the Gospel" in African tradition manifests itself in "this intensely religious life of the African... who is and has been religiously ready for many centuries".[158] Consequently,

"Christianity in our continent has no greater service to render than to transpose the existence of this religious man of Africa into the existence brought about by the Gospel light, by Jesus Christ, so that the entire life of Africa can proclaim Christ as Lord and King. In that road, the man of Africa will not have very far to go before he begins to walk on familiar ground..."[159]

It is obvious in much of the discussion above that Mbiti has here taken his distinction between Christianity as a particular cultural embodiment of the Christian Faith on the one hand, and the inner meanings of the Faith, on the other, to its farthest yet. By doing so, he is able to place his emphasis, appropriately, on Jesus Christ, who brings "not a *religion*, but the life whose quality and full realisation lie in the eternal order".[160] Accordingly, the encounter between the Christian Faith and African religious tradition is the meeting of African man in his religiosity and Jesus Christ, whose presence in the world (as Mbiti describes it elsewhere, in reference to *John* 8:58), "is not a historical [i.e. chronological] but a geographical presence of Christ in the world made by and through Him".[161]

It might seem as though Mbiti's approach to the subject of Christ's relation to the African heritage suggests that the missionary background of the modern African Church ceases to have any historical significance. Such a reading of Mbiti's outlook would be mistaken. However, Mbiti's approach does mean that the missionary background is seen from the perspective of its place within a religious history which belongs to African tradition. Since God is One,[162] Mbiti maintains that "God the Father of our Lord Jesus Christ is the same God who for thousands of years has been known and worshipped in various ways within the religious life of African peoples", and who, therefore, "was not a stranger in Africa prior to the coming of missionaries".[163] If the proclamation of the Gospel through missionary agency "brought Jesus Christ", its significance is that:

"... the Gospel enabled people to utter the name of Jesus Christ... that final and completing element that crowns their traditional religiosity and brings its flickering light to full brilliance."[164]

It is this affirmation of the ultimate and irreplaceable significance of Jesus Christ for African religious tradition and experience,[165] as for every religious tradition and experience, which gives to Mbiti's theological thought what John W. Kinney calls its "elevated christological perspective".[166]

V. Conclusion

John Mbiti has had, perhaps, the most varied theological career among African theologians of his generation, from the literary point of view. A member of the prestigious Society for New Testament Studies (*Studiorum Novi Testamenti Societas*), it is in the field of African Traditional Religion that his influence has been most deeply felt. In this sense, Mbiti's career illustrates more eloquently than most, that the theological enterprise within the Christian Church in modern Africa was not likely to follow the patterns forged in the history of Western theology. Having acquired their character within the context of European post-Constantinian Christendom, the norms and methods of the theological traditions of Europe (and eventually of North America) were not likely to prove the most helpful in the modern African context of religious pluralism. Mbiti, as we have seen, considered "Christian Theology from the major traditions of Christendom" as essential for putting African theologians in "the mainstream of ecumenical and apostolic heritage" and "the Catholicity of the Church".[167] He has probably gone the farthest in articulating a Christian theological consciousness which, precisely because it is African, may have done more for the catholicity of the Church than would otherwise have been the case.

Furthermore, if it is true that all African theologians who have been "forced to study and lecture on African Traditional Religion... approach this topic, not as historians of religions do, nor as anthropologists do", but as "Christian theologians",[168] here also, Mbiti's work illustrates the principle to a high degree. Mbiti makes no apologies for looking at Africa's pre-Christian heritage in religion from the standpoint of his Christian commitment, nor does he see any contradiction in finding that insights from the African heritage provide interpretative clues to the Gospel, and vice versa. For Mbiti, both realities are integral to the one unified experience of the history of African religiosity and spirituality. Probably no other major African theologian uses the expression "Christian Africa" as freely as Mbiti.[169]

This is what makes his thesis that the African pre-Christian

heritage in religion constituted a *praeparatio evangelica* so significant in his overall theological scheme; it is this thesis and its
outworking that may perhaps be his most enduring contribution
to the theology of the Church in twentieth-century Africa. When
Mbiti's works on African Traditional Religion are seen from this
perspective, that is, as an attempt to articulate the African
preparedness for the Gospel, which, in turn, helps to interpret the
Gospel in African experience, these writings take on an entirely
new significance. As a "hermeneutical tool", the thesis is very
important; it confers a "personality" on the pre-Christian tradition
as an active ingredient, and not just a passive component, in the
making of the Christian experience of the modern African. Accordingly, the development of African religious self-consciousness,
from the pre-Christian past into the Christian present, becomes
the unfolding of *one* story, through the one and the same Christ
who illuminates and crowns all comparable histories anywhere in
the world.[170] Thus Mbiti, as John W. Kinney rightly observes,
"tends to reject ethnicity as a theological category";[171] instead he
removes the history of African religious tradition from the realm of
the exotic (and one might add, the "anthropological"), and integrates
it firmly into the Christian theological category of a universal salvation-history.

However, Mbiti's effort at a theological interpretation of African
religious tradition has also had its critics. His postulate of the
essential and fundamental religiousness of the totality of African
existence has been rejected by an African lay theologian and
philosopher like Joshua Kudadjie (of Ghana), who maintains that
"religion is very important in the life of the African, but it is not
the whole of his life".[172] More important has been the rejection, by
some writers on African Religion, of Mbiti's theological approach
to his subject. In this regard, a representative and significant
viewpoint is that of Benjamin Ray, on Mbiti's *Concepts of God in
Africa:*

> "As in his previous work, *African Religions and Philosophy*,
> Mbiti's primary purpose is theological. Like Idowu and other
> contemporary African theologians, Mbiti is attempting to lay
> the basis for a distinctively African theology by blending the
> African past with the Judaeo-Christian tradition."[173]

Ray, here, interprets Mbiti rightly, though he disapproves of
what he finds; and P.R. McKenzie regards *The Prayers of African
Religion* "a difficult, even unsatisfactory book", not least because

Mbiti "tends to blur the distinctiveness of African spirituality" by seeking a *praeparatio evangelica* rather than "the integrity of the cult-group".[174]

Valuable as these comments are, the more fundamental question they raise is that of who decides on what in the African heritage of religion and culture belongs or does not belong to the African Christian consciousness. In this connection, it is hard to avoid the conclusion that the kind of synthesis which Mbiti's books have attempted to demonstrate, has found an echo in those whose concern with African religious tradition is not only academic, but, like his own, is both academic *and* existential.[175] So it is only appropriate that the last word on how the African heritage in religion relates to the Gospel of Jesus Christ, should go to the one whose major achievement has been the demonstration that these two realities belong together within the one redemptive process in the history of African religious experience:

"The meeting of the Christian Faith and African Religion affirms the word of the Scriptures which says: 'In past generations He (God) allowed all the nations to walk in their own ways; yet He did not leave Himself without witness' (*Acts* 14:16f). African Religion reflects God's witness among African peoples through the ages. It has been a valuable and indispensable lamp on the spiritual path. But, however valuable this lamp has been, it cannot be made a substitute for the eternal Gospel which is like the sun that brilliantly illuminates that path. Yet, it is a crucial stepping stone, towards that ultimate light. As Christianity develops in our continent, answering African needs and being firmly rooted in our culture, it will derive great benefits from the work already done by African Religion. The Gospel has come to fulfil and complete African religiosity. African Religion has taught us the basic religious vocabulary by means of which we may stammer, but we nevertheless say something behind that stammering; the Gospel teaches us how to speak with maturity and confidence. For both we thank God."[176]

Notes

1. John S. Mbiti, *Poems of Nature and Faith*, Nairobi: East African Publishing House, 1969, p.42. The line quoted begins "A Birthday Wish".

2. It has proved difficult to trace all the writings of Dr Mbiti. But the volume of what can be easily "salvaged" is impressive. See details in our Bibliography.

3. See, for the First World Festival of Negro Arts, held at Dakar, Senegal in April, 1966, John S. Mbiti, "La litérature orale africaine", in *Colloque sur l'Art nègre*, Paris: Présence Africaine, 1967, pp.255-279.

4. For the Second Festival held at Lagos, Nigeria, in 1977, see John Mbiti, "African oral literature" in *Festac '77: Second World Black and African Festival of Arts and Culture*, Lagos, London: Africa Journal Ltd, 1977, pp.96-97; "African Cosmology", *ibid.*, pp.40-49

5. Published by Oxford University Press, London, 1974.

6. Mbiti was born in 1931.

7. Adrian Hastings, *A History of African Christianity 1950-1975*, Cambridge: Cambridge University Press, 1979, p.232.

8. As an indication of Prof. Mbiti's standing in the wider Christian world, see his tribute to Pope John XXIII, "Pope John XXIII: a man of vision", in the collective volume published under the auspices of the (predominantly Roman Catholic inspired) Society for African Culture, *Un hommage à africain à Jean XXIII*, Paris: Présence Africaine, 1965, pp.99-102; see also his "African Answer" to the Symposium question: "Why did God make me (man)?" in the Roman Catholic publication *Concilium*, vol.108, 1977, pp.88-90.

9. John S. Mbiti, *African Religions and Philosophy*, London: Heinemann, 1969, p.233.

10. John Mbiti, "Faith, Hope and Love in the African Independent Church Movement" (An Ecumenical discussion with John Mbiti), in *Study Encounter*, 63, vol.10, no.3, 1974, p.19.

11. In the preface to *Poems of Nature and Faith*, Mbiti expresses himself quite clearly on this point: "It is with a deep Christian Faith that I feel conscious of myself, that I respond to the universe and that I try to make something out of life" (p.7).

12. John W. Kinney is right when he notes that "His [Mbiti's] perspective suggests that African theology should first and foremost address itself to the positives of the Christian faith and that the vast agenda of African theology ill affords wasting time with constant litanies about the foreignness of the church and the mistakes of the missionaries." See John W. Kinney, "The Theology of John Mbiti: His Sources, Norms and Method", in *Occasional Bulletin of Missionary Research*, vol.3, no.2, April, 1979, p.66.

13. With characteristic charitableness, Mbiti draws attention not only to the weaknesses of mission Christianity – "It bears the stigma of colonialism, foreignness, Westernism and paternalism", but also to its strengths – "the potentialities and strength of organisation, institutionalism, links with the historic traditions of Christendom, financial resources, personnel from overseas, an increasing ecumenical concern, and a deliberate attempt to relate Christianity to modern problems in Africa". See his *African Religions and Philosophy*, pp.236f.

14. John Mbiti, "The Future of Christianity in Africa, 1970-2000" in *Communio Viatorum*, vol.13, no.102, p.19. Cf. *African Religions and Philosophy*, pp.229ff.

15. John S. Mbiti, *African Religions and Philosophy*, p.229.

16. *Ibid.*, p.229.

17. *Ibid.*, p.239. Cf. John Mbiti, "The Growing Respectability of African Traditional Religion" in *Lutheran World*, vol.19, no.1, 1972, p.54.

18. See John Mbiti, "Faith, Hope and Love in the African Independent

Church Movement", p.9: "The Independent Church movement is an African opportunity to mess up Christianity".

19. *Ibid.*, pp.6f. Cf. David B. Barrett, *Schism and Renewal in Africa: An analysis of six thousand contemporary religious movements*, London, Nairobi: Oxford University Press, 1968.

20. John Mbiti, "Faith, Hope and Love in the African Independent Church Movement", p.7.

21. John Mbiti, "The Future of Christianity in Africa 1970-2000", pp.34f. Cf. A.F. Walls, "The Anabaptists of Africa? The Challenge of the African Independent Churches", in *Occasional Bulletin of Missionary Research*, vol.3, no.2, April, 1979, pp.48-51.

22. Mbiti has observed, in somewhat quaint and anecdotal style: "We can add nothing to the Gospel, for this is an eternal gift of God; but Christianity is always a beggar seeking food and drink, cover and shelter from the cultures it encounters in its never-ending journeys and wanderings. " See his "Christianity and Traditional Religions in Africa", *IRM*, vol.59, no.236, October, 1970, p.438.

23. *Ibid.*, pp.430, 437: "Christianity has christianised Africa, but Africa has not yet africanised Christianity... Energy, effort, wisdom and grace should now be concentrated on africanising Christianity in our continent... Now the African world should be given an opportunity to flow into Christianity, if we are to be serious about africanising Christianity." Also, "The Growing Respectability of African Traditional Religion", p.56: "Africa is becoming Christian so rapidly that Christianity has hardly had time to become 'naturalised', psychologically indigenised and emotionally assimilated into the natural points of reference." Cf. "African indigenous culture in relation to evangelism and church development", in R. Pierce Beaver (ed) *The Gospel and Frontier Peoples* (A Report of a Consultation, December, 1972), Pasadena: William Carey Library, 1973, p.93: "African Christianity is emerging, wearing an imprint of our cultures and simultaneously its universal dimension is uplifting what otherwise have been local values. Indigenous cultures are localising, indigenising and temporalising the universality of Christianity."

24. See John W. Kinney, *op.cit.*, p.66, where Kinney quotes from a personal correspondence with Mbiti. These same sentiments were confirmed to me in an interview with Mbiti in August, 1980.

25. Mbiti's "Response" to John Kinney, quoted in John W. Kinney, *op.cit.*, p.66.

26. John Mbiti, "Faith, Hope and Love in the African Independent Church Movement", p.7.

27. Professor Mbiti informed me that "at home" in Kenya, he still finds acceptance and a welcome in the Africa Inland Church.

28. For the explanation given in this section of my work, I am indebted to Professor Mbiti, who kindly agreed to provide the information I requested. I trust that in the manner I have reported him, I have respected his wishes for modesty on the whole subject. For a study of the AIM's operations and its relationship with the African church under its auspices, see John Alexander Gration, *The Relationship of the Africa Inland Mission and its National Church in Kenya between 1895 and 1971* (New York University Ph.D, 1974), Ann Arbor: University Microfilms, 1974. See especially, his evaluation of the "areas of tension", pp.348-353.

29. John S. Mbiti, *African Religions and Philosophy*, p.232. Cf. his obser-

vation elsewhere, "New Testament Eschatology and the Akamba of Kenya", in David B. Barrett (ed), *African Initiatives in Religion* (21 Studies from Eastern and Central Africa), Nairobi: East African Publishing House, 1971, p.27: "Can one speak of a theological system emerging or being initiated in the Church of Africa which, apart from the Orthodox and Coptic branch in Ethiopia and Egypt, has so far no theology? This theology-less situation is not only precarious but it almost negates the very existence of the Church in Africa."

30. Distinguishing between the motivations of American Black Theology and African Theology, Mbiti comments: "The latter [African Theology] grows out of our joy in the experience of the Christian faith, whereas Black Theology emerges from the pains of oppression". See his "An African views American Black Theology", in *Worldview*, vol.17, no.8, August, 1974, pp.41-44. Quotation is on p.43.

31. Johannes Verkuyl, *Contemporary Missiology – An Introduction* (translated and edited by Dale Cooper), Grand Rapids: Eerdmans, 1978, p.277.

32. John Mbiti, "The Ways and Means of Communicating the Gospel", in C.G. Baëta (ed), *Christianity in Tropical Africa* (Studies presented and discussed at the seventh International African Seminar, University of Ghana, April, 1965), London: Oxford University Press, 1968, pp.329-350.

33. Dr Richard Gray, of the University of London School of Oriental and African Studies, who introduced Mbiti's paper for discussion, appears to have seen the value of the paper basically in these terms. See C.G. Baëta (ed), *op.cit.*, p.146.

34. *Ibid.*, pp.148f.

35. John Mbiti, "The Ways and Means of Communicating the Gospel", p.329.

36. *Ibid.*, p.339.

37. *Ibid.*, p.329: "There is too much preaching and too little teaching in our churches all over the continent. In traditional Africa, there was plenty of teaching and no preaching. Why have we allowed this principle to become practically reversed in communicating the Gospel? Preaching alone will not deepen the Faith in Africa, and what the majority of Christians require is a clearer picture of Biblical knowledge, the life and mission of the Church in the world".

38. *Ibid.*, pp.329f.

39. *Ibid.*, p.337.

40. Elsewhere, Mbiti has noted, on African conversion to Christianity: "... conversion... does not mean simply a clear, sudden forsaking of one religious system and a simulataneous embracing of another – in a given point of time. Conversion is a process both theological and psychological. For African Christians in fact, it means a blending of Christianity (or Islam) and traditional religion, in a creative way, in which Christianity makes sense only when seen, experienced and understood in the light of traditional religion". See his "The Growing Respectability of African Traditional Religion", in *Lutheran World*, vol.19, no.1, 1972, p.57.

41. John Mbiti, "The Ways and Means of Communicating the Gospel", pp.341-342.

42. In an article written in 1967, Mbiti commented: "[The Church in Africa is] a Church without a theology, without theologians, and without theological concern". See his "Some African concepts of Christology", in Georg F. Vicedom (ed), *Christ and the Younger Churches*, London: S.P.C.K., 1972, p.51. (Collec-

tion originally published in German as *Theologische Stimmen aus Asien, Afrika und Lateinamerika*, München: Chr. Kaiser Verlag, 1968). Several years later, in 1971, Mbiti again observed concerning the dearth of theological awareness in the Church in Africa: "The tragedy goes further back, in that, with only a few exceptions, missionaries who established Christianity in the past one hundred to two hundred years have not been theologians. The Church has now come into existence evangelistically but not theologically". See his *New Testament Eschatology in an African Background – A Study of the Encounter between New Testament Theology and African Traditional Concepts*, London: S.P.C.K., 1978, p.188. (First published in 1971, by Oxford University Press.)

43. John S. Mbiti, *The Crisis of Mission in Africa*, Mukono: Uganda Church Press, 1971, p.5.

44. John Mbiti, "The Ways and Means of Communicating the Gospel", p.332.

45. See especially, John Mbiti, "African Indigenous Culture in relation to Evangelism and Church Development", pp.79-95; and "Christianity and Culture in Africa", also, "Christianity and African Religion", in Michael Cassidy and Luc Verlinden (eds), *Facing the New Challenges – the message of PACLA* (i.e. Pan-African Christian Leadership Assembly, December 9th-19th, 1976), Nairobi, Kisumu: Evangel Publishing House, 1978, pp.272-284; 308-313.

46. Whilst urging that the African Church should see the Gospel as fulfilling the aspirations of African cultural values, Mbiti adds: "It demands first that we isolate the very essence of Christianity from its peripherals. What is it which, in spite of cultural alienation [i.e. of European Christianity] has found its way through and reached African people who have embraced Christianity?" See his "African Indigenous Culture in relation to Evangelism and Church Development", p.90.

47. John Mbiti, "The Biblical Basis of Present Trends in African Theology" in Kofi Appiah-Kubi and Sergio Torres (eds), *African Theology en Route* (Papers from the Pan-African Conference of Third-World Theologians, December 17th-23rd, 1977, Accra, Ghana), New York: Orbis Books, 1979, p.83.

48. It is interesting that Charles Kraft of Fuller Theological Seminary, who was assigned to respond to Mbiti's paper on "Christianity and Culture in Africa" at the Pan-African Christian Leadership Assembly, felt able to "applaud his [Mbiti's] freedom to take the risks that must be taken in attempting to contextualise Christian theology in Africa..." See Michael Cassidy and Luc Verlinden (eds), *op.cit.*, p.286.

49. See, for example, Mbiti's studies on Christology and Soteriology respectively, "Some African Concepts of Christology" in Georg F. Vicedom (ed), *op.cit.*, pp.51-62, and "ὁ σωτὴρ ἡμῶν as an African Experience" in Barnabas Lindars and Stephen Smalley (eds), *Christ and the Spirit in the New Testament* (Essays in honour of C.F.D. Moule), Cambridge: Cambridge University Press, 1973, pp.397-414; as well as his major work *New Testament Eschatology in an African Background*, in which Mbiti interacted with the major currents of traditional (i.e. hitherto Western) New Testament scholarship.

50. The book is a modified version of his doctoral thesis presented to the University of Cambridge, England, in 1963, and the "African background" involved is his own native Ukambani region, and the experience of the Akamba people in their encounter with Christian missionary work under the auspices of the Africa Inland Mission and other missions, "though the Africa Inland Mission and the Africa Inland Church are numerically by far the largest" (p.20).

51. John S. Mbiti, *New Testament Eschatology in an African Background*, p.185.

52. *Ibid.*, p.189.

53. *Ibid.*, p.189.

54. *Ibid.*, p.189. Cf. John Mbiti, "The Future of Christianity in Africa, 1970-2000", p.32: "It is primarily in the third and fourth of these areas [i.e. in a list of items identical to those mentioned and enumerated in the same order] that African theology will, probably, make a uniquely African contribution to Christian theology in general."

55. John S. Mbiti, *New Testament Eschatology in an African Background*, pp. 189-190.

56. See John Mbiti, "On the article of John W. Kinney: A Comment", in *Occasional Bulletin of Missionary Research*, vol.3, no.2, April, 1979, p.68.

57. In a personal communication, Mbiti explained further his increased interest in history. The significance of history lies in the Biblical concept of divine activity in history. This activity of God in history does not exclude Africa. Thus, in his view, the agonies of African people must not be excluded from the universal divine activity, quipping, "if God has taken 500 years to liberate Angola and Mozambique, we can hope for similar activity in due time in South Africa!"

58. Published in R. Pierce Beaver (ed), *op.cit.*, pp.79-95.

59. Published in Michael Cassidy and Luc Verlinden (eds), *op.cit.*, pp.272-284.

60. H. Richard Niebuhr, *Christ and Culture*, New York: Harper & Row, 1951.

61. John Mbiti, "African Indigenous Culture in relation to Evangelism and Church Development", p.86.

62. *Ibid.*, p.86.

63. John Mbiti, "The Future of Christianity in Africa..." p.36. My emphasis.

64. It is revealing that Mbiti, who generally makes scant reference to particular individuals for their derogatory views on African peoples, is forced to mention that "as recently as 1959, a theologian as great and 'ought-to-have-been-knowledgeable' as the late Paul Tillich could advise, in his *Theology of Culture,* that 'what we do with primitive peoples in the mission field' should be the same as what he advises to be done with children..." See John Mbiti, "African Indigenous Culture in relation to Evangelism and Church Development", p.81.

65. A.F. Walls, "The Gospel as the Prisoner and Liberator of Culture", in *Faith and Thought* vol.108, nos.1-2, 1981, pp.39-52. Quotation on p.49; also published in *Missionalia*, vol.10, no.3, November, 1982, pp.93-105.

66. The career of Professor Harry Sawyerr, of Fourah Bay College, University of Sierra Leone, Freetown, is another interesting example of a comparable "enforced" shift from Biblical (New Testament) specialisation into African Religion. Of Harry Sawyerr's writings, see especially *Creative Evangelism – Towards a New Christian Encounter with Africa*, London: Lutterworth Press, 1968; *God: Ancestor or Creator? Aspects of traditional belief in Ghana, Nigeria and Sierra Leone*, London: Longman, 1970; and numerous articles in the *Sierra Leone Bulletin of Religion*. Of particular interest is the collection of essays in honour of Sawyerr, Mark Glasswell & E. Fasholé-Luke (eds), *New Testament Christianity for Africa and the World* (Essays in honour of Harry Sawyerr),

London: S.P.C.K., 1974.

67. See Okot p'Bitek, *African Religions in Western Scholarship,* Nairobi, Kampala, Dar-es-Salaam: East African Literature Bureau, n.d.

68. See H.W. Turner, "The Way Forward in the Religious Study of African Primal Religions", in *JRA,* vol.12, fasc.1, 1981, p.11.

69. John S. Mbiti, *African Religions and Philosophy,* p.1.

70. *Ibid.,* preface, p.xii.

71. *Ibid.,* p.1.

72. Benjamin C. Ray, *African Religions – Symbol, Ritual and Community,* Englewood Cliffs, New Jersey: Prentice Hall, Inc. 1976, p.14. In this connection, Ray's criticism of Mbiti's *African Religions and Philosophy* (and Parrinder's *African Traditional Religions),* in my view, misses the point. "They try to be exhaustive and to cover too many societies and too many types of religious phenomena. Consequently, those surveys present little more than superficial catalogues of examples extracted in Frazerian fashion from concrete socio-religious contexts. For the most part, they concentrate upon 'beliefs' without giving due recognition to the socio-cultural and ritual fabric within which they are embedded. Thus they reduce African religions to a set of 'doctrines' analogous in structure to Western faiths..." (pp.13-14).

73. John S. Mbiti, *African Religions and Philosophy,* preface, p.xii

74. *Ibid.,* p.276.

75. *Ibid.,* p.277.

76. *Ibid.,* p.277. My emphasis.

77. *Ibid.,* p.14: "My approach in this book is to treat religion as an ontological phenomenon with the concept of time as the key to reaching some understanding of African religions and philosophy." In view of the particular and innovative character of Mbiti's theory about time, I have chosen to reserve it for the *excursus* which follows in the next section.

78. John S. Mbiti, *Concepts of God in Africa,* London: S.P.C.K., 1970, p.xiii.

79. Thus chapters 4 to 7 in *African Religions and Philosophy* on "The Nature of God", "The Works of God", "God and Nature", and "The Worship of God" respectively, make reference to the appropriate sections of *Concepts of God in Africa.*

80. John S. Mbiti, *Concepts of God in Africa,* p.xiii.

81. *Ibid.,* pp.xiii-xiv.

82. *Ibid.,* pp.45ff.

83. *Ibid.,* pp.91ff.

84. See chapters 16 to 19.

85. Cf. Mbiti's statement in his textbook for schools and colleges, *Introduction to African Religion,* London: Heinemann, 1975, p.9: "Religion is part of the cultural heritage... It is by far the richest part of the African heritage. Religion is found in all areas of human life. It has dominated the thinking of African peoples to such an extent that it has shaped their cultures, their social life, their political organisations and economic activities. We can say, therefore, that religion is closely bound up with the traditional way of African life, while at the same time, this way of life has shaped religion as well."

86. John S. Mbiti, *Concepts of God in Africa,* p.219. Mbiti quotes from K.A. Busia, "The Ashanti" in Daryll Forde (ed), *African Worlds – Studies in the*

Cosmological Ideas and Social Values of African Peoples, London: Oxford University Press, 1954, p.192.

87. See John S. Mbiti, African Religions and Philosophy, p.1.

88. John S. Mbiti, The Prayers of African Religion, London: S.P.C.K., 1975, p.x.

89. Mbiti considers that "at least ninety per cent of the prayers are addressed to God. Therefore he emerges as the clearest and most concrete spiritual reality" (ibid., p.4). The remaining ten per cent are addressed to spirits mainly family and ancestral, and to lesser divinities.

90. Adrian Hastings, African Christianity – An essay in interpretation, London: Geoffrey Chapman, 1976, p.51.

91. It is interesting that Aylward Shorter, working on a smaller number of African prayer texts, and relating them more closely to the wider issues in the phenomenology of prayer, arrives at essentially similar conclusions about the value of the tradition of prayer in African religious experience. See his Prayer in the Religious Traditions of Africa, Nairobi: Oxford University Press, 1975. For an appreciation of the "Christian" value of these "traditional" prayer texts, see the review of both books by K.E. Amos Lyiomo in ATJ, vol.6, no.2, 1977, pp.71-73. Lyiomo concludes: "No doubt the present Christian Church in Africa has a lot to learn from the philosophy of these prayers and litanies. These could be Christianised and be included in our liturgical books" (p.73). Cf. the review of The Prayers of African Religion by Desmond Tutu, in JTSA, no.17, December, 1976, pp.68-69.

92. John Mbiti, Prayer and Spirituality in African Religion (The Charles Strong Memorial Lecture, Australia, August, 1978), Bedford Park: Australian Association for the Study of Religions, 1978.

93. Ibid., p.14.

94. Ibid., p.14. My emphasis. This prayer is cited by Mbiti in Concepts of God in Africa, p.23, as an important illustration of an African concept of God as Spirit. See also his Prayers of African Religion, pp.134f., 144. Aylward Shorter (op.cit., p.34) describes this same prayer as "an example of pure theism, the multiple and all-embracing experience of the Supreme Being".

95. John S. Mbiti, The Prayers of African Religion, p.1.

96. Ibid., p.1.

97. John Mbiti, Prayer and Spirituality in African Religion, pp.7ff. Also The Prayers of African Religion, passim.

98. Cf. the observation by Aylward Shorter, op.cit., p.4, that prayer constitutes "the central phenomenon in the religious traditions of Africa". Also, Adrian Hastings, African Christianity – An essay in interpretation, p.49: "It is in the experience of vernacular prayer, both public and private, both formal and informal, and in the spirituality which grows up from such experience that the true roots for an authentic African Christianity will most surely be found." Cf. Desmond Tutu, in his review of Mbiti's The Prayers of African Religion (op.cit, p.69): "Some of the prayers reveal a remarkable sublimity. One only asks again why if African spirituality was of this kind, those who brought the Gospel to this so-called dark continent should have missed the golden opportunity of employing this for conveying the Christian verities."

99. John S. Mbiti, African Religions and Philosophy, p.14.

100. See John Mbiti, "The African Concept of Time", in ATJ, no.1, February 1968, pp.8-20. The subject was also treated in substantially identical terms

under the title, "Afrikanische Begriffe der Zeit, Geschichte und des Todes", in *Afrika Heute*, vol.3, no.1, 1967, pp.38-42, and found in the French and English versions of the same publication; for the English, see in *Afrika: German Review of Political, Economic and Cultural Affairs in Africa and Madagascar*, vol.8, no.2, 1967, pp.33-38; the major parts of the article in *ATJ* were also serialised in *Pro Veritate*, under the following titles: "Traditional African Thinking (1): Religion" (June, 1972, p.3); "Traditional African Thinking (2): The Essence of things" (July, 1972, p.14); "Traditional African Thinking (3): Concept of Time" (August, 1972, p.11); "Traditional African Thinking (4): Concept of Chronology" (September, 1972, p.11); "Traditional African Thinking (5): Concept of History" (November, 1972, p.23). Also see his "Hope, Time and Christian Hope" (Some Reflections of African Experiences of 'Accounting for the hope that is in us'), in *Lumen Vitae*, vol.30, no.1, 1975, pp.93-104. For some responses to Mbiti, see Nimrod Mkele, "Time Concept of Blacks" in *Pro Veritate*, November, 1972, p.16; D. Chidiebele Okeke, "African Concept of Time" in *CRA*, vol.7, no.14, juillet, 1973, pp.297-302; Francis Gillies, "The Bantu Concept of Time", in *Religion*, vol.10, Spring 1980, pp.16-30.

101. See Stanley P. Saunders, "Christian Eschatology: The Ground and Impetus for Mission" in *Gospel in Context*, vol.2, no.4, October, 1979, pp.3-10; for Mbiti's response, see *ibid.*, pp.13-14.

102. *Ibid.*, p.14.

103. In a personal communication, Mbiti confirmed that "the concept of Time" was simply "an academic device for an attempt to understand the African world-view", and that he was willing to try other concepts and points of reference.

104. Francis Gillies, *op.cit.*, p.16. Useful though Gillies' observation is, it is worth noting that Alexis Kagame, also of Bantu culture (like Mbiti), who has written on the Bantu understanding of time, has little difficulty in seeing corroborative evidence in Sudanic Africa: "Our study relates expressly to the Bantu area and virtually to the Sudanese area as well. Although the linguistic system of Sudanese civilisation differs from that of the Bantu area, some information obtained by surveys allows us to state that the two zones are united on many points of profound thought. We are therefore convinced that our conclusions, at least on the whole, are equally valid for Sudanese culture." Therefore, it may still be possible to speak of an *African* concept of time, meaning at least, Black Africa. See Alexis Kagame, "Aperception empirique du temps et conception de l'histoire dans la pensée bantu" in Paul Ricoeur (ed), *Les Cultures et le Temps*, Paris: Payot/UNESCO, 1975, pp.103-133. Quotation on p.104.

105. John Mbiti, "Hope, Time and Christian Hope", p.98.

106. See John S. Mbiti, *African Religions and Philosophy*, p.18; also, "African Concept of Time", p.11.

107. See John S. Mbiti, *New Testament Eschatology in an African Background*, pp.24-32.

108. Cf. John Mbiti, "Hope, Time and Christian Hope", p.98: "The most fundamental issue in 'accounting for the hope that is in us' in the African setting, lies in the area of reconciling traditional concepts of time and hope with the Christian hope interpreted on a three-dimensional scale of time." In an earlier article on the subject of "eschatology", Mbiti considered that the effort "to link up African and Christian eschatology" as "the most crucial", even if also "the most difficult" part of the discussion. See his "Eschatology", in Kwesi A. Dickson and Paul Ellingworth (eds), *Biblical Revelation and African Beliefs*,

London: Lutterworth Press, 1969, pp.159-184. Quotation on p.180.

109. John S. Mbiti, *African Religions and Philosophy*, p.17; also "African Concept of Time", p.10.

110. John Mbiti, "African Concept of Time", p.12.

111. John S. Mbiti, *African Religions and Philosophy*, p.19.

112. *Ibid.*, p.23.

113. For a discussion of the meanings of *Zamani* and *Sasa*, see John S. Mbiti, *African Religions and Philosophy*, pp.22-23. For similar use of Kikamba words *Tene* and *Mituki*, see his *New Testament Eschatology in an African Background*, chapter 2: "Time, History and Eschatology".

114. John S. Mbiti, *African Religions and Philosophy*, p.23.

115. The most sustained critique of Mbiti's three points, as far as I am aware, is provided by Francis Gillies, *op.cit.*

116. *Ibid.*, p.21.

117. Alexis Kagame, *op.cit.*

118. Francis Gillies, *op.cit.*, p.21. It is worth noting, though, that Kagame's view does not amount to a denial of the concept of time as determined by events: "In traditional Bantu culture... time is a colourless, indifferent entity as long as no concrete deed is performed to mark it out, to stamp an impression on it. That event can be the action of the Pre-existing One, of Man, of the animal world, or of a natural phenomenon... From the moment that the action or event occurs time is marked, stamped, individualised, rescued from anonymity, and it becomes *the time of that event.*" See Alexis Kagame, *op.cit.*, p.114. My emphasis.

119. Kagame *(op.cit.*, p.117), after quoting the relevant passage from Mbiti *(African Religions and Philosophy*, p.17) on the virtual absence of the future dimension of time in African (Bantu) consciousness, then comments: "We, therefore, share the opinion of this excellent author, although we do not start from the same point of view. Since the 'future' does not have the possibility of being marked out by real events, it does not correspond to a recognisable concept of time. The man who projects his forecasts into it is not even sure of being there the following day..." And he further adds: "Given that Bantu culture limits any extension of the year's round, one realises that an individual cannot form any plans going beyond this span of time divided into twelve months." It is only by making a distinction between the "individual" and the "nation" that Kagame is able to posit the consciousness of an "indefinite future" in the case of the latter.

120. John S. Mbiti, *African Religions and Philosophy*, p.15.

121. *Ibid.*, p.16.

122. Alexis Kagame, *op.cit.* p.111.

123. John S. Mbiti, "African concept of time", p.9.

124. John S. Mbiti, *African Religions and Philosophy*, p.24.

125. *Ibid.*, p.25: "Death is a process which removes a person gradually from the *Sasa* period to the *Zamani.*"

126. *Ibid.*, p.23: "The people neither plan for the distant future nor 'build castles in the air'." Francis Gillies *(op.cit.*, p.23) responds, accordingly, by referrring to Mbiti's call for "a theology of dreams... in the light of the seriousness with which Africans take some of their dreams". See John S. Mbiti, "God, Dreams and African Militancy", in J.S. Pobee (ed), *Religion in a Pluralis-*

tic Society. Leiden: E.J. Brill, 1976, p.38.

127. See Nimrod Mkele, *op.cit.;* also D. Chidiebele Okeke, *op.cit.*

128. Alexis Kagame, *op.cit.*, p.116: "Dans la culture bantu, le passé revêt une importance capitale..."

129. *Ibid.*, p.227.

130. *Ibid.*, p.128.

131. John S. Mbiti, *African Religions and Philosophy*, p.28.

132. It is interesting that Mbiti sees in "the political instability of our [African] nations" a possible indication of the painful process of African accommodation of "this new discovery of the future" (*ibid.*, p.28).

133. John S. Mbiti, *New Testament Eschatology in an African Background*, p.57.

134. *Ibid.*, p.61.

135. *Ibid.*, pp.51-56.

136. John S. Mbiti, "New Testament Eschatology and the Akamba of Kenya", p.21. Cf. *New Testament Eschatology in an African Background*, p.57.

137. Francis Gillies, *op.cit.*, p.18.

138. See John S. Mbiti, *New Testament Eschatology in an African Background*, p.183.

139. *Ibid.*, p.182.

140. John S. Mbiti, *African Religions and Philosophy*, p.19. Cf. Alexis Kagame, *op.cit.*, p.114.

141. See John S. Mbiti, *New Testament Eschatology in an African Background*, p.183: "Newness is the word in Christian Eschatology, and it is newness in Christ."

142. *Ibid.*, p.191.

143. *Ibid.*, p.190.

144. See above, "Towards an African Theology (2): The pre-Christian heritage as *praeparatio evangelica*", pp.385ff. Also John S. Mbiti, *African Religions and Philosophy*, p.277.

145. *Ibid.*, p.277.

146. In a personal communication, Mbiti revealed that he projected a study on Christology as a sequel to his work on New Testament Eschatology. One wishes that he will have the strength and opportunity to bring this project to fruition.

147. See John S. Mbiti, "Some African Concepts of Christology", in Georg F. Vicedom, *op.cit.*, pp.51-62; and "ὁ σωτὴρ ἡμῶν as an African Experience", in Barnabas Lindars and Stephen Smalley, *op.cit.*, pp.397-414.

148. John S. Mbiti, "ὁ σωτὴρ ἡμῶν as an African Experience", p.400.

149. See A.F. Walls, "The Anabaptists of Africa? The Challenge of the African Independent Churches", pp.48-51.

150. John S. Mbiti, "Christianity and East African Culture and Religion" in *Dini na Mila* (Revealed Religion and Traditional Custom), vol.3, no.1, pp.106. [A slightly abridged version of this article is also published as "Our stand towards African Traditional Religion" in *Write!* vol.1, no.1, 1973, pp.9-17,21 (African Literature Centre, Kitwe, Zambia, 1973).]

151. *Ibid.*, pp.2-3.

152. *Ibid.*, p.3.

153. *Ibid.*, p.4.

154. *Ibid.*, p.4.

155. See Rudolf Otto, *The Idea of the Holy. An inquiry into the non-rational factor in the idea of the divine and its relation to the rational* (ET by John Harvey), London: Oxford University Press, 1950 (2nd ed).

156. See John S. Mbiti, "Christianity and East African Culture and Religion", p.1: "The whole of African life is a religious phenomenon, and every person who comes into this world is, *ipso facto*, a religious being: he cannot run away from that, and he cannot reject it because he belongs to a religious phenomenon and a religious community. Long before he is born, at his birth, through his initiation rites, in marriage and procreation, at death and burial, and in the life after death – all through this long journey, he is involved in a religious drama. His vocabulary, his thought-forms, his actions, and every portion of his life, is a participation in a religious experience".

157. *Ibid.*, p.5.

158. *Ibid.*, p.4.

159. *Ibid.*, p.4.

160. *Ibid.*, p.6.

161. John Mbiti, "On the article of John W. Kinney: A Comment", p.68.

162. See John S. Mbiti, *Concepts of God in Africa*, p.xiii; cf. *Romans* 3:29f.

163. John Mbiti, "On the article by John W. Kinney: A Comment", p.68. In a personal communication, Mbiti made the same point, in the happy expression: "Missionaries did not bring God to Africa, God brought them".

164. John Mbiti, "On the article by John W. Kinney: A Comment", p.68.

165. *Ibid:* "Without Him [i.e. Jesus Christ] the meaning of our religiosity is incomplete."

166. John W. Kinney, *op.cit.*, p.66.

167. John S. Mbiti, *New Testament Eschatology in an African Background*, p.189.

168. A.F. Walls, "The Gospel as the Prisoner and Liberator of Culture", p.49.

169. See John Mbiti, "Church and State: A Neglected Element of Christianity in contemporary Africa", in *ATJ*, no.5, December, 1972, pp.31-45; and even when the exact expression is not used, the thought is often present. Cf. "The Future of Christianity in Africa, 1970-2000", *passim*; also, *African Religions and Philosophy, passim*. Furthermore, as early as 1961, Mbiti felt able to write on "The Protestant contribution to the cultural expression of the African personality"; see the collective work, published under the auspices of the Society for African Culture, *Colloque sur les Religions* (Abidjan, 5-12 avril, 1961), Paris: Présence Africaine, 1962, pp.137-145.

170. In a personal communication, Mbiti expressed this same outlook in the following remarkable statement, on the "presence" of God in African tradition and on African preparedness for the Gospel: "As if they waited without knowing it, but not in darkness; there was a light which was divine revelation, and that light led Africans to the Gospel. The Gospel did not originate among African peoples, but when they heard it, it was not an offence to their spiritual sensibilities. They said Amen, and that Amen had already been worked out by the wisdom of God. The Gospel did not contradict what

they already knew; it affirmed it, and in that affirmation, people found new religious life in the Gospel of Jesus Christ".

171. John W. Kinney, *op.cit.*, p.67. Kinney refers to Mbiti's article, "An African views American Black Theology".

172. J.N. Kudadjie, "Does Religion Determine Morality in African Societies? A Viewpoint" in J.S. Pobee (ed) *Religion in a Pluralistic Society*, pp.60-77. Quotation on p.73, emphasis in original.

173. Benjamin C. Ray, *op.cit.*, p.15.

174. P.R. McKenzie, "Review of *Prayers of African Religion* by John S. Mbiti" in *The Expository Times*, vol.87, 1975-76, pp.220-221.

175. See the reviews of *The Prayers of African Religion* by Desmond Tutu and K.E. Amos Lyiomo; also, review of *Concepts of God in Africa* by Eliewaha E. Mshana in *ATJ*, no.5, 1972, pp.73-75.

176. John Mbiti, "Christianity and African Religion", p.313. Cf. John Mbiti, "The Encounter between Christianity and African Religion", in *Temenos: Studies in Comparative Religion*, vol.12, 1976, pp.125-135, especially, pp.131-132.

Chapter Nine

A Variety of African Responses (3): Mulago gwa Cikala Musharhamina, or The Entry of Africa into the *Catholica*

I. "For long enough people have been thinking our problems for us, without us, and even in spite of us."[1]

It is appropriate that we should begin our examination of the work of this eminent francophone African theologian with a reference to that collection of "wide-ranging and hard-hitting essays [to which he contributed] which was to have a considerable impact"[2] in the development of theological self-confidence among Africans of the Roman Catholic communion. The essays were published under the auspices of "Présence Africaine", the publishing agency of the Paris-based Société Africaine de Culture. This was perhaps significant. For it indicated the extent to which this manifestation of African theological self-consciousness was related to the wider and intensifying "cultural crisis of conscience" which had taken place among African francophone intellectuals in the previous two decades under the aegis of the Négritude movement.[3] It is therefore not surprising that the word *négritude* appears in several of the essay titles. This convergence of the quest for an African theological identity on the one hand, and the more pervasive affirmation of an African cultural personality on the other, through Présence Africaine and the Société Africaine de Culture, has continued, imparting a heightened degree of cultural awareness generally to the writings of francophone African theologians.

Described by Adrian Hastings as the work of "a movement of Young Turks",[4] *Des Prêtres noirs s'interrogent* was asking questions which had not hitherto been raised about Catholic Christianity in Africa, or else had not been heard from African Catholics. The gentle warning and reminder by the Archbishop of Dakar in his preface, to the effect that "nothing can nor should be done without the Church",[5] gives an indication of what the African and Caribbean contributors to the volume were about. But if the Apostolic Delegate for French Africa was somewhat concerned lest the fundamental structure and teaching of the Roman Catholic Church should be infringed in the interest of some "African habits and customs",[6] his fears were unfounded. For whilst every author dealt with one or other aspect of the cultural implications of the Roman Catholic presence in African or "black" society, each did so "as a son of the Church".[7] The various writers, brought together by their theological studies in Europe, questioned neither the rightness of their belonging within the Roman Catholic Church, nor the validity of the ecclesiastical traditions which they had inherited. It is doubtful whether any of the essays could be faulted for straying beyond what Archbishop Lefebvre called "the framework of ecclesiastical discipline".[8]

And yet, the book, in a profound and unprecedented way, was interrogating the Roman Catholic Church, by asking that African sense of self-worth be respected, and that room be made for African genius and contribution in the establishment of the *Catholica*, not only among the peoples of Africa and in communities of African origin in the Caribbean and Americas, but also in the wider world as a whole.[9] In his poem *La Vierge Noire*, which figures with other poems as appendix to the essays, Albert Abble addresses the one who has traditionally been the focus of Catholic affection and devotion:

> "See now, Mother,
> The yellow people have given you
> Their yellow colour.
> The redmen have made you
> Look like their women.
> The whites have depicted you
> As a western girl –
> Are you going to refuse
> To take on our colour?"[10]

In similar vein, Jérôme Bala, in one of his poems, *A Notre Mère*, declares:

> "Pictures of you may be black or white without any trouble."[11]

For a work of its kind, *Des Prêtres noirs s'interrogent* is remarkable for its mildness of tone and the avoidance of frequent and sustained criticism of European missionary practice in Africa.[12] Instead, the writers concentrate their efforts on providing positive evidence that African cultural values possess a character of their own, and offer a valid basis for constructing vigorous Catholic communities which would not be passive recipients of the Christian message.[13] The volume, therefore, was a serious attempt by young African Catholic clergy to respond to the assumption that Africa represented a cultural and religious *tabula rasa* for the implantation of a Christian civilisation from Europe. That assumption had already been seriously challenged a decade earlier by the Belgian Franciscan missionary, Placide Tempels.[14] In *Philosophie Bantoue*, a work that was destined to exert considerable influence subsequently, Tempels had argued that Africans possessed deeply held indigenous religious and ethical concepts within coherent philosophy and world-view, and that it was only upon the basis of this cultural *substratum* that a viable and vigorous Christian community could develop.[15] The significance of *Des Prêtres noirs s'interrogent* lies in the fact that it represents the first concentrated effort by a group of African writers to enter that discussion, and, according to their own statement, "... to add our word also to the debate which has been going on for so long about Africa".[16]

An indication of the importance of Mulago in this venture is the fact that he alone contributed two essays to the volume.[17] The article entitled "Nécessité de l'adaptation missionnaire chez les Bantu du Congo", is clearly the keynote piece of the entire collection, and appropriately constitutes the first chapter. While his second article and many of the others, which, on the whole, treat specific applications of the interaction of the Roman Catholic presence with some aspects of African and Caribbean reality, "Nécessité de l'adaptation missionnaire...", tackles some of the basic theoretical questions thrown up by the Catholic missionary enterprise which produced the African and Caribbean Catholic communities.

Mulago begins by posing the important missiological question as to whether the phenomenal numerical success of the Catholic missionary enterprise in his native Congo (now Zaire), was matched by a sufficiently deep rooting of the Christian faith in the African soul:

"Is what we see flourishing rooted in the African soul, or is it simply an expression of the general Europeanisation of the black continent? Is our missionary method complete? Has

Christ been 'incorporated' into the African?"[18]

Behind these queries lay Mulago's criticism of the theory of *tabula rasa* as the underlying assumption in the missionary enterprise which meant logically:

"... destroying, demolishing, flattening everything in order to be in a position to build a new civilisation on the ruins, as western, Christian civilisation."[19]

As evidence that such a practice was, in fact, bound to fail, Mulago cites cases of African converts, especially among those educated in European values – the "developed people" – who, being at once neither fully at home in the new *civilisation occidentale chrétienne*, nor able to abandon completely what amounted, in some missionaries' eyes, to "superstitions", became thereby virtually "a class of displaced persons".[20]

Mulago identifies with the opposite persuasion – in his view *plus profond, plus juste* – which affirmed the existence in every human being, on the basis of a common human nature:

"... what the old church called *Logos spermatikos*, the remnants of a primitive revelation..., a spark which has to be fanned into life and raised above the human in order to become the clear, glowing flame of the *lumen Christi*."[21]

Mulago pursues the discussion along the same lines, and comes to similar conclusions when he examines the teachings of papal missionary encyclicals and other official documents, from *Maximum Illud* (1919) of Pope Benedict XV, to *Evangelii Praecones* (1951) of Pope Pius XII.[22] Essentially, missionary activity of the Church involves an elevation and improvement of human nature, which possesses "a naturally Christian basis (Tertullian)[23] which, illuminated by divine light and nourished by grace, may rise to authentic virtue and superhuman life".[24]

It is extraordinary that by invoking the traditional Catholic categories of "nature" and "grace" and their interrelations, Mulago actually exposes the "unCatholic" character of the theory of *tabula rasa*, and beats its protagonists at their own game. For he shows that he is no less concerned than they are to preserve inviolate the high status of the Gospel which the Church brings. However, he differs from them by stressing that the Church never builds on emptiness. By this argument, it becomes self-evident that Christian theology is always constructed on the basis of a "natural" theology which, far from being its opponent, is in fact its pre-supposition.[25] It is thus quite consistent for Mulago to integrate, as he does here, the need to appreciate the character of the particular "natural" theology which the missionary activity encounters, into the total process of Christianisation:

> "You cannot Christianise a people until you have begun to understand them, unless you are willing to be content with a superficial Christianity... After penetrating the mentality of the people whom you wish to conquer, you must 'graft' the Christian message into the soul of the proselyte. This is the only method which will give lasting results."[26]

In these statements, one already finds anticipations of what will become a major preoccupation of Mulago's in his subsequent academic career, namely, his meticulous study of the "traditional religion" of the Bantu peoples as a properly theological concern. For it is his theological interpretation of the Bantu religious tradition and world-view that provides some of the essential elements in his sustained pursuit of theological "adaptation" which has become virtually synonymous with him in the mainly Catholic theology of francophone Africa.[27] But unlike Idowu, whose interests are the nearest equivalent in the Protestant theology of anglophone Africa,[28] Mulago's concern with the theological significance of the Bantu religious heritage is motivated not so much by a desire to vindicate the rights of African religious consciousness, as by a conviction that there exists a deep harmony between the authentic religious aspirations of the Bantu and the Christian message proclaimed by the Catholic Church. One needs to give due weight to this fundamental presupposition in order properly to appreciate what Mulago understands by "adaptation".

II. *"Un visage africain du Christianisme"* (1): the principle of "adaptation"

Two years before the appearance of *Des Prêtres noirs s'interrogent*, Mulago had successfully sustained his doctoral thesis in theology at the University of the Congregation for the Propagation of the Faith (*Propaganda Fide*) in Rome. It was a revised version of this thesis[29] which, published ten years later,[30] was to become Mulago's most representative writing. In the meantime, parts of the thesis had already been published as articles and short studies,[31] including the two chapters already referred to in *Des Prêtres noirs s'interrrogent*.

The theoretical discussion of theological adaptation which forms the third part of the leading essay in *Des Prêtres noirs s'interrogent*, is further refined and clarified in the preliminary chapter of *Un visage africain du Christianisme*, and this is our reason for withholding treatment of it till now. What Mulago does in *Un visage africain du Christianisme* is to provide a wider context for understanding the necessity for, and the nature of, theological "adaptation" in African Catholicism. This wider framework embraces a discussion of theological responsibility in the Church and the community, an updated examination of papal and other official teachings on the subject, including this time the declarations of Pope John XXIII, and a fuller theological argument for the very principle of "adaptation" itself.

By invoking the Gospel illustration of the scribe in the kingdom of heaven who is adept at bringing from his storeroom things old and new,[32] Mulago clearly indicates the nature of the theological task he was proposing. In the context of the social and cultural revolution which post-colonial Africa was then beginning to undergo, Mulago saw the theologian, particularly the "missionary theologian" – by which he meant, not necessarily foreign personnel, but "primarily genuine sons of the missionary field of action"[33] – playing a decisive role. Mulago saw African societies, emerging from colonial tutelage, as poised between two dangers, "ancient paganism and modern paganism."[34] and unsure of their bearings for the future. But Mulago is thoroughly convinced about the relevance of the Christian message for African self-understanding and he casts the Christian theologian in an all-important integrating role:

> "The remedy for averting this double danger cannot be a surface Christianity, but a Christianity which has been comprehended and lived through, an incarnated and involved Christianity, a Christianity which has become more deeply rooted than the old ancestral beliefs and is more alive than all the forms of modern civilisation.

> "The theologian's role must lie in fulfilling this programme. He has to undertake a laborious journey to the source of the peoples' customs and practices and try to discover there the kernel and centre of their organisations and traditions. Once he has discovered this centre of gravity he can graft into it the message of the Christian mystery."[35]

What is immediately significant about Mulago's outlook is that he sees the task of the (African) theologian in fundamentally missiological terms, that is, involving an encounter between "the message of the Christian mystery" and what constitutes "the centre of gravity" in the religious heritage of a particular people.[36]

It is conceivable that this missiological perspective may owe something to the well-established Catholic concept of "the missionary phase" of relatively young Catholic communities – the phase of the *Plantatio Ecclesiae*.[37] Nevertheless, Mulago displays this missiological emphasis with sufficient consistency in much of his other writing that it is hard not to conclude that one is dealing with an aspect of his overall theological understanding. It is interesting therefore that well before Pope Paul VI called upon African Catholic clergy to be their own missionaries in Africa,[38] Mulago had already urged his fellow African priests to assume the role of missionary theologians to their own various peoples.[39]

Mulago represents one of the finest instances of this sense of theological responsibility for one's cultural community, an attitude which is found among modern African theological writers as a whole. But what Mulago also exemplifies, as a committed Catholic scholar, is a high degree of fidelity to Catholic magisterial tradition. This pronounced fidelity to Catholic tradition, paradoxically, seems to reinforce and deepen, rather than to diminish, his sense of accountability to his cultural roots, and one gets the impression that there is no *hiatus* in Mulago's thinking on these points. For instance, it might seem to other interpreters that the relaxation in what seemed like a rigid Catholic missionary policy with regard to encouraging the cultural personality of non-Western Catholic communities, began in earnest only under the pontificate of John XXIII.[40] Mulago, however, finds convincing antecedents of this development under earlier pontiffs. Citing the missionary teaching of Popes Benedict XV and Pius XI on the development of local clergy,[41] he observes:

"The attentive reader will not fail to notice that the purpose of the indigenous clergy is to penetrate the thinking, the heart and the soul of the people who are to be evangelised. The indigenous priest, who knows his people better than anyone, will in fact find ways of instilling the faith into their souls, because he has easy access to territory where a stranger is not permitted to set foot."[42]

Whatever the merits of Mulago's claim as to the consistency of Catholic magisterial teaching on the extent to which local cultures should determine new Catholic communities outside of Europe,[43] his own conviction is unambiguous. The Catholic Church, by virtue of its very self-understanding as a universal entity, must present itself in every cultural context with a recognisable face, recognisable, that is, both to itself and to the particular environment in which it takes root; in Africa, this means "an African face":

> "The Catholic Church should always be presented with its true face. It is not a stranger to any people nor to any culture, because it is universal and transcends them all."[44]

To understand properly Mulago's argument for "adaptation", one must appreciate the centrality of this fundamental conviction he holds about the nature of the Church. For it is his perception of the Church – his ecclesiology – rather than simply a desire to vindicate an African cultural personality which really constitutes the *force motrice* of his argument. The same can be said of his eventual advocacy of an "African Theology", which, in effect, is only an extension of his earlier concern with "missionary adaptation".

Mulago agrees with the statement by Bossuet, the seventeenth-century French Catholic prelate, that the Church is "Jesus Christ distributed and communicated".[45] Accordingly, in the course of what André Seumois calls "the extension in space of the universal church" – the "starting theology" of the Church's mission[46] – the Church rehearses the process whereby the Word Incarnate assumed humanity, transforming and conferring upon mankind a new, elevated character:

> "The paradoxical mission of the Church is the continuation of that of its divine founder. It is the mystical body of Christ, thus it should enter into and transfigure everything it touches by giving it a new value."[47]

However, by its very nature, this transfiguring and renewing activity has its converse, namely, a discerning and discriminating activity. "Adaptation", as the mark *par excellence* of the Church's missionary enterprise, also implies the necessity to distinguish between what conforms to the Gospel and what is opposed to it in every new cultural context which the Church encounters:

> "Missionary activity will therefore consist in distinguishing what can be purified from what is essentially opposed to the spirit of the Gospel... If it is a question of instilling Christianity into things which are good or indifferent and offering them to Christ, it is no less a question of eliminating and rejecting everything false..."[48]

This twofold nature of "adaptation" as a missionary and theological activity answers to and continues the work of the Incarnate Word, who as "the restoration and consummation of all things... is already enlightening every man that comes into the world".[49] It is understandable, therefore, that, for Mulago, the speech of St Paul – "the perfect type of Gospel herald and mission-ary theologian"[50] – to the Athenians on Mars Hill,[51] provides the most eloquent demonstration of what, in his view, the proclama-tion of the Christian Gospel is meant to achieve: to reveal to a people their own treasures, whilst also bringing to them that fullness which is found only in the Gospel itself. For, in the final analysis, those treasures are intrinsic to the universal Gospel entrusted to the Church whose mission it is to set forth "the divine treasure of which she (the Church) is the sole trustee".[52] Whatever light human beings possess and however faint this may be, "it is still the light of Christ and an attempt to reach him".[53]

"Adaptation" as the missionary activity of the Church is thus "the extension of the incarnation of the Word, the adaptation of God to man", and operates following the analogy with the Incar-nate Word. The Saviour assumed humanity without loss to His essential Deity; similarly, the Church's "adaptation" to the diver-sity of human cultures does not involve a diminution or a mutila-tion of the truth of the Christian message.[54] On the contrary, such "adaptation" belongs to the very essence of the Church in the world; it is the way of ensuring that the Church assimilates such new elements as will help bring it that bit closer to the fullness of catholicity and unity which is the goal for it in the plan of God.[55] Through "adaptation", the Church participates in the *assimilation vitale* of new and fresh elements and insights provided by different cultures, a necessary factor in its own organic growth – "its on-going growth"[56] – as the *Catholica*.

For Mulago, therefore, "adaptation" is an entirely positive con-cept, even in what it rejects, for it does so with good reason and to a rightful end:

> "This work of cleaning up and setting free, of entering in and transfiguring can open up the peoples of Africa to hear the Christian message. The will find in what they already possess the very reason for accepting the fullness which the Catholic religion is offering them."[57]

III. *"Un visage africain du Christianisme"* (2): The application of "adaptation"

From our discussion above, it becomes evident that Mulago's theological self-understanding is deeply rooted in his Catholic commitment.[58] But the Catholicism in which he feels so thoroughly at home is one which is "transcendent", that is, "neither Western, nor Asian, nor African, and... in spite of that, everywhere at home".[59] In other words, for Mulago, Catholicism must be in *manifestation* what it is in essence, namely, universal; and the universality meant is not one of uniformity, but one which embraces different cultural expressions of the life of the one universal Church:

> "The local churches should be able to express the life of the universal Church, to particularise or localise it. It is quite normal for the Church in Africa to wear African dress and have African colour, and for each local Church to 'localise', so to speak, the face of the *Catholica*."[60]

How Mulago proposes that such "particularisation" and "localisation" of the universal Church might be achieved in the African context provides one of the most interesting instances of a comprehensive programme of theological indigenisation to come from one writer in modern African theology.

The theological method of Mulago has been rightly described as "stepping-stone theology",[61] an expression favoured by Mulago himself,[62] who uses it to indicate that there are, in the particular African cultural and religious tradition which he treats, providential "stepping-stones" to the meanings inherent in Christian formulations. But fellow Zairean theologian, Ngindu Mushete, considers that this method of seeking "stepping-stones" in African cultural and religious values for Christian doctrines and life makes very little serious contribution to a properly scientific theology. He criticises Mulago's approach for what he regards as its "attempts to achieve agreement, which consist in confusing Christian revelation with the systems of thought which have served to expound it in the course of history". And he poses the question:

> "What depth of Christian truth can be reached by comparing Christianity, considered in the absolute as a fixed system of truths, and certain African cultural elements isolated from their global context?"[63]

An even more scathing criticism of the entire concept and approach of theological "adaptation" is made by the Haitian writer, Laënnec Hurbon, who is quoted by Ngindu Mushete:

> "The adaptation to cultural values which is so much talked about is often no more than a process of indigenising the Roman Church, which keeps a firm hold on its previous position and is entitled to do so 'by means of the indications of its preceding history (which itself is rendered history in view of that subsequent entitlement), this instance being at one and the same

time defined, definitive and defining'."[64]

These criticisms, as applied to Mulago's work, seem to me to be excessive. Whilst some of Mulago's proposals for "adaptation" in *Un visage africain du Christianisme* may be considered rather tame, especially in the light of the decisions of the Second Vatican Council, it is far from certain that even those suggestions have had no impact on the emergence of bolder initiatives.[65] Furthermore, it does less than adequate justice to Mulago's theological perspective to reduce his efforts to a mere "comparison" between Christianity conceived of as an abstract system on the one hand, and isolated African cultural values on the other. What Mulago considers to be universally relevant, is not the Roman Church as such, but rather the Christian message. A closer study of Mulago's application of his principle of adaptation will show that his approach has a more radical edge to it than appears on the face of it. This interpretation, it seems to me, can still hold good, even if one also accepts the view that Mulago has continued to operate with a largely ecclesiocentric conception of Christian mission and theology. But here the problem lies at the heart of Catholic missiology as a whole,[66] and is not peculiar to Mulago and those of his "school".[67]

As we have already noted, Mulago considers that a fundamental aspect of the integrating task of the "missionary theologian" – like himself – has to do with discovering what constitutes "the centre of gravity"[68] in the religious and social life of the particular people with whom he is concerned. It is when this preliminary stage of the task has been satisfactorily carried out that the theological enterprise proper – which involves a correlation of one aspect or other of the Christian Gospel with the longings and aspirations discovered in the preliminary enquiry – can be seriously entered upon. In "Nécessité de l'adaptation missionnaire..." Mulago stated

"It is incumbent on the theologian to discover that aspect of Catholic dogma which best answers the people's expectations. But this work presupposes a deep and methodical study of the cultural values which constitute the wealth of the people who are to be evangelised. Adaptation aims to meet the aspirations both of the people and of the Christian message."[69]

This "deep and methodical study" is certainly what Mulago pursues in the first and second parts of *Un visage africain du Christianisme*. From a wide-ranging study of the family life, the socio-political organisation and the religious ideas of three Bantu peoples of Central Africa – the Bashi, the Banyarwanda and the

Barundi – Mulago distils the concept of "vital union" or "unity of life" as the integrating principle, "the centre of gravity", of the Bantu world-view. This dynamic concept, arising from a sense of vital participation in the same life and of sharing in the same life-resources (*moyens vitaux*) – ultimately derived from God, *Nyamuzinda Imana* – and with tremendous implications for relationships and participation within the universe of the living, the deceased, creatures animate and inanimate, is what Mulago identifies as the essential ingredient of the "philosophical wisdom"[70] of the Bantu. But whilst Mulago's study is limited to the three Bantu groups named above, "in order to avoid gratuitous generalisations",[71] he has little doubt that his findings have a relevance for the vast majority of African societies. By the same token, the theological application which follows in the third part of the book, though made within the context of Bantu ideas and experiences, is not restricted in relevance to that context alone.

In accordance with the methodological principle enunciated above, the isolation of the concept of *union vitale* as, in some sense, the interpretative key to Bantu life, is only preparatory and a means to an end, namely, to discover "theological approximations between the vital principle which unites members of the Bantu community and that which unites members of the mystical body".[72] In other words, to the Bantu concept with its well-known implications, Mulago finds in the tradition of the Church a corresponding concept, what he calls "church unity, that is to say, the actuality formed as a result of participation by the members of the Church in the mystery of the unique and very life divine of Christ".[73] Thus the entire theological argument in the book, which is aimed at demonstrating how the African Christian may "think and live Christ and Christianity with his own soul"[74] is pursued as an exploration of the analogies between the two realities, namely, the Clan and the Church.

One would see the point of the criticism of Mulago's theology for all its alleged *concordisme*[75] were it the case that Mulago contents himself with simply correlating received Christian dogma with facets of African life without any expectation of affecting, in the process, the way in which the Christian tradition is understood. Mulago expresses himself quite clearly on this point in the first chapter of *Un visage africain du Christianisme*:

> "It is necessary that the Bantu, the African converts, should be able to find their secular aspirations in Catholicism. Those who aspire to the unity and intensity of life will not fail to seize upon

the mystery of the Church and perhaps bring into it some elements for a better understanding of the mystery."[76]

Furthermore, his oft-repeated conviction that the longings and aspirations implied in the Bantu concept of *union vitale* find their crowning response and fulfilment in the Church,[77] seems to me to give a clue as to what Mulago is seeking to achieve in *Un visage africain du Christianisme*, as in subsequent writings.

It has already been noted that Mulago operates with a conception of Christian mission which is essentially ecclesiocentric. Within such a missiological frame of reference, whereby the implantation of the Church – of the *Catholica* as a visible entity, "a real society, ... a human society"[78] – is the chief end of missionary activity, it is to be expected that missionary theology should face up to the kind of issues that inform the social experience of a people, particularly at the institutional level of its existence. Accordingly, it is arguable that Mulago's choice of the Bantu concept of *union vitale* – "vital union, the kernel and centre of their organisations and traditions"[79] – as the "meeting point" between Bantu society and the Church's proclamation, answers to the missiological perspective that has shaped his own thinking. If the Church presents itself as a total socio-religious reality, then it cannot ignore the socio-religious experience of the people it seeks to bring within its ambit. The Church in that case must meet, satisfy and transcend the socio-religious aspirations of the people concerned. In other words, the Church must address itself to questions which belong to the socio-religious experience of the people, and communicate its message in terms and categories not extraneous to that experience, but rather derived from it. Only when this is seen to be happening can genuine "adaptation" be said to be taking place:

"It is necessary to get down to basics and to work out a presentation of dogma and morality suited to the Bantu mind; we must manage to turn the liturgy into a true expression of the African soul before *its own* God in community worship; pastoral and social action must be rethought in terms of our faithful, thus rejecting a pure and simple transposition of western forms, and Catholic action will be conceived as a task of spiritual fertilisation, flowing from our state as children of God and incumbent on all members for the expansion and diffusion of the family; discipline, far from being regarded as submission to established authority because this is right and proper, should be regarded as a demand of fruitfulness in the community. *Then and only*

then will Africans begin to understand that the Church is not
foreign to them; they will understand that it is a living com-
munity in which each person, as in the Bantu community, has
work to do as a son or daughter, a father or mother."[80]

This comprehensive programme involving a cultural rethinking
of the Church's message and how it is communicated, is required
not only so that "everyone may feel at home in the Church".[81] It
answers also to a fundamental theological necessity which arises
from Catholicism's own self-understanding. If, indeed, the Church
is the continuation of the Incarnation of the Word in the world,
then surely the existence of an African Catholicism makes the
assumption of African experience and interpretation of reality only
a matter of course, and follows the logic of the faith. For,

"Christ wants to prolong his presence and his redeeming work
in every one of his faithful people. The same Christ who, two
thousand years ago, showed himself to mankind by conde-
scending to take on human form as a Jew, he who permitted his
message to flow for centuries into a world of Graeco-Latin
culture – today, when his Church has broken out of the
geographical limits confining it to the Mediterranean basin, he
will not disdain *the new opportunities to manifest himself and*
to bear witness which Bantu culture offers him."[82]

Interestingly, the kind of new possibilities which, in Mulago's
view, the African context was offering the Church, seem to have
been anticipated by Placide Tempels. In *Philosophie Bantoue*,
Tempels had argued that some important aspects of the Church's
doctrine had what he described as "a striking analogy in the
ontological thought of the Bantu".[83] What Tempels was referring
to here was the Bantu idea of reinforcement of life through the
participation in, and communication of "life-resources" (*moyens*
vitaux). It was this concept which Tempels discovered to be
remarkably analogous to the Catholic understanding of the operation of divine grace within the Christian believer and in the
Christian community. Tempels, therefore, found himself as a
Christian missionary, on common ground with the "pagan" Bantu,
against European rationalist thinking:

"What for rationalist Western science remains an hypothesis, a
theory which cannot be demonstrated, namely, the inward,
intrinsic growth of the being in the manner taught by the Bantu,
is precisely the same as is taught by Christian doctrine about
grace based on the certainty of revelation."[84]

In what follows, Tempels is almost interpreting the Church's dogma, as Mulago will eventually suggest that it ought to be, from the perspective of the Bantu "view of the world":

"The Church does not cease to teach and profess this reality (the reinforcement of a life) and Christians continue to aspire towards reinforcement of life, ennoblement of life, participation in the life of God himself. The Church believes in constant participation in a life eternal, in inward growth through union with God... Catholic spirituality teaches that God created humanity by means of his own vital riches, by goodness, to permit his creatures to take part in his own divine life, in his blessedness... that is to say, that on earth there exists an opportunity for vital growth which is inward, intrinsic and eternal. This high spiritual doctrine, which inspires and nourishes souls in the bosom of the Catholic Church, finds a striking analogy in the ontological thought of the Bantu. We thus arrive at the extraordinary conclusion that Bantu paganism, ancient Bantu wisdom is at the bottom of its Bantu soul striving towards the very soul of Christian spirituality. It is only in Christianity that the Bantu can find relief for their secular nostalgia and full satisfaction of their deepest aspirations."[85]

There could hardly be a clearer statement of what Mulago would take as his theological agenda! He quotes part of this passage at the outset of the third and theological part of *Un visage africain du Christianisme*,[86] and this may be an indication of the extent to which Tempels' intuition may have served as an important foothold for his own efforts.[87] Since Mulago explicitly denies any suggestion that his work is specifically based on Tempels' book[88] (though he admits to taking up the earlier writer's call to test his findings[89]), the most that one can say is that what *Philosophie Bantoue* does is to provide a significant literary and missiological precedent for Mulago's own achievement, which is to bring a Christian theological perspective to bear on the interpretation of his Bantu religious heritage. Whatever measure of truth one accords to Alexis Kagame's view that European missionary "theologicising" of Bantu wisdom and philosophy distorted the latter's "ultimate aim",[90] there can be little doubt concerning Mulago's own reading of the evidence.[91] Setting aside as inadequate and false any suggestion that the new reality of the Christian Church in Bantu society and the religious and cultural heritage of the Bantu represent two irreconcilable entities, he seeks to demonstrate instead that "the wisdom of our Bantu seems to be a providential stepping-stone to the doctrine of the mystery of the

Church".[92]

To do this, Mulago systematically takes up themes and aspects of Christian doctrine and practice relating to the Church, and seeks to show how an approach in terms of Bantu ideas renders these doctrines and practices meaningful to Bantu experience. Some of his analogies are relatively self-evident, and indicate a high degree of convergence in understanding. This is seen, for example, in his treatment of the analogies between the Church's sacraments and Bantu symbolic acts and ritual within the frame of reference of the concept of *union vitale*.[93] But Mulago is also capable of some remarkable *tours de force* and of producing some very illuminating insights into traditional Church dogma in the process. One such instance is his discussion of the dynamics of "participation" as applied to the Christian life and to the Church as a community that shares in a common life – albeit a supernatural one, derived and motivated by the Triune God – and its analogies with the Clan and its solidarity at the "natural" level.[94] A further interesting feature of Mulago's treatment of especial interest to us is his regular reference to and use of patristic insights. Cyril of Alexandria, Gregory of Nyssa and Augustine, in particular, figure quite prominently in the discussion of some of his themes.[95] However, by appealing to the Fathers as part of Catholic tradition and as dogmaticiahs rather than as witnesses to the cultural task of Christian theology in the Graeco-Roman context, Mulago unfortunately reduces their significance for the purposes of this study. On the other hand, it goes to show to what extent Mulago considers the central affirmations of dogma in Catholic tradition to be in harmony with his suggested "adaptation" in his African context.

"Participation" lies at the heart of the experience of *union vitale* as the means, through symbolic action, whereby the reinforcement of life in community as in individual life is achieved.[96] Mulago begins by distinguishing three ideas which are implied by the term "participation": these are, first, the reality which is being participated in, or the content of the experience; second, the participating subject; and third, the resultant relationship between the reality participated in, and the participating subject, as well as the relationship between several participating subjects. He then relates those three ideas to their various applications in the community. The "reality" participated in, which provides the content of the experience of *union vitale* is twofold: it is on the one hand, the unity of life derived from a common clan-ancestor (the unity of life, the identity with and indivisibility from the blood of the founding father); and on the other hand, the life-resources which sustain this unity of life (everything which sustains life and the life-resources).[97] The participating subjects comprise each and all of those who share in the twofold "reality" of common ancestral blood and common life-resources, while the resultant relationships emerge in the form of family-relations, the wider socio-political organisation and the community's religious life. The intense emphasis on community and on relationships in the experience of *union vitale* means that:

"For the Muntu, to live is to exist in the bosom of a community, to participate in the life of his ancestors he is called to be an extension of his forebears and to perpetuate himself in his descendants. The Muntu cannot conceive of life outside his community, he does not possess his *ntu* (i.e. his 'being') except in common..."[98]

From this description of the nature of "participation" in Bantu community, it is not hard to predict how he will develop the analogy with the Church, which is also "... a life community, in the sense that there is the same life principle in all its members", and so, "a community based on participation", though "in a manner more true and transcendent".[99] Accordingly, unlike the "natural" community which derives its unity of life from ancestral blood, the Church derives its unity of life from the very life of the Triune God, Father—Son—Holy Spirit:

"The reality shared in the Church is the divine nature, the very life of God, made human in the Word and spread abroad in our hearts by the Holy Spirit."[100]

The participants in this supernatural life become "a new people, the Church of the Incarnate Word", and share in the experience of sonship, being "really and not metaphorically, ... sons of God by sharing in the life of the only Son".[101]

In the light of these observations, Mulago then goes on to develop a concept of the "participation" of the Church in the Trinity in a way that shows how, from the perspective of a primal world-view, the Christian account of the relationship of the human to the divine can acquire some new and interesting insights.[102] If, through the Holy Spirit, the "new people, the Church of the Incarnate Word" become participants in the divine nature, the life of God, then these human participants, by virtue of the unique Son, become reproductions of the Son of God. This is brought about by the Father causing the Son to be reproduced in the believers, who receive from the Spirit, proceeding from the Father and the Son, the imprint by grace of their (i.e. Father and Son) image.[103] Hence, on the human level, participation in the divine nature and in the divine life is the reflection of the community of nature and life within the Trinity.[104]

But the relationship of the life of the Christian community to the Trinity is more intricate than would be suggested by the analogy of an "original" to its "image". The Trinity, Christ and the Church exist in a relationship which Mulago describes as "reciprocal interiority".[105] They interpenetrate each other; for since Jesus is in the Trinity, those who are united to Jesus are also in the Trinity, and through the divine grace imparted by the Son believers are brought into the presence of the Father as adopted children.

This does not mean that Mulago obliterates the distinction between the divine and the human. Rather, the assumption of human nature by the Incarnate Word means that human nature has become sanctified and divinised;[106] those who respond to His redeeming love constitute:

"A new people, regenerated humanity (in actual fact), the mystical body of Christ, which has as its head the Son of God himself, as its soul the Spirit, and as members all those touched by the vital influence, both internal and external, of Christ's grace."[107]

By "internal influence" Mulago means the divine grace of salvation which is imparted internally in the Christian, whilst "external influence" describes the "hierarchical government" of the Catholic Church which, in his scheme of ideas, is integral to the essential character and life of the mystical body of the "horizontal" dimension of the Christian community's participation in the divine life. Here, the analogy of the Church to the family/clan becomes of special significance. The redemptive love of God for mankind takes the form of the creation of a family in which all who share in the divine nature live and experience their new status as God's children. The unique Son of God assumes human nature in order to become both brother and sanctifier of the new sanctified family of God: "for he, the Sanctifier and we, the sanctified, have the same Father".[108] By the same token, he is born of a woman, like his brethren,[109] and so partakes of their flesh and blood.[110]

At this point, the manner of the Redeemer's Incarnation by human birth provides Mulago with an opportunity to make a highly colourful contribution, from the perspective of Bantu thinking, to the special Catholic dogma concerning the "mother of God". What Mulago does is to invoke the tradition of associating a "queen-mother" with the reigning monarch, to fulfil the symbolic role of mother of the ruler as well as of the community as a whole.

> "The queen-mother, *omwamikasi* – royal woman of the Bashi; *umugabekazi*, 'she who distributes' of the Banyarwanda and the Barundi – is primarily a *mother*, mother of the king, and by the same token mother of all the subjects in the kingdom: her motherhood covers all those who come under the sway of the sceptre of her son the king. The *mwami* (king) is the universal father, the queen-mother is the universal mother. The queen-mother's royalty is no more than the normal outcome of her motherhood."[111]

It is therefore on the grounds of an analogy between the queen-mother in a context of sacral kinship and Mary's role in relation to the Lord from heaven, that Mary's place in Christian devotion is vindicated:

> "By the fact of her royal motherhood the queen-mother obtains a special place in the kingdom; she is drawn by her son into the privileged ranks which divide the *mwami* from ordinary mortals. She is no longer a subject... Mary too, by the fact of her divine motherhood, belongs to a special order in the Church; she is raised to the edge of divinity. In both cases the position of the mother means sharing as a subordinate in that of the son."[112]

As if in one bold stroke, a modern African theologian seems to sweep away all the thorny exegetical and historical problems which attach to a development in Christian doctrine that continues to divide the wider Christian community.[113] It is indeed extraordinary that what emerged in the course of Christian history in other climes, as an outcome of simple, popular piety,[114] is now validated in an African setting as the crowning fulfilment of a pre-Christian tradition!

> "The converted Muntu will discover in Mary the perfect, transcendent realisation of the idea which he has of the *mwamikazi* or *mugabekazi*, and his devotion to the supernatural Mother cannot but be the more secure for it, because it is better grounded theologically."[115]

By the kind of argument used, therefore, it follows that the doctrine of the bodily resurrection and Assumption of Mary, queen of heaven and earth, can also be found meaningful, "... so that Christ the King in heaven should not be a king without a mother."[116]

In this theological "adaptation" through analogies, some of the associations that Mulago attempts to establish may appear a little contrived. For instance, later in the book, he vindicates the primacy of the bishop of Rome on the grounds of a striking analogy between the person and role of the Roman Pontiff and the sacral *mwami*, who as the focus of the community's life-resources, is also its symbol of unity.[117] It would, however, be wrong to consider these analogies as entirely fortuitous, so far as Mulago is concerned. To the extent that they indicate valid and meaningful connections between Bantu concepts and Christian ideas, they show not only that the socio-religious reality of the Church answers to Bantu aspirations, but, more important, that they form a continuum which derives from the unified purpose of God in self-revelation:

> "The vital unity of the Church is the true answer to Bantu aspirations, a transcendent, supernatural answer, not in the sense that nature could in any way be prepared to receive supernatural gifts, but in the sense that, in God's plan, man has since his creation been raised up to the supernatural order, freely and without any merit on his part."[118]

"Bantu aspirations" and the "Christian response" share, therefore, a more profound community of meaning than would appear. Every positive aspect of the Bantu (or African) world-view is owed to the same Source as has given the Christian revelation.[119] This view of the harmonious relation of Bantu pre-Christian experience to Christian understanding may help explain why it is that in seeking to portray "the African face of Christianity", Mulago appears hardly to question seriously the nature of the "Christianity" with which he is dealing. Rather, the impression one gets is that as a Catholic scholar and a Catholic churchman, Mulago is prepared to accept the received tradition and to find ways to make sense of it for himself, and for other fellow African Catholics. To that extent, "adaptation", for Mulago, is essentially an "Africanisation" of an existing tradition. On the other hand, such Africanisation cannot leave the received tradition in its pristine form, because the process necessitates making room in the tradition for what had, hitherto, been regarded as extraneous to it. Thus, when we see Mulago's concern for "missionary adaptation" transformed into a more vigorous affirmation of the necessity of an "African theology", we ought to see the two sets of interests as being strictly in continuity. The development, in point of fact, involves only a sharpening of focus; the essential content of the arguments remain the same.

IV. "We claim the right to be allowed to express ourselves as Africans, even in the sphere of theology..."[120]: the case for an "African Theology".

It is an indication of Mulago's stature in the quest for a self-conciously African theological outlook and point of view in the last two decades, that at some of the early ecumenical gatherings of African churchmen, it was Mulago who seemed to represent and articulate the mainly Catholic experience of francophone Africa. He was a contributor both at the 7th International African Seminar held at Accra, Ghana in 1965 to study Christianity in Tropical Africa,[121] and at the Consultation of African Theologians which took place at Ibadan, Nigeria, the following year.[122]

The papers which Mulago presented at those two meetings[123] show that the kind of concerns which he had expressed in *Un visage africain du Christianisme* were to remain with him for a long time to come. Some of the same terms and concepts would continue in use with much the same meanings. In fact, the article on "Vital participation..." offers hardly any new ideas, and relies heavily, as Mulago points out, on the relevant portions of *Un visage africain du Christianisme*.[124] However, in several subsequent articles and studies, those early concerns would now be persistently urged as being fundamental to the development of an entirely legitimate African standpoint for understanding the Christian message.[125]

Our interest, at this point, is to follow through some of the arguments elaborated in favour of an "African theology" by one who even his critics concede is "one of the great inspirers and promoters of African theology".[126]

In "*Christianisme et culture africaine: apport africain à la théologie*", Mulago states his viewpoint in an almost matter-of-fact manner:

"By the very fact that African Christians, having their own mentality and culture and drawing certainty and light from their faith, are endeavouring through the operation of reason to understand and explain revealed mysteries and their consequences, they are creating an African theology."[127]

Mulago's insistence on Africans having and presumably drawing upon their own thought-forms and culture in theological activity is important; for what he means is more than cultural self-consciousness. Behind these terms, Mulago sees essentially religious categories. He is fully persuaded that it is religion, in particular the "traditional religion" that constitutes the main axle of life and self-understanding in most, if not all, African societies, even when Christianisation has made significant strides. At least, this was so in the community he had studied most deeply.[128] If this was indeed the case, then "African Theology" would have to integrate the interpretation of African pre-Christian religious tradition which, being the focus of fidelity to the past, is therefore essential to the identity of the African Christian. For the Christian authenticity of the African implies to no less a degree a sense of fidelity to one's pre-Christian tradition than to one's commitment to the Church. It is the quest for the synthesis which affirms this kind of authenticity which underlies the process Mulago describes by the term "African Theology":

"On the one hand we claim the right to be able to express ourselves as Africans even in the sphere of theology, but on the other hand we want this language to have all the richness and depth of our African nature. And that comes not out of a desire to preserve our ancestral past at all costs, *but so that we might be authentic Christians, faithful to our origins and to the Church.*: *Real adaptation is fidelity to the law of the incarnation of the God-Man.*"[129]

The keen interest which Mulago has continued to show in what may initially appear to be "non-Christian" themes,[130] finds its rationale here. By approaching the conception of "African theology" from the perspective of the religious history and the cultural identity of the African Christian, Mulago avoids the kind of problem which causes J.K. Agbeti (of Ghana) to posit a distinction between an "African Christian or 'indigenised' theology" on the one hand, and the "Theology of African religions" on the other; for according to Agbeti, both concepts have equal and legitimate right to the expression "African theology".[131] However, as we have already noted, Mulago takes the view that the socio-religious aspirations of Bantu people (as of all Africans) find their full and "transcendent" fulfilment in the experience of what the Christian message offers.[132] What Mulago therefore requires of "African Theology" is, *mutatis mutandis*, what has always been required of theology, namely, the interpretation of life as a unified experience.[133] In other words, African Theology, without renouncing its Christian identity, has to encounter, interrogate and clarify the

African religious heritage and to incorporate whatever is not incompatible with the Christian Gospel. In fact, this essentially integrating activity of theology is what gives it its truly *Christian* character. Thus African Theology is to provide a framework in which Africans and African society will understand African tradition in the light of Christ who is a universal reality. This explains why, elsewhere,[134] at the end of a lengthy study of the possible parallels between the symbolism in Bantu socio-religious life and the Christian sacraments, Mulago is able to conclude:

"... it is not a question of rediscovering the meaning and role of the symbols, but of living them; since they are there, they speak a living, intelligible language. It is a question of taking them up and, after having purified them should that be necessary, of christianising and integrating them... In the liturgy, there are divine elements which the Church is not free to change. But there are also human elements which are contingent, attached to the socio-cultural environments which gave rise to them. These elements are not immutable. *Africa has therefore the right to substitute its own values for these contingent elements, if this substitution can help her to be more Christian, more true to the spirit of Christ.*"[135]

Since Mulago operates with an organic and unified conception of African religious tradition and experience, it is not surprising that when he comes to discuss the basal elements of an African contribution to Christian theology,[136] he locates these elements in what can only be described as the "traditional religion". The two foundation-ingredients, namely, belief in a Supreme God and the innate sense of participation, are both realities "which could be called 'pre-Christian'".[137] But it is evident from Mulago's treatment of the subject that he does not consider that what African pre-Christian tradition brings to Christian theology consists in sets of beliefs. If it was a matter of "beliefs" as such, then the belief in God would hardly be worth mentioning. Rather what African tradition brings is an approach and an attitude of the mind – perhaps better still, a posture of the total personality – towards the existence and activity of God in human life and in the world. In other words, African experience brings a sense of God which informs the understanding of God's attributes as these impinge on the human predicament. An indication that this is what Mulago seeks to convey is the extent to which his discussion of ideas such as, God as the source of all life, His transcendence, God as Creator of all things, Divine Providence, the Fatherhood of God, is shot through with the concept of participation, which constitutes his second foundation-element. From the discussion on God, it emerges that what explains the Bantu (African) view of God is, in fact, the concept of participation. Thus, on the Bantu sense of the Fatherhood of God, Mulago writes:

> "... among the Bantu, to say that God is Father is to say everything. This divine fatherhood is communicated to men through creation, which is participation in the life of God and his fatherhood; it is a synthesis of God's attributes."[138]

This statement is perhaps less important for what it affirms about Bantu belief in God as Father than for the way in which that conviction is conceived. For the significance of the approach described here is that Bantu religious concepts are fundamentally relational in character, and as such are much more statements of the human experience of the transcendent than they are attempts at defining an objective reality.[139] This is what emerges quite distinctly from Mulago's effort to show what form an "Africanisation in theology" "grafted" on to the two foundation-elements noted above, might possibly take.[140] Thus, for example, the doctrine of creation is approached as not only a manifestation of the outgoing divine life and love to the creature,[141] but also as a divine condescension which invites the creature to participate in the kind of intimate fellowship that brings together Father, Son and Holy Spirit within the trinitarian relationship. The fruitfulness of human love, therefore, becomes a reflection, on the human level, of the divine intimacy which produces the created order:

> "Thus man is made a participant in divine fruitfulness; he becomes a fellow worker with God in continuing creation. All mankind and all human families issued from that first couple."[142]

Divine grace is also a product of the intimate fellowship within the Trinity, so that the Incarnation of the Son is, in effect, a divine participation in humanity with a view to re-establishing the human participation in the divine love which the first couple forfeited, dragging their descendants down with them.[143]

If the concept of participation can thus be employed to illuminate the "inner" mysteries of the Trinity and the Incarnation, it stands to reason that the concept comes into its own when it is applied to the doctrine of the Church and the significance of the Church's sacraments. Accordingly, the sacraments become the means of maintaining and reinforcing the reciprocal human relations, and the relation with Christ, who is conceived of as Head of a "community of partners – in life eternal":[144]

"Through the sacraments the Bantu will realise their longing for vital union with God, with the invisible world and with their brothers in the Faith... The sacraments make our life merge with Christ's life and cause divine energies to flow in us. Thus they bring about just that which the Bantu were trying to produce with their symbols and they surpass it in a marvellous and divine fashion. It is God himself who condescends to enter into contact with us, so that we may become *one* with him and with all his children."[145]

It is evident therefore, that for Mulago, to speak of "African Theology" implies to make space in the process of Christian formulation for African inspiration, African experience and insight, and African personality:

"Christ does not ask the African to divest himself of his personality in order to become his disciple. *But on the contrary the African who has become a disciple in the Kingdom is called to bring his 'Africanness' into that Kingdom to enrich it and to contribute to its varieties of beauty*."[146]

Much of the argumentation in "Christianisme et culture africaine: apport africain à la théologie" is found, in substantially identical form, in an important contribution he made to the 4th annual *Semaine théologique* organised by the Faculty of Theology of Lovanium University, Kinshasa, in July, 1968.[147] The theme was "African Theology."[148]

Whilst much of Mulago's paper rehearses and reaffirms many of the ideas and positions which we have met elsewhere among his writings, a significant feature of his discussion is the fact that this time he draws extensively on the decisions of the Second Vatican Council to establish his case. Taking a firm stand in favour of an "African theology", he opposes the views of the Belgian Catholic dogmatician Alfred Vanneste (also on the staff of the Faculty of Theology at Lovanium), who had challenged the very idea of the possibility of an African theology.[149] Mulago rejects the view that theology is valid only as universal, since that kind of argument often hides the fact that what is meant by universal is also what is Western.[150] Mulago insists, therefore, on the right of African Christians to develop such intellectual and conceptual categories as are appropriate for grasping and articulating the revealed data of the Christian message in a theology "which is not foreign to our environment nor to our tradition of thought, our sensibilities, our mentality or our culture".[151]

In Mulago's view, then, far from being excluded from the process of incarnating the Church itself in human cultures, such theological "naturalisation"[152] of the Christian message in every human culture, is what must undergird and determine that process. If, therefore, the Conciliar decisions as well as major magisterial declarations were unambiguous in pointing to the need to respect the diverse cultures in which the Church was planted,[153] then Mulago would insist firmly on having the principle applied to African Catholicism. "Africanisation" in the theology of the African Church is only the necessary corollary of Africanisation in its hierarchy and institutional life; and in stating this conviction, Mulago produces one of his most felicitous statements:

> "The Africanisation of the Church is the acceptance of Africa into the bosom of the Church, and it will happen in proportion as the Africanisation of theology opens the way for it."[154]

One can hardly miss the point that for Mulago, even the argument for theological plurality in the Church may also be a dimension of "participation"! For, after all, is the *Catholica* not a "community of partners – in life eternal"?

V. Conclusion

It may appear now that the terms in which Mulago has sought to make a case for a specific African viewpoint in religious apprehension and theological idiom have become out-of-date.[155] At least, this would seem to be the case since the Catholic bishops of Africa, at the Roman Synod of 1974, "repudiated 'the theology of adaptation' in no uncertain terms and opted for what they called 'the theology of incarnation'".[156] But, as this study has attempted to show, Mulago's use and understanding of "adaptation" in no sense presupposes the perpetuation of "Western superiority and domination",[157] either in religious insight or in theological formulation. On the contrary, Mulago has consistently held that a positive and unshackled African contribution to Christian theology would undoubtedly enrich the universal tradition of the Church.[158] Furthermore, what the concept of "adaptation" is supposed to have excluded, namely, "religious dialogue with African tradition",[159] is precisely what lies at the heart of Mulago's concerns. Meanwhile, Mulago has continued to argue for "adaptation" in a sense hardly distinguishable from the supposedly more progressive meaning of "incarnation",[160] which is generally associated with the aftermath of the Second Vatican Council.[161] Sometimes Mulago uses both terms in relation to the same body of material and with evidently similar meaning.[162] There is a consistency both in Mulago's usage of "adaptation", and in the remarkably "progressive" meaning he has given to the term, well before the significance of the Second Vatican Council for the emergent non-Western theologies was recognised.[163] Consequently, the least that can be said is that Mulago's work represents a genuine instance of African initiative in the forging of the theological agenda of African Christianity. It is perhaps significant that Mulago's early career was intimately linked with that movement of young African and Caribbean Catholic priests who, as early as the mid-1950s, considered that the time had come to raise some very serious questions about the European missionary planting of Christianity in Africa.[164]

But if the value of Mulago's work cannot be settled on the basis of a choice between two catchwords, does the fact of social change in Africa make his use of African "traditional" categories of thought and socio-religious ideas irrelevant? Is it really the case that Mulago's work is of scant theological significance for being based, allegedly, on "a view of the world which is in the process of passing away"?[165] Neckebrouck criticises Mulago's attempt to establish an analogy between the office of Pope and that of the Bantu ruler (*Mwami*) on the grounds that not only has the monarchy ceased to exist in Rwanda and Burundi, and is of little import among the Bashi, but also the concept of an authoritarian papacy is itself now called into question.[166] Neckebrouck concludes therefore that "the actual theological value of such attempts is practically nil".[167]

Similarly Deogratias Mbonyinkebe, in a review of *Un visage africain du Christianisme*, though avoiding the extreme views of Neckebrouck, yet observes:

"... we are now no longer in the world context described by Professor V. Mulago. Contacts with foreign cultures have intro-duced faults into our adherence to the values of our cul-tures..."[168]

But Mbonyinkebe is also careful to note – singling out what he calls "the sense of solidarity and participation" – that not every feature of Mulago's "traditional" world-view has disappeared from modern Africa. Furthermore, in view of what he describes as Africa's "treasures of ritual and symbolic sensibility",[169] Mbonyinkebe admits that hardly sufficient use has been made of African inspiration in Christian liturgy and worship.[170]

And yet, granted that the criticisms just noted may have some validity, it is doubtful whether the critics have adequately grasped the properly *theological* intent behind Mulago's writings. When allowance has been made for what is of purely transitory value in Mulago's analogies between Bantu custom and ideas on the one hand, and Catholic dogma and practice on the other, much still remains which is of exemplary significance within his total frame of reference. On some specific points of theological application in relation to Africa, Mulago echoes concepts and ideas found in Christian thinkers of other contexts. For instance, his concept of the Church as a Clan whose members descend from a common ancestor and share in the life transmitted from him, is not as outlandish as it might seem. Already in early Christian thought, Aristides and Justin are witnesses to the idea that Christ might conceivably be said to be "ancestor" of the Christian "third race".[171] Furthermore, his concept of the interpenetration of the Trinity, Christ, Church and the Christian believer without injury to the individuality of each, represents an interesting and valuable insight into the nature of the spiritual life. Aylward Shorter has noted that one area (among others) in which African Theology can probably make a contribution to the universal Christian Church would be to "help the world rediscover the relativity of such terms as 'sacred' and 'profane' and encourage the typically African vision of 'wholeness' or integration".[172] Mulago's entire theological outlook, so heavily invested as it is with the tremendous concepts of *union vitale* and *participation*, would seem to point clearly in the direction of what a "wholistic" African theology begins to look like.

But there is a more important sense in which Mulago's "adaptation" responds to the nature of the problem that faces African theology. Neckebrouck, who would rather see African theology address itself to religious questions thrown up by modern Western culture on the grounds that these are universally relevant,[173] is justly criticised by Aylward Shorter for his tendency, thereby, to "minimise the element of continuity between the theology of traditional African religions and indigenised Christian theology".[174] Behind the scepticism about the possibility of an "African theology" in the fullest sense of the term, there seems to lurk the spectre of the old theory about Africa being a cultural and religious *tabula rasa* upon which an entirely new theological system is to be constructed, using ingredients derived virtually entirely from the Western Christian tradition. Here, Mulago and those who share his outlook, resist the imposition of such a programme upon the modern African conscience. In their view, the identity of modern

Africa, including Christian Africa, will not be shaped independently of the religious forces that have operated in African
societies through countless generations of African history. The
importance attached to understanding the "traditional" heritage
of Africa finds its rationale here, and Mulago states this firmly in
the preface to *La Religion traditionnelle des Bantu et leur vision
du monde*:

> "Our project is a humble contribution to the question of tradi-
> tional, black African religions, particularly the *Bantu*, and a
> proof of their relevance with regard to the civilisation which
> Africa is in the process of forging, which cannot be solid and
> viable except in proportion as it remains faithful to ancestral
> traditions and as it manages to be judicious in its contact with
> the civilisations of other peoples and of revealed religion."[175]

The significance of the problem of identity in modern African
theological thinking can hardly be described more clearly, nor with
greater incisiveness. In specifically *theological* terms, what
Mulago's work has consistently sought to argue is that there is in
African tradition, a theology, a *natural* theology, the product of a
natural revelation, which is the only valid and sure basis for an
adequate Christian theological integration in modern Africa.[176]
The depth and the seriousness of Mulago's own personal Christian
commitment are hardly ever in doubt, and neither is his conviction
as to the relevance of the Christian message for Africa. However,
if he would be a Catholic theologian, he would insist on being so as
an African, and as a *Muntu*. What this means for the African
Catholic consciousness and indeed for the *Catholica* as a whole,
Mulago stated in the conclusion of *Un visage africain du Christianisme*:

> "At this point black Africa has made its entry into the history
> of the Church, and nothing more can be done in the new
> Jerusalem without the participation and contribution of the
> black world."[177]

It can hardly be said that Mulago has made an exaggerated
claim for the place of Africa in modern Christian history.[178]

Notes

1. *Des Prêtres noir s'interrogent*, Paris: Les Editions du Cerf, 1957, p.16.

2. Adrian Hastings, *A History of African Christianity: 1950-1975* (African
Studies series, 26), Cambridge: Cambridge University Press, 1979, p.119.

3. On the rise and impact of the "Négritude" movement, see Lilyan Kesteloot, *Les Ecrivains noirs de langue française: naissance d'une littérature* (4th
edition), Bruxelles: Editions de l'Institut de Sociologie, Université Libre de

Bruxelles, 1971.

4. Adrian Hastings, *A History of African Christianity: 1950-1975*, p.119.

5. *Des Prêtres noirs s'interrogent*, p.13.

6. *Ibid.*, p.13.

7. *Ibid.*, p.11.

8. *Ibid.*, p.14.

9. See, for instance, Meinrad Hebga, "Christianisme et Négritude", pp.189-203.

10. *Des Prêtres noirs s'interrogent*, p.279.

11. *Ibid.*, p.274.

12. See, however, R. Dosseh and R. Sastre, "Propagande et Vérité", pp.137-152.

13. See, for instance, J.-C. Bayeux, "Mentalité noire et mentalité biblique", pp.57-82.

14. Placide Tempels, *La Philosophie Bantoue* (Traduit du Néerlandais par A. Rubbens), Paris: Présence Africaine, 1949.

15. *Ibid.*, p.112: "The discovery of Bantu philosophy exercises a disturbing effect on those concerned with the education of the Blacks. We often found ourselves facing them as if it were all against nothing. In our mission of educating and civilising we had the impression of starting with a clean sheet; we thought we had at the very most to eliminate non-values in order to build sound foundations on bare ground. We were convinced that we had to despise stupid customs and empty beliefs which were completely ridiculous, essentially evil and void of all sense... We thought we were educating children, 'big children'... and that seemed quite easy. Now, all of a sudden, it seems that we are dealing with adult human beings, conscious of their wisdom and moulded by their own universal philosophy."

16. *Des Prêtres noirs s'interrogent*, p.16.

17. *Ibid.*, pp.19-40, "Nécessité de l'adaptation missionnaire chez les Bantu du Congo", and pp.171-187, "Le Pacte du Sang et la communion alimentaire, pierres d'attente de la communion eucharistique".

18. *Ibid.*, p.21.

19. *Ibid.*, p.22.

20. *Ibid.*, pp.21f.

21. *Ibid.*, p.23.

22. *Ibid.*, pp.24-31. For a discussion of the missionary teaching contained in these documents, see André Seumois, *Théologie Missionnaire* (vol.1: Délimitation de la Fonction missionnaire de l'Eglise), Rome: Bureau de Presse, OMI, 1973, pp.31-33. Also, André Rétif, *Introduction à la doctrine pontificale des missions*, Paris: Editions de Seuil, 1953, and Edouard Loffeld, *Le problème cardinal de la missiologie et des missions catholiques*, Rhenen, Holland: Editions "Spiritus", 1956, pp.205ff.

23. *Apologeticum*, 17.

24. Mulago, "Nécessité de l'adaptation missionnaire...", p.29. Mulago here quotes from *Evangelii Praecones*, in *AAS*, 43, 1951, p.336. For English translations of the various documents (except *Maximum Illud*), see the relevant volumes by Claudia Carlen, *The Papal Encyclicals*, Raleigh: McGrath Publishing Co., 1981.

25. For a defence of a similar principle, albeit in different terms, by a Protestant theologian, and ostensibly to correct "Roman Catholic misunderstanding", see Emil Brunner, *Revelation and Reason – the Christian Doctrine of Faith and Knowledge* (ET by Olive Wyon), London: SCM Press, 1971, p.262: "The original revelation is not a historical entity. Like the Creation, it is the presupposition of every individual and collective existence." Men know something of God – γνόντες τὸν θεόν – because "God has revealed it unto them". Thus revelation is not something that took place long, long ago, and has now been relegated to the far-distant past, but as Paul says, it is a present reality – even when men turn its reality into illusion. Behind all religion, therefore, there lies, on the side of God, truth, communication, the testimony of the Creator-God to himself."

26. Mulago, "Nécessité de l'adaptation missionnaire..." p.23.

27. See Ngindu Mushete, "L'Histoire de la théologie en Afrique. De la polémique à l'irénisme critique", in K. Appiah Kubi *et al.*, *Libération ou Adaptation: La théologie africaine s'interroge* (Le Colloque d'Accra), Paris: Librairie-Editions Harmattan, 1979, p.36.

28. Not unlike the concerns of E. Bolaji Idowu, Mulago's protracted interest in "African Traditional Religion" has led to his book, *La Religion Traditionelle des Bantu et leur vision du monde*, 2me edition (*Bibliotèque du Centre d'Etudes des Religions Africaines*, 5), Kinshasa: Faculté de Théologie Catholique, 1980.

29. The thesis title was *L'Union vitale "bantu" chez les Bashi, les Banyarwanda, et les Barundi face à l'Unité ecclésiale* (July, 1955).

30. Published as *Un visage africain du Christianisme: L'Union vitale bantu face à l'Unité vitale ecclésiale*, Paris: Présence Africaine, 1965.

31. See Vincent Mulago, "L'Union vitale bantu ou le principe de cohésion de la communauté chez les Bashi, les Banyarwanda et les Barundi" in *Annali Lateranensi*, vol.20, 1956, pp.61-263; "L'Union vitale bantu" in *Rythmes du monde*, vol.4, 1956, nos. 2-3, pp.133-141; "Dialectique existentielle des Bantu et sacramentalisme" in *Aspects de la culture noire*, pp.146-171; "La théologie et ses responsabilités" in *Présence Africaine*, vols.27-28, August-November, 1959, pp.188-205.

32. *Matt.* 13:52.

33. V. Mulago, "Nécessité de l'adaptation missionaire..." p.28.

34. V. Mulago, *Un visage africain du Christianisme*, p.17.

35. *Ibid.*, pp.17-18.

36. V. Mulago, "Nécessité de l'adaptation missionnaire..." p.38: "Adaptation aims at bringing about the meeting of the people's aspirations and the Christian message."

37. See for instance, André Seumois, *op.cit.* (vol.2), pp.123ff.

38. Pope Paul VI, "Address to Symposium of African Bishops" (31st July, 1969), text in *AAS*, 1969, pp.572-591. Cited in André Seumois, *op.cit.* (vol.1), p.39. See also Hubert Jedin *et al* (eds), *History of the Church* (vol.10: *The Church in the Modern Age*), London: Burns and Oates, 1981, pp.793-794.

39. V. Mulago, "Nécessité de l'adaptation missionnaire..." p.28.

40. See Adrian Hastings, *A History of African Christianity 1950-1975*, pp.167f. André Seumois, *op.cit.* (vol.1), points out, interestingly, that it is with John XXIII's *Princeps Pastorum* (28th Nov. 1959), that there emerges something approaching a clear statement regarding a plurality-within-unity in Catholic magisterial missionary teaching: "The idea of mission is defined by

various expressions which relate to the concept of particular churches to be founded (*ad novas condendas communitates christianas, AAS*, 1959, 855) to cause new seeds of the Church to grow (*ut novella Ecclesiae germina succrescant, AAS*, 1959, 835), *in this manner improving older official texts which had been content to speak of 'founding the Church'*" (p.35). My emphasis.

41. For Benedict XV, see his apostolic letter *Maximum Illud* (in *AAS*, 11, 1919); and for Pius XI, his encyclical *Rerum Ecclesiae* in *AAS*, 1926, pp.65ff).

42. V. Mulago, *Un visage africain du Christianisme*, pp.19-20.

43. *Ibid.*, p.24: "It is interesting to establish the doctrinal unity of the Holy See with regard to missionary methodology from the beginnings of the Congregation for the Propagation of the Faith up till today."

44. *Ibid.*, p.25. Mulago appropriately recalls the declaration by Pope John XXIII to the 2nd Congress of Black Writers and Artists, in Rome, April, 1959: "The Church... is not identified with any culture, even with Western culture, with which its history is, however, closely intertwined." For the full text of the Pope's address, see the volume assembled by the Société Africaine de Culture, *Un hommage africain à Jean XXIII*, Paris: Présence Africaine, 1965, pp.11-13.

45. Quoted in V. Mulago, "Nécessité de l'adaptation missionnaire..." pp.31f. Cf. V. Mulago, *Un visage africain du Christianisme*, p.24: "The Church is the mystical continuation and extension of Christ."

46. André Seumois, *op.cit.* (vol.2), p.7.

47. V. Mulago, *Un visage africain du Christianisme*, p.29.

48. *Ibid.*, p.29.

49. *Ibid.*, p.31; cf. *John* 1:9.

50. V. Mulago, *Un visage africain du Christianisme*, p.30.

51. *Acts* 17:22ff.

52. V. Mulago, *Un visage africain du Christianisme*, p.32.

53. *Ibid.*, p.31.

54. *Ibid.*, p.30; cf. "Nécessité de l'adaptation missionnaire..." p.33.

55. V. Mulago, *Un visage africain du Christianisme*, p.34; also, "Nécessité de l'adaptation missionnaire..." p.40: "This will be the flowering and consummation of unity, because Christ will be totally and completely all in all." Mulago refers to *Colossians* 3:11.

56. V. Mulago, *Un visage africain du Christianisme*, p.24; "Nécessité de l'adaptation missionnaire..." pp.30f.

57. V. Mulago, *Un visage africain du Christianisme*, p.30.

58. Cf. V. Mulago, "Nécessité de l'adaptation missionnaire..." p.37: "Catholicism is not one religion among others; it is religion plain and simple, 'the form which must clothe humanity so that it can be itself at last'". Mulago here quotes Henri de Lubac, *Catholicisme = Catholicism − A Study of Dogma in relation to the corporate destiny of mankind* (ET from 4th French edition, 1947, by Lancelot C. Sheppard) London: Burns, Oates and Washbourne, 1950, p.153.

59. V. Mulago, *Un visage africain du Christianisme*, p.223.

60. *Ibid.*, p.227.

61. See Ngindu Mushete, *op.cit.*, p.36.

62. See for instance, *Des Prêtres noirs s'interrogent*, p.171; V. Mulago, *Un visage africain du Christianisme*, p.12.

63. Ngindu Mushete, *op.cit.*, p.37.

64. *Ibid.*, p.38; Laënnec Hurbon, *Dieu dans le Voudou haitien,* Paris: Payot, 1972, p.33. See also Laënnec Hurbon, "Racisme et théologie missionnaire" in *Présence Africaine*, vol.71, no.3, 1969, p.40. Hurbon refers to Henri Desroche, *Sociologies religieuses*, Paris: Presses Universitaires de France, 1968, p.189 = *Jacob and the Angel: An Essay in Sociologies of Religion* (ET by John K. Savacool), Amherst: University of Massachussetts Press, 1973, p.134.

65. For an indication of the kind of "bold" initiatives which have increasingly emerged in African Catholic theology, including the call for an African Catholic Council, see the collection of essays published under the title *Civilisation noire et Eglise catholique* (Colloque organisé par la Société Africaine de Culture sous le haut patronage du gouvernement de la Republique de Côte d'Ivoire et sous la tutelle du Ministère ivorien des Affaires Culterelles, Abidjan, 12-17 September, 1977), Paris: Présence Africaine, 1978.

66. Pierre Charles, *Etudes Missiologiques,* Bruxelles Desclée de Brouwer, 1956. Cf. André Rétif, "Evolution of the Catholic idea of mission" in *History's Lessons for Tomorrow's Mission: Milestones in Missionary Thinking,* Geneva: W.S.C.F., n.d., pp.262-271.

67. Cf. F.-M. Lufuluabo, "La Conception bantoue face au christianisme" in *Personalité africaine et catholicisme*, Paris: Présence Africaine, 1963, pp.115-130.

68. V. Mulago, *Un visage africain du Christianisme*, p.18.

69. V. Mulago, "Nécessité de l'adaptation missionnaire..." p.38.

70. V. Mulago, *Un visage africain du Christianisme*, p.148; cf. pp.117ff. Elsewhere Mulago has defined *union vitale* clearly, as follows: "By unity of life or vital unity we understand (a) a relationship of being and life between each man and his descendants, his family, his brothers and sisters in the clan, his ancestors and finally God, the ultimate source of all life... (b) an analogous ontological relationship of each man with his patrimony, his background, with all that it contains, with what lives and grows there. If you like, vital union is the unifying link between them, vertically and horizontally, people-living and dead; it is the life-giving principle to be found in all of them. It is the result of a communion or participation in the same reality, the same vital principle which joins several people together." See Mulago, *La religion traditionnelle des Bantu et leur vision du monde*, p.133. On this whole subject, see the authoritative works by Alexis Kagame, *La philosophie bantu-rwandaise de l'être*, Bruxelles, Academie royale des Sciences coloniales (d'outre-mer), Classe des Sciences morales et politiques, vol.12, 1958; *La Philosophie bantu comparée*, Paris: Présence Africaine, 1976.

71. V. Mulago, *Un visage africain du Christianisme*, p.222.

72. *Ibid.*, p.159.

73. *Ibid.*, p.159.

74. *Ibid.*, p.30.

75. See Ngindu Mushete, *op.cit.*, p.37.

76. V. Mulago, *Un visage africain du Christianisme*, p.33.

77. *Ibid.*, pp.12, 33, 161ff.

78. Pierre Charles, *op.cit.*, pp.27f. This eminent Belgian Catholic missiologist considered the concept and practice of mission as based "on the very nature of the visible Church" and assigned as the "formal object" of such mission "the setting up of the visible Church in countries where it does not yet

exist" (pp.26f). Charles went on with evident self-assurance, to distinguish between the Protestant and Catholic approaches: "... for them [Protestants], the Church is no more than a society of the spirit, for us it is a society of souls, for us it is a society of men and is thus concerned with bodies, by its rights as a church." (pp.27-28). He concludes, accordingly, "mission, being founded on the Church, not immediately on the universality of redemption or on the uniqueness of God or on any other truth – the only true mission is Catholic mission and the Pope is its only head." (p.28). It is doubtful whether Mulago, in the ecumenical context of African Christian life, shares Pierre Charles' exclusivist views. However, cf. his comment in "Nécessité de l'adaptation missionnaire..." (p.37): "Catholicism is not one religion among others, it is religion plain and simple, the form which must clothe humanity so that it can be itself at last." Nevertheless, it is more likely that by "Catholicism", Mulago meant little more than the Christian message. For a thorough discussion of the concept of "implantation of the Church", in Catholic missiology, see André Seumois, *op.cit.* (vol.2), ch.3, "L'implantation ecclésiale".

79. V. Mulago, *Un visage africain du Christianisme*, p.18.

80. *Ibid.*, pp.225-226. My emphasis.

81. *Ibid.*, p.223.

82. *Ibid.*, p.226. My emphasis. Cf. pp.30f: "adaptation is by no means a propaganda tactic, it is not a stratagem but an aspect of fidelity to the mission of the Church, which is involved entirely in prolonging the incarnation of the Word, the adaptation of God to man. 'The apostle is guided not primarily by a propaganda interest but by the logic of his faith'." Mulago quotes from Henri de Lubac, *op.cit.*, p.259 = ET, p.156.

83. Placide Tempels, *op.cit.*, p.123.

84. *Ibid.*, p.123.

85. *Ibid.*, þ.123.

86. V. Mulago, *Un visage africain du Christianisme*, p.161.

87. *Ibid.*, p.157. It is worth noting, though, that Mulago rejects Tempels' basic equation of the Bantu concept of "being" (*l'être*) with "power" (*force*). See Placide Tempels, *op.cit.*, pp.33ff. For Mulago, "power" (*force*), far from constituting the totality of "being" (*l'être*), is only a modal category of being: "power does not exhaust the categories of the *ntu* or created being; it is not the being, the *ntu* pure and simple, but of the being. Power finds its place in the category *kuntu*, the category of way of being." (p.157). Thus Tempels' interpretation which tends towards portraying an impersonal universe pervaded by "power(s)", is replaced by a more "relational" concept. This highlights appropriately the importance of "participation" and "communication" in Mulago's thinking.

88. V. Mulago, *Un visage africain du Christianisme*, p.156.

89. *Ibid.*, p.158; cf. Placide Tempels, *op.cit.*, p.125.

90. See Alexis Kagame, *La philosophie bantu-rwandaise de l'être*, pp.410ff; see also Kagame's two studies on "La place de Dieu et de l'homme dans la Religion des Bantu" in *CRA*, vol.2, no.4, July 1968, pp.213-222. and vol.3, no.5, January 1969, pp.5-11. For Kagame, at the centre of Bantu religious thought is the belief that man is himself centre of God's universe, and so at the heart of religion; but not man as individual, but rather as humanity, i.e. "the perpetuation of humankind." and that this perpetuation of the human is what constitutes the centre of Bantu religious consciousness: "the ultimate aim of man is procreation, a limitless process" (p.10), and thus he concludes: "...tradi-

tional Bantu religion groups its truths/beliefs around two vital centres: *God* and *Man*. The high place which this religion reserves for God is nevertheless regarded as a necessary presupposition for the entire plan fixed beforehand by the Creator, who has directed everything towards the perpetuation of his best piece of work – *the human race*". (In *CRA*, vol.3, no.5, January, 1969, p.11)

91. It is an indication of the eminently *theological* concerns of Mulago (as against Kagame's more strictly *philosophical* interests), that while he also accepts Bantu religion to be "essentially anthropocentric", Mulago reaches beyond the "phenomenological" observation to give a "theological" account of it: "In order better to understand the religious attitude of Africans we must get rid of the dualist dialectic which characterises Western thought and according to which the exaltation of man means the rejection of God. No, African religion revolves around two truths/beliefs as around two vital centres: God and man." See Mulago, *La Religion Traditionnelle des Bantu et leur vision du monde*, p.166. Mulago, in a note, refers to Kagame's two articles.

92. V. Mulago, *Un visage africain du Christianisme*, p.158.

93. *Ibid.*, pp.195-219.

94. *Ibid.*, pp.177-194; cf. pp.161-176.

95. For Cyril of Alexandria and Augustine, on the Incarnation of the Word and its implications for the Church as continuation of the Incarnation, see pp.168-171; cf. pp.213-214, for Cyril of Alexandria on the Eucharist. For Gregory of Nyssa, on the unity of mankind through participation in the image of God, see pp.183-184.

96. Cf. V. Mulago, "Vital Participation: the cohesive principle of the Bantu community" in Kwesi A. Dickson and Paul Ellingworth (eds), *Biblical Revelation and African Beliefs,* London: Lutterworth Press, 1969, pp.137-158.

97. V. Mulago, *Un visage africain du Christianisme*, p.177.

98. *Ibid.*, p.178.

99. *Ibid.*, p.178.

100. *Ibid.*, pp.178f. Mulago, in a note, refers to *2 Peter* 1:3-4.

101. V. Mulago, *Un visage africain du Christianisme*, p.179.

102. See the very engaging article by Greek Orthodox churchman, Anastasios Yannoulatos, "Growing into an awareness of primal world-views" in John B. Taylor (ed), *Primal World-views: Christian Involvement in Dialogue with Traditional Thought Forms,* Ibadan: Daystar Press, 1976, pp.72-78.

103. V. Mulago, *Un visage africain du Christianisme*, pp.179f. Mulago, in a note, refers to *Romans* 8:15-18,29.

104. V. Mulago, *Un visage africain du Christianisme*, p.180.

105. *Ibid.*, p.181.

106. *Ibid.*, p.182.

107. *Ibid.*, p.182.

108. *Ibid.*, p.187. Mulago refers appropriately to *Hebrews* 2:11-13,17.

109. V. Mulago, *Un visage africain du Christianisme*, p.188. Mulago refers to *Galatians* 4:4.

110. *Hebrews* 2:14.

111. V. Mulago, *Un visage africain du Christianisme*, p.188.

112. *Ibid.*, p.189. The "divine motherhood" of Mary as the principle of her "royal dignity" was also underscored by Pope Pius XII in his encyclical *Ad Caeli*

Reginam, to which Mulago, appropriately, refers. See English text in Claudia Carlen, *op.cit.*, p.274. The special point of interest in Mulago's application, however, is the fact that he develops his thinking on Mary's "divine motherhood" directly from Bantu tradition!

113. See Raymond E. Brown, *et al.*, *Mary in the New Testament* (*A Collaborative Assessment by Protestant and Roman Catholic scholars*), Philadelphia: Fortress Press; New York: Paulist Press, 1978.

114. Maurice Wiles, *The Making of Christian Doctrine: A Study in the principles of early doctrinal development*, Cambridge: Cambridge University Press, 1967, p.89: "There is one area of doctrine in Christian history where development is unquestionably due to the successful influence of popular devotion – the sphere of Mariological doctrine."

115. V. Mulago, *Un visage africain du Christianisme*, p.189. It is interesting that Mulago, in fact, suggests that his discussion on the analogy between the *reine-mère* and Mary could be developed into a full treatment of Mariological doctrine on the basis of the Bantu concept of participation (*ibid.*, p.188, note 31).

116. *Ibid.*, p.190.

117. *Ibid.*, p.203: "Like the *mwami* and even more so than he, the Sovereign Pontiff is the father of his people, the sign and almost the incarnation of the invisible world, the true 'bearer of power' and the ultimate symbol of unity, since in him all lower authorities converge, in him the powers of Peter are carried on and in him Christ, the Word of God, the Founder of the Church, lives on and continues to act on earth."

118. *Ibid.*, p.222.

119. Cf. Mulago, *La religion traditionelle des Bantu et leur vision du monde*, pp.169f: "... for those who know both Christianity and African religious values from the inside and in essence there do not seem to be *two* realities opposed to one another. God who is the source of all that is positive in our cultural heritage is at the same time Author of the Christian Revelation. True to himself, he cannot contradict himself. For through the centuries God, as a provident Father, has been preparing the way for the Gospel."

120. Mulago, "Christianisme et culture africaine: apport africain à la théologie" in C.G. Baëta (ed), *Christianity in Tropical Africa* (Studies presented and discussed at the seventh International African Seminar, University of Ghana, April, 1965), London: Oxford University Press, 1968, p.308.

121. See C.G. Baëta (ed), *op.cit.*

122. See Kwesi A. Dickson and Paul Ellingworth (eds), *op.cit.*

123. These were, respectively, "Christianisme et culture africaine: apport africain à la théologie", pp.308-328, and "Vital Participation: the cohesive principle of the Bantu community", pp.137-158.

124. Mulago, "Vital Participation: the cohesive principle of the Bantu community", p.137.

125. Many of these studies appear in two important journals on religion published in Zaire: *Revue du Clergé Africain (RCA)*, which is edited from the major seminary at Inkisi and *Cahiers des Religions Africaines (CRA)*, issued by the Centre d'Etudes des Religions Africaines, which is headed by Mulago. See bibliography for details. It has not been possible for me to gain access to all of Mulago's articles in these journals. However, I consider that a sufficient number have been available to me, and that I have been enabled to form a reasonable opinion of his theological thinking.

126. See Ngindu Mushete, *op.cit.*, p.36.

127. Mulago, "Christianisme et culture africaine..." p.318.

128. See Mulago, "La Religion traditionnelle, élément central de la culture Bantu" in *Les Religions africaines comme source de valeurs de civilisation* (Colloque organisé par la Société Africaine de Culture avec l'aide et sous le haut patronage du Gouvernement du Dahomey et avec le concours de l'UNESCO, Cotonou, 16-22 aout, 1970), Paris: Présence Africaine, 1972, pp.115-155, esp. pp.150ff. See also his *La Religion traditionnelle des Bantu et leur vision du monde*, pp.165-169. Cf. E. Bolaji Idowu's observation, "African Traditional Religion is the master-key to the understanding of Africans who in all things are religious"; see his "The Study of Religion with special reference to African Traditional Religion", in *Orita*, vol.1, no.1, June, 1967, p.11.

129. Mulago, "Christianisme et culture africaine..." p.308. My emphasis.

130. See, for example, the titles of some of his essays and articles listed in our bibliography.

131. J.K. Agbeti, "African Theology: What it is", in *Presence,* vol.5, no.3, p.7, quoted in Aylward Shorter, *African Christian Theology – Adaptation or Incarnation?* London: Geoffrey Chapman, 1975, p.27.

132. See previous section, *"Un visage africain du christianisme* (2): The application of 'adaptation'".

133. J.V. Langmead Casserley, lamenting the dearth of this all-important aspect of the task of theology in the Western tradition of the 20th century, points out: "the subject matter of theology is life, the life of the universe and the life of man considered in their relation to the will and purpose of the Creator." See his *The Retreat from Christianity in the Modern World* (The Maurice Lectures for 1951), London: Longmans, Green & Co., 1952, p.73.

134. Mulago, "Symbolisme dans les Religions traditionnelles africaines et Sacramentalisme" in *RCA*, vol.27, nos.4/5, July 1972, pp.467-502.

135. *Ibid.*, p.501. My emphasis.

136. Mulago, "Christianisme et culture africaine..." pp.308-317.

137. *Ibid.*, p.309.

138. *Ibid.*, p.313. Cf. Mulago, "Le Dieu des Bantu" in *CRA*, vol.2, no.3, January, 1968, pp.23-64.

139. Cf. Martin Buber's declaration: "In the beginning is relation". It is interesting to see that Martin Buber associates his relational concept with "the speech of 'primitive' peoples, that is of those that have a meagre stock of objects, and whose life is built up within a narrow circle of acts highly charged with presentness." (He names the Zulu). See Martin Buber, *I and Thou* (ET by Ronald Gregor Smith), Edinburgh: T. & T. Clark, 1937, p.18.

140. Mulago, "Christianisme et culture africaine..." pp.317-324

141. *Ibid.*, p.319; Mulago refers to and expounds *Genesis* 1:26f, 2:7 and 2:18-24.

142. Mulago, "Christianisme et culture africaine..." p.320.

143. *Ibid.*, pp.320f.

144. *Ibid.*, pp.321ff.

145. *Ibid.*, pp.323-324.

146. *Ibid.*, p.324. My emphasis.

147. For this assessment of Mulago's contribution, see Alphonse Ngindu

(Mushete), "La quatrième semaine théologique de Kinshasa et la problèmatique d'une théologie africaine" in *CRA*, vol.2, no.4, July 1968, pp.353-372; on Mulago, pp.361-363. The papers are published under the title *Renouveau de l'Eglise et Nouvelles Eglises, Colloque sur la théologie africaine*, under the auspices of the *Revue du Clergé Africain*. See also *RCA*, March/May, 1969.

148. See Mulago, "Le problème d'une théologie africaine revu à la lumière de Vatican II" in *Renouveau de l'Eglise et Nouvelles Eglises*, pp.115-152.

149. See "Débat Th. Tshibangu – A. Vanneste" in *RCA*, July 1960, pp.333-352. Tshibangu, at the time a pupil of Vanneste, was destined to become the first Zairean *Recteur* of Lovanium University of Kinshasa.

150. Mulago, "Le problème d'une théologie africaine..." pp.119f. See also Alfred Vanneste, "Théologie universelle et théologie africaine" in *Renouveau de l'Eglise et Nouvelles Eglises*, pp.162-174. Vanneste admits to the rightness of Mulago's criticism: "I am very willing to admit that by insisting continually on the fact that all theology must aim at universality in order to be true, I am inclined to underline the unity of the science of theology rather than its plurality. And it is perhaps not completely wrong to reproach the partisans of unity with conceiving it primarily as a Western unity." (p.173).

151. Mulago, "Le problème d'une théologie africaine..." p.125.

152. This is another term favoured by Mulago for the process of theological adaptation. See his "'Naturalisation' du christianisme en dehors de l'Occident à la lumière de Vatican II" in *Euntes Docete* 20, 1967, pp.241-262.

153. Mulago, "Le problème d'une théologie africaine..." p.125. Cf. Mulago, *La Religion traditionnelle des Bantu et leur vision du monde*, p.176, where he refers specifically to three documents of the Second Vatican Council: *Lumen Gentium* (par.13); *Ad Gentes* (par.22) on missionary activity; and *Nostra Aetate* (par.12) on the Church's relations with other religious traditions.

154. Mulago, "Le problème d'une théologie africaine..." p.121.

155. See Aylward Shorter, *African Christian Theology: Adaptation or Incarnation?* pp.150f.

156. *Ibid.*, p.150. Shorter quotes the relevant section of the Bishops' declaration.

157. *Ibid.*, p.150.

158. Mulago, "Christianisme et culture africaine..." p.324.

159. Aylward Shorter, *op.cit.*, pp.150.

160. Cf. Mulago, "Christianisme et culture africaine..." p.308: "True adaptation is fidelity to the law of the Incarnation of the God-man ."

161. Cf. Aylward Shorter, *op.cit.*, pp.149f.

162. Cf. Mulago, "Le problème d'une théologie africaine..." pp.126-127. Referring to the decisions of the Second Vatican Council, Mulago writes: "Nevertheless, Vatican II did not rest with formulating the principle of the embodiment of Christianity in the culture of every people, it applied it to various areas of manifestation of the Christian life." Then later in the same section of the article, "The legislators of Vatican II are so aware of the need for adaptation that, even when it is a question of the formation of priests, they are unwilling to give more than general principles, leaving it to the bishops of each country to adopt a special programme of priestly formation."

163. Mulago does acknowledge the importance of the Second Vatican Council for the developments he has for so long sought to promote. See his "Le

problème d'une théologie africaine..." p.132: "...it is right to acknowledge that this Council is opening a new way to liberation for us. The outcome will be a *confessio africana* which would not have to formulate a new profession of faith, but starting from the Gospel and the traditional Creed, would provide an answer to the particular problems of the modern African Christian."

164. See *Des Prêtres noirs s'interrogent.*

165. V. Neckebrouck, *L'Afrique noire et la crise religieuse de l'Occident,* Tabora, Tanzania: T.M.P. Book Department, 1971, p.242.

166. *Ibid.,* pp.240-241.

167. *Ibid.,* p.241.

168. Deogratias Mbonyinkebe, review of *Un visage africain du Chris-tianisme,* in *CRA,* vol.3, no.5, January, 1969, pp.143-147. Quotation from p.146.

169. *Ibid.,* p.146.

170. Mbonyinkebe expresses this viewpoint in the happy and hopeful statement: "From this point of view we are living below our real potential." (*ibid.,* p.146).

171. See Justin, *Dialogue with Trypho,* 123,9: "We from Christ, who begot us unto God, ... are called and are the true sons of God"; cf. Aristides, *Apology,* 2 (Syriac version): "The Christians then trace the beginning of their religion from Jesus Christ." Both references follow Edgar J. Goodspeed (ed), *Die ältesten Apologeten,* Göttingen: Vandenhoek & Ruprecht, 1914.

172. Aylward Shorter, *op.cit.,* p.34.

173. V. Neckebrouck, *op.cit.,* pp.242f. Neckebrouck singles out especially the problematic of faith in a personal God in the modern West.

174. Aylward Shorter, *op.cit.,* p.28; cf. p.34.

175. Mulago, *La Religion traditionnelle des Bantu et leur vision du monde,* p.7.

176. Cf. Mulago, *Un visage africain du Christianisme,* pp.222f: "... the value which the Church can confer on the aspirations of the Bantu *will not be an addition, but a new way of being,* a new creation, at once a death and a resurrection; in a word, involvement, a *state of being taken up into Christ and taken over by him, and likewise with the Church.*" (My emphasis) For an engaging and sympathetic study of the whole subject by a Catholic missionary author with African experience, see Henri Maurier, *The Other Covenant: A Theology of Paganism* (ET by Charles McGrath), Glen Rock, New Jersey: Newman Press, 1968. (Originally, *Essai d'une théologie du paganisme,* Paris: Editions de l'Orante, 1965). See also, Henri Maurier's contribution to the 1968 Lovanium Conference on "African theology", "Insertion de l'Eglise dans le monde africain et problèmatique de la doctrine chrétienne" in *Renouveau de l'Eglise et Nouvelles Eglises,* pp.153-161.

177. Mulago, *Un visage africain du Christianisme,* p.227.

178. See A.F. Walls, "Towards understanding Africa's place in Christian history" in J.S. Pobee (ed), *Religion in a Pluralistic Society* (Essays presented to Professor C.G. Baëta in celebration of his retirement from the service of the University of Ghana, September 1971, by friends and colleagues scattered over the globe), Leiden: E.J. Brill, 1976, pp.180-189.

Chapter Ten

A Variety of African Responses (4): Byang Kato, or Theology as Bibliology[1] I. The emergence of a dissenting voice

It is fitting that we should examine last of all the theological thought and outlook of an African theologian, who, equally alive in his own way to the legacy of the "Third Opportunity", yet has sought to deal with the identity problem of the modern African Christian in ways which are quite at variance on most points with the responses offered by our other writers. For though he was the last to come to prominence and had the shortest career of all,[2] Byang Henry Kato came to embody the very antithesis of the basic positions enunciated by the African theologians we have studied so far. Virtually everything he wrote was intended as a reaction to, and a rebuttal of, much that went to constitute the "African theology" of the last two decades. For this, if for no other reason, Byang Kato's work compels attention.[3]

Moreover, Kato presents the remarkable instance of one who, though trained in theology on a Western model like his fellow African theologians of modern times, yet unlike them, retained that model for his theological reflection in his African context. Whilst it cannot be said that Kato was entirely lacking in critical discernment regarding the theological models and viewpoints he espoused, it is nonetheless the case that there is little in his outlook which does not stem from his deep roots in the conservative evangelical tradition – particularly the North American variant – of Christianity.[4] It is understandable, therefore, that Timothy Njoya should rebuff Kato's criticism of "African theology" in the terms he employs:

"Byang Kato's fear of African religion and philosophy is genuinely rooted in his evangelical tradition. Evangelicalism in Africa claims itself to be cultureless, timeless, and unhistorical in order to cover up the fact that it is American and conservative."[5]

But even if the evangelicalism that Kato embodied was "American and conservative", his generally negative attitude to "African [traditional] religion and philosophy" cannot be so easily imputed to fear. No major African theological figure so resolutely took on the proponents of what Kato called "an integral Christianity" – integral in the sense that it incorporated elements from African pre-Christian tradition, and involved "the peaceful evolution of Africans from pagan to Christian beliefs and ways"[6] – as Kato did. To appreciate adequately Kato's outlook, one has to understand his own perception of his religious and spiritual background.

Nowhere was Byang Kato's dissenting voice more clamant than in relation to what became the chief element in the agenda of most other African theologians, namely, the pre-Christian religious traditions of Africa. In a revealing statement which is intended to be a criticism of John Mbiti's positive theological evaluation of African pre-Christian religious tradition, Kato indicated also what lay behind his own negative attitude:

"His [Mbiti's]... limitation comes from the fact that he was born and brought up in a Christian home. Thus he is not able to understand the background of African traditional religion as well as one who has been raised in a thoroughly traditional way."[7]

Whilst one can readily appreciate the implied suggestion that "a thoroughly traditional" upbringing has some value for assessing the African pre-Christian religious tradition from the standpoint of the Christian present, Kato shows no awareness of the effect that his fundamentally unsympathetic and even disdainful attitude to "non-Christian religions"[8] may have on his understanding of those religions, including his own religious past. As a result, his case study of his native Jaba religion,[9] becomes less useful than it might have been. Since Kato was so overwhelmingly committed to ensuring that this "non-Christian religion" was not elevated "to the same status as Biblical Christianity",[10] he was unable to provide the kind of theological interpretation and insight into the religion and spirituality of the Jaba people, which a more eirenical approach might conceivably have done. Through the various sections of the study – The Jaba concept of a Supreme Being, Jaba concepts of the spirit world, The Jaba concept of salvation, The Jaba concept of revelation – Kato's one overriding concern was to demonstrate that "there is neither redemption nor evidence of direct divine revelation to individuals in Jaba religion".[11]

Thus, when Kato came upon evidence which seemed to point in the direction of a convergence between Jaba religious ideas and Biblical teaching, he was forced to the expedient of finding ways to minimise the significance of such evidence. A notable example is the view that Jaba understanding of sin "boils down to only social ills". Kato recognised that this "is comparable to the view of sin as conceived by the prophets of Israel", adding: "Justice to one's neighbour is what God requires from His people (*Amos* 5:24)".[12] However, in order to maintain his basic viewpoint on the relative positions of Jaba traditional religion and the Christian Gospel, Kato then minimised the importance of this social dimension of sin in the Bible:

> "But sin against the society is only a minor manifestation of the basic sin of rebellion against God. The challenge, therefore, goes forth to Israel, 'He has told you, O man, what is good; and what does the Lord require of you but to do justice, to love kindness, and to walk humbly with your God?' (*Mic.* 6:8). David declares, 'Against Thee, Thee only, have I sinned, and done what is evil in Thy sight, so that thou art justified when thou dost speak and blameless when thou dost judge' (*Psa.* 51:4)."[13]

Kato seemed not to realise that of the three divine precepts announced by the prophet Micah, the first two were couched in essentially *social* terms, and that the kind of distinction which he was making between "individualistic" and "societal" views of sin was not easily sustained from his Biblical proof-texts. And yet, Kato went on to criticise Jaba people for having a "wrong conception of sin..."[14]

Perhaps an even more pertinent illustration of Kato's basic stance towards Jaba traditional religion is seen in his treatment of spirit-possession. This is particularly significant since the instances which Kato chose to highlight had an important bearing on the eventual establishment of Christianity in the community:

> "The spirits bring not only harm to the community. They possess certain ladies in the society and enable them to predict good

things to come. When a lady is possessed, she speaks in tongues, prophesies, and performs miracles. Gwamna Awon has related that a possessed woman predicted several years earlier that some white people would come to Kagoro and tell them about Gwaza, the Supreme Being. This prediction was of course fulfilled. Kagoro today is about sixty per cent 'Christian' because of active missionary effort. The same lady consoled the bereaved mother of the Chief of Kagoro with this prophecy, 'Do not weep. You will bring forth another son who will become a chief'. Awon has been a chief for 28 years and has been one of the best chiefs in the Northern States of Nigeria."[15]

What is significant about Kato's study at this point is that whilst Kato was prepared to link the sizeable "Christian" segment of the Jaba population with "active missionary effort", he seemed to have no place in his interpretative framework for the "prophetess" who, through spirit-possession, not only predicted the event in the first place, but also exercised a ministry of consolation in the community prior to the coming of *Christian* ministry! Neither does Kato explain how "the spirits" who "are always associated with 'Kuno', Satan",[16] can be responsible for such an evidently beneficent development in the religious history of the community. It becomes hard to avoid the conclusion that Kato's generally negative estimation of African pre-Christian religious tradition was not only the result of observation and previous participation, but also a necessary corollary of the kind of theological presuppositions with which he operated. In other words, one effect of his intense commitment to preserving the integrity of "Biblical Christianity" was that "non-Christian religions" appeared to manifest little more than "weak clues" to the awareness of the Supernatural, "only the faint steps that man is more than flesh and blood", and offered virtually no help towards answering the fundamental human "craving after the Supreme Being", and "search for reality in life..." Accordingly,

"The beliefs of African traditional religions only locate the problem; the practices point away from the solution; the Incarnate risen Christ is the answer. Christianity is a radical faith and it must transform sinners radically."[17]

What Byang Kato's understanding of the relationship between the African heritage in religion and the Christian faith amounted to, was that the two constituted quite distinct and discontinuous entities, different religious systems with little or no common ground between them. From Kato's standpoint, therefore, there was no theological validity for the very basis on which the African theological enterprise was being constructed, namely, that the "perennial religions and spiritualities of Africa" were the chief realities with which the African Christian scholar needs in the first place, to come to terms, and to interpret.[18] In Kato's words, "Christianity cannot incorporate any man-made religion",[19] and he criticised other African theologians for their "great enthusiasm about African religions", and for their failure "to see the unique nature of Biblical revelation".[20]

It is therefore not surprising that Kato emphatically rejected the statement issued by the Ibadan Consultation of African Theologians in 1965, to the effect that "God's self-revelation in Jesus Christ... is not totally discontinuous with our people's previous traditional knowledge of Him".[21] Kato would allow only the continuity of a weak "general revelation... through nature and conscience". On the substantial issue of revelation in Jesus Christ, he declared:

> "Redemptive salvation of Christ, first prefigured in the Old Testament, is a new thing. Thus Christ is the fulfilment of the Old Testament and of the deep spiritual need of the human hearts, *but He is not the fulfilment of African traditional religions or any other non-Christian religion.*"[22]

The closest that Kato came to a positive evaluation of the African pre-Christian heritage in religion was in a brief discussion on the salvability of the dead who never heard the Gospel proclaimed. Responding favourably to the suggestion by J.N.D. Anderson that a person in that category, in "whose heart the God of all mercy had been working by His Spirit, who had come in some measure to realise his sin and need for forgiveness, and who had been enabled, in the twilight as it were to throw himself on the mercy of God",[23] might be presumed saved on the basis of God's mercy, Kato added the interesting comment:

> "It should be noted that Anderson isolates certain ones whose heart the Lord might have touched somehow. Such persons, if there were any, would not be ardent religious worshippers. Rather they might be 'atheists' in regard to pagan worship, like Socrates."[24]

Here, one might have thought, Kato was dealing with a highly significant idea which, as we have seen, not only had an important place in early Christian apologetics[25], but also might have some relevance for the understanding of the African story.[26] But Kato's generally negative estimation of African pre-Christian religious tradition prevented him from considering as worthy of further investigation what might well have been a useful theological and historical insight.

It is in this postulate of radical discontinuity between African tradition and Christian faith that Kato's real significance as a dissenting voice in modern African theology lies. For, by conceiving of the relationship between Christianity and the African religious past in such starkly negative terms, Kato reproduced an important ingredient in the nineteenth-century missionary view of Africa, a view which, as we have already noted, was crucial in the making of an identity problem for the African Christian conscience of modern times.[27] By claiming that African theological reflection could not have any positive links with African religious tradition and experience of the past, Kato was, in fact, confirming the earlier missionary perception of Africa as a "*tabula rasa* on which a wholly new religious psychology was somehow to be imprinted".[28] Thus, whereas most other African theologians felt an inner compulsion to "... vindicate Africa before a critical European audience, one that is largely without understanding of the continent",[29] Byang Kato, on the other hand, tended to see as his opponents fellow African theologians, who, perhaps more aware than he was that the Western value-setting for the Christian faith was no longer tenable, were concerned to seek new foundations for an African Christian self-identity which took account of the African religious past. Since, for his part, Kato was convinced that the religious past had no significance for African Christian self-consciousness except as darkness in relation to light,[30] it stands to reason that he saw those who held a divergent viewpoint on the subject as detractors of the Christian faith who needed to be exposed.[31]

II. " Tying together the feet of a cat and a pig..." The Evangelical-Ecumenical Divide

It is quite consistent with Kato's outlook and theological stance that he described the distinction between "Evangelicals" and "Ecumenicals" in the following terms:

"The unity of believers and those who are not sure that they are believers cannot produce fellowship. Such a unity may be compared with the unity that results from tying together the feet

of a cat and a pig and pushing them into the mud. There can be
no fellowship in that mud. Evangelicals believe only in the kind
of unity that also produces genuine fellowship in the Word of
God."[32]

In the graphic imagery used, it is obvious which groups are
represented by the proverbially *clean* cat and the equally proverbially *dirt-loving* pig! The sort of uncompromising divide that Kato
thus postulated between what were to him two *kinds* of Christians,
pervaded virtually everything that Kato wrote in his brief theological career. Whether the distinction was between "Bible-believing
Christians" and "liberals", between "conservative evangelicals"
and "ecumenicals" or "liberals", between "evangelicals" and
"ecumenists", the thought remained the same: the one term represents those who "hold to the true doctrine" and the other describes
those who "do not adhere to the true doctrine", and "have now fallen
by the wayside".[33] In his one major work, *Theological Pitfalls in
Africa*, Kato devoted three whole chapters to the subject of
"Ecumenism" and the dangers it posed to the development of
"Biblical Christianity" in Africa.[34]

In attacking "Ecumenism" Kato was not decrying Christian
unity as such, and he was keen not only to point out that "Jesus
Christ did pray for both spiritual and visible unity (*John* 17:21)",
but also that Evangelicals had every cause "to pull together" if only
because "unity is strength even in the Lord's work".[35] His real
target was "the solidly institutionalised movement incarnated in
the World Council of Churches".[36] By introducing a specific comparison between what he called "historical ecumenism" (of the
undivided Church of the Patristic era), and the "modern
ecumenism" of the World Council of Churches, Kato intended to
indicate what he felt was wrong with the "ecumenism" of his day:

"Unlike the true type of early ecumenical councils, present-day
ecumenism plays down doctrinal issues. Their thesis is that
doctrine divides, but service unites... To the ecumenicals, unity,
almost at any cost, is the greatest thing that could happen to
the Christian Church..."[37]

By isolating doctrinal consensus as the hallmark of the true
type of Christian ecumenism, Kato was setting up a criterion with
which to judge the history of the modern ecumenical movement.
Using this criterion, Kato challenged the link usually made between "current ecumenism" and the Edinburgh World Missionary
Conference of 1910, which has been described as "the crucial event

in the history of the ecumenical movement".[38] In Kato's view this link could be shown to be a "weak one", for two reasons which had to do with two objectives of the Edinburgh Conference, namely, "the concern for salvation of individual souls", and "the difference between Christianity and non-Christian religions".[39] Since, according to Kato, the World Council of Churches had departed from each of these points which he considered crucial for Christian commitment, the Council as the embodiment of "current ecumenism" could not claim continuity with the Edinburgh Conference.

On the other hand, the Council was in continuity with what Kato saw as the "weaknesses" of the Edinburgh Conference. The first and "major weakness of the Edinburgh Conference was the absence of doctrinal considerations", since "it was resolved at the outset that 'questions of doctrine or church policy with regard to which the Churches and Societies taking part... differ among themselves' would not be discussed".[40] The other weakness of Edinburgh 1910 consisted in "the exclusion of Latin America among the areas to be evangelised..." as a move to conciliate Roman Catholics who considered the continent already Christian. On each of these points of "weakness", Kato saw "features which today's ecumenicals can justifiably claim for heritage". However,

> "On other counts, Edinburgh was soundly evangelical. To bring salvation to people as individuals was their goal. The utter lostness of man without Christ was their Biblical presupposition. There was no doubt at all in their minds as to the meaning of salvation. Their mission was clear. Their message was unadulterated."[41]

Kato therefore concluded that there were "poisonous elements" in the "theology of ecumenism"[42] – basically "syncretism" and "universalism" – at both the world-wide level of the World Council of Churches (WCC), and the local level of its African manifestation in the All Africa Conference of Churches (AACC). Thus, in his study of the evolution of the AACC, from its formation in 1963 at Kampala (Uganda) to its third General Assembly in 1974 at Lusaka (Zambia),[43] Kato's major concern was to show how the "poisonous elements" in the "theology of ecumenism" were progressively replacing what he saw as "the essential basic doctrines of the Church".[44] Since Kato considered these basic doctrines to relate to belief in the "inerrancy" of the Bible,[45] the uniqueness of Christianity over against "non-Christian religions" and the affirmation of the centrality of individual salvation from sin – "the fundamental dilemma of man" – conceived in essentially individualistic and spiritual terms,[46] he could accept neither the quest for a theological synthesis between the pre-Christian heritage and the Christian faith, nor the politicisation of African theological thought to deal with issues of social injustice and political oppression.[47] These developments amounted to a betrayal of the Gospel and a misconception of the Christian calling as he understood them.[48]

Even if it is granted that Kato's attacks upon theological views he could not accept stemmed from his own particular theological presuppositions, one may still wonder how deeply Kato understood some of the positions he assailed. A case in point is his discussion of South African "Black Theology" in a public lecture delivered at the University of Nairobi in September, 1975.[49] In an attempt to demonstrate that "Black Theology" was, among other things, "relativistic or situational", after recalling that "for the Christian, the Bible is the absolute authority on which to base all theological and ethical formulations", Kato then continued:

"Black Theology, however, has human experience as the basic term of reference. Basil Moore writes, 'Black Theology is a situational theology. And the situation is that of the black man in South Africa.' Biko in rejecting absolutes writes, 'It [Black Theology] grapples with existential problems and does not claim to be a theology of absolutes. It seeks to bring back God to the Black man and to the truth and reality of his situation.' Says Pityana, 'Blackness gives a point of reference, an identity and a consciousness'."[50]

In discussing this sampling of statements by some of those who, in the harsh realities of South African existence, were seeking to articulate the nature of a relevant faith in the God of the Bible, Kato displayed not only a lack of appreciation for the context of "Black Theology", but also an inability to recognise the *theological* significance of the human predicament as such. His concluding comments are revealing of his whole approach and outlook:

"A popular motto found on many lorries in Nigeria is, 'No condition is permanent'. This is an apt description of the human condition. Man comes and goes. Human struggles consistently shift. Empires rise and fall. If a theology is based on human experience, rather than human experience seeking answers from the absolute Word of God, that theology is as good as a sail boat without sails. John Robinson's situation ethics which allows immorality provided that love dictates the situation, has been firmly rejected as being out of line with the absolute teaching of the Scriptures. Bible believing Christians should reject Black Theology on the same basis. The absolute Word of God must be the measuring rod of the varying, fleeting situations."[51]

Three times Kato stressed the *absolute* character of the Scriptures as the Word of God; yet at no point does his statement really respond to the theological method and viewpoints he attacked. Perhaps the clue to Kato's response is given by the introduction into his answer of "John Robinson's situation ethics". The only reason for mentioning this seems to be the fact that Basil Moore describes Black Theology as "a situational theology". Accordingly, the term "situational" acts as a sort of operative catchword which evokes a comparison between ("situational") Black Theology and "situation ethics". Thus, in the final analysis, Black Theology is judged not on the basis of its *theological* response to the situation of Black existence in South Africa, but on the grounds of the unacceptability of "John Robinson's *situation* ethics".

To Kato's concern to safeguard the Scriptures as "the absolute authority" for all theological formulations, we shall come presently. However, his treatment of Black Theology already indicates that the affirmation of the centrality of the Word of God need not always be taken to mean that Kato had worked out how that principle applied meaningfully in concrete situations. Furthermore, Kato's criticism of "Ecumenism" and "Ecumenicals" was sometimes of such a nature that it even raised questions about his disposition to appreciate viewpoints which he did not share. An instance of this was his attack on the doctrinal basis of the WCC (as of the AACC), for what he considered its lack of precision:[52]

"It is praiseworthy for the WCC Constitution to include 'according to the Scriptures'. But what Scriptures? Is it Buddhist, Muslim or Hindu Scriptures? If it is Christian Scriptures, as the context shows, is it the mutilated, errant Scriptures of the liberals or the inspired, inerrant Word of God of the conservative evangelicals?"[53]

According to Kato, elaborating on the same criticism:

"Obviously, the minimal nature of the statement provides room for the easy accommodation of various theological positions. The Scriptures are left undefined so they can accommodate theologians who reject the doctrine of the infallibility of the

Bible."[54]

Whatever the demerits of the WCC and the AACC regarding their doctrinal commitments, Kato's observations and queries almost suggest that St Paul himself might not have been blameless when he stated that both the death and resurrection of the Lord Jesus Christ took place "according to the Scriptures".[55]

For one who felt so profound an antipathy towards "modern ecumenism" and its various manifestations, Kato's presence at gatherings of "Ecumenicals" might be considered somewhat unusual. Kato attended both the third General Assembly of the AACC in Lusaka (Zambia) in May, 1974, and the fifth Assembly of the WCC in Nairobi (Kenya) in December, 1975 – though, admittedly, as an observer.[56] On both meetings Kato produced and published reports which were generally unfavourable and unsympathetic to the gatherings themselves, as well as the two bodies which had organised them.[57] And yet, a close reading of Kato's writings would seem to suggest that for all his stress on the priority of purely spiritual concerns and individual salvation, he was not indifferent to institutional realities. He had a keen awareness of the material and other resources to which Africa's "Ecumenicals" had access through their affiliation to "Ecumenical" networks, and he sometimes displayed a ready willingness to use that kind of information to generate interest in the cause of Africa's "Evangelicals" (that is, the Association of Evangelicals of Africa and Madagascar, AEAM), and to solicit aid for "evangelical" structures intended to counteract the institutional advances of "ecumenism" in Africa.[58] It is evident that to Kato's way of thinking, the rationale for the existence of the AEAM consisted in its being an "evangelical" counterblast to the "ecumenical" AACC. The difference between the two institutions, in keeping with Kato's outlook, was that "Evangelical" organisational structures were to be based "on doctrinal agreements".[59] Since the unity of the "Ecumenicals" amounted to "unity in the dark",[60] "the most desirable alternative" for Africa's "Evangelicals", according to Kato, "is membership in the Evangelical Fellowship in each country and also membership in the African Evangelical Association", that is, the AEAM, which alone offered the basis of "true unity". For,

"This kind of unity among those who truly know the Lord and are seeking to serve Him is a Biblical unity. It does not enforce any compromise of the truth; in fact, it promotes the emphasis of Bible truth."[61]

In the light of this perspective, it is not surprising that some early promotions of the AEAM should have described the Association as "the strength of God's work in Africa".[62]

III. " How far can we go without changing the content of the inspired, eternal Word of God? " An unresolved question

It is on the status and meaning of the Bible as the Word of God that Kato saw the Evangelical-Ecumenical divide at its deepest. Reporting a debate involving representative figures from the WCC, the AACC and Kato himself as spokesman for the AEAM, Kato stated his perception of the distinction between "Ecumenicals" and "Evangelicals" on this issue. The "Ecumenicals" comprise:

"... that section of 'Christians' who are so concerned for Church unity that the matter of doctrine becomes of secondary importance. For example, some modern ecumenicals claim that the Bible is full of mistakes and the words of men which should be disregarded, and ecumenism today calls for the inclusion of those who hold this position.

"Evangelicals may be described as Bible-believing Christians who believe that the Bible IS God's Word in its entirety, without errors. It is the final authority in all that it affirms. What the Bible teaches about God, Jesus Christ, man and sin, future resurrection and judgments, is true. All miracles such as the virgin birth of Christ, His supernatural acts and His physical resurrection did happen as the Bible says. Prophetic events, some of which are still future, will take place as the Bible says they will. There are differences in the details of interpretation among evangelicals, but all submit to the final authority of God's Word."[63]

Again and again, Kato's rallying call was an affirmation of the centrality and absolute authority of the Bible with "Evangelicals" consistently defined as those Christians who were the most seriously concerned to "stand... for the truth of the Word of God".[64] Indeed, on the basis of this one all-decisive test, Kato was willing, as the passage just quoted implies, to cast doubt on the quality of *Christian* commitment professed by "Ecumenicals". If he devoted a vast proportion of his *Theological Pitfalls in Africa* to a critique of the works of John Mbiti, Bolaji Idowu, and what he described as the "theology of ecumenism", it was because Kato genuinely believed that those whom he criticised had departed from a prin-

ciple which he considered vital, and which he believed that he
upheld.

Adequately to understand Kato's theological outlook, one must
appreciate what this insistence on the centrality of the Bible meant
to him. To Kato, the "absolute authority" of the Bible meant the
"absolute authority" of the Bible as *inerrant*. Kato considered
"inerrancy" so important that he would not accept *infallibility* as
an adequate description of the trustworthiness of the Bible.[65]
Kato's understanding of inerrancy included the usual implications
affecting the absence of any sort of error in the text of the Scriptures (that is, in the original autographs),[66] but it also involved
more. For Kato, the content of the Bible constituted not only "the
basic source", but also virtually the only subject-matter of theology. In his criticism of "theological trends in Africa" it was "the
use of sources other than the Scriptures as in equal standing with
the revealed Word of God"[67] that he considered the first major
feature of the "African Theology" of which he disapproved. In
Kato's view, the investigation of African pre-Christian religious
tradition for a possible contribution to African Christian thought
amounted to a denial of "the sufficiency of the Scriptures as the
sole authority for faith and practice".[68] It is an indication of how
far Kato was prepared to go to affirm the importance of the Bible
that he would not accept as adequate Mbiti's statement that "the
uniqueness of Christianity is Jesus Christ":[69]

> "The uniqueness of Christianity must cover more than the
> uniqueness of Jesus Christ. How can I know for sure about
> Jesus Christ in an errant Bible? The Scriptures that speak
> about Jesus Christ must be accepted as God's final and special
> revelation. Inerrant authoritative Scriptures alone can give us
> reliable facts about Jesus Christ and man's relationship to
> Him."[70]

The result of thus channelling every facet of Christian doctrine
and affirmation into the defence of Biblical inerrancy was that the
Bible itself became for Kato almost the whole subject-matter of
theology. Kato brought the two ideas together in a later article
which also rehearsed most of the arguments advanced in
"Theological trends in Africa today":

> "That Africans have a unique contribution to make to theologi-
> cal debates is undeniable, but theology as such must be left in
> its essence. The Bible must remain the basic source of Christian
> theology. Evangelical Christians know of only one theology –

Biblical theology – though it may be expressed in the context of each cultural milieu."[71]

Thus, what Kato's understanding of African "contribution to theological debates" amounted to was "a mode of expression of [Biblical] theology in African terms".[72] From much else that Kato wrote and said, it becomes clear what this "mode of expression" meant in relation to the Bible, which, for Kato, was not only the content of divine revelation, but also the content of theology itself. In a criticism of what he regarded as an unwarranted "proliferation of ethnic or regional theologies based on human experience", Kato wrote:

> "While the Bible should speak to every people within their own situation in the language they can understand, there is no need to create particular theologies for each situation. The theological systems being hatched today have man's experience as their frame of reference. The struggle to overcome economic oppression in Latin America becomes the basis for the Theology of Liberation. The suffering of the black man forms the basis for Black Theology, etc. *This is a clever way of destroying the objective and supernatural nature of God's revealed truth. In the face of this, evangelical Christians must oppose the devil and he will flee. The old-time cry of the Reformers, 'Sola Scriptura, sola fide' (Scripture alone, faith alone), must continue to be our vanguard.*"[73]

Kato expressed a similar thought in an even more significant context, where he was discussing, specifically, the content of revelation and its way of expression:

> "The content of the Bible is inspired. It cannot be changed. 'Scripture cannot be broken' (*John* 10:35). As the Bible moves from culture to culture it remains the same. It is the culture that must change. If the Bible did not remain the same, Christianity would have changed so much from country to country and generation to generation that it would hardly be recognisable today. Jesus Christ remains the same as He was in the past and will ever be (*Heb.* 13:8). His Word remains unchanged in the same way (*Psalm* 119:89).

> "Although the content of the Bible remains the same, the way of expressing it is changeable. This is because the way of expressing it is not inspired. God may take one instrument on some occasion and use it for the spreading of His unchanging Word, and take another kind of instrument on other oc-

casions."[74]

Kato went on to discuss ways of expressing the content of revelation, such as music, musical instruments, the language used for worship, and church architecture, all of which should be of such a kind that "African Christians" are enabled to remain "Christian Africans". But it is evident that the really substantial issue had to do with safeguarding the content of the Bible as the Word of God, and in this connection the reference to *Psalm* 119:89 in the earlier part of the passage quoted above is important. This Scriptural text is cited by Kato frequently enough to indicate how deeply, in his mind, the whole question of theology was tied to his essentially Biblicist understanding of the Word of God.[75] In this sense one must understand his criticism of the fifth Assembly of the WCC for its "lack of theological content" as meaning the lack of Bible content, and this explains the importance he attached to the observation that some of the Bible study groups "made no reference to the Scriptures".[76]

The fundamental tie-up between the content of the Bible and the content of theology becomes clearer still when one understands Kato's conception of divine revelation. Using traditional Protestant Reformed categories, Kato distinguished a "general (or natural) revelation" from a "special revelation".[77] Referring to Eric Sauer,[78] Kato located "general revelation" in the areas of nature (or the created universe), human conscience and the universal primeval history portrayed in the early chapters of the book of *Genesis*. However, in each of these areas, the fall of the human race has entailed a fundamental distortion of apprehension, thus eliminating any possibility of accurate perception of divine truth. To make his point, Kato quoted the Reformed theologian G.C. Berkouwer:

"Accordingly, when we speak of insufficiency, we certainly do not intend to cast any reflection on the divine act of revelation in this general revelation. On the contrary, it only points to human guilt and blindness. This insufficiency is not a deficiency of revelation, but it is a deficiency which is historically determined, i.e. in connection with the fall of man."[79]

With "general revelation" firmly set aside, Kato could then indicate the full significance of the "special revelation" in the "Christ-event" which constituted the only "clear and final revelation to any people".[80]

"This final and unique revelation in Jesus Christ is not a

fulfilment of other religions. It is decisive and final in the sense that it provides the only answer for which human endeavour has been searching. It is conclusive that the Scriptures know of only one way of approach to God, that is, through the Living Word, Jesus Christ. Natural revelation may give hints about the Supreme Being, but it is the Incarnate Christ alone who has truly revealed God to man finally and decisively. Natural revelation does indeed have its place, but special revelation bridges the infinite chasm which separates God and man."[81]

By introducing such ideas as separation between God and humanity, and the way of approach to God, Kato here indicated what the motivating element of his thought was; for behind the issue of revelation, there lay in Kato's mind the question of salvation. On this "crucial question" as he described it elsewhere,[82] as on much else, Kato's view was categorical, and the distinction between "general revelation" and "special revelation" came to have a far-reaching effect, as we shall see. In the first place, by completely ignoring the explicit Scriptural declaration that from the creation of the world, what may be known of God has always been plain to all who love rather than suppress the truth,[83] Kato denied any salvific element whatsoever in "general revelation". In Kato's view, "God's design for natural revelation" was for it "to be only a pointer to the Creator rather than soteriological", and Kato appealed to the foreordination of the Lamb of God to redemptive sacrifice as further support for this view:

"... natural revelation was never given for the purpose of salvation. That was why the plan for the Lamb *to be slain* (*Rev.* 13:8) was included from the beginning. There was always something wanting, this lack was provided for through the Incarnation."[84]

Kato reiterated this view, with further amplification of the relative purposes of "general revelation" and "special revelation" in his article, "Evangelisation and Culture":

"General revelation was never meant to point the way to God Himself, who has planned the way of salvation through Jesus Christ. That is why Jesus Christ is called the Lamb of God who was ordained *to be killed* before the foundation of the world (*Rev.* 13:8). Man was supposed to see the hand of God in creation, and using the dim light of General Revelation, follow on to what God will show him more clearly in Special Revelation."[85]

The crux of Kato's argument at this point is not what he says about "General Revelation" and "Special Revelation" as distinctive modes of divine operation, but his use of *Revelation* 13:8. It is worth noting that, of the two alternative readings of the passage, Kato accepts the one which connects the expression "before the foundation of the world" not to the election of the redeemed, but to the foreordination of the Lamb of God to redemptive sacrifice. However, by choosing practically to rewrite the Scriptural text the way he did, Kato obviated the possible implication which the perfect participle of the verb (killed, slain) carried in the original, namely, that the divine sacrifice, in a mysterious sense, had been wrought from all eternity.[86]

Kato's procedure at this point is somewhat puzzling. For one who insisted so firmly on the principle that "Scripture cannot be broken" and appeared to mean it literally, his approach to the Scriptures on such an important issue seems to be a departure from his own rule. And yet, what explains Kato's interpretation of *Revelation* 13:8 may not be his lack of interest in the fine points of New Testament syntax, but rather his Christology.

There is no doubt that Kato's radical and polemical distinction between "general revelation" and "special revelation" helps to explain his understanding of the redemptive sacrifice of Christ as being operative only since the Saviour's Incarnation.[87] Possibly this means merely that Kato conceived of the divine activity of revelation and salvation in essentially linear and chronological terms. However, it would seem that behind Kato's rigid chronological schematisation of the divine operation lay also his inability to conceive of any redemptive activity by the pre-Incarnate Saviour. Occasionally one comes upon expressions and statements which might suggest that Kato understood the redemptive work of Christ to be truly universal *and* eternal in its significance.[88] However, these statements do not carry any implication that the efficacy of the saving work of Christ has positive value for human existence prior to the Incarnation. Conclusive evidence of Kato's virtual lack of understanding in this whole area of the question of salvation is provided by his uncompromising rejection of Justin Martyr's theory regarding the redemptive presence and activity of the pre-Incarnate Word in the pre-Christian past. Kato summarily dismissed what was a central element in the attempt by this eminent early Christian thinker both to vindicate the universality of the revelatory and redemptive work of Christ and to account for righteous conduct in Hellenistic pre-Christian tradition. In Kato's estimation, Justin "succumbed to the subtlety of the devil" by giving "erroneously, ... the heathen philosophers the credit of worshipping the same God Christians worship".[89] And yet, when Kato applied the same stringent criticism to "an African theologian" (whom he did not name), Kato, in turn, came close to "Arianising" views:

> "I once had a brief discussion with an African theologian who firmly stated that the *Logos* spirit was operative in African traditional religions. Therefore, to deny salvation to these wor- shippers is to deny the working of God in their midst. Second- century gnosticism has come back to life. As Christ has been depersonalised in liberal theology (e.g. Schleiermacher, Ritschl), the same tendency is rising in Africa today as some African theologians seek to glorify African traditional religions. But it must be maintained that Jesus Christ became incarnate as a particular person in time and history. John's use of *Logos* (*Jn* 1:1-7) was in that particular sense. The Word became flesh by assuming not only the form of man in general (*Phil.* 2:5-8), but of (*sic*) being born as a particular person in Bethlehem. This was necessary in view of the work He was going to do. He could be crucified in time and history only as a particular man. He died and rose as an individual to save the sinner as an in- dividual. So the question of incarnation also settles the question of salvation of individuals, although individuals cannot be saved in isolation since they are engrafted into the Body of Christ with other persons (*1 Cor.* 12:3; *Eph.* 4:11-16)."[90]

In seeking to "particularise" Christ in terms of His incarnation as "a particular person in Bethlehem" who "could be crucified in time and history as a particular man", who "died and rose as an individual", it is evident that Kato was concerned to safeguard and to affirm the full historicity of the Saviour against a possible "docetic" interpretation of Christ. On the other hand, it is not obvious from Kato's account that a declaration of the pre-incarnate activity of the *Logos* as expounded by the "African theologian" in question, necessarily implied a "docetic" view of the Incarnation of the Saviour, and the passage illustrates the extent to which the polemical attitude which Kato so consistently adopted in theologi- cal discussion tended to becloud rather than illumine the central issues involved. Accordingly, Kato seems to have failed to recognise that the prologue of the *Gospel according to John* certainly con- veyed more about the *Logos* than the mere announcement of His incarnation "as a particular person in time and history".

Nowhere is Kato's inability to conceive of Christ and His redemptive work in any other than purely temporal terms more glaring than in his discussion of the standing before God of those "ancestors who died before they ever had the opportunity to hear the Gospel".[91] On this question, Kato's "particularist" under-standing of Christ, his contention that "special revelation" alone was the realm of salvation and his radical and exclusivist Biblicism came together to give an answer which provides probably the single most important insight into his uniformly negative evaluation of African pre-Christian religious tradition.

It is perhaps revealing that Kato considered the question of the salvation of the ancestors as a "sentimental issue in Africa".[92] In a brief survey of some of the solutions offered, Kato dismissed as devoid of "Scriptural basis" the view of those who on the one hand, "affirm that they [the ancestors] are in heaven because they were good or religious people", and of those on the other, who "call for prayer by the living Christians with the hope that there is still chance for the dead".[93] We have already noted Kato's response to the suggestion by J.N.D. Anderson to the effect that salvation for some dead ancestors on the basis of God's mercy could not be entirely ruled out of consideration.[94] While Kato did not completely dismiss Anderson's argument, he yet insisted:

"The more Scriptural basis would rather be that if God had been dealing with any person apart from the gospel witness, He would provide the way for that would-be Christian to hear the Gospel and accept it to be born again. The case of Cornelius is the precedent (*Acts* 10:35)."[95]

Whilst one can readily understand Kato's concern not to reach beyond the boundaries of the explicit declarations of the Scriptures, the effect of thus absolutising Biblical incidents in themselves was to render Kato incapable of appreciating the nuances of the very Scrip-tures he was so intent on safeguarding. Consequently, Kato's state-ment of his conviction, though obviously derived from the Bible, did not amount to the full-orbed balance of the true Biblical doctrine of human redemption:

"For the rest of the heathen who died before the advent of Christian evangelism, it is humanly wished that they found their place in eternal bliss. But the Word of God gives no warrant for such a view. Since the original fall, the total race of Adam has been condemned to death (*Rom*. 3:23; 6:23). Salvation in the Biblical sense is the passing out of this death dungeon

(*John* 5:24) into the dimension of life. The members of the Adamic race are all stillborn (*Rom.* 5:12). Not one of them deserves to live. But the undeserving favour of God has made salvation possible through the death and resurrection of Jesus Christ. The death and resurrection of the Second Adam is described as to only "abound to many" (*Rom.* 5:15). Christ is universally available to all men everywhere at any time. But its effectiveness applies *only to those who receive the offer.*"[96]

Since those who did not and do not hear the preaching of the Gospel, by Kato's definition, were not and are not in a position to receive the offer of salvation, the meaning that Kato attached to the final qualifying phrase brought him perilously near to saying that it needed human authentication for the divine act in human redemption to become effective. It is doubtful whether Kato would have accepted the criticism that he ever changed "the content of the inspired, eternal Word of God". But he may also have been unaware that he was seeking to define the limits of divine sovereignty and freedom more sharply than they are presented in the same "inspired, eternal Word of God" when he wrote:

"The Biblical answer to the question concerning those who died before hearing the Gospel seems to be that they go to hell. There is no clear basis for optimism in this case. No one deserves to be saved in any case. So the question of God's partiality does not arise. Humanly speaking, one would wish that all men will be saved. But there is no scriptural warrant for that position. God's omnipotence must be matched with His omniscience and judicious action. His grace and love must not overshadow His justice and holiness."[97]

Perhaps an even more pervasive feature of Kato's handling of the Scriptures was that in spite of his pronounced claim to let the Bible be "the final infallible rule of faith and practice",[98] he operated with "a canon within the Canon". We have already noted his inability to fully appreciate the social dimensions of sin as found in the Old Testament prophetic teaching.[99] Elsewhere, Kato criticised "Ecumenicals" who "see salvation in the same terms as the deliverance of Israel from Egypt. That is why instead of turning to the book of *Romans* for salvation, their favourite passage is the book of *Exodus*".[100] In Kato's view:

"This is, of course, a distortion of the meaning of salvation preached by Christ and His followers. Jesus Christ said, 'Come to me, all you who are weary and burdened, and I will give you rest' (*Matt.* 11:28). This invitation was to all men and not just to the people oppressed politically and/or economically."[101]

Whilst one can readily appreciate Kato's concern to safeguard the spiritual character of God's salvation, it is also evident that Kato did not recognise that there could be other concepts of salvation which had just as much validity within the overall teaching of the Scriptures. Consequently, Kato tended to minimise the value of those dimensions of Biblical teaching which did not seem to suit his "individualistic" and "spiritual" conception of Biblical salvation. A case in point is his treatment of the words of Jesus in *Luke* 4:18-19:

"The Spirit of the Lord is upon me, because He has anointed me to preach good news to the poor. He has sent me to proclaim release to the captives and recovering of sight to the blind, to set at liberty those who are oppressed, to proclaim the acceptable year of the Lord."[102]

Taking exception to the view that "the oppressed are the sole object of Christ's mission", Kato criticised "the liberal ecumenicals" who "go on to limit the goal of Christ's mission to social, political and economic liberation". And yet, in the final analysis, Kato's own way of dealing with the passage was to resort to an *ad hominem* response to his opponents which left the dominical saying unexplained:

"If this is taken in the narrow sense of Christ coming only for the downtrodden, why did He have any dealings at all with the religious leaders – the Pharisees; the aristocrats – the Sadducees; the wealthy businesswomen – Mary and Martha; the well-to-do fishermen – the sons of Zebedee; the successful civil servants – Matthew and Zacchaeus? Why did God allow His Son to be buried in the tomb of 'capitalistic' Joseph of Arimathea – If Christ's mission was for political liberation, why did He not organise a gang-resistance to the Roman oppressors instead of urging His followers to go the extra mile (*Matt.* 5:41)?"[103]

Kato rightly insisted that "liberation in terms of what Christ came to do must be understood as meaning liberation from man's fundamental dilemma, which is sin",[104] but he did not shed any fresh light on the hermeneutical problem posed by *Luke* 4:18-19, in the context of the socio-political questions of the twentieth century. Thus the weakness in Kato's view of the Bible in its relation to theology lay in his failure to grasp sufficiently that there was a hermeneutical problem to be resolved.

Kato's approach to the meaning of the Bible for the modern African context was determined essentially by two fixed points, namely, the Biblical text itself, and the modern context; between these two points the current flowed only in one direction, from the Biblical text to the African context with its problems and questions to be met and answered with Biblical solutions.[105] Kato would not allow that there could be a reverse current, bringing African insights and experience to bear on the interpretation of the Scriptures. If he saw such a possibility, he saw it as one of the "pitfalls" into which some African theologians were heading, and he warned appropriately:

> "Express Christianity in a truly African context, allowing it to judge the African culture and never allow the culture to take precedence over Christianity. To do otherwise would isolate African Christianity from historical Christianity, Biblically based. This can be done by creating an 'African Theology' as understood by some African theologians today..."[106]

Whilst Kato's persistent concern to affirm the integrity of the Bible must be given its due weight as a positive contribution to African Christian thought, his conception of that integrity made it virtually impossible to pose *new* questions to the Scriptures from within the African context in any meaningful sense. In other words, Kato could not conceive of what René Padilla has called "the hermeneutical circle", characterised by

> "a new open-ended reading of Scripture with a hermeneutic in which Gospel and culture become mutually engaged in a dialogue whose purpose is to place the Church under the lordship of Jesus Christ in its historical situation."[107]

Believing that there did exist a pure and universally valid "Biblical Christian Theology", [108] Kato tended to fail to recognise the "pitfall" which consists in the assumption that the task of theology (in the African context) was "simply to extract the message directly from the biblical text and to transmit it to the hearers... with no consideration of the role of culture in the whole interpretative process".[109] Conceived in this way, a theology which ignores serious cultural engagement with the context for which it is intended, easily becomes, as René Padilla further points out, "reduced to the repetition of doctrinal formulations borrowed from other latitudes".[110] Thus, though Kato was by no means indifferent to the question of cultural relevance, his very concept of theology as essentially "Bibliology" made the issue of relevance itself problematic for him.

IV. "Christianity as an African religion": Cultural relevance as a problem

It is an indication of Kato's sensitivity to the question of cultural relevance[111] that he sought to show that one could properly claim Christianity to be an African religion. Kato not only wrote an article bearing the specific and significant title, "Christianity as an African religion",[112] he also produced a booklet, *African Cultural Revolution and the Christian Faith*,[113] which tackled the wider issues raised for the Christian Church in Africa by the quest for a new cultural identity in independent Africa.

Earlier, in 1974, at the International Congress on World Evangelisation held at Lausanne, Switzerland, Kato had presented a seminar paper on the subject of "The Gospel, cultural context and religious syncretism".[114] It is perhaps significant that of the three themes treated, it was "religious syncretism" which received the greatest amount of space in Kato's presentation. Furthermore, Kato contended strongly that "even some of the most outstanding theologians in Africa" – pointing particularly to John Mbiti and Bolaji Idowu – had "syncretistic and/or universalistic tendencies".[115] By this description, Kato evidently meant the efforts by these theologians towards a positive theological evaluation of the pre-Christian religious heritage and the integration of its insights into the African understanding of the Christian faith. It stands to reason, therefore, that Kato, whose main concern was to safeguard what he called "the clear-cut... unadulterated Gospel of Jesus Christ",[116] had relatively little to say on the subject of cultural context which he discussed under the designation "contextualisation".[117] It is obvious from Kato's treatment that he considered the subject of questionable importance; whilst efforts to seek cultural relevance for Christianity in Africa were commendable, his more fundamental concern was to stress that such efforts were not to entail the destruction of Christianity's "ever-abiding message":[118]

> "Not only should the message be preached in the language best understood by the congregation, but terminology of theology should be expressed the way common people can understand. But theological meaning must not be sacrificed at the altar of comprehension. Instead of employing terms that would water down the Gospel, the congregation should be taught the meaning of the term as originally meant."[119]

The example that Kato chose to clarify his point is revealing, and is a good illustration of his own response to his agonising question as to how far the quest for cultural relevance could go "without changing the content of the inspired, eternal Word of God".

"One instance is the mustard seed. This is a crop not found in America or Africa. Instead of substituting it with a local grain, the term should be employed and the explanation given. While the content of God's Word should remain what it is, the expression of it in teaching, preaching and singing should be made relevant."[120]

Kato hardly raised the question regarding "the content of God's Word" in the process of translation,[121] and it is perhaps significant that, at the end of his paper, he suggested that "the subject of cultural relevance belongs to another presentation".[122]

In the spirited defence of "Christianity as an African religion", Kato appealed essentially to the ancient and deep historical connections between Christianity and Africa, reaching into Biblical times, and also to the massive evidence of African profession of the Christian faith. However, in Kato's view, this important and unignorable African Christian profession was in fundamental discontinuity with the pre-Christian heritage. He therefore concluded that:

"Africans [like everyone else] have the right to change their religion from heathen worship to Christianity. Having done so, Christianity can become an African religion. This is what has happened.

"Historically Christianity was thriving in Africa before it reached North America and the British Isles where most of the Protestant missionaries [to Africa in modern times] come from. We can therefore rightly call Christianity an African religion."[123]

In the final analysis, Kato's thesis came to rest on the "universal nature of Christianity"; so that, on the basis of *Galatians* 3:28:

"No one racial class or sex group has a monopoly on the claims of Christ's Church. Christianity is an African religion to its African adherents, just as it is European to the European, American to the American, or Asian to the Asian followers of Christ."[124]

Whilst Kato was prepared to recognise that in the practice of

Christianity in Africa there were "alien [that is, non-African and non-Christian] beliefs and/or practices mingled with Christianity", he remained considerably more conscious of what he called "the unchanging biblical faith".[125] Correspondingly, Kato showed much less awareness of the possibility that the Christianity which he evidently believed was relevant to the African, might also have "a foreign sound, or no sound at all, in relation to many of the dreams and anxieties, problems and questions, values and customs of people".[126]

Kato's most sustained effort in dealing with the question of culture in relation to the Christian Gospel came in *African Cultural Revolution and the Christian Faith*.[127] Behind the production of the booklet lay two events which Kato described as "outstanding" but which he also regarded as potentially harmful to "the evangelical truth 'once and for all delivered to the saints'",[128] as he understood it. The two events were the Second World Black and African Festival of Arts and Culture, scheduled to take place in Lagos, Nigeria,[129] and the fifth Assembly of the WCC in Nairobi, Kenya. In Kato's view, these two events posed the threat of the "secularisation of Christianity in the Third World in general, but in Africa in particular",[130] by which he meant the danger of displacing the "spiritual" content of Christianity by "temporal" concerns. The Festival would achieve this end by seeking "to promote the unity of the black race and the identity of the African irrespective of religious conviction", whilst the WCC Assembly would, in turn, "seek to minimise differences between Christianity and other religions, promote their erroneous view of evangelism and salvation, and capitalise on the already great desire for cultural revolution".[131] The booklet was, therefore, as much an attempt to deal with the relationship of Gospel to Culture in its own right, as it was intended to warn "Evangelicals" of the "pitfalls" to avoid "as the Gospel is indigenised".[132]

Kato stated his fundamental outlook on the question of the relationship of Gospel to culture in the first chapter by taking "the view that not only is religion part of culture but it is the heart of it".[133] Accordingly, for Africa's Christians:

> "Because they have assumed a new religion, Christianity, they have to abide by the principles laid down in the Book of their religion, the Bible. The Bible becomes the final judge of their culture."[134]

Kato based his study of the Gospel and culture question upon the analysis of "levels of culture" proposed by missionary anthropologist Donald Jacobs.[135] Working from "philosophical" (that is, the deepest and most intimate) level, through to the "mythical", "value" and "formal" levels of culture, Kato sought to show how in the event of genuine Christian conversion, the convert received "a new philosophy of life",[136] which, in turn, was to produce corresponding transformations at the other levels of cultural existence.

Kato maintained that "this basic core of culture",[137] in the case of Christians, was constituted by their Christian commitment; he also indicated that, at the other levels of cultural existence, there were "valuable concepts in African culture which can be employed as a vehicle for presenting the unchanging Gospel of Christ".[138] Thus, at the "mythical" level, which is the level of "the accepted beliefs of a people", Kato considered that the "African interest in the life beyond can be given true meaning only in the Christian faith", in that, "the reality of conscious existence and the future resurrection for judgment or retribution can be found in the Bible".[139] Similarly, "the (traditional African) respect for the elder falls in line with what the Bible teaches", and quoting *Romans* 13:9, Kato opined accordingly that "Christians should be the most loyal citizens".[140]

However, Kato was in no doubt regarding Christian conduct in the event of conflict "between God's laws and man's laws". Mindful of the trials that Christians in Chad and Zaire were then undergoing in the *Kulturkampf* of Presidents Tombalbaye and Mobutu respectively, Kato used vivid incidents from the responses of Christians in the two situations of conflict, which he prefaced symbolically with the ancient account of the martyrdom of Polycarp, to further establish his basic viewpoint:

> "As Christians we plead with African political leaders to understand this. A rejection of certain aspects of African culture must not be taken for disloyalty to our culture or our leaders. Since religious beliefs have to conform to the ruling of God, the new Master of their (*sic*) philosophical level, they have to obey Him."[141]

Kato applied to the "value" and "formal" levels the same two-fold approach; strengthening and enriching through the "newly found faith" what Kato called the "valuable concepts" on the one hand, and adjusting or even rejecting those which were contrary to the Bible on the other. Kato's treatment at this point and on most of the subjects discussed shows him in probably the best light: practical, wise and pastorally concerned. Kato is perhaps most helpful on issues related to the impact of Christian commitment and discipleship on what is "considered good and beneficial in marriage in African society".[142] And his perspective on the whole range of questions in connection with the Gospel's relation to culture is well summed up in his closing statement:

> "A converted Christian receives a new basic philosophy of life. His religious practices will have to fall in line with what his new basic faith is. This new basic faith obtained from Jesus Christ through the Holy Spirit, is based on the Bible. The Christian will have to examine his whole life-style or culture by the Bible. *The Bible is the final judge of every culture.*

> "The heart that has undergone change through conversion has assumed a new philosophy of life. This new philosophy of life, based on the Bible, is the basis for examining mythical values, or the formal level of a culture.

> "Any practice that does not agree with what the Bible teaches must be dropped. The concept or practice that fits biblical principles may be employed for the use of Christianity. African Christians do not need to wear European clothes or bear foreign names to be Christians. Neither do they have to do away with everything European to be truly Africans or Christians.

> "Christians should be willing to go along in adapting African culture as long as it does not conflict with Scripture. When such a conflict does arise, such as worship of pagan gods, wearing of indecent clothing, Christians must choose to obey God rather than men."[143]

The importance of this statement consists not only in its clarity as an expression of Kato's conception of the relation of the Christian Gospel to culture and of the nature of Christian existence in the world; the passage also reveals what was probably most characteristic of Kato as a Christian thinker, namely, an essentially *practical* mind.[144] It is interesting that whilst Kato found "valuable concepts" at the "mythical", "value" and "formal" levels of culture to serve as vehicles "for the use of Christianity", Kato did not raise this possibility with regard to the "philosophical" level from which "every other aspect of life receives direction".[145] At this level of culture which "answers the question as to what really gives meaning to life",[146] in Kato's view, "the new philosophy of life based on the Bible" comes in as an entirely self-explanatory entity in its own right, and independent of the cultural realities which have shaped the individual and the community at this most profound and intimate level of culture. For Kato, therefore, there could be, strictly speaking, no *cultural* reading or apprehension of the Gospel in the sense that no cultural factors had any part in the shaping of one's understanding of the Christian Faith as such, since the Gospel itself was cultureless. Kato had stated this viewpoint quite emphatically in his seminar at the International Congress on World Evangelisation:

> "The inspired, inerrant Word of God gives us the Gospel and its working power in a nutshell in *1 Cor.* 15:1-4. It is not a part of any people's culture. It is not indigenous to any soil. It is revealed propositionally and must be declared accordingly."[147]

It is possible to see in Kato's postulate of the *acultural* nature of the Gospel, a further dimension of his exclusivist Biblicism. But it is equally possible to discern in it the outlook of a Christian who was deeply mistrustful of speculative thinking,[148] and therefore unwilling to venture beyond what he considered to be the certainties of explicit Scriptural declarations. In Kato's terms, "the worldview of the traditional [that is, non-Christian] African was that of a natural man",[149] with obvious reference to the language of St Paul: the natural person is incapable of apprehending the things of the Spirit of God.[150] By removing the Gospel and its apprehension from the most intimate realm of "natural" cultural perception, Kato was affirming the same kind of distinction which he consistently made between "natural revelation" and "special revelation", between "non-Christian religions" and "Christianity". However, the particular significance of the distinction as it related to the issue of Gospel and culture is that from Kato's perspective, not only was the quest for cultural relevance firmly limited to the peripherals of culture, but by the same token, any theology which availed itself of insights from culture became suspect. Theology conceived as a synthesis of "old" and "new" in a unified frame of reference dealing with "culturally rooted questions,[151] became impossible.

V. Conclusion

Byang Kato's persistent affirmation of the centrality of the Bible for the theological enterprise in the Church in Africa must surely be reckoned to have been his most important contribution to modern African Christian thought.[152] By championing so intrepidly the "Biblicist" principle, Kato directed the attention of the practitioners of "African Theology" to the need to secure the emergent theology to "its rootage in the Biblical traditions".[153] On this issue, Kato's position would have found endorsement from one[154] whom, strangely enough, Kato relentlessly criticised for departing from the Biblical tradition, and yet who, in turn, has publicly given a warm commendation of Byang Kato's place in African theological thinking.[155] It is, therefore, not accurate to isolate Byang Kato as the lone voice in modern African theological debate intent on seeking an African Christianity which is informed by a theology that is both "truly African and truly Biblical".[156]

Furthermore, Kato's perception of the concerns of "African Theology" cannot be accepted without question. Not only was his negative and unsympathetic posture towards the African pre-Christian religious heritage based on outdated assumptions about the nature of African "traditional" religion, but also his very attitude rendered him incapable of appreciating and discerning some of its crucial and positive dimensions. Consequently, though Kato sought to argue that the Christian faith was "as much an African religion as it is a European religion",[157] he did not have an integrating framework for rooting the Christian faith in African tradition. In Kato's schema of the relationship between the Christian Gospel and the African heritage in religion, Africans, in practice, come to the Christian faith religiously and spiritually empty.

Kato genuinely believed that his viewpoint on the question of the relationship between African "traditional" religion and the Christian faith was the most biblically valid in comparison with the solutions of most other African theologians. It is only such a conviction that explains the fierceness of his criticism of the works of John Mbiti and E. Bolaji Idowu in particular, in his *Theological Pitfalls in Africa*. Yet Kato's own interpretation of the Bible, as we have seen, is not without its "pitfalls"; neither is his criticism of Mbiti and Idowu compelling.[158] My investigation of the writings of Mbiti and Idowu in earlier chapters of the present study[159] has led me to quite different conclusions from Kato's view of the two writers. Furthermore, it is interesting that an evangelical reviewer of *Theological Pitfalls in Africa* felt able to suggest that "an attempt to evaluate the positive contributions of their [Mbiti's and Idowu's] theological viewpoints would make his [Kato's] analysis more balanced".[160] Accordingly, I have not included Kato's critique of

Mbiti and Idowu in this study of his work. I have preferred instead to seek to understand Kato's thought in terms of his own theological presuppositions and commitment, and to assess his contribution towards an African theological tradition that engages seriously with the question of identity faced by the modern African Christian conscience.

Looked at from this angle, Byang Kato's legacy to African theological thought would seem to be more problematic than, perhaps, has been realised in Evangelical circles.[161] In a recently published article, the present Executive Secretary of the Theological Commission of the AEAM complained about fellow Evangelicals:

> "Some evangelicals claim to have no theology but the Word of God. Theologians, they say, complicate God! In these circles the 'spiritual' thing to do is to hold to the pure and simple Gospel – as if the Gospel was that simple!"[162]

One may venture to ask whether Kato's fundamental outlook does not lend weight to the "evangelical" attitude described here; whether, in fact, Kato's negative posture towards "African Theology" was not also an indication of a mistrust of theology itself. It is ironical that Kato chose to compare the context of the Christian Church in twentieth-century Africa to that of the nascent Christian movement in the second century. For while Kato was eminently aware of "the challenge of syncretistic universalism"[163] which faced the early Christian Church as it proclaimed a unique revelation of God, he seems to have been much less conscious of the kind of bold and "risky" initiatives that the apologists took in order to vindicate the claims to that unique character of their faith. Thus, Kato, who considered "conservative evangelicals" to be the "spiritual descendents" of the "early apologists",[164] yet failed to appreciate the significance of the *theological* insights of Justin Martyr for the eventual triumph of the Christian Gospel as a unique *and* universal faith.[165] It is doubtful, therefore, whether Kato sufficiently understood the cultural, intellectual, as well as the spiritual dynamics that motivated the very apologetic movement with which he was so eager to make common cause.

It is possible to see in Kato's view of the concerns of "African Theology" the evidence of a similar misconception. Having an essentially unspeculative mind, Kato tended to see "syncretism" where others found material for a "synthesis". Since Kato considered the African pre-Christian heritage in religion as of little or no theological value, he was faced with the task of seeking African rootage for what, from his perspective, amounted to a religious irruption which had virtually no basis in the African religious past. Given his evangelical commitment to the centrality of the Bible for theology, Kato's tendency to conceive of the task of theology in terms of what I have described as "Bibliology", followed almost as a matter of course from his religious and theological presuppositions.

It is hard to see how an outlook which so persistently made light of the deep religious heritage of African peoples, and even went so far as to pontificate on the state of those who died without having heard the Gospel, could provide a sufficient foundation for a creative theological tradition among Africa's Evangelicals. Paul Bowers has suggested that *Theological Pitfalls in Africa* "should not be taken as Kato's intended paradigm for the theological task awaiting African evangelicalism". Instead, according to Bowers, the book should be seen as "a ground-clearing exercise in preparation for the positive task" which would have followed had Kato been spared.[166] If Bowers is right, then it is heartening that already there are among Africa's Evangelicals, some who, without denying their commitment to the centrality of the Bible for theology, have begun to seek more positive ways of letting the Christian Gospel encounter African tradition.[167]

Notes

1. I have come upon the word "Bibliology" in the literature of a theological institution in North America, as a term for "the study of the doctrines that relate to the Bible..." with particular reference to "the importance of belief in the inerrancy of Scripture". See the *1982-83 Catalogue of the School of Theology,* International Christian Graduate University, Arrowhead Springs, San Bernardino, California, p.91. Without implying any connection between Byang Kato and this institution, I have nonetheless found in the word "Bibliology", and what it denotes, a helpful description of Kato's theological position and viewpoint on the issues relevant to this study.

2. Kato, born in June, 1936, died suddenly and accidentally by drowning off the coast of Kenya in December, 1975, only two years after becoming the first African General Secretary of the Association of Evangelicals of Africa and Madagascar (AEAM), and the Executive Secretary of the Association's Theological Commission.

3. Byang Kato produced only one major work, *Theological Pitfalls in Africa,* Kisumu (Kenya): Evangel Publishing House, 1975. But Kato was a prolific writer of articles, reports and essays, many of which have been published posthumously by the AEAM in the Association's bulletin, *Perception.* A few of these articles have also been published in *ERT.* Reference will be made to the various sources at the appropriate places in this study.

4. Kato himself uses "conservative evangelical" as a term of self-definition.

See his *Theological Pitfalls in Africa*, p.178. Kato's academic background indicates the dominant influence of this tradition within Christianity. Converted to the Christian Faith at the age of 12 under the auspices of the Sudan Interior Mission (SIM) related Evangelical Churches of West Africa in Nigeria, Kato began theological studies at the SIM Seminary at Agbaja. After earning a BD degree (University of London) through London Bible College, England, (1966), he pursued studies for STM (1971), and Th.D (1974) at Dallas Theological Seminary, Texas, U.S.A. It is his Th.D thesis presented to Dallas Theological Seminary, which forms the substance of his *Theological Pitfalls in Africa*.

5. Timothy M. Njoya, *Dynamics of Change in African Christianity: African theology through historical and socio-political change*, Princeton Theological Seminary (Ph.D), 1976; Ann Arbor: University Microfilms, 1976, p.60.

6. See Byang H. Kato, *Theological Pitfalls in Africa*, p.38. Kato quotes the expression from J.B. Schuyler, "Conceptions of Christianity in the context of Tropical Africa: Nigerian reactions to its advent" in C.G. Baëta (ed), *Christianity in Tropical Africa*, London: Oxford University Press, 1968, p.219.

7. Byang H. Kato, *Theological Pitfalls in Africa*, p.60.

8. In the fourth of his "ten point proposal" for "safeguarding Biblical Christianity in Africa", Kato suggests that "African traditional religions as well as other religions" be studied "carefully", but "only secondarily to the inductive study of God's Word. The New Testament writers and the early church evangelists did not consider it worth while to spend too much of their energy in the study of non-Christian religions. All non-Christians belong to one and the same group – "unsaved; the sinful nature needs no study analysis as its outworking is clearly manifested in daily life". See his *Theological Pitfalls in Africa*, p.183. No statement, perhaps, indicates so clearly how far apart Kato stood from the dominant emphasis in the Christian theological scholarship of modern Africa.

9. *Ibid.*, chapter 3: "African Traditional Religions: A Case study", pp.27-46. The Jaba people live in the North Central State of Nigeria.

10. *Ibid.*, p.45. In this consists his basic criticism of the proponents and practitioners of "African Theology".

11. *Ibid.*, p.44.

12. *Ibid.*, p.42.

13. *Ibid.*, p.42.

14. *Ibid.*, p.42.

15. *Ibid.*, p.36.

16. *Ibid.*, p.37.

17. *Ibid.*, p.38.

18. See Adrian Hastings, *African Christianity – An Essay in interpretation*, London: Geoffrey Chapman, 1976, pp.50f. Dr Hastings' judgment has been abundantly borne out by our studies of the work.

19. Byang H. Kato, *Theological Pitfalls in Africa*, p.17.

20. Byang Kato, "Theological Trends in Africa", in *Perception*, no.1, March, 1974, p.5. It is important to note that Kato's criticism of "African Theology" appears to depend rather unduly on the view of J.K. Agbeti (of Ghana) that "African Theology", strictly, "should mean the interpretation of the pre-Christian and pre-Moslem African people's experience of their God". (See J.K. Agbeti, "African Theology, what it is" in *Presence*, vol.5, no.3, 1972, p.6.) Cf. Byang Kato, "Black Theology and African Theology" in *Perception*, no.6, October 1976, pp.7-8; also *Theological Pitfalls in Africa*, pp.53ff. Agbeti's view

would certainly not be shared by all practitioners of "African Theology".

21. See Kwesi A. Dickson and Paul Ellingworth (eds), *Biblical Revelation and African Beliefs*, London: Lutterworth Press, 1969, p.16, quoted in Byang H. Kato, *Theological Pitfalls in Africa*, pp.154f.

22. Byang H. Kato, *Theological Pitfalls in Africa*, p.155; emphasis in original.

23. J.N.D. Anderson, *Christianity and Comparative Religion*, London: Inter-Varsity Press, 1970, p.102.

24. Byang H. Kato, *Theological Pitfalls in Africa*, p.180.

25. See especially chapter four above: "Christ and the Hellenistic Heritage (1): Justin, or, Christ as 'The Expectation of the Nations'".

26. See our chapter six above: "The Legacy of 'the Third Opportunity' and the making of a modern identity problem".

27. *Ibid.*

28. Adrian Hastings, *Church and Mission in Modern Africa*, London: Burns & Oates, 1967, p.60.

29. Philip Turner, "The Wisdom of the Fathers and the Gospel of Christ: Some notes on Christian adaptation in Africa", in *JRA*, vol.4, fasc.1, 1971, p.65.

30. In response to a statement by Canon Burgess Carr (of Liberia), then General Secretary of the All Africa Conference of Churches (AACC), deploring "the total rejection of the African past, especially our traditional religious life", Kato declared: "Is this rejection of non-Christian religions merely a Western prejudice? Does the Lordship of Jesus Christ not call for total, unreserved devotion to the Lord of lords and King of kings (*Matt.* 6:24)?" See Byang H. Kato, "Evangelical evaluation of Lusaka Conference" (i.e. of AACC Third General Assembly, in Lusaka, Zambia, 11-24 May, 1974), in *Perception*, no.2, July, 1974, p.7.

31. It is this polemical frame of mind which explains his scathing attack on the writings and views of John Mbiti and Bolaji Idowu, whom he accuses not only of syncretism, but also universalism, by which he means "the belief that all men will eventually be saved whether they believe in Christ now or not". See Byang H. Kato, *Theological Pitfalls in Africa*, pp.53-128 (quotation on p.11.

32. Byang Kato, "Ecumenicals and Evangelicals" in *Perception*, no.16, May, 1979, p.8.

33. *Ibid.*, p.6.

34. See Byang H. Kato, *Theological Pitfalls in Africa*, chapters 10-12, pp.129-171.

35. *Ibid.*, p.170.

36. *Ibid.*, p.130.

37. *Ibid.*, p.130. My emphasis.

38. Ruth Rouse and Stephen Neill, *A History of the Ecumenical Movement, 1517-1948*, London, 1954, p.355; quoted in Barry Till, *The Churches Search for Unity*, Harmondsworth, Penguin Books, 1972, p.193.

39. Byang H. Kato, *Theological Pitfalls in Africa*, p.132.

40. *Ibid.*, p.132; cf. Barry Till, *op.cit.*, p.196.

41. Byang H. Kato, *Theological Pitfalls in Africa*, p.132.

42. *Ibid.*, pp.140f.

A Variety of African Responses (4)   419

43. *Ibid.*, pp.138-169.

44. *Ibid.*, p.149.

45. *Ibid.*, p.141.

46. *Ibid.*, pp.163f.

47. *Ibid.*, pp.154ff.

48. *Ibid.*, p.179: "The Christian may feed all the hungry people in the world, and pay all the bills of liberation movements of the society. His primary task is not done. His primary task is preaching the gospel of soul salvation."

49. See Byang H. Kato, "Black Theology and African Theology" in *Perception*, no.6, October, 1976, pp.1-8; also in *ERT*, issue no.1, October, 1977, pp.35-48.

50. *Ibid.*, p.3. The quotations are from Basil Moore (ed), *Black Theology: The South African Voice*, London: Hurst & Co., 1973, pp.5,43,63.

51. Byang H. Kato, *Black Theology and African Theology*, p.3.

52. The AACC, like the WCC, defines its doctrinal basis for membership in the following terms: "The All Africa Conference of Churches is a fellowship of Churches which confess the Lord Jesus Christ as God and only Saviour according to the Scriptures and therefore, seek to fulfil together their common calling to the glory of the one God, Father, Son and Holy Spirit". See Byang H. Kato, *Theological Pitfalls in Africa*, p.138.

53. *Ibid.*, p.141.

54. *Ibid.*, p.139.

55. *1 Corinthians* 15:3-4.

56. Kato attended the AACC Assembly in Lusaka, Zambia, at the invitation of the (then) General Secretary of the AACC, Canon Burgess Carr. See Byang H. Kato, *Theological Pitfalls in Africa*, p.159. I have, so far, been unable to ascertain in what capacity Dr Kato attended the WCC Assembly, but I have presumed that he was invited as observer to represent the AEAM.

57. For Kato's report on the Lusaka meeting, see Byang H. Kato, "Evangelical evaluation of Lusaka Conference" in *Perception*, no.2, July, 1974, pp.1-14; on the Nairobi Assembly, the report compiled from his notes, "The World Council of Churches Nairobi Assembly and Africa" in *Perception*, no.5, March, 1976, pp.1-12. (The notes for this report were among the last things Kato wrote before he died.)

58. See Byang H. Kato, *Theological Pitfalls in Africa*, pp.15, 139, 154; also, "Aid to the National Church: when it helps, when it hinders", in *EMQ*, vol.8, no.4, 1972, pp.193-201; "We are at the turning point in Africa's church history", in *Africa Now*, September/October, 1974, pp.6-7; "Africa: Prudence and Promise – a candid survey of current opportunity and dangers facing evangelicals and missionary strategy in Africa" in *United Evangelical Action*, Summer 1975, pp.17-20, 26, 34; "Africa's Christian Future" (part 2), in *Christianity Today*, 10th October, 1975, pp.10-14.

59. Cf. Kato's sixth proposal "for safeguarding Biblical Christianity in Africa": "Consolidate organisational structures based on doctrinal agreements. Fraternal relationship such as is being shaped by the Association of Evangelicals of Africa and Madagascar (AEAM) is strongly urged. The gregarious nature of the African calls for a fellowship so much needed; yet it does not need to be an organic union, neither does it need to be a unity at any cost". See his *Theological Pitfalls in Africa*, p.183.

60. *Ibid.*, p.169.

61. *Ibid.*, p.170.

62. See publicity brochure, "The Association of Evangelicals of Africa and Madagascar" issued in 1974.

63. Byang H. Kato, "Ecumenicals-Evangelicals debate in Germany" in *Perception*, no.3 (= vol.2, no.1), April, 1975, p.1. The debate was at the request of the "Evangelicals" (i.e. evangelical "Evangelicals", as "evangelische" in German simply means "Protestant") of the Lutheran Synod of Southern Germany, and was held on 13th-15th February, 1975.

64. In a rousing conclusion to his report, Kato declared: "While we do recognise that there are elements of evangelical Christianity evident in ecumenical groups in Africa, for example in the AACC and the National Councils of Churches, we must realise that there are unbiblical trends in ecumenism that are spreading rapidly. Evangelicals should present a united voice through an Evangelical Fellowship in their countries. The AEAM, which is the recognised voice of evangelicals in Africa today, deserves moral and financial support from all Africa (*sic*) Evangelicals. If you are an evangelical, why not take an open and positive stand with other evangelicals for the truth of the Word of God?" (*ibid.*, p.8)

65. See Byang H. Kato, *Theological Pitfalls in Africa*, p.141. Kato quotes the following passage from E.J. Young, *Thy Word is Truth*, Grand Rapids: Eerdmans, 1970, p.5: "Despite all that is being said and has been said to the contrary, the doctrine of inspiration is of the utmost significance and importance. If the Bible is not infallible, then we can be sure of nothing. The other doctrines of Christianity will then one by one go by the board. The fortunes of Christianity stand or fall with an infallible Bible. Attempts to evade this conclusion can only lead to self-deception." Kato then comments interestingly: "Young's statement can hardly be improved upon, except to redeem the word 'infallible' from the erroneous understanding of even some evangelicals today. When Young uses 'infallible', he means 'inerrant', rather than an errant Bible being infallible notwithstanding."

66. *Ibid.*, p.182. The Bible as "propositional revelation is fully inspired, inerrant in the original manuscripts, and faithfully transmitted (2 *Timothy* 3:16; *John* 10:35)." For the classic statement of this view of the Bible, see B.B. Warfield, *The Inspiration and Authority of the Bible* (edited by S.G. Craig, with introduction by Cornelius van Til), Philadelphia: The Presbyterian and Reformed Publishing Co., 1948 (reprinted in 1970). See also the recent "Chicago Statement on Biblical Inerrancy" in *ERT*, vol.4, no.1, April, 1980, pp.8-19.

67. Byang H. Kato, "Theological Trends in Africa Today", in *Perception*, no.1, March, 1974, p.4.

68. *Ibid.*, p.4.

69. John S. Mbiti, *African Religions and Philosophy*, London: Heinemann, 1969, p.277.

70. Byang H. Kato, "Theological Trends in Africa Today", p.5.

71. Byang H.Kato, "We are at a turning point in Africa's church history", p.6.

72. Byang H. Kato, "Theological Trends in Africa Today", p.5.

73. Byang H. Kato, "Ecumenicals-Evangelicals Debate in Germany", p.7. My emphasis.

74. Byang H. Kato, "Evangelisation and Culture", in *Perception*, no.12, April, 1978, p.6. See also, his *African Cultural Revolution and the Christian Faith*, Jos, Nigeria: Challenge Publications, 1975, pp.49-50.

75. See Byang H. Kato, "Africa: Prudence and Promise..." p.26: "We believe that the content of Christianity is inspired, but the mode of expression is not

inspired. By this I mean the instrument played rather than the music. Or, in the method of preaching, I don't see anything inspired in insisting on a three-point sermon in order to communicate... We can tell stories, we can hold dramas. We can find effective methods which can communicate adequately to people, but when we are doing this, we dare not tamper with the content of God's message to man. Because it is inspired and unchanging to whatever culture it goes, the Word of God remains forever. 'O Lord, your Word is settled in heaven' (*Ps.* 119:89)." Also, "The Christian Surge in Africa" (part 1), an interview given to the North American evangelical journal, *Christianity Today*, 26th September, 1975. In a criticism of "African Theology", Kato declared: "It [African Theology] argues that Africa has been Christianised, so now it is time to Africanise Christianity. African traditional religions are being revived on the theory that the worship they represent is of God, and only the means of worship is different. The gods being worshipped are even said to have been instituted by God. The idea is to pick out some elements of African religions and include them in Christianity. Syncretism is a real danger. My position is that I do see the point of expressing biblical Christianity in the context of every people. Biblical Christianity should be expressed in Africa in such a way that the African can feel at home in the Church of Jesus Christ. But we must realise that 'forever, O Lord, your word is settled in heaven' (*Ps.* 119:89)." For further references to *Ps.* 119:89, see Byang Kato, "Evangelical evaluation of Lusaka Conference", p.13; cf. *Theological Pitfalls in Africa*, p.169.

76. Byang H. Kato, "The World Council of Churches Nairobi Assembly and Africa", pp.9f.

77. See Byang H. Kato, *Theological Pitfalls in Africa*, pp.115ff.

78. Eric Sauer, *The Dawn of World Redemption*, Grand Rapids: Eerdmans, 1971, p.82. See Byang H. Kato, *Theological Pitfalls in Africa*, pp.122f.

79. G.C. Berkouwer, *General Revelation*, Grand Rapids: Eerdmans, 1955, p.132. Berkouwer's passage is incorrectly quoted in *Theological Pitfalls in Africa*, p.123, but correctly quoted elsewhere. See Byang Kato, "The Theology of Eternal Salvation" in *Perception*, no.14, October, 1978, p.4.

80. Byang H. Kato, *Theological Pitfalls in Africa*, p.123.

81. *Ibid.*, pp.123-124.

82. Byang H. Kato, "The Theology of Eternal Salvation", p.4: "The crucial question which confronts us is whether there can be salvation in general revelation, as it is admittedly different from special revelation. Going back farther, how clear are the 'heathen' in their interpretation of God's revelation?"

83. See *Romans* 1:18ff.

84. Byang H. Kato, *Theological Pitfalls in Africa*, p.123. My emphasis.

85. Byang H. Kato, "Evangelisation and Culture", p.6. In the same article Kato defined "Special Revelation" as "... God making Himself known through Jesus Christ and the Bible. It is through Special Revelation that we know the absolute way of salvation" (p.6).

86. See R.H. Charles, *A Critical and Exegetical Commentary on the Revelation of St John* (vol.1), Edinburgh: T. & T. Clark, 1920, p.354: "What has been foreordained in the counsels of God is in a certain sense a fact already. The principle of sacrifice and redemption is older than the world: it belongs to the essence of the Godhead." Cf. G.R. Beasley-Murray, *The Book of Revelation* (New Century Bible), London: Oliphants, 1974, p.214: "The sacrifice of the Lamb of God lay hidden in the heart of God from all eternity, and expresses the very nature of God." On the meaning of the Greek perfect tense, see C.F.D. Moule, *An Idiom-Book of New Testament Greek*, Cambridge: Cambridge University Press (2nd edition), 1959, p.13. Moule describes the perfect as expressing "punctiliar event in the past, related in its effects to the present".

87. Cf. Byang H. Kato, *Theological Pitfalls in Africa*, p.124: "If general revelation is kept in its proper place, the temptation of exalting any non-scripturally revealed concepts to the soteriological status will be considerably reduced. Jesus Christ alone will stand tall and unique above all other religions. He alone will be the Saviour of those who accept the *sola fide* (by faith alone) contingency of salvation. This is the remedy for universalism."

88. For instance, in "The Theology of Eternal Salvation" (p.7), Kato states: "The work of Christ is sufficient. He shed His blood for the redemption of sinners of all ages (*Mark* 10:45; *1 Cor.* 15:2-3)", and also "... the work of Christ is both cosmic and personal. In his vicarious sacrificial death, He has made salvation potentially possible for all men (*Jn* 1:29; *2 Cor.* 5:17-19), but only those who actively partake of the redemptive banquet can benefit from it (*Acts* 13:38,39; *Jn* 20:31)".

89. Byang H. Kato, *Theological Pitfalls in Africa*, p.121. Cf. "The Theology of Eternal Salvation", pp.5f.

90. Byang H. Kato, "The Theology of Eternal Salvation", p.6.

91. Byang H. Kato, *Theological Pitfalls in Africa*, pp.179ff.

92. *Ibid.*, p.179.

93. *Ibid.*, p.179.

94. See above, p.390-391.

95. Byang H. Kato, *Theological Pitfalls in Africa*, p.180.

96. *Ibid.*, pp.180-181. Emphasis in original. Kato then cites *Romans* 5:17 as support for his final qualifying phrase.

97. *Ibid.*, p.181.

98. *Ibid.*, p.182; cf. his "Black Theology and African Theology", p.3: "For the Christian, the Bible is the absolute authority on which to base all theological and ethical formulations."

99. See above, p.388.

100. Byang H. Kato, *African Cultural Revolution and the Christian Faith*, p.41.

101. *Ibid.*, p.41.

102. See Byang H. Kato, "Black Theology and African Theology", p.6.

103. *Ibid.*, p.6.

104. *Ibid.*, p.6.

105. Byang H. Kato, *Theological Pitfalls in Africa*, p.182: "The African problems of polygamy, family structure, spirit world, liturgy, to mention a few, need to be tackled by evangelical African theologians and Biblical answers presented."

106. *Ibid.*, p.182.

107. C. René Padilla, "Hermeneutics and Culture – a theological perspective" in John R.W. Stott and Robert Coote (eds), *Down to Earth: Studies in Christianity and Culture* (The papers of the Lausanne Consultation on Gospel and Culture), Grand Rapids: Eerdmans, 1980, pp.63-78; quotation on p.78.

108. Cf. Byang H. Kato, "The Church in the Closing Years of the Twentieth Century", in *World Vision Magazine*, December, 1974, p.9: "How far can we go without changing the content of the inspired, eternal Word of God? Attempts are already being made on fragmentation of Biblical Christian Theology into Theology of Liberation, Theology of Evolution [?], Black Theology and African Theology..."

109. C. René Padilla, *op.cit.*, p.77.

110. *Ibid.*, p.73.

111. See Paul Bowers, "Evangelical Theology in Africa: Byang Kato's Legacy", in *ERT*, vol.5, no.1, April, 1981, pp.35-39. However, if as Bowers argues, "the terms... in which the fundamental questions of contemporary African Christian thinking are posed demand a continually nurtured orientation not only upon the query 'Is it African?' but also upon the query, 'Is it Christian?'" (p.39), it is somewhat misleading for Bowers, then, to place Kato virtually alone and solely on the "Christian" side of the debate. On the other hand, it may also indicate that "the fundamental questions of contemporary African Christian thinking" need not be posed in such antithetical terms in the first place.

112. See Byang H. Kato, "Christianity as an African Religion", in *Perception*, no.16, May, 1979, pp.1-6. (This article is reprinted in *ERT*, vol.4, no.1, April, 1980, pp.31-39.)

113. B.H. Kato, *African Cultural Revolution and the Christian Faith.*

114. Byang H. Kato, "The Gospel, Cultural Context and Religious Syncretism", in J.D. Douglas (ed), *Let the Earth Hear His Voice* (International Congress on World Evangelisation, Lausanne, Switzerland; Official reference volume: *Papers and Responses*), Minneapolis: World Wide Publications, 1975, pp.1216-1223.

115. *Ibid.*, p.1222.

116. *Ibid.*, pp.1216,1222.

117. *Ibid.*, pp.1217f.

118. *Ibid.*, p.1223.

119. *Ibid.*, p.1217.

120. *Ibid.*, p.1217.

121. See Jacob A. Loewen, "The Gospel: its Content and Communication – an anthropological perspective", in John R.W. Stott and Robert Coote (eds), *op.cit.*, p.123.

122. Byang H. Kato, "The Gospel, Cultural Context and Religious Syncretism", p.1223.

123. Byang H. Kato, "Christianity as an African religion", p.4.

124. *Ibid.*, p.5.

125. *Ibid.*, p.5.

126. C. René Padilla, *op.cit.*, p.77. Cf. a revealing statement by Kato, "Christianity as an African religion", p.2: "In these challenging days there are many voices being heard both within and outside the Church for relevancy. Some people call it the Africanisation of Christianity. Despite the fact that 150 million out of the 360 million people of Africa call themselves 'Christians', there are still voices denying the fact that Christianity is an African religion. What we need in today's Africa is not a return to the old traditional religions, or even a borrowing of some of the pagan practices to add to Christianity. Our greatest need is to live up to the claims we make as Christians and promote the Christian message to all areas of life and everywhere possible as true ambassadors of Christ."

127. B.H. Kato, *African Cultural Revolution and the Christian Faith*, pp.13-31.

128. *Ibid.*, p.46.

129. This Festival, after being rescheduled, took place in 1977.

130. B.H. Kato, *African Cultural Revolution and the Christian Faith*, p.45.

131. *Ibid.*, pp.45-46.

132. *Ibid.*, p.54.

133. *Ibid.*, p.10.

134. *Ibid.*, p.12.

135. *Ibid.*, pp.13-31. For a further treatment of the subject of Gospel and Culture with particular reference to African experience, see Donald Jacobs, "Conversion and Culture – an anthropological perspective with reference to East Africa", in John R.W. Stott and Robert Coote (eds), *op.cit.*, pp.131-145.

136. B.H. Kato, *African Cultural Revolution and the Christian Faith*, p.17.

137. *Ibid.*, p.15.

138. *Ibid.*, p.19.

139. *Ibid.*, p.19.

140. *Ibid.*, p.20.

141. *Ibid.*, p.20; cf. p.24: "A Zairean in a sense may be a Zairean before a Christian chronologically... But when he accepts Christ, his first loyalty is to Jesus Christ, the Lord of Glory. Where there is a clash of loyalties, Christ comes first."

142. *Ibid.*, pp.24-25; see also Kato's "'The Christian Leader and his Family" in *Perception*, no.9, June, 1977, pp.1-8.

143. B.H. Kato, *African Cultural Revolution and the Christian Faith*, pp.30-31.

144. See for instance, the "Guidelines on Questionable Practices" which conclude the work under discussion, pp.54-56.

145. *Ibid.*, p.15.

146. *Ibid.*, p.15.

147. Byang H. Kato, "The Gospel, Cultural Context and Religious Syncretism", p.1216.

148. It is interesting that in commenting on J.N.D. Anderson's suggestion regarding the possibility of salvation for some of those who died without having heard the Gospel preached, Kato observed: "Anderson's position may be granted on the basis of deductive speculation", whilst he himself preferred "the more Scriptural basis..." See Byang H. Kato, *Theological Pitfalls in Africa*, p.180.

149. B.H. Kato, *African Cultural Revolution and the Christian Faith*, p.28.

150. *1 Corinthians* 2:14f.

151. See C. René Padilla, *op.cit.*, p.69.

152. See Paul Bowers, *op.cit.*

153. *Ibid.*, p.39.

154. See John Mbiti, "The Biblical Basis for Present Trends in African Theology" in Kofi Appiah-Kubi and Sergio Torres (eds), *African Theology en Route* (Papers from the Pan-African Conference of Third World Theologians, December, 17-23, 1977, Accra, Ghana), New York: Orbis Books, 1979, p.91: "As long as African theology keeps close to the Scriptures, it will remain relevant to the life of the Church in Africa and it will have lasting links with the theology of the church universal. African theologians must give even more attention to the Bible than is sometimes the case. As long as we keep the Bible close to our minds and our hearts, our theology will be viable, relevant, and of lasting service to the church and glory to the Lord to whom be honour, dominion, and power unto the ages of ages. Amen."

155. *Ibid.*, p.85. After recalling that in *Theological Pitfalls in Africa*, Kato launched "a most bitter attack on myself, Professor E.B. Idowu and

ecumenism... " Mbiti continued: "Dr Kato's passionate attack on fellow theologians and the ecumenical movement arose partly out of insufficient understanding on his part. I had the opportunity of discussing with him some of the issues on December 9, 1975. At the end he apologised to me for having unjustifiably attacked me and promised to rewrite and change the relevant parts of his book. Ten days later, on December 19, 1975, Dr Kato drowned on the shores of the Indian Ocean in Kenya. I learned a year later that before his tragic death Dr Kato had actually written the parts he promised to revise, and the publisher of the book undertook to incorporate them into subsequent printings of the book. I give this personal note about Dr Kato as an indication that he had no malicious intentions in his book; he apologised to me and in the same spirit I am sure he would have made personal apologies to those others whom he had attacked. His death was certainly a major loss for African theology... and may God rest his soul in peace."

For a report which seems to minimise the extent to which Kato modified his earlier views on Mbiti's theology, see Richard Bekulumpagi Kabazzi, "PACLA – Part of a movement or cornerstone of a monument?" in *Perception*, no.8, April, 1977, p.5.

156. Paul Bowers, *op.cit.*, pp.35,39.

157. See Byang Kato, "Christianity as an African religion", p.5.

158. Paul Bowers (*op.cit.*, p.37) admits: "To be sure the analysis is not always accurate, the polemic not always just, the demonstration not always persuasive, the organisation not always clear."

159. See above, chapters 7 and 8.

160. See John F. Robinson's review of *Theological Pitfalls in Africa* by Byang Kato, in *EMQ*, vol.12, no.4, October, 1976, pp.243f, reprinted in *ERT*, vol.1, no.1, October, 1977, pp.167.

161. See Paul Bowers, *op.cit.*

162. Tite Tienou, "Threats and Dangers in the Theological Task in Africa", in *ERT*, vol.5, no.1, April, 1981, pp.40-47; quotation on p.41.

163. Byang H. Kato, *Theological Pitfalls in Africa*, p.173.

164. *Ibid.*, p.178.

165. *Ibid.*, pp.121f.

166. Paul Bowers, *op.cit.* p.38.

167. See for instance, Tite Tienou, "Biblical Foundations for African Theology", in *Missiology*, vol.10, no.4, October, 1982, pp.435-448.

Chapter Eleven

Conclusion
Africa and the Fathers: The Relevance of the Achievement of Early Hellenistic Christian Theology for the Theological Enterprise in Modern Africa

The Ancient as Analogue of the Modern

Our study so far has proceeded along parallel lines. The thought and viewpoints of each of the writers selected for the purpose have been expounded primarily in terms of the particular writer's own perspective and agenda. Furthermore, the two different cultural and historical contexts to which the writers belong have been preserved in their distinctness, and there has been no attempt to read off the problems and issues of one context from the other; neither has a modern writer been treated as little more than a copy of an ancient model. I have sought to let the theological ideas and responses of each writer reflect as far as possible the questions and problems of that writer's own world of thought and concerns.

Yet it was also part of the initial impulse for this study to test the explicit suggestion that the question of identity with its significance for the development of theological self-consciousness, constitutes a shared presumption of the formative phase of Hellenistic Christian thought in the second century AD on the one hand, and the early flowering of Christian theology in the post-missionary Church in twentieth-century Africa on the other.[1] According to this argument, the question of identity constitutes a "hermeneutical key" which, by granting access to the kind of concerns exhibited by Christian writers in the two contexts, leads to a deeper understanding of the modern situation in particular, and shows how the modern context manifests features which are identifiable elsewhere in Christian history. It is now time to assess the extent to which the patristic evidence examined not only helps to clarify the modern context, but also contributes positive insights towards a solution of the modern problems.

The point of the kind of correlation being suggested here is not that the ancient and the modern contexts are in any sense interchangeable; nor is it implied that the questions and issues involved in the modern situation have been formulated in the same terms as in the earlier context; it is evident that the solutions from the past do not have a direct and unmediated relevance for the problems of the present. Rather, the perspective from which early Hellenistic Christian thought may be said to be relevant for modern African Christian reflection is, *mutatis mutandis*, as was stated by Richard A. Norris in *God and World in Early Christian Theology*:

> "The problems of modern Christian thought have no exact parallels in the theology of the Early Church. One cannot appeal to the past either for ready-made solutions to contemporary questions or for precise definitions of the questions themselves. Yet it remains true... that modern problems have their analogues and, even more important, their roots in the events and in the thought of the past."[2]

Thus, whilst we cannot turn to the past for solutions to the problems of the present, it is possible to find in the past analogues to the situations and circumstances in the present which raise some of the perennial questions that Christian reflection in every age is required to handle. By the same token, the answers that were given in the past may illuminate the path of the modern inquirer after solutions to the problems of the present.

"Continuity" and "Discontinuity": Problems of meaning

E.W. Fasholé-Luke, at the end of a wide-ranging survey of the quest for an appropriate Christian theological idiom in modern Africa, summed up the evidence as follows:

> "... the quest for African Christian theologies which has been vigorously pursued in the last decade, amounts to attempting to make clear the fact that conversion to Christianity must be coupled with cultural continuity. Furthermore, if Christianity is to change its status from that of resident alien to that of

citizen, then it must become incarnate in the life and thought of Africa and its theologies must bear the distinctive stamp of mature African thinking and reflection. What African theologians have been endeavouring to do is to draw together the various and disparate sources which make up the total religious experience of Christians in Africa into a coherent and meaningful pattern."[3]

In this important statement, Dr Fasholé-Luke clarifies a significant point of convergence between the circumstances surrounding the birth of modern African theology and those that attended the rise of the Christian theological tradition in Graeco-Roman culture. For it was the interaction of a heightened sense of Christian self-consciousness on the one hand, and the awareness of a shared intellectual heritage in a common culture on the other, which provided the major motivating force for the positive vindication of Christianity in the Graeco-Roman world by the early Christian writers we have studied. This must be said even of Tatian and Tertullian. In the case of Justin and Clement of Alexandria, the point is quite obvious; and yet it has to be maintained with regard to Tatian and Tertullian also, because it is the only basis on which sufficient communication with the cultural context could take place. It is true that in terms of the value placed on the insights derived from the common culture they shared with their non-Christian contemporaries, these four early Christian writers fall into two groups with some considerable differences between them. However, these differences are as much the product of temperament, education and background, as of varying perceptions of their cultural world. On the fundamental issue of Christian convictions, their views are strikingly similar.

In spite of the differences between them in terms of the approach to the "cultural witness" of the Church, these early Christian writers remained remarkably unanimous in the essentials of what they affirmed theologically with regard to what Gregory Dix described as the "Syriac" content of the Gospel which had come to them through the religious history of Israel – with its *Barbarian* elements.[4] It is conceivable that the more Hellenically-minded among them could have chosen the Gnostic solution to the problem of identity and "the cultural witness" of the Church. This would have involved a radical Hellenisation by jettisoning such Barbarian elements as Old Testament history and religion; the doctrine of the absolute reality and sovereignty of the one and only

Living God at the centre of the universe – the *monarchia* as against
the rule of the many, *polykoirania*, which is postulated from
human experience; the doctrine of the Incarnate God; a drastic
eschatology and bodily resurrection; the opposition of history to
myth in matters of religion – *diegema* as against *mythos*; divine
revelation as against human speculation. It is extraordinary that
this "Hellenistic" solution did not find favour with Christian
thinkers who were as self-consciously Hellenistic as were the
Gnostics. The repudiation by the Great Church of both the Mar-
cionite solution to the problem of the canon of Scripture and the
Valentinian theology of *aeons* and *ogdoads* is therefore significant.
One can even pursue the distinctions into the controversies of later
times. For what became recognised as orthodoxy at Nicaea in AD
325 and found full ratification at Constantinople in AD 381 by a
predominantly Hellenistic Church, speaking Greek and thinking
in Greek, was in fact, the *Barbarian* philosophy of the Living God
of "Syriac" origin. "The unknown God" of pre-Christian Athens,[5]
was now affirmed as the "One God, Father Almighty, Maker of all
things, visible and invisible..."

Looked at from the angle of the dynamics of early Christian
thought amid Graeco-Roman culture, concepts such as "continuity"
and "discontinuity" may even be misleading. In other words, it is
not enough to see Justin and Clement as protagonists of "continuity" whilst Tatian and Tertullian represent the opposite tendency of "discontinuity". All four writers are clear on the
importance of fidelity to the Scriptures and to Christian tradition
as this had been handed on from apostolic times. What is even more
remarkable, in the context of the conflict of cultures between
Hellenism and Barbarism, is the fact that all – including the most
Greek of them, Clement of Alexandria – were utterly convinced of
the Barbarian character and origins of the Christian revelation,
the true and only effectual philosophy; so that what was, in Werner
Jaeger's phrase, "the headway made in history by the Greek
mind",[6] they explained in terms of borrowings from the more
ancient Scriptural tradition, or else, as simply the data of God's
self-revelation in Hellenistic tradition. Tatian, from his vantage
point as an Assyrian, and finding the supposed Barbarian
philosophy a powerful tool for warding off the alien imposition of
a culture in which he did not believe, understandably exploited the
argument about borrowings most intensely of all. But Tatian does
not therefore become simply a champion of "discontinuity" as such;

he affirmed another kind of "continuity", though not with Hellenistic tradition. His concern was a continuity with Barbarism as the essential character of the Christian faith. It is most unlikely that Christians of Hellenistic culture would have followed Tatian in his polemic. And yet, paradoxically, what in Tatian's schema was the heart of his anti-Hellenistic polemic, namely, the chronological argument for the priority of Moses and the Old Testament tradition, became his most enduring contribution to the Greek-speaking Church. With the tools that Tatian thus provided, a writer like Clement of Alexandria was able to argue for the antiquity of the Christian tradition, and so to secure for it "continuity" with a truly ancient and ancestral heritage within a culture that had great respect for pedigree.

Tertullian is the genuine enigma. We noted the view of Joseph Lortz[7] that Tertullian must not be set apart from the Greek Apologists, since he and they form an intellectual unity. Tertullian's advance on his Greek counterparts consists in the greater vehemence of his response to the hostile environment and of his defence of Christian self-identity. Besides, when it is recognised that the "discontinuity" which Tertullian postulated was that between the divine revelation granted in Christian tradition on the one hand, and all human speculative systems on the other, then his position too becomes all the more complex. For Tertullian also affirms a form of "continuity", but one, as he understood it, of the Christian's unsullied conscience. There is perhaps no more vigorous exponent of what has been called, with reference to Christian self-understanding, "the pilgrim principle", which consists in defining Christian authenticity in terms of factors lying outside of one's natural culture and society.[8] However, it is doubtful whether Tertullian would have described his response to his cultural context in *cultural* terms; from Tertullian's standpoint, the Christian's response to the sinful world could only be religious because Christian self-understanding was essentially religious in character. Since all that was of the world (*saecularia*) was of demons, it followed that the entire outfit which sustained the cultural and political life of the Empire – in other words, everything which lay outside of Christian self-consciousness and of the Christian community thus conceived – was to be rejected. Instead, the Christian was to maintain the "continuity" of a radical alternative religious system and *vision du monde* which ought to be entirely *Christian*.

If the development of early Hellenistic Christian thought on this issue has any value for subsequent Christian history, it may be in what it shows about the complexities that attach to the "continuity" or "discontinuity" with every form of pre-Christian tradition. The subject has tended to be oversimplified where the Christian story of modern Africa is concerned. G.C. Oosthuizen, referring to H. Richard Niebuhr's classic treatment of the subject,[9] has commented:

> "The viewpoint of Tertullian the Montanist has been accepted with regard to the indigenous culture [of Africa] while with regard to the Western culture that of Abelard and the early European approach has been accepted."[10]

Our own study of Tertullian allows us to modify somewhat the traditional perception of his approach, by giving due weight to the essentially *religious* character of his outlook. However, when the traditional view of Tertullian's position – described as "Christ against culture"[11] – is set beside that of Abelard and the early European approach – described as "Christ of culture",[12] then Oosthuizen's point becomes clear: the presumption that the Christian Gospel is somehow intrinsically "part of the Western way of life" has the effect of making suspect all serious attempts at theological indigenisation in Africa (and, for that matter, in any non-Western context). This explains why the efforts of Africa's theologians to "draw together the various and disparate sources which make up the total religious experience of Christians in Africa into a coherent and meaningful pattern"[13] have tended to be met with scepticism. And yet, as our ancient analogues in early Hellenistic Christian thought show, a positive evaluation of the pre-Christian tradition and an attempt to derive insights from it for the declaration of Christian convictions need not imply a theological syncretism. Of the African writers we have studied – all committed churchmen – none, in giving a positive evaluation of the pre-Christian African tradition, sees it as antithetical to the significance of the Christian Gospel for Africa. In the case of Byang Kato, the one writer who maintained a negative and unsympathetic approach to every form of "non-Christian" religion, we have had reason to question the theological basis of his outlook.

Some specific areas of relevance: (a) The possibility of synthesis

It follows therefore, that one aspect of the relevance of the achievement of early Hellenistic Christian thought for the modern

African context has to do with the possibility of a genuine theology
which seeks a synthesis between Christian religious commitment
and cultural continuity. This conclusion was clearly stated by
André Benoit who included a discussion of the value of patristic
studies for the "Younger Churches" of Africa, Asia and Oceania in
his discussion of the relevance of the Church Fathers for the
Church in the twentieth century. According to Benoit, the
"Younger Churches", confronted with the task of indigenising the
Gospel rather than perpetuating Western modes of thought and
expression, would find more helpful models in the efforts of the
Church Fathers than in more recent Western theology, in which it
is difficult, if not impossible "to distinguish between what is
authentically Christian and what is just a cultural contribution".
Consequently, for the "Younger Churches",

> "It is a question for them of rethinking Christianity within the
> framework of a non-Western culture without, however, betray-
> ing or twisting it. That is to say that they must recover the
> usable elements in the native civilisations and reject the others.
> The Fathers did the same. As bearers of the Gospel they had to
> express it within the framework of Hellenistic culture; they
> preserved the usable elements of that culture and left aside
> what was without value. Studying the Fathers would in this
> case render appreciable service in emphasising the fundamen-
> tal elements of all Christian theology and in showing the neces-
> sity for a certain amount of adaptation as well as the limits to
> it."[14]

If Benoit is right that the theology of the Fathers manifests
some of the "fundamental elements of all Christian theology", then
one such element is the fact that no Christian theology in any age
is ever simply a repetition of the inherited Christian tradition; that
all Christian theology is a synthesis, an "adaptation" of the inherited Christian tradition in the service of new formulations of
the problem of "the life of the universe and the life of man considered in their relation to the will and purpose of the Creator" –
which is the subject matter of theology.[15]

(b) The Challenge of Pluralism

The ancient achievement in early Hellenistic Christianity is
also significant for our modern concerns in view of the context in
which it took place. Benoit noted this point as well in his discussion,
though he limited its value to the similarities he saw between the
"paganism" which confronted the Early Church and the

"paganism" that the "Younger Churches" have to encounter in their cultural world:

"Never since Christian antiquity have the Church and paganism confronted each other with such vigour. It is thus right to wonder whether a study of the reactions of the Fathers faced with the paganism of those days could not contribute elements of a solution to the problem of the present struggle between Christianity and paganism in mission territories."[16]

John Foster, writing in 1942, had stated a similar viewpoint, arguing not only that "the Younger Churches are the Early Church of our day", but also that:

"... there is hardly a problem, a situation, a task, belonging to the history of the Church in the first four centuries which is not a chief preoccupation to the men of the missionary movement today."[17]

It is possible, in the light of studies in the phenomenology of religion, to clarify even further these suggestions about the similarities in the respective "paganisms" in the contexts of early Hellenistic Christianity and the modern "Younger Churches". Not only has the expansion of Christianity registered its most marked responses in "societies with primal religious systems"[18] (which will include the Mediterranean world of the early Christian centuries, Northern and Western Europe and the lands of the "Younger Churches" of Africa, Asia and Oceania), but also this peculiar historical connection between this form of "paganism" and Christianity raises questions about possible "affinities between the Christian and primal traditions"[19] which have hitherto not been taken seriously. In other words, the fact that it is *primal* religions which "underlie therefore the Christian faith of the vast majority of Christians of all ages and all nations",[20] is of more than episodic interest, and may carry far-reaching significance for the understanding of the nature of the Christian faith itself.

However, what both Benoit and Foster failed to indicate was that the really important point of convergence between the ancient and the modern contexts in question, consisted in the fact and the experience of pluralism. Long before pluralism – religious as well as cultural – became a subject of serious discussion in the Western world, many of the Christian communities of Africa had been living, witnessing and learning to survive and grow in the context of religious pluralism. Unlike Western Europe, "generally speaking, Africa has avoided *Christian* ontocracies"[21] whereby throne and altar were integrated. In the modern African "pluralism of Christian and Muslim, or of Christianity and adherents of the old religion, or of different and sometimes competing forms of Christianity..."[22], it is evident that theology cannot be done, studied and taught in quite the same way in which it has been in the Western European tradition, where the challenge of pluralism was virtually unknown or else was minimal for a very long time. It also means that the intellectual framework as well as the kind of questions that will be posed, will differ from those that have characterised the Western European tradition in theology.

(c) Theology as Indigenisation

The shifts in interests that almost every one of Africa's theologians trained in theology according to a Western model, has been "forced" to make is only symptomatic of the fact that both the *content* of theological study, and the *agenda* for the African theological enterprise were developing along lines which could not have been anticipated in view of the Western missionary background of the Christian Churches in Africa. An indication of the radically new situation which the African pluralistic context now presented is the fact that the university Faculties of Divinity or Theology which had developed within European Christendom with their attention directed mainly towards the investigation of the traditional fields of Biblical, historical and dogmatic studies, have had to make way for Departments of Religious Studies with a more pronounced interest in the phenomenology and theology of religions. No self-respecting theological institution in Africa can now avoid the study of African Traditional Religions, for it is they which "are now at the very centre of the academic stage".[23] Consequently, Byang Kato's proposal that "African Traditional Religions as well as other religions" should be studied "carefully... but only secondarily to the inductive study of God's Word",[24] is unlikely to prove realistic in "the conditions of a plural society where religion is a massive, unignorable fact of life".[25] Paradoxically, what this also means is that for modern Africa's theologians, inheritors of nearly twenty centuries of Christian scholarship, the theological task becomes "... more rather than less, exacting."[26]

In this regard also, the achievement of early Hellenistic Christian theology has a relevance for the modern African context. It has been noted that the Apostolic Fathers were witnesses to the traditional faith rather than interpreters of it.[27] But from Justin Martyr onwards, this attitude could no longer remain undisturbed.

New questions and issues were now forced upon the growing, largely Hellenistic Church: How did the Gospel relate to the Hellenistic past? What was the nature of the saving activity of the one Living God through the centuries prior to the Incarnation of the Saviour and the inauguration of the Christian era, or (as Clement of Alexandria chose to call it) the "common tradition", the era of "the universal calling to salvation by the one Lord and Saviour of all mankind"? Justin was convinced that there were Christians *before* Christ, and he was prepared to offer names as evidence for the truth of his intuition. Clement went even further, and argued that some philosophers and thoughtful persons of the past had in fact found justification through their genuine quest after nobler conceptions of the divine, and excellence in conduct; that the philosophical tradition itself was a divine gift bestowed upon Hellenistic culture to lead to Christ and so to serve much the same purpose as the Old Testament revelation in the religious history of the Hebrews.

Some elements in this new Christian thinking about the pre-Christian tradition seemed far removed from the New Testament, and some Christians sought to remind Clement of St Paul's warning about the dangers of philosophy.[28] Clement had a ready response: the apostle did not mean all philosophy, but only the Epicurean sort, which had no room for God and exalted pleasure as the fundamental principle of life. Therefore, *all* philosophical tenets were to be tested, and those that approximated to Christian beliefs integrated into Christian theology; in fact, in so far as they approximated to Christian convictions, they were borrowings from the Scriptures, or else were the outcome and evidence of direct inspiration by God in Hellenistic tradition.

The really striking feature in this patristic reinterpretation of the pre-Christian religious tradition is the extent to which the entire enterprise was rooted in the quest for an integral picture of the redemptive activity of God, in view of the fact that God is One and universal; but this integral picture of the divine activity was also necessary for an integrated Christian self-consciousness within Hellenistic culture. Therefore the effort to trace a salvific dimension in the pre-Christian tradition and so by implication to identify "Christian" antecedents in it, answered to a single urge, namely, to articulate a unified world-picture in which the God of Christian revelation was seen to be Who He really is; the one and only God of all mankind. In this, the patristic thought was the authentic heir of the theology of St Paul.[29]

(d) The pre-Christian heritage as a "tradition of response"

By adopting this open and inclusive approach to the pre-Christian tradition, Justin and Clement were refusing to treat Christian revelation and the "non-Christian" tradition as mutually exclusive *systems*. Rather, in their thinking, the encounter between the two realities took place on quite different terms, that is, "in the things that pertain to the spirit",[30] and they were prepared to argue for the operation of the pre-incarnate Word in the "non-Christian" tradition no less than in the Christian. Looked at from this angle, the pre-Christian tradition became a "tradition of response" to the reality of the Transcendent,[31] and so could be probed not so much for the measure of truth it contained, as for the truth of the human response to the divine action within the tradition. Consequently, what we described earlier as the postulate of "two traditions" within the Hellenistic heritage, namely, the true and the false, may equally well be called the postulate of "two responses". The early Christian apologists' instinct to welcome and identify with the philosophical tradition and to reject the popular religion and its mythology, finds its deepest meaning here. However, it is worth noting that in making common cause with philosophy, they were still operating within a unified framework of the religious quests of their time, since the philosophy they meant was virtually a religion – the religion of the educated and thoughtful people. Therefore the fact that the African heritage does not seem to have produced a distinct tradition of "philosophy" independently of religion[32] need not hamper the usefulness of the relevant patristic insights at this point. This may be just one indication that the crucial question for theology in the two contexts cannot be reduced to identical formulations in all cases. On the other hand, it is evident that the efforts made by Idowu, Mbiti and Mulago to demonstrate, on the basis of the oneness of God and the pre-Christian African sense of God, that African Christian experience is not totally discontinuous with the pre-Christian heritage, fall within the kind of approach adopted by Justin and Clement to their Hellenistic heritage. Besides, the fact that in both the early Hellenistic and modern African contexts, the solution of the problem posed by the pre-Christian tradition is invariably related to the question of identity, shows the extent to which the two contexts shed light on each other.

Nevertheless, it remains true that the positive evaluation of the

African pre-Christian heritage has, on the whole, said "little... about the failings of the past (on the African side)".[33] Even though John Mbiti has acknowledged the existence of "deadness and rottenness in our traditional religiosity" which must be purged by the Christian faith as professed by Africans,[34] the theme is not developed by him, nor by any of the other writers who give a positive interpretation of Africa's "old" religions. A possible explanation may be that African Theology so far has been concerned mainly to respond to the derogatory European evaluation of African tradition by seeking to achieve a genuinely sympathetic interpretation of the religious past. In the process, Africa's theologians were in fact providing the kind of "theological and scholarly stiffening for the new African Church which was important in the establishment of confidence".[35] On the other hand, it may also indicate something of a methodological problem in "African Theology" that the blemishes of the religious past have not so far been adequately clarified and set in perspective. Unlike the Fathers who inherited from their pre-Christian background a tradition of intellectual critique of the old religion which was thus affirmative of their cultural identity, Africa's theologians received a critique, which by being extraneous and Eurocentric, could only be alienating for them and destructive of the very concept of an African theology of synthesis. Here the weakness noted in the theological outlook of Byang Kato finds its deepest significance. Here also, we find the reason why the task of articulating the theological significance of the pre-Christian religious tradition is likely to remain a preoccupation of African Theology for some time yet.[36] In the process, it may be that the patristic experiments in the early centuries of the Christian movement will find a more prominent place in the consciousness of Africa's theologians, and the "Tertullianic" tendency that Byang Kato represented may need to be taken more seriously, even if his own solution was far from adequate.

Indeed, it is curious that those of Africa's theologians who have sought to give a positive evaluation of the pre-Christian heritage, have hardly made any conscious or systematic use of the kind of patristic insights that we have been considering. John Mbiti, whose outlook and approach come the closest to those of Justin and Clement, nowhere mentions them in this connection. Mulago, whose Catholic theological training has exposed him to the patristic literature most intimately of all, merely treats the Fathers as part of the *magisterium* of the Church and does not draw upon their historical significance for his own concern with a theology of synthesis. Interestingly, it was Byang Kato who noted the parallels between the context of the Hellenistic Church of the second century and that of the African Church of the twentieth century; but Kato then went on to reject the theological achievement of early Hellenistic Christianity. Thus, whilst African Theology has been wrestling with essentially the same problems as confronted early Hellenistic Christian theology,[37] African theologians, it appears, have pursued their agenda, so far at least, in virtual isolation from the most relevant analogue in the history of Christian thought to their modern efforts.[38]

In one sense, this is a disturbing state of affairs; it obscures the true character of the achievement of African Theology which is thereby consigned to a sort of limbo, with no clear links to the historical tradition of Christian theological reflection. As a consequence, African Theology's properly *theological* concern with the African pre-Christian heritage has tended to be assessed by the criteria of social anthropology, and so has been generally misunderstood. It is, however, the history of Christian theological thought, and the early patristic phase of that history in particular, which most adequately clarifies its intuitions and illuminates its insights.

Agenda for the future: (a) African Theology and its African critics

It is also the early patristic experiments we have examined which most helpfully identify some of the crucial areas which may still require attention in modern African Theology. In concluding the "Prolegomena" to the present study we indicated the significance of the non-Christian African writer Okot p'Bitek, who, glorying in the African pre-Christian past, "speaks the authentic voice of Celsus"[39] in our modern context. The fact that African Theology has yet to produce a full-scale response to Okot p'Bitek and other African non-Christian critics of the African theological enterprise may be an indication of the strength of his criticism that by seeking to "christianise" the African religious past, African Theology is merely "continuing the missionary misrepresentation of the past".[40] But the absence of a major *theological* response to Okot p'Bitek may also reveal a more fundamental lack which needs to be addressed in the agenda of the future.

African Theology has now overturned virtually every negative verdict passed on African tradition by the ethnocentricism of the Western missionary enterprise. In the process, African Theology has provided the theoretical validation for the "massive and unavoidable fact and factor" of Christianity "in the African scene" as a genuinely African reality.[41] But African Theology is perhaps now called upon to engage creatively with the developing African intellectual opinion which interprets African reality differently to the point of setting aside the very principle of religion itself.[42] Here a basic postulate of the entire modern African theological enterprise is challenged, namely, the view that African existence and African interpretation of that existence are essentially and totally *religious*. How African Theology responds to this *African* philosophical and intellectual atheism must certainly be one of the most crucial issues in the theology of the future.

(b) The Christian Faith as "a historical category" in the African Experience

However, the response to this new *African* challenge will form part of a much wider task which involves clarifying in the African Experience what Marcel Simon meant when he described the emergence of Christianity in the ancient world as the "birth of a historical category".[43] For the response to Celsus in early Hellenistic Christian theology which came through Origen was the culmination of a process of Christian self-definition in Graeco-Roman culture.[44] In much the same way, it is as the modern African Christian identity problem is fully thought through that the definitive response to the non-Christian African critics of African Theology can be given.

Here, the relevance of the patristic achievement points, among other things, to how they managed to preserve the Christian revelation intact against those who would have divested it of its "Barbarian" character, and yet were able to vindicate for the Christian conscience a place to feel at home in the common culture they shared with their non-Christian contemporaries. But at the heart of that achievement was their perception of the Gospel itself – how they understood what Simon called "the specific nature of Christianity".[45] In this regard, our ancient analogue shades into an ancient model and reveals the Fathers as truly our masters. For in the thinking of the early Christian writers whom we have studied, the Christian Gospel came to constitute an intellectual and historical category in its own right; it not only provided them with a precious interpretative key for discerning the religious meanings inherent in their heritage, so that they could decide what to accept and what to reject; in the Gospel they also found an all-encompassing reality and an overall integrating principle which enabled them to understand themselves and their past, and face the future, because the Gospel of Jesus Christ became for them the heir to all that was worthy in the past, whilst it held all the potential of the future. Something of this realisation seems to lie behind Prof. C.G. Baëta's observation on the impact of Christianity in Africa in the twentieth century:

> "In numberless institutions of many different kinds as well as in the equally numerous and diverse voluntary organisations and free associations of men, women and children; in the pervasive influence and challenge of its message to men and demand upon their individual lives and their relationships with one another; in countless personal and group decisions made, and lives actually lived very differently from what they would otherwise have been; in the new high hopes and aspirations for individual and social destiny which it has awakened; in the sheer excellence of human performance in devotion and courageous, self-sacrificing service to others, and yet in other ways, Christianity... plays a role and exerts a force in tropical Africa which is none the less real or significant because it eludes full and conclusive analysis."[46]

The truth of Baëta's observation may well be illustrated in the following incident of religious encounter reported from Ghana:

> "A sharp conflict recently erupted between the Christian churches and the traditional authorities in the Ghanaian town of Akim Tafo over violation by the churches of a ban on drumming during a traditional religious festival.

> "During the two weeks preceding the 'Ohum' religious festival, drumming, clapping of hands, wailing, firing of musketry, and any other noises likely to disturb the gods is not permitted.

> "But Christian churches in the town ignored the ban and continued to allow drumming during their worship services, arguing that drumming was an essential part of the Ghanaian form of worship."[47]

It is evident that from a religious point of view, the most striking thing about this incident is that the controversy took place in the context of worship. Here, then, is a classic instance of power-encounter, a meeting of experiences, an interaction of apprehensions of reality. What is even more interesting about this religious conflict is the fact that the Christians, as concerned as their non-Christian opponents to affirm their cultural integrity, insist that their *Christian* worship with the aid of drums, even though it may be in violation of a traditional religious ban, has an equal right to being recognised as authentic *Ghanaian* worship.

Here, Christian history comes full circle, and, as in our ancient analogue, the "tradition of response" bifurcates, not because the Gospel introduces an entirely new religious *system* which is unrelated to the cultural heritage (otherwise the Christians of Akim Tafo could hardly claim against the devotees of the "old" gods that their Christian worship was in any real sense Ghanaian). Rather, the Gospel of Jesus Christ, turning as it does "on grace and personality" and having "to do with men as men, their sins and their fears, and not with Jews as Jews, or Greeks as Greeks",[48] introduces "a historical category" which by transcending the stubborn human divisions of race, culture and lineage, not only provides a means of making manifest the dynamic of spirituality for what it is, but also clarifies in a new way the nature of identity as ultimately rooted in God and Christ. An anticipation of what the fuller African theological response may be was given by John Mbiti when he wrote in 1972:

> "Cultural identities are temporary, serving to yield us as Christians to the fullness of our identity with Christ. Paradoxically, culture snatches us away from Christ, it denies that we are His; yet when it is best understood, at its meeting with Christianity, culture drives us to Christ and surrenders us to Him, affirming us to be permanently, totally and unconditionally His own."[49]

Perhaps nothing demonstrates more clearly that the theological achievement of early Hellenistic Christianity in the second century and the emergent theological self-consciousness of African Christianity in the twentieth century, belong to one and the same story.

Notes

1. See above, "Introduction: The question of identity as a key to understanding the concerns of Christian thought in the 2nd century AD and in 20th century Africa", pp.1ff.

2. Richard A. Norris, *God and World in early Christian Theology – A Study in Justin Martyr, Irenaeus, Tertullian and Origen*, London: A. & C. Black, 1966, p.vii.

3. E.W. Fasholé-Luke, "The Quest for an African Christian Theology", in *The Ecumenical Review*, vol.27, no.3, July 1975, pp.267-268.

4. Gregory Dix, *Jew and Greek – A Study in the Primitive Church*, London:

Dacre Press, Westminster, 1953.

5. *Acts* 17:23.

6. Werner Jaeger, *Early Christianity and Greek Paideia*, London: Oxford University Press, 1961, p.35.

7. Joseph Lortz, *Tertullian als Apologet* (1 Band), Munster: Aschendorffsche Verlagsbuchhandlung, 1927.

8. See A.F. Walls, "The Gospel as the Prisoner and Liberator Of Culture" in *Faith and Thought*, 108 (1-2), 1981, pp.30-52; especially pp.45f.

9. See H. Richard Niebuhr, *Christ and Culture*, New York: Harper and Row, (Harper Colophon Books), 1951.

10. G.C. Oosthuizen, *Post-Christianity in Africa – A Theological and Anthropological Study*, London: Hurst and Co., 1968, p.4.

11. H. Richard Niebuhr, *op.cit.*, pp.51ff.

12. *Ibid.*, pp.83ff.

13. E.W. Fasholé-Luke, *op.cit.*, p.268.

14. André Benoit, *L'actualité des Pères de l'Eglise* (Cahiers théologiques, 47), Neuchâtel: Editions Delachaux et Niestlé, 1961, p.79.

15. J.V. Langmead Casserley, *The Retreat from Christianity in the Modern World* (The Maurice Lectures for 1951), London: Longmans, Green and Co., 1952, p.73.

16. André Benoit, *op.cit.*, pp.78-79.

17. John Foster, *Then and Now – The Historic Church and the Younger Churches*, London: SCM Press, 1942, p.65; cf. also his *After the Apostles – Missionary Preaching of the First Three Centuries*, London: SCM Press, 1951.

18. See A.F. Walls, "Africa and Christian Identity", in *Mission Focus*, vol.4, no.7, November 1978, pp.11-13.

19. See H.W. Turner, "The Primal Religions of the World and their Study", in Victor Hayes (ed), *Australian Essays in World Religions*, Bedford Park, South Australia, 1977, p.37.

20. A.F. Walls, "Africa and Christian Identity", p.11.

21. A.F. Walls, "Towards Understanding Africa's Place in Christian History" in J.S. Pobee (ed), *Religion in a Pluralistic Society* (Essays presented to Professor C.G. Baëta), Leiden: E.J. Brill, 1976, p.187. My emphasis. For the word "ontocracy", see Arend Th. van Leeuwen, *Christianity in World History: The Meeting of the Faiths of East and West* (ET by H.H. Hoskins), London: Edinburgh House Press, 1964.

22. A.F. Walls, "Towards Understanding Africa's Place in Christian History", p.187.

23. Adrian Hastings, *African Christianity – An essay in interpretation*, London: Geoffrey Chapman, 1976, p.183.

24. Byang H. Kato, *Theological Pitfalls in Africa*, Kisumu (Kenya): Evangel Publishing House, 1975, p.183.

25. A.F. Walls, "A Bag of Needments for the Road: Geoffrey Parrinder and the study of religion in Britain", in *Religion*, vol.10, Autumn 1980, p.144. It is interesting, as Professor Walls points out, that it was in such conditions and through the work of Geoffrey Parrinder that "Departments of Religious Studies as we know them in Britain were born..." i.e. in West Africa.

26. A.F. Walls, "Towards Understanding Africa's Place in Christian His-

tory", p.184.

27. See J.N.D. Kelly, *Early Christian Doctrines* (4th edition), London: A. & C. Black, 1968, p.90.

28. Cf. *Colossians* 2:8.

29. See *Romans* 3:29f; 10:11-13. For a study of the thinking of the Church Fathers which stresses this quest for integration and points to the significance of the patristic achievement for a modern understanding of all forms of pre-Christian tradition, see A. Luneau, "Pour aider au dialogue: les Pères et les religions non chrétiennes", in *NRT*, September-November, 1967, pp.821-841.

30. *Ibid.*, p.836: "On the level of this present life, there is no gap between Christianity and paganism, or *rather, it is situated on another plane, on the level of the spirit.*" (My emphasis.)

31. See John V. Taylor, *The Go-Between God – The Holy Spirit and the Christian Mission*, London, SCM Press, 1972, pp.182f. It seems to me that the concept of "religion as a people's tradition of response to the reality of the Holy Spirit..." describes very accurately what I think Justin and Clement were trying to express in their approach to their Hellenistic heritage, and I use it freely for that reason.

32. One recalls to mind here the title of John Mbiti's well-known volume *African Religions and Philosophy*. African traditional "philosophy" is essentially a religious philosophy.

33. Adrian Hastings, *African Christianity – An essay in interpretation*, p.52.

34. See John S. Mbiti, "Christianity and Traditional Religions in Africa" in *IRM*, vol.59, no.236, October, 1970, pp.436-437.

35. Adrian Hastings, *A History of African Christianity 1950-1975*, Cambridge: Cambridge University Press, 1979, p.231.

36. See T. Tshibangu, "Les tâches de la théologie africaine" in K. Appiah-Kubi *et al* (eds), *Libération ou Adaptation: La Théologie africaine s'interroge*, (Le Colloque d'Accra), Paris: Editions Harmattan, 1979, pp.92-102.

37. See A.F. Walls, "The Gospel as the prisoner and liberator of culture", p.50.

38. See, for instance, Patrick Kalilombe, "The Salvific Value of African Religions", in *AFER*, vol.21, no.3, June 1979, pp.143-157; this article is reprinted in Gerald H. Anderson and Thomas F. Stransky (eds), *Faith meets Faith* (Mission Trends, no.5), New York: Paulist Press, Grand Rapids: Eerdmans, 1981, pp.50-68. In this illuminating and very interesting discussion, Bishop Kalilombe neither mentions nor explicitly makes use of patristic insights.

39. A.F. Walls, "The Gospel as the prisoner and liberator of culture", p.49.

40. *Ibid.*, p.49. See Okot p'Bitek, *African Religions in Western Scholarship*, Kampala: East African Literature Bureau, 1970; also his long poem, *Song of Lawino*, Nairobi: East African Publishing House, 1966.

41. See C.G. Baëta (ed), *Christianity in Tropical Africa* (Studies presented and discussed at the Seventh International African Seminar, University of Ghana, April, 1965), London: Oxford University Press, 1968, p.xii.

42. See, for instance, the work of the Ghanaian philosopher Kwasi Wiredu, *Philosophy and an African Culture*, Cambridge: Cambridge University Press, 1980.

43. Marcel Simon, "Christianisme: naissance d'une catégorie historique" in *Revue de l'Université de Bruxelles*, 5, 1966, pp.1-24. The article is quoted here as in Marcel Simon, *Le Christianisme et son contexte religieux – Scripta varia* (vol.1), Wissenschaftliche Untersuchungen zum Neuen Testament, 23), Tübingen: J.C.B. Mohr, 1981, pp.312-335.

44. See Henry Chadwick, *Origen: Contra Celsum*, Cambridge: Cambridge University Press, 1956, 1980, p.ix. Origen's "*Contra Celsum* stands out as the culmination of the whole apologetic movement of the 2nd and 3rd centuries".

45. Marcel Simon, *op.cit.*, p.335.

46. C.G. Baëta, *op.cit.*, pp.xii-xiii.

47. "Drumbeat in Church", in *Voice Weekly*, 3-9, September, 1980, p.6. My emphasis. I am indebted to Prof. A.F. Walls of the University of Aberdeen for drawing my attention to this interesting report.

48. Kenneth Cragg, *Christianity in World Perspective*, London: Lutterworth Press, 1968, p.48.

49. John Mbiti, "African Indigenous Culture in relation to Evangelism and Church Development" in R. Pierce Beaver (ed), *The Gospel and Frontier Peoples* (A Report of a Consultation, December 1972), Pasadena: William Carey Library, 1973, p.94.

Bibliography

A. Primary Christian texts used for this study

I. Patristic Sources

The works of the patristic authors studied here are all translated in the *Ante-Nicene Fathers* (Grand Rapids: Eerdmans, 1978f), being the American reprint of the Edinburgh edition of the *Ante-Nicene Christian Library*, edited by Alexander Roberts and James Donaldson. However, I occasionally have varied the translation to obtain improved renderings. My indebtedness to other translators is also indicated in the footnotes to the appropriate chapters.

i. Tatian

Oration addressed to the Greeks

The text of Tatian's *Oration* used in this study is as edited by E. Schwartz and published in *TU*, vol.4, part 1, 1888. Passages are cited following the chapter divisions, page and line as in this edition. Occasionally reference has been made to the edition by J.C.T. Otto, published in *Corpus Apologetarum Christianorum Saeculi Secundi (CACSS)*, vol.6, Jena, 1854.

ii. Tertullian

Of Tertullian's numerous extant works, it is those of an apologetic character which have been used particularly in this study. Among these, the *Apologeticum* has pride of place. Full details of passages used are given in the footnotes to the chapter on Tertullian. The edition of Tertullian's writings used is as established in vols.1 and 2 of *Corpus Christianorum, Series Latina (CCL)*, Turnhout, 1954, with passages cited following the chapter arrangements and paragraph divisions in the appropriate volumes of *CCL*. Occasionally reference is made to T. Herbert Bindley, *Tertullian – Apologeticus adversus gentes pro Christianis*, Oxford: Clarendon Press, 1889, and to J.P. Waltzing, *Tertullien: L'Apologétique* (Apparat critique et traduction littérale revue et corrigée), Liège: H. Vauillant-Carmane, 1919, and to other critical editions of individual works.

iii. Justin

1 Apology
2 Apology (or *Appendix*)
Dialogue with Trypho

The text used of Justin's writings generally acknowledged to be genuine is as established by E.J. Goodspeed, *Die ältesten Apologeten: Texte mit kurzen Einleitungen*, Göttingen: Vandenhoek und Ruprecht, 1914. Occasionally reference is made to J.C.T. Otto's edition in *CACSS* (vol.1), and to A.W.F. Blunt, *The Apologies of Justin Martyr*, Cambridge: Cambridge University Press, 1911.

iv. Clement of Alexandria

Protreptikos (Address to the Greeks)
Paidagogos (1-3) (The Tutor)
Stromateis (1-8) (The Miscellanies)

The text of Clement's writings used is as established by Otto Stählin and revised by Ludwig Früchtel and Ursula Treu, in the series *Die Griechischen Christlichen Schriftsteller der ersten drei Jahrhunderte (GCS)*, Berlin, 1960ff. On the *Protreptikos*, reference has occasionally been made to G.W. Butterworth's edition in the *Loeb Classical Library (LCL)*.

II. Modern African sources

(Only works of direct relevance to the present study are cited here)

i. E. Bolaji Idowu

a) Books

Olódùmarè – God in Yoruba Belief, London: Longman, 1962.

Towards an Indigenous Church, London: Oxford University Press, 1965.

African Traditional Religion – A Definition, London: SCM Press, 1973.

b) Articles

"The Study of Religion with special reference to African Traditional Religion" in *Orita* 1/1, June 1967, pp.3-12.

"Religion, Magic and Medicine – with special reference to Africa" in *Orita*, 1/1, June 1967, pp.62-77.

"The Challenge of Witchcraft" in *Orita*, 4/1, June 1970, pp.3-16.

"Faiths in Interaction" in *Orita*, 4/2, December 1970, pp.85-102.

"Religions on Peace" in *Orita*, 5/2, December 1971, pp.83-92.

"Man: an Enigma" in *Orita*, 6/2, December 1972, pp.67-74.

"Nation Building" in *Orita*, 8/2, December 1974, pp.87-96.

"Religion and Cultural Renewal" in *Orita*, 9/2, December 1975, pp.75-83.

ii. John S. Mbiti

a) Books

Poems of Nature and Faith, Nairobi: East African Publishing House, 1969.

African Religions and Philosophy, London: Heinemann, 1969.

Concepts of God in Africa, London: SPCK, 1970.

New Testament Eschatology in an African Background – A Study of the Encounter between New Testament Theology and African Traditional Concepts, London: Oxford University Press, 1970; republished by SPCK, London, in 1978.

Crisis of Mission in Africa, Mukono: Uganda Church Press, 1971.

The Prayers of African Religion, London: SPCK, 1975.

Introduction to African Religion, London: Heinemann, 1975.

Prayer and Spirituality in African Religion (The Charles Strong Memorial Lecture, Australia, August 1978), Bedford Park: Australian Association for the Study of Religions, 1978.

b) Articles

"Ways and Means of Communicating the Gospel" in C.G. Baëta (ed), *Christianity in Tropical Africa*, London: Oxford University Press, 1968, pp.329-350.

"Some African Concepts of Christology" in Georg F. Vicedom (ed), *Christ and the Younger Churches*, London: SPCK, 1972, pp.51-62; published earlier in German as "Afrikanische Beiträge zur Christologie" in Georg F. Vicedom (ed), *Theologische Stimmen aus Asien, Afrika und Lateinamerika* (vol.3), München: C. Kaiser Verlag, 1968.

"Christianity and East African Culture and Religion" in *Dini na Mila: Revealed Religion and Traditional Custom*, vol.3, no.1, May 1968 (Makerere University, Uganda), pp.1-6.

"Eschatologie und Jenseitsglaube" in H. Bürkle (ed), *Theologie und Kirche in Afrika*, Stuttgart: Evangelisches Verlagswerk, 1968; published in English as "Eschatology" in Kwesi A. Dickson and Paul Ellingworth (eds), *Biblical Revelation and African Beliefs*, London: Lutterworth Press, 1969, pp.159-184.

"African Concepts of Human Relations" in *Ministry: Theological Review*, no.9, October 1969, pp.158-162.

"The Future of Christianity in Africa (1970-2000)" in *Communio Viatorum: Theological Quarterly*, vol.13, 1-2, 1970, pp.19-38.

"Christianity and Traditional Religions in Africa" in *IRM*, vol.59, no.236, October 1970, pp.430-440.

"New Testament Eschatology and the Akamba of Kenya" in D.B. Barrett (ed), *African Initiatives in Religion*, Nairobi: East African Publishing House, 1971, pp.17-28.

"African Names of God" in *Orita*, 6/1, June 1972, pp.3-14.

"The Growing Respectability of African Traditional Religion" in *Lutheran World*, vol.19, no.1, 1972, pp.54-58.

"ὁ σωτὴρ ἡμῶν as an African Experience" in Barnabas Lindars and Stephen Smalley (eds), *Christ and the Spirit in the New Testament* (Studies in honour of C.F.D. Moule), Cambridge: Cambridge University Press, 1973, pp.397-414.

"African Indigenous Culture in relation to Evangelism and Church Development" in R. Pierce Beaver (ed), *The Gospel and Frontier Peoples* (Report of a Consultation, December 1972), Pasadena: William Carey Library, 1973, pp.79-95.

"An African Views American Black Theology" in *Worldview*, vol.17, no.8, August 1974, pp.41-44.

"Theological Impotence and the Universality of the Church" in *Lutheran World*, vol.21, no.3, October 1974, pp.251-260; reprinted in Gerald H. Anderson and Thomas F. Stransky (eds), *Third World Theologies* (Mission Trends, 3), New York: Paulist Press; Grand Rapids: Eerdmans, 1976, pp.6-18.

"Some Current Concerns of African Theology" in *The Expository Times*, vol.87, no.6, March 1976, pp.164-168.

"God, Dreams and African Militancy" in J.S. Pobee (ed), *Religion in a Pluralistic Society* (Essays presented to Professor C.G. Baëta), Leiden: E.J. Brill, 1976, pp.38-47.

"Christianity and African Culture" in *JTSA*, no.20, September 1977, pp.26-40; also in Michael Cassidy and Luc Verlinden (eds), *Facing the New Challenges – the Message of PACLA* (Pan African Christian Leadershp Assembly, 9-19 December, 1976, Nairobi), Kisumu: Evangel Publishing House, 1978, pp.272-284.

"Christianity and African Religion" in Michael Cassidy and Luc Verlinden (eds), *op.cit.*, pp.308-313.

"The Encounter between Christianity and African Religion" in *Temenos: Studies in Comparative Religion*, vol.12, 1976, pp.125-135.

iii. Mulago Gwa Cikala Musharhamina

a) Books

Un visage africain du Christianisme: l'Union vitale bantu face à l'unité vitale ecclésiale, Paris: Présence Africaine, 1965.

La Religion traditionnelle des Bantu et leur vision du monde (second edition), (Bibliothèque du Centre d'Etudes des Religions Africaines, 5), Kinshasa: Faculté de Théologie Catholique, 1980.

b) Articles

"L'union vitale bantu ou le principe de cohésion chez les Bashi, les Banya-rwanda et les Barundi" in *Annali Lateranensi*, vol.20, 1956, pp.61-263.

"L'union vitale bantu" in *Rythmes du monde*, vol.4, no.2-3, 1956, pp.133-141.

"La théologie et ses responsabilités" in *Présence Africaine*, vols.27-28, August-November, 1959, pp.188-205.

"La Nécessité de l'adaptation missionnaire chez les Bantu du Congo" and "Le pacte de sang et la communion alimentaire, pierres d'attente de la communion eucharistique" in *Des Prêtres noirs s'interrogent*, Paris: Les Editions du Cerf, 1957, pp.19-40; 171-187.

"'Naturalisation' du Christianisme en dehors de l'Occident à la lumière de Vatican II" in *Euntes Docete*, 20, 1967, pp.241-262.

"Christianisme et culture africaine: apport africain à la théologie"

450   Bibliography

in C.G. Baëta (ed), *Christianity in Tropical Africa*, London: Oxford University Press, 1968, pp.308-328.

"Vital participation: the cohesive principle of the Bantu community" in Kwesi A. Dickson and Paul Ellingworth (eds), *Biblical Revelation and African Beliefs*, London: Lutterworth Press, 1969, pp.137-158.

"Le Dieu des Bantu" in *CRA*, vol.2, no.3, January 1968, pp.23-64.

"La religion traditionnelle, élément central de la culture bantu" in *Les religions africaines comme source de valeurs de civilisation*, Paris: Présence Africaine, 1972, pp.115-155.

"Symbolisme dans les Religions traditionnelles africaines et Sacramentalisme" in *RCA*, vol.27, nos.4/5, July 1972, pp.467-502.

"Le problème d'une théologie africaine revu à la lumière de Vatican II" in *Renouveau de l'Eglise et Nouvelles Eglises* (Colloque sur la théologie de l'Université Lovanium, 22-27, juillet, 1968), *RCA*, May, 1968, pp.115-152.

iv. Byang H. Kato

a) Books

Theological Pitfalls in Africa, Kisumu (Kenya): Evangel Publishing House, 1975.

African Cultural Revolution and the Christian Faith, Jos (Nigeria): Challenge Publications, 1975.

b) Articles

"Theological Trends in Africa today" in *Perception*, No.1, March 1974, pp.1-9.

"Evangelical Evaluation of the Lusaka Conference", in *Perception*, no.2, July 1974, pp.1-14.

"The Gospel, Cultural Context and Religious Syncretism" in J.D. Douglas (ed), *Let the Earth Hear His Voice* (International Congress on World Evangelisation, Lausanne, Switzerland. Official Reference volume: Papers and Responses), Minneapolis: World Wide Publications, 1975, pp.1216-1223.

"Ecumenicals – Evangelicals Debate in Germany" in *Perception*, no.3, April 1975, pp.1-8.

"The World Council of Churches Nairobi Assembly and Africa" in *Perception*, no.5, March 1976, pp.2-10. (This report was compiled by the AEAM staff from Dr Kato's notes.)

"Black Theology and African Theology" in *Perception*, no.6, October, 1976, pp.1-8; reprinted in *ERT*, vol.1, no.1, October, 1977, pp.35-48.

"The Christian and his Family" in *Perception*, no.9, June 1977, pp.1-8.

"Evangelisation and Culture" in *Perception*, no.12, April 1978, pp.1-8.

"The Theology of Eternal Salvation" in *Perception*, no.14, October 1978, pp.1-8.

"Christianity as an African Religion" in *Perception*, no.16, May 1979, pp.1- 6; reprinted in *ERT*, vol.4, no.1, April 1980, pp.31-39.

"Ecumenicals and Evangelicals" in *Perception*, no.16, May 1979, pp.6-8.

"Aid to the National Church: When it Helps, When it Hinders" in *EMQ*, vol.8, no.4, 1972, pp.193-201.

"We are at the Turning Point in Africa's Church History" in *Africa Now*, September/October, 1974, pp.6-7.

"Africa: Prudence and Promise – a candid survey of current opportunity and dangers facing evangelicals and missionary strategy in Africa" in *United Evangelical Action*, Summer 1975, pp.17-20,26.

"The Christian Surge in Africa, part 1" (report of an interview with Dr Kato), in *Christianity Today*, 26th September, 1975, pp.4-7.

"Africa's Christian Future, part 2" (report of an interview with Dr Kato), in *Christianity Today*, 10th October, 1975, pp.12-16

B. Other Literature Consulted

ABRAHAM, W., "The Life and Times of Anton Wilhelm Amo" in *Transactions of the Historical Society of Ghana*, vol.8, Legon, 1965, pp.60-81.

AGBETI, J.K., "African Theology: What it is" in *Presence*, vol.5, no.3, 1972.

AJAYI, J.F.À., *Christian Missions in Nigeria 1841-1891: The Making of a New Elite*, London: Longman, 1965.

ALFONSI, L., "La 'Consuetudo' nei 'Protrettici'", in *VC*, vol.18, 1964, pp.32-36.

ALLIER, Raoul, *La Psychologie de la conversion chez les peuples non-civilisés*, Paris: Payot, 1925.

ALLMEN, Daniel von, "The Birth of Theology: Contextualisation as the dynamic element in the formation of New Testament Theology" in *IRM*, vol.64, January 1975, pp.37-52.

ALTANER, B., *Patrology* (ET by H.C. Graef), Freiburg: Herder: London: Nelson, 1960.

ANDERSON, G.H. (ed), *The Theology of the Christian Mission*, London: SCM Press, 1961.

ANDRESEN, Carl, "Justin und der mittlere Platonismus" in *ZNW*, 44, 1952-1953, pp.157-195.

Logos und Nomos: Die Polemik des Kelsos wider das Christentum, Berlin: Walter de Gruyter, 1955.

APPIAH-KUBI, K., and TORRES, Sergio, *African Theology en Route* (Papers from the Pan-African Conference of Third World Theologians, December 17-23, 1977, Accra, Ghana), New York: Orbis Books, 1979. French language version: *Libération ou Adaptation – La théologie africaine s'interroge* (Le Colloque d'Accra) Paris: Librairie-Editions l'Harmattan, 1979.

AYANDELE, E.A., *The Missionary Impact on Modern Nigeria, 1842-1914 – A Political and Social Analysis*, London: Longman, 1966.

BACKER, Emile de, *Sacramentum: Le mot et l'idée représentée par lui dans les oeuvres de Tertullien,* Bruxelles: Albert Dewi, Paris: A. Picard et Fils, 1911.

BAËTA, C.G., (ed) *Christianity in Tropical Africa* (Studies presented and discussed at the Seventh International African Seminar, University of Ghana, April 1965), London: Oxford University Press, 1968.

BARDY, G, "Aux origines de l'école d'Alexandrie" in *RSR*, vol.27, pp.65-90.

"Saint Justin" in *DTC*, vol.8, coll. 2228-2277.

"Tatien" in *DTC*, vol.15, coll.59-66.

"Tertullien" in *DTC*, vol.15, coll.130-171.

BARNARD, L.W., *Justin Martyr: His Life and Thought*, Cambridge: Cambridge University Press, 1967.

BARNES, T.D., *Tertullian: A Historical and Literary Study*, Oxford: Clarendon Press, 1971.

BARRE, A. de la, "L'école chrétienne d'Alexandrie" in *DTC*, vol.1, coll. 805-824.

BARRETT, David B. (ed), *African Initiatives in Religion* (21 Studies from East and Central Africa), Nairobi: East African Publishing House, 1971.

Schism and Renewal in Africa – An analysis of six thousand contemporary religious movements, Nairobi: Oxford University Press, 1968.

BASTIDE, Roger, "Sociologies des Missions Protestantes" in *Les Missions Protestantes et l'Histoire* (Actes du 11e Colloque, 4-9 octobre, 1971, Université Paul Valéry, Montpellier, Etudes des Colloque, vol.2), Paris: Société de l'Histoire du Protestantisme français (n.d.), pp.47-62.

BAUER, Walter, *Orthodoxy and Heresy in Earliest Christianity* (ET), London: SCM Press, 1972 (Original German published in 1934).

BEASLEY-MURRAY, G.R., *The Book of Revelation (NCB)* London: Oliphants, 1974.

BEAVER, R. Pierce (ed), *The Gospel and Frontier Peoples* (A report of a Consultation, December, 1972), Pasadena: William Carey Library, 1973.

BEECHAM, J., *Ashantee and the Gold Coast, Being a sketch of the History, Social State and Superstition of the inhabitants of these countries with a notice of the state and prospects of Christianity among them* (with introduction and notes by G.E. Metcalfe), London: Dawson's of Pall Mall, 1968 (first published 1841).

BENOIT, André, *L'Actualité des Pères de l'Eglise* (Cahiers théologiques, 47), Neuchâtel: Editions Delachaux et Niestlé, 1961

BENZ, Ernst, "Christus und Sokrates in der alten Kirche" in *ZNW*, vol.43, 1950-1051, pp.195-224.

BERG, J. van den, *Constrained by Jesus' Love – An inquiry into the motives of the missionary awakening in Great Britain in the period between 1695 and 1815*, Kampen: J.H. Lok, 1956.

BERKOUWER, G.C., *General Revelation*, Grand Rapids: Eerdmans, 1955.

BEVAN, Edwyn, "Greeks and Barbarians" in F.S. Marvin (ed), *Western Races and the World* (Unity Series, 5), London: Oxford University Press, 1922.

BIGG, Charles, *The Christian Platonists of Alexandria*, Oxford: Clarendon Press, 1886.

BINDLEY, T. Herbert, *Tertullian: Apologeticus adversus gentes pro Christianis*, Oxford: Clarendon Press, 1889.

p'BITEK, Okot, *African Religions in Western Scholarship*, Kampala: East African Literature Bureau, 1970.

   Song of Lawino, Nairobi: East African Publishing House, 1966.

BLAUW, J., *The Missionary Nature of the Church – A Survey of the Biblical Theology of Mission* (Foundations of the Christian Mission Series), London: Lutterworth Press, 1962.

BLUNT, A.W.F., *The Apologies of Justin Martyr*, Cambridge: Cambridge University Press, 1911.

BOAS, G., and LOVEJOY, A.O. (eds), *Primitivism and Related Ideas in Antiquity* (Contributions to the history of primitivism), New York: Octagon Books, 1973.

BOER, W. den, "Hermeneutic problems in early Christian literature" in *VC*, vol.1, 1947, pp.150-167.

BOISSIER, Gaston, *La Fin du Paganisme (Etude sur les dernières luttes religieuses en occident au quatrième siècle)* (tome 1), Paris: Hachette, 1894.

BOUSSET, W., "Jüdisch-christlicher Schulbetrieb in Alexandria und Rom – Literarische Untersuchungen zu Philo und Clemens von Alexandria, Justin und Irenaeus" in *FRLANT*, vol.6, 1915 (pp.155-271 on Clement).

BOWERS, Paul, "Evangelical Theology in Africa: Byang Kato's Legacy" in *ERT*, vol.5, no.1, April 1981, pp.35-39.

BRAY, G.L., *Holiness and the Will of God: Perspectives on the Theology of Tertullian* (Marshall's Theological Library), London:

Marshall, Morgan and Scott, 1979.

BRIGHAM, F.H., "The Concept of *New Song* in Clement of Alexandria's *Exhortation to the Greeks*" in *Classical Folia* (New York), vol.16, 1962, pp.9-13.

BROWN, R.E. *et al.* (eds), *Mary in the New Testament* (A collaborative assessment by Protestant and Roman Catholic scholars), Philadelphia: Fortress Press, New York: Paulist Press, 1978.

BRUCE, F.F., *The Acts of the Apostles* (the Greek text with Introduction and Commentary), London: Inter-Varsity Press (second edition), 1952.

BRUNNER, Emil, *Revelation and Reason – The Christian Doctrine of Faith and Knowledge* (ET by Olive Wyon), London: SCM Press, 1971.

BUTTERWORTH, G.W., "Clement of Alexandria and Art", in *JTS*, vol.17, 1916, pp.68-76.

CADOUX, C.J., *The Early Church and the World (A history of the Christian attitude to pagan society and the State down to the time of Constantinus)*, Edinburgh: T. & T. Clark, 1925.

CAMELOT, Pierre, "Clément d'Alexandrie et l'utilisation de la philosophie grecque" in *RSR*, vol.21, 1931, pp.541-569.

"Les idées de Clément d'Alexandrie sur l'utilisation des sciences et de la littérature profane", in *RSR*, vol.21, 1931, pp.38-66

CAMPENHAUSEN, Hans von, *Die Idee des Märtyriums in der alten Kirche*, Göttingen: Vandenhoek und Ruprecht, 1936.

Fathers of the Greek Church (ET), London: A. & C. Black, 1963.

Fathers of the Latin Church (ET by Manfred Hoffmann), London: A. & C. Black, 1964.

CAREY, William, *An Enquiry into the Obligations of Christians to Use Means for the Conversion of the Heathen* (reprinted from the edition of 1792), London: Hodder and Stoughton, 1891.

CARLEN, Claudia, *The Papal Encyclicals* (4 vols), Raleigh: McGrath Publishing Co. 1981.

CARPENTER, H.J., "Popular Christianity and the Theologians in the Early Centures" in *JTS* (n.s.), 14, 1963, pp.294-316.

CARRINGTON, Philip, *Christian Apologetics of the Second Century (in their relation to modern thought)*, London: SPCK, 1921.

The Early Christian Church (vol.2) – *The Second Christian Century*, Cambridge: Cambridge University Press, 1957.

CASEY, Robert P., "Clement of Alexandria and the Beginnings of Christian Platonism" in *HTR*, vol.18, 1925, pp.39-101.

CASPARI, W., and GILMORE, Geo. W., "Renunciation of the Devil in the Baptismal Rite" in *The New Schaff-Herzog* vol.9, pp.488-489.

CASSERLEY, J.V. Longmead, *The Retreat from Christianity in the Modern World* (The Maurice Lectures for 1951), London: Longman, Green and Co, 1952.

CASSIDY, Michael, and VERLINDEN, Luc (eds), *Facing the New Challenges – The Message of PACLA* (Pan African Leadership Assembly, Nairobi, December 9th-19th, 1976), Kisumu: Evangel Publishing House, 1978.

CHADWICK, Henry, *Early Christian Thought and the Classical Tradition: Studies in Justin, Clement and Origen*, London: Oxford University Press, 1966.

"Justin Martyr's Defence of Christianity" in *BJRL*, 47, 1964-1965, pp.274ff.

Origen: Contra Celsum, Cambridge: Cambridge University Press, 1953.

CHARLES, Pierre, *Etudes Missiologique*, Bruxelles: Desclée de Brouwer, 1956.

CHARLES, R.H., *A Critical and Exegetical Commentary on the Revelation of St. John* (vol.1), Edinburgh: T. & T. Clark, 1920.

"Chicago Statement on Biblical Inerrancy" in *ERT*, vol.4, no.1, April 1980, pp.8-19.

CHRISTALLER, J.G., *A Dictionary of the Asante and Fante Language called Tshi (Chwee, Twi), with a grammatical introduction and appendices on the geography of the Gold Coast and other Subjects*, Basel: Evangelical Missionary Society, 1881.

Christian Life and Message in Relation to Non-Christian Systems of Thought and Life (vol.1 - Reports of Meeting of the International

Missionary Council at Jerusalem, Easter, 1928), London: Oxford University Press, 1928.

Church in Changing Africa, The (Report of the All-Africa Church Conference, Ibadan, January 1958), New York: International Missionary Council, 1958.

Civilisation noire et Eglise Catholique (Colloque organisé par la Société Africaine de Culture sous le haut patronage du gouvernement de la République de Côte d'Ivoire et sous la tutelle du Ministère ivoirien des Affaires Culturelles, Abidjan, 12-17 septembre, 1977), Paris: Présence Africaine, 1978.

COCHRANE, C.N., *Christianity and Classical Culture – A Study of Thought and Action from Augustus to Augustine*, London: Oxford University Press, 1939.

CONGAR, Yves M.-J., *The Catholic Church and the Race Question*, Paris: UNESCO, 1953.

CRAGG, Kenneth, *Christianity in World Perspective*, London: Lutterworth Press, 1968.

"Conversion and Convertibility, with special reference to Muslims" in John R.W. Stott and Robert Coote (eds), *Down to Earth – Studies in Christianity and Culture*, Grand Rapids: Eerdmans, 1980, pp.193-208.

CROSS, F.L., *The Early Christian Fathers*, London: Duckworth, 1960.

CURTIN, Philip, *The Image of Africa: British Ideas and Actions, 1780-1850*, Madison: University of Wisconsin Press, 1964.

D'ALÈS, Adhémar, *La Théologie de Tertullien* (Bibliothèque de théologie historique), Paris: Beauchesne et Cie, 1905.

DANIÉLOU, Jean, *Gospel Message and Hellenistic Culture* (ET by J.A. Baker), London: Darton, Longman and Todd, 1973.

The Origins of Latin Christianity (ET by David Smith and John Austin Baker), London: Darton, Longman and Todd, 1977.

DANQUAH, J.B., *The Akan Doctrine of God* (second edition), London: Frank Cass, 1968.

DAVIDSON, Basil, *Black Mother – Africa and the Atlantic Slave Trade* (revised and expanded edition), Harmondsworth: Penguin Books, 1970, 1980.

DAVIDSON, H.R. Ellis, *Gods and Myths of Northern Europe*, Harmondsworth: Penguin Books, 1964.

DAVIES, W.D., *Paul and Rabbinic Judaism – Some Rabbinic Elements in Pauline Theology* (fourth edition with new preface), Philadelphia: Fortress Press, 1980.

DECHARME, P., *La Critique des traditions religieuses chez les Grecs – des origines au temps de Plutarque*, Paris: A. Picard et Fils, 1904.

DE BROSSES, Charles, *Du culte des dieux fétiches, ou Parallèle de l'ancienne religion de l'Egypte avec la religion actuelle de Nigritie* (1760), republished by Gregg International Publishers Ltd, Westmead, Farnborough, 1972.

DE CLERCQ, V.C., "The Expectation of the Second Coming of Christ in Tertullian" in *Studia Patristica*, 11,2, 1972 (= *TU*, 108, 1972, pp.146-151).

DE FAYE, Eugène, *Clément d'Alexandrie: Etude sur les rapports du Christianisme et de la philosophie grecque au 2ème siècle* (second edition), Paris: Ernest Léroux, 1906.

DE STE. CROIX, G.E.M., "Why were the Early Christians Persecuted?" in *Past and Present*, 26, November, 1963, pp.6-38.

Des Prêtres noirs s'interrogent, Paris: Les Editions du Cerf, 1957.

DICKSON, Kwesi A., and ELLINGWORTH, Paul, *Biblical Revelation and African Beliefs*, London: Lutterworth Press, 1969.

"'Hebrewisms in West Africa': The Old Testament and African Life and Thought" in *Legon Journal of the Humanities*, vol.1, 1974, pp.23-34.

DIELS, Hermann, *Doxographi Graeci*, Berlin, 1879.

DILL, Samuel, *Roman Society from Nero to Marcus Aurelius*, London: Macmillan, 1904, 1910.

DIX, Gregory, *Jew and Greek – A Study in the Primitive Church*, London: Dacre Press, Westminster, 1953.

DODDS, E.R., *Pagan and Christian in an Age of Anxiety – Some Aspects of Religious Experience from Marcus Aurelius to Constantine*, Cambridge: Cambridge University Press, 1965.

DUCHESNE, Louis, *Early History of the Christian Church (from its foundation to the end of the third century)* (ET), London: John Murray, 1910.

DUPONT, J., *Etudes sur les Actes des Apôtres*, Paris: Les Editions du Cerf, 1967.

DYKES, Eva B., *The Negro in English Romantic Thought – A Study of Sympathy for the Oppressed*, Washington DC: The Associated Publishers, 1942.

ELZE, Martin, *Tatian und seine Theologie*, Göttingen: Vandenhoek und Ruprecht, 1960.

EVANS-PRITCHARD, E.E., *Nuer Religion*, London: Oxford University Press, 1956

Theories of Primitive Religion, Oxford: Clarendon Press, 1965.

FARMER, H.H., *Revelation and Religion*, London: Nisbet, 1954.

FASHOLÉ-LUKE, E.W. *et al.* (eds), *Christianity in Independent Africa*, London: Rex Collings, 1978.

"The Quest for an African Christian Theology" in *The Ecumenical Review*, vol.27, no.3, 1978, pp.259-269.

FESTUGIÈRE, A.-J., *L'idéal religieux des Grecs et l'Evangile* (preface by M.-J. Lagrange), Paris: Gabalda et Cie, 1932.

Personal Religion among the Greeks, Berkeley: University of California Press, 1954.

FINAN, Thomas, "Hellenism and Judaeo-Christian History in Clement of Alexandria" in *Irish Theological Quarterly*, vol.28, 1961, pp.83-114.

FOERSTER, Werner, art. Δαίμων in *TDNT*, 2, pp.1-20.

FOSTER, John, *After the Apostles – Missionary Preaching of the First Three Centuries*, London: SCM Press, 1951.

Then and Now – The Historic Church and the Younger Churches, London: SCM Press, 1942.

FREDERIKSEN, Linwood, *A Christian Witness in a Non-Christian Culture according to Clement of Alexandria* (State University of Iowa, Ph.D, 1965), Ann Arbor: University Microfilms, 1965.

FRÉDOUILLE, Jean-Claude, *Tertullien et la Conversion de la*

Culture Antique, Paris: Etudes Augustiniennes, 1972.

FREEMAN, Kathleen, *Ancilla to the Pre-Socratic Philosophers* (A complete translation of the Fragments in Diels' *Fragmente der Vorsokratiker*), Oxford: Basil Blackwell, 1952.

FREEMAN, T.B., *Journal of Two Visits to the Kingdom of Ashanti in Western Africa*, London: John Mason, Wesleyan Conference Centre, 1843.

FREND, W.H.C., *Martyrdom and Persecution in the Early Church – A study of a conflict from Maccabees to Donatus*, Oxford: Blackwell, 1965.

FRIEDLÄNDER, Moriz, *Geschichte der jüdischen Apologetik als Vorgeschichte des Christentums*, Amsterdam: Philo Press, 1973 (first published, Zurich, 1903).

FULLER, J.M., "Tatianus" in *DCB*, vol.4. pp.782-804.

"Tertullianus" in *DCB*, vol.4, pp.818-864.

GAIRDNER, W.H.T., *Edinburgh 1910 – An Account and Interpretation of the World Missionary Conference*, London: Oliphant, Anderson and Ferrier, 1910.

GARDINER, Alice, "Superstition" in *ERE*, vol.12, pp.120-122.

GÄRTNER, Bertil, *The Areopagus Speech and Natural Revelation*, Uppsala: C.W.K. Gleerup, 1955.

GEFFKEN, J., *Der Ausgang des Griechisch-Römischen Heidentums*, Heidelberg: Carl Winter, 1929.

GEMERY, H., and HOGENDORN, J.S. (eds), *The Uncommon Market – Essays in the Economic History of the Atlantic Slave Trade* (Studies in Social Discontinuity Series), New York: Academic Press, 1979.

GEORGE, P.J., "Racist Assumptions of the 19th century Missionary Movement", in *IRM*, vol.19, 1970, pp.271-284.

GIBBON, Edward, *The History of the Decline and Fall of the Roman Empire*, vol.2 (edited by J.B. Bury), London: Methuen and Co., 1897.

GILLIES, Francis, "The Bantu Concept of Time" in *Religion*, vol.10, Spring 1980, pp.16-30.

GLOVER, T.R., *The Conflict of Religions in the Early Roman*

Empire (eighth edition), London: Methuen, 1919.

GOODENOUGH, E.R., *The Theology of Justin Martyr*, Jena: Verlag Frommansche Buchhandlung, 1923.

GOODSPEED, E.J., *A History of Early Christian Literature* (revised and enlarged by R.M. Grant), Chicago: Phoenix Books, 1966.

GRANT, R.M., *Augustus to Constantine – the Thrust of the Christian Movement into the Roman World*, London: Collins, 1971.

"Aristotle and the Conversion of Justin" in *JTS* (n.s.), 7, 1956, pp.246-248.

Early Christianity and Society, London: Collins, 1978.

"Justin Martyr" in *The New Schaff-Herzog* (suppl. vol.14), p.620.

"Studies in the Apologists: Tatian's Theological Method" in *HTR*, 51, 1958, pp.123-134.

"Tatian and the Bible" in *TU*, 63, 1957, pp.297-306.

"The Chronology of the Greek Apologists" in *VC*, vol.9, 1955, pp.25-33.

"The Heresy of Tatian" in *JTS*, n.s. vol.5, 1954, pp.63ff.

GROVES, C.P., *The Planting of Christianity in Africa* (4 vols), London: Lutterworth Press, 1948ff.

GUIGNEBERT, Charles, *Tertullien: Etude sur ses sentiments à l'egard de l'Empire et de la société civile*, Paris: Ernest Léroux, 1901.

GUTERMAN, Simeon L., *Religious Toleration and Persecution in Ancient Rome*, London: Aiglon Press, 1951.

GUTHRIE, W.K.C., *A History of Greek Philosophy* (vol.3 – The Fifth-Century Enlightenment), Cambridge: Cambridge University Press, 1969.

GUTIERREZ, Gustavo, *A Theology of Liberation – History, Politics and Salvation* (ET by Sister Caridad Inda and John Eagleson), London: SCM Press, 1974.

HAHN, F., *Mission in the New Testament* (Studies in Biblical

Theology, 47; ET by Frank Clarke), London: SCM Press, 1968.

HARGREAVES, J.D., *Prelude to the Partition of West Africa*, London: Macmillan 1963.

HARNACK, Adolf, "Die Überlieferung der griechischen Apologeten des zweiten Jahrhunderts in der alten Kirche und im Mittelalter" in *TU*, 1, 1-2, 1882, pp.199ff.

History of Dogma, vol.1 (ET, from third German edition, by Neil Buchanan), London: Williams and Norgate, 1894.

History of Dogma, vol.2 (ET, from third German edition, by Neil Buchanan), London: Williams and Norgate, 1896.

The Mission and Expansion of Christianity in the First Three Centuries (2 vols), (ET by J. Moffatt), London: Williams and Norgate, 1908.

HASTINGS, Adrian, *African Christianity – An essay in interpretation*, London: Geoffrey Chapman, 1976

A History of African Christianity, 1950-1975, Cambridge: Cambridge University Press, 1979.

Church and Mission in Modern Africa, London: Burns and Oates, 1967.

HATCH, Edwin, *The Influence of Greek Ideas and Usages upon the Christian Church* (Hibbert Lectures, 1888), London: Williams and Norgate, 1890.

HAY, Denys, *Europe – The Emergence of an Idea*, Edinburgh: Edinburgh University Press, 1957.

HENGEL, Martin, *Jews, Greeks and Barbarians – Aspects of the Hellenisation of Judaism in the Pre-Christian Period* (ET by John Bowden), London: SCM Press, 1980.

HENNECKE, E., and SCHNEEMELCHER, W., (eds), *New Testament Apocrypha* (2 vols) (ET edited by R. McL.Wilson), Philadelphia: Westminster Press, 1963.

HILL, J. Hamlyn, *The Earliest Life of Christ Ever Compiled from the Four Gospels, being the Diatessaron of Tatian*, Edinburgh: T. & T. Clark, 1910.

HOLTE, Ragnar, "*Logos Spermatikos*: Christianity and ancient

Philosophy according to Saint Justin's *Apologies*" in *Studia Theologica*, 12, 1958.

Hommage africain à Jean XXIII, Un, Paris: Présence Africaine, 1965.

HORNUS, Jean-Michel, "Etude sur la pensée politique de Tertullien" in *RHPR*, 38, 1958, pp.1-38.

HORT, F.J.A., *Six Lectures on the Ante-Nicene Fathers*, London: Macmillan and Co, 1895.

HORT, F.J.A., and MAYOR, J.B. (eds), *Clement of Alexandria: Miscellanies Book 7* (The Greek text, with Introduction, translation, notes, dissertations and indexes), London: Macmillan and Co., 1902.

HURBON, Laënnec, "Racisme et Théologie missionnaire" in *Présence Africaine*, vol.71, part 3, 1969, pp.35-47.

INGE, W.R., "Alexandrian Theology" in *ERE*, vol.1, pp.313-319

JACOB, Edmond, *Theology of the Old Testament* (ET by Arthur W. Heathcote and Philip J. Allcock), London: Hodder and Stoughton, 1958 (originally published 1955).

JACOBSEN, S., *Am I Not a Man and a Brother? British Missions and the Abolition of the Slave Trade in West Africa and the West Indies, 1786-1838*, Uppsala: Gleerup, 1972.

JAEGER, Werner, *Early Christianity and Greek Paideia*, London: Oxford University Press, 1961.

JANZEN, John M., and MacGAFFEY, Wyatt (eds), *An Anthology of Kongo Religion: Primary Texts from Lower Zaire* (University of Kansas Publications in Anthropology, 5), Lawrence, Kansas: University of Kansas, 1974.

JEDIN, Hubert, *et al.* (eds), *History of the Church* (ET), (10 vols, vol.1 = Karl Baus, *Handbook of Church History, 1, From the Apostolic Community to Constantine*), London: Burns and Oates, 1965-1981.

JOLY, Robert, *Christianisme et Philosophie – Etudes sur Justin et les Apologistes grecs du deuxième siècle*, Bruxelles: Editions de l'Université de Bruxelles, 1973.

The Origins of Modern African Thought – Its development in West Africa during the 19th and 20th centuries, London: Faber and

Faber, 1968.

KAGAME, Alexis, *La philosophie bantu-rwandaise de l'être,* Bruxelles: Académie Royale des Sciences Coloniales (d'Outre-mer), Classe des Sciences Morales et Politiques, vol.13, 1958.

"Aperception empirique du temps et conception de l'histoire dans la pensée bantu" in Paul Ricoeur (ed), *Les Cultures et le Temps,* Paris: Payot/UNESCO, 1975, pp.103-133.

La philosophie bantu comparée, Paris: Présence Africaine, 1976.

KALILOMBE, Patrick, "The Salvific Value of African Religions" in *AFER,* vol. 21, no.3, June, 1979, pp.143-157.

KAUFMANN-BÜHLER, D., "Eusebeia" in *RAC,* vol.6, coll. 986-1023.

KELLY, J.N.D., *Early Christian Doctrines,* London: A. & C. Black, (4th edition), 1968.

KENDALL, Elliott, *The End of an Era – Africa and the Missionary,* London: SPCK, 1978.

KESTELOOT, Lilyan, *Les Ecrivains noirs de langue française: naissance d'une littérature* (fourth edition), Bruxelles: Editions de l'Institut de Sociologie, Université de Bruxelles, 1971.

KIBICHO, Samuel G., "The Continuity of the African Conception of God into and through Christianity: A Kikuyu case study" in Edward Fasholé-Luke *et al.* (eds), *Christianity in Independent Africa,* London: Rex Collings, 1978, pp.370-388.

KINNEY, John W., "The Theology of John Mbiti: His Sources, Norms and Method" in *Occasional Bulletin of Missionary Research,* vol.3, no.2, April 1979, pp.65-67.

KOEHLER, L., and BAUMGARTNER, W., *Lexicon in Veteris Testamenti Libros,* Leiden: E.J. Brill, 1958.

KRAEMER, H., *The Christian Message in a Non-Christian World,* London: Edinburgh House Press, 1938.

KRUGER, Paul, *Philo und Josephus als Apologeten des Judentums,* Leipzig: Verlag der Dürr'schen Buchhandlung, 1966.

LABRIOLLE, Pierre de, *Tertullien: De Praescriptione Haereticorum* (Textes et Documents), Paris: A. Picard et Fils, 1907

La Crise Montaniste, Paris: Ernest Léroux, 1913.

History and Literature of Christianity – from Tertullian to Boethius (ET by Herbert Wilson), London: Kegan Paul, Trench and Trubner, and Co, 1924.

La Réaction païenne: Etude sur la polémique anti-chrétienne du 1er au 6ème siècle, Paris: L'Artisan du Livre, 1948 (first published 1943).

LANG, Andrew, *The Making of Religion* (second edition), London: Longmans, Green and Co, 1900.

LATOURETTE, K.S., *A History of the Expansion of Christianity* (7 vols), New York: Harper and Row, 1937ff.

LEBRETON, J., "Le désaccord de la foi populaire et de la théologie savante dans l'Eglise chrétienne du 3ème siècle" in *RHE*, 19, 1923, pp.481-506; 20, 1924, pp.5-27.

Histoire du dogme de la Trinité (2 vols), Paris: Beauchesne et Cie, 1927-1928.

"La théorie de la connaissance religieuse chez Clément d'Alexandrie" in *RSR*, vol.18, 1928, pp.457-488.

"L'Apologétique chrétienne au 2ème siècle" in A. Fliche and V. Martin (eds), *Histoire de l'Eglise depuis ses origines jusqu'à nos jours* (tome 1, *L'Eglise Primitive*), Paris: Bloud et Gay, 1946, p.454.

"L'école chrétienne d'Alexandrie avant Origene" in A. Fliche and V. Martin (eds), *Histoire de l'Eglise depuis ses origines jusqu'à nos jours* (tome 2), Paris: Bloud et Gay, 1946, pp.226f.

LEEUWEN, Arend Th. van, *Christianity in World History – The Meeting of the Faiths of East and West* (ET by H.H. Hoskins), London: Edinburgh House Press, 1964.

LEITH, John H., *The Creeds of the Churches – A Reader in Christian Doctrine from the Bible to the Present*, Richmond: John Knox Press, 1973.

LÉVY-BRUHL, L., *Les Fonctions Mentales dans les sociétés inférieures*, Paris: Félix Alcan et Guillaumin, 1910.

La Mentalité Primitive, Paris: Félix Alcan, 1922.

LIEBESCHUETZ, J.H.W.G., *Continuity and Change in Roman*

Religion, Oxford: Clarendon Press, 1979.

LIENHARDT, Godfrey, *Divinity and Experience – The Religion of the Dinka,* Oxford: Clarendon Press, 1961.

LIGHTFOOT, J.B., and HARMER, J.R., *The Apostolic Fathers,* London: Macmillan, 1898.

LILLA, Salvatore R.C., *Clement of Alexandria – A Study in Christian Platonism and Gnosticism,* London: Oxford University Press, 1971.

LOCHNER, N., "Anton Wilhelm Amo: A Ghana Scholar in 18th Century Germany" in *Transactions of the Historical Society of Ghana,* vol.3, part 3, Achimota, 1958.

LOEWEN, Jacob, "The Gospel, its Content and Communication – an anthropological perspective" in John R.W. Stott and Robert Coote (eds), *Down to Earth – Studies in Christianity and Culture,* Grand Rapids: Eerdmans, 1980, pp.115-130.

LOFFELD, Edouard, *Le problème cardinal de la missiologie et des missions catholiques,* Rhenen, Hollande: Editions "Spiritus", 1956

LORTZ, Joseph, *Tertullian als Apologet* (1), Munster: Aschendorffsche Verlagsbuchhandlung, 1927.

LOVEJOY, A.O., *The Great Chain of Being – A Study of a History of an Idea,* Cambridge, Mass: Harvard University Press, 1936.

LOVETT, R., *The History of the London Missionary Society, 1795-1895* (vol. 1), London: Henry Frowde, 1899.

LUBAC, Henri de, *Catholicism – A Study of Dogma in Relation to the Corporate Destiny of Mankind* (ET from fourth French edition, 1947, by Lancelot C. Sheppard), London: Burns, Oates and Washbourne, 1950.

LUFULUABO, F.-M., "La conception bantoue face au Christianisme" in *Personalité africaine et Catholicisme,* Paris: Présence Africaine, 1963, pp.115-130.

LUNEAU, A., "Pour aider au dialogue: les Pères et les religions non chrétiennes" in *NRT,* September-November, 1967, pp.821-841.

LYIOMO, K.E., Amos, "Review of Aylward Shorter, *Prayer in the Religious Traditions of Africa,* and John S. Mbiti, *Prayers of African Religion*", in *ATJ,* vol.6, no.2, 1977, pp.71-73.

McKENZIE, P.R., *Inter-Religious Encounters in West Africa:*

Samuel Adjai Crowther's Attitude to African Traditional Religion and Islam, Leicester: Study of Religion Sub-Department, 1976.

"Review of John S. Mbiti, *Prayers of African Religion"* in *The Expository Times*, vol.87, 1975-76, pp.220-221.

McMULLEN, R., *Enemies of the Roman Order*, London: Oxford University Press, 1967.

McVEIGH, Malcolm J., *God in Africa: Conceptions of God in African Traditional Religion and Christianity*, Cape Cod, Mass. and Hartford, Vermont: Claude Stark, 1974.

MARKUS, R.A., *Christianity in the Roman World*, London: Thames and Hudson, 1971.

"The Problem of Self-Definition: From Sect to Church" in E.P. Sanders (ed), *Jewish and Christian Self-Definition* (vol.1) – *The Shaping of Christianity in the Second and Third Centuries*, London: SCM Press, 1980, pp.1-15.

Saeculum: History and Society in the Theology of Saint Augustine, Cambridge: Cambridge University Press, 1970.

MARMARDJI, A.-S., *Diatessaron de Tatien – Texte arabe établi, traduit en français, collationné avec les anciennes versions syriaques, suivi d'un evangéliare diatessarique syriaque et accompagné de quatre planches hors texte*, Beyrouth: Imprimerie Catholique, 1936.

MARROU, Henri-Irénée, *Saint Augustin et la Fin de la Culture Antique*, Paris: E. de Boccard, 1938.

Histoire de l'Education dans l'Antiquité, Paris: Editions du Seuil, 1948

MAURIER, Henri, *The Other Covenant: A Theology of Paganism* (ET by Charles McGrath), Glen Rock, New Jersey: Newman Press, 1968 (originally, *Essai d'une théologie du Paganisme*, Paris: Editions de l'Orante, 1965).

MBONYINKEBE, Deogratias, "Review of Mulago, V., *Un visage africain du Christianisme*" in *CRA*, vol.3, no.5, January 1969, pp.143-147.

MERRILL, E.T., *Essays in Early Christian History*, London: Macmillan, 1924.

METUH, Emefie Ikenga, *God and Man in African Religion – A case study of the Igbo of Nigeria*, London: Geoffrey Chapman, 1981

"Religious Concepts in West African Cosmogonies" in *JRA*, vol.13, fasc.1, 1982, pp.11-23.

Missionary Message in Relation to Non-Christian Religions: The World Missionary Conference 1910 – Report of Commission IV, Edinburgh and London: Oliphant, Anderson and Ferrier, 1910.

MKELE, Nimrod, "Time Concept of Blacks" in *Pro Veritate*, November 1972, p.16.

MOLLAND, Einar, "Clement of Alexandria on the Origin of Greek Philosophy" in *Symbolae Osloenses*, fasc. 15-16, 1936, pp.57-85.

The Conception of the Gospel in the Alexandrian Theology, Oslo: Jacob Dybwab, 1938.

MONCEAUX, Paul, *Histoire Littéraire de l'Afrique Chrétienne (depuis les origines jusqu'à l'invasion arabe)*, (tome 1, *Tertullien et les origines*), Paris: Ernest Léroux, 1901.

MONDÉSERT, Claude, *Clément d'Alexandrie: Introduction à l'etude de sa pensée à partir de l'Écriture*, Paris: Aubier, 1944.

MOODY, Campbell N., *The Mind of the Early Converts*, London: Hodder and Stoughton, 1920.

MORTLEY, Raoul, "The Past in Clement of Alexandria: A study in an attempt to define Christianity in socio-cultural terms" in E.P. Sanders (ed), *Jewish and Christian Self-Definition* (vol.1) *The Shaping of Christianity in the Second and Third Centuries*, London: SCM Press, 1980, pp.186-200.

MOULE, C.F.D., *An Idiom-Book of New Testament Greek*, Cambridge: Cambridge University Press (second edition), 1959.

MSHANA, Eliewaha E., "Review of John Mbiti, *Concepts of God in Africa*", in *ATJ*, no.5, 1972, pp.71-75.

MUNCK, J., *Untersuchungen über Klemens von Alexandria*, Stuttgart: Verlag von W. Kohlhammer, 1933.

MURRAY, Gilbert, *Five Stages of Greek Religion*, London: Watts and Co., 1935.

MUSURILLO, H., *The Acts of the Christian Martyrs*, Oxford: Clarendon Press, 1972.

NECKEBROUCK, V., *L'Afrique Noire et la Crise Religieuse de l'Occident*, Tabora, Tanzania: T.M.P. Book Department, 1971.

NEIL, William, *The Acts of the Apostles* (*NCB*), London: Marshall, Morgan and Scott, 1973.

NEILL, Stephen, *A History of Christian Missions* (The Pelican History of the Church, 6), Harmondsworth: Penguin Books, 1964.

NIEBUHR,   H. Richard, *Christ and Culture*, New York: Harper and Row (Harper Colophon Books), 1975.

NILSSON, M.P., *The History of Greek Religion* (ET by F.J. Fielden with preface by J.G. Frazer), Oxford: Clarendon Press, 1925.

   Greek Piety (ET by H.J. Rose), Oxford: Clarendon Press, 1948.

NISBET, R., *History of the Idea of Progress*, New York: Basic Books, 1980.

NJOYA, Timothy M., *Dynamics of Change in African Christianity: African theology through historical and socio-political change* (Ph.D. thesis, Princeton Theological Seminary, 1976), Ann Arbor: University Microfilms, 1976.

NOCK, A.D., *Early Gentile Christianity and its Hellenistic Background*, New York: Harper and Row (Harper Torchbooks), 1964 (first published in A.E.J. Rawlinson (ed), *Essays on the Trinity and the Incarnation*, London: Longmans, Green and Co, 1928, pp.51-156.

   Conversion – Old and New in Religion from Alexander to Augustine, Oxford: Clarendon Press, 1933.

NORRIS, F.W., "The Social Status of Early Christianity" in *Gospel in Context* (Abington: Partnership in Mission), vol.2, no.1, January 1979, pp.4-14.

NORRIS, Richard A., *God and World in Early Christian Theology: A Study in Justin Martyr, Irenaeus, Tertullian and Origen*, London: A. & C. Black, 1965.

OAKSMITH, John, *The Religion of Plutarch*, London: Longman, Green and Co., 1902.

ODAMTTEN, S.K., *The Missionary Factor in Ghana's Development up to the 1880s*, Accra: Waterville Publishing House, 1978.

OKEKE, Chidiebele, "African Concept of Time" in *CRA*, vol.7, no.14, juillet 1973, pp.297-302.

OOSTHUIZEN, G.C., *Post-Christianity in Africa – A theological and anthropological study*, London: Hurst and Co., 1968.

OPPENHEIM, Ph., "Apotaxis Lossagung im Taufritus" in *RAC*, vol.1, coll.559-562.

OSBORN, E.F., *The Philosophy of Clement of Alexandria*, Cambridge: Cambridge University Press, 1957.

  Justin Martyr (Beiträge zur historischen Theologie, 47), Tübingen: J.C.B. Mohr, 1973.

OTTO, Rudolf, *The Idea of the Holy – An inquiry into the non-rational factor in the idea of the divine and its relation to the rational* (ET by John Harvey) (second edition), London: Oxford University Press, 1950.

PADILLA, C. René, "Hermeneutics and Culture" in John R.W. Stott and Robert Coote (eds), *Down to Earth – Studies in Christianity and Culture*, Grand Rapids: Eerdmans, 1980, pp.63-78.

PAGE, Jesse, *The Black Bishop, Samuel Adjai Crowther*, London: Hodder and Stoughton, 1908.

PARRINDER, Geoffrey, *West African Religion (A Study of the Beliefs and Practices of Akan, Ewe, Yoruba, Ibo and Kindred Peoples)* (third edition), London: Epworth Press, 1969.

  Religion in Africa, London: Pall Mall Press, 1969.

  "Monotheism and Pantheism in Africa" in *JRA*, vol.3, 1970, pp.81-88.

PATRICK, John, *Clement of Alexandria* (The Croall Lecture, 1899-1900), Edinburgh and London: Blackwood and Sons, 1914.

PATTERSON, L.G., *God and History in Early Christian Thought – A Study in themes from Justin Martyr to Gregory the Great*, London: A. & C. Black, 1967.

PAYNE, E.J., and BEAZLEY, C.R. (eds), *Voyages of the Elizabethan Seamen: Select Narratives from the 'Principal Navigations' of Hakluyt*, Oxford: Clarendon Press, 1907.

PEEL, J.D.Y., "The Christianisation of Africa: Some Possible Models" in Edward Fasholé-Luke *et al.* (eds), *Christianity in Independent Africa*, London: Rex Collings, 1978, pp.443-454.

PELIKAN, Jaroslav, *The Emergence of the Catholic Tradition, AD 100-600* (The Christian Tradition – A history of the development of doctrine, vol.1), Chicago: University of Chicago Press, 1971.

Personalité africaine et Catholicisme, Paris: Présence Africaine, 1963.

PHILLIPS, C.J., *Protestant America and the Pagan World: the first half century of the American Board of Commissioners for Foreign Missions, 1810-1860,* Cambridge, Mass: Harvard University Press, 1969.

POBEE, J.S. (ed), *Religion in a Pluralistic Society* (Essays presented to Prof. C.G. Baëta), Leiden: E.J. Brill, 1976.

PORTER, Andrew, "Evangelical Enthusiasm, Missionary Motivation and West Africa in the late 19th century: the career of G.W. Brooke" in *JICH,* vol.6, 1977, pp.23-46.

POWELL, Douglas, "Tertullianists and Cataphrygians" in *VC,* 29, 1975, pp.33-54.

PREUSCHEN, E., "Tatian" in *The New Schaff-Herzog,* vol.11, pp.274-275.

PRIGENT, P., *Justin et l'Ancien Testament,* Paris: Gabalda et Cie, 1964.

PUECH, Aimé, *Recherches sur le Discours aux Grecs de Tatien suivies d'une traduction française du Discours avec Notes,* Paris: Félix Alcan, 1903.

Les Apologistes grecs du deuxième siècle de notre ère, Paris: Hachette, 1912.

QUASTEN, J., *Patrology* (vol.2, *The Ante-Nicene Literature after Irenaeus*), Utrecht-Antwerp: Spectrum Publishers, 1964.

RAY, Benjamin C., *African Religions – Symbols, Ritual and Community,* Englewood Cliffs, New Jersey: Prentice Hall Inc., 1976.

Renouveau de l'Eglise et Nouvelles Eglises – Colloque sur la théologie africaine (La quatrième semaine théologique de Kinshasa, 22-27 juillet, 1968).

RÉTIF, André, *Introduction à la doctrine pontificale des missions,* Paris: Editions du Seuil, 1953.

"The Evolution of the Catholic Idea of Mission" in *History's*

Lessons for Tomorrow's Mission – Milestones in Missionary Thinking, Geneva: WSCF, n.d., pp.262-271.

RICHARDSON, Don, *Peace Child*, Ventura, California: Regal Books, G.L. Publications, 1974.

RIDDLE, D.W., "Environment as a Factor in the Achievement of Self-Consciousness in Early Christianity" in *Journal of Religion*, 9, 1927, pp.146-163.

ROBINSON, J.A., "The Remains of the Original Greek of the *Apology* of Aristides" in *Texts and Studies* 1 (i), Cambridge: Cambridge University Press, 1891, pp.86ff.

ROBINSON, John F., "Review of Byang Kato, *Theological Pitfalls in Africa*", in *EMQ*, vol.12, no.4, October 1976, pp.243-244; reprinted in *ERT*, vol.1, no.1, October 1977, p.167.

RODNEY, Walter, *How Europe Underdeveloped Africa*, London: Bogle-L'Ouverture; Dar-es-Salaam: Tanzania Publishing House, 1972.

ROUSE, Ruth, "A Study of Missionary Vocation" in *IRM*, vol.6, 1917, pp.244-257.

RYAN, Patrick J, "'Arise, O God!' The Problem of 'Gods' in West Africa" in *JRA*, vol.11, fasc.3, 1980, pp.161-171.

SAMUEL V., and SUGDEN, C. (eds), *Sharing Jesus in the Two Thirds World* (The papers of the first Conference of Evangelical Mission Theologians from the Two Thirds World, Bangkok, Thailand, March 22-25, 1982), Bangalore, India: Partnership in Mission-Asia, 1983.

SAUER, Eric, *The Dawn of World Redemption*, Grand Rapids: Eerdmans, 1971.

SAUNDERS, Stanley P., "Christian Eschatology: the Ground and Impetus for Mission" in *Gospel in Context*, vol.2, no.4, October 1979, pp.3-10.

SAWYERR, Harry, *Creative Evangelism – Towards a New Christian Encounter with Africa*, London: Lutterworth Press, 1968

SCHLIER, Heinrich, "Religionsgeschichtliche Untersuchungen zu den Ignatius-briefen" in *ZNW*, 8, 1929.

SCHMIDT, Wilhelm, *The Origin and Growth of Religion* (ET, second edition), London: Methuen and Co, 1935.

SCHOEDEL, William R., "Christian 'Atheism' and the Peace of the Empire" in *Church History*, vol.42, no.3, 1973, pp.309-319.

SCHÜRER, Emil, *A History of the Jewish People in the Time of Jesus Christ* (3 vols) (ET by Sophia Taylor and Peter Christie), Edinburgh: T. & T. Clark, 1885ff.

SEMISCH, Karl, *Justin Martyr: His Life, Writings and Opinions*, (2 vols) (ET by J.E. Ryland), Edinburgh: T. & T. Clark, 1843.

SETILOANE, G.M., *The Image of God among the Sotho-Tswana*, Rotterdam: A.A. Balkema, 1976.

"How the Traditional World-View Persists in the Christianity of the Soth-Tswana" in E.W. Fasholé-Luke, *et al.* (eds), *Christianity in Independent Africa*, London: Rex Collings, 1978, pp.402-412.

SEUMOIS, André, *Théologie Missionnaire* (2 vols), Rome: Bureau de Press, OMI, 1973.

SEVENSTER, J.N., *Paul and Seneca* (Supplement to *Novum Testamentum*, vol.4), Leiden: E.J. Brill, 1961.

SHARPE, Eric J., *Comparative Religion – A History*, London: Duckworth, 1975.

SHORTER, Aylward, *African Christian Theology: Adaptation or Incarnation?* London: Geoffrey Chapman, 1975.

Prayer in the Religious Traditions of Africa, Nairobi: Oxford University Press, 1975.

SHOTWELL, W.A., *The Biblical Exegesis of Justin Martyr*, London: SPCK, 1965.

SIDER, Robert Dick, *Ancient Rhetoric and the Art of Tertullian*, London: Oxford University Press, 1971.

SIMON, Marcel, *St Stephen and the Hellenists in the Primitive Church*, London: Longmans, Green and Co., 1958.

Verus Israel – Etude sur les relations entre Chrétiens et Juifs dans l'empire romain (AD 135-425), Paris: E. de Boccard, 1964.

Le Christianisme et son contexte religieux – Scripta Varia (2 vols) (Wissenschaftliche Untersuchungen zum Neuen Testament, 23), Tübingen: J.C.B. Mohr, 1981.

SKARSAUNE, Oskar, "The Conversion of Justin" in *Studia*

Theologica, 30, 1976, pp.53-73.

SMITH, E.W., *The Christian Mission in Africa: A study based on the work of the international conference at Le Zoute, Belgium, September, 14-21, 1926,* London: Edinburgh House Press, 1926.

African Ideas of God – A Symposium (second edition revised and edited by E.G. Parrinder), London: Edinburgh House Press, 1950.

SMITH, Noel, *The Presbyterian Church of Ghana, 1825-1960,* Accra: Ghana Universities Press, 1966.

SMITH, Wilfred Cantwell, *The Meaning and End of Religion,* London: SPCK, 1978 (first published in 1962 by Macmillan, New York).

SÖDERBLOM, Nathan, *The Living God: Basal Forms of Personal Religion* (Gifford Lectures, 1931), London: Oxford University Press, 1933.

SPANNEUT, Michel, *Le Stoïcisme des Pères de l'Eglise – De Clément de Rome à Clément d'Alexandrie,* Paris: Editions du Seuil, 1957.

SPEIGL, J., *Der römische Staat und die Christen,* Amsterdam: Verlag A.M. Hackert, 1970.

STEVENSON, J. (ed), *A New Eusebius – Documents Illustrative of the History of the Church to AD 337,* London: SPCK, 1957.

STOCK, E., *The History of the Church Missionary Society – Its environment, its men and its work* (vol.1), London: CMS, 1899.

STOTT, John R.W., and COOTE, Robert (eds), *Down to Earth – Studies in Christianity and Culture,* Grand Rapids: Eerdmans, 1980.

SUNDKLER, Bengt, *The Christian Ministry in Africa,* London: SCM Press, 1962.

SWINNY, S.H., "The Humanitarianism of the 18th Century and its Results" in F.S. Marvin (ed), *Western Races and the World,* London: Oxford University Press, 1922, pp.121-145.

TASIE, G.O.M., *Christian Missionary Enterprise in the Niger Delta, 1864-1918,* Leiden: E.J. Brill, 1978.

TAYLOR, John B. (ed), *Primal World Views: Christian Involvement in Dialogue with Traditional Thought-Forms,* Ibadan: Daystar Press, 1976.

TAYLOR, John V. *The Growth of the Church in Buganda – An Attempt at Understanding,* London: SCM Press, 1958.

The Primal Vision – Christian Presence amid African Religion, London: SCM Press, 1963.

The Go-Between God – The Holy Spirit and the Christian Mission, London: SCM Press, 1972.

TEMPELS, Placide, *La Philosophie Bantoue,* Paris: Présence Africaine, 1949; ET as *Bantu Philosophy,* by Colin King, with foreword by Margaret Read, Paris: Présence Africaine, 1959.

TIENOU, Tite, "Threats and Dangers in the Theological Task in Africa" in *ERT,* vol.5, no.1, April 1981, pp.40-47

"Biblical Foundations for African Theology" in *Missiology,* vol.10, no.4, October 1982, pp.435-448.

TILL, Barry, *The Churches Search for Unity,* Harmondsworth: Penguin Books, 1972.

TOLLINTON, R.B., *Clement of Alexandria: A Study in Christian Liberalism* (2 vols), London: Williams and Norgate, 1914.

TRENCH, R.C., *Plutarch, his Life, his Parallel Lives and his Morals,* London, 1873.

TURNER, Harold W., "The Primal Religions of the World and their Study" in Victor Hayes (ed), *Australian Essays in World Religions,* Bedford Park, South Australia, 1977, pp.27-37.

"The Way Forward in the Religious Study of African Primal Religion" in *JRA,* vol.12, fasc.1, 1981, pp.1-15.

TURNER, H.E.W., *The Pattern of Christian Truth,* London: Mowbray and Co, 1954 (reprinted, New York: AMS Press, 1978).

TURNER, Philip, "The Wisdom of the Fathers and the Gospel of Christ: Some notes on Christian adaptation in Africa", in *JRA,* vol. 4, fasc.1, 1971, pp.45-68.

TUTU, Desmond, "Review of John S. Mbiti, *Prayers of African Religion*" in *JTSA,* no.17, December 1976, pp.68-69.

"Whither African Theology?" in E.W. Fasholé-Luke *et al.* (eds), *Christianity in Independent Africa,* London: Rex Collings, 1978, pp.364-369.

TYLOR, E.B., *Primitive Culture – Researches into the Development of Mythology, Philosophy, Religion, Art and Custom* (2 vols), (third edition revised), London: John Murray, 1891 (first published in 1871).

VERKUYL, Johannes, *Contemporary Missiology – An Introduction* (translated and edited by Dale Cooper), Grand Rapids: Eerdmans, 1978.

VICEDOM, Georg F. (ed), *Christ and the Younger Churches*, London: SPCK, 1972 (Originally published in German as *Theologische Stimmen aus Asien, Afrika und Lateinamerika*, München: Chr. Kaiser Verlag, 1968).

VIDLER, A.R., *The Church in an Age of Revolution, 1789 to the Present Day* (Pelican History of the Church, 5), Harmondsworth: Penguin Books (revised edition), 1977.

VOGT, J., *Zur Religiosität der Christenverfolger im römischen Reich*, Heidelberg: Carl Winter, 1962.

VÖLKER, Walther, "Der wahre Gnostiker nach Clemens Alexandrinus" in *TU*, 57, 1952.

WALLS, A.F., "The First Chapter of the Epistle to the Romans and the Modern Missionary Movement" in W. Gasque and R. Martin (eds), *Apostolic History and the Gospel: Biblical and Historical Essays presented to F.F. Bruce*, Exeter: Paternoster Press, 1970, pp.346-357.

"Missionary Vocation and the Ministry: the First Generation" in M.E. Glasswell and E.W. Fasholé-Luke (eds), *New Testament Christianity for Africa and the World* (Essays in honour of Harry Sawyerr), London: SPCK, 1974, pp.141-156.

"A Colonial Concordat: Two Views of Christianity and Civilisation" in D. Baker (ed), *Church, Society and Politics* (Studies in Church History), Oxford: Blackwell, 1975, pp.293-302.

"Africa and Christian Identity" in *Mission Focus*, vol.6, no.7, November, 1978, pp.11-13.

"Towards Understanding Africa's Place in Christian History" in J.S. Pobee (ed), *Religion in a Pluralistic Society* (Essays presented to Professor C.G. Baëta), Leiden: E.J. Brill, 1976, pp.180-189.

"Black Europeans, White Africans: Some Missionary Motives in West Africa" in D. Baker (ed), *Religious Motivation: Biographical and Sociological Problems of the Church Historian*, Cambridge: Cambridge University Press, 1978, pp.339-348.

"A Bag of Needments for the Road: Geoffrey Parrinder and the Study of Religion in Britain", in *Religion*, vol.10, part 2, Autumn 1980, pp.141-150.

"The Anabaptists of Africa? The Challenge of the African Independent Churches" in *Occasional Bulletin of Missionary Research*, vol.3, no.2, April, 1979, pp.48-51.

"Ruminations on Rainmaking: the Transmission and Receipt of Religious Expertise in Africa", in J.C.Stone (ed), *Experts in Africa* (Proceedings of a Colloquium at the University of Aberdeen, March 1980), Aberdeen: Aberdeen University African Studies Group, 1980, pp.146-151.

"The Gospel as the Prisoner and Liberator of Culture" in *Faith and Thought*, 108 (1-2), 1981, pp.39-52; reprinted in *Missionalia* vol.10, no.3, November 1982, pp.93-105.

WALTZING, J.P., *Tertullien: L'Apologétique* (Apparat critique et traduction littérale revue et corrigée), Bibliothèque de la Faculté de Philosophie et Lettres, Université de Liège: H. Vaillant-Carmane, 1919.

WALZER, R., *Galen on Jews and Christians*, London: Oxford University Press, 1949.

WARFIELD, B.B., *The Inspiration and Authority of the Bible* (edited by S.G. Craig, with Introduction by Cornelius van Til), Philadelphia: The Presbyterian and Reformed Publishing Co, 1940 (reprinted in 1970).

WARNECK, Johannes, *The Living Forces of the Gospel – Experiences of a Missionary in Animistic Heathendom* (ET, from third German edition, by Neil Buchanan), Edinburgh and London: Oliphant, Anderson and Ferrier (n.d.)

WARREN, M., *The Missionary Movement from Britain in Modern History*, London: SCM Press, 1965

WASZINK, J.H., *"Pompa Diaboli"* in *VC*, 1, 1947, pp.13-14.

Quinti Septimi Florentis Tertulliani: De Anima, Amsterdam: J.M. Meulenloff, 1947.

"Varro, Livy and Tertullian on the History of Roman Dramatic Art" in *VC*, 2, 1948, pp.224-242.

WEBSTER, J.B., *Christian Churches among the Yoruba, 1888-1922*, Oxford: Clarendon Press, 1964.

WENDLAND, Paul, *Die hellenistisch-römische Kultur in ihren Beziehungen zu Judentum und Christentum*, Tübingen: J.C.B. Mohr, 1912 (originally, 1907).

WESTCOTT, B.F., "Clement of Alexandria" in *DCB*, vol.1, pp.559-567.

WESTERMANN, D., "The value of the African's Past" in *IRM*, vol.15, 1926, pp.418-437.

Africa and Christianity (Duff Lectures, 1935), London: Oxford University Press, 1937.

WEY, Heinrich, *Die Funktionen der bösen Geister bei den griechischen Apologeten des zweiten Jahrhunderts nach Christus*, Winterthur: Verlag P.G. Keller, 195.

WILES, Maurice, *The Making of Christian Doctrine – A Study in the Principles of Early Doctrinal Development*, Cambridge: Cambridge University Press, 1967.

WILKEN, Robert L., "Towards a Social Interpretation of Early Christian Apologetics" in *Church History*, vol.39, no.4, 1970, pp.437-458.

"The Christians as the Romans (and Greeks) saw them" in E.P. Sanders (ed), *Jewish and Christian Self-Definition* (vol.1) – *The Shaping of Christianity in the Second and Third Centuries*, London: SCM Press, 1980, pp.100-125.

WILLIAMS, A. Lukyn, *Justin Martyr: The Dialogue with Trypho* (Translation, Introduction and Notes), London: SPCK, 1930.

WILLIAMSON, S.G., *Akan Religion and the Christian Faith*, Accra: Ghana Universities Press, 1965.

WINDEN, J.C.M. van, *An Early Christian Philosopher – Justin's Dialogue with Trypho, Chapters One to Nine* (Introduction, Text and Commentary), Leiden: E.J. Brill, 1971.

WIREDU, Kwasi, *Philosophy and an African Culture*, Cambridge: Cambridge University Press, 1980.

WITT, R.E., "The Hellenism of Clement of Alexandria" in *The Classical Quarterly*, vol.25, nos.3-4, July/October, 1931, pp.195-204.

WOLFSON, H.A., *The Philosophy of the Church Fathers* (third edition revised), Cambridge, Mass: Harvard University Press, 1970.

WUILLEUMIER, P., *Tacite: Annales 13-16*, Paris: Editions Belles Lettres, 1978.

ZAHN, Theodor, *Forschungen zur Geschichte des neutestamentlichen Kanons und der altkirchlichen Literatur* (3 Theil: Supplementum Clementinum), Erlangen: Andreas Deichert, 1884.

ZELLER, E., *A History of Greek Philosophy: From the Earliest Period to the Time of Socrates*, vol.2 (ET by S.F. Alleine), London: Longmans, Green and Co, 1881.

Index of Modern Authors

Abble, Albert 348
Abelard 431
Abraham, W. 451
Agbeti, J.K. 5, 12, 368, 383, 417, 451
Ajayi, J.F.A. 258-259, 451
Akerman, Malte 128
Alfonsi, L. 215, 452
Allcock, Philip J. 96, 463
Alleine, S.F. 170, 479
Allen, Roland 265-266
Allier, Raoul 235, 260-261, 452
Allmen, Daniel von 297, 452
Altaner, B. 60, 129, 136, 452
Amo, Anton Wilhelm 227, 253, 451, 466
Anderson, Gerald H. 243, 263, 443, 448, 452
Anderson, J.N.D. 390, 404, 418, 424
Anderson, Rufus 259
Andresen, Carl 12, 55, 63, 138, 147-148, 161-162, 167-169, 452
Angus, S. 56
Appiah-Kubi, Kofi 262, 296, 299, 338, 377, 424, 452
Ashcroft (Niger) 259
Awolalu, J. Omosade 290, 301
Awon, Gwamna 389
Ayandele, E.A. 259, 452

Backer, Emile de 131-132, 452
Baëta, C.G. 268, 294-298, 308, 337, 382, 385, 417, 440, 443-444, 447, 450, 452
Baker, D. 258, 261, 296, 476-477
Baker, John Austin 56, 129, 161, 457
Bala, Jerome 348
Bardy, Gustave 90, 101, 126, 160, 170, 208-210, 452
Barnard, L.W. 148, 161-163, 168, 171, 453
Barnes, T.D. 126-128, 453
Barre, A. de la 208, 209, 453
Barrett, David B. 336-337, 448, 453
Bastide, Roger 236, 261, 453
Bauer, Walter 133, 179, 210-211, 453
Baumgartner, W. 216, 464
Baus, Karl 12, 128, 463

Bayeux, J.-C. 376
Beasley-Murray, G.R. 421, 453
Beaver, R. Pierce 259, 336, 339, 444, 448
Beazley, C.R. 253, 470
Beecham, John 246-247, 255, 264
Benedict XV, Pope 350, 353, 378
Benoit, André 8, 12, 161, 432-433, 442, 453
Benz, Ernst 62, 158-159, 165-166, 171-172, 453
Berg, Johannes van den 241, 259, 262, 453
Berkouwer, G.C. 400, 421, 454
Bevan, Edwyn 87-88, 98-99, 454
Bigg, Charles 209-210, 454
Biko, Steve 394
Bindley, T. Herbert 132, 445, 454
p'Bitek, Okot 9-10, 12, 340, 438, 443, 454
Blaise, Albert 127
Blauw, Johannes 242, 263, 454
Blunt, A.W.F. 158, 165-167, 169, 172, 446, 454
Boas, George 95, 454
Boer, W. den 218, 454
Boissier, Gaston 130, 454
Bonhoeffer, Dietrich 271
Bossuet, J.B. 354
Bousset, W. 179, 181, 209, 211-212, 454
Bowden, John 58, 462
Bowers, Paul 416, 423-425, 454
Braun, René 126
Bray, G.L. 101-104, 126-128, 454
Brigham, F.H. 215, 455
Brooke, G.W. 471
Brown, Raymond E. 382, 455
Bruce, F.F. 51, 166, 455
Brunner, Emil 377, 455
Buber, Martin 383
Buchanan, Neil 97, 135, 161, 209, 462, 477
Bürkle, H. 448
Bury, J.B. 50, 460
Busia, K.A. 340
Butterworth, G.W. 194, 217, 222, 446,

455
Buxton, Sir Thomas Fowell 227-228, 254-255, 259

Cadoux, C.J. 128, 455
Camelot, Pierre 186, 210-211, 214, 216-217, 221, 455
Campenhausen, Hans von 101, 126, 160, 164-165, 173, 222, 455
Carey, William 229, 255, 455
Carlen, Claudia 376, 382, 455
Carlyle, E. Irving 254
Carpenter, H.J. 122, 134-136, 455
Carr, Burgess 418-419
Carrington, Philip 58-59, 456
Casey, Robert P. 208, 456
Caspari, W. 129, 456
Casserley, J.V. Langmead 383, 442, 456
Cassidy, Michael 338-339, 449, 456
Chadwick, Henry 43-44, 55, 61-63, 98-99, 127, 132, 135, 141, 146, 162-164, 167-171, 181, 210, 212-213, 218, 444, 456
Charles, Pierre 379-380, 456
Charles, R.H. 421, 456
Christaller, Johannes G. 292, 302, 456
Christie, Peter 91, 473
Clarke, Frank 265, 462
Cochrane, C.N. 53, 55, 57, 93, 457
Congar, Yves M.-J. 258, 457
Cooper, Dale 337, 476
Coote, Robert 11, 298, 422-424, 457, 466, 470, 474
Conford, E.T. 56
Cragg, Kenneth 4, 11, 171, 239-241, 244, 262-264, 298, 444, 457
Craig, S.G. 420, 477
Cross, F.L. 57, 59, 208, 457
Crowther, Samuel Ajayi 234, 259, 296, 470
Curtin, Philip 226, 233, 252-254, 256, 259-260, 457

d'Alès, Adhémar 130, 132, 134-135, 457
Daniélou, Jean 42, 46, 56-57, 61-62, 99, 116-117, 129, 132, 149, 153, 161, 168, 170-171, 215, 218, 457
Danquah, J.B. 299, 457
Davidson, Basil 227, 253, 457
Davidson, H.R. Ellis 291, 302, 458
Davies, W.D. 264, 458
de Brosses, Charles 256, 458

de Clercq, V.C. 127, 458
de Faye, Eugène 179, 183, 203, 206, 208, 210-213, 218-221, 458
de Gobineau, Arthur 254
de Ste Croix, G.E.M. 56, 458
Decharme, P. 212, 458
Desroche, Henri 379
Dickson, Kwesi A. 1-2, 11, 294-295, 297-299, 342, 381-382, 418, 448, 450, 458
Diels, Hermann 170, 221, 458, 460
Dill, Samuel 24, 53, 458
Dix, Gregory 50, 91, 249, 264-265, 428, 441, 458
Dodd, C.H. 270, 295
Dodds, E.R. 63, 164-165, 214, 458
Donaldson, James 445
Dosseh, R. 376
Douglas, J.D. 423, 450
Duchesne, Louis 61, 93, 126, 134, 166, 262, 458
Dupont, J. 264, 459
Dych, William V. 302
Dykes, Eva B. 253, 459

Eagleson, John 167, 461
Ellingworth, Paul 294-295, 297-299, 342, 381-382, 418, 448, 450, 458
Ellis, A.B. 299
Ellis, William 255
Elze, Martin 65, 67-70, 75, 81, 90-92, 94-97, 99, 459
Erasmus, Desiderius 247
Evans-Pritchard, E.E. 256, 261, 288, 301, 459

Farmer, H.H. 299, 459
Fasholé-Luke, Edward W. 11-12, 259, 294, 296-297, 339, 427- 428, 441-442, 459, 464, 470, 473, 475-476
Festugière, A.-J. 170, 175, 208-209, 212, 459
Fielden, F.J. 469
Finan, Thomas 219-221, 459
Fliche, A. 90, 210, 221, 465
Foerster, Werner 166, 459
Forde, Daryll 340
Foster, John 8, 12, 161, 433, 442, 459
Fowler, H.N. 218
Frazer, J.G. 170, 230, 256, 469
Fredericksen, Linwood 209, 221-222, 459
Frédouille, Jean-Claude 107, 126-29,

132, 134-135, 459
Freeman, Kathleen 170, 460
Freeman, Thomas B. 245-247, 260, 264, 460
Frend, W.H.C. 16, 50-52, 460
Friedländer, Moriz 91, 98, 460
Früchtel, Ludwig 446
Fueter, P.D. 296
Fuller, J.M. 90, 99-101, 126, 460

Gairdner, W.H.T. 231, 257-258, 460
Gardiner, Alice 53, 460
Gårtner, Bertil 166, 460
Gasque, W. Ward 63, 168, 257, 476
Geffken, J. 50, 57-58, 460
Gemery, Henry 226, 252, 460
George, P.J. 258, 460
Gibbon, Edward 15, 18, 50-51, 460
Gillies, Francis 324-325, 327, 342-344, 460
Gilmore, G.W. 129, 456
Glasswell, M.E. 259, 339, 476
Glover, T.R. 52-55, 58, 99, 127, 144, 165, 460
Godley, A.D. 216
Goodenough, E.R. 155, 161, 164, 171, 461
Goodspeed, E.J. 44, 58, 61, 92, 144, 166, 385, 446, 461
Goreham, Norman J. 263
Graef, H.C. 60, 452
Grant, R.M. 17, 50-51, 58, 75, 80, 89-90, 92, 94-97, 162, 164, 461
Gration, J.A. 336
Gray, Richard 337
Greenslade, S.L. 134
Groves, C.P. 252, 461
Guignebert, Charles 128-132, 139, 461
Guterman, Simeon L. 56, 461
Guthrie, W.K.C. 170, 461
Gutierrez, Gustavo 167, 461

Hahn, Ferdinand 249, 262, 265, 461
Hardy, E.R. 90, 169
Hargreaves, J.D. 253, 462
Harmer, J.R. 58-59, 466
Harnack, Adolf von 19, 35, 40, 50-51, 58-60, 90, 97, 135, 161, 172, 209-211, 221, 241, 262-263, 462
Harvey, John 345, 470
Hastings, Adrian 1-2, 5, 11, 225, 238, 252, 260-261, 295, 300, 302, 335, 341, 347, 375-377, 417-418, 442-

443, 462
Hatch, Edwin 221, 462
Hawkins, Sir John 253
Hay, Denys 255, 462
Hayes, Victor 442, 475
Heathcote, Arthur W. 96, 463
Hebga, Meinrad 376
Hengel, Martin 58, 462
Hennecke, E. 211, 219, 462
Hill, J. Hamlyn 90, 462
Hoffmann, Manfred 126
Hogendorn, Jan 226, 252, 460
Holte, Ragnar 148, 163, 167-170, 462
Hondius, J. 255
Hornus, Jean-Michel 131-132, 463
Hort, F.J.A. 204, 207, 220-222, 463
Hoskins, H.H. 53, 465
Hunt, James 258
Hurbon, Laënnec 258, 356, 379, 463
Hutchinson (*Niger*) 259
Hyldahl, Niels 162-163

Idowu, E. Bolaji 10, 237-238, 261, 267-302, 312, 333, 351, 377, 383, 397, 408, 414-415, 418, 424, 436,446
Ikenga-Metuh, Emefie 299, 302, 467
Inda, Caridad 167, 461
Inge, W.R. 210, 463

Jacob, Edmond 96, 463
Jacobs, Donald 411, 424
Jacobsen, Stiv 253, 463
Jaeger, Werner 44, 58, 61-63, 89, 99, 134, 209, 429, 442, 463
Janzen, John M. 293, 302, 463
Jedin, Hubert 12, 377, 463
John XXIII, Pope 335, 352-353, 377-378
Joly, Robert 91, 97, 133, 162-163, 259, 463
Jones, Thomas Jesse 260

Kabazzi, R.B. 425
Kagame, Alexis 325-327, 342-344, 361, 379-381, 464
Kalilombe, Patrick 443, 464
Kato, Byang H. 10, 261, 386-425, 431, 434, 437-438, 442, 450- 451, 454, 472
Kaufmann-Bühler, D. 52-53, 464
Kelly, J.N.D. 95-96, 159, 167, 172, 443, 464
Kendall, Elliott 265, 464

Kestleloot, Lilyan 375, 464
Kibicho, Samuel G. 8, 12, 294, 464
King, Colin 260, 475
Kinney, John W. 332-333, 335-336, 339, 345-346, 464
Knox, Robert 254
Koehler, Ludwig 216, 464
Korinchi, Chief 245-247
Kraemer, H. 464
Kraft, Charles 338
Kranz, W. 170
Kruger, Paul 99, 464
Kudadjie, Joshua N. 333, 346

Labriolle, Pierre de 102-106, 126-128, 132, 215, 464
Lagrange, M.-J. 208-209, 459
Lampe, G.W.H. 91
Lang, Andrew 282, 299, 465
Latourette, K.S. 252, 465
Lebreton, J. 65. 90, 134-135, 163, 168, 209-210, 221, 465
Lee, Sidney 254
Leeuwen, Arend Th. van 53, 57, 442, 465
Lefebvre, Archbishop Marcel 348
Leith, John H. 167, 465
Lévy-Bruhl, Lucien 235-236, 260-261, 465
Liebeschuetz, J.H.W.G. 24, 53-54, 465
Lienhardt, Godfrey 301, 466
Lietzmann, H. 57
Lightfoot, J.B. 52, 58-59, 102, 211, 466
Lilla, Salvatore R.C. 206, 219-221, 466
Lindars, Barnabas 338, 344, 448
Lochner, Norbert 253, 466
Loewen, Jacob A. 423, 466
Loffeld, Edouard 376, 466
Lortz, Joseph 106, 128, 430, 442, 466
Lovejoy, Arthur O. 95, 253, 454, 466
Lovett, Richard 254, 466
Lubac, Henri de 378, 380, 466
Lubbock, John (Lord Avebury) 230, 256
Lufuluabo, F.-M. 379, 466
Luneau, A. 443, 466
Lyiomo, K.E. Amos 341, 346, 466

MacGaffey, Wyatt 293, 302, 463
McGrath, Charles 467
McKay, A.M. 263
McKenzie, P.R. 259, 333, 346, 466
McMullen, R. 50-51, 467
McVeigh, Malcolm J. 260, 293, 302, 467

Mansfield, Lord Chief Justice 253
Maran, Dom 93
Markus, R.A. 55, 57-58, 60, 116, 126, 132, 136, 211, 215, 219, 467
Marmardji, A.-S. 64, 90, 467
Marrou, H.-I. 189, 208, 215, 221, 467
Martin, Ralph P. 63, 168, 257, 476
Martin, V. 90, 210, 221, 465
Marin, F.S. 98, 253, 255, 454, 474
Maurier, Henri 385, 467
Mayor, J.B. 204, 220-221, 463
Mazrui, Ali 9-10
Mbiti, John S. 9-10, 12, 237-238, 260-261, 264-265, 296, 301, 303-346, 387, 397-398, 408, 414-415, 418, 420, 424-425, 436-437, 441, 443-444, 447, 464, 466-468, 475
Mbonyinkebe, Deogratias 373, 385, 467
Merrill, E.T. 52, 467
Metcalfe, G.E. 255, 453
Metuh, Emefie Ikenga 299, 302, 468
Mleke, Nimrod 342, 344, 468
Mobutu, President 411
Moffat, Robert 232, 257, 263
Moffatt, James 50, 210, 462
Molland, Einar 200, 203-204, 214, 219-220, 468
Monceaux, Paul 468
Mondésert, Claude 176, 199, 208-209, 211, 213, 218, 220, 468
Moody, Campbell N. 8, 12, 161, 468
Moore, Basil 394-395, 419
Mortley, Raoul 188, 215, 220, 468
Moule, C.F.D. 421, 468
Mshana, Eliewaha E. 346, 468
Mulago, Vincent 10, 347-385, 436-437, 449, 467
Munck, J. 209-210, 468
Murray, A.T. 216
Murray, Gilbert 130, 164, 170, 468
Mushete, Ngindu 296, 356, 377-379, 383
Musurillo, H. 56, 60, 165, 468

Neckebrouck, V. 373-374, 385, 469
Neil, William 51, 469
Neill, S.C. 259-260, 418, 469
Ngindu, Alphonse (Mushete) 383
Niebuhr, H. Richard 31, 33, 49, 57-58, 62-63, 136, 221, 314, 339, 431, 442, 469
Nilsson, M.P. 165, 170, 469

Nisbet, R. 256, 469
Njoya, Timothy M. 265, 386, 417, 469
Nketia, J.H. 296
Nock, A.D. 13, 29, 32, 55-57, 99, 129, 140, 163-164, 209, 469
Norris, F.W. 469
Norris, Richard A. 60, 118, 120-121, 123-124, 133-136, 160, 169-170, 173, 212, 427, 441, 469

Oaksmith, John 54, 469
Odamtten, S.K. 296, 469
Okeke, D. Chidiebele 342, 344, 469
Oliver, Roland 293, 302
Oosthuizen, G.C. 240, 248, 262, 264, 297, 431, 442, 470
Oppenheim, Ph. 129, 470
Osborn, E.F. 140, 161, 163-165, 168-171, 173, 211, 470
Otto, J.C.T. 61, 69, 88, 92-93, 95-97, 99, 144, 162, 172, 445- 446,
Otto, Rudolf 330, 345, 445, 470

Padilla, C. René 407, 422-424, 470
Page, Jesse 234, 259, 470
Parrinder, Geoffrey 260, 265, 267, 285, 290, 292-294, 299-302, 340, 442, 470, 474, 477
Patrick, John 207-209, 211-213, 217, 220, 222, 470
Patterson, L.G. 208, 470
Paul VI, Pope 353, 377
Payne, E.J. 253, 470
Peel, J.D.Y. 8, 12, 470
Pelikan, Jaroslav 170, 471
Peters, George 263
Phillips, C.J. 254, 259, 471
Pityana 394
Pius XI, Pope 353, 378
Pius XII, Pope 350, 381
Pobee, J.S. 12, 343, 346, 385, 442, 449, 471, 476
Porter, Andrew 258, 471
Powell, Douglas 101-102, 126-127, 471
Preuschen, E. 94, 471
Prigent, P. 162, 173, 471
Puech, Aimé 59, 61, 65-66, 68-70, 78, 83, 85-87, 90-99, 138, 161, 164, 167-168, 471

Quasten, J. 139, 212-213, 471

Rackham, H. 52

Radice, Betty 52
Rahner, Karl 302
Rawlinson, A.E.J. 99, 469
Ray, Benjamin C. 11, 333, 340, 346, 471
Read, James 254
Read, Margaret 260, 475
Rétif, André 376, 379, 471
Richardson, Don 472
Ricoeur, Paul 342, 464
Riddle, D.W. 50, 472
Ritschl, F.W. 493
Roberts, Alexander 445
Robinson, J. Armitage 59-60, 472
Robinson, John A.T. 271, 394-395
Robinson, John F. 425, 472
Rodney, Walter 253, 472
Rose, H.J. 94, 165, 469
Rouse, Ruth 241, 262, 418, 472
Rubbens, A. 376
Ryan, Patrick J. 292, 300, 302, 472
Ryland, J.E. 161

Samuel, V. 472
Sanders, E.P. 50, 60, 215, 467-468, 478
Sastre, R. 376
Sauer, Eric 400, 421, 472
Saunders, Stanley P. 342, 472
Savacool, John K. 379
Sawyerr, Harry 11, 297, 339, 472
Schleiermacher, F.E.D. 403
Schlier, Heinrich 91, 472
Schmidt, Wilhelm 282, 299, 301, 472
Schneemelcher, W. 211, 219, 462
Schoedel, William R. 27, 55, 473
Scholefield, Alan 253
Schürer, Emil 91, 99, 473
Schuyler, J.B. 417
Schwartz, E. 90, 95-97, 134, 445
Seaton, R.C. 216
Semisch, Karl 159, 161, 172, 473
Setiloane, Gabriel M. 262, 294-295, 299, 301, 473
Seumois, André 354, 376-378, 380, 473
Sevenster, J.N. 54, 473
Sharpe, E.J. 256, 473
Sheppard, L.C. 378, 466
Shorter, Aylward 12, 341, 374, 383-385, 466, 473
Shotwell, W.A. 169, 473
Sider, R.D. 473
Simon, Marcel 34, 58, 211, 262, 439, 444, 473
Skarsaune, Oskar 140, 142-143, 157,

163-166, 171, 473
Smalley, S.S. 338, 344, 448
Smith, David 129, 457
Smith, Edwin W. 260-261, 265, 291-292, 301-302, 474
Smith, Noel 264, 474
Smith, Roland Gregor 383
Smith, Wilfred Cantwell 281, 298, 474
Söderblom, Nathan 246-247, 264, 282, 299, 474
Somersett, James 253
Spanneut, Michael 96, 136, 474
Speigl, J. 56, 63, 474
Stählin, Otto 196, 208, 216-217, 221, 446
Stevenson, J. 52, 57, 61, 164, 474
Stewart, Zeph 99
Stock, Eugene 254, 259, 474
Stone, J.C. 264, 477
Stott, John R.W. 11, 298, 422-424, 457, 466, 470, 474
Stransky, Thomas F. 443, 448
Sugden, C. 472
Sundkler, Bengt 3, 11, 474
Swinny, S.H. 253, 474

Tasie, G.O.M. 258-259, 474
Taylor, John B. 381, 474
Taylor, John V. 12, 242, 263, 265, 269, 294, 443, 475
Taylor, Sophia 91, 473
Tempels, Placide 260, 265, 349, 360-361, 376, 380, 475
Thompson, Thomas 254
Tienou, Tite 425, 475
Til, Cornelius van 420, 477
Till, Barry 418, 475
Tillich, Paul 271, 339
Tollinton, R.B. 175, 178, 181, 205-206, 208-212, 221-222, 475
Tombalbaye, President 411
Torres, Sergio 262, 299, 338, 424, 452
Tränkle. H. 128
Trench, R.C. 54, 475
Treu, Ursula 446
Tshibangu, Debat Th. 384, 443
Turner, H.E.W. 133, 475
Turner, Harold W. 5-6, 11-12, 300, 340, 442, 475
Turner, Philip 297, 418, 475
Tutu, Desmond 2, 11, 341, 346, 475
Tylor, E.B. 230-232, 256-258, 293, 302,

476

Vanneste, Alfred 371, 384
Venn, Henry 259
Verkuyl, Johannes 307, 337, 476
Verlinden, Luc 338-339, 449, 456
Vicedom, Georg F. 262, 337-338, 344, 447, 476
Vidler, Alec R. 254, 476
Vogt, Joseph 28-29, 52, 55, 476
Völker, Walter 214, 476

Waddell, Hope 256
Walls, Andrew F. 8, 11-12, 46, 62, 116, 132, 168, 223, 238, 243-245, 257-265, 294, 296, 316, 336, 339, 344-345, 385, 442-444, 476
Waltzing, J.P. 98, 129, 132, 445, 477
Walzer, R. 57, 61, 164, 477
Warfield, B.B. 420, 477
Warneck, Johannes 231-233, 257-258, 477
Warren, Max 239, 254-255, 259, 262-263, 477
Waszink, J.H. 108, 129, 133, 477
Webster, J.B. 259, 478
Wendland, Paul 170, 478
Westcott, B.F. 198, 208, 218, 478
Westermann, Dietrich 260, 264, 295, 478
Wey, Heinrich 166, 478
Wiles, Maurice 382, 478
Wilken, Robert L. 28, 41-42, 50, 55, 60-61, 261, 478
Williams, A. Lukyn 161-162, 172, 478
Williamson, S.G. 247-248, 264, 478
Wilson, Herbert 127, 465
Wilson, R. McL. 211, 219, 462
Winden, J.C.M. van 161-164, 478
Wiredu, Kwasi 443, 478
Witt, R.E. 208, 479
Wolfson, H.A. 134, 139, 479
Wood, H.G. 255
Wuilleumier, P. 20, 52, 479
Wyon, Olive 377, 455

Yannoulatos, A. 381
Young, E.J. 420

Zahn, Th. 178, 208, 210-211, 213, 479
Zeller, E. 170, 479

Index of Classical Names

Abraham 59, 98-99, 156-158, 160, 191
Achilles 72
Adam 216, 404
Admetus 72
Aecus 214
Aeneas 22
Agamemnon 72, 84
Aion 97
Alexander the Great 97
Amosis 98
Amphion 190
Ananias, Azarias & Mishael 156-158
Antiochus of Askelon 168
Antiochus IV Epiphanes 54
Antoninus Pius, emperor 38
Apion 91
Apollo 72
Apollonius Rhodius 216
Apuleius of Madaura 55-56
Arion 190
Aristides 38, 41, 59, 374, 472
Aristodemus 54
Aristotle 56, 120, 189, 215, 254
Artapanus 103
Asclepius, god of healing 157
Athenagoras 55, 61-62, 92-94, 171, 184, 213
Athene 72
Augustine 43, 52-54, 56, 61, 86, 93-94, 98, 129, 189, 215, 362, 381, 467
Augustus, emperor 16-17, 22, 25, 53
Aurelius, Marcus 21, 52, 96, 242

Bacchanalia 40
Bacchus 110
Balbus 21-24
Bar Kochba, Simon 34
Basilides 210
Berosus 83
Buddha 213

Caecilius 51, 60
Caesar, C. Julius 17
Callimachus of Cyrene 93
Callistus 102
Caracalla, emperor 52
Catiline 20, 52

Celsus 10, 21, 28-29, 48, 55, 57, 62-63, 86, 97, 99, 104, 127, 132, 140, 168, 188, 206, 212, 215, 220, 438-439
Chrysostom, John 95, 132
Cicero 21-24, 27, 42, 52-54, 56, 147, 167-168, 189, 209, 215
Claudius, emperor 18, 51
Clement of Alexandria 10, 36, 41, 45, 47, 49, 56-57, 59-63, 66, 74, 86, 91,93, 95, 97-98, 133, 166, 174-222, 245, 428-430, 435-437, 443, 446, 454-456, 458-459, 463, 465-466, 468, 470, 475-476, 478-479
Clement of Rome 159
Confucius (Kong-fu-tse) 247
Cornelius 404
Cotta 53
Crescens the Cynic 93, 143
Cyprian 130
Cyril of Alexandria 362, 381

Danaus 94
Daniel 113, 131
David 159
Deiphobus 72
Didymus the Blind 126
Diogenes Laertius 94
Dionesus, god of wine 157
Dionysius II of Sicily 92

Elijah 156-158
Elizabeth, mother of John the Baptist 192
Ennius, Quintus 129
Ephraem Syrus 65
Epictetus 172
Epicurus 157, 171, 213
Epiphanius 208
Esau 80
Eunomus 190
Euripides 195
Eusebius 50, 57-59, 61, 64-65, 86, 90-91, 98-99, 160, 162, 168, 173, 177-178, 207-211, 474
Eve 216

Fronto, Marcus Cornelius 60

Galen 56, 61, 164, 477
Gallienus 55
Gallio 50
Glaucon 93
Gregory of Nyssa 362, 381
Gregory Thaumaturgus 209

Hadrian, emperor 59
Hector 72
Hellenos 59
Hera 170
Heraclitus 149-150, 156-158, 171, 194
Hermes 170
Hermias 61
Herodotus 216
Hesiod 45, 84, 153-154
Hierax 60
Hippolytus 102
Hiram 83
Homer 45, 83-84, 93, 153-154, 190, 216

Ignatius 58, 96, 472
Inachos of Argos 83, 98
Irenaeus 64-65, 89, 121-122, 134-135,
    148-149, 168, 179, 454, 469
Isaac 59
Isis 56
Israel 159

Jacob 59, 159
James, brother of Jesus 34
James Zebedee 406
Jerome 90, 130, 174, 207
John the Baptist 192-193
John Zebedee 406
Joseph of Arimathea 406
Joseph (*Genesis*) 99, 113, 131, 159
Josephus 51, 54, 57, 60, 67, 86, 91, 464
Joshua 114
Judah 159
Justin Martyr 10, 31, 34, 38, 41-47, 49,
    51, 55-58, 60-63, 65-66, 74, 82, 86-
    87, 90-95, 97-88, 130, 135, 137-173,
    177-179 194, 204-205, 207, 210,
    212, 215-217, 221, 245, 247, 374,
    402-403, 415, 428-429, 434-437,
    443, 446, 452-454, 456, 461, 463,
    469-471, 473, 478

Kronos 59

Lactantius 57, 86, 98, 129

Livy 55, 60, 478
Lucian of Samosata 28, 51, 55, 62, 94,
    164
Lucius 56

Maecenas 25
Marcion 64
Martha of Bethany 406
Mary, mother of Jesus 365, 381-382,
    454
Mary of Bethany 406
Matthew 406
Metrodorus of Lampsacus 93
Midas 54
Minucius Felix 51, 55, 50
Molo, Apollonius 60
Moses 33, 73, 83-87, 93, 98-99, 114,
    150, 155, 184, 188, 203-204, 220,
    430
Musonius Rufus, Stoic
    philosopher 156-158, 172, 247

Narcisssus 51
Nebuchadnezzar 83, 158
Nero, emperor 17, 19-20, 24, 158
Nicias 54
Noah 255
Numa 53
Numenius of Apamaea 164, 204

Octavian (Augustus) 23
Origen 47, 51-52, 55, 57-58, 86, 97-99,
    168, 177, 208-210, 212, 215, 439,
    444, 456, 469
Orosius 57
Orpheus 190

Pantaenus 166, 174, 177, 205, 207-210
Paul 19, 35, 50, 59, 145-146, 166, 171,
    181, 184-185, 197, 239-241, 244-
    245, 248-250, 265, 355, 377, 396,
    413, 435-436, 473
Peregrinus (Proteus) 62, 94
Perseus 157
Peter 114, 382
Philo 161, 215, 454, 464
Photius 221
Pilate 18, 51
Pindar 215
Piso 158
Plato 44, 56, 62, 92-93, 98, 120, 142,
    145, 150, 152, 154-155, 165-170,
    195, 204, 215, 218

Pliny the Elder 50
Pliny the Younger 20-21, 52, 55-56, 60
Plotinus 208
Plutarch 25-27, 42, 54-55, 144, 165, 469, 475
Polybius 22-23, 52-53
Polycarp 411
Poppaea 17
Porphyry 50
Ptolemy of Mendes 97

Rabbula, bishop of Edessa 65
Rhea 59
Rhodo 91
Rubellius Plautus 158
Rusticus 56

Sallust 20, 52
Sardanapalus 157, 171
Saturninus 64
Scaevola, Publius 53
Seneca 24, 27, 42, 47, 53-54, 56, 61, 63, 97, 109, 129, 473
Sextus Empiricus 96
Silas 19
Simon Magus 160
Socrates 41, 43, 45-46, 56, 62, 143-145, 149, 154-158, 165-166, 171, 247, 390, 453
Solomon 83, 117
Solon 98
Stephen 473
Stesimbrotus of Thasos 93

Suetonius 18, 20, 50-52, 55, 94
Suidas 172

Tacitus 17, 19-20, 50-52, 55, 60, 158, 172, 479
Tatian 10, 43-45, 47, 49, 51, 56-57, 61-62, 64-101, 121, 130, 134, 150, 184, 428-430, 445, 452, 459-462, 467, 471
Tertullian 10, 39-41, 43, 45, 47, 49, 51, 53-54, 56-58, 60-62, 86, 89, 93, 98, 100-136, 140, 178, 350, 428-431, 445, 452-454, 457-461, 463-464, 466, 468-469, 473, 477-478
Theodoret of Cyrrhus 65
Theophilus of Antioch 57, 86, 98
Thraesea Paetus 17
Tiberius, emperor 51
Trajan, emperor 20
Trypho 34, 137, 139-140, 162, 172-173

Valentinus 64, 210
Varro 23, 52, 54, 478
Venus 110
Vergil 22, 25, 53
Victorinus, Marius 43, 61

Xenophanes of Colophon 153-154

Zacchaeus 406
Zechariah, father of John the Baptist 192-193
Zeus 59, 157, 170, 190

Index of Ancient References

Acts of Justin and Companions
5.8   56
Apollonius Rhodius
 Argonautika
  4.264   216
Aristides
 Apology   38, 41, 59
259, 385
  3-7   59
  8-9   59
  12-13   59
  14   59
  15ff   59
Aristotle
 Protreptikos   56
Athenagoras
 Legatio
  4-30   55
  7   62
  8.1   213
  11.32-33   61
  17   93
  31   62
  33   94
  33-34   92
Augustine
 Confessions
  3.2   93
  3.4   56, 215
  8.2   61
 De civitate Dei
  4.27   52, 53
  6.5   52, 53
  6.10   54, 129
  14.20   94
  18.37   98
Aurelius, Marcus
 Meditations
  11.3   52
  12.3   96
Epistle of Barnabas 178
Callimachus of Cyrene
 Hymn (2) to Apollo
  9.11.47-49   93
Caracalla
 Constitutio
  Antoniana   52

Celsus
 Alethes logos (True Doctrine) 10,
  28, 48, 220
Cicero
 De finibus bonorum et malorum
  4.7.17-18   167
 De legibus
  2.8.19   52
  2.10.23   53
 De natura deorum 209
  1.2.3-4   54
  1.2-4   53
  2.3.8   52
  2.28.72   53
  3.2.6   53
 Hortensius 56, 189, 215
 Paradoxa Stoicorum 215
Clement of Alexandria
 Didaskalos   213
 Hypotyposeis 208
 Paidagogos 56, 61, 179-181, 198,
  213
  1.1   213
  1.1.3.3   212
  1.6.37.3   222
  1.7.54.3   221
  1.9.83.3   218
  2.2   61
  3.4   93
  3.12.97.3-98.1   212
 Hymn to Christ 56, 218
 Protreptikos 175, 179-181,188, 189,
  193, 203, 206, 207, 212, 214
  1.2.1   216
  1.2.3   216
  1.3.1   216
  1.3.2   216
  1.4.2   216
  1.4.3   216
  1.5.4   216
  1.6.3   216
  1.6.4-5   216
  1.7.3   216
  1.7.5f   216
  1.7.6   217
  1.8.1-2   217
  1.9.1ff   217

1.9.83.3	216	1.1.7.3	213
1.10.1	217	1.1.8.2	213
1.10.3	217	1.1.11.1-2	208, 209
2	217	1.1.11.3	213
2.11.1	217, 218	1.1.15.3	213
2.12.2	216	1.1.15.4-16.1	213
3	217	1.1.16.2	214
4	93, 194, 217	1.1.17.2	214
4.46.1	217	1.1.18.1	214
4.50.4f	217	1.2.19.3	214
4.51.2ff	217	1.2.19.4	214
4.51.6	217	1.2.20.2	212
4.57.1	217	1.2.21.2	213
4.59.2	217	1.3	214
5	62, 63	1.5	61
6	62	1.5.7	219
6.68.1	217	1.5.28.2	219
6.68.2-3	217	1.5.32.4	219
6.70.1	220	1.6.9-10.20	214
6.72.3	218	1.7.37.6	212
6.72.5	218	1.11.14-16, 21-29	220
7	63, 217	1.11.53.2	220
7.73.1	217	1.12	214
7.74.2	217	1.13.57.1	211, 212
7.74.7	218	1.13.57.6	211, 212,
7.76.3	217	1.13.57-58	214
8	196	1.15-16	213
8.77.1	218, 220	1.15.21	57
8.77.2-81.8	218	1.15.71.6	213
8.77.7	218	1.19.91.5	219
8.81.2	218	1.20	214
9	196	1.20.97.1-2	220
9.86.2	218	1.20.97.4	220
9.88.2	218	1.20.99.1	219
10.89.1	215, 218	1.20.100.1-2	214
10.89.2	218	1.21-29	215
10.89.3	218	1.21	98
10.90.2	218	1.21.101.1	219
10.98.4	217	1.21.101.2	213
10.110.1	218	1.22.150.2	220
10.110.3	218	1.22.150.4	220
11.112.1	212, 214	1.24.158.1	220
11.112.2	212	1.28.176.1	219
11.113.1	212	1.29	98
11.114.2	212	1.29.180.2	220
11.114.3f	212	1.29.181.4	215
12.118.1	218	2.1.2.1	211
12.120.1-5	217	2.1.3.1-2	214
Stromateis		2.2	62, 97
1.1	182, 211	2.2.5.1	219
1.1.1.2	213	2.2.6.11	213
1.1.4.3	213	2.5.18	220
1.1.5.4	213	2.5.22.3	219

2.6.29.1	217
2.6.31.2	211
2.11	214
2.11.48.1	219
2.20.116.3	211
3.2	95
3.13	91
4.8.69.2-4	213
5.1	214
5.1-3	213
5.1.10-12, 14	220
5.3	133
5.14.138.2	213
6.2-6	220
6.2	62
6.2.4.3	220
6.2.28.5	214
6.5	59, 62, 219
6.5.39.1	219
6.5.39.5	219
6.5.41.7	219
6.5.42.1-2	219
6.5.42.3	219
6.6	219
6.6.44	217
6.6.44.2ff	219
6.6.46.4	219
6.6.47.2	220
6.6.47.4	219
6.7	219
6.7.54.1	220
6.7.56.2	228
6.8	219
6.8.67.1	212, 219
6.8.67.2	213
6.11.91.1f	214
6.17	60, 63, 205, 219
6.17.157.4-5	217
6.17.159.9	221
6.56.1-2	209
7.2	219
7.6.34.2	220
7.16.95.3	214
7.16.102.3	216

Clement of Rome
1 Corinthians
6.1	52
45.4ff	158

Cyprian
Epistle to Donatus
5	130

Didymus the Blind
De Trinitate

3.41	126

Dio Chrysostom
Discourses
10.29-30	95
To Diognetus	37, 41
1	59
5	59, 61
6	59
7	59
9	59
10	59

Epiphanius
Haereses
32.6	208

Eusebius
Ecclesiastical Canon 178
Historia ecclesiastica 64
1.4.6	173
2.23	58
4.3	59
4.11.8	162
4.16.7	61
4.18	168
4.28-29	90
4.29	90, 98
5.10	207, 209
5.11	208
5.13	91
6.13	208, 211
6.15	210
6.19.13	209

Praeparatio Evangelica
1.2	50, 86
9.18	99
9.23	99
9.27	99
10.11	57, 98

Gospel of the Egyptians 211
Gospel of the Hebrews 211

Gregory Thaumaturgus
Panegyric
6-15	209

Hermias
Irrisio 61

Herodotus
Histories
2	216

Homer
Iliad 84
22.11.224-231	83, 93
Odyssey	190
4.217f	216

Ignatius

Magnesians
10   58
Philadelphians
6   58
Irenaeus
  Adversus Haereses 121, 179
    1.28.1   89
    2.26.1   134
    3.3   134
    3.23(8)   89
    5.26.2   168
  Adversus Valentinianos
    5.1   135
Jerome
  Commentary on Titus
    intro.   90
  Liber de viris illustribus
    36   207
  Translatio hom. Origenis in Ezech.
    13   130
Josephus
  Antiquities
    12.6.2   54
    20.8.11   51
  Contra Apionem 60
    2.148   57, 91
Justin Martyr
  1 Apology   137, 140, 152, 171
    1.1   160, 162
    2.1   164
    4   51
    5   55, 62
    5.2   171
    5.3   165, 166, 171
    5.4   166
    5.46   62
    5.46.2   61
    10   163
    10.1-2   172
    10.2   167
    14.5   161
    15.6   162
    15.29   61
    18-19   163
    19   92
    20.3   169
    20.4-5   169
    21.4-6   171
    22   171
    26   168
    27   95
    31ff   163

31.7   162
32.4   162
32.104   172
44   57, 98
44.8   169
44.9-10   169
44.10   167
46   61
46.2   168
46.3   165, 168, 169, 171
46.3-4   171, 173
46.4   172
53   58
53.3   161, 217
53.5   172
54.1   171
54.2-4   171
54.5-6   171
56   168
59   57, 98
59.1   169
59.1-5   169
60   51, 57, 98
60.1ff   169
60.10   167
60.11   169
2 Apology   140, 146, 152, 171
  1.6   61
  2   92
  3.1.6   165
  3.6   165
  5.3   166
  7   61
  7.3   169, 171
  7.10   62
  8.1   168, 171
  8.2   172
  8.2-3   169
  8.3   166, 168
  10   51, 60, 62, 169
  10.1   166
  10.1-3   168
  10.2f   169
  10.5-6   166
  10.5.8   165
  10.6   166, 170
  10.13.2   61
  12.1   142, 164
  13   56, 62, 63
  13.2   167
  13.2-6   169, 170

13.3   166
13.4   167
13.5   169
13.6   169
15.1   160
Dialogue with Trypho 137, 139,
              140, 152, 162, 171
1.3f   169
1.4   162
1.4-5   164
2   130, 161
2.1   212
2.1-2   163
2.6   169
3   97, 130
6   142
7   142, 161
7.1   163
7.2   163
7.3   162, 165
8   56, 62, 97, 161
8.1   142, 162
8.1-2   140, 164
9   56, 91
9.1   163
11.4   172
11.5   172
12   58
23.3   166
28.2   161
29.1   172
29.2   173
35.2   172
40.1   216
41.3   161
52.2.4   172
52.4   162
80   163
109   162
119.5-6   172
120.3.5   172
120.6   160
123   60
123.7   172
123.9   172, 385
131.5   162
On the Resurrection 172
Lactantius
  Divine Institutes
  1.11   129
  4.5   58, 98
Livy
  Annals

39.8-19   55
39.13-14   60
Lucian of Samosata
  Death of Peregrinus 62, 94
11   55
12.13   51
  Martyrdom of Justin & Companions
  4.8   60
Minucius Felix
  Octavius
  5.8.12   51, 60
  9   55
  9.6   60
  31.2   60
Origen
  Contra Celsum   444, 456
  1-2   99
  1.2   57, 97, 212
  1.9   55, 57
  1.27   51
  1.28   57
  1.28ff   55
  1.47   58
  1.69ff   55
  2.13   58
  2.55   55
  3.44   57
  3.55   57, 127
  4.23   57
  4.25   168
  5.14   55
  5.34   215
  5.40   215
  6.1   97
  8.65   52
  8.67   55
  8.68   57, 132
  8.69   55, 57, 132
  8.73   55, 57
  8.75   51
Orosius
  Historiarum adversus paganos
  5.2   57
Philo
  Moses
  1   215
Photius
  Bibliotheca
  110   221
Plato
  Apologia
  11.24B   166

Ion *(On the Iliad)*93
Protagoras   215
Republic
    2.377   170
    10.595   165, 170
    260D   165
    518D   56
Symposium
    202E   165
Theaetetus
    176B   218
Timaeus   150
    22B   98
    32B-C   169
    36B-C   167
Pliny the Elder
    Natural History
    13.4   50
Pliny the Younger
    Letters
    96   52, 60
Plutarch
    Adversus Colotem (Moralia 14)
    31(112-15)   54
    Amatorius
    13(756)   54
    De defectu oraculorum (Moralia 5)
    9.414E   165
    9.414F   54
    13.416E   165
    De fortuna Romanorum
    (Mor. 4)   54
    De Iside et Osiride (Moralia 5)
                       54
    ·26.361C   165
    De superstitione (Moralia 2)
                       25, 54
    1.164E   54
    3.166B   54
    4.166D   54
    8.168F   54
    8.169D   54
    9.169D   54
    10.169F   54
    11.170E   54
    14.171F   54
    Non posse... Epicurum (Mor. 14)
    21.1101-2   54
    Praecepta gerendae Republicae
    (Moralia 10)   54
Polybius
    History
    6.56   52, 53

Preaching of Peter   36-38, 40, 41, 62,
    201
Pseudo-Cyprian
    De pascha computus   40, 41, 58
Pseudo-Justin
    Cohortatio   61
Pseudo-Plato
    Epistle
    2   167, 169
Sallust
    War with Cataline
    37.3   52
Seneca
    De superstitione 54, 129
    Epistulae morales
    12.11   63
    16.7   63
    89.4-8   53
    90.3   24, 54, 61, 97
Suetonius
    The Deified Augustus
    43   50
    The Deified Claudius
    25.4   51
    Life of Nero
    16.2   52, 55
Tacitus
    Annals
    13-16   52
    14.59   172
    15.44   51, 52, 55, 60
    15.71   172
    16.22   50
    Histories
    5.4   50
    5.5   51, 52
    5.8   50, 60
Tatian
    Diatessaron   65, 88
    Living Creatures 91
    On the Nature of Demons 91
    On Perfection   91
    Oration to the Greeks   44, 64-99
    1 (p.2.9)   91-92
    2-3   94
    2 (p.2.22f)   92
    3 (p.4.7f)   92
    4 (p.5.2-12)   95
    4 (p.5.15)   92
    5   95
    5 (p.5.16)   92
    6   92
    7   93, 95

7 (p.7.6-19)	95	23 (p.26.4)	93
7 (p.7.30f)	95	24 (p.26.16)	93
7 (p.8.2)	95	25	94
8	93	25 (p.26.18)	94
8 (p.10.9)	92	25 (p.26.25)	93
12 (p.12.19f)	95	25 (p.27.4)	91
12 (p.12.21)	95	26	92
12 (p.12.26ff)	95	26 (p.27.19)	94
12 (p.13.13-14)	95	26 (p.27.20f)	94
12 (p.13.19-21)	95	26 (p.27.22-28)	94
12 (p.13.31-14.1)	95	26 (p.27.27f)	94
12 (p.14.4)	92	26 (p.28.3ff)	91
12 (p.14.5-9)	97	26 (p.28.4)	94
12 (p.14.7)	95	26 (p.28.5f)	93
12 (p.14.8)	92, 95	26 (p.28.9ff)	94
13 (p.14.4)	95	26 (p.28.14f)	94
13 (p.14.10-12)	95	27 (p.29.13-17)	94
13 (p.14.14)	95	28	94
13 (p.14.16f)	95	28 (p.29.20f)	95
13 (p.14.31-15.3)	96	28 (p.29.22f)	95
13 (p.15.5f)	96	29	56, 61, 92, 94, 130
14	96		
15	91	29 (p.29.26)	92
15 (p.16.6)	95	29 (p.30.3ff)	91
15 (p.16.10-13)	96	29 (p.30.4-16)	97
15 (p.16.13)	95	29 (p.30.11-13)	98
15 (p.16.13-16)	96	30	92, 96
15 (p.16.14-16)	96	30 (p.31.2)	92
15 (p.16.20ff)	96	31	57
15 (p.16.23)	96	31-33	91
15 (p.16.24f)	96	31 (p.31.4f)	96
15 (p.16.30f)	96	31 (p.31.5)	92, 97
15 (p.16.31)	96	31 (p.31.8)	98
15 (p.17.1-3)	96	31 (p.31.11-16)	97
15 (p.17.7f)	96	31 (p.32.15-23)	97
16	91	32 (p.33.5)	97
17 (p.18.21)	91	32 (p.33.13)	92
17 (p.18.22)	91	32 (p.33.27)	97
18	61	32-33	51, 61
18 (p.20.15f)	90	33 (p. 34.2)	92
20 (p.22.29-23.3)	96	33 (p.37.19f)	97
21	71	34 (p.36.23f)	92
21 (p.23.6)	96	35	56, 61, 91
21 (p.23.7f)	92, 93	35 (p.36.25-p.37.4)	92
21 (p.24.2)	93	35 (p.36.26)	92
21 (p.24.10ff)	93	35 (p.37.6f)	91
21 (p.24.15f)	92, 93	35 (p.37.7f)	91, 97
21 (p.24.16)	93, 95	35 (p.37.12)	92
21 (p.25.15)	93	36ff	57
22-24	93	36 (p.38.9)	92, 97
22 (p.24.19ff)	93	36 (p.39.6)	97
22 (p.24.23f)	93	38	97, 98
22 (p.25.2)	93	39 (p.39.24)	98

39 (p.40.27)	98
40	91,134
40 (p.41.1-10)	98
40 (p.41.2ff)	98
40 (p.41.4ff)	93
40 (p.41.5f)	98
40 (p.41.7ff)	98
40 (p.41.11f)	92
42	91
42 (p.43.9f)	97
42 (p.43.12f)	97
Tertullian	
Ad martyras	106, 128
2.5	136
3.1	130
4	106
Ad nationes	40, 106, 128, 133
1.3	51
1.4	62
1.8	60
1.18	106
1.20	60
4.1	53
Ad Scapulam	105
3	105
Ad uxorem	
1.3	128
Adversus Judaeos	105
1	128
9-14	128
13	58
Adversus Praxean	101, 105, 134, 135
3.1	135
5.3	127
Apologeticum	40,104-106, 108, 109, 115, 119, 120, 128
3	51
4.55ff	129
10-11	129
10.2	129
12	54, 129
12.7	129
14	62
15	93
15.8	129
17.4-6	135
17.6	128
18.4	127, 130, 136
18.9	135
19	98
19.47	57
21	134, 135

21.11-12	128
21.15	128
22	129
22.2	130
22.4	130
22.12	130
23	129, 130
27.1	105
33.1	132
37	61, 128
37.4	132
38.1	116
38.3	132
38.4	128, 130
38.5	132
39	60
39.14-19	51
42.3	132
46.2	128
46.5	133
46.10-16	133
46.18	133
47	98, 133
47.1	133
47.3	134
47.4	134
47.5-8	133
47.9	128, 134
47.10	134
50	56, 106, 128
De anima	135
3.1	136
20	56
De baptismo	
18.5	136
De carne Christi	
5	133
De corona	114, 115
3-4	131
7	131
7.8	131
11.1	131
11.2-4	131
11.4	131
12.4	132
13.4	132
De fuga in persecutione	106
2.2	128
De idolatria	105, 111, 114, 115, 130
1.1	130
1.5	130
5	130

8	130
9.5	131
10.6	130, 131
11.2	130
11.8	131
12	130
13.1	130
17.3	131
18.3	131
18.4	131
18.5	131
18.6	131
18.7	131
18.8	131
19.2	131
19.3	131
20-23	131

De ieiunio adversus Psychicos
7.1	135
15	98

De monogamia
9.8	126
11.2	126

De pallio 107, 128
4.2	128
6.2	128

De patientia
13.6	128

De praescriptione haereticorum 105, 117, 120-122, 132, 133
7	61
7.5	134
7.9-13	133
8.1	133
9.4	133
10.1-4	133
11.6	133
12.5	135
13	133, 135
13.1	135
14.1-5	134
19.2	136
36	134
39.1	134
41	133

42.6	133
43	133
47.11	134

De pudicitia
19.5	127
21.17	126

De spectaculis 105, 111, 115, 130
1.4	129
4.1	129
4.3	129
5.3	129
7.2	130
8.9	131
10	93, 130
10.6	130
10.12	130
11.1	130
15.8	130
24.2	130

De testimonio animae 105, 123, 136
1.2	135
1.4	135
1.5	135
1.6-7	135
1.7	136
5.1-2	135
5.7	136
6.3	135
6.4f	135

De virginibus velandis
1.1	129
17.3	126

Scorpiace
10	60
10.10	128

Theophilus of Antioch
Ad Autolycum
2.30	57, 98
3.20	57, 98

Vergil
Aeneid
6.791ff	53

Index of Bible References

Old Testament

Genesis 400
1 150
1.26 383
2:7 383
2:18-24 383
3 95, 216
6:2 166
49:10ff 157, 172

Exodus 405
7:3 217
13:21 217
30:34-36 204

Numbers
21:5ff 169

Deuteronomy
32:8 217

1 Kings
18-19 171

Psalms
8:5 80
32:2-4 215
39:3-4 215
51:4 388
95:7 94
97:1-3 215
104:29-30 283
109:3 216
119:89 399, 400, 421
143:9-10 215
149:1 215

Isaiah
2:3 216
7:9 183
42:6 215
54:1 58, 192

Jeremiah
9:26 58
31.31ff 36, 219

Daniel
3 157-158, 171

Amos
5:24 388

Micah
6:8 388

New Testament

Matthew
2:1-12 131
3:7 216
3:9 216
5:41 406
6:24 418
7:7 133
8:5 131
11:28 406
13:3ff 148
13:44ff 96
13:52 377
19:24 219
21:33 214
28:19 243

Mark
10:25 219
10:45 422
15:12 51
15:26 51

Luke
1:7-13 217
4:18-19 406
18:25 219
18:42 134

John
1:1 216
1:1-7 403
1:1-14 148, 168, 403
1:5 78
1:9 378
1:29 422
4:21ff 36
4:23 58
4.24 95
5:24 405
8:58 331
10:35 399, 420
17:21 392
19:15 51
20:31 422

Acts

7.22	98
7:36	217
9:2	51
10:34	219
10:35	404
11:19-26	262
11:26	58
11:27ff	263
13:26ff	264
13:38-39	422
14:15ff	59, 167, 264
14:16f	334
15:1-21	294
15:1-33	265
17	136
17:6	19, 50
17:18	166
17:22ff	59, 167, 264, 378
17:23	166
17:28	283
18:2	18
18:12-17	50, 51
18:13	50
19:9	51
19:23	51
22:4	51
24:14	51
24:22	51
24-25	51
28:15	19
28:22	51

Romans 405

1	244
1:1	130, 131
1:14	58
1:18ff	421
1:20	95
1:20ff	197
1-2	167
2:11	219
2:11ff	264
2:14ff	59
2:24	173
3:23	404
3:29f	167, 345, 443
5:12	405
5:15	405
5:17	422
6:23	404
7:15-18	381
8:24ff	216

8:29	381
9-11	51
10:11-13	443
13:9	411
16:11	51

1 Corinthians

1:22	213
1:24	214
1:26f	19, 263
2:14f	80, 96, 121, 424
3:16	96
6:19	96
7:23	113
9:20-21	213
10:32	58
11:18ff	134
12:3	403
15:1-	413
15:2-3	422
15:3-4	419
15:44	95

2 Corinthians

5:1	96
5:17	58
5:17-19	422
6:16	96
8-9	263

Galatians

2:1-10	265
2:10	263
2:11-21	265
3:28	59, 409
4:4	381
4:21-31	249
4:27	192
5:1	249
5:2ff	265
6:6	58
6:15	212
6:16	265

Ephesians

1:4	216
1:10ff	264
2:2	217
2:11ff	264
2:14ff	58
2:22	96
3:3ff	264
4:11-16	403
4:13	220
6:12	134

Philippians
1:1   131
2:5-8   403
3:3   58, 59
3:9   104
4:22   51

Colossians
1:15ff   264
1:27   264
1:28   185, 213
2:8   62, 136, 443
3:11   58, 378

1 Thessalonians
4.9   220

1 Timothy
4.1   144
6:11   216

2 Timothy
3:15   197, 220
3:16   420

Titus
2:11-13   216

Hebrews
1:1   214
1:3   96
1:14   217
2:11-13   381
2:14   81
2:17   381
3-4   94
12:17   80
13:8   399

1 Peter
2:9ff   58
3:19   202

2 Peter
1:3-4   381

Revelation
5:9   215
13:8   401, 402
14:2   215

General Index

adaptation principle
  and African religious consciousness
    351, 356, 358, 361, 368-370
  analogies 365-366, 369, 371
  application 355-367
  criticised 356-357, 372-373
  and culture 353-357, 360
  defined 355
  ecclesiology 354-355, 359, 361
  and Gospel message 351-352, 354-
    355, 357, 369
  and liturgy 369, 373
  missiology 352-354, 357
  as theological task 352-354, 357
  union vitale 358-359
  value 372-375
adhesion, and religious frontiers 30
African Independence Churches 305-
  306, 315, 329
African Inland Mission 306, 327, 338,
  n50
African theology
  and Bible 2, 277, 280, 313, 398, 414
  celebrating life 315, 322
  and Christian tradition 5-10, 276
  and church, world-wide 312-313,
    332, 348, 352-356, 371
  contribution of 369-375, 439
  critics of, African 9-10, 333, 438-
    439
  emergence 1, 250, 306-328
  and experience of history 313
  future task 438-441
  Graeco-Roman parallels 9-10, 251-
    252
  and Hellenistic Christianity 7-8,
    240, 438
  indigenisation 272-279, 284, 304-
    305, 434-436
  interpreting, in post-missionary era
    1-3, 225, 252, 270, 279, 284,
    352, 368, 437
  literature, growth 250, 303
  missiology 280, 304-305, 352-353
  need for 237-238, 306-312, 367-372
  and patristics 434-439

possibility challenged 371, 386-387
  and Western theology 1-6, 243,
    248, 271, 313, 316, 332, 348,
    371, 374, 434
  see also: religious tradition, African
Akan religion 247-248, 292
Alexandria 174, 177, 181, 205, 207 n1,
  208 n8, 210
All Africa Conference of Churches 272,
  393, 395-397, 419-420
Animism 230-233, 243
apologetics, early Christian
  conversion experience 31-32, 110,
    129 n82, 196
  and Hebrew Bible 33, 119, 189
  and Hellenism 154-155, 176, 436
  literature 36-48, 59 n168, 67-71,
    88, 104-106, 181
  missionary purpose 87
  theology 78-79, 123, 144, 415
Aristides, Apology of, significance 38
Asante (Ashanti) 245-247, 321
Association of Evangelicals of Africa
  and Madagascar (AEAM) 396- 397,
    416, 419-420
atheism, in Graeco-Roman understanding 25-28, 55 n98, 60 n191
Athens 174, 245
Bacchanalia 40, 55 n100, 60 n198, 216
  n164
Bantu religion 324-326, 349, 351, 357-
  376, 380-381
  barbarism
    as Christian heritage 32-33, 44, 66-
      68, 71, 188, 191, 202-203,
      439
    and Graeco-Roman world 24-26
Buganda, church in 242, 305
Carthage, Church Council (AD 225) 102
Christianity
  as African religion 304-312, 408-
    409, 414
  and barbarian heritage 32-33, 44,
    66-68, 188, 191, 202-203,
    439
  equated with civilisation 227-228,

233, 238, 251, 255 n32
as European religion 228, 235-238,
271, 305, 349, 412, 414
exclusiveness, a problem to Romans
56 n116
foreignness 10, 240, 268-273, 285,
290, 304, 318, 360, 371, 410
Gentile conversions 19, 34-36, 42,
48, 199, 240-242
historical roots 34-35
and Judaism 19, 34, 179, 240
and paganism, Graeco-Roman 18-
33, 37, 48-49
spread 19-20, 44, 48, 58 n150, 115,
175, 433
as superstition 18-21, 27-29
as threat to society 17-21, 29, 188
uniqueness 319-320
Church Missionary Society 234, 259
n74
Church of Scotland, and missions 254
n23, 276
civilisation, and moral conscience 232,
236
Clement of Alexandria
antiquity of Christianity 188, 191,
202-203
background 174-177
Bible, use of 178, 182, 185-204
Christian identity 188
and conversion 189-191, 196, 207
covenant 200-201, 204
custom, challenge of 188-190, 197
demonology 190, 192, 195
evaluation 205-207
faith 183-187
Fall 192
Gospel 176, 180-191, 195, 197, 200-
202, 207
Hellenism 47, 174-207, 435
idolatry 193-197, 201
Incarnation 176, 191-192, 198-199,
201
Jews 178-179
Logos doctrine 176-180, 183, 190-
193, 195-196, 199, 436
Moses 184, 188, 203-204
New Song concept 189-193
Paidogogos 179-186
philosophy 47, 175-176, 180-189,
194-196, 199-206, 435-436
Protreptikos 179-181, 188-193 206
salvation, universal 175, 177, 180,

185, 191-193, 197-199, 202,
204, 207, 435
Stromateis 179-183, 188
tradition, on deadliness of 187-199
truth 179-182, 186-187, 195-196
writings 178-180
Constantinople, Council of (AD 381)
429
Consultation of African Theologians
(Ibadan, 1966) 367, 390
continuity/discontinuity 427-431
conversion
in African situation 236, 245, 337
n40, 411-412
novelty confronting Graeco-Roman
culture 29-33, 188
converts, Gentile
parallels with modern Africa 8,
240-245
problem of identity 34-36, 42, 48,
199
proportion in early church 34, 48
converts, Jewish, identity problem 16,
34-35
culture, African
basis for Christian community 349
and Christianity 3, 7-8, 234, 312,
355, 408-413
identity quest 16, 31-32, 347-348,
428-430
and Roman Catholic Church 348-
349, 353-356
culture, Graeco-Roman
and Christian conversion 29-33
and Christian expansion 44
and Christian identity 15-21, 48-50
and Gospel 8
and Jews 15-16
Romanitas 22, 24
social order 15-18, 21, 29
and *superstitio* 20-29
and third race 34-41
demonology
Clement of Alexandria 190, 192,
195
Justin martyr 144-145, 149, 156-
158, 166 n73
Plutarch 26, 54 n82
Tatian 71-73, 77-78, 80-81, 84
Tertullian 105-117, 120, 124, 430
De pascha computus 40-41
Dinka religion 301 n139
Diognetus, Epistle to, significance 37

divine names, African
  monotheism 287-289, 291-293
  among Nuer 288
  polytheism 286, 292-293
  Supreme God 287-289, 292, 295
    n23
  in West Africa 283, 287, 291-293,
    322
  among Yoruba 279, 288-289, 292,
    299-301
Epicureanism 22, 25, 171 n181, 183,
  213 n94, 435
eschatology 78, 316, 324-328
fetishism 256 n46; *see* Animism
Gentile mission, Paul's, and African
  situation 8, 240-245, 248- 251
Ghana, Christian Council of 272
God, African sense of
  creation 270, 282, 330
  European misunderstandings 270,
    282-284, 291
  and Old Testament 321
  prayer 321-322
  pre-missionary 2-3, 279-281, 287-
    288
  Traditional Religion 284-289, 330-
    331, 345 n170, 361, 366, 436
  see also African theology; divine
    names; time
God, Western sense of, lost 242, 271,
  295 n23
Honest to God 271
humanitarianism 227, 233, 250, 253-
  254
identity, African-Christian
  and culture 347-350, 427, 432,
    439, 441
  and European values 237-239, 251,
    271-279, 350, 391
  and Hellenistic Christian analogies
    240-242, 427, 439-441
  nature 3-6, 10, 248, 350
  and patristic insights 427-433, 436
  theological problem 237-239, 251-
    252, 288, 312, 319, 368, 375,
    428, 436, 439
identity, early Christian
  and barbarianism 32, 428-430
  and conversion 31-33
  and culture 16, 31-32, 347-348,
    428-430
  and Gnosticism 428-429
  in Graeco-Roman world 16, 31-33,

46, 48, 70-71, 201, 428-430
  and Hellenism 43, 187, 191, 199,
    429-430
  pilgrim principle 430
  problem of 16, 31-36, 41-42, 48-50,
    199, 436
  and religious history of Israel 33,
    428, 430
  third race 34-41, 45, 88, 374
Idowu, Bolaji 267-293
  achievements 293
  and African theology 277-279, 285
  and African traditional religion
    279-293
  background 267-268, 284
  Bible translation 277
  Christology 275-279
  criticised 397, 414, 418 n31, 424
    n155
  God, doctrine of 279-289
  God in pre-Christian tradition 270-
    271, 279-288
  and identity problem 288
  indigenous church 272-279, 284
  and liturgy 276
  post-missionary presence in Africa
    268-272
  religion, understanding of 280-282
  revelation 281-282
  universality of Gospel 271, 275-
    279, 282
  Western theology 271, 278
International African Seminar (Accra,
  1965) 308, 367
International Congress on World Evangelisation (Lausanne, 1974) 408
Islam 229, 252 n1, 280, 285, 292, 318-
  319, 434
Jaba religion 387-389
Jerusalem Conference (1928) 243, 258
  n65
Jews
  and Christians, relation 15-16, 34
  conversion, need for 30
  in Graeco-Roman world 15-16, 18,
    34
  and superstition 26
Justin Martyr 137-173
  background 137-141, 147, 160 n2
  "Christians" before Christ 41-42,
    153-160, 435
  chronological priority of Moses 150
  conversion 137, 139-145

demonology 144-145, 149, 156-158,
   166 n73
Dialogue with Trypho 139-140
faith and reason 138-141
and Hellenism 46, 138-141, 146,
   148, 153-155, 159-160
and Jews 138, 172 n204
Logos, seminal Word of God 42,
   146-153, 156-160, 436
and martyrs 143, 158
Old Testament 139-141, 150-152,
   158-160
philosophy 42-47, 138, 141-149,
   155, 436
and Socrates 41, 43, 45-46, 143-
   145, 156-158
truth 143-146, 149, 151-152, 155-
   158
vocabulary 147-148, 166 n73
Kato, Byang 386-416
   *African Cultural Revolution and
      the Christian Faith* 408,
      410
   African theology, disapproves 398,
      407, 415
   background 386-387, 416 n4
   on Bible innerrancy, not infal-
      libility 398, 420 n65
   biblical translation 409
   bibliology 388-390, 392-393, 395-
      400, 405-407, 410-413, 416
      n1
   Black Theology 394-395, 399
   on Christianity as African religion
      408-409, 414
   Christology 398, 401-406
   contribution 413-416
   and conversion 411
   culture 408-413
   dead ancestors 390, 404-405, 416
   death 416 n2
   ecumenism 391-397, 405-406, 410
   Gospel 394, 408, 410-413
   Jaba religion 387-389
   Liberation Theology 399, 406
   Logos 403
   pre-Christian religions 387-391,
      393-394, 402-403, 408
   prophecy 389
   revelation, general/special 390,
      399-404, 413
   salvation 390, 393, 396, 401-406
   significance 391

situation ethics 394-395
spirit-possession 388-389
syncretism 408, 415, 421 n75
Theological Pitfalls in Africa 392,
   397, 414, 416
uniqueness of Christianity 398,
   400
unity 392, 396, 410
Le Zoute Conference (1926) 260 n86,
   265 n191
Logos doctrine
   Clement of Alexandria 176-180,
      183, 190-193, 199, 436
   Justin Martyr 42, 146-153, 156-
      160, 436
   Kato, Byang 403
   Mulago, Vincent 350
martyrdom 52, 56-57, 106, 143
martyrs, African 305
Mbiti, John 303-334
   African culture 307, 312-314, 321
   African history 313
   African identity 312, 319, 331
   African Religions and Philosophy
      316-320, 322-323, 333
   African theology 306-328
   Anglicanism 306
   background 303, 306, 332
   biblical theology 313, 316, 321
   on Christianity as African 304-312,
      315, 319
   Christology 306, 310-311, 319-320,
      323, 327-332
   community 309-310, 321, 325-326
   Concepts of God in Africa 320-322,
      333
   criticised 9, 387, 397-398, 408, 414,
      418 n31, 424 n155
   Gospel 305-314, 324, 329-334
   indigenisation, rejects 305-306
   on missionary shortcomings 304-
      307, 335 n13
   *New Testament Eschatology in an
      African Background* 316,
      324
   Prayers of African Religions 321-
      322, 333
   on religious ontology 325-328
   traditional religions 237-238, 304,
      310, 313-323, 329-334
   uniqueness of Christianity 319-320
   Western theology 313, 316, 320,
      324, 332

works 303-304, 316-323
missionary perception of Africa 225-252
   civilisation needed before Gospel 227-228
   degradation 225, 227, 232, 235, 251, 255 n39
   ethnocentricism 227, 232-239
   European value-setting 235, 238, 251, 269, 314
   savagery 227-228, 233
   as *tabula rasa* 349-350, 374, 391
   theological misunderstanding 225, 243, 269-270, 280, 286, 437
   traditional religion, failure to appreciate 245, 269-270, 291-293, 304-307, 314, 322, 349
   universality of Gospel, failure to grasp 240-248, 251, 269
missionary vocation, motives 241, 243
monotheism 280, 287-289, 291-293
Mulago, Vincent 347-375
   adaptation 351-375: *see* adaptation principle
   African theology 367-372
   Bantu religion 351, 357-366, 368-371, 373-375, 380-382
   Catholic tradition 353, 355-358, 362, 364-366, 372
   Catholic missiology, questions 349-350
   community 362-364, 371
   criticised 356-357
   ecclesiology 354-355, 358-359, 362-364, 370, 374
   Gospel 354-355, 369
   identity problem for converts 350
   Incarnation 364, 368, 370, 372
   indigenisation 356, 368
   Logos spermatikos 350
   Mariology 365-366, 382
   missiology 352-354, 359
   natural theology 350-351
   participation 362-364, 369-372, 374
   patristics 362
   Des Prêtres noirs s'interrogent 347-349, 351
   sacraments 369-371
   tabula rasa theory, criticises 350-351
   Trinity 363-364, 370, 374
   union vitale 358-359, 362, 371, 374,

   379 n70
   Un visage africain du Christianisme 352, 357-359, 361, 367, 373, 375
mystery religions 24, 28-29, 69, 190, 193
Négritude movement 347, 375 n3
Nigeria 234, 237, 267-268, 271-280, 284
Nuer religion 288
Orita (Ibadan Journal of Religious Studies) 267-268, 280, 284 n5
paganism, and early Christianity 17-32, 47-48, 433
paternalism 234, 242
Paul's missionary methods, relevance to Africa 240-251
persecution
   in Africa 305, 411
   in early Church 15, 19-20, 29, 31, 105-106, 113, 142
Philosophie Bantoue 349, 360-361
philosophy
   Clement of Alexandria 47, 175-176, 180-189, 194-196, 199-206, 435-436
   and educated Graeco-Romans 30, 42, 45-46
   Justin martyr 42-47, 138, 141-149, 155, 436
   morality 24, 42
   Tatian 44, 66, 69, 74, 81-84
   Tertullian 43-45, 105-108, 117-124
Platonism 142, 150
Pluralism, challenge of religious 432-434
polemic, anti-Christian
   by Africans 9, 438
   by Celsus 10, 28-29, 48, 57 n138, 188
polemic, anti-Judaistic 35, 38, 105
polytheism 38, 286, 292-293, 302 n170
Preaching of Peter, significance 36-37
Présence Africaine 347
religio
   defined 22-23
   philosophical defence of 22-24
   place in ancient world 21-32, 53-55
   and superstition 21-29
religion, comparative, evolutionary view of 230
religious consciousness, dynamics 236
religious tradition, African

academic study 312-323, 332, 349,
    434
Christian response 7, 237-239, 304,
    351-355, 361, 408
and Gospel 2, 6, 237, 241, 245, 270
rejected 387-391
missionary misunderstanding of
    237-245, 251, 284, 304, 350
pre-Christian 1-6, 247, 270, 312-
    323, 333-334, 368, 409, 436-
    438
as theological problem 234-239,
    279-293, 352
religious tradition, Graeco-Roman 153-
    154
and Christianity 17-18
Roman Catholic Church in Africa 347-
    375
missiology 349, 353, 357
Roman state
ancestral piety 27
and Christianity 16, 18-20, 27, 56
    n116
emperor worship 17, 22, 29
gods, reverence for 22-24, 52 n53
Romanitas (Roman values) 22, 24
Rome, Christian community in 18-19
Scriptures, Hebrew, in apologetic
    literature 33
Sierra Leone 234, 259 n77, 261 n104,
    273, 296 n28
slavery 225-227, 249, 253-254
Société Africaine de Culture 347
Sophists 154, 186
spirituality, African 321-322, 332-334
Stoicism 22, 24, 44, 53, 76, 79, 95, 124,
    147, 151-152, 177
superstition (superstitio)18-29, 39, 42,
    53 n65
tabula rasa theory 349-351, 374, 391
Tacitus, and Christians 51-52
Tatian 64-99
Barbarian background 66, 71, 429
Barbarian priority over Hellenism
    82-88, 430
Bible, use of 64, 66, 69, 75-86, 89
chronological argument for Chris-
    tianity 81-86
creation 77-79
demonology 71-73, 77-78, 80-81, 84
Diatessaron 65, 68
doctrine of two Spirits 76-81
eschatology 78

Fall 77-80
Graeco-Roman tradition, rejects
    44, 61 n230, 64, 66-86, 91
    n25
Greek scholar 64, 71, 75, 89
Greek theology, assails 71-72
importance 86-89
man, nature of 77, 79
Oration to the Greeks 65-89
orthodoxy 69
philosophy, Christian faith as 44,
    66, 69, 74, 81-84
reputation under suspicion 64-65,
    90 n11
salvation 76, 78-80
soul 77-80
Syriac background 64-66, 88, 90
    n7, 91 n19
truth, understanding of 67, 71-72,
    75, 81-82
writings 90 n16
Tertullian 100-126
Apologeticum 104-106, 115-116,
    119
baptism 108, 125, 127 n16, 129n73
Bible 119, 121-122, 125
Christ's example 113-114
on conversion 104, 110, 125
demonology 105-117, 120, 124, 430
Graeco-Roman tradition 104-105,
    109, 111, 121
heresy 119-122
idolatry 109-112
on martyrdom 106
and military service 112, 114-115,
    131-132
Montanism 100-103, 106, 126 n14,
    127
orthodoxy 101
pallium 107-108
and persecution 113
philosophy 43-45, 105-108, 117-
    124
on political life 116
pompa diaboli 108-117
and psychici 102, 125
reputation, unsound 103
Roman civil religion 110, 114-117
rule of faith 118-123, 125
sanctification 103
and spiritales 102-103
third race 39-41
Trinitarian doctrine 105, 126 n7,

134 n180
and truth 117-120, 123-125
works 105-106
third opportunity in Africa 235, 250,
    252 n1, 304, 386
third race, Christians as 34-41, 45, 88,
    374
time, African concept 323-328, 341-343
union vitale 358-359, 362, 371, 374, 379
    n70
universality of Gospel 177, 198, 202,

207, 240-251, 269-271, 275-279,
    282, 435
Vatican II 357, 371-373, 384-385
World Council of Churches 392-393,
    395-397, 400, 410, 415
World Missionary Conference (Edin-
    burgh, 1910) 231, 235, 243, 392-
    393
Yoruba religion 279, 286-289, 292, 299-
    300
Zaire (Congo) 349, 411

REGNUM BOOKS

Vinay Samuel and Chris Sugden (eds)
SHARING JESUS IN THE TWO-THIRDS WORLD
Papers from the first conference of the International Fellowship of Evangelical Mission Theologians with contributions from Orlando Costas, Rene Padilla, Kwame Bediako, Michael Nazir Ali and others on Christology in the Two-Thirds World
432 pages

Michael Nazir Ali
FRONTIERS IN CHRISTIAN MUSLIM ENCOUNTER
The General Secretary of the Church Missionary Society considers Christology in an Islamic context, the Cross as a bridge to Muslim and Christian understanding, and the relationship between faith in Christ and non-Christian religions
176 pages

Vinay Samuel and Albrecht Hauser (eds)
PROCLAIMING CHRIST IN CHRIST'S WAY
Studies in Integral Evangelism

Essays on wholistic mission from David Gitari, Raymond Fung, Vinay Samuel, John Stott, Ron Sider, Kwame Bediako and others.
228 pages

Chris Wright and Chris Sugden (eds)
ONE GOSPEL, MANY CLOTHES
Case-studies and reflection on evangelism from five continents, among nomads in Kenya and decision-makers in Australia, on housing estates in England and in slums in India, among Jews and among women.
190 pages

Vinay Samuel and Chris Sugden (eds)
AD 2000 AND BEYOND - A MISSION AGENDA
A Festschrift for John Stott

Essays from scholars in Africa, Asia, Latin America and Europe on holistic mission, including landlessness, good news to the poor, and mission in the context of world religions.
166 pages

Regnum Studies in Mission and Development

Forthcoming titles in this series, published by Regnum Books in association with Lynx Communications

Eugenia Adoyo
AN AFRICAN PLEA FOR INDEPENDENCE
Reflections on the Call for a Missionary Moratorium

David W. Bennett
BIBLICAL IMAGES FOR LEADERS AND FOLLOWERS

Klaus Fiedler
THE FAITH MISSIONS
The Story from the Beginning to Today

Graham Kings
GOD'S LOVE TO A WHOLE COMMUNITY
A Kenyan Diocese in Mission

Anne-Marie Kool
THE FOREIGN MISSION MOVEMENT IN HUNGARY - AN UNTOLD STORY

Vinay Samuel and Chris Sugden
TRANSFORMATION
Development in a Kingdom Perspective

TRANSFORMATION JOURNAL – a quarterly international evangelical dialogue on mission and ethics edited by Tokunboh Adeyemo (Nigeria), Vinay Samuel (India) and Ron Sider (USA) published by the Oxford Centre for Mission Studies.

Regnum Books,
Oxford Centre for Mission Studies,
P.O. Box 70,
Oxford, OX2 6HB, UK.
Phone: 44-865-56071; Fax: 44-865-510823